JAVA™ WEB SERVICES

IN A NUTSHELL

Other Java™ resources from O'Reilly

JAVA™ WEB SERVICES

IN A NUTSHELL

Kim Topley

Beiji  ebastopol · Taipei · Tokyo

O'REILLY®

Java™ Web Services in a Nutshell
by Kim Topley

Copyright © 2003 O'Reilly & Associates, Inc. All rights reserved.
Printed in the United States of America.

Published by O'Reilly & Associates, Inc., 1005 Gravenstein Highway North, Sebastopol, CA 95472.

O'Reilly & Associates books may be purchased for educational, business, or sales promotional use. Online editions are also available for most titles (*safari.oreilly.com*). For more information, contact our corporate/institutional sales department: 800-998-9938 or *corporate@oreilly.com*.

Editors:	Brett McLaughlin and Robert Eckstein
Production Editor:	Mary Brady
Cover Designer:	Hanna Dyer
Interior Designers:	Ellie Volckhausen and David Futato

Printing History:

June 2003:	First Edition.

ISBN: 0-596-00399-4
[M]

Table of Contents

Part II. API Quick Reference

Part III. Appendix

Preface

This book is a desktop quick reference for programmers writing web services or web service clients using the Java™ programming language. Part I offers a fast-paced but comprehensive tutorial covering the web service APIs that are part of the J2EE 1.4 platform and the Java Web Services Developer Pack (JWSDP), both of which provide all of the software needed to develop and test web services using Sun's reference implementations of these technologies. These chapters are followed by a quick-reference section that details each class and interface in the web service APIs covered in the tutorial.

This book is intended to be used in conjunction with the best-selling O'Reilly titles *Java in a Nutshell*, by David Flanagan and *Java Enterprise in a Nutshell*, by William Crawford, Jim Farley, and David Flanagan. *Java in a Nutshell* introduces the Java programming language and provides an API quick reference for the core packages and classes of the Java 2 Standard Edition (J2SE) platform, while *Java Enterprise in a Nutshell* does the same for the APIs in the Java 2 Enterprise Edition (J2EE). Web services leverage technology that is provided by J2EE (including XML, servlets, and Enterprise JavaBeans™) and therefore at least a basic working knowledge of the Java programming language and its enterprise features is required in order to get the best from this book.

Contents of This Book

Part I, which is the first eight chapters of this book, provides an introduction to web services and tutorial material for the APIs and command-line tools that are provided by the J2EE 1.4 platform and the Java Web Services Developer Pack (JWSDP):

Chapter 1, *Introduction*
  This chapter is a short but practical introduction to web services in general and to the support provided for web services by both the JWSDP and the J2EE 1.4 platform. The second part of this chapter provides a quick overview of the JAX-RPC API and shows how you might use it to create a client that can browse through the books available at Amazon.com, using that company's store-browsing web service.

Chapter 2, *JAX-RPC*

For most web service developers, JAX-RPC is the most important of the APIs covered in this book. This chapter provides a basic introduction to JAX-RPC and shows you how to create a simple service and a client that can be used to access it, starting from a Java definition of the interface that the service provides. This chapter also discusses the use of both servlets and Enterprise JavaBeans (EJBs) to host JAX-RPC services and the tools that you need to build and deploy them.

Chapter 3, *SAAJ*

While JAX-RPC is probably the most commonly used web service API, the SOAP with Attachments API for Java (or SAAJ) is the API that appeals most to those who like to see and understand what goes on "under the hood." SAAJ provides the means to create and receive raw SOAP messages. It requires you to build and decode each message at the XML element level. This chapter covers all of the SAAJ API, including the use of MIME attachments, which allow you to transfer arbitrary content, such as images and sound files.

Chapter 4, *JAXM*

JAXM is a development of SAAJ that provides asynchronous messaging and more reliable delivery. In this chapter, you'll see how to make use of these features and how to configure the reference implementation so that your JAXM clients can communicate with each other. This chapter also looks at the two SOAP message profiles, SOAP-RP and ebXML TRP, that are supported by the reference implementation.

Chapter 5, *WSDL*

The Web Service Description Language (WSDL) is an application of XML that lets you describe the interface to a web service in implementation-independent terms. One of the most useful features of WSDL is that it can be both created and consumed easily by software tools; as a result, you can use it to publish the interface to a web service implemented in Java or a different programming language, and create from the WSDL definition artifacts that allow clients for that service to be written in any language on any platform that has support for web services. Chapter 5 looks at the grammar of a WSDL document, preparing the way for the application of WSDL in Chapter 6.

Chapter 6, *Advanced JAX-RPC*

This lengthy chapter starts by showing you how to use JAX-RPC to import a WSDL definition of a web service and then generate the Java interface and other classes required to let you build a client for that service. It goes on to demonstrate the wide range of powerful features that the JAX-RPC API provides, including support for both document- and RPC-based services, the use of MIME attachments with JAX-RPC web services, and SOAP message handlers, which let you process and extract data from or insert data into a SOAP message without modifying the code for the client or server that will generate or consume the message.

Chapter 7, *JAXR*

> This chapter covers the Java API for XML-based Registries (JAXR). Registries allow organizations to publish their services so that would-be clients can discover them, learn how to access them and, eventually, do business using them. The JAXR API supports both the UDDI and ebXML registries in such a way as to make it possible to write a registry client application that can work with either of them without requiring any registry-specific code, while still allowing applications that need access to features that are offered by only one registry or the other to be created.

Chapter 8, *Web Service Tools and Configuration Files*

> Both the JWSDP and J2EE 1.4 provide a number of tools that you need to use when creating web services. This chapter documents both the tools themselves and the configuration files that are required to control them.

Part II (Chapters 9 to 20) forms the API quick reference, which is a succinct but detailed API reference formatted for optimum ease of use. Please be sure to read *How to Use This Quick Reference*, which appears at the beginning of the reference section; it explains how to get the most out of these chapters.

Related Books

O'Reilly and Associates, Inc. publishes an entire series of books on Java programming. You can find a complete list of Java books from O'Reilly and Associates at *http://java.oreilly.com*. Books that are of particular interest to Java developers working with web services include:

Java in a Nutshell by David Flanagan

> A Java language tutorial and complete API reference for the core Java classes.

Java Enterprise in a Nutshell by Jim Farley, William Crawford, and David Flanagan

> A tutorial and API reference for many of Java's enterprise API's, including EJBs and servlets, both of which can be used to host Java web services.

Java and XML by Brett McLaughlin

> Although it is possible to create and use simple web services without much understanding of XML, a proper grounding in this important subject is required to make use of the more advanced features. Brett McLaughlin's *Java and XML* provides both an introduction to XML and good coverage of many of the XML-based technologies that are relevant to web services.

XML Schema by Eric van der Vlist

> This book provides detailed coverage of the XML schema language, a knowledge of which is useful if you want to be able to read web service definitions written using WSDL, or if you intend to use the lower-level web service APIs, such as SAAJ.

Ant: the Definitive Guide by Jesse Tilly and Eric M. Burke

> Provides comprehensive coverage of Ant, which is now the tool that is most commonly used by development teams to build their software, and which is required to compile and run the example source code for this book.

Web Services Programming Resources Online

This book is a quick reference designed for speedy access to frequently needed information. It does not, and cannot, tell you everything you need to know about developing web services in Java. In addition to the books just listed, there are several valuable (and free) electronic sources of information about web services:

The World Wide Web Consortium (W3C) web site
> Although much of the existing technology underpinning web services was developed independently by groups of companies such as Sun Microsystems, IBM, and Microsoft working together, most of those technologies have now been adopted and are being standardized by the W3C. You can find the latest drafts of the specifications currently being worked on, plus technical reports that document the earlier work, including the specifications for SOAP and WSDL, on the W3C web site at *http://www.w3c.org*.

The OASIS web site
> The Organization for the Advancement of Structured Information Standards (OASIS) is a not-for-profit organization that is leading the development of standards in the e-business arena. OASIS is one of the sponsors for ebXML, which uses SOAP as its underlying message transport mechanism, and is also undertaking web service–related work in the areas of distributed management, interactive applications, reliable messaging, and services for remote portals. You can find the current state of this work at *http://www.oasis-open.org*.

Web Services Interoperability Organization (WS-I) web site
> WS-I is a relatively new organization whose aim is to promote cross-platform web service interoperability by defining profiles that reduce the number of choices that web service vendors need to make when creating their infrastructure. Sun recently announced that the web service support in J2EE 1.4 conforms to the WS-I Basic Profile Version 1.0, which covers the construction of SOAP messages, WSDL documents, and service publication in XML-based registries. The WS-I web site is at *http://www.ws-i.org*.

Apache Web Services Project web site
> The Apache Software Foundation has a project dedicated to web services, the web site of which can be found at *http://ws.apache.org*. Apache Axis, which can be downloaded from this site, is an implementation of SOAP that claims to comply to both the JAX-RPC 1.0 and SAAJ 1.1 specifications and can therefore be used as an alternative to Sun's reference implementations of these APIs. There is also an implementation of WS-Security, a W3C standard that is not currently part of either J2EE 1.4 or the JWSDP.

XMethods web site
> The XMethods web site at *http://www.xmethods.com* provides links to many publicly available demonstration web services, some of which also have example clients that you can use to try out the service or see how to use it.

Examples Online

The examples in this book are available online and can be downloaded from the book's home page at *http://www.oreilly.com/catalog/javawsian/*. You may also want to visit this site to see if any important notes or errata about the book have been published there. Once you download the example source code, you need to install it, together with either the Java Web Services Developer's Pack (JWSDP) or the J2EE Version 1.4 reference implementation.

The JWSDP is a standalone package that contains everything that you need to get started with web service development, including the reference implementations of the web services APIs, a version of the Tomcat web server that has been preconfigured with web services, and the Ant build tool for compiling and running web service applications. The JWSDP requires J2SE Version 1.3.1 or later. The example source code for this book has been tested with JWSDP Version 1.1 and J2SE versions 1.4.0 and 1.4.1.

Most of the web services technologies from the JWSDP have been incorporated into the J2EE 1.4 platform. The examples have been tested with the beta release of the J2EE 1.4 reference implementation and should work unchanged with the final release, unless unexpected changes are made. Following the FCS release of J2EE 1.4, refer to the book's web site where any necessary updates to the example source code will be posted.

You can obtain the JWSDP from *http://java.sun.com/webservices/webservicespack. html*. After completing the download, follow the instructions that are supplied with the distribution to install it. Alternatively, download and install the reference implementation of J2EE 1.4, which is available at *http://java.sun.com/j2ee/ download.html*. If you choose to use the examples in this book with J2EE 1.4, you will not need to download the JWSDP.

Installing the Example Source Code

The example source code is supplied as a ZIP file that can be unpacked into a directory of your choice, which we'll refer to throughout this section as *c:\ JWSNutshell\examples*. Beneath this directory, you'll find the examples for each chapter organized into separate directories. The example source code contains buildfiles for the Ant utility, which is supplied with both the JWSDP and the J2EE 1.4 reference implementation and, throughout this book, you'll find specific instructions for building and running each example along with the text that describes it.

Once you unpack the examples, copy the files *jwsnutExamples.properties* and *jwsnutJaxrExamples.properties* to your home directory. These files need to be tailored to suit your environment before you can run any of the examples, as described in the following sections.

Tailoring the jwnutExamples.properties file

Before you start editing the *jwsnutExamples.properties* file, you need to decide whether you will be using the example source code with the JWSDP or with J2EE 1.4. To use the JWSDP with the Tomcat web server, uncomment and set the following properties that appear near the top of the file:

```
USING_JWSDP=true
WSROOT=c:/jwsdp-1.1
```

The WSROOT property should be set to point to the directory in which you installed the JWSDP. Since this file is read by the Ant build utility, it is acceptable to use forward slashes in pathnames on all operating system platforms, although Windows users may use backslashes if preferred. To use the example source code with J2EE 1.4, uncomment and set the following properties instead:

```
USING_J2EE14=true
J2EEROOT=c:/j2sdkee1.4
WSROOT=${J2EEROOT}
```

You should ensure that the property definitions in only one of these two blocks are uncommented.

The settings for the remainder of the properties in this file do not depend on your choice of web container and should be set as described in Table P-1. In most cases, the values that you'll find in the file will work for your system; therefore, only a small number of these properties will need to be changed.

Table P-1. Properties defined in the jwsnutExamples.properties file

Property	Description
EXAMPLES_ROOT	The directory in which you have installed the example source code — for example, *c:/JWSNutshell/examples*.
USERNAME PASSWORD	Some of the examples in this book make use of HTTP basic authentication to demonstrate how you can apply basic security to your web service. These examples require you to supply a username and password, which are referred to within the text as JWSUser and JWSPassword respectively, but which may have any values you choose. The username and password must also be registered with the web container, as described later in this section.
AMAZON_TAG	Chapter 1 contains an example that makes use of a web service provided by Amazon.com. If you want to run this example for yourself, you will need to register at Amazon.com's web site and obtain a developer tag, the value of which you should supply here. To register, visit the URL *https://associates.amazon.com/exec/panama/associates/join/developer/application.html*.
CONNECTED	Some of the examples in Chapter 7 are fully functional only when used on a machine that has an Internet connection. If your machine has such a connection, set this property to true.
TARGET_HOST	The name of the host on which the Tomcat or J2EE 1.4 web container is running. In most cases, the value localhost, which is the default, is appropriate.
TOMCAT_WEBPORT J2EE14_WEBPORT	The port number used by the web container. The values that you'll find in the file as installed are correct for the default installations of the JWSDP and J2EE 1.4
TOMCAT_WEBSVCPORT J2EE14_WEBSVCPORT	The JWSDP installs a small number of services in the Tomcat web container. These services are accessed at a different port, which must be supplied using the TOMCAT_WEBSVCPORT property. The value supplied in the file as installed is correct for the default configuration of the JWSDP and for J2EE 1.4.
TOMCAT_WEBHTTPSPORT J2EE14_WEBHTTPSPORT	The port number that the web container uses for secure HTTP (HTTPS). The initial settings are correct for the default installations of JWSDP and J2EE 1.4.
HTTP_PROXY_SERVER HTTP_PROXY_PORT HTTPS_PROXY_SERVER HTTPS_PROXY_PORT	If you need to run the client parts of the example source code in this book through a proxy server, you may do so by setting these properties to point to the server and port number of the proxy that you are using. The HTTPS properties need to be set only if the example uses a secure connection. These properties must not be set if you do not need to use a proxy.

Tailoring the jwsnutJaxrExamples.properties file

The *jwsnutJaxrExamples.properties* file contains settings that are used with the examples for JAXR (covered in Chapter 7). The appropriate values are described in Chapter 7 alongside the text for the examples that use them.

Environment variables

Some of the utilities in the JWSDP and the J2EE reference implementation rely on environment variables to locate libraries, configuration files, and other utilities. Table P-2 lists the variables that you need to set, along with typical values.

Table P-2. Environment variable settings

Variable	Description
JAVA_HOME	The installation directory of the J2SE SDK. A typical value is *c:\j2sdk1.4.1*.
J2EE_HOME	The installation directory of the J2EE reference implementation. This is required only if you are using J2EE 1.4. A typical value is *c:\j2sdkee1.4*.
JWSDP_HOME	The installation directory of the JWSDP. A typical value is *c:\jwsdp-1.1*. Does not need to be set if you are using J2EE 1.4.
JAXRPC_HOME	The home directory for JAX-RPC. This is required only if you are using the JWSDP and should be set to point to the JAX-RPC directory directly below JWSDP_HOME. For JWSDP 1.1, this would be *%JWSDP_HOME%\jaxrpc-1.0.3*
JAXR_HOME	The home directory for JAXR. This is required only if you are using the JWSDP and should be set to point to the JAXR directory directly below JWSDP_HOME. For JWSDP 1.1, this is *%JWSDP_HOME%\jaxr-1.0_03*
ANT_HOME	The home directory for the Ant build tool. If you are using the JWSDP, set this to *%JWSDP_HOME%\jakarta-ant-1.5.1*. For J2EE 1.4, set it to the value of J2EE_HOME. You can also set this variable to point to a separately installed version of Ant if you prefer.
PATH	This variable must include the following: • The *bin* directory of the J2SE SDK (e.g. *c:\j2sdk1.4.1\bin*) • The *bin* directory of the J2EE installation, if you are using J2EE 1.4 (e.g., *c:\j2sdkee1.4\bin*) If you are using the JWSDP, the *bin* directories for the JWSDP itself, then Ant, JAX-RPC, and JAXR must also be added: • *%JWSDP_HOME%\bin* • *%JWSDP_HOME%\shared\bin* • *%ANT_HOME%\bin* • *%JAXRPC_HOME%\bin* • *%JAXR_HOME%\bin*

Using the Example Source Code with the JWSDP

To use the example source code with the Tomcat web container that is supplied with the JWSDP, you need to add a role name and two usernames and passwords to the web container's authentication information, which you'll find in the file *%JWSDP_HOME%\conf\tomcat-users.xml*. The lines that should be added to this file are highlighted in Example P-1.

Example P-1. Adding authentication information to the tomcat-users.xml file

```
<?xml version='1.0'?>
<tomcat-users>
```

Example P-1. Adding authentication information to the tomcat-users.xml file (continued)

```
    <role rolename="admin"/>
    <role rolename="manager"/>
    <role rolename="provider"/>
    <role rolename="JWSGroup"/>
    <user username="JWSUserName" password="JWSPassword"
    roles="admin,manager,provider,JWSGroup"/>
    <user username="AnotherUser" password="Pwd"
            roles="admin,manager,provider,JWSGroup"/>
</tomcat-users>
```

Note that the values JWSUserName and JWSPassword shown here must match the USERNAME and PASSWORD properties set in the *jwsnutExamples.properties* file. If you have substituted your own username and password, then you must use the same values in the *tomcat-users.xml* file.

Using the Source Code with J2EE Version 1.4

If you intend to use J2EE 1.4, you need to add two usernames and a group to the application server's authentication information. The commands required to do this are shown next, where it is assumed that the *bin* directory of the J2EE installation has been added to your PATH environment variable:

```
realmtool -addGroup JWSGroup
realmtool -add JWSUserName JWSPassword JWSGroup
realmtool -add AnotherUser Pwd JWSGroup
```

Note that the values JWSUserName and JWSPassword shown here match those of the USERNAME and PASSWORD properties set in the *jwsnutExamples.properties* file. If you have substituted your own username and password, then you must use the same values here.

Using the Examples with a TCP Monitor Utility

It is sometimes useful to be able to see the SOAP messages that a web service client sends and receives. There are various monitoring utilities available that can be interposed between the client and the server to catch and print these messages as they are exchanged. One such utility is tcpmon, which is part of the Apache Axis distribution and can be downloaded from *http://ws.apache.org/axis*. A file in this distribution, *axis.jar*, contains the class files for tcpmon. To monitor the examples in this book using this utility, you need to select a free port on which tcpmon will listen and from which it will forward all messages to the server. Assuming you select port 5050 for tcpmon, you can start it using the following command:

```
java -classpath axis.jar org.apache.axis.utils.tcpmon 5050 localhost 8000
```

This command will display any messages sent to port 5050 and pass them on to port 8000 on localhost, which is the port on which the J2EE 1.4 reference implementation listens by default. If you are using the JWSDP, then you should forward the messages to port 8080 instead. Next, you need to ensure that the examples connect to port 5050 instead of the port assigned to the web container. To do this, edit the *jwsnutExamples.properties* file in your home directory and set either TOMCAT_WEBPORT (for the JWSDP) or J2EE_WEBPORT (for J2EE 1.4) to 5050. With these changes, you'll see all of the SOAP messages sent and received by most of the examples in this book displayed in the tcpmon window. To revert to normal operation, just reset the value of TOMCAT_WEBPORT or J2EE_WEBPORT and stop tcpmon.

Conventions Used in This Book

We use the following formatting conventions in this book:

Italic

Used for emphasis and to signify the first use of a term. Italic is also used for commands, email addresses, web sites, FTP sites, file and directory names, and newsgroups.

Bold

Occasionally used to refer to particular keys on a computer keyboard or to portions of a user interface, such as the Back button or the Options menu.

Constant Width

Used in all Java code and generally for anything that you would type literally when programming, including keywords, data types, constants, method names, variables, class names, and interface names.

Constant Width Italic

Used for the names of function arguments and generally as a placeholder to indicate an item that should be replaced with an actual value in your program.

Constant Width Bold

Used occasionally for emphasis in code.

Franklin Gothic Book Condensed

Used for the Java class synopses in the quick-reference section. This very narrow font allows us to fit a lot of information on the page without a lot of distracting line breaks. This font is also used for code entities in the descriptions in the quick-reference section.

Franklin Gothic Demi Condensed

Used for highlighting class, method, field, property, and constructor names in the quick-reference section, which makes it easier to scan the class synopses.

Franklin Gothic Book Condensed Italic

Used for method parameter names and comments in the quick-reference section.

Request for Comments

Please address comments and questions concerning this book to the publisher:

O'Reilly & Associates, Inc.
1005 Gravenstein Highway North
Sebastopol, CA 95472
(800) 998-9938 (in the United States or Canada)
(707) 829-0515 (international/local)
(707) 829-0104 (fax)

There is a web page for this book, which lists errata, examples, or any additional information. You can access this page at:

http://www.oreilly.com/catalog/javawsian

To comment or ask technical questions about this book, send email to:

bookquestions@oreilly.com

For more information about books, conferences, Resource Centers, and the O'Reilly Network, see the O'Reilly web site at:

http://www.oreilly.com

Acknowledgments

When Bob Eckstein suggested the idea of writing a book in the Nutshell series to cover the web service APIs in the Java Web Services Developer's Pack, I must admit to not having been immediately inspired by the idea. My feelings changed, however, when I saw the number of sessions devoted to this subject at the 2002 JavaOne conference in San Francisco, most of which were extremely well attended. Soon after the conference, I agreed to write the book you are now holding in your hands. My thanks for providing me with the opportunity to do so go to Bob as well as to Mike Loukides, who also had a hand in the process of persuasion that ultimately lead to me making the right decision.

When Bob moved on to other things in O'Reilly, the editorial job was taken over by Brett McLaughlin, a man known to write books at a speed that mere mortals such as I can only simultaneously disbelieve and envy. Brett had the unenviable task of making sense of the first draft of this manuscript, which was in the process of being hastily overhauled following the release of the beta version of the J2EE 1.4 reference implementation. I am extremely grateful to Brett for his comments on the technical content of the book and for working so hard to edit and push the book through its production process in time for a fixed release date that we all wanted to meet. Thanks also to Kyle Hart for the part she played in making sure the book met this very important deadline.

The production team at O'Reilly have turned some very ordinary-looking text and diagrams into a real book under considerable time pressure. My thanks go to Mary Brady as production editor and to the rest of the team, whose names you will find in the Colophon at the end of this book, for a job well done. Thanks also to David Flanagan for his help with the preparation of the API reference material and for his general advice on the content of this part of the book.

Java Web Services in a Nutshell has taken the best part of a year to produce. For various reasons, this has been one of the most difficult years of my professional career. I am grateful, as ever, for the support of my family, Berys, Andrew, and Katie, who have made the last year more bearable than it otherwise would have been. Without your support, I would not have been able to finish this book at all.

I

Introduction to the Java Web Services API

Part I is an introduction to writing web services using Java. These chapters provide enough information for you to get started using the J2EE web services APIs right away:

1

Introduction

This book is an introduction to, and a quick reference for, the Java APIs for web services as implemented in the J2EE 1.4 platform. This chapter begins with a high-level overview of web services, using a real-world example to show why you might need to create one and how it would differ from a traditional HTML-based web application. It then moves on to introduce the technologies that have been developed to enable web services and describes how those technologies have been made available to Java developers. The chapter closes by demonstrating the steps required to build a client application that can communicate with and present information from the web service interface provided by the online bookseller Amazon.com.

What Is a Web Service?

In early 2002, Sun Microsystems released the first version of their Java Web Services Developer's Pack (JWSDP). This large download contained everything that a developer needs to begin creating web services using the Java platform. When it appeared, the questions that most developers immediately asked were just exactly what is a web service and why should I be interested in finding out how to build or use one? If, at that time, you looked around the bookstores and the Internet for an answer to these questions, your conclusion would most likely have been that there was plenty of hype, promise, and marketing talk from those companies interested in promoting web services to other companies (and in particular to their Chief Technology Officers), but very little that would be of real use to hands-on developers trying to come to terms with a new technology. Even today, a full year later, it is still difficult to find a consistent definition of what constitutes a web service. The most useful definition that I have been able to find is the following, which appears in the Web Services Architecture document published by the World Wide Web Consortium (W3C), available for download from their web site at *http://www.w3.org/TR/ws-arch*:

A web service is a software system identified by a URI, whose public interfaces and bindings are defined and described using XML. Its definition can be discovered by other software systems. These systems may then interact with the Web service in a manner prescribed by its definition, using XML-based messages conveyed by Internet protocols.

In essence, then, a web service is something that provides an interface defined in terms of XML messages and that can be accessed over the Internet (or, of course, an Intranet). What about looking at some real examples of web services to see what they are actually being used for? This is where it gets a little bit harder. At the present time, there aren't many real web services deployed and available on the Internet, although it is expected that this situation will change as web service standards, in particular those related to security, are published and start being implemented over the next year or so.

A good place to look for example web services is the XMethods web site at *http://www.xmethods.com*, which describes itself as a "virtual laboratory" for developers, allowing them to showcase the ways in which web services can be used. Here, you'll find a wide range of services implemented using various technologies; for example:

- A route finder that provides an optimal route between two or more locations in the form of directions or a map
- A service that locates synonyms for a given word
- A stock quote service that provides stock prices, updated every 15 minutes
- An online dictionary
- A weather service
- A POP3 client that allows you to access your mailbox

If you go to the XMethods web site and follow a link to any of these services, you won't find yourself directly connected to the service itself. Instead, you'll be presented with a page that tells you, among other things, where to get a service definition and who to contact for further information. If you want to actually use the service, you'll need to write your own client application. Services like these are, of course, already freely available to anyone with a web browser and a connection to the Internet (or even a cell phone!). Why bother to invent a new way of delivering them, which also puts the onus on the service consumer to write or obtain the client-side software? The answer to this question goes to the very heart of the movement towards web services—the need to perform business-to-business transactions using open but secure protocols over the Internet.

Web Services and Web Applications

To see why the current web application model is not sufficient for business-to-business commerce and why it is also quite limiting when your client is a human consumer, consider the case of the online bookstore Amazon.com. Amazon.com has one of the best-known web sites on the Internet. Book buyers use its facilities to browse for and purchase books (and, these days, a wide range of other products), while publishers and authors use its sales ranking and reader reviews to get a feel for public reaction to their work. If you want to find a good Java book, all you have to do is use the site's search facilities to locate a few titles, read the reviews, and place your order. At each stage, the site sends you a page of HTML that your browser renders for you, and you respond by clicking a link or filling in a form to move to the next stage.

Although this is convenient for low-volume searches conducted by humans, it is not quite as useful if you want to extract and collate information from the site. Suppose, for example, that you are a publisher (or an author) wanting to keep track of the sales rankings of a group of books on a daily basis. To achieve this using the HTML-based interface provided by Amazon's web site, you need to bookmark the page for each book you are interested in, reload each of those pages every day, and manually extract the sales ranking and the latest customer reviews. If you are a little more technically minded, you could automate this process somewhat by writing a client application that reads the HTML and extracts the information using screen-scraping techniques.* While this is perfectly feasible, it is less than ideal, due to the following:

- Amazon.com web pages contain a lot of content. This makes them large documents—often in excess of 10 kilobytes. In reality, you need only a very small portion of the information that each of them contains.

- Screen-scraping programs, by their nature, are very reliant on the layout of the information source that they are analyzing—in this case, the HTML produced by Amazon.com's web servers. Unfortunately, web site designers have a habit of changing their page layouts from time to time, and these changes can invalidate the algorithm that your application uses to locate the small part of the information buried in the HTML markup that it actually needs.

The root cause of these problems is the use of HTML to convey data. HTML is, of course, reasonably good at the job it was designed for—combining raw data with markup that specifies how it is to be presented and links that allow related information to be obtained. If you're only looking for the sales ranking of your book, all you really want is a single number—you certainly don't need lots of additional tags that tell you how to present the information. This is exactly the kind of situation in which, if you had control over the server, you would choose to use XML rather than HTML to encapsulate the data, so that a client that is interested only in the raw content would not need to concern itself with stripping out the markup.

If you look back at the definition of a web service cited earlier in this chapter, you'll see that if Amazon.com provided a web service interface to its bookstore and exposed the appropriate information in XML form, authors and publishers would have an easier way to find out how their books are performing. In fact, in mid-2002, Amazon.com did exactly that. The Amazon.com web service is one of the few commercial web services currently available on the Internet. As well as writing private client applications to extract specific book-related information, web service developers can use this service to create their own web sites that incorporate information obtained from Amazon.com, without having to present it in the same way as it appears on the Amazon.com web site. Figure 1-1 shows an example software architecture that might be used to do this.

---

* You'll find an example that demonstrates how to write such a client for a cell phone in *J2ME in a Nutshell*, by Kim Topley (O'Reilly).

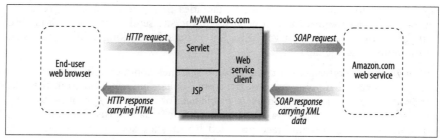

Figure 1-1. Using XML-based web services to obtain information from a web service provider

In this diagram, an end user using a web browser visits the web site of MyXML-Books.com, a fictional company that, amongst other things, is a member of the Amazon.com Associates program. This allows MyXMLBooks.com to earn royalties on sales of books made via its own web site. MyXMLBooks.com has previously used click-through links that will display Amazon.com's own web pages when the user selects a book advertised on its web site, but now wants to make use of Amazon's web service to obtain raw information and present it in a way that is more consistent with the other pages on its site. When the user selects a book from one of MyXMLBooks.com's web pages, the HTTP request generated is routed via a controlling servlet on the MyXMLBooks.com web server, which determines that it needs to retrieve raw book data from Amazon.com. The servlet obtains this data by using a web service client implemented by MyXMLBooks.com's developers. This client uses the web service interface published by Amazon.com to invoke a method on its server that returns the required information. The method invocation is performed by creating an XML message that contains the method name and any required parameters and then sending it to Amazon.com's server using the SOAP protocol, which is discussed later in this chapter. The value (or values) returned by the method call are then wrapped in another XML message and sent back to the MyXMLBooks.com's web client, which extracts the information that it needs and uses a JSP to render it as HTML. The HTML is then returned to the client's browser.[*]

Figure 1-1 represents what will probably be a fairly typical use of a web service. Notice in particular that the direct user of the web service is not a human, but a web server. In fact, this diagram shows both a Business-to-Consumer (B2C) transaction performed using HTML over HTTP, and a Business-to-Business (B2B) transaction, which is the domain of web services and uses XML-based messaging.

Once MyXMLBooks.com adopts this architecture, which separates the presentation of information from the means by which it is obtained, it is relatively simple for it to add additional features. For example, if other online booksellers begin to offer a web service interface, MyXMLBooks.com could provide a consolidated service that routes user requests to the vendor that provides the best price or

---

[*] Although this example uses a web browser as the client, it is equally possible to create a rich client (using Swing, for example) that would connect directly to the web service and present the results on the user's desktop rather than via a browser.

shortest delivery time for the items that the user wants to buy, or could query all of the available providers for their prices and delivery time commitments and then allow the user to make the choice. Although all of this could be done using screen scraping, the advantages of using a web service instead are:

- Less data will need to be transferred because the useful information does not need to be accompanied by presentation markup.
- The code required to make a request of a web service is much simpler than that required to extract data from an HTML page.
- If, in the future, a standard interface were to be defined for online booksellers, MyXMLBooks.com needs only to write a single client in order for it to be able to talk to multiple booksellers.

The SOAP Protocol

The web service definition cited earlier in this chapter stated that a web service communicates using "XML-based messages conveyed by Internet protocols." Although it is expected that there will be a choice of web service protocols in the future, at the present time, web services communicate using Simple Object Access Protocol (SOAP). SOAP is an XML-based protocol that can be carried over any transport mechanism capable of delivering a byte stream. In practice, SOAP messages are usually exchanged between clients and services that are resident in web containers and are typically encapsulated inside an HTTP request or response message. However, nothing in the SOAP 1.1 specification (which can be obtained from the W3C web site at *http://www.w3c/org/TR/SOAP**) prevents the use of other transport mechanisms, such as FTP, SMTP or even JMS; in fact, both Apache SOAP and its successor, Axis, support the use of SMTP as the carrier for SOAP messages.

A basic SOAP message consists of an envelope that may contain any number of headers plus a body. These parts are delimited by XML elements called Envelope, Header, and Body, which belong to a namespace defined by the SOAP specification. Although the specification defines rules that implementations must follow when creating the structure of a SOAP message, it says nothing about the application-dependent information that the message may contain, apart from the fact that any content conveyed within the envelope must be valid XML. Example 1-1 shows a typical SOAP message.

Example 1-1. A SOAP message

```
<env:Envelope xmlns:env="http://schemas.xmlsoap.org/soap/envelope/"
              xmlns:xsd="http://www.w3.org/2001/XMLSchema"
              xmlns:xsi="http://www.w3.org/2001/XMLSchema-instance"
              xmlns:enc="http://schemas.xmlsoap.org/soap/encoding/"
```

---

* Like most web service specifications, SOAP was originally defined by a group of cooperating businesses and has now been taken under the wing of the W3C. The next version of the SOAP specification (Version 1.2) is being produced by the W3C and can be obtained from *http://www.w3c.org*.

Example 1-1. A SOAP message (continued)

```
            xmlns:ns0=
                "urn:jwsnut.chapter6.headerbookservice/types/HeaderBookQuery"
            xmlns:ns1=
                "urn:jwsnut.chapter6.headerbookservice/wsdl/HeaderBookQuery"
            env:encodingStyle="http://schemas.xmlsoap.org/soap/encoding/">
    <env:Header>
        <ns1:auth xsi:type="ns0:Authentication">
            <UserName xsi:type="xsd:string">JWSUserName</UserName>
            <Password xsi:type="xsd:string">JWSPassword</Password>
        </ns1:auth>
    </env:Header>
    <env:Body>
        <ns1:getBookAuthor>
            <String_1 xsi:type="xsd:string">Java in a Nutshell</String_1>
            <String_2 xsi:type="xsd:string" xsi:nil="1"/>
        </ns1:getBookAuthor>
    </env:Body>
</env:Envelope>
```

As you can see, the message consists of an Envelope element that wraps both a Header element and a Body element. This particular Envelope element declares a bewildering number of XML namespaces, the meaning of which will be explained in Chapter 3, as will the rules that govern the way in which the message is constructed. In this case, the message has a single SOAP header that contains a username and a password, and a single element in the body that represents a request to the receiver to return the name of the author of the book *Java in a Nutshell*. The interpretation of the information in the header and the body is generally determined by the application itself, although in this case the body contains a remote procedure call (RPC) request that is formed according to rules laid down in the SOAP specification and was actually generated by JAX-RPC, which is the subject of the next chapter. In other cases, the body might contain an arbitrary XML document formed according to a schema that both the sender and the receiver have agreed to use. Similarly, although some SOAP headers will be standardized, others are not. In this example, the authentication information is conveyed in a very insecure way using an XML structure defined by the application itself. There is, of course, work in progress to define the standards for web service security that is standardizing the way in which information like this is carried in SOAP messages, but the results of that work are not yet visible in either J2EE 1.4 or the JWSDP.

In many cases, limiting an application to XML is too restrictive. As an example, MyXMLBooks.com might like to include book cover images on its web site. One way to achieve this is to return a URL in the SOAP message and have the client application fetch the image directly using HTTP (i.e., without involving a SOAP message). This approach is not mandatory, however, because there is an extension to the SOAP specification called SOAP with Attachments that allows a SOAP message to have associated MIME attachments that can carry any data with a recognized (or even application-private) representation. Both the SOAP and SOAP with Attachments specifications are covered in detail in Chapter 3, which also contains an example that shows how to use an attachment to return a book cover image to a web service client.

Web Service Profiles

The SOAP specification provides encoding rules for the XML data and attachments that make up an application-level message, but it leaves much in the hands of the application itself. For example, it defines a framework for placing information that might need to be processed alongside the actual message data into message headers. These headers may be directed at either the system containing the web service itself or intermediaries that the message might need to pass through en route to its destination. What it does not do, however, is specify what those headers are or what information they should contain. This flexibility is deliberate because it allows SOAP to be used at one end of the scale as the basis for a private distributed application, where the header and data content need be known only to the implementor of the application, or at the other end as a building block for more open web services, such as that provided by Amazon.com.

In the real world, it is necessary to reduce the level of flexibility available to service implementors in order to make it less likely that incompatible implementations, either of SOAP itself or of the applications it supports, are developed. For this reason, several different web service profiles have been proposed or developed. A profile consists of rules, in addition to those imposed by SOAP, that all participants in that profile agree to abide by to ensure that their implementations can interwork with each other. Three examples of such profiles follow:

The WS-Routing profile
> The WS-Routing profile (originally known as SOAP-RP) defines a set of SOAP headers that allow the specification of a route to be followed by a SOAP message as it is being sent from the client application to the server. The specification also allows a reverse path to be constructed as the message is being passed between the intermediary systems that form its output route. Since this profile is concerned only with message routing, it does not specify any standard body content.

The ebXML Transport, Routing, and Packaging profile (ebXML-TRP)
> This profile defines a message format for applications engaged in various forms of electronic business. Like WS-Routing, it includes a definition of a set of headers and prescribes their meanings. Unlike WS-Routing, it also includes a set of standard XML elements that can be included in the message body. See "The ebXML Profile" in Chapter 4 for a discussion of this profile.

The Web Services Interoperaibility (WS-I) profile
> WS-Routing and ebXML-TRP are narrow standards that confine themselves to specific aspects of SOAP messaging. Indeed, ebXML-TRP itself applies only to a particular vertical marketplace. By contrast, the WS-I profile, introduced early in 2003, is a broad profile that aims to maximize the potential for interworking across a range of applications by ensuring that the messaging systems on which they are built obey certain specific rules that cover not only SOAP, but also some of the other technologies that you'll see elsewhere in this book. The WS-I profile creates a greater probability of successful interworking by reducing the number of choices that implementors can make from the wide range allowed by individual specifications to a much smaller number—often just one. Sun Microsystems recently announced that the web services support provided by the J2EE 1.4 platform is WS-I conformant; therefore, developers using J2EE 1.4 do not need to do anything in order to comply with this specification.

Describing and Discovering Web Services

One of the clauses in the W3C definition of a web service states that its "definition can be discovered by other software systems." In order to make this possible, the web service standards include:

- A language used to define the interfaces provided by a web service, in a manner that is not dependent on the platform on which it is running or the programming language used to implement it
- A provision for a registry within which these definitions can be placed

Since all access to web services uses XML messaging, it is appropriate that the language used to describe a web service should itself be XML-based. The Web Service Description Language (WSDL) was originally defined by Microsoft, IBM, and Ariba, and is now subject to standardization by the W3C consortium. W3C recently published a draft of its official variant of WSDL (Version 1.2), which can be downloaded from its web site at *http://www.w3c.org*. At the time of this writing, however, most existing WSDL-aware software (including that provided by Sun Microsystems) is based on WSDL Version 1.1.

As you'll see in Chapter 5, WSDL describes a web service by defining the messages that it accepts and the reply messages that it returns. These messages are actually defined first in abstract terms and then bound to one or more message and transport protocols. Today, of course, web services use SOAP as the messaging protocol, and therefore almost all WSDL files will define a binding of the service to SOAP messages delivered over the HTTP protocol. WSDL is not a difficult metalanguage to learn, and it is useful to be able to glance at a WSDL file to get an overview of the interface of a service. However, you don't really need to be able to do much more than this because WSDL definitions are usually both created and consumed by software tools. As you'll see later in this chapter, once you obtain the WSDL definition of a service, the first thing to do is generate a Java interface from it that provides the same operations as the service itself. Not only is a Java interface much easier to understand than the corresponding WSDL, but you can also use the interface when writing your client application, or when creating an implementation of the service itself, if that is your assigned task.

Given that WSDL definitions are central to web services, how would you go about finding such a definition? One way to do so is to contact the service owner and ask for it. WSDL definitions are plain-text XML documents and can be readily exchanged using email or placed at a known URL for download from the Internet (most tools that consume WSDL let you specify its location either as a URL or as a file in an accessible filesystem). In many cases, however, you might not know who owns a service or even exactly what services are available. You might, for example, want to find out which organizations provide online book-selling services and then examine their service definitions to see if any of them provide the facilities that you need. To make this possible, WSDL definitions can be published in a registry. There are two major registry standards in use today, both of which can store web service information—the ebXML registry/repository and the UDDI registry. Both of these registry types, which are discussed in Chapter 7, allow the service owner to advertise service information that includes the location of a WSDL definition plus associated documentation and contact numbers that will be of use to potential consumers of the service. A registry can also contain classification information that can make services easy to find. For example, a service provider can specify that it is a bookseller operating in the United States. A potential client for a bookseller's web service based in the United States can locate all such providers by searching the registry using these specific criteria. Not surprisingly, both the ebXML and UDDI registries are themselves XML-based web services.

J2EE Web Service APIs

Java web services are one of the major new features in the J2EE 1.4 platform, which has integrated versions of some of the APIs that Sun Microsystems released as part of the Java Web Services Developer's Pack in 2002. Figure 1-2 shows the various web service APIs (represented by the shaded areas) and how they fit together.

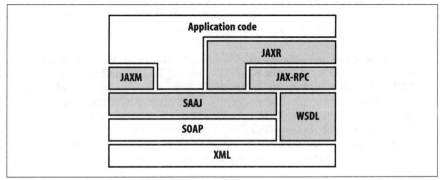

Figure 1-2. The J2EE 1.4 and JWSDP web service APIs

Working up from the bottom of the diagram, by definition, all web services depend on XML, since the messages exchanged between the service provider and the service consumer are encoded in XML. At the present time, these messages are carried using the SOAP protocol, which is itself based on XML. It is generally accepted, however, that SOAP is only the current state of the art and need not be the only web service protocol. Layered above SOAP and XML are the various web service APIs, which are summarized in the following sections:

WSDL
>As described earlier, WSDL is an XML vocabulary used to describe the interface provided by a web service. Both J2EE 1.4 and JWSDP support the use of WSDL 1.1 to specify service interfaces, but do not provide an API for application code to directly manipulate WSDL. At the time of this writing, a standard API (called JWSDL) that provides this functionality is under development by the JSR 110 expert group. See *http://jcp.org/jsr/detail/110.jsp* for details. WSDL is discussed in Chapter 5.

SAAJ

SAAJ (SOAP with Attachments API for Java) provides a direct programming interface to the SOAP protocol. If you are used to low-level protocol handling and don't mind building your own SOAP messages, then you will likely find SAAJ quite simple to use, but for most application developers it is probably not the right place to start. You'll find detailed coverage of the API in Chapter 3.

JAXM

SAAJ provides a basic SOAP messaging service, but it is lacking some features required by more advanced applications. The Java API for XML Messaging (JAXM), which is layered on top of SOAP, provides some additional functionality that many developers will find useful, including asynchronous messaging, support for the ebXML and WS-Routing profiles, and a limited facility to retransmit messages that are not successfully delivered when first sent. A reference implementation of JAXM, which is the subject of Chapter 4, is available in the JWSDP, but was not formally adopted as part of the J2EE 1.4 platform. There is, however, the possibility that some vendors will nevertheless provide JAXM support in their products.

JAX-RPC

For most developers, the Java API for XML-based RPC (JAX-RPC) is the most important web service API in the J2EE 1.4 platform (and in the JWSDP). JAX-RPC provides a relatively simple way to access web services using Java programming language constructs, thereby entirely shielding the underlying SOAP- and XML-based infrastructure from those who do not wish to see it. The JAX-RPC API is relatively small, but still manages to provide such a large number of features that it requires two chapters in this book (Chapter 2 and Chapter 6) to provide complete coverage.

JAXR

The Java API for XML-based Registries (JAXR) provides an interface to both UDDI and ebXML registries. Although this API can be used by any application, it is most likely to be of use to developers who wish to create tools that allow easy access to registries or provide custom searches. JAXR allows both the publication of information to registries and information retrieval. Full coverage of this API can be found in Chapter 7.

The most obvious omission from the suite of web service APIs included with the J2EE 1.4 platform is anything relating to security. Although the use of HTTPS is supported, this is not a complete solution for applications that have high security requirements, and there are several working groups currently engaged in the specification of security mechanisms for XML-based messaging. These efforts are being tracked by JCP expert groups and, no doubt, over the next year additional packages will be released that can be added to the J2EE 1.4 platform to incorporate these features.

An Example Web Service

Although it might appear from Figure 1-1 that there is a lot to learn before you can properly make use of web services, in practice, this is not true. Even though the technology is still relatively new, there are already tools in existence that simplify life for both the end user and the developer. To illustrate this, let's look at how you might go about the task of developing a client application for the web service provided by Amazon.com.

First of all, how would you know that Amazon.com offers a web service? One way to find out is to visit their web site. In general, though, when looking for web services, you won't know in advance all of the companies that might offer the service that you need, so you will most likely go to an electronic business registry and perform a search based on criteria such as industry sector, country of residence, etc. In Chapter 7, you'll see exactly how businesses can publish information to a registry and attach classifications to it so that you can, indeed, perform a search based on various criteria, much as you would when looking for a business in the Yellow Pages.

Figure 1-3 shows the result of performing a search for Amazon.com in a UDDI business registry, which in this case is hosted by IBM.* As it happens, Amazon.com has not applied any meaningful criteria to its entry in this registry (at least at the time of writing), so I did not find it by looking for booksellers. However, in an ideal world, this would be possible and, no doubt, for many other businesses, a search using reasonable criteria would produce the desired results. As you can see, the information on this page includes the URL of the WSDL definition of the service.

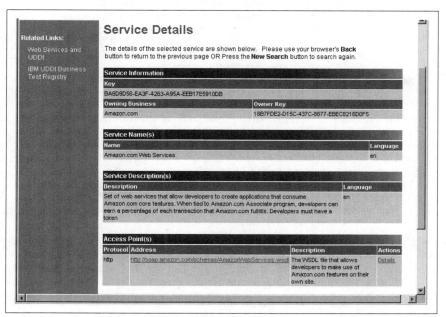

Figure 1-3. Results of looking for details of the Amazon.com web service in a UDDI registry

---

* In fact, you have to go through several steps before reaching this screen. Refer to Chapter 7 for a description of the complete process.

The WSDL definition can be downloaded using a web browser and, since it is an XML document, can be inspected to determine the details of the service interface. However, there is a simpler way. Using a tool called wscompile that is supplied with both the JWSDP and the J2EE 1.4 reference implementation, you can obtain a definition of the service in the form of a Java interface. You'll see exactly how to perform this conversion in the chapters of this book that deal with JAX-RPC. The result is shown in Example 1-2.

Example 1-2. A Java version of the Amazon.com web service interface

```
public interface AmazonSearchPort extends java.rmi.Remote {
    public ora.jwsnut.chapter1.amazon.ProductInfo keywordSearchRequest(
        ora.jwsnut.chapter1.amazon.KeywordRequest keywordSearchRequest)
            throws java.rmi.RemoteException;
    public ora.jwsnut.chapter1.amazon.ProductInfo browseNodeSearchRequest(
        ora.jwsnut.chapter1.amazon.BrowseNodeRequest browseNodeSearchRequest)
            throws java.rmi.RemoteException;
    public ora.jwsnut.chapter1.amazon.ProductInfo asinSearchRequest(
        ora.jwsnut.chapter1.amazon.AsinRequest asinSearchRequest)
            throws java.rmi.RemoteException;
    public ora.jwsnut.chapter1.amazon.ProductInfo upcSearchRequest(
            ora.jwsnut.chapter1.amazon.UpcRequest upcSearchRequest)
            throws java.rmi.RemoteException;
    public ora.jwsnut.chapter1.amazon.ProductInfo authorSearchRequest(
        ora.jwsnut.chapter1.amazon.AuthorRequest authorSearchRequest)
            throws java.rmi.RemoteException;
    public ora.jwsnut.chapter1.amazon.ProductInfo artistSearchRequest(
        ora.jwsnut.chapter1.amazon.ArtistRequest artistSearchRequest)
            throws java.rmi.RemoteException;
    public ora.jwsnut.chapter1.amazon.ProductInfo actorSearchRequest(
        ora.jwsnut.chapter1.amazon.ActorRequest actorSearchRequest)
            throws java.rmi.RemoteException;
    public ora.jwsnut.chapter1.amazon.ProductInfo manufacturerSearchRequest(
        ora.jwsnut.chapter1.amazon.ManufacturerRequest
            manufacturerSearchRequest) throws java.rmi.RemoteException;
    public ora.jwsnut.chapter1.amazon.ProductInfo directorSearchRequest(
        ora.jwsnut.chapter1.amazon.DirectorRequest directorSearchRequest)
            throws java.rmi.RemoteException;
    public ora.jwsnut.chapter1.amazon.ProductInfo listManiaSearchRequest(
        ora.jwsnut.chapter1.amazon.ListManiaRequest listManiaSearchRequest)
            throws java.rmi.RemoteException;
    public ora.jwsnut.chapter1.amazon.ProductInfo similaritySearchRequest(
        ora.jwsnut.chapter1.amazon.SimilarityRequest similaritySearchRequest)
            throws java.rmi.RemoteException;
}
```

The Java interface is much easier to understand than the WSDL version, which you'll find in the file *chapter1\amazon\AmazonWebService.wsdl* relative to the installation directory of the example source code for this book. The interface uses several classes, such as asinSearchRequest, which are passed to the methods that represent the web service operations, to supply the criteria for a product search. Each of these methods returns a ProductInfo object that contains the results of the search. These classes are all defined, in XML terms, in the WSDL document and are converted to Java form by the wscompile utility.

Given the interface definition in readable and compilable form, it only remains to write an application to use it. At this point, you would probably be looking for some documentation that would tell you what the method parameters mean, what each method does, and how to interpret the results. Usually, a company would publish a link to relevant documentation along with the service entry in the registry. It so happens that, at least when I looked, Amazon.com had not done this. You can, however, obtain documentation from the Amazon.com web site, where you will also discover that you need to obtain a "developer token" to make use of the service.

The example source code for this book contains a simple GUI application that uses the Amazon.com web service by collecting search parameters from the user, and using authorSearchRequest( ), asinSearchRequest( ), and keywordSearchRequest( ) to perform the search. If you look at the source code for this example, which you'll find in the directory *chapter1\amazon\client\ora\jwsnut\chapter1\client*, you'll see that almost all of it is concerned with managing the user interface. In fact, only three lines of code are required to set up the JAX-RPC library in preparation for a call to be made to the service:

```
AmazonSearchService service = new AmazonSearchService_Impl( );
amazonSearch = service.getAmazonSearchPort( );
((Stub)amazonSearch)._setProperty(Stub.ENDPOINT_ADDRESS_PROPERTY, address);
```

What is convenient about JAX-RPC is that all of the classes required by the client application are generated for you from the WSDL. All you have to do is supply the service address, which can also be found in the WSDL file:[*]

```
<!-- Endpoint for Amazon Web APIs -->
<service name="AmazonSearchService">
    <port name="AmazonSearchPort" binding="typens:AmazonSearchBinding">
        <soap:address location="http://soap.amazon.com/onca/soap"/>
    </port>
</service>
```

Actually calling the web service and obtaining the results requires the construction of a SOAP message containing the query parameters, transmitting it, receiving the response message, and converting it back from XML to Java objects. If you were to code this using the low-level SAAJ API, you would probably end up with a couple of pages of code. However, JAX-RPC reduces this to something much simpler. Here, for example, is how you might perform a search for a book based on author name:

```
AuthorRequest authorReq = new AuthorRequest(newKey, String.valueOf(page),
MODE, WEBSERVICE, TYPE, devtag, VERSION);
result = amazonSearch.authorSearchRequest(authorReq);
```

At the moment, it's not necessary to worry about what all of the method arguments mean. The important point is that obtaining information from a web service is no more complex in programming terms than making a local method

---

[*] Although this code explicitly supplies the web service address, you'll see in Chapter 6 that you can also create JAX-RPC applications that obtain the service address directly from the WSDL document.

call. The tools provided by JAX-RPC handle the details of parsing the service's WSDL definition, and the use of SOAP and XML to encode the content of the message ensures that you don't need to be concerned about either the nature of the platform on which the service itself is running or the programming language used to implement it.

You can try out the Amazon web service for yourself by obtaining a developer tag from the Amazon.com web site, including it in the *jwsnutExamples.properties* file in your home directory as the value of the AMAZON_TAG property, making *chapter1\ amazon* your working directory, and typing the following commands:

```
ant compile
ant run-client
```

The user interface that appears allows you to choose a search based on Author, Keyword, or ISBN, and a search string of your choice. To start the search, press the Go button. The books (up to 10 of them) that match your search criterion appear in the form of a list. If you select an entry from this list, the sales ranking for that book, together with any available customer reviews, appears, as shown in Figure 1-4.

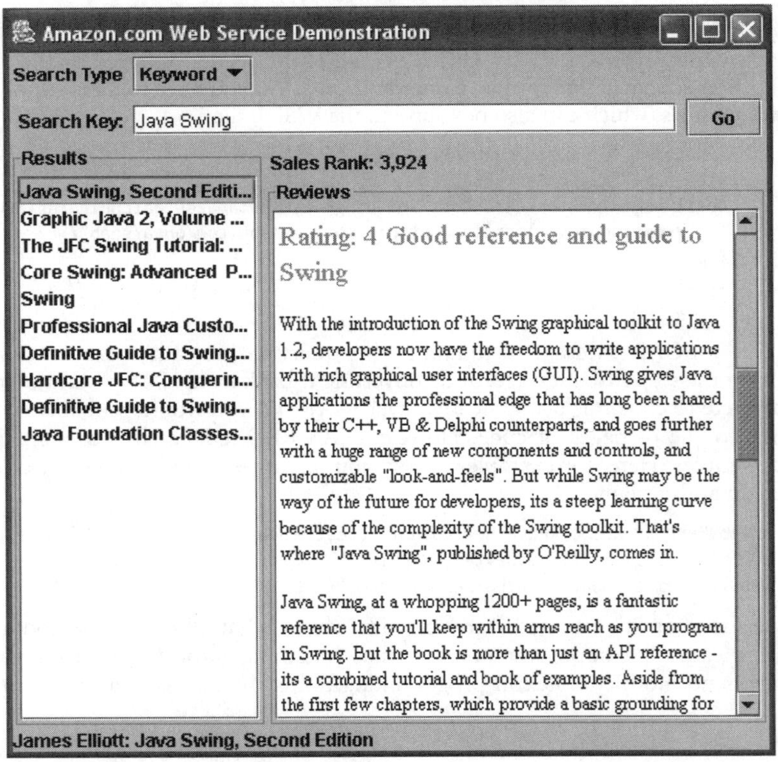

Figure 1-4. The results of a book search using the Amazon web service

The Amazon.com web service is one of a small but growing number of commercial web services that are now becoming available on the Internet. At the moment, many of these services are more experimental than serious, and there are still minor interoperability issues between SOAP implementations from different vendors. It is likely that real business transactions over the Internet using web services will not take place in any volume until the security features are fully defined, implemented, and deployed. However, as you'll see in the rest of this book, there is already a lot of functionality available for use and for developers to become familiar with.

2

JAX-RPC

The *Java API for XML-based RPC* (JAX-RPC) is designed to provide a simple way to create remote procedure call–based web services in which either the client or the server (or both) run on the Java platform without requiring the developer to be aware of the way that the SOAP messages that carry the procedure call request and response are encoded. Because JAX-RPC is based around remote procedure calls, the programming model will be very familiar to Java developers who have used RMI or CORBA.

In order to use the more powerful features of JAX-RPC, you need to have some understanding both of SOAP and of WSDL, an XML-based language that describes the interface to a web service. These topics are covered in Chapter 3 and Chapter 5, respectively. However, you don't need to know anything about either of them in order to become a JAX-RPC programmer. This chapter provides a straightforward introduction to JAX-RPC by demonstrating how to create and deploy a simple JAX-RPC web service and a client application that calls it, using familiar-looking Java code and only a very small amount of XML. The more advanced features of JAX-RPC will be covered in detail in Chapter 6, once the details of SOAP and WSDL are explained.

The JAX-RPC specification was developed under the Java Community Process as JSR 101 and is available for download from *http://jcp.org/jsr/detail/101.jsp*.

JAX-RPC Overview

JAX-RPC was designed to provide a simple way for developers to create web services and web service clients using techniques that are not very different from those used in nondistributed Java programming. Programming with JAX-RPC is very similar to using RMI to create a distributed application, in the sense that client code appears to be making ordinary method calls on local objects. In reality, however, the infrastructure handles these calls by converting them to messages that are sent over a network to the server, where they cause a local call to be made on the actual method implementation. The results of this call are used to create a reply message that is sent back the client, where they are extracted and presented as return values from the client application's method call.

Although there are similarities between RMI and JAX-RPC, the major difference arises from the fact that the messages exchanged between JAX-RPC clients and services are encoded using an XML-based protocol and can potentially be carried by a range of transport-level protocols, including HTTP (or its more secure variant HTTPS), SMTP, or even FTP. JAX-RPC allows a client written in the Java programming language to access a service implemented on, for example, the Microsoft .NET platform, whereas RMI clients and servers must both be written in Java (although it is possible to expose an RMI/CORBA hybrid service written in any language that has a binding to CORBA IIOP). In other words, it can communicate with foreign services without needing to be aware of the technology that its peer is actually using.

One of the benefits of using JAX-RPC over a lower-level web services technology such as SAAJ or JAXM (both of which will be covered later in this book) is that it doesn't require you to know much about XML before you can start building a distributed application. This is because, with a few exceptions that fall into the advanced category, the programming interfaces are completely independent of both the underlying messaging infrastructure and the transport protocol that is used to carry the XML messages. The JAX-RPC specification requires every implementation to support at least the use of SOAP over HTTP 1.1, but, as a developer, you can use JAX-RPC without having to be an expert in XML, SOAP, or HTTP. On the other hand, if these technologies are more than acronyms to you, as you'll see in Chapter 6, it is possible to use some of the more advanced JAX-RPC features to gain access to the lower levels. Here, you can directly handle SOAP headers or extend the set of data types that the client and server can exchange beyond those supported transparently by JAX-RPC.

The JAX-RPC Programming Model

This section introduces the JAX-RPC API by examining its programming model. At first, some of the concepts described here may seem a little abstract, especially if you are not familiar with another distributed programming technology, such as CORBA or RMI. In order to make things a little clearer, the following section will illustrate these concepts by relating them to a simple example.

Services, ports, and bindings

JAX-RPC uses web services terminology to describe some of its concepts. The meaning of some of these terms is represented in a diagram in Figure 2-1. A *web service* consists of a *service endpoint interface* (which is often referred to simply as an endpoint) that defines one or more operations that the web service offers. In order to promote portability and independence from the underlying communications mechanisms, web services are thought of as entities in their own right, separate from the protocol stacks used to gain access to them. Access to an endpoint is provided by *binding* it to a protocol stack through a *port,* which has an address that a client can use to communicate with it and invoke its operations.*

Since the JAX-RPC specification requires that all implementations support the use of SOAP 1.1 messaging over HTTP 1.1 as the underlying transport protocol, the most common binding uses SOAP and HTTP, as shown in Figure 2-1. Bindings to other messaging systems and protocols are neither required nor precluded by the specification. In Figure 2-1, for example, port 1 provides access to the web service through a SOAP 1.1/HTTP protocol stack, port 2 uses SOAP 1.1 over HTTPS,† and port 3 exposes the same endpoint via a different (unspecified) protocol and messaging system.

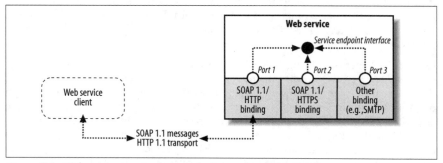

Figure 2-1. Web service terminology: endpoint, port, and binding

The nature of a port address depends partly on the protocol to which the endpoint is bound and partly on the JAX-RPC implementation. We'll see how the JAX-RPC reference implementation handles port addressing later in this chapter. In the case of an HTTP or HTTPS binding, port addresses are based on URLs. It is important to note that when you implement a web service using JAX-RPC, (provided that you don't use some of the more advanced features described in Chapter 6) your code will be independent of both the port address and the binding used by the client to access it, and therefore will not contain any SOAP- or HTTP-specific details.

JAX-RPC web service clients and servers

In terms of Java programming, JAX-RPC maps a web service operation to a Java method call and maps a service endpoint to a Java interface. One way to begin the implementation of a web service with JAX-RPC, therefore, is to create a Java interface that contains a method for each operation that the service will provide, along with a class that implements that interface. There are certain rules that need to be followed when defining both the interface and the methods that it contains. As we'll see in Chapter 6, JAX-RPC also allows you to import the definition of an

---

* The terms introduced in this section are based on those used by the Web Service Description Language (WSDL), which is covered in detail in Chapter 5.

† Support for HTTPS is not required by the JAX-RPC specification, but very often is required by real-world operation; it is included in the JAX-RPC reference implementation.

existing web service in the form of a WSDL document and then generate from it the corresponding Java interface definition, in order to create either your own implementation of the service itself or a client that will use the service.

In a nondistributed programming environment, method calls are handled entirely by the Java virtual machine. For example, suppose you were to create a simple class like the one shown in Example 2-1, and another one that uses it, as shown in Example 2-2.

Example 2-1. A simple "service"

```
import java.util.Date;

public class DateService {
    public Date getDate( ) {
        return new Date( );
    }
}
```

Example 2-2. A simple "client"

```
import java.util.Date;

public class Test {
    public static void main(String[] args) {
        DateService  instance = new DateService( );
        Date date = instance.getDate( );
        System.out.println("The date is " + date);
    }
}
```

If you were to run the main( ) method of the class shown in Example 2-2, the getDate( ) method would be invoked directly within the same Java virtual machine as the main( ) method. In a distributed environment, however, the service implementation—that is, the DateService class and its getDate( ) method— would reside in a different Java virtual machine (and usually a different physical host) than the service client, which is the main( ) method in the Test class in this case. In these circumstances, the getDate( ) method call could not be dispatched directly by the client's virtual machine. Instead, a layer of software must be used to convey the method call from the client program to the server, carrying with it any arguments provided by the method caller (although in this case there are none) and returning the method call result (the Date object) to the client. This layer of software is provided by the JAX-RPC runtime system, as shown in Figure 2-2, in which the client application represents the Test class and the service implementation is the DateService class.

Although Figure 2-2 implies that the JAX-RPC runtime system is present on both the client and server systems, this will not always be the case. JAX-RPC supports interoperation with other XML-based RPC implementations, provided that they implement the SOAP 1.1 messaging protocol and use the same transport layer binding. The following list describes the supported software combinations.

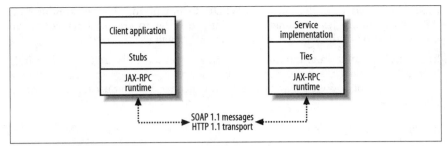

Figure 2-2. Clients, services, and the JAX-RPC runtime system

- JAX-RPC client implementation connecting to a JAX-RPC service implementation, as shown in Figure 2-2
- JAX-RPC client implementation connecting to a third-party SOAP 1.1–based RPC product, as shown in Figure 2-3
- Third-party SOAP 1.1-based RPC client implementation connecting to a JAX-RPC service implementation, as shown in Figure 2-4

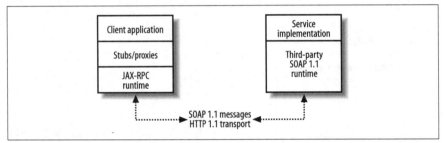

Figure 2-3. JAX-RPC client interoperability with services implemented using a third-party product

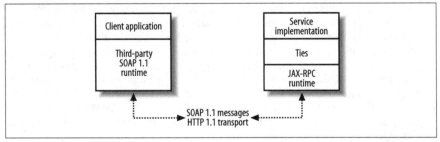

Figure 2-4. JAX-RPC service interoperability with a client implemented using a third-party product

At the time of this writing, there are several SOAP 1.1 development environments available in addition to JAX-RPC, including Apache SOAP, Apache Axis, and GLUE, which are all Java-based, and SOAP::Lite for Perl developers. Perhaps most significantly, however, the Microsoft Visual Studio .NET development environment makes the creation of SOAP-based web services and web service clients for the Microsoft .NET platform relatively simple. As a result, web services created with JAX-RPC are easily accessible to clients written in Visual Basic or C# and running on .NET and vice versa.

JAX-RPC service creation

As a developer, you may find yourself in one of several possible roles when working with web services:

1. Creating a web service together with the corresponding client or clients for in-house use
2. Creating a web service to be made available locally or on the Internet
3. Creating a client for an existing web service implemented by somebody else, possibly in a different organization

In the first case, where you will develop both the service and the client software that will be used to access it, it may be possible to use JAX-RPC on both the client and server systems. In the second case, the service itself may be implemented using JAX-RPC, but the clients, developed by other groups within your company or by users in other companies, could be built on the .NET platform or using a different Java SOAP implementation. Finally, in the third case, a client for an existing web service can be written using JAX-RPC, provided that the service is RPC-based and uses only data types that JAX-RPC can support or for which you can write extensions.*

In all three cases, there needs to be a definition of the web service that describes the operations that it provides and the data types that they require as arguments and provide as return values. In addition, but of less interest in this chapter, it is necessary to define how the information that moves between the client and the server when operations are performed is mapped onto the protocols to which the JAX-RPC (or third party) implementation is bound—that is, how the SOAP 1.1 messages that are exchanged are to be constructed. Service definitions that contain all of this information are typically made available as a document written using the *Web Service Description Language* (WSDL), which is covered in Chapter 5.

From the client developer's point of view, having a WSDL description of someone else's service to work with is useful even if you don't know very much about WSDL, because JAX-RPC can read such a document and generate from it the Java code required to link your client code to the service, leaving you to write only the business logic of the client application itself. Since WSDL is a standardized language based on XML, JAX-RPC can do this for any web service, whether it was originally implemented using JAX-RPC, on the .NET platform, or in any other way. If you'd like to know what a WSDL document looks like, flip forward to the

---

* In order to support new data types, you need to write a custom serializer that knows how to convert between the data type and a corresponding XML representation. At the time of this writing, the JAX-RPC specification does not provide a framework for writing serializers that are portable between JAX-RPC implementations, and the API used by the reference implementation to create them is, therefore, not part of the specification. Consequently, you should consider creating custom serializers only if there is no other choice.

Appendix at the back of this book, which contains a couple of representative examples.

For the benefit of the server developer, having defined your service as a Java interface, you can avoid the tedious task of manually creating the corresponding WSDL document by using a tool provided by JAX-RPC. Once the WSDL is created, it is typically advertised at a well-known URL or in a registry so that client implementors can find and import it. WSDL file publication and discovery can be handled using facilities provided by another J2EE technology called the Java API for XML Registries (JAXR), which is described in Chapter 7.

JAX-RPC client and server programming environments

JAX-RPC supports the creation of clients that are implemented either as freestanding J2SE applications, as J2EE client applications (that is, applications that operate within the J2EE client container), or within a web or EJB container. A freestanding JAX-RPC client application is typically a rich GUI client implemented with Swing or AWT, while a container-based client might be embedded in a servlet or an Enterprise JavaBean (EJB) that is part of a J2EE-hosted web application. In the future, support will be provided for freestanding JAX-RPC clients on small devices that host the Java 2 Micro Edition (J2ME) platform.

On the server side, the JAX-RPC specification envisages that a JAX-RPC service will be implemented as either a servlet or an EJB, although the specification itself covers only the programming model for a service hosted by a servlet. In support of this, the JAX-RPC reference implementation provides a servlet that can be used to direct SOAP messages received over an HTTP transport to the actual web service implementation. The details of this mechanism will be covered later in this chapter. The implementation of a JAX-RPC service within an EJB is outside of the scope of the JAX-RPC specification itself. However, support for EJB-hosted web services is an integral part of the J2EE 1.4 platform and is discussed later in this chapter. For the most part, however, you don't need to care too much about which environment your service is running in, since most of the details are the same in both cases.

The classes that form the JAX-RPC API—many of which are available to both client- and server-side code—are distributed over the small set of packages listed in Table 2-1.

Table 2-1. Packages in the JAX-RPC API

Package name	Description
javax.xml.rpc	Core classes that provide the client-side programming model.
javax.xml.rpc.encoding	Classes that perform the conversion of Java primitives and other supported data types to and from the XML representation used in SOAP messages.
javax.xml.rpc.handler javax.xml.rpc.handler.soap	Classes that process the XML messages sent and received during request and response handling. Developers can create custom handlers that may be invoked during message processing on both the client and server sides to perform specialized tasks such as data encryption or other security services. Creation of message handlers requires an understanding of SOAP. This is covered in Chapter 6.

Table 2-1. Packages in the JAX-RPC API (continued)

Package name	Description
javax.xml.rpc.holders	Classes that support the use of output or input-output parameters in JAX-RPC method calls. Since Java does not directly support the notion of parameters whose value can be changed as the result of a method call (i.e., parameters that have call-by-reference semantics), these classes can be used to wrap the actual parameters in order to provide that capability.
javax.xml.rpc.server	This package contains the minimal API (only two interfaces) provided by JAX-RPC for the use of web service implementation classes.
javax.xml.rpc.soap	This package contains the JAX-RPC classes that are specific to the SOAP binding of the JAX-RPC API. At the time of this writing, it consists of a single exception class (SOAPFaultException).

Stubs and ties

When a JAX-RPC client invokes an operation provided by a web service, the method that it calls is not the one that will actually perform the operation, since, as shown in Figure 2-2, the service implementation does not reside in the same Java virtual machine as the client. Instead, the client-side JAX-RPC runtime converts the call into a message that is sent to the server-side JAX-RPC runtime to be dispatched to the actual service class method implementation. For simplicity, however, it is desirable for the client code to look as similar as possible to that shown in Example 2-2, even though it cannot directly invoke a method on the actual implementation class.

To make this possible, JAX-RPC provides a *stub* object that has the same methods as the service implementation class.* The client application is linked with the stub and invokes a stub method, which is then delegated to the client-side JAX-RPC runtime so that the appropriate SOAP message can be sent to the server. When the method call is completed on the server, the result is sent back to the client-side JAX-RPC runtime and then forwarded to the client stub, which returns it as the result of the client application's method call. Figure 2-2 shows where stubs reside in the client-side JAX-RPC implementation.

Similarly, on the server side, the message received as a result of a client's method call must be converted into a method call on the actual service implementation. This functionality is provided by another piece of glue software, called a *tie*, that knows how to extract the method name and parameters from an incoming SOAP 1.1 message and use them to invoke the required service method. The tie also converts the result of the method call back into a response message to be returned to the client JAX-RPC runtime system.

Since the stub and tie classes have to be able to handle the same methods as the service endpoint that the client wishes to use, they depend on the definition of the service endpoint created by the web service developer. They also need to be coded to use the underlying JAX-RPC runtime to create, send, and receive SOAP 1.1 messages. Fortunately, the developer does not have to write these classes— instead, JAX-RPC implementations are required to provide tools that generate

---

* If you are familiar with CORBA or RMI programming, you'll recognize that the same stub and tie programming model is being used here.

them. The details of this process are not part of the JAX-RPC specification; therefore, vendors are free to implement this functionality in any way that they see fit. As you'll see shortly, the JAX-RPC reference implementation includes command-line programs that can be used to create stubs and ties from either a WSDL document or a Java interface definition. Other vendors might include this functionality as part of an integrated development environment (IDE), and generate the stub and tie classes automatically as part of the normal process of running an application or deploying a service from within the IDE.

Client invocation modes

JAX-RPC provides two different modes of operation that client applications may use when invoking service methods. The first and most familiar mode is *synchronous request-response*, illustrated in Figure 2-5. This mode works exactly like an ordinary Java method call, in that once the client has invoked the method, it blocks until the service performs the requested operation and either returns the results or throws an exception. In terms of message exchanges, once the client JAX-RPC runtime has generated and sent the request message, it waits for its counterpart on the server-side to return a response message and then delivers the results to the client application.

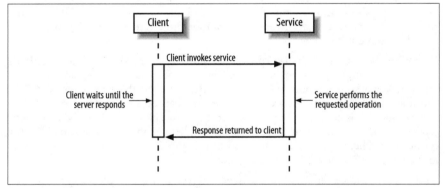

Figure 2-5. Synchronous method invocation

JAX-RPC also supports a less coupled mode of operation referred to as a *one-way RPC*. In this mode, shown in Figure 2-6, the client does not expect a reply from the service and therefore does not block after the request has been sent. Note that a one-way RPC is *not* represented by the following style of Java method call:

```
public void request(int arg1, int arg2);
```

Even though a method defined in this way does not return a value to the caller, if it appeared in a web service interface definition, it would actually be mapped to a synchronous request-response RPC and not a one-way RPC. A response from the server is required even though the method return type is void because, even though it would not contain a return value, it might still need to indicate that an exception should be thrown to the client. A one-way RPC, by contrast, cannot result in an exception being thrown from the service implementation and therefore cannot report an error condition to the initiating client.

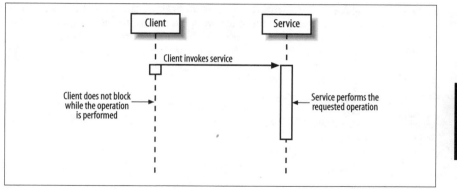

Figure 2-6. One-way RPC invocation

There is no Java method call syntax that correctly reflects the semantics of a one-way RPC call. For this reason, client stubs support only the synchronous request-response mode. In order to make a one-way RPC call, an application has to bypass the stubs and make a Dynamic Invocation Interface (DII) call. DII calls are discussed in Chapter 6.

A Simple JAX-RPC Example

Now that you've seen the basic concepts of JAX-RPC, it's time to see how it works in practice by looking at a simple example that shows how to define a web service endpoint, deploy the server implementation, and, finally, invoke it from a client application. In this section, we're not going to look in much detail at the JAX-RPC API itself or the code that implements either the client or the service—instead, the focus is on demonstrating how to use the JAX-RPC reference implementation to quickly create a web service from scratch. The details will be covered later in the chapter.

Defining the service interface

Since WSDL is the universally understood language for describing web services, the JAX-RPC specification requires all implementations to provide a mechanism to convert a WSDL document into the corresponding Java interface definition, together with the stubs and ties that allow you to implement the service itself and client applications that will invoke it. From a developer's viewpoint, though, having to create a WSDL definition of a new web service as the first step is far from convenient. Fortunately, although it is not mandatory, the specification also allows implementations to support other ways of specifying a web service. As already mentioned, the JAX-RPC reference implementation accepts service definitions in the form of class files that contain compiled Java interfaces. From these class files, it creates not only the stubs and ties, but also a WSDL file that represents the web service. This is convenient because it means that you don't need to learn to write WSDL documents before you can get started writing web services.

We'll use this approach to demonstrate the steps necessary to create a simple web service that provides information about books. Given the title of a book, the service can return specific attributes such as its price or the name of its author. It also provides a way to get a listing of all available books, together with full information for each of them. A Java interface that represents the service endpoint interface definition for the book web service is shown in Example 2-3.

Example 2-3. The BookQuery interface

```
package ora.jwsnut.chapter2.bookservice;

import java.util.HashMap;
import java.rmi.Remote;
import java.rmi.RemoteException;

/**
 * The interface definition for the book
 * web service.
 */
public interfaceBookQuery extends Remote {
    // Gets the number of books known to the service
    public abstract int getBookCount() throws RemoteException;

    // Gets the author of a book given its title
    public abstract String getAuthor(String name) throws RemoteException;

    // Gets the editor of a book given its title
    public abstract String getEditor(String name) throws RemoteException;

    // Gets the price of a book given its title
    public abstract double getPrice(String name) throws BookServiceException,
                                                         RemoteException;

    // Gets information for  all books known to the service in
    // the form of an array
    public abstract BookInfo[] getBookInfo() throws RemoteException;

    // Gets information for all books in the form of a HashMap in which the key
    // is the book's title in upper case and the value is a BookInfo object
    public abstract HashMap getBookMap() throws RemoteException;
}
```

The first point to notice about this definition is that the interface extends java. rmi.Remote. This is a requirement of all JAX-RPC service endpoint interface definitions. The second important point is that every method in the interface is defined to throw a java.rmi.RemoteException. This is also a mandatory requirement and it allows the JAX-RPC runtime to use this exception to report communication problems that might occur during the exchange of SOAP messages required to complete a method call.

Aside from these requirements, the methods are declared in the same way as they would be if they were intended to be implemented by a class in the local Java virtual machine. As you'll see later, there are some restrictions on the types of arguments that can be used and on the values that can be returned. In this case, most of the methods use only Java primitive types and Strings. The getBookInfo( ) and getBookMap( ) methods, however, are slightly different.

The getBookMap( ) method returns all of the books that the service knows about in the form of a HashMap. Here, we are using an extension that is part of the JAX-RPC reference implementation, because support for Java collections as method arguments and return values is not required by the JAX-RPC specification.

The getBookInfo( ) method is defined to return an array of objects of type BookInfo, a simple class that is part of the web service interface definition. JAX-RPC supports the use of certain types of developer-defined Java objects, both as method parameters and return values, provided they meet certain simple criteria that are discussed later. If you need to use an object of a type that does not meet these criteria, you need to write a custom serializer, which is a nontrivial task that is not supported in a portable manner at the present time.

The definition of the BookInfo class is shown in Example 2-4.

Example 2-4. The BookInfo class

```
package ora.jwsnut.chapter2.bookservice;

/**
 * A class that holds information relating
 * to a book known to the book web service.
 */
public class BookInfo {

    private String title;
    private String author;
    private String editor;
    private double price;

    // Constructs an uninitialized BookInfo object.
    public BookInfo( ) {
    }

    // Constructs a BookInfo object initialized with given attributes.
    public BookInfo(String title, String author, String editor, double price) {
        this.title = title;
        this.author = author;
        this.editor = editor;
        this.price = price;
    }

    // Gets the title of the book
    public String getTitle( ) {
        return title;
    }

    // Gets the author of the book
    public String getAuthor( ) {
        return author;
    }

    // Gets the name of the editor the book
```

Example 2-4. The BookInfo class (continued)

```
    public String getEditor( ) {
        return editor;
    }

    // Gets the price of the book in USD
    public double getPrice( ) {
        return price;
    }

    // Sets the title of the book
    public void setTitle(String title) {
        this.title = title;
    }

    // Sets the author of the book
    public void setAuthor(String author) {
        this.author = author;
    }

    // Sets the name of the editor the book
    public void setEditor(String editor) {
        this.editor = editor;
    }

    // Sets the price of the book in USD
    public void setPrice(double price) {
        this.price = price;
    }
}
```

This class is simply a holder for information returned from the web service to its clients. Aside from providing methods to set and retrieve its attributes, it has no useful behavior. To use a term that is familiar to J2EE developers, this is an example of a *value type*. Value types are one of the types of method arguments and return values that JAX-RPC supports.

Since the client application is not expected to modify the content of a `BookInfo` object, it seems inappropriate to incorporate public methods such as `setAuthor( )` that seem to encourage this behavior. Unfortunately, for reasons that we'll cover later, JAX-RPC requires you to declare these public mutator methods, or make the attributes themselves public, which is an even worse alternative.

Notice that, in addition to `RemoteException`, the `getPrice( )` method of the `BookQuery` interface shown in Example 2-3 is declared to throw a `BookServiceException`. JAX-RPC allows methods to throw service-specific exceptions that are derived from `java.lang.Exception`, but not errors (i.e., subclasses of `java.lang.Error`). In this case, `BookServiceException` is derived directly from `java.lang.Exception`, as shown in Example 2-5.

Example 2-5. A JAX-RPC service-specific exception

```
package ora.jwsnut.chapter2.bookservice;

/**
 * A service-specific exception that reports
 * problems while executing methods of the book
 * web service
 */
public class BookServiceException extends Exception {

    // Constructs a BookServiceException with an associated message
    public BookServiceException(String message) {
        super(message);
    }

    // Gets the message associated with this exception
    public String getMessage( ) {
        return super.getMessage( );
    }
}
```

Notice that this exception class defines a getMessage( ) method that returns the message set in the constructor, even though a method with the same name and signature is inherited from its superclass. If this were not done, a BookServiceException thrown by the service implementation would not be translated to a BookServiceException on the client side. The exact conditions that must be met when defining an exception class in order for the exception to be properly reported to a client application are:

- Each parameter supplied to the constructor must have a corresponding accessor method defined in the exception class itself (and *not* inherited from its superclass). This condition requires BookServiceException not only to have a getMessage( ) method, but to provide it for itself rather than rely on the one inherited from java.lang.Exception.

- Each accessor method must have a corresponding parameter in the constructor.

- The parameter type of each argument of the constructor must match that of the return type of its accessor method. In this case, both are of type String.

- There must be only one accessor method with a given return type. This means that BookServiceException could not define another accessor method that would return a String.

If any of these conditions is not met, then a SOAPFaultException will be thrown in the client instead of the application-specific exception thrown by the service.

You have now seen all of the source code that makes up the definition of the book web service. There are a couple of points to note about this code:

- Although we created an interface that contains the operations provided by the service, you haven't yet seen anything that ties this interface into the web service itself. As you'll see in Chapter 4, when a web service is defined in a WSDL file, the association between the service and the operations that it provides is obvious because of the structure of the XML. When you start with a Java interface, however, the mechanism used to link the service to the interface is implementation-dependent. For this purpose, the reference implementation uses a separate XML configuration file that you'll see when we take a closer look at this example later in this chapter in "Converting the Service Interface Definition to Client-Side Stubs."

- Both of the classes that make up the definition of the web service have been declared to be in the package ora.jwsnut.chapter2.bookservice. Later in this chapter, you'll see a recommended source code structure that clearly separates the files that represent the interface definition from those that make up the service implementation and the code for the application client. Neither the JAX-RPC specification nor the reference implementation requires a particular source code structure or package organization, but it is a good idea to keep related pieces together (and separate from other pieces) for the sake of clarity.

Implementing the service

Having defined the service endpoint interfaces, the next step is to write the code for the service itself. The service implementation can be spread over as many classes as you like, provided that there is at least one class, usually referred to as a *servant*, that meets the following conditions:

- It must have a public, no-argument constructor.
- It must implement the methods of the service endpoint interface.

 The JAX-RPC specification requires not only that the servant provide implementations of the methods defined in the service interface, but also that it declares, using the Java implements keyword, that it implements that interface. However, the J2EE Web Services specification (JSR 109) relaxes this requirement, making it optional for the servant class to make this declaration, subject to the proviso that if it chooses not to, then the methods themselves must not be final. At the time of this writing, the JWSDP imposes the requirement of the JAX-RPC specification and therefore, for the sake of compatibilty, the servant classes for all of the examples in this book declare that they implement the service endpoint interface. J2EE 1.4 follows JSR 109 and does not insist on this declaration.

Provided you follow these rules, there is nothing special about writing a JAX-RPC servant class. In fact, apart from a couple of interfaces defined in the javax.xml.rpc.server package that allow a servlet-based servant to interface to the servlet container within which it is running, there is no server-side JAX-RPC API. These interfaces will be covered in Chapter 6.

The JAX-RPC specification does not specify how the methods of the servant class are invoked in response to a method call made by an application client. For services that are hosted in a web container, the reference implementation provides a servlet that uses the tie classes to extract the method arguments from a call message, invokes the appropriate servant method, and then builds the reply message. A similar arrangement is provided for EJB-hosted web services. Since these details are all handled by the JAX-RPC runtime, you don't need to concern yourself with them when creating the service implementation.

The implementation of the book web service consists of two Java classes and a text file that contains the list of books that the service knows about, together with the information to be provided in the BookInfo objects for each book. Since much of the code is concerned with reading the text file and building the book list, I'm not going to include all of it here. If you download the example source code and install it as described in the section "Examples Online" in the Preface, you'll find all of the code for these classes in the folder *chapter2\bookservice\server\ora\ jwsnut\chapter2\bookservice*. The code for the servant class, BookServiceServant, which actually implements the service endpoint interface, is shown in Example 2-6.

Example 2-6. Implementation of the book web service

```
package ora.jwsnut.chapter2.bookservice;
import java.util.HashMap;

/**
 * Implementation class for the book web service
 */
public class BookServiceServant implements BookQuery {

    public int getBookCount( ) {
        return BookServiceServantData.getBookInfo( ).length;
    }

    public String getAuthor(String name) {
        BookInfo book = findBook(name);
        return book == null ? null : book.getAuthor( );
    }

    public String getEditor(String name) {
        BookInfo book = findBook(name);
        return book == null ? null : book.getEditor( );
    }

    public double getPrice(String name) throws BookServiceException {
        BookInfo book = findBook(name);
        if (book == null) {
            // No such book - throw an exception
            throw new BookServiceException("No matching book for '" +
                name + "'");
        }
        return book.getPrice( );
    }

    public BookInfo[] getBookInfo( ) {
        return BookServiceServantData.getBookInfo( );
    }
```

Example 2-6. Implementation of the book web service (continued)

```
    public HashMap getBookMap( ) {
        return BookServiceServantData.getBookInfoHashMap( );
    }

    /* -- Implementation details -- */
    private BookInfo findBook(String name) {
        BookInfo[] books = BookServiceServantData.getBookInfo( );
        for (int i = 0; i < books.length; i++) {
            if (books[i].getTitle( ).equalsIgnoreCase(name)) {
                // Found a match
                return books[i];
            }
        }
        return null;          // No match
    }
}
```

The important things to note about this class are:

- It looks like an ordinary Java class, in the sense that it does not contain any JAX-RPC–specific code. The fact that JAX-RPC does not require the service code to be written in any particular way (other than as mentioned in the following paragraphs) means that you don't need to learn a new API to create the server-side parts of a web service. It also makes it easier to convert existing code into a web service.

- The JAX-RPC runtime does not require this class to have any particular name or be derived from a fixed base class. It does, however, require that this class has a public no-argument constructor. In this case, since there is nothing for the constructor to do, the default constructor inserted by the compiler satisfies this requirement.

- The servant class is required to implement the methods of the service endpoint interface. As noted earlier, it is optional for the class to use the implements keyword to declare that it implements this service endpoint interface. The interface methods may not be final if the servant class does not declare that it implements the service endpoint interface.

- Although the operation methods are declared to throw RemoteException in the endpoint interface definition shown in Example 2-3, the actual method implementations do not do so. The interface definition is required to declare that a RemoteException might be thrown because the service methods are invoked through the JAX-RPC runtime, including the client-side stubs and the server-side tie classes, which might encounter various types of errors that are reported by throwing a RemoteException.

- By contrast, the getBookPrice( ) method, which is declared to throw the service-specific BookServiceException in the interface definition in Example 2-3, also makes this declaration in the implementation class and throws the exception in the normal way if it cannot find a book that matches the title supplied as its argument.

The data for this service is managed in a separate helper class called BookServiceServantData, the implementation of which is uninteresting apart from the code shown in the following extract:

```
InputStream is = BookServiceServantData.class
  .getResourceAsStream("booklist.txt");
BufferedReader reader = new BufferedReader(
  new InputStreamReader(is));
String line;
while ((line = reader.readLine()) != null) {
    StringTokenizer st = new StringTokenizer(line, "!");
    if (st.countTokens() == 4) {
        list.add(new BookInfo(st.nextToken(),
                    st.nextToken(),
                    st.nextToken(),
                    Double.parseDouble(st.nextToken())));
    }
}
```

The significant point here is that the book data is kept in a file called *booklist.txt* that resides in the same package as the BookServiceServantData class itself. Because there is nothing special about a JAX-RPC service implementation, this file can be treated as a resource and therefore can be located at runtime in the usual way, using the getResourceAsStream( ) method of java.lang.Class.

Since JAX-RPC services will ultimately be deployed in a web or EJB container of a J2EE-based application server, another way to obtain initialization data is from the container's JNDI environment or, for a servlet-based implementation, from the initialization parameters of the servlet that invokes the service's methods. You'll see how to get access to the servlet's initialization parameters as part of the discussion of the ServletLifecycle interface in Chapter 6.

Writing the client code

For the purposes of demonstrating the book web service, the example code contains a freestanding J2SE client application that invokes the methods of the BookQuery interface and displays the results that it receives. The source for this application can be found in the file *chapter2\bookservice\client\ora\jwsnut\ bookservice\client\BookServiceClient.java* relative to the installation directory of the example source code for this book.

To invoke the methods of a service endpoint interface, a client application needs to get a reference to an object that implements that interface. Obviously, it cannot simply instantiate the BookServiceServant class in order to do this—instead, as you can see from Figure 2-2, it has to get a reference to a generated stub object that implements the service endpoint interface. Unfortunately, the JAX-RPC specification does not fully specify the naming convention to be used for stub classes. Instead, it makes the following statement:

> The name of a generated stub class is either <BindingName>_Stub or is implementation specific.

As a result of this rather loose requirement, it is not possible to write portable code that refers directly to generated stub classes. If you need to write fully portable code, then you have two choices:

- Write a J2EE application client and deploy it into your J2EE application server. A J2EE application client runs in a container generated at deployment time by the application server. This container provides the means to get statically generated stubs in a portable way. The disadvantage of this approach is that the client must be deployed separately into each application server whose web services it needs to access. See "JAX-RPC and J2EE 1.4 Application Clients" in Chapter 6 for an example of this technique.

- Use the Dynamic Invocation Interface or a dynamic proxy, both of which are discussed in Chapter 6. Be aware, however, that both of these are likely to incur much more runtime overhead than using a statically generated stub.

If you are using the JAX-RPC reference implementation, you can obtain and use a stub using the following code:

```
// Get a reference to the stub and set the service address
BookService_Impl  service = new BookService_Impl( );
BookQuery  bookQuery = (BookQuery)service.getBookQueryPort( );
((Stub)bookQuery)._setProperty(Stub.ENDPOINT_ADDRESS_PROPERTY, args[0]);

BookInfo[] books = bookQuery.getBookInfo( );
```

As you'll see in "Programming with JAX-RPC" later in this chapter, BookService_Impl is one of the classes that is generated along with the stubs themselves. The BookService_Impl class contains a generated method that allows an instance of the stub for the service endpoint interface to be obtained. The stub object implements both the BookQuery service endpoint interface and the interface javax.xml.rpc.Stub, which is part of the JAX-RPC client-side API. This latter interface provides a method (called _setProperty( )) that allows the information that the stub needs in order to communicate with a server that contains the actual service implementation to be supplied. The only information that the stub requires is the address to which the call message should be sent, which must be set using the stub's ENDPOINT_ADDRESS_PROPERTY. We'll look in more detail at the properties of stubs and the exact format of the address in "Converting the Service Interface Definition to Client-Side Stubs," later in this chapter.

Once the address is set, the stub can be used to make any number of method calls, which look exactly like local calls:

```
BookInfo[] books = bookQuery.getBookInfo( );
```

Looking at this code, it is natural to think of the object referenced by bookQuery as being a single object at the server on which method calls can be made. However, this is not necessarily the case. If you make two separate method calls using the same bookQuery reference, those calls *might* actually be dispatched to two different server-side objects, depending on the way in which the JAX-RPC server-side environment is implemented. In this example, that isn't important, since the service endpoint interfaces defined here simply query the state of a static set of books. However, it is important if we attempt to define an interface that requires several method calls to set up conditions within the target object followed by a call that performs some operation based on those conditions, since not all of the conditions will necessarily be set on the same server-side object instance. In other words, the server-side object that implements the service cannot be assumed to maintain state relating to any of its clients.*

Example source code organization

When you create a web service, you need to write the source code for the interface definition and the service implementation classes and, at least for testing purposes, you will most likely also create a client application. As well as your own source code, the build process creates class files and (optionally) source code for the stub and tie classes. For the sake of clarity, the example source code for this chapter is organized into a directory structure, shown in Figure 2-7, that reflects the function of each class and its relationship to the other components of the overall system. It is clearly desirable to separate the client application from the service implementation, for example, because in the real world the client and the service may be developed independently and possibly by different developers working in different companies. Similarly, the source code that defines the service endpoint interface should be maintained separately from the service implementation.

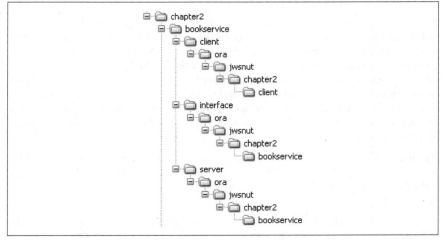

Figure 2-7. Example source code organization

The top-level directory, *chapter2*, contains a subdirectory called *bookservice* that contains all of the source code for this example. The Java source file for the service endpoint interface definition is placed beneath the *interface* subdirectory, in a directory hierarchy organized according to the usual package naming conventions and, similarly, the service implementation is held below the *server*

---

* The server-side JAX-RPC API includes a provision for a servlet-hosted web service implementation to preserve per-client state across web service method calls, provided that the client allows it. See "Session Management" in Chapter 6 for an example that demonstrates this feature.

subdirectory. For this example, both the interface definition and the service implementation code are in the same package (ora.jwsnut.chapter2.bookservice), although this is not required by JAX-RPC—in fact, JAX-RPC does not place any restrictions on the mapping of classes to packages when you create your own service endpoint interface.* The client code is held separately in the *client* subdirectory and also resides in a separate package (ora.jwsnut.chapter2.client). Again, this is done for the sake of clarity.

Compiling and running the book web service example

Once the code is written, deployment and testing of a web service requires that the following steps are performed:

1. The service endpoint interface and the service implementation classes must be compiled.
2. The server-side code must be bundled into a Web Archive (WAR) file, together with the appropriate tie classes.
3. The WAR must be deployed into the target web container or J2EE-based application server.
4. Client-side stubs must be generated.
5. The client code must be compiled.

To simplify this process, the examples in this book are all built and run using the Ant build tool, which is included in both the J2EE 1.4 reference implementation and the Java Web Services Developer Pack.† Before you can run the examples, you need to set up environment variables used by the JAX-RPC reference implementation as well as create a file called *jwsnutExamples.properties* in your home directory that contains information specific to your system that will be used by the Ant buildfile to locate source files and deploy the web service. If you have not already done so, refer to "Examples Online" in the Preface for a description of what is required.

To use the example source code, open a command window and make the *bookservice* directory your working directory. Here, you will find three files that are relevant to the build process, as shown in Figure 2-8:

build.xml
> This is the build control file for Ant. This XML file contains a set of targets that you can use to build the interface definitions, the service implementation, and the client, as well as use to run the example.

---

* If you start with a WSDL file instead of Java service definitions, all of the generated classes are placed in the same package by default. However, it is possible to force some of the generated classes to be placed in different packages based on the XML namespace within which they are defined. For more details, refer to Chapter 6.

† You don't need to know anything about Ant to be able to run the example source code in this book. However, Ant is an extremely useful tool for all kinds of Java development. If you're not familiar with it (or even if you are), I recommend getting a copy of *Ant: The Definitive Guide*, by Jesse Tilly and Eric M. Burke (O'Reilly).

---

config.xml

> This file tells the command-line utility wscompile (which will generate client-side stubs that will be used to access the web service) where to find the definition of the service endpoint interface for the book web service. We'll look at this file in detail in "Converting the Service Interface Definition to Client-Side Stubs" later in this chapter.

example.properties

> Because many of the tasks involved in building and deploying web services are common, most of the content of the *build.xml* file is actually stored in a separate location from which it is imported when it is read by Ant. The *example.properties* file contains settings that tailor the common build process for this particular example.

Figure 2-8. Build-related files for the book web service

There are also some files that are related to the server-side deployment process, which you'll find in the *deploy* and *deploy-j2ee14* subdirectories. There are two sets of files because the deployment process required for J2EE 1.4 is different from that used with the JWSDP. These files are discussed in "The Server-Side Implementation," later in this chapter.

The *build.xml* file contains a number of targets that can be used to perform selected parts of the build process, to deploy the web service, or to run the client application. To call one of these targets, use a command such as:

```
ant target
```

where target is one of those listed in Table 2-2.

Table 2-2. Targets in the Ant buildfile for the book web service

Target	Description
compile-interface	Compiles the service endpoint interface definitions from the *interface* subdirectory.
compile-server	Compiles the classes in the *server* subdirectory that make up the service implementation.
generate-client	Runs wscompile to generate the client stub classes.
compile-client	Compiles the classes in the *client* subdirectory that make up the application clients for this web service.
compile	Compiles both the service implementation and the application clients.
portable-web-package	Packages the service implementation as a WAR file.
web-package	Uses the file created by the portable-web-package target to create a deployable WAR file by generating and adding tie classes and the WSDL file for the service.

Table 2-2. Targets in the Ant buildfile for the book web service (continued)

Target	Description
deploy	Compiles, packages, and deploys the book web service in the J2EE reference implementation application server or the Tomcat web container included with the Java Web Services Developer Pack.
undeploy	Removes the book web service from the web container.
redeploy	Replaces the current version of the book web service in the web container by undeploying it and deploying the most recently packaged version.
run-client	Runs one of the application clients.
run-client-bookmap	Runs the other application client.
clean	Deletes all generated and compiled files and output directories, leaving only the original source files.

In most cases, these targets invoke other targets as necessary to complete their tasks so that, for example, if you use the compile-server target, it will automatically invoke the compile-interface target that creates the inputs that it requires.

The easiest way to run the book web service example is to start by generating the files required for the server-side deployment using the following command:

    ant web-package

This target causes Ant to compile the service interface definitions and the service implementation classes, and create a web archive containing everything necessary to deploy the service.* During this process, two extra directories are created beneath the *bookservice* directory:

- The *generated* directory holds the Java source code for the client-side stubs created from the service endpoint interface definitions.
- The *output* subdirectory contains all of the compiled class files, including those corresponding to the generated stubs. In order for you to see where each class file comes from, they are organized into subdirectories called *output/interface*, *output/server*, and *output/client*.

Compiling the interface definitions and the service implementation files is a simple matter of running the Java compiler in the usual way, specifying the appropriate location in which to store the class files beneath the *output* directory. The only point to note is that the CLASSPATH passed to the compiler needs to include the classes that make up the JAX-RPC API. For the J2EE 1.4 platform, these classes are bundled into the file *lib\j2ee.jar,* which contains the entire J2EE API, whereas for JWSDP 1.1, they can be found in the JAR file *jaxrpc-api.jar* in the *jaxrpc-1.0.3\lib* directory. The Ant buildfile takes care of setting the correct CLASSPATH, but you will need to ensure that you include the appropriate JAR files if you intend to compile JAX-RPC services or applications from the command line.

Having created the web archive, which will be written to the file *chapter2\ bookservice\Books.war*, the next step is to make the service available by deploying it either in a web container or in a J2EE-compatible application server. There are

---

* The details of this process will be described in more detail in "The Server-Side Implementation," later in this chapter.

several different ways to perform the deployment, but the simplest approach is to use the deploy target in the Ant buildfile:

```
ant deploy
```

Having deployed the service, if you want to make changes to it, some containers (including Tomcat) require you to undeploy the existing instance before you can install a new one. The Ant buildfile provides a target called undeploy that will do this for you, as well as a target called redeploy that combines the undeployment and deployment steps.

A quick way to check that the service is properly deployed is to open a browser and point it at the URL

http://hostname:port/Books/BookQuery?WSDL

where hostname and port correspond to the HTTP port of the J2EE application server or the Tomcat web container for the JWSDP. If you are using J2EE 1.4, the appropriate URL is:

http://localhost:8000/Books/BookQuery?WSDL

whereas if you have installed the JWSDP with the default setup, the web container uses port 8080 instead of port 8000; therefore, the URL is:

http://localhost:8080/Books/BookQuery?WSDL

If the service is properly deployed, then in the case of the JWSDP, this URL will return a page of XML tags like that shown in Figure 2-9, which is actually the WSDL definition for the deployed web service. WSDL is described in detail in Chapter 5 of this book.

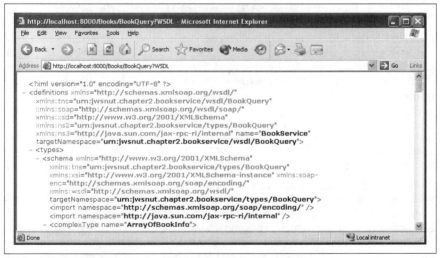

Figure 2-9. WSDL definition for a deployed web service

The next step is to build the application client code, which can be done using the compile-client target of the Ant buildfile:

```
ant compile-client
```

There are actually two application clients, which you can run by using the run-client or run-client-bookmap targets. The client run by the run-client-bookmap target, for example, uses the getBookMap( ) method of the BookQuery interface to fetch the complete set of books known to the service in the form of a HashMap, in which the key to each entry is the book title in uppercase and the associated value is the BookInfo object for that book. Having retrieved the HashMap, it prints the key and value for each of its entries. Type the following command:

```
ant run-client-bookmap
```

You should see output that looks like this (only a subset is actually shown):

```
    [java] KEY: [JAVA IN A NUTSHELL], value = Java in a Nutshell by David
Flanagan, edited by Paula Ferguson, Robert Eckstein, price USD 39.95
    [java] KEY: [J2ME IN A NUTSHELL], value = J2ME in a Nutshell by Kim
Topley,  edited by Robert Eckstein, price USD 29.95
    [java] KEY: [JAVA I/O], value = Java I/O by Elliotte Rusty Harold,
edited by Mike Loukides, price USD 32.95
    [java] KEY: [JAVA 2D GRAPHICS], value = Java 2D Graphics by Jonathan
Knudsen, edited by Mike Loukides, price USD 29.95
    [java] KEY: [JAVA SWING], value = Java Swing by Robert Eckstein et al,
edited by Mike Loukides, price USD 44.95
    [java] KEY: [JAVA SERVLET PROGRAMMING], value = Java Servlet
Programming by Jason Hunter, William Crawford, edited by Paula Ferguson,
price USD 32.95
```

The other client can be used to invoke any of the remaining methods of the BookQuery interface, depending on the arguments supplied on its command line. The client's command line looks like this:

```
java ora.jwsnut.chapter2.bookservice.BookServiceClient  url    command
    title
```

Here, url is the address of the BookQuery service endpoint interface, command indicates which interface operation is to be called, and title is the book title to be supplied as the argument to the operation. If the command and title arguments are omitted, the client uses the getBookInfo( ) method to get a book list and prints the result. You can try this out using the command:

```
ant run-client
```

This produces a result that is similar to that shown earlier, except that the key values are not present because the return value is an array of BookInfo objects instead of a HashMap.

The allowable values for the command argument are author, editor, and price. Selecting one of these values causes the application client to invoke the BookQuery interface's getAuthor( ), getEditor( ), or getPrice( ) method, passing the book title obtained from the remaining command-line arguments as its parameter. The BookInfo object that is returned is then printed. To supply command-line arguments to this client using Ant, set the CLIENT_ARGS property from the command line and execute the run-client target. To get the name of the editor of the book *Java Swing*, for example, use the following command:

```
ant -DCLIENT_ARGS="http://localhost:8000/Books/BookQuery  editor Java Swing"
run-client
```

This command produces the following result:

```
run-client:
    [java] NAME = [Java Swing]
    [java] Mike Loukides
```

The URL used in this command:

http://localhost:8000/Books/BookQuery

indicates that the method to be called belongs to the BookQuery interface of a web service deployed in a web application called Books. The fact that such a simple and obvious address exists for this service endpoint interface is determined by configuration information supplied among the deployment files for this service, the details of which will be shown in "The Server-Side Implementation," later in this chapter.*

In order to run the application client, the Ant buildfile sets up the appropriate CLASSPATH so that all of the JAR files that the JAX-RPC reference implementation relies on are available. The CLASSPATH required to run a client application is larger than that required to compile it because it is necessary to include the classes for a specific JAX-RPC implementation, whereas the compilation step requires only the implementation-independent JAX-RPC API classes. If you are using the JWSDP, the complete set of files required is quite large:

jaxrpc-api.jar	jaxrpc-ri.jar	saaj-api.jar	saaj-ri.jar
activation.jar	commons-logging.jar	dom4j.jar	mail.jar
jaxp-api.jar	dom.jar	sax.jar	xalan.jar
xercesImpl.jar	xsltc.jar		

These JAR files can be found in various subdirectories of the JWSDP installation. In the case of the J2EE 1.4 platform, the CLASSPATH needs only to include the *lib\ j2ee.jar* file and a small number of additional JAR files that can be found in the *lib/ endorsed* subdirectory of the reference implementation.

Programming with JAX-RPC

Now that you've seen a simple example of JAX-RPC programming, this section lifts the hood a little and looks more closely at some of the details that were skimmed over in the first part of this chapter. Although much of what follows is completely generic, it isn't possible to give a complete description of JAX-RPC programming without going beyond the bounds of the specification, since there are certain aspects of the programming model that vendors are permitted to implement in any convenient manner. Where this is the case, we'll make it clear

---

* Almost all of the web service URLs that you'll see in this book use port number 8000, since this is the default HTTP port for the web container in the J2EE 1.4 reference implementation. If you are using the examples with the JWSDP, you should use port 8080 instead. In most cases, however, you won't need to concern yourself with this difference because the Ant buildfile targets that run the example applications handle this difference for you by obtaining the port number from the *jwsnutExamples.properties* file.

that what is being described is not covered by the specification, and we'll use the JAX-RPC reference implementations in the J2EE 1.4 platform and the JWSDP as typical examples.

The JAX-RPC Service Interface

Web service development with JAX-RPC begins either with the definition of the service itself as a Java interface or by importing a service definition in the form of a WSDL document. In this chapter, for the sake of simplicity, we consider only the first case and defer discussion of WSDL and of using WSDL as the starting point for JAX-RPC development to Chapter 5 and Chapter 6, respectively. As noted earlier, using Java to define the service endpoint interface is not sufficient if you want to publish the service so that it can be used by clients written in other programming languages. In order to be truly open, the service definition has to be exported as a WSDL document. However, using Java as the definition language is convenient at this stage since we haven't yet described WSDL. Therefore, we will continue to discuss JAX-RPC service definitions and the rules that apply to them in terms of their bindings to the Java language for the rest of this chapter.

Interface method definitions

A Java web service endpoint interface must obey the following rules:

- The interface must extend `java.rmi.Remote`.
- Each interface method must declare that it throws `java.rmi.RemoteException`.
- A method may additionally throw service-dependent exceptions, as long as they are checked exceptions derived from `java.lang.Exception`.
- Method name–overloading is permitted, subject to the usual rules of the Java language.
- Service endpoint interfaces may be derived by extension from other interfaces.

Arguments passed to the methods of an endpoint interface are passed to the service implementation by value. Where an argument is an object, its value is copied before being sent to the server. Return values that are objects are newly created during the processing of the reply message from the server. The copying and creation of objects in this way by the JAX-RPC runtime requires certain restrictions to be placed on the types of objects that can be used as arguments and return values, as described in the later section "Value types."

Service endpoint interface definitions cannot include static fields, and, as a result, constants declared using the usual Java syntax (i.e., using the `public static final` modifiers) are not allowed.

Supported data types

JAX-RPC allows a limited range of data types to be used as method arguments or as the return value. The types for which support is required by the JAX-RPC specification are listed in Table 2-3.

Table 2-3. Java data types that can be used as JAX-RPC method arguments and return values

Data type	Description
Java primitive types	boolean, byte, short,int, long, float, double
Wrapper classes for Java primitive types	Boolean, Byte, Short, Integer, Long, Float, Double
Standard Java classes	The specification requires support for the following: • java.lang.String • java.util.Calendar • java.util.Date • java.math.BigDecimal • java.math.BigInteger
Value types	Arbitrary classes that meet certain conditions can be used as method arguments and return types. The BookInfo class is an example of a value type. See the later section "Value types" for further details.
Holder classes	Holder classes may be used as method arguments to provide a form of "pass by reference" semantics that is not directly supported by the Java programming language. See the later section "Holder classes" for further information.
Arrays	Single- and multidimensional arrays, in which the elements are all JAX-RPC–supported types, can be used both as method arguments and for the return value.

Implementations may also provide built-in support for additional types, use of which would, of course, reduce the vendor-independence of a JAX-RPC web service. The reference implementation, for example, allows the use of the following collection classes from the java.util package:

- ArrayList
- HashMap
- HashSet
- Hashtable
- LinkedList
- Properties
- Stack
- TreeMap
- TreeSet
- Vector

If you need to use data types that are not directly supported by JAX-RPC, you can do so by creating a custom serializer and deserializer that together convert an object of that type to and from its XML representation. However, the current JAX-RPC specification does not provide a framework for creating serializers and deserializers that are portable between different JAX-RPC implementations; therefore, using this feature may compromise your ability to port your service to a different JAX-RPC implementation—that is, between application servers from different vendors.

Support is *not* provided for the passing of objects by remote reference in the manner of RMI. Objects used as method arguments and return values are therefore not permitted to implement the java.rmi.Remote interface, which is necessary to implement object-by-reference semantics, since the SOAP 1.1 specification does not provide the support required for true remote method invocation.

There is little difference between the use of a Java primitive type such as int and its object wrapper, so that the following method declarations are both valid:

```
public void methodName(int value) throws RemoteException;
public void methodName(Integer value) throws RemoteException;
```

However, the second form makes it possible to use null as a distinguished value that might be of special significance to the method being invoked. Similarly, a method that is declared to return a wrapper object can also return a null value. So, for example, if a service interface method were defined to return the number of copies of a named book that a publisher has in stock in the form of an Integer, a return value of null could be reserved to mean that the book title is not recognized, as an alternative to throwing an exception.

Notice that the list of supported types in Table 2-3 does not include java.lang.Object. This means that it is not possible to define an operation with an argument or return type whose runtime type is not specified. This restriction is, however, relaxed in the reference implementation, making it possible (if portability is not an issue) to use a method defined like this:

```
public Object sendAnObject(Object arg);
```

However, even though arg is declared as being of type Object, its runtime type must still be one of those listed in Table 2-3, or a type for which a custom serializer has been created. The same restriction applies to the return value. When using this feature, it is important to realize that the actual runtime type of the argument used by the sender is not known by the receiver. Hence, in some cases, the object that is delivered to the service implementation class may not be of the same type as the one supplied by the client application. This situation can arise when more than one data type uses the same representation in the XML messages that are exchanged by the client and the service. Consider the following example:

```
Object result = stub.sendAnObject(new Date());
```

This method call requires that a Date object be transmitted to the server. However, JAX-RPC maps both the Date class and the GregorianCalendar class to the XML schema data type xsd:dateTime, which is what therefore appears in the SOAP message that the client sends. Lacking any specific type information, the server-side JAX-RPC runtime has to choose which representation to use for an xsd:dateTime element in an incoming message. In the reference implementation, it happens to be the case (at least at the time of this writing) that it chooses to create a GregorianCalendar object and not the Date object that was originally supplied. This results in a ClassCastException if the service class implementation assumes that it will receive a Date object. This feature should, therefore, be used only with great caution.

As mentioned earlier, all objects used as method arguments or return values need to have an associated serializer so that they can be converted to and from their XML representations during the method call. JAX-RPC supplies serializers for the data types listed in Table 2-3. Therefore, in most cases, when the method signature specifies the actual object type, the JAX-RPC runtime system can arrange for appropriate serializers to be available to the stubs and ties that are generated from the interface definition. However, when you declare a method that uses Object as an argument or return value, the actual type will not be known until runtime; therefore, the required set of serializers cannot be created from the endpoint interface definition alone. The same is true if the method signature references an abstract class, an interface type, or in the case where a method is declared to use a base class (such as Calendar) but is actually passed an instance of a derived class (such as GregorianCalendar). In these examples, the developer must list the actual types that are used at runtime in a configuration file used when the stubs and ties are generated. This topic is covered in more detail in Chapter 6.

Method arguments and return values may be single- or multidimensional arrays of any supported JAX-RPC data type. Note, however, that because a JAX-RPC method call operates on a copy of its argument, assignment to a member of an array does not have the same effect as it would in the case of a local call. Suppose, for example, that you want to define a method in a service endpoint interface that reverses the order of the elements in an array of integers. In the case of a local call, the following code accomplishes this:

```
public void reverse(int[] values) {
    for (int i = 0; i < values.length/2; i++) {
        int temp = values[i];
        values[i] = values[values.length - 1 - i];
        values[values.length - 1 - i] = temp;
    }
}
```

If this method is called like this:

```
int[] values = new int[] {1, 2, 3, 4, 5};
reverse(values);
```

then the order of elements in the values array is reversed in-situ, because the reverse( ) method has direct access to the array. If this same method is included in a service endpoint interface and called from a client application, the elements of the array are reversed on the server, but this has no effect on the client's copy. One way to implement this functionality in JAX-RPC is to return the re-ordered array:

```
public int[] reverse(int[] values) {
    for (int i = 0; i < values.length/2; i++) {
        int temp = values[i];
        values[i] = values[values.length - 1 - i];
        values[values.length - 1 - i] = temp;
    }
    return values;
}
```

and invoke the method like this:

```
int[] values = new int[] {1, 2, 3, 4, 5};
int[] reversedValues = reverse(values);
```

so that the JAX-RPC runtime returns (a copy of) the server's reversed integer array from the reverse( ) method.

Holder classes

Although Java itself does not provide pass-by-reference semantics for method call arguments, JAX-RPC includes a set of *holder* classes that can be used to simulate something similar to pass-by-reference arguments. The set of standard holder classes, which reside in the `javax.xml.rpc.holders` package, is shown in the following table:

BigDecimalHolder	BigIntegerHolder	BooleanHolder
BooleanWrapperHolder	ByteArrayHolder	ByteHolder
ByteWrapperHolder	CalendarHolder	DoubleHolder
DoubleWrapperHolder	FloatHolder	FloatWrapperHolder
IntegerWrapperHolder	IntHolder	LongHolder
LongWrapperHolder	ObjectHolder	QNameHolder
ShortHolder	ShortWrapperHolder	StringHolder

Each of the supported JAX-RPC data types has its own holder class. The name of the holder class for a Java primitive type is formed by taking the type name, capitalizing the first letter, and appending `Holder` so that, for example, an `IntHolder` is a class that holds a value of type `int`. The corresponding object wrapper classes use a similar naming convention, except that they append `WrapperHolder` instead of `Holder`. Therefore, the holder class for an object of type `java.lang.Integer` is called `IntegerWrapperHolder`.

All of the holder classes implement the `javax.rpc.xml.holders.Holder` interface. This interface is simply a marker to indicate that classes that implement it are holders—it does not declare any methods. Instead, holders follow a coding pattern, exemplified by the public API of the `IntHolder` class, which consists of two constructors and a public field:

```
public int value;
public IntHolder( );
public IntHolder(int value);
```

The value associated with the holder is held in the value field, where it can be set before a method call and retrieved when the call completes. The initial value can also be set at construction time. If the no-argument constructor is used, the associated value will be zero, or false for a Boolean value. In the case of an object-value holder such as `IntegerWrapperHolder`, the default value is `null`.

Holder classes provide another way to implement the reverse( ) method shown in the previous section. Recall that, since the array of ints passed to this method is passed by copy, we declared the method to return an array of ints so that we could retrieve them in reverse order. In fact, what we really need is to provide copy-by-reference semantics for the integer array, so that the service can (appear to) update it in-place. This is exactly the purpose of a `Holder` class. However, since there is no standard `Holder` for an array of integers, we need to define one. The code for this very simple class is shown in Example 2-7.

Example 2-7. A custom holder class for an array of integers

```
import javax.xml.rpc.holders.Holder;

/**
 * A class that acts as a holder for an array of integers.
```

Example 2-7. A custom holder class for an array of integers (continued)
```
*/
public class IntArrayHolder implements Holder {

    // The actual int[] value
    public int[] value;

    // Constructs an IntArrayHolder with a null value
    public IntArrayHolder( ) {
    }

    // Constructs an IntArrayHolder initialized with the given array
    public IntArrayHolder(int[] value) {
        this.value = value;
    }
}
```

To make use of this holder, replace the reverse( ) method in the service endpoint interface definition with the following:
```
public void reverse(IntArrayHolder holder);
```
Then, provide the following code in the service implementation:
```
public void reverse(IntArrayHolder holder) {
    int[] values = holder.value;
    for (int i = 0; i < values.length/2; i++) {
        int temp = values[i];
        values[i] = values[values.length - 1 - i];
        values[values.length - 1 - i] = temp;
    }
}
```
Aside from the change in the method signature, the only difference between this implementation and the original is that the integer array containing the values to reverse is obtained from the values field of the holder, rather than directly as a method argument. Notice that, since the array is updated in-situ, there is no need to change the values field at the end of the method call or to return a value.

The client-side code to invoke this method is also very simple:
```
int[] values = new int[] {0, 5, 10, 15, 20};
IntArrayHolder  holder = new IntArrayHolder(values);
bookQuery.reverse(holder);
values = holder.value;   // NOTE THIS LINE (SEE  BELOW)
for (int i = 0; i < values.length; i++) {
    System.out.println(values[i]);
}
```
The line of code shown in bold is very important in this example. Although an IntArrayHolder passes an array of integers to the JAX-RPC runtime and allows another array holding the results of the method call to be passed back, the returned array is not actually the one that was originally supplied. The JAX-RPC runtime creates a new array to contain the method call results and assigns it to the value field of the Holder object. This is necessary in the general case because the returned integer array need not contain the same number of elements as the one supplied; therefore, reuse of the original array is not possible.

All of the standard holder classes and our custom IntArrayHolder store the associated value in a public field. When implementing custom holders, it is very important to use the name value for this field, since the stubs generated by the reference implementation use this name to access the content of the holder.

Holder classes are used by the JAX-RPC runtime to represent parameters with "out" or "in-out" semantics (also known as *parameter modes*) in code generated from a web service described by a WSDL document. See Chapter 5 for a description of WSDL and Chapter 6 for further discussion of parameter modes.

Value types

Although you cannot use arbitrary Java classes as method arguments without writing a custom serializer and deserializer, JAX-RPC does provide support for the use of *value types*, which are classes having the following characteristics:

- This class has a public, no-argument constructor. It may also have other constructors for the use of application code, but these will not be used by the JAX-RPC runtime.
- The class may be derived by extending any other class, may contain static and instance methods, and may implement any Java interfaces apart from java.rmi.Remote or any interface that has java.rmi.Remote as an ancestor.
- The class may contain static fields and instance fields that are public, protected, package private, or private. Each of these fields must be either another value type (allowing nesting of value types to any depth), a type for which a custom serializer or deserializer is available, or one of the other supported JAX-RPC types listed in Table 2-3.

It might at first appear that almost any Java class could be considered to be a value type. However, the important point about these objects is that, when used as method arguments or a return value, JAX-RPC only copies those parts of the object state that it can get access to, either directly or by using accessor and mutator methods. When a call involving a value-type argument is made, the following steps are taken:

1. The accessible state of the object is extracted and included as part of the SOAP message sent to the server-side JAX-RPC runtime.

2. The server-side JAX-RPC runtime creates an instance of the value type using its public, no-argument constructor, then uses the values in the received message to initialize the object state either by writing directly to public fields or using mutator methods for those fields that are not public.

The same process is used when a method has a return value that is a value type object or its argument list includes a Holder class that references one. Therefore, in order for an element of the object state to be transferred from the client to the server, it must satisfy one of the following requirements:

- It must be a public, nonfinal, and nontransient static or instance field. Clearly, a final field does not need to have its state copied because it is fixed and will be set either when the class is first loaded (for static state) or before or during execution of the constructor. Transient state is not transferred because, by definition, it is not required to be preserved during the process of object transfer by serialization and deserialization.

- If the field is not public, it must have both an accessor and a mutator method that can be used to retrieve and set its value. These methods must follow the usual JavaBeans naming conventions.

The BookInfo class used in the book web service example and shown in Example 2-4 is an example of a value type. Here, all of the instance fields are private, but their values can be obtained for inclusion in the message sent from the client by calling the accessor methods getTitle( ), getAuthor( ), getEditor( ), and getPrice( ), and can be set in the object passed to the service implementation using the mutator methods setTitle( ), setAuthor( ), setEditor( ), and setPrice( ). When the state of the the object is being set from a received message, the order in which the mutator methods are called is undefined; therefore, care should be taken when implementing the value type to ensure that there are no unintended side-effects resulting from the order in which the mutator methods are invoked.

The requirement that the JAX-RPC runtime be able to set these values means that value type classes must have mutator methods, even though this might not be desirable from the point of view of the object model. The BookInfo class is a case in point, since we would prefer that it were an immutable object from the client's viewpoint, but the JAX-RPC runtime requires the presence of mutator methods.

The case in which a class has both a public field and a pair of accessor and mutator methods that correspond to a JavaBeans property that has the same name is considered to be an error:

```
public class ValueType {
    public int value;      // Error - name clash. OK if not public.

    public int getValue( ) {
        return value;
    }

    public void setValue(int value) {
        this.value = value;
    }
}
```

In the reference implementation, this error is detected when the stub and tie classes are being generated, and results in an error message from the generation process.

When a value type is derived from another (non-Object) class, all of the public and nonpublic fields accessible via public accessor and mutator methods, both in the value type class itself and all of the classes in its inheritance hierarchy, are included in the state transferred between the client and the server.

Inner classes

The JAX-RPC specification does not mention the subject of inner classes, but the reference implementation supports their use, provided that they are declared as static. For example, suppose you want to extend the book web service so that the

BookInfo object contains a type value that indicates whether the subject matter of the book is most closely related to the J2EE, J2SE, or J2ME platform. To do this, you might subclass the value type BookInfo to create a new class called ExtendedBookInfo, for example, that contains the new book type attribute, and then extend the service endpoint interface definition to provide a method that returns instances of the subclass instead of BookInfo itself. Since the book type is a constant that can have only a limited number of fixed values, it is natural to define it as a static inner class of ExtendedBookInfo and then define three static constants that represent the three types. Example 2-8 shows how this might be implemented.

Example 2-8. Using an inner class with JAX-RPC

```
public class ExtendedBookInfo extends BookInfo {

    // The type of this book
    private BookType bookType;

    public ExtendedBookInfo( ) {
    }

    public ExtendedBookInfo(String title, String author, String editor,
                            double price, BookType bookType) {
        super(title, author, editor, price);
        this.bookType = bookType;
    }

    public BookType getBookType( ) {
        return bookType;
    }

    public void setBookType(BookType bookType) {
        this.bookType = bookType;
    }

    // Inner class -- must be static and a value type
    public static class BookType {

        public static final BookType J2EE_TYPE = new BookType("J2EE");
        public static final BookType J2SE_TYPE = new BookType("J2SE");
        public static final BookType J2ME_TYPE = new BookType("J2ME");

        private String type;

        public BookType( ) {
        }

        public BookType(String type) {
            this.type = type;
        }

        public String getType( ) {
            return type;
        }
```

Example 2-8. Using an inner class with JAX-RPC (continued)

```
        public void setType(String type) {
            this.type = type;
        }

        public String toString() {
            return type;
        }

        public int hashCode() {
            return type.hashCode();
        }

        public boolean equals(Object o) {
            return o instanceof BookType &&
                    type.equals(((BookType)o).type);
        }
    }
}
```

Here, BookType is the inner class that represents the type of the book. This class defines three constant values: BookType.J2EE_TYPE, BookType.J2SE_TYPE, and BookType.J2ME_TYPE, which can be passed to the ExtendedBookInfo constructor or its setBookType( ) method to associate the type with a book. The important points to note about this class are:

- It is a public, static inner class.
- It is a value type and therefore must have a public, no-argument constructor and accessor and mutator methods for the type property, which is a human-readable description of the type.

This class also overrides the equals( ) and hashCode( ) methods inherited from Object so that expressions like this are possible:

```
ExtendedBookInfo info = ....; // Get an instance (not shown)
if (info.getBookType( ).equals(ExtendedBookInfo.BookType.J2ME_TYPE)) {
    // This is a J2ME book...
}
```

Note that the following plausible alternative does not work:

```
if (info.getBookType( ) == ExtendedBookInfo.BookType.J2ME_TYPE) {
```

because the value returned by the getBookType( ) method is an instance created by the JAX-RPC runtime on receipt of a reply message and not the constant instance defined in the BookType class. In general, the direct comparison of objects returned by JAX-RPC method calls should be avoided and equals( ) used instead.

Other data types

In addition to those already covered in this section, JAX-RPC provides mechanisms for the use of two other classes of data types:

- Data that can be represented using a MIME encoding. Objects of this type are carried as an attachment in the SOAP messages that implement the remote procedure call.

- XML documents or fragments of XML documents. Arbitrary XML fragments can be passed as method arguments or as a method return value using classes provided by the SAAJ API, which is covered in Chapter 3.

The JAX-RPC API that allows these data types to be used is discussed in Chapter 6.

Converting the Service Interface Definition to Client-Side Stubs

The JAX-RPC specification does not specify how service endpoint interface definitions are converted into the stubs and ties required by the JAX-RPC runtime. It also doesn't place any constraints on how the stubs and ties operate. Both the conversion mechanism and the resulting classes are, therefore, entirely dependent on the JAX-RPC implementation that you use. We have already seen (in "Writing the client code" earlier in this chapter) that the client code is dependent on the names of the generated stub classes. Although the design of portable stubs is an aim for a future revision of the specification, at the present time, if you want to change your JAX-RPC software vendor, you need to regenerate the stubs (for the client application) and modify your client code. In this section, we assume that you are using the JAX-RPC reference implementation.*

The reference implementation provides a command-line utility called wscompile that, given either a WSDL file or a service endpoint interface definition written in Java, can generate the following:

- The compiled class files and, optionally, the Java source files, for the stubs required to interface with the reference implementation's client-side JAX-RPC runtime.
- The compiled class files and, optionally, the corresponding source files, for the ties required by the JAX-RPC server-side runtime, together with configuration information that is used to link these artifacts to the web or EJB container that will dispatch incoming service requests. In practice, however, wscompile is usually not used directly to create these artifacts. Instead, for the J2EE 1.4 platform, they are created using either the deploytool or j2eec utilities, whereas the JWSDP provides a different utility called wsdeploy. For further information on generating ties, refer to the later section "The Server-Side Implementation."
- If the service is presented as a Java interface (as is the case in this chapter), a WSDL file that is equivalent to the interface definition.
- If the service is presented in the form of a WSDL document (as will be the case for some of the examples in Chapter 6), the Java interface definition that corresponds to the service endpoint that it defines, together with Java classes for any value-type objects that it references.

---

* As well as being vendor-dependent, stubs and ties are specific to the underlying messaging service and transport protocol in use. The stubs created by the reference implementation work only for SOAP 1.1 messages carried by HTTP 1.1. If support is provided at some future point for alternatives, then using a different communications infrastructure would involve creating and linking different stubs and ties, even if the same JAX-RPC implementation is used.

- A *model* file that describes the service in an internal form that can be processed more quickly than either compiled Java class files or WSDL documents. Having created a model file using wscompile, you can use it next time
you run wscompile for improved performance. Model files can also be used
when creating the server-side artifacts, as you'll see later.

The wscompile utility has many command-line arguments, which are described in
detail in Chapter 8. You need only to use a small number of these to create the
client-side stubs. The following command line generates the stubs, compiles
them, and places them below the directory *output*, which must already exist:

```
wscompile -gen:client -d  output/client -classpath classpath config-file
```

The classpath argument is a colon-separated (for Unix) or semicolon-separated
(for Windows) list of JAR files or directories that contain the class file for the
endpoint interface definition for which the stubs are to be generated and any
supporting classes on which they depend. In most cases, this argument contains a
single directory name, since it is desirable to keep all of the classes that make up
the interface in the same package. The actual name of the class that represents the
endpoint interface is specified in the configuration file given as the last argument
to wscompile and described next.

The command line just shown creates the source files for the stubs in a temporary
location and deletes them once they are compiled. You can arrange to retain the
Java source files for inspection by using the –keep argument and supplying the
name of the directory below which they will be placed (which must already exist),
using the –s argument:

```
wscompile -gen:client -keep -s  generated/client  -d  output/client
    -classpath classpath config-file
```

The Ant buildfile for the example shown in this chapter provides a target called
generate-client that runs wscompile to create the client stubs and retains the Java
source files for inspection so that you can get a feel for how they work. The generated source files and the class files are stored in directories that make clear that
they are client-side artifacts. The pathnames of these directories, relative to the
installation directory of the example source code, are:

Java source code	*chapter2\bookservice\generated\client*
Compiled class files	*chapter2\bookservice\output\client*

The format of the configuration file required by wscompile depends on whether it
is being given a WSDL document, a model file, or a service defined by Java interfaces as its starting point. You'll find a complete specification of this file in
Chapter 8. The configuration information for the book web service can be found
in the file *chapter2\bookservice\config.xml*. The content of this file is shown in
Example 2-9, in which the line numbers shown on the left are for reference
purposes only and do not exist in the file itself.*

---

* The use of the name *config.xml* for this file is consistent with the naming conventions used by the
  documentation supplied with the JWSDP, but it is only a convention. You can choose any name
  you like for this file.

Example 2-9. wscompile configuration file for the book web service

```
1   <?xml version="1.0" encoding="UTF-8" ?>
2   <configuration xmlns="http://java.sun.com/xml/ns/jax-rpc/ri/config">
3       <service name="BookService"
4           targetNamespace="urn:jwsnut.chapter2.bookservice/wsdl/BookQuery"
5           typeNamespace="urn:jwsnut.chapter2.bookservice/types/BookQuery"
6           packageName="ora.jwsnut.chapter2.bookservice">
7
8           <interface name="ora.jwsnut.chapter2.bookservice.BookQuery"/>
9       </service>
10  </configuration>
```

The outermost element of this file, called configuration, specifies that this is a wscompile configuration file, the format of which is defined by the XML schema document that can be found at the URL *http://java.sun.com/xml/ns/jax-rpc/ri/config*. If you want to look at this document offline and have installed the JWSDP tutorial, you'll find a copy in the file *docs\tutorial\examples\jaxrpc\common\jax-rpc-ri-config.xsd*. If you are not familiar with XML schema documents, you can find a tutorial at *http://www.w3c.org/TR/xmlschema-0*, or else pick up a copy of *XML Schema*, by Eric van der Vlist (O'Reilly). Since XML schema files and the data types defined by the W3C XML schema documents are used extensively by JAX-RPC, it is advantageous to have at least some familiarity with this subject.

The configuration element may contain one of the following nested elements:

service
> Defines a web service in terms of Java interface definitions

wsdl
> Defines a web service using a WSDL document

modelfile
> Defines a web service from a model file

In this chapter, we look only at the use of the service element, which has four associated attributes that are listed in Table 2-4. Typical values for these attributes are shown in Example 2-9.

Table 2-4. Attributes of the config.xml service element

Attribute name	Description
name	The name to be used for the web service. This value of this attribute determines the names of some of the generated files, including the Java source file that represents the service itself. By convention, this name is also part of the URL used to reference the web service and, in the example code used in this book, it is also the name of the WAR file used to deploy the server-side components.
targetNamespace	The XML namespace that will be used in the generated WSDL file for the names associated with the service itself, the port type (i.e., the endpoint interface definition), the operations (i.e., the methods), and the definitions of the SOAP messages exchanged by the client and service JAX-RPC runtimes. This namespace also appears in the code that is generated by wscompile. It is important that the value of this attribute is set correctly — see "JWSDP configuration files and XML namespaces" at the end of this chapter for more information.

Table 2-4. Attributes of the config.xml service element (continued)

Attribute name	Description
typeNamespace	This is the XML namespace that will be used in the generated WSDL file for any data types that are declared by the web service definition. In the book service example, BookInfo is an example of a data type that would be associated with this namespace. It is important that the value of this attribute is set correctly — see "JWSDP configuration files and XML namespaces" at the end of this chapter for more information.
packageName	The name of the Java package in which the classes generated by wscompile for the service itself will be placed (see Table 2-5). The stub classes generated from the endpoint interface definition appear in the same package as the service endpoint interface and are therefore not affected by this setting. In the book web service example, we use ora.jwsnut.chapter2.bookservice, which is the same package used by the endpoint interfaces; therefore, all of the generated classes appear in the same package.

The service element must have a nested interface element. An interface element may have several attributes, of which only the name attribute is mandatory.* This attribute gives the the fully qualified name of the Java class that contains the service endpoint interface definition, and, in the case of the web service, it has the value ora.jwsnut.chapter2.bookservice.BookQuery.

Using this book's example source code, type the following command:

```
ant generate-client
```

This runs wscompile to generate the client-side stubs, writing the Java source files to the directory *chapter2\bookservice\generated\client* and the compiled class files to *chapter2\bookservice\output\client*. As noted before, we deliberately place client-related files in a separate directory hierarchy from those related to the interface definition and the service implementation so that you can easily see which files relate to which part. Below these directories, the files are arranged according to their package location. Since the interface class (shown in Example 2-3) is in the package ora. jwsnut.chapter2.bookservice and the packageName attribute in the *config.xml* file (shown on line 6 of Example 2-9) has the same value, all of the generated source files will be in the directory *chapter2\bookservice\generated\client\ora\jwsnut\ chapter2\bookservice*, while the compiled classes will be written to *chapter2\ bookservice\output\client\ora\jwsnut\chapter2\bookservice*. If you examine the set of files created, you will find that there are several different groupings, a selection of which are shown in Table 2-5.

Table 2-5. Some of the client-side source files generated by wscompile

Source	Generated files
Service	*BookService.java*
	BookService_Impl.java
	BookService_SerializerRegistry.java
Exception	*BookServiceException_SOAPSerializer.java*
	BookServiceException_SOAPBuilder.java

---

* Refer to Chapter 8 for a more complete desccription of the elements and attributes in the wscompile configuration file.

Table 2-5. Some of the client-side source files generated by wscompile (continued)

Source	Generated files
Value type	BookInfo_SOAPSerializer.java
	BookInfo_SOAPBuilder.java
BookQuery interface	BookQuery_Stub.java
	BookQuery_getAuthor_RequestStruct.java
	BookQuery_GetAuthor_ResponseStruct.java
	BookQuery_getAuthor_RequestStruct_SOAPBuilder.java
	BookQuery_GetAuthor_ResponseStruct_SOAPBuilder.java
	BookQuery_getAuthor_RequestStruct_SOAPSerializer.java
	BookQuery_GetAuthor_ResponseStruct_SOAPSerializer.java
	BookQuery_getBookCount_RequestStruct.java
	BookQuery_GetBookCount_ResponseStruct.java
	BookQuery_getBookCount_RequestStruct_SOAPSerializer.java
	BookQuery_GetBookCount_ResponseStruct_SOAPSerializer.java

If you choose a different package name for the packageName attribute in the *config.xml* file, only the three service-related files shown in Table 2-5 will be generated in that package. The package location for all of the other files is determined by the package lines in the Java interface definitions themselves.

The Client-Side JAX-RPC API

Most of the files in Table 2-5 handle the details of interfacing with the JAX-RPC runtime to convert client method calls to SOAP messages and extract the return value, if there is one, from the reply message. To use the client-side JAX-RPC API, you need only to concern yourself with the service-related files and the stubs.

The file *BookService.java* contains the definition of an interface that represents the book web service itself. In other words, it corresponds directly to the service element in the wscompile configuration file. The content of this file is shown in Example 2-10.

Example 2-10. The BookService.java file, generated by xrpcc

```
package ora.jwsnut.chapter2.bookservice;

import javax.xml.rpc.*;

public interface BookService extends javax.xml.rpc.Service {
    public ora.jwsnut.chapter2.bookservice.BookQuery getBookQueryPort( );
}
```

The BookService interface extends javax.xml.rpc.Service, which, despite its name, is actually a JAX-RPC client-side interface. Most of the methods of the Service interface are concerned with the details of the dynamic invocation interface (DII), which will be covered in Chapter 6. The single generated method in the

BookService interface allows you to get a reference to the stub object for the endpoint interface for this service. The value returned by the getBookQueryPort( ) method is of type `ora.jwsnut.chapter2.bookservice.BookQuery`, which corresponds to the service endpoint interface itself, rather than the actual runtime type of the generated stub. This makes the code that uses the stub more portable, since it does not need to refer to the stub class using an implementation-dependent name.

When writing an application, you need to get a reference to the stub. In order to get one, you need an object that implements the BookService interface so that you can call its getBookQueryPort( ) method. The only way to get such an object is to instantiate BookService_Impl, which is another class generated by wscompile that implements the BookService interface. This is unfortunate, because the JAX-RPC specification does not require the name of the implementation class for the service interface to be formed by adding _Impl to the service interface name as it is in this case—it recommends only that it should be. As a result, the code required to access the service is dependent on a particular JAX-RPC implementation:

```
// Get a reference to the stub and set the service address
BookService_Impl  service = new BookService_Impl( );
```

 The client-side JAX-RPC API includes an interface called ServiceFactory, which is intended to allow Service objects to be created without requiring prior knowledge of the implementation class involved. Ideally, it should be possible to obtain a Service object by calling a method of ServiceFactory, passing it the name of the service that you require. Unfortunately, this works only if your service is described by a WSDL document, or if you want to use the dynamic invocation interface; ServiceFactory is of no use when using statically created client-side stubs. The ServiceFactory interface is described in Chapter 6.

Given an instance of the Service implementation class, you can get a reference to an object that implements the service endpoint interface:

```
BookQuery  bookQuery = (BookQuery)service.getBookQueryPort( );
```

Using this reference, you can call any of the methods of the BookQuery interface:

```
String  editorName = bookQuery.getEditor(bookTitle);
```

However, this does not work yet, because nowhere have you told the JAX-RPC runtime how to connect to the host containing the service implementation. In order to do this, you have to *configure* the stub. As well as implementing the methods of service endpoint interface, the stub returned by the getBookQueryPort( ) method implements the interface javax.xml.rpc.Stub, which is part of the client-side JAX-RPC API.[*] This interface is particularly simple, consisting of only three methods:

```
public interface Stub {
    public abstract Object _getProperty(String name) throws JAXRPCException;
```

---

[*] In fact, the object returned by the getBookQueryPort( ) method is an instance of the generated BookQuery_Stub class that was listed in Table 2-5.

```
    public abstract Iterator  _getPropertyNames();
    public abstract void  _setProperty(String name, Object value)
        throws JAXRPCException;
}
```

These methods allow a Stub to be configured using a set of properties, a small number of which are defined by the JAX-RPC specification and are therefore portable across different JAX-RPC implementations. Vendors are also permitted to define their own properties, which the application code may use at the risk of reducing application portability. The names of the standard properties, which are described in Table 2-6, are all constants defined by the Stub interface.

Table 2-6. Standard Stub properties

Property name	Type	Description
ENDPOINT_ADDRESS_PROPERTY	String	The address of the service to which the stub should connect. The format of this address depends on the protocol used to carry the messages to the server.
SESSION_MAINTAIN_PROPERTY	Boolean	Specifies whether the client wishes to enter into and maintain a session with the service endpoint. By default, this property is false and session management is not performed. Refer to "Client and Server Context Handling" in Chapter 6 for more information on the use of this property.
USERNAME_PROPERTY PASSWORD_PROPERTY	String	These properties can be used to specify a username and password if the server requires client authentication. Support for basic HTTP authentication is required by the specification when HTTP is used as the underlying message transport mechanism. Authentication is described in more detail in "JAX-RPC Authentication" in Chapter 6".

The _getPropertyNames() method returns an Iterator whose values are the names of the properties for which the stub has configured values. The _getProperty() method returns the value associated with a single named property, while _setProperty() changes a given property's value. The last two methods throw a JAXRPCException if they detect an error, which might be caused by one of the following:

- Using an invalid property name.
- Attempting to associate a value with a property that is not of the type expected by that property.
- Attempting to associate a value with a property that is of the correct type but is illegal for some other reason. Note, however, that not all property values are necessarily verified at the time that they are set. For example, the value of the ENDPOINT_ADDRESS_PROPERTY might not be checked by the _setProperty() method because its validity can only be determined by attempting to use it. In this case, an illegal value instead leads to an exception during the invocation of a remote method.

JAXRPCException is defined in the javax.xml.rpc package. It may have an associated error message and/or refer to another Throwable that describes the initial cause of an error. These values can be obtained using the getMessage() and getLinkedCause() methods, respectively. Since JAXRPCException is a RuntimeException, application code is not obliged to catch and handle it.

The address of the service to which the Stub should connect is configured by setting the property ENDPOINT_ADDRESS_PROPERTY, the value of which must be a String. The way in which the address is interpreted depends on the transport mechanism and the implementation of the server-side JAX-RPC runtime. The book web service application client avoids any knowledge of the format of the address by obtaining it from the command line and then calling the _setProperty( ) method of the Stub object obtained from the getBookQueryPort( ) method to configure it:

```
((Stub)bookQuery)._setProperty(Stub.ENDPOINT_ADDRESS_PROPERTY, args[0]);
```

You'll see how the appropriate value for the address is actually constructed in the next section.

The Server-Side Implementation

As you saw earlier in this chapter, the server-side implementation of the book web service is not at all dependent on JAX-RPC—it is simply a set of classes, one of which implements the methods of the BookQuery interface. In fact, there really isn't very much that can be termed a server-side JAX-RPC API. The javax.xml. rpc.server package, which contains what API there is, consists only of two interfaces, both of which deal with accessing the servlet environment from which the methods of the servant class will be invoked. Neither of these interfaces is relevant to a web service hosted by an EJB, so there really is no service-side JAX-RPC API at all for EJB-hosted services. Since the book web service (which is initially implemented within a servlet) doesn't need to access the servlet environment, we defer discussion of the javax.xml.rpc.server package to Chapter 6.

Server-side architecture

In order to understand how a JAX-RPC service is deployed, it is useful to review how the methods of the service implementation class are invoked by the server-side JAX-RPC runtime. Figure 2-10 shows the server-side architecture for the case in which the service is deployed in a web container. The alternative, in which the service is provided by a stateless session bean, is covered separately in "Using EJBs to Implement Web Services" later in this chapter.

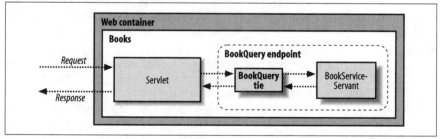

Figure 2-10. The server-side JAX-RPC runtime environment as implemented in a web container

SOAP messages for a service deployed in a web container are handled first by a servlet that is registered to receive HTTP requests directed to URLs that begin with the context path of the web application in which the service is deployed, plus an additional part that identifies the web service itself. The way in which these URL parts are determined depends on the details of the deployment, which are described in the later section "Deployment of a JAX-RPC Service in a Web Container." For example, the URL for the book web service, when deployed on the J2EE 1.4 platform using deployment information supplied with the example source code, is *http://localhost:8000/Books/BookQuery*. Here, the context path is *Books* and the part of the URL that corresponds to the book web service itself is *BookQuery*. In terms of Figure 2-10, the entire URL maps to the single servlet instance shown at the top-left of the diagram, within the Books web application.

On receipt of a SOAP message, the servlet locates the generated tie class for the service endpoint interface and passes it the message, from which the tie extracts the name of the method to be invoked, together with the XML-encoded representations of its parameters. The tie decodes the method parameters and uses them to invoke the target method of the servant class. The return value and any output parameters are then encoded into XML and used to build a reply message that the servlet returns to the calling client.

The JAX-RPC specification does not describe in detail how the servlet itself is to be implemented. Vendors are free to provide their own implementation or may generate one during the deployment process. The information that determines the URL of the servlet is provided at deployment time, along with details that allow the servlet to find the service endpoint interface, the tie class, and the service implementation class. The information required to deploy a web service on the J2EE 1.4 platform is defined by the J2EE Web Services specification (JSR 109). There is no formal specification that covers other possible deployment targets (such as the Tomcat web container with the JWSDP, which defines its own set of deployment files as described in the later section "Deploying a JAX-RPC Service with the JWSDP").

Service implementation threading model

If a servlet receives a client request for a web service while that service is already handling an earlier request, it needs to decide whether to dispatch the new request immediately or to defer it until handling of the existing request is completed. The JAX-RPC specification does not define what should happen in this case, but there is a precise definition for the case in which the web service is deployed on the J2EE 1.4 platform. The rules are as follows:

Service hosted by a servlet on the J2EE 1.4 platform
> In this case, the behavior depends on whether the servant class implements the javax.servlet.SingleThreadModel interface. If it does not, the servlet may dispatch the request immediately to an existing instance of the servant class. As a result, there may be multiple threads of execution within the servant class at any given time, and it must therefore be implemented in a thread-safe manner. On the other hand, if the servant class implements SingleThreadModel, the servlet ensures that only one thread of execution is active in any one instance of the servant class. It may do this by serializing all requests through a single instance of the class or by creating as many instances as are necessary to service all outstanding requests (probably subject to a maximum number of instances) and dispatch each request to a dedicated instance.

Service hosted by a stateless session bean on the J2EE 1.4 platform

Like all EJBs, stateless session beans are inherently single-threaded, and therefore the container must ensure that only one web service request at a time is active within any given EJB. Should another request be received while an earlier one is active, the container may choose to create a new instance of the bean to service the request, or may queue the request for later processing by an existing instance.

Service hosted by the JWSDP in a Tomcat web container

The JWSDP behaves as if the servant class did not implement the SingleThreadModel interface. In other words, all requests are dispatched to a single servant instance, which must therefore be implemented so that it is thread-safe.

An important point to note is that the servant class, whether it is hosted in a servlet or a stateless session bean, cannot hold client-specific state in its instance variables. Attempting to do so would lead to undefined effects, since the same instance might be used first to service a method call from one client and then to handle a call from another client, thereby changing the state created for the first client. Alternatively, if the server-side implementation adopts a pooled model, two successive method calls from the same client might be dispatched to different instances of the servant class, which would also result in the client state set up by the first method called being unavailable for the second call. The bottom line is that all operations in web service interfaces must supply all the necessary information as method parameters, and the operation cannot have any side effects.[*]

Deployment of a JAX-RPC Service in a Web Container

To deploy a servlet-hosted web service, create a web archive (WAR) file containing the classes and resources required to define a J2EE web application.[†] The files that you might expect to have to place in this archive include:

- The Java class file for the service endpoint interface
- The Java class files for the service implementation and any resources that it relies on, such as the *booklist.txt* file
- A *web.xml* file that contains deployment information for the web application
- The class files for the JAX-RPC tie classes

The responsibilty for creating the files in the first three categories lies with the developer. However, the generated tie classes are dependent on a specific JAX-RPC implementation, so, if you create a WAR file that includs them, you would only be able to deploy the file into a container hosting the JAX-RPC implementation used to generate them. In order to clearly separate the duties of the

---

[*] In fact, as we'll see in Chapter 6, it is possible to use HTTP sessions to pass client-specific state between a JAX-RPC client and the servant class, provided that the service is hosted in a web container. There is no such facility for EJB-hosted web services.

[†] The deployment of a web service hosted by an EJB is described separately in "Using EJBs to Implement Web Services" later in this chapter.

application developer or assembler from those of the person performing the actual deployment, the process is actually divided into two steps:

1. The developer or application assembler creates an archive that contains the components that have no dependency on the JAX-RPC runtime. The result of this step is a portable WAR file.

2. The deployer processes the portable WAR file to create a separate, implementation-specific archive or archives that can be deployed into a specific web container. This processing is performed by a tool provided by the vendor of the target JAX-RPC environment.

The details of both of these steps depend on whether your deployment target is the J2EE 1.4 reference implementation (or a commercial product derived from it) or a Tomcat web container hosting the JWSDP. These two cases are described separately in the following sections.

In the case of the book web service, the content of the portable WAR file includes those files listed in Table 2-7, which are clearly not dependent on the deployment platform.

Table 2-7. Content of the portable WAR file for the book web service

Category	Filename
Service Definition	*WEB-INF/classes/ora/jwsnut/chapter2/bookservice/BookQuery.class*
	WEB-INF/classes/ora/jwsnut/chapter2/bookservice/BookServiceException.class
	WEB-INF/classes/ora/jwsnut/chapter2/bookservice/BookInfo.class
Implementation	*WEB-INF/classes/ora/jwsnut/chapter2/bookservice/BookServiceServant.class*
	WEB-INF/classes/ora/jwsnut/chapter2/bookservice/BookServiceServantData.class
Resources	*WEB-INF/classes/ora/jwsnut/chapter2/bookservice/booklist.txt*

In addition, the developer is required to include one or more files that contain information required by the tools that will perform the actual deployment. The requirement to include these files appears to make the archive nonportable. However, this is not strictly true, for the following reasons:

- A portable archive that will eventually be deployed onto the J2EE 1.4 platform requires a set of files that are defined by the J2EE Web Service specification. Such an archive is, therefore, portable amongst all implementations of that specification. In practice, additional deployment information will likely need to be supplied in vendor-specific files within the archive. As long as these are named differently by each vendor, it should still be possible to create a single portable archive that can be targeted at a range of J2EE 1.4 platform implementations by including the additional vendor-specific files for all of them.

- The JWSDP also requires additional deployment information. Unfortunately, at the time of this writing, the JWSDP requires the developer to include in the portable WAR file a version of the *web.xml* file that is not compatible with the requirements placed on the same file by J2EE 1.4. It is therefore not practical to build a portable web archive that can be deployed both to a J2EE 1.4 platform and to a web container hosting the JWSDP reference implementation. In practice, it is unlikely that the JWSDP will be used as a deployment target in production environments; therefore, the incompatibility with J2EE 1.4 is not really important.*

As a result of the differences between these two cases, the deployment targets in the Ant buildfiles for the example source code for this book can be used to build a portable WAR file that can be deployed either to J2EE 1.4 or to the JWSDP (but not to both). The two deployment processes are described separately in the next two sections.

Deploying a JAX-RPC Service onto the J2EE 1.4 Platform

Deployment of a JAX-RPC web service onto the J2EE 1.4 platform requires the creation of a portable web archive and processing of that archive by utilities provided by the target platform. This section describes the steps required to deploy a service using the tools provided by this J2EE 1.4 reference implementation.

Creating the portable WAR file

The portable WAR file for the J2EE 1.4 platform requires the files listed in Table 2-7, plus a number of other files that contain deployment information. The content of these files is completely described by the J2EE Web Services specification, so you can rely on the fact that the same files should work with all conforming implementations. Vendors are, however, free to require additional information to be provided in files that are specific to their own implementations of the J2EE 1.4 platform. To create the deployable WAR file for the book web service, use the command:

```
ant portable-web-package
```

which results in an archive called *Books-portable.war* being created in the directory *chapter2\bookservice*.

The required deployment files are listed in Table 2-8.

---

* It happens to be the case that, despite the apparent incompatibility between J2EE 1.4 and the JWSDP, it is possible to create a single *web.xml* file that can be used for both deployments; therefore, a single portable WAR file can be built that is suitable for both. However, after processing, the *web.xml* file in the deployable WAR file for the JWSDP contains content that should not, strictly speaking, be legal, even though it happens to work when deployed to the Tomcat web container. This should be considered good luck and should not be relied upon in the real world.

Table 2-8. Deployment files required by the J2EE 1.4 platform

File	Description
WEB-INF/web.xml	Maps web application URLs to the servlets hosting the web service and contains environment settings and parameters for those servlets, together with security constraints that may be used to restrict access only to authorized users.
WEB-INF/webservices.xml	Describes the web services contained in the archive and how they map to servlets or EJBs.
WSDL files	Definitions for each web service in the *webservices.xml* file.
Mapping file	Defines the mapping from the WSDL definition of the web services to the Java classes that implement the service.

The easiest way to describe these files is to look at those used to deploy the book web service. The *web.xml* file for this service is shown in Example 2-11 and a copy of it, together with the other deployment files, can be found in the directory *chapter2\bookservice\deploy-j2ee14* relative to the book's example source code.

Example 2-11. The web.xml file for the book web service for deployment on the J2EE 1.4 platform

```xml
<?xml version="1.0" encoding="UTF-8"?>

<!DOCTYPE web-app
    PUBLIC "-//Sun Microsystems, Inc.//DTD Web Application 2.3//EN"
    "http://java.sun.com/j2ee/dtds/web-app_2_3.dtd">

<web-app>
  <display-name>JAX-RPC Book Service</display-name>
  <description>JAX-RPC Book Service</description>
  <servlet>
    <servlet-name>BookQueryServlet</servlet-name>
    <servlet-class>ora.jwsnut.chapter2.bookservice.BookServiceServant
        </servlet-class>
    <load-on-startup>0</load-on-startup>
  </servlet>
  <servlet-mapping>
    <servlet-name>BookQueryServlet</servlet-name>
    <url-pattern>/BookQuery</url-pattern>
  </servlet-mapping>
  <session-config>
    <session-timeout>60</session-timeout>
  </session-config>
</web-app>
```

This is a standard *web.xml* file that declares a single servlet called BookQueryServlet, which can be accessed using the path BookQuery relative to the context path of the web application itself. If the web application is deployed with the context path Books, then the URL *http://localhost:8000/Books/BookQuery* can be used to send SOAP messages to this web service. The following rules apply to the servlet-mapping element in the *web.xml* file when the servlet it relates to is the host for a J2EE web service.

- It is not mandatory to include a `servlet-mapping` for the servlet. If this element is omitted, the deployment tools will determine a suitable mapping and include the appropriate `servlet-mapping` element in the deployed version of the *web.xml* file.*

- If a `servlet-mapping` is specified, then the `url-pattern` must not be a wildcard path. In other words, values such as /* and /BookQuery* are not valid.

- Only one `servlet-mapping` may be specified for each servlet that hosts a web service.

Once the service is deployed, its URL is used to update the `address` element in the WSDL definition so that clients can use this file to locate the web service. See Chapter 5 for a discussion of WSDL files and the addressing information that they contain.

The servlet name assigned using the `servlet-name` tag should be unique within the web archive. It is used to link the servlet to the ports in the *webservices.xml* file (shown later) for the service endpoint interfaces that it hosts. The `servlet-class` element contains the name of the service implementation class rather than a servlet class. At deployment time, this name is replaced by a reference to a servlet provided or generated by the target container to create a valid *web.xml* file.

The portable WAR file must include a WSDL file that describes the web service being deployed. The book service example used in this chapter is specified using a Java interface definition, so a WSDL description is not immediately available. However, you can use the command-line utility `wscompile` to create a suitable WSDL file, using a command line like the following:

```
wscompile -define -classpath output\interface -d output\server config.xml
```

where the *config.xml* file is as shown in Example 2-9, and gives the name of the service and the class name of the Java interface that defines the service endpoint. The `-classpath` option points to the directory beneath which the compiled interface class file can be found. The WSDL file is written to the directory supplied with the `-d` option and is typically copied to the root directory or the *WEB-INF* directory of the portable archive. The exact location of this file within the archive is not critical because it is specified in the *webservices.xml* file.

The *webservices.xml* file contains definitions for the web services that appear in the portable WAR file. The content of this file for the book service is shown in Example 2-12. This file *must* reside in the *WEB-INF* directory of the archive. For a complete description of the elements that may appear in this file, refer to Chapter 8.

Example 2-12. The webservices.xml file for the book web service

```
<?xml version="1.0" encoding="UTF-8"?>

<!DOCTYPE webservices
    PUBLIC "-//IBM Corporation, Inc.//DTD J2EE Web services 1.0//EN"
    "http://www.ibm.com/standards/xml/webservices/j2ee/j2ee_web_services_1_0.dtd">
```

---

* Although this requirement appears in the J2EE Web Services specification, at the time of this writing it is not implemented in the J2EE 1.4 reference implementation.

Example 2-12. The webservices.xml file for the book web service (continued)

```
<webservices>
  <webservice-description>
    <webservice-description-name>JAX-RPC Book Service
    </webservice-description-name>
    <wsdl-file>BookService.wsdl</wsdl-file>
    <jaxrpc-mapping-file>WEB-INF/model</jaxrpc-mapping-file>
    <port-component>
      <port-component-name>BookQueryPort</port-component-name>
      <wsdl-port>
        <namespaceURI>urn:jwsnut.chapter2.bookservice/wsdl/BookQuery
        </namespaceURI>
        <localpart>BookQueryPort</localpart>
      </wsdl-port>
      <service-endpoint-interface>ora.jwsnut.chapter2.bookservice.BookQuery
      </service-endpoint-interface>
      <service-impl-bean>
        <servlet-link>BookQueryServlet</servlet-link>
      </service-impl-bean>
    </port-component>
  </webservice-description>
</webservices>
```

A WAR file may contain implementations of any number of web services; for each, there is a corresponding `webservice-description` element in the *webservices.xml* file. Each such element must contain at least the following child elements:

`wsdl-file`

Points to the WSDL document that describes the web service represented by the containing `webservice-description` element. The value of this element is a path that is taken to be relative to the root of the archive. There is no fixed location for this file. In Example 2-12, the WSDL definition is in a file called *BookService.wsdl* located in the root of the archive. It is not necessary to include a leading "/" to indicate that the path begins with the archive root.

`jaxrpc-mapping-file`

A file that describes a mapping between the WSDL definition and the Java interfaces that represent the service endpoints of the web service. There is no fixed name or location within the web archive for this file. Its content is used by the deployment tools when creating the tie and serializer classes for the deployed web service. This is a complex file that is described in more detail in Chapter 8. In the simplest cases, it is only necessary to indicate how the namespaces within the WSDL file for the service are mapped to Java packages. The J2EE 1.4 reference implementation allows a model file to be supplied instead of a JAX-RPC mapping file. This is convenient, because a model file can be generated automatically from either a Java interface definition or a WSDL file. The examples in this book all take advantage of this feature in order to minimize the work required to deploy a web service on the J2EE 1.4 platform. Vendor implementations are not required to support this, but are likely to provide a tool that will allow a default mapping file to be created with minimal effort. In Example 2-12, the `jaxrpc-mapping-file` element points to a model file held within the *WEB-INF* directory of the archive.

port-component

> A `webservice-description` element must contain a `port-component` element for each port in its associated WSDL file. A mismatch between the set of ports in the WSDL file and the `port-component` elements in *webservices.xml* causes an error at deployment time. Recall from the beginning of this chapter that a port represents a binding of a service endpoint interface to a particular combination of messaging and transport protocols at a specific transport address. The child elements of the `port-component` element contain the information necessary to identify the WSDL port and the way in which it is implemented within the web container.

The `port-component` element has several optional child elements that allow the inclusion of descriptive information, plus an optional `handler` element that allows SOAP message handlers to be configured. (SOAP message handlers are an advanced feature that is described in Chapter 6.) The following child elements must appear exactly once, in the following order, in each `port-component` element:

port-component-name

> Provides a name for the port. This name is not necessarily related to the name port that appears within the WSDL definition for the web service, but it must be unique among all `port-component` elements in the *webservices.xml* file.

wsdl-port

> Specifies the port within the WSDL definition that the `port-component` is associated with, in terms of the port name and its namespace URI (refer to Example 2-12). The quickest way to determine the values to be used within this element is to locate the definition of the port in the WSDL file and transcribe the name and namespace URI from there.

service-endpoint-interface

> Gives the fully qualified Java class name of the class that represents the service endpoint interface.

service-impl-bean

> This element is the link from the port definition to its actual implementation. The `service-impl-bean` element must contain either a nested `servlet-link` or a nested `ejb-link` element, depending on whether the service is hosted within a servlet or a stateless session bean. In the former case, the value of the `servlet-link` element is the `servlet-name` of a servlet defined in the *web.xml* file in the same web archive. In Example 2-12, for instance, this element has the value `BookQueryServlet`, which indicates that the web service is hosted by the servlet of the name defined in the *web.xml* file shown in Example 2-11. This, in turn, means that the URL associated with this port will be */BookQuery* relative to the context path of the web application. For a description of the alternative `ejb-link` element, refer to "Using EJBs to Implement Web Services," later in this chapter.

Note that the J2EE Web Services specification requires that only one `port-component` element be associated with any particular servlet, which means that one servlet can only implement a single service endpoint interface.

Deploying the JAX-RPC service

Once you have a portable WAR file, there are several ways to deploy it to a J2EE application server. The most direct approach is to use the -deployModule option of the deploytool utility:

```
deploytool -server localhost -deployModule -id Books Books-portable.war
```

This command causes the web service in the file *Books-portable.war* to be deployed on the application server running on localhost. During the deployment, the appropriate tie classes are generated and the linkage between the servlet, the tie classes, and the web service implementation class (as shown in Figure 2-10) are created. The id argument supplies the context path of the web application hosting the web service, so that the BookQuery port of the service is available at the URL *http://localhost:8000/Books/BookQuery*. This method also works if the portable WAR file is wrapped into an Enterprise Archive (EAR) in order to allow EJBs to be deployed at the same time.

As an alternative, you can perform the deployment in two stages. The first step uses the j2eec utility to create the ties required by the web service and saves them in a separate JAR file, along with the appropriate serializers, the client-side stubs, and the generated Service class for the service:

```
j2eec -o Books-generated.jar Books-portable.war
```

The second step uses the deploytool -deployGeneratedModule option to complete the deployment:

```
deploytool -server localhost -deployGeneratedModule -id Books
Books-portable.war Books-generated.jar
```

The -deployGeneratedModule option differs from -deployModule in that it requires a JAR file containing the pregenerated ties to be supplied as a command-line argument, whereas the -deployModule option generates the ties each time it is used. During development, it may be faster to use the -deployGeneratedModule option because it avoids the overhead of tie class generation for each deployment, provided that you don't change the web service interface in any way that would require a change in the generated classes.

Deploying a JAX-RPC Service with the JWSDP

This section describes the steps needed to deploy a JAX-RPC web service into a web container hosting the JWSDP reference implementation. Before attempting to deploy the book web service into the JWSDP, you should edit the *jwsnutExamples.properties* file in your home directory so that the USING_JWSDP property is set, as described in "Examples Online" in the Preface. These settings determine how the Ant buildfile targets perform the deployment.

Creating the portable WAR file

As noted earlier, the portable WAR file for the JWSDP is portable only between implementations of the JWSDP. To create a portable WAR file for the book web service, with *chapter2\bookservice* as your working directory, type the command:

```
ant portable-web-package
```

which creates a file called *Books-portable.war* in the same directory. If you look at the content of this file, you'll find that it contains the three files shown in Table 2-9 in addition to those listed in Table 2-7.

Table 2-9. Additional portable WAR files required for JWSDP deployment

Name	Description
WEB-INF/web.xml	Web application deployment descriptor
WEB-INF/jaxrpc-ri.xml	JWSDP-specific deployment information
WEB-INF/model	Model file generated by `wscompile`

A *web.xml* file typically contains information that describes the servlets that make up a web application, together with the URL mappings for those servlets. It may also contain initialization parameters and security constraints that must be applied to protect some or all of the web application's resources. The *web.xml* file for the book web service example, which can be found in the directory *chapter2\ bookservice\deploy*, is shown in Example 2-13.

Example 2-13. The web.xml file for the book web service for deployment with the JWSDP

```
<?xml version="1.0" encoding="UTF-8" ?>

<!DOCTYPE web-app
    PUBLIC "-//Sun Microsystems, Inc.//DTD Web Application 2.3//EN"
    "http://java.sun.com/j2ee/dtds/web-app_2_3.dtd">


<web-app>
    <display-name>JAX-RPC Book Service</display-name>
    <description>Book Service Web Application using JAX-RPC</description>
</web-app>
```

As you can see, this file contains only a description of the web application. Information relating to the deployment of the service, such as the servlet to use and the URL mapping, is not included. Instead, the JAX-RPC reference implementation in the JWSDP generates this information based on the content of the *jaxrpc-ri.xml* file when it creates the deployable WAR file.

In most cases, it would not be strictly necessary to include a model file in the portable archive. If you choose not to do so, then during the process of creating a deployable WAR file, a WSDL definition for the service is created based on the Java interface that defines the service endpoint, whereas if the model file is included in the archive and referenced from the *jaxrpc-ri.xml* file (as shown next), the WSDL definition is built from the information in the model file. The difference between these two approaches is as follows:

- If the model file is used, the service name in the WSDL file is as specified to `wscompile`, which in this case is `BookService`. If it is not specified, the service name is the name of the Java interface file—in this case, `BookQuery`. In many cases, this is not significant, because it is not visible to a client that uses statically generated stubs. It may be considered relevant if, as will be shown in

Chapter 6, the client stubs are created from the WSDL definition rather than from the Java interface definition, since the name of the service class will not match that used in the static client.

- In some cases, it is essential to include the model file because the Java interface definition alone does not convey everything about the way in which the service should behave. Some examples of this will be given in Chapter 6.

All of the JAX-RPC examples in this book include the model file in the deployable web archive.

Creating a deployable WAR file

To create a deployable WAR file for deployment in the JWSDP, use a command-line utility called `wsdeploy`. The basic form of this command requires only the names of the portable WAR file and deployable WAR file that is to be created:

```
wsdeploy -o targetFileName portableWarFileName
```

You'll find a more complete description of `wsdeploy` in Chapter 8. To create the deployable WAR file for the book web service, you can use the `web-package` target of the `Ant` buildfile:

```
ant web-package
```

This command writes its output to the file *chapter2\bookservice\Books.war*. Note that, despite its name, the `wsdeploy` command simply creates the deployable WAR file and does *not* actually deploy it to an application server.

The process of creating the deployable archive is driven mainly by the content of the *jaxrpc-ri.xml* file, which is described later. The archive will contain the following:

- The class files and resources that were supplied in the portable WAR file.
- A compiled class file for the implementation-dependent tie required by the service endpoint interface. In the case of the `BookQuery` interface, this class is called `BookQuery_Tie`.
- Compiled class files for the serializers required to encode the method calls and data types used by the service into SOAP messages and to decode them. These files are the same as those created by `wscompile` when generating the client-side stubs. This makes sense, because each serializer contains the code to both encode and decode a data type or an RPC message; therefore, the same classes can be used by both the client and the server.
- A WSDL file that describes the web service in a form that can be used by other developers to create clients that can use the service. This file is placed in the *WEB-INF* directory of the archive and is created either from the Java interface representing the service endpoint or from the model file, if it is included.
- A copy of the JAX-RPC model file for the service, placed in the *WEB-INF* directory. This is either a copy of the model file that is included in the portable archive or, if it is not included, a compressed binary file built by inspecting the Java service interface definition. For the book web service, if this file is generated by `wsdeploy`, it would be called *BookQuery_model.xml.gz*. For more information on the use of a model file, refer to the description of the `wscompile` command in Chapter 8.

- A modified version of the *web.xml* file.
- A file called *jaxrpc-ri-runtime.xml*, which is based on the content of the *jaxrpc-ri.xml* file supplied in the portable WAR file.

When the web service is deployed as a web application, SOAP messages addressed to the URLs that correspond to the application will be delivered to a servlet (as shown in Figure 2-10) based on a servlet-mapping element in the *web.xml* file. This element, together with the name of servlet itself, was not supplied in the original *web.xml* file shown in Example 2-13, but is added by wsdeploy. Example 2-14 shows the version of *web.xml* that appears in the deployable archive.

Example 2-14. The modified web.xml file included in the Books.war file

```
<?xml version="1.0" encoding="UTF-8"?>
<!DOCTYPE web-app PUBLIC "-//Sun Microsystems, Inc.//DTD Web Application 2.3//EN"
        "http://java.sun.com/j2ee/dtds/web-app_2_3.dtd">
<web-app>
  <display-name>JAX-RPC Book Service</display-name>
  <description>Book Service Web Application using JAX-RPC</description>
  <listener>
    <listener-class>com.sun.xml.rpc.server.http.JAXRPCContextListener
    </listener-class>
  </listener>

  <servlet>
    <servlet-name>BookQuery</servlet-name>
    <display-name>BookQuery</display-name>
    <description>JAX-RPC endpoint - BookQuery</description>
    <servlet-class>com.sun.xml.rpc.server.http.JAXRPCServlet</servlet-class>
    <load-on-startup>1</load-on-startup>
  </servlet>

  <servlet-mapping>
    <servlet-name>BookQuery</servlet-name>
    <url-pattern>/BookQuery</url-pattern>
  </servlet-mapping>
</web-app>
```

The servlet element causes a servlet called JAXRPCServlet (which is part of the JWSDP reference implementation) to be loaded when the web application is started, while the servlet-mapping element causes all URLs that have the string BookQuery immediately following the context part, such as *http://localhost:8080/Books/BookQuery*, to be delivered to it. The *web.xml* file does not, of course, contain the information that the servlet will need to locate the correct tie and servant classes for the web service, which will be needed in order to handle SOAP messages. This information is supplied in the *jaxrpc-ri.xml* file, which the developer creates and includes in the portable WAR file. The content of this file, as used to deploy the book web service, is shown in Example 2-15.

Example 2-15. The jaxrpc-ri.xml file for the book web service

```
<?xml version="1.0" encoding="UTF-8"?>
<webServices
  xmlns="http://java.sun.com/xml/ns/jax-rpc/ri/dd"
```

```
version="1.0"
targetNamespaceBase="urn:jwsnut.chapter2.bookservice/wsdl/"
typeNamespaceBase="urn:jwsnut.chapter2.bookservice/types/">

    <endpoint
        name="BookQuery"
        displayName="BookQuery Port"
        description="Book Query Port"
        model="/WEB-INF/model"
        interface="ora.jwsnut.chapter2.bookservice.BookQuery"
        implementation="ora.jwsnut.chapter2.bookservice.BookServiceServant"/>

    <endpointMapping
        endpointName="BookQuery"
        urlPattern="/BookQuery"/>
</webServices>
```

The `webServices` element in this file may contain any number of `endpoint` elements, followed by any number of `endpointMapping` elements.[*] Each `endpoint` element describes a single service endpoint interface that will be managed by the servlet. The `name` attribute provides a symbolic name that links it to an `endpointMapping` element that has an `endpointName` attribute with the same value. When such an `endpointMapping` element exists, its `urlPattern` attribute is used to create the `url-pattern` element of the `servlet-mapping` for the service endpoint in the *web.xml* file, which in this case is */BookQuery*. If more than one `endpoint` is included in the `webServices` element, then there will be a `servlet-mapping` in the *web.xml* file for each of them. This means that more than one web service can be managed by a single servlet.

It is not necessary to include an `endpointMapping` element for each `endpoint` element. If you choose not to provide such an element, however, you must add an additional attribute to the `webServices` element that will be used to create the URL pattern for that endpoint. Example 2-16 shows an alternative to the *jaxrpc-ri.xml* file shown in Example 2-15 that does not use an `endpointMapping` element.

Example 2-16. A jaxrrpc-ri.xml file with no endpointMapping element

```
<?xml version="1.0" encoding="UTF-8"?>
<webServices
    xmlns="http://java.sun.com/xml/ns/jax-rpc/ri/dd"
    version="1.0"
    targetNamespaceBase="urn:jwsnut.chapter2.bookservice/wsdl/"
    typeNamespaceBase="urn:jwsnut.chapter2.bookservice/types/"
    urlPatternBase="/base">

    <endpoint
        name="BookQuery"
        displayName="BookQuery Port"
```

---

[*] The `targetNamespaceBase` and `typeNamespaceBase` attributes of the `webServices` element are not described here, because they are not relevent to this discussion. They are, however, covered in "JWSDP configuration files and XML namespaces," later in this chapter.

```
    description="Book Query Port"
    model="/WEB-INF/model"
    interface="ora.jwsnut.chapter2.bookservice.BookQuery"
    implementation="ora.jwsnut.chapter2.bookservice.BookServiceServant"/>
</webServices>
```

Since there is no endpointMapping element corresponding to the BookQuery endpoint element, wsdeploy uses the urlPatternBase attribute of the webServices element to create a default mapping using the pattern:

```
    urlPatternBase + '/' + endpoint name
```

In this case, this produces the result:

```
    /base/BookQuery
```

Using this setup, assuming that the web application is deployed with the context path Books, a client program needs to use the URL *http://localhost:8080/Books/base/BookQuery* to access the book web service, instead of *http://localhost:8080/Books/BookQuery*. As you can see from Example 2-15, you don't need to supply a value for urlPatternBase if every endpoint element has a matching endpointMapping.

Two other attributes in the endpoint element supply the other information that is required when decoding a URL from a client request. The interface attribute names the Java service endpoint interface that corresponds to the endpoint, while the implementation attribute provides the class name of the servant class. When wsdeploy processes this file, it creates a modified version of the file (called *jaxrpc-ri-runtime.xml*) that includes the name of the tie class that it generates for this endpoint (which is the information that the servlet really needs, together with the servant class name). Example 2-17 shows the *jaxrpc-ri-runtime.xml* file generated for the book web service, with the interesting attributes of the endpoint element highlighted in bold. Since this file is private to the JAX-RPC reference implementation, its format may change at any time. Fortunately, you will never have to create one of these files by hand.

Example 2-17. The jaxrpc-ri-runtime.xml file for the book web service

```
<?xml version="1.0" encoding="UTF-8"?>
<endpoints xmlns='http://java.sun.com/xml/ns/jax-rpc/ri/runtime' version='1.0'>
  <endpoint
    name='BookQuery'
    interface='ora.jwsnut.chapter2.bookservice.BookQuery'
    implementation='ora.jwsnut.chapter2.bookservice.BookServiceServant'
    tie='ora.jwsnut.chapter2.bookservice.BookQuery_Tie'
    model='/WEB-INF/BookQuery_model.xml.gz'
    wsdl='/WEB-INF/BookQuery.wsdl'
    service='{urn:jwsnut.chapter2.bookservice/wsdl/BookQuery}BookQuery'
    port='{urn:jwsnut.chapter2.bookservice/wsdl/BookQuery}BookQueryPort'
    urlpattern='/BookQuery'/>
</endpoints>
```

The *jaxrpc-ri-runtime.xml* file is placed in the *WEB-INF* directory of the deployable archive, where it can be located and read by the servlet during initialization.

Deploying the service implementation

Once you have the deployable WAR file, there are several ways in which you can deploy it. The context path associated with the web application that is created depends on the deployment method, as described in the following paragraphs.

Manually

If you are using the JWSDP with the Tomcat web container, a manual deployment can be performed by stopping the web server, copying the *Books.war* file into its *webapps* directory, and then restarting the web server. This is all that is required to complete the deployment. Although this is very simple, it is inconvenient because it involves manually stopping and starting the server each time you make a change to the service. The context path for the web application in this case is taken from the name of the web archive file with the *.war* suffix removed, and will therefore be *Books* in this case.

Using the Ant buildfile

The Tomcat web server includes a built-in web application called manager that can be used to programmatically deploy another web application. The JWSDP includes Ant tasks that use the manager application to automate the tasks of deployment and undeployment. The Ant buildfile for the example source code provides targets called deploy, undeploy, and redeploy, that take advantage of these tasks, the use of which is described in "Compiling and running the book web service example," earlier in this chapter. In this case, the context path for the web application is explicitly provided as a parameter to the Ant task.

Special handling for the HTTP GET request

Although SOAP messages from JAX-RPC clients are sent using HTTP POST requests, it is worth noting that JAXRPCServlet provides some useful behavior when it receives an HTTP GET request for the URL corresponding to a service endpoint. The information returned in response to these requests is intended for display in a browser and can be used to check that the service is properly deployed, or by developers that need to get a copy of the WSDL document that describes your service.

If, for example, you point your browser at the URL for the book web service, you get the result shown in Figure 2-11. You'll notice that the web page shown in the figure contains two further URLs that are directly derived from the URL of the service itself:

http://localhost:8080/Books/BookQuery?WSDL

Returns the WSDL document for the service. When you define a web service in terms of Java interfaces, the WSDL is created and deployed for you by wsdeploy. In Chapter 6, you'll see how to create the client stubs needed to allow a JAX-RPC client to access an existing web service given a WSDL document that describes it. The result of using this URL was shown in Figure 2-9 earlier in this chapter.

http://localhost:8080/Books/BookQuery?model

Fetches a compressed binary file that contains an internal representation of the web service as created by wsdeploy. As noted in "Converting the Service Interface Definition to Client-Side Stubs," earlier in this chapter, you can supply the content of this file to wscompile as another way to create the JAX-RPC client-side stubs for an existing web service.

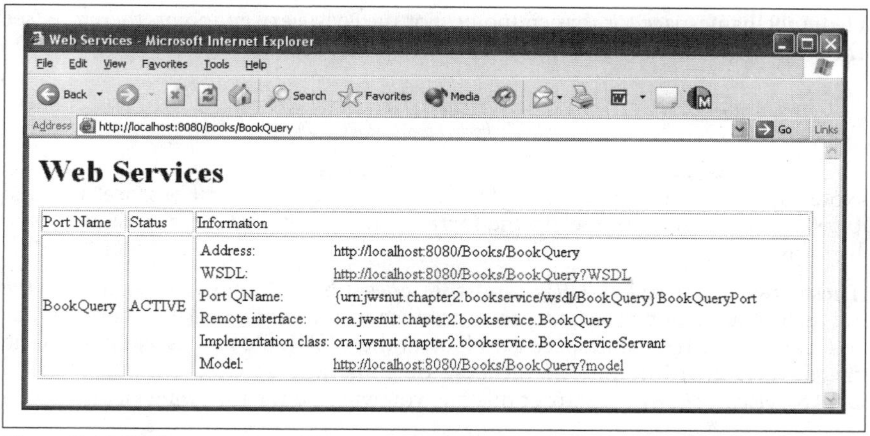

Figure 2-11. Web page returned by a GET request on the book service URL

JWSDP configuration files and XML namespaces

If you compare the content of the *config.xml* file used to generate the client-side stubs in Example 2-9 with the *jaxrpc-ri.xml* file for the server-side deployment shown in Example 2-15, you'll notice that they both have elements that contain namespace-related attributes. In the case of the *config.xm*l file, these attributes are associated with the service element:

```
<service name="BookService"
    targetNamespace="urn:jwsnut.chapter2.bookservice/wsdl/BookQuery"
    typeNamespace="urn:jwsnut.chapter2.bookservice/types/BookQuery"
    packageName="ora.jwsnut.chapter2.bookservice">
```

while in *jaxrpc-ri.xml* they appear with the webServices element:

```
<webServices
    xmlns="http://java.sun.com/xml/ns/jax-rpc/ri/dd"
    version="1.0"
    targetNamespaceBase="urn:jwsnut.chapter2.bookservice/wsdl/"
    typeNamespaceBase="urn:jwsnut.chapter2.bookservice/types/">
```

In Chapter 6, you'll see exactly how the namespaces specified by these attributes are used when building the SOAP messages that are exchanged by the client and server. For now, it is important to ensure that they specify consistent values—otherwise the server will not be able to decode messages sent to it by the client.

The key to using the correct value is to start by choosing the values of targetNamespaceBase and typeNamespaceBase in the *jaxrpc-ri.xml* file, which fixes their values for the server-side implementation. A namespace can be any valid URI; here, we chose to use a URN that clearly indicates that the service is part of the example source code for this chapter. By convention, the suffixes wsdl and types are added to indicate the different uses that are made of these namespaces.

As their names imply, these attributes are just base values. When the ties and the WSDL document for each service endpoint interface in the *jaxrpc-ri.xml* file are generated, wsdeploy appends the name of the endpoint to each base name to create the namespace for that endpoint. For the BookQuery endpoint, therefore (see the endpoint element in Example 2-15), the namespaces are:

Types namespace	urn:jwsnut.chapter2.bookservice/wsdl/BookQuery
Target namespace	urn:jwsnut.chapter2.bookservice/types/BookQuery

Note that it is necessary to add the "/" to the targetNamespaceBase and typeNamespaceBase attributes in the *jaxrpc-ri.xml* file in order for these names to be formed correctly.

These two namespace URIs are the ones that should be used for the targetNamespace and typeNamespace attributes in the *config.xml* file. Another way to locate the correct namespace is to look at the WSDL file that wsdeploy places in the deployable WAR file. In the case of book web service, this file is called *BookService.wsdl.** At the start of this file, you will find the following elements:

```
<?xml version="1.0" encoding="UTF-8"?>

<definitions name="BookService"
    targetNamespace="urn:jwsnut.chapter2.bookservice/wsdl/BookQuery"
    xmlns:tns="urn:jwsnut.chapter2.bookservice/wsdl/BookQuery"
    xmlns="http://schemas.xmlsoap.org/wsdl/"
    xmlns:soap="http://schemas.xmlsoap.org/wsdl/soap/"
    xmlns:xsd="http://www.w3.org/2001/XMLSchema"
    xmlns:ns2="urn:jwsnut.chapter2.bookservice/types/BookQuery"
    xmlns:ns3="http://java.sun.com/jax-rpc-ri/internal">
  <types>
  <schema targetNamespace=
      "urn:jwsnut.chapter2.bookservice/types/BookQuery"
        xmlns:xsi="http://www.w3.org/2001/XMLSchema-instance"
        xmlns:tns="urn:jwsnut.chapter2.bookservice/types/BookQuery"
        xmlns:soap-enc="http://schemas.xmlsoap.org/soap/encoding/"
        xmlns:wsdl="http://schemas.xmlsoap.org/wsdl/"
        xmlns="http://www.w3.org/2001/XMLSchema">
```

The correct values to use for the typeNamespace and targetNamespace attributes in the *config.xml* file are given by the targetNamespace attributes of the schema and definitions elements, respectively. This technique can also be used when you need to create a client to communicate with an existing service for which you only have a WSDL definition. You'll find more about WSDL in Chapter 5.

Using EJBs to Implement Web Services

So far, you have seen how to implement a web service and arrange for it to be hosted by a servlet in a web container. J2EE 1.4 extends this model by allowing you to implement web services as stateless session beans in the EJB container or, if you want to view it another way, to advertise the remote interface of an existing stateless session bean as a web service, provided that the interface methods meets the requirements of a JAX-RPC service endpoint interface.

---

* This name is used only if you include a model file in the deployable web archive and reference it from *jaxrpc-ri.xml*. If you do not, then the WSDL file will be called *BookQuery.xml* and the name attribute in the definitions element will be *BookQuery*.

Web Service Session Bean Requirements

Session beans typically have a combination of the following:

- A remote interface that contains the service methods that remote clients can invoke. This interface is required to extend `javax.ejb.EJBObject`.

- A local interface that contains the methods available to clients that reside with the session bean. This may be the same set of methods as those in the remote interface, but this is not required. The local interface extends `javax.ejb.EJBLocalObject`.

- A home interface that remote clients use to manage their view of the lifecycle of the session bean, including obtaining an instance of it and releasing it when it is no longer required. The home interface must extend `javax.ejb.EJBHome` and is required to exist if the session bean provides a remote interface.

- A local home interface, which is the equivalent of the home interface for clients that are local to the bean and extends `javax.ejb.EJBLocalHome`. The local home interface is required only if the bean provides a local interface.

- An implementation class or classes that provide the bean's code. One of these classes is considered to be the main implementation class of the bean and must implement the `javax.ejb.SessionBean` interface.

Session beans that host web services must provide and implement a service endpoint interface like the `BookQuery` interface defined for the book web service described in this chapter. This interface must, of course, satisfy the usual JAX-RPC requirements described in "Defining the service interface," earlier in this chapter, and will ultimately be published to clients in the form of a WSDL definition. The session bean may also have remote and/or local interfaces and the corresponding home and local home interfaces. However, a bean that is implemented simply in order to host a web service is not required to be accessible to either local or remote clients as an EJB and therefore is not required to provide the local and remote interfaces (or their home interface counterparts). Thus, although it is possible to extend an existing session bean so that it can be exposed as a web service by defining a service endpoint interface that advertises some or all of its existing business methods, it is not necessary to invent a local or remote interface or home interfaces for a new bean that is only intended to be used as a web service.

A web service session bean must provide a public no-argument constructor and all of the methods of the `SessionBean` interface. As you'll see later in this section, if the bean is purely providing a web service interface, most of these methods can be empty stubs. The bean must also provide implementations of all of the methods in the web service endpoint interface. However, the bean implementation class is not required to declare that it implements the endpoint interface.

EJB Web Service Programming Model

The lifecycle of a web service session bean is exactly the same as that of an ordinary stateless session bean. When a web service client invokes one of its methods, the container creates an instance and delegates the method invocation to it. Since the bean is stateless, the container is free to create a pool of bean instances to which it directs web service method invocations as required. The lifecycle of the bean is, therefore, decoupled from the lifecycle of the client applications that invoke its methods.

The overall lifecycle is as follows:

1. The container invokes the bean implementation class's zero-argument constructor.

2. The container calls the bean's setSessionContext( ) method, passing it a SessionContext object that gives it access to the container environment.

3. The container calls the bean's ejbCreate( ) method. Since the bean is created by the container rather than in response to a create( ) call from a home interface, and there is no state available that could be passed as method arguments, the bean is required to provide a zero-argument ejbCreate( ) method.

4. The container calls one or more methods from the web service endpoint interface as a result of receiving and decoding SOAP messages from clients.

5. After some time, the container may choose to destroy the bean instance. At this point, it calls its ejbRemove( ) method, after which no further web service calls will be delegated to it.

6. Eventually, the bean is garbage-collected. However, the implementation class is not permitted to override the finalize( ) method and cannot, therefore, use this method to tidy up its state. Any required cleanup should, therefore, be performed in the ejbRemove( ) method.

The fact that the container calls the ejbCreate( ) and ejbRemove( ) methods makes it possible for the bean to manage resources at the beginning and end of its lifecycle. By contrast, the implementation class for a servlet-hosted bean does not have direct access to the lifecycle of that servlet, and therefore, it must use its constructor and finalize( ) method to allocate and release resources unless it also implements the optional ServiceLifecycle interface, which will be discussed in Chapter 6.

The container's call to the setSessionContext( ) method provides the bean with a SessionContext object, which allows it access to its execution context, such as the java.security.Principal object that identifies the caller of its service endpoint methods. A servlet-hosted service implementation must implement the ServiceLifecycle interface to obtain the same information. Of course, the caller identity is valid only if the container has authenticated the caller. For further discussion of this topic, refer to Chapter 6. Note that the bean may not attempt to use the SessionContext getEJBHome( ) and getEJBLocalHome( ) methods to access the home or local home interfaces if it does not define those interfaces. Similarly, the bean may not call the getEJBObject( ) and getEJBLocalObject( ) methods during the execution of the methods that implements its service endpoint interface. This remains true even if the bean provides a local or remote client view outside the scope of its web service role.

A web service implemented in a session bean can assume that it is single-threaded, since this restriction applies to all session beans. EJB-based web services, therefore, have a slightly simpler programming model than those hosted by servlets, where multithreading is the norm.

The Book Web Service Implemented as a Stateless Session Bean

It is extremely simple to convert the servant class for the book web service shown in Example 2-6 into a session bean implementation of the same service. Since web service beans don't need to have home interfaces or even remote interfaces, you need only to build the session bean class itself, although nothing prevents you from providing these interfaces if you also want to expose your web service to EJB clients. Example 2-18 shows part of the bean implementation class for the book web service.

Example 2-18. Implementing the book web service as a stateless session bean

```
package ora.jwsnut.chapter2.ejbbookservice;

import java.util.HashMap;
import javax.ejb.EJBException;
import javax.ejb.SessionBean;
import javax.ejb.SessionContext;
import ora.jwsnut.chapter2.bookservice.BookInfo;
import ora.jwsnut.chapter2.bookservice.BookServiceException;

/**
 * Implementation class for the books web service
 * hosted by a stateless session bean.
 */
public class BookServiceEJB implements SessionBean {

    private SessionContext sessionContext;

    /**
     * Provides the bean with access to state
     * from the container.
     */
    public void setSessionContext(SessionContext sessionContext)
      throws EJBException {
        this.sessionContext = sessionContext;
    }

    // SessionBean methods
    public void ejbCreate() throws EJBException {
        // Nothing to do in this example
    }

    public void ejbRemove() throws EJBException {
        // Nothing to do in this example
    }

    /**
     * Activation/passivations methods are also no-ops
     */
    public void ejbActivate() throws EJBException {
    }
```

Example 2-18. Implementing the book web service as a stateless session bean (continued)

```
    public void ejbPassivate( ) throws EJBException {
    }

    /**
     * Gets the number of books known to the service
     * @return the number of books known to the service.
     */
    public int getBookCount( ) {
        return BookServiceServantData.getBookInfo( ).length;
    }

    // All other code unchanged
}
```

As you can see, the BookServiceEJB class implements the SessionBean interface, which requires it to provide the setSessionContext( ), ejbActivate( ), ejbPassivate( ), and ejbRemove( ) methods. In this case, there is nothing to do in any of these methods, although a more complex bean might use the ejbRemove( ) method, for example, to deallocate any resources that the bean uses during its life-cycle. In order to expose a session bean as a web service, it is also necessary to provide a no-argument ejbCreate( ) method, which could be used to perform initial resource allocation or to use JNDI to access configuration information specified in the *ejb-jar.xml* file and stored in the bean's environment, but which in this case also does nothing. The rest of the code consists of the implementation of the web service interface, which is not shown here because it is unchanged from Example 2-6.

The bean also has to provide a service endpoint interface class, which defines its web service view and provides the methods that its clients can use. In this case, the bean will simply reuse the BookQuery interface as defined in Example 2-3. Note, however, that the BookServiceEJB class does not state that it implements the BookQuery interface, because the Web Services for J2EE specification does not require it to do so. As you'll see later in this chapter, the connection between the bean class and the service endpoint interfaces that it implements is made in a deployment descriptor rather than in code. As a matter of fact, the bean implementation of this service can refer to exactly the same compiled class file for the service interface as the servlet-hosted variant. This means that a single application client could load the same service endpoint interface class file to access either the servlet- or the session bean–hosted variant of the service and not be able to tell them apart. More realistically, however, a client application will not have access to the original class file created by the service developer. Instead, it will use an interface class generated from the service's WSDL definition. Since both implementations offer the same service interface, they can share the same WSDL definition; therefore, no client that imports that definition will be aware of which implementation choice was made by the service developer.

EJB Web Service Deployment

Of course, writing the code is not the end of the story—you also need to deploy the service, which means creating the deployment descriptors and packaging them with the code. Writing deployment descriptors is a tedious task that is best dele-gated to a tool. Nevertheless, it is useful to know what they look like and how they depend on each other, so that you know where to look and what to expect should anything go wrong with your deployment.

You can compile and deploy the web service EJB by making *chapter2\ejbbookservice* your working directory and typing the command:

```
ant ejb-deploy
```

This command creates an EJB JAR file, wraps it in an Enterprise Archive, and deploys it to the J2EE 1.4 server. The EJB JAR file contains the files shown in Table 2-10.

Table 2-10. Files required to deploy the session bean-hosted book web service

File type	File name
Service endpoint interface	ora/jwsnut/chapter2/bookservice/BookInfo.class
	ora/jwsnut/chapter2/bookservice/BookQuery.class
	ora/jwsnut/chapter2/bookservice/BookServiceException.class
Bean implementation classes	ora/jwsnut/chapter2/ejbbookservice/BookServiceEJB.class
	ora/jwsnut/chapter2/ejbbookservice/BookServiceServantData.class
	ora/jwsnut/chapter2/ejbbookservice/booklist.txt
WSDL file	BookService.wsdl
Deployment information	META-INF/ejb-jar.xml
	META-INF/mapping.xml
	META-INF/model
	META-INF/webservices.xml
Manifest file	META-INF/MANIFEST.MF

The *mapping.xml* and model files perform the same function for the EJB as they did for the servlet-hosted version of the service shown earlier in this chapter. The two files of most interest in the archive are *ejb-jar.xml* and *webservices.xml*. The first file contains standard deployment information for a stateless session bean, as shown in Example 2-19.

Example 2-19. ejb-jar.xml file for the book web service session bean

```
<?xml version="1.0" encoding="UTF-8"?>
<ejb-jar version="2.1"
        xmlns="http://java.sun.com/xml/ns/j2ee"
        xmlns:xsi="http://www.w3.org/2001/XMLSchema-instance"
        xsi:schemaLocation="http://java.sun.com/xml/ns/j2ee
        http://java.sun.com/xml/ns/j2ee/ejb-jar_2_1.xsd">
  <display-name>EJB Book Service</display-name>
  <enterprise-beans>
    <session>
      <ejb-name>BookQueryBean</ejb-name>
      <service-endpoint>ora.jwsnut.chapter2.bookservice.BookQuery
      </service-endpoint>
```

```
        <ejb-class>ora.jwsnut.chapter2.ejbbookservice.BookServiceEJB</ejb-class>
        <session-type>Stateless</session-type>
        <transaction-type>Container</transaction-type>
      </session>
    </enterprise-beans>
</ejb-jar>
```

There are a couple of points worth noting in this file. First, since this bean offers only a web service interface, it does not require either a remote or a home interface, and therefore the elements of the deployment descriptor that correspond to these classes have been omitted from *ejb-jar.xml*. Second, for a web service bean, you have to include an additional element that declares the service endpoint interface that the bean implements. The line containing the service-endpoint element appropriate for this bean is highlighted in Example 2-19.

The content of the *webservices.xml* file for this archive is shown in Example 2-20.

Example 2-20. The webservices.xml file for the book web service session bean

```
<?xml version="1.0" encoding="UTF-8"?>
<!DOCTYPE webservices
    PUBLIC "-//IBM Corporation, Inc.//DTD J2EE Web services 1.0//EN"
    "http://www.ibm.com/standards/xml/webservices/j2ee/j2ee_web_services_1_0.dtd">

<webservices>
  <webservice-description>
    <webservice-description-name>EJB-Based JAX-RPC Book Service
    </webservice-description-name>
    <wsdl-file>BookService.wsdl</wsdl-file>
    <jaxrpc-mapping-file>META-INF/model</jaxrpc-mapping-file>
    <port-component>
      <port-component-name>BookQueryPort</port-component-name>
      <wsdl-port>
        <namespaceURI>urn:jwsnut.chapter2.bookservice/wsdl/BookQuery
        </namespaceURI>
        <localpart>BookQueryPort</localpart>
      </wsdl-port>
      <service-endpoint-interface>ora.jwsnut.chapter2.bookservice.BookQuery
      </service-endpoint-interface>
      <service-impl-bean>
        <ejb-link>BookQueryBean</ejb-link>
      </service-impl-bean>
    </port-component>
  </webservice-description>
</webservices>
```

This file is almost the same as that deployed with the version of the service shown in Example 2-12, with the exception of the service-impl-bean element. Here, this element contains a nested ejb-link element instead of the servlet-link that is used when the service is hosted by a servlet. The value contained within the ejb-link element is the name of the session bean that provides the service and must match the value of the ejb-name element in the *ejb-jar.xml* file in Example 2-19.

The EJB Web Service URL

To be accessible to a client, a web service must have a URL. A web service port implemented in a servlet has a URL that is derived from that of the servlet itself, as described earlier in this chapter. Session beans, of course, do not have associated URLs. One of the steps required to deploy a session-bean hosted web service, therefore, is to define the URL to be used to access the bean's web service interface. The deployment tools and the container are responsible for ensuring that SOAP messages sent to the assigned URL are decoded and converted to calls on the session bean's service endpoint interface methods. Although the means by which this is achieved are container-dependent, a natural implementation involves generating a servlet and registering it to respond to the bean's URL.

In the J2EE 1.4 reference implementation, the URL for a session bean–hosted web service is declared in the file *sun-j2ee-ri.xml*, which is placed in the *META-INF* directory of the EAR file. The content of the file used in the deployment of the book web service session bean is shown in Example 2-21.

Example 2-21. The sun-j2ee-ri.xml file for the book web service session bean

```
<?xml version="1.0" encoding="UTF-8"?>

<!DOCTYPE j2ee-ri-specific-information
    PUBLIC '-//Sun Microsystems Inc.//DTD J2EE Reference Implementation 1.3//EN'
    'http://localhost:8000/sun-j2ee-ri_1_3.dtd'>

<j2ee-ri-specific-information>
    <enterprise-beans>
        <module-name>EJBBooks.jar</module-name>
        <unique-id>0</unique-id>
        <ejb>
            <ejb-name>BookQueryBean</ejb-name>
            <gen-classes/>
            <webservice-endpoint>
                <port-component-name>BookQueryPort</port-component-name>
                <endpoint-address-uri>webservice/EJBBookQuery
                </endpoint-address-uri>
            </webservice-endpoint>
        </ejb>
    </enterprise-beans>
</j2ee-ri-specific-information>
```

The content of enterprise-beans element applies to a bean called BookQueryBean that will be found in the file *EJBBooks.jar* within the EAR. This name matches the value of the ejb-name element in the *ejb-jar.xml* file in the JAR, as shown in Example 2-19. The nested webservice-endpoint element names the specific port of the web service for which the URL is to be defined and the URL itself, and the value of the port-component-name element must match that of a port-component-name element in the *webservices.xml* file in *EJBBooks.jar* (see Example 2-20). The URI given by the endpoint-address-uri element is appended to the URL of the server itself to become the full URI of the web service endpoint. To verify this, and to show that you can use the same web service client to access an EJB-hosted web service and one implemented in a servlet, you can run the book service client shown earlier in this chapter against the session bean by making *chapter2\ bookservice* your working directory and typing the command:

```
ant -DCLIENT_ARGS=http://localhost:8000/webservice/EJBBookQuery run-client
```

For the steps required to deploy a session-bean hosted web service to a different J2EE application server and specify its URL, consult the server vendor's documentation.

3

SAAJ

In the last chapter, you saw how to use JAX-RPC to create web services based around the use of remote procedure calls. Even though JAX-RPC uses an XML-based protocol, there was hardly any XML in evidence in Chapter 2. For the most part, JAX-RPC does a very good job of hiding the details of messages that are exchanged between a web service and its client during a remote procedure call. However, most of the more advanced JAX-RPC features require an understanding of SOAP, the XML-based protocol on which JAX-RPC in particular, and web services in general, are based. This chapter paves the way for a more in-depth examination of JAX-RPC by introducing SOAP, together with SAAJ, which is a Java API for creating, sending, and receiving SOAP messages.

Introduction to SAAJ

SAAJ, which stands for *SOAP with Attachments API for Java*, provides a convenient API for constructing SOAP messages without having to directly create the XML yourself. SAAJ was originally part of the *Java API for XML Messaging* (JAXM), which was developed by the JSR 67 expert group. The final release of this specification (JAXM Version 1.0) provided two different but related facilities:

- Core functionality concerned with manipulating SOAP messages in a generic way, together with the ability to send a SOAP message from one entity to another.

- A higher-level messaging facility that included reliable delivery of messages and support for *messaging profiles*, which require SOAP messages to be constructed in specific ways.

During the maintenance cycle for JSR 67, it was decided to unbundle the low-level SOAP message creation features into a separate specification, thus creating SAAJ 1.1, leaving the higher-level features to form JAXM Version 1.1. At the same time, minor modifications were made to the API to remove a dependency that would otherwise have had the undesirable effect of making SAAJ 1.1 dependent on JAXM 1.1. The result is that it is possible to use SAAJ as a lightweight library for building and exchanging SOAP messages, without requiring the inclusion of JAXM 1.1, which provides facilities that go beyond the requirements of many web service clients. JAX-RPC, in particular, uses SAAJ to construct and decode SOAP messages, but it does not require reliable messaging and therefore is not dependent on the presence of a JAXM implementation.

The formal specifications for both SAAJ 1.1 and JAXM 1.1 can be downloaded from *http://jcp.org/jsr/detail/67.jsp*. This chapter looks only at SAAJ and uses it as a convenient means of introducing SOAP messages; the more advanced messaging facilities provided by JAXM are covered in Chapter 4.

SAAJ Programming

Whereas JAX-RPC is concerned with allowing a client program to make a remote procedure call to a web service without exposing the underlying XML-based protocols that are used, SAAJ is a much lower-level API that is entirely concerned with the messages exchanged between the web service and its clients. Furthermore, while JAX-RPC applications look, for the most part, like ordinary Java applications making local method calls, an application that uses SAAJ needs to construct SOAP messages piece by piece and extract information from response messages. Using SAAJ requires much more work on the part of the developer than JAX-RPC, so why would you bother to use it? Here are some of the circumstances in which you might want to use SAAJ and its close relative JAXM instead of JAX-RPC:

- JAX-RPC is convenient for accessing web services that present an RPC-like interface. However, the RPC model is not suitable for all services. In many cases, it is more convenient to simply send an XML message to a service, which the service interprets and then generates an XML response. The most commonly quoted example of this is a business-to-business service where the client sends a purchase order in the form of an XML document to which the service responds with a confirmation and an invoice, also encoded as an XML document. A simple service like this does not require method calls or arguments—all that is necessary is to exchange fragments of XML. SAAJ represents a convenient way to encode and decode the SOAP messages that will carry these XML documents.

- Most services accessed using JAX-RPC are likely to be synchronous in nature, so that the service immediately processes the request and returns a reply to the client, which is blocked until the call completes. However, it is not always convenient or appropriate for the service to handle the request and reply immediately. Using the purchase order example again, the business that receives the purchase order may not be able to respond with a confirmation or an invoice immediately—perhaps not until the goods are in stock, or until it is verified that the initiator of the request has an account against which the goods can be ordered and that sufficient credit is available. For this type of business model, which is likely to be very common in the real world, it is more appropriate to think of the whole process as two separate operations that are not tightly coupled to each other and that the responding business might take anything from several seconds to several days to reply. To implement this type of loosely coupled messaging, it is appropriate to use JAXM, which is built on top of SAAJ and provides the ability to send and receive messages asynchronously.

- JAX-RPC works only when the client and the service are active at the same time and also assumes that there is an available network path that directly connects them. If the service is not available when the client initiates the request, or there are good reasons (perhaps security-related) why the client cannot be directly connected to the server, then you can't use JAX-RPC. JAXM, on the other hand, provides a reliable delivery service without requiring the client application to be involved in how the reliability is provided and can also support routing of SOAP messages between hosts that cannot be directly connected.

SAAJ and JAXM provide a complete solution for XML-based messaging. The major differences between SAAJ and JAXM are as follows:

- SAAJ provides the API for the generic handling of SOAP messages; JAXM builds on this by adding the capability to create SOAP messages with preset content as required by messaging standards such as SOAP-RP and ebXML-TRP.

- SAAJ can be used to create a freestanding Java client that communicates directly with a web service. JAXM adds the concept of a messaging provider, which acts as an intermediary between the client and the eventual recipient of the message. The message provider can provide a reliable delivery service and can route messages to other intermediaries without the involvement of the client. JAXM clients that use a messaging provider must be hosted in a web container or an application server.

- SAAJ clients (and JAXM clients that choose not to use a messaging provider) can only engage in synchronous request/response message exchanges. However, JAXM clients using a messaging provider have access to additional message exchange modes, including asynchronous delivery and receipt of messages. See Chapter 4 for further details.

The classes and interfaces that provide the SAAJ and JAXM APIs reside in different packages, and, to emphasize the fact that SAAJ does not require JAXM, they are distributed in separate JAR files, as shown in Table 3-1.

Table 3-1. Packaging of the SAAJ and JAXM APIs

API	Package	JAR file
SAAJ	javax.xml.soap	*saaj-api.jar* (API)
		saaj-ri.jar (reference implementation)
JAXM	javax.xml.messaging	*jaxm-api.jar* (API)
		jaxm-runtime.jar (reference implementation)

In the case of J2EE 1.4, JAXM is not supported and the SAAJ classes appear in *lib\ j2ee.jar*, which contains almost all of the packages in the reference implementation.

Although we have used the terms "client" and "server" to describe the participants in a SAAJ message exchange, the programming model for both SAAJ and JAXM does not make a strong distinction between these two roles, because most of the API is concerned with the details of handling the messages rather than actually sending and receiving them. In fact, SAAJ messaging represents more of a peer-to-peer model in which it might be more appropriate to use the terms "sender" and "receiver" instead of "client" and "server." In this chapter, however, all of the examples use SAAJ and are therefore limited to synchronous request/reply exchanges. For the sake of clarity, I will continue to use the term "client" to refer to the initiator of a service request, which will always be a freestanding J2SE application, and I will use "server" to mean the entity that receives and replies to the request.

For the JWSDP, to compile client applications that use SAAJ, your CLASSPATH needs to include only the *saaj-api.jar* file. However, the CLASSPATH required to run a client application is much larger, consisting of the following JAR files, which can be found in various subdirectories of the JWSDP installation:

saaj-api.jar	*saaj-ri.jar*	*activation.jar*	*commons-logging.jar*
dom4j.jar	*mail.jar*	*jaxp-api.jar*	*dom.jar*
sax.jar	*xalan.jar*	*xercesImpl.jar*	*xsltc.jar*

To run a SAAJ client application with J2EE 1.4, your CLASSPATH needs to include *lib\j2ee.jar*, together with the following four files from the endorsed directory:

dom.jar	*sax.jar*	*xalan.jar*	*xercesImpl.jar*

Aside from the handling of SOAP messages, SAAJ includes the ability to synchronously send a completed message to a given destination using HTTP as the underlying transport mechanism[*] and receive the reply (see "Creating and Sending a SOAP Message Using SAAJ," later in this chapter), but no specific provision is made for receiving a SOAP request in the server role. Servers are expected to reside in web containers or application servers, and need to make their own arrangements to receive SOAP messages. The JAXM specification includes a servlet (javax.xml.messaging.JAXMServlet) that can be used as the basis for a web container–based message receiver, but service providers are not required to use it. The example source code in this chapter uses a servlet that is very similar to JAXMServlet, so that we can demonstrate SAAJ without introducing a dependency on JAXM. This servlet is described later in this chapter in the section "Receiving a SOAP Message."

SOAP Messages

The format of SOAP messages is defined by a note submitted to the World Wide Web Consortium (W3C) in May 2000 by a group of companies including

---

[*] Support of HTTP as the transport mechanism for SOAP messages is mandatory for all SAAJ implementations. Vendors are free to provide other transport mechanisms, but are not required to do so.

Microsoft and IBM. This note, which describes Version 1.1 of SOAP and can be downloaded from *http://www.w3.org/TR/SOAP*, is not a formally adopted W3C specification but it is, nevertheless, the specification on which all existing SOAP implementations, including SAAJ, are based. The W3C is working on a formal definition of the next revision of SOAP, to be called Version 1.2. At the time of this writing, the SOAP 1.2 specification is available for public review, and Sun plans to include support for SOAP 1.2 in SAAJ (and JAX-RPC) when the specification is finalized.[*]

SOAP defines a way to wrap information represented in XML so that it can be transmitted between peer entities that know how to interpret that information and, presumably, act on it to provide a service. Other than the fact that the useful content of the message (which is known as the *payload*) must be encoded in XML, SOAP does not mandate a particular set of XML elements and attributes to be used to represent primitive items of data (such as integers, floating-point numbers, and strings) in terms of XML constructs, although it does specify an encoding mechanism for these data types and others, the use of which is encouraged. In practice, these encoding rules, commonly referred to as "SOAP section 5 encoding," have become a *de facto* standard and are the default encoding used by JAX-RPC to represent method arguments and return values. Although detailed coverage of these encoding rules is outside the scope this book, there are several examples of their use in this chapter; you'll find a complete discussion of the SOAP encoding rules in *Java and SOAP*, by Robert Englander (O'Reilly). Applications are free to use privately defined encodings instead of the SOAP section 5 rules if they wish.

What SOAP *does* specify is the overall structure of a message, together with rules for wrapping SOAP messages when the underlying transport protocol is HTTP. There are two slightly different ways to construct a SOAP message depending on whether the message has any attachments (the meaning of which is defined later). The SOAP Version 1.1 specification covers only the case where there are no attachments and requires that a message be constructed as shown in Figure 3-1. The outermost layer of the message is a protocol-specific wrapper, the nature of which is defined in the specification only for HTTP and which we'll see later in this chapter. Inside this wrapper is the SOAP message itself, consisting of an envelope, a header part, a body part, and optional additional content.

The SOAP *envelope* is, as its name suggests, a top-level XML element that acts as a container for the rest of the message. The SOAP header is optional but, if present, must be the first element in the envelope. It is intended to be used to carry information that can be used in the processing or routing of the message payload, such as a digital signature to guarantee the integrity of payload data or authentication information to validate the identity of the message sender. There are specifications, referred to in the JAXM documentation as profiles, that define specific SOAP headers to be used to communicate information to applications that are

---

[*] The acronym SOAP originally stood for "Simple Object Access Protocol." In SOAP Version 1.2, the letters no longer have any meaning. This is probably a good idea, because the original name is arguably not really an accurate description of what SOAP is: although the S and the P could be justified, there is really nothing in SOAP that provides object access, at least not in any sense that would be acceptable to an object-oriented programmer.

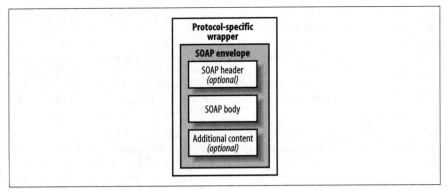

Figure 3-1. A SOAP message with no attachments

aware of the profile. The reference implementation of JAXM includes messaging providers that can create SOAP messages that have pre-installed headers as required by the SOAP-RP or ebXML TRP specifications. For further information on these two profiles, see Chapter 4.

The SOAP *body* is the only mandatory part of the envelope and contains the actual payload intended for the ultimate recipient of the message. It must either follow the SOAP header or, if the header is omitted, be the first element in the envelope. Following the body, it is possible to include additional content, the interpretation of which, like the payload itself, is entirely dependent on the sending and receiving entities.

Everything within the SOAP envelope *must* be encoded in XML. For many applications, this is not an acceptable restriction. For example, an online book store offering a web service interface might want to supply book details that include a photograph of the book's cover, scanned copies of pages from the book, or a sample chapter in the form of a PDF document. In order to enable applications such as this, Microsoft and Hewlett Packard created an additional specification called "SOAP Messages with Attachments," which can be downloaded from *http:// www.w3.org/TR/SOAP-attachments*. Like the SOAP 1.1 document, this specification has been submitted to the W3C, and although it has not been approved by W3C, it has become the *de facto* standard for packaging SOAP messages that require some element of non-XML content.

A SOAP message that has attachments is formatted as shown in Figure 3-2. *Attachments* typically contain non-XML data, such as images, audio, or plain text. The first part of the message contains the SOAP envelope and its content, constructed as described by the SOAP 1.1 specification. Each object to be attached is then added as MIME content, and the whole message is packaged as a MIME `Multipart/Related` message as defined by RFC 2387 (which can be found at *http://www.ietf.org/rfc/rfc2387.txt*). Each separate message part has its own MIME wrapper that specifies, among other things, the type of data that it contains—it may contain an identifier that can be used within the SOAP envelope to refer to it. Using SAAJ, you can construct SOAP messages with attachments that contain any type of data that has a MIME encoding. This topic is discussed in more detail in "SOAP with Attachments," later in this chapter, where you'll also see exactly what a typical message with attachments looks like when bound to the HTTP protocol.

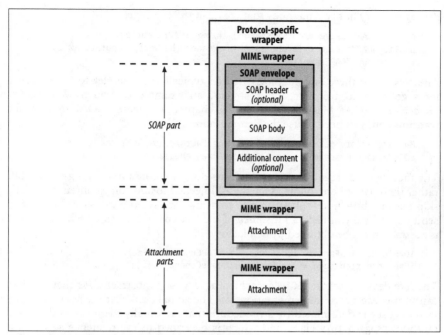

Figure 3-2. A SOAP message with two attachments

Creating and Sending a SOAP Message Using SAAJ

In order to allow vendors to supply their own implementations, almost all of the SAAJ API is made up of interfaces and abstract classes. In particular, the SOAPMessage class, which represents a SOAP message, is abstract and therefore cannot be directly instantiated. To create a SOAP message, you need to use a MessageFactory. MessageFactory, which is part of the javax.xml.soap package, is itself an abstract class, an instance of which can be obtained using its static newInstance( ) method:

```
public static MessageFactory newInstance( ) throws SOAPException;
```

To permit vendors to plug in their own implementations of MessageFactory, this method looks at the system property javax.xml.soap.MessageFactory and in a couple of other places to select the subclass of MessageFactory that will be used. Refer to the description of javax.xml.soap.MessageFactory in the reference section of this book for a complete description of the steps taken to find a MessageFactory.

If a problem is encountered while instantiating the MessageFactory, a SOAPException is thrown. SOAPException, which is one of only four concrete classes in the javax.xml.soap package, is a checked exception that is thrown by many of the methods in the SAAJ API. It contains a message describing the reason for the exception and, for cases where the root cause is an exception thrown from a lower level, provides a getCause( ) method to provide access to the original exception.

`MessageFactory` has two methods that create SOAP messages:

```
public SOAPMessage createMessage( ) throws SOAPException;
public SOAPMessage createMessage(MimeHeaders headers, InputStream is)
    throws SOAPException;
```

The second of these two methods is used typically in a servlet to deserialize a message received from an input stream, an example of which we'll see in "Receiving a SOAP Message," later in this chapter. To create a SOAP message for transmission, you need to use the first method:

```
MessageFactory messageFactory = MessageFactory.newInstance( );
SOAPMessage message = messageFactory.createMessage( );
```

The message that `createMessage( )` returns does not contain anything useful, but rather than pause here to introduce the API needed to add some content to it, let's skip ahead a little and look at how to transmit the skeleton message. In order to send a message, you need an instance of the `SOAPConnection` class, which, since it is abstract, must be obtained from a factory:

```
SOAPConnectionFactory connFactory = SOAPConnectionFactory.newInstance( );
SOAPConnection conn = connFactory.createConnection( );
```

Just like `MessageFactory`, `SOAPConnectionFactory` is an abstract class that vendors can supply their own implementations of. The actual class that the `newInstance( )` method uses is determined by a procedure that is virtually identical to that used by the `MessageFactory` class, and which is described in the reference section for `javax.xml.soap.SOAPConnectionFactory`, later in this book. If all else fails, the reference implementation returns its own implementation of `SOAPConnectionFactory` (or throws a `SOAPException` if this class is not available).[*]

Once you have a `SOAPConnection`, you can use its `call( )` method to transmit a message:

```
public abstract SOAPMessage call(SOAPMessage request, Object destination)
    throws SOAPException;
```

The destination object determines where the message will be sent. The SAAJ specification requires that the following types be supported as valid destination arguments:

- An instance of the `java.net.URL` class.

- An instance of `String`, provided that its value can be converted to a valid URL using its `URL(String url)` constructor.

- An instance of the class `javax.xml.messaging.URLEndpoint`. This class, which wraps a URL, is part of the JAXM API and is therefore not likely to be used by pure SAAJ applications. It is accepted as a valid destination because Version 1.0 of the JAXM specification, which did not have SAAJ separated out as a freestanding API, defined the destination parameter of this method as being

---

[*] Despite its name, `SOAPConnection` does not actually represent a connection to a message receiver. Instead, think of it as representing a connection between application code and the SAAJ runtime that can be used to send SOAP messages. In Chapter 4, we'll see that JAXM has a similar class, called `ProviderConnection`, which provides an association between a JAXM application and a messaging provider, but similarly does not imply that an immediate network connection is made.

of type `javax.xml.messaging.Endpoint`. This is an abstract base class of which `URLEndpoint` is the only concrete implementation; therefore, supporting a destination of type `URLEndpoint` provides backward-compatibility.

The reference implementation supports all of these possibilities; vendor implementations are free to add their own destination types as required. All of these destination types resolve to a URL, but the structure of this URL depends entirely on the implementation of the receiver and the environment in which it is hosted. We'll see a typical example in "Receiving a SOAP Message," later in this chapter.

As noted earlier in this section, a SAAJ client can only use a synchronous request/ response programming model; therefore, the `call( )` method blocks having sent the message until a reply sent to the message is received, or until an error causes it to throw a `SOAPException`. The reply is returned to the method caller. Having received a reply, if you don't need to make further use of the `SOAPConnection` object, you should use its `close( )` method to release it; this method can be called only once. Once it is, any further invocations of `call( )` method result in a `SOAPException`.

The example source code for this chapter includes a client that creates a SOAP message, prints its content, and then sends it to a servlet that echoes it straight back. To run this example, start your web server or application server, open a command window and make *chapter3\echoservice* your working directory, and then use the following command to build and deploy the servlet:

```
ant deploy
```

Next, compile and run the client application using the command:

```
ant compile-client run-client
```

In the command window, you'll see quite a lot of output, including the XML for the `SOAPMessage` that was transmitted (which has been reformatted to make it more readable):

```
1   <soap-env:Envelope xmlns:soap-env=
        "http://schemas.xmlsoap.org/soap/envelope/">
2       <soap-env:Header/>
3       <soap-env:Body/>
4   </soap-env:Envelope>
```

This is what the basic message returned by the `createMessage( )` method looks like if you don't make any changes to it. Lines 1 and 4 contain the XML elements that represent the SOAP message envelope. As you can see, the element name is `Envelope` and it is qualified using the namespace prefix `soap-env`, which is associated with the URL *http://schemas.xmlsoap.org/soap/envelope*. This URL identifies the entire SOAP message as being formatted according to the rules of SOAP Version 1.1. If a SOAP message whose envelope is qualified with any other namespace is received, then it should be treated as a SOAP version mismatch, and the receiver is required to reject the message by generating a SOAP fault (as described in "SOAP Fault Handling," later in this chapter).

Inside the envelope are the header and body elements, for which the element names are `Header` and `Body`, respectively. These two elements are also qualified with the same namespace tag as the envelope. In this case, since we didn't actually add anything to the message returned by the `MessageFactory` `createMessage( )`

method, the header and body parts are both empty. Under normal circumstances, if you do not need any header content, you completely remove the header part. You'll see how to do this later in this chapter.

 SOAP messaging makes heavy use of XML namespaces and XML schema. A detailed discussion of these topics is outside the scope of this book and, although we'll explain the use of namespaces and schemas as we encounter them, for a full treatment of XML namespaces and XML schema, refer to *XML In a Nutshell,* Second Edition, by Elliotte Rusty Harold and W. Scott Means (O'Reilly).

Receiving a SOAP Message

The SOAPConnection class provides the call( ) method to allow a SOAP message to be transmitted, but there is no corresponding API that takes care of receiving a message. The example just shown uses a servlet as the target of the message. This is convenient because the SOAPConnection class uses HTTP as the default protocol when transmitting messages, and the servlet API contains everything that you need to handle a payload delivered over an HTTP connection, including a convenient API to handle the HTTP headers.

The java.xml.messaging package includes a servlet called JAXMServlet that can be used to receive and handle SOAP messages. However, since this package is part of the JAXM API, using it would introduce a dependency on JAXM as well as SAAJ, which is not desirable because JAXM is not part of the J2EE 1.4 platform. To avoid this, the servlet used in the echoservice example is based on a slightly simpler version of JAXMServlet that is provided in the sample code supplied with the JWSDP. The source code for this servlet can be found in the file *chapter3\ servlet\ora\jwsnut\saaj\SAAJServlet.java* relative to the installation directory of the example code for this book. Most of the code is also shown in Example 3-1.

Example 3-1. A servlet that can receive SOAP messages

```
package ora.jwsnut.saaj;

import java.io.IOException;
import java.io.OutputStream;
import java.util.Enumeration;
import java.util.Iterator;
import java.util.StringTokenizer;
import javax.servlet.ServletConfig;
import javax.servlet.ServletException;
import javax.servlet.http.HttpServlet;
import javax.servlet.http.HttpServletRequest;
import javax.servlet.http.HttpServletResponse;
import javax.xml.soap.MessageFactory;
import javax.xml.soap.MimeHeader;
import javax.xml.soap.MimeHeaders;
import javax.xml.soap.SOAPException;
import javax.xml.soap.SOAPMessage;

/**
 * A servlet that can be used to host a SAAJ
```

Example 3-1. A servlet that can receive SOAP messages (continued)

```java
 * service within a web container. This is based
 * on ReceivingServlet.java in the JWSDP tutorial
 * examples.
 */
public abstract class SAAJServlet extends HttpServlet {

    /**
     * The factory used to build messages
     */
    protected MessageFactory messageFactory;

    /**
     * Initialisation - create the MessageFactory
     */
    public void init(ServletConfig config) throws ServletException {
        super.init(config);
        try {
            messageFactory = MessageFactory.newInstance();
        } catch (SOAPException ex) {
            throw new ServletException("Failed to create MessageFactory", ex);
        }
    }

    /**
     * Handles a POST request from a client. The request is assumed
     * to contain a SOAP message with the HTTP binding.
     */
    public void doPost(HttpServletRequest request, HttpServletResponse response)

throws ServletException, IOException {

        try {
            // Get all the HTTP headers and convert them to a MimeHeaders object
            MimeHeaders mimeHeaders = getMIMEHeaders(request);

            // Create a SOAPMessage from the content of the HTTP request
            SOAPMessage message = messageFactory.createMessage(mimeHeaders,
                                            request.getInputStream());

            // Let the subclass handle the message
            SOAPMessage reply = onMessage(message);

            // If there is a reply, return it to the sender.
            if (reply != null) {
                // Set OK HTTP status, unless there is a fault.
                boolean hasFault = reply.getSOAPPart().getEnvelope()
                                    .getBody().hasFault();
                response.setStatus(hasFault ?
                                HttpServletResponse.SC_INTERNAL_SERVER_ERROR :
                                HttpServletResponse.SC_OK);

                // Force generation of the MIME headers
                if (reply.saveRequired()) {
```

Example 3-1. A servlet that can receive SOAP messages (continued)

```
                    reply.saveChanges( );
                }

                // Copy the MIME headers to the HTTP response
                setHttpHeaders(reply.getMimeHeaders( ), response);

                // Send the completed message
                OutputStream os = response.getOutputStream( );
                reply.writeTo(os);
                os.flush( );
            } else {
                // No reply - set the HTTP status to indicate this
                response.setStatus(HttpServletResponse.SC_NO_CONTENT);
            }
        } catch (SOAPException ex) {
            throw new ServletException("SOAPException: " + ex);
        }
    }

    /**
     * Method implemented by subclasses to handle a received SOAP message.
     * @param message the received SOAP message.
     * @return the reply message, or <code>null</code> if there is
     * no reply to be sent.
     */
    protected abstract SOAPMessage onMessage(SOAPMessage message)
        throws SOAPException;

    // HEADER HANDLING CODE NOT SHOWN.....

}
```

When SAAJServlet receives a SOAP message, it hands it to the abstract onMessage( ) method and sends the reply message returned by this method to the message sender. To provide specific message handling, subclass SAAJServlet and implement the required processing in the onMessage( ) method.

The doPost( ) method of this servlet demonstrates how to receive a SOAP message from an HTTP connection. When transmitted over HTTP, the protocol-specific wrapper shown in Figure 3-1 and Figure 3-2 is represented as HTTP headers, and the rest of the message is written out as a stream of XML or, if the message has attachments, as a Multipart/Related MIME payload containing the XML and the encoded attachment data. Example 3-2 shows what an empty SOAP message looks like when bound into an HTTP request message.

Example 3-2. An empty SOAP message bound to the HTTP protocol

```
Content-Length: 17 1
SOAPAction: ""
User-Agent: Java1.4.0
Host: localhost:5050
Accept: text/html, image/gif, image/jpeg, *; q=.2, */*; q=.2
Connection: keep-alive
```

```
<?xml version="1.0" encoding="UTF-8"?>
<soap-env:Envelope xmlns:soap-env="http://schemas.xmlsoap.org/soap/envelope/">
    <soap-env:Header/>
    <soap-env:Body/>
</soap-env:Envelope>
```

When this HTTP request message is delivered to a servlet, the HTTP headers are automatically stripped off and made available via the HttpServletRequest object, while the rest of the data, namely the XML itself, can be obtained by reading the InputStream provided by the HttpServletRequest getInputStream( ) method. To convert the XML back into a SOAPMessage, the servlet uses a MessageFactory that it creates when it is initialized, and calls the second variant of the createMessage( ) method that we saw in "Creating and Sending a SOAP Message Using SAAJ" earlier in this chapter, passing it the HTTP headers and the input stream containing the XML-encoded SOAP message:[*]

```
// Create a SOAPMessage from the content of the HTTP request
SOAPMessage message = messageFactory.createMessage(mimeHeaders, request.
getInputStream( ));
```

The first argument supplied to this method is an object of type javax.xml.soap. MimeHeaders, which encapsulates the HTTP headers that were received as part of the HTTP binding. We'll look at this class and the way in which it is populated from the HTTP request in "SOAP Messages and MIME Headers." later in this chapter.

Once the SOAPMessage is created, it is passed to the onMessage( ) method. If this method returns a reply, it needs to be sent back to the caller in the servlet's HTTP response message. Naturally, the reply needs to be wrapped in HTTP in the same way that the request was when it was transmitted by the sender. The original message was created as a result of calling the SOAPConnection call( ) method, which opens an HTTP connection to the servlet and takes care of building the HTTP wrapper for the message. Here, however, we can't use this method because we want to return the message using the HTTP connection originally created by the client, so we have to create the HTTP binding for the reply message ourselves. This requires three steps:

1. Get any HTTP headers to be sent with the reply message from the message itself. This can be done by calling the SOAPMessage getMimeHeaders( ) method, which returns them in the form of a MimeHeaders object.

2. Use the methods of the servlet's HttpServletResponse object to install the HTTP headers in the reply.

3. Get the XML representation of the SOAPMessage itself and write it to the OutputStream obtained from the HttpServletResponse getOutputStream( ) method.

---

[*] In case you are wondering why the createMessage( ) method needs access to the HTTP headers as well as the XML content, it is because it uses the Content-Type header to decide whether the SOAP message has attachments, and decodes the rest of the HTTP request appropriately.

Before we can start this process, however, we need to ensure that the HTTP headers for the SOAPMessage have been created. As you'll see later, a newly created SOAPMessage object does not actually contain any XML or any of the HTTP headers that will eventually be used when transmitting it over HTTP. Instead, it consists of a hierarchy of objects that represents the envelope, the header, the body, and so on, in much the same way as a DOM model represents an XML document. In order to force the headers to be created, we use the following code:

```
if (reply.saveRequired()) {
    reply.saveChanges();
}
```

The saveChanges() method creates not only the headers, but also the XML representation of the message itself. The saveRequired() method is used to discover whether it is actually necessary to perform this step—once saveChanges() is called, it does not need to be called again, and saveRequired() returns false until some change is made to the SOAPMessage that causes either the headers or the XML to need to be updated. The actual code that gets the HTTP headers from the reply SOAPMessage and installs them in the HTTP response is shown in the later section "SOAP Messages and MIME Headers."

The XML representation of a SOAPMessage can be written to an OutputStream using the following SOAPMessage method:

```
public void writeTo(OutputStream os);
```

It is not necessary to call saveChanges() before invoking this method, since writeTo() calls it for itself (if necessary). Hence, the following code is all that is necessary to write the reply message back to the caller:

```
// Send the completed message
OutputStream os = response.getOutputStream();
reply.writeTo(os);
os.flush();
```

Incidentally, the writeTo() method is a useful debugging aid because you can use code like the following to dump the XML represented by a SOAPMessage to the standard output stream:

```
message.writeTo(System.out);
```

Note, however, that this method writes only the XML—it does *not* include the MIME headers, which must be obtained separately by calling getMimeHeaders().

This leaves only one open issue regarding the handling of SOAP messages in a servlet: what destination URL should the client application supply to the SOAPConnection call() method to arrange for the message to be delivered to the servlet? The simple answer is that it depends on how the servlet is deployed. In the case of the echoservice example used here, the message echoing is provided by a simple servlet that is derived from SAAJServlet and overrides its onMessage() method to return the SOAPMessage that it is called with, having first written its content to the web containers log for debugging purposes, as shown in Example 3-3.

Example 3-3. A servlet that logs and echoes a received SOAP message

```
public class EchoServlet extends SAAJServlet {

    /**
     * Output stream used to save a SOAP message
     * for logging.
     */
    private ByteArrayOutputStream os = new ByteArrayOutputStream( );

    /**
     * Handles a received SOAP message by simply
     * returning it.
     */
    public SOAPMessage onMessage(SOAPMessage message) {

        // Convert the message to string representation
        // and log it.
        try {
            message.writeTo(os);
            log("Received SOAP message:\n" + os.toString( ));
            os.reset( );
        } catch (Exception ex) {
            log("Exception", ex);
        }

        // Return the received message to the caller.
        return message;
    }
}
```

This servlet (together with its base class, SAAJServlet) is wrapped in a WAR file and then deployed as a web application called SAAJEchoService. The web application's *web.xml* file looks like this:

```
<web-app>
    <display-name>SAAJ Echo Service</display-name>
    <description>SAAJ Message Echo Service</description>

    <servlet>
        <servlet-name>EchoService</servlet-name>
        <display-name>Servlet for the SAAJ Message Echo Service
        </display-name>
        <servlet-class>ora.jwsnut.chapter3.echoservice.EchoServlet
        </servlet-class>
    </servlet>

    <servlet-mapping>
        <servlet-name>EchoService</servlet-name>
        <url-pattern>/*</url-pattern>
    </servlet-mapping>
</web-app>
```

The url-pattern element means that all URLs that map to the web application SAAJEchoService are directed to the servlet. Assuming that the web application is deployed in a web server listening at port 8000 on your local machine, the client application may therefore use the following URL to send SOAP messages to the servlet:

http://localhost:8000/SAAJEchoService

If the url-pattern element looks like this:

```
<url-pattern>/EchoServlet/*</url-pattern>
```

the result is that the required URL is:

http://localhost:8000/SAAJEchoService/EchoServlet

If you are writing a SAAJ client that is intended to communicate with an existing server, then the URL that you need to use should be obtained from the service provider. In some cases, the address of a service is not fully specified by a URL. An example of this might be a server implementation where all requests are initially handled by a single servlet and then routed internally to the appropriate web service based on something in the message itself. In order to aid with such an arrangement, the SOAP 1.1 specification defines an HTTP header called SOAPAction that can be used to provide a string that holds further information that can be used to identify the target web service. If a service does not require SOAPAction, its value should be set to the empty string. This is, in fact, the default value for the SOAPAction header when you create a new SOAPMessage, as you can see from Example 3-2. If the service you need to communicate with requires a specific SOAPAction value, you can install it using the MimeHeaders setHeader( ) method:

```
message.getMimeHeaders( ).setHeader("SOAPAction", "ServiceInfo");
```

The Anatomy of a SAAJ SOAP Message

Although a SOAP message is transmitted as a set of characters encoded in UTF-8, holding the message in character form would make it difficult to manipulate. Instead, SOAPMessage contains a hierarchy of objects that represent the various parts of the message and the XML elements and text (if any) that it contains. The message is kept in this form until it is ready to be transmitted, at which point a UTF-8 byte stream is created from its content. Figure 3-3 shows a typical hierarchy of elements that might make up a SOAPMessage object.

A SOAPMessage object consists of a single SOAPPart and zero or more AttachmentParts. The default message returned by the MessageFactory createMessage( ) method contains a SOAPPart but no attachments. AttachmentParts, if they are required, must be explicitly created and added to create a SOAP with attachments message. The SOAPPart, in turn, contains a SOAPEnvelope object, which represents the envelope shown in Figure 3-1 and Figure 3-2. Within the envelope is the SOAP message header, represented by an object implementing the SOAPHeader interface and the SOAP message body in the form of a SOAPBody object. Both the body and the header contain XML markup that constitutes, respectively, the message payload and any information required to qualify or process the payload, represented by SOAPElements or Text nodes.

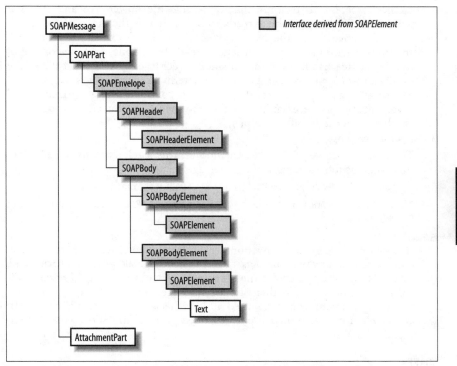

Figure 3-3. Component parts of a SOAPMessage object with a single attachment

SOAPMessage

SOAPMessage is an abstract class that represents the whole SOAP message. It contains methods that deal with the following:

MIME headers

When a SOAP message is wrapped in a MIME-aware transport protocol such as HTTP or SMTP, MIME-related information must be included to identify the data being carried as an XML message. A SOAPMessage object supplies default values for the MIME Content-Type, Content-Length, and SOAPAction headers, but it also provides a method that returns the underlying MimeHeaders object that contains the associated MIME headers. You can use this object to retrieve the headers for a received message or to add additional ones for an outgoing message. See "SOAP Messages and MIME Headers" later in this chapter, for details.

SOAPMessage also provides a convenience method to set or retrieve the value of the optional Content-Description header, which is used to attach descriptive text to the message.

Conversion between object and byte format

A SOAP message is created and manipulated by application code as a tree of objects like that shown in Figure 3-3. For transmission, however, it must be converted to a byte stream that represents the XML itself. The saveChanges( )

method creates a byte array that represents the object tree and stores it within the SOAPMessage object ready to be written by the writeTo( ) method. Since the creation of the byte representation is an expensive process, it should be performed only if it has not already been done, or if the content of the object tree has been modified since saveChanges( ) was last called. The saveRequired( ) method can be used to determine whether it is necessary to call saveChanges( ). The writeTo( ) method calls both saveRequired( ) and saveChanges( ) as necessary, so it is rarely necessary for client code to do anything other than call writeTo( ).

Access to the SOAPPart object

The SOAPMessage getSOAPPart( ) method returns a reference to the SOAPPart that contains the XML parts of the message:

```
public SOAPPart getSOAPPart( ) throws SOAPException;
```

Note that it is not possible to replace the SOAPPart associated with a SOAPMessage.

Attachments

A SOAPMessage can have any number of attachments, each of which may contain data of any type that has a MIME encoding. SOAPMessage provides the methods necessary to create the AttachmentPart objects that represent individual attachments, add them to the message, retrieve them, and remove them. Attachments must be used if it is necessary to include non-XML content in a message; their use is described in detail in "SOAP with Attachments," later in this chapter.

SOAPPart

The SOAPPart object is a wrapper for the SOAP envelope and therefore contains the part of the message that must be represented in XML. For simple SOAP messages, SOAPPart does not really add anything other than the ability to access the SOAPEnvelope object, but for a SOAP message with attachments, it provides the ability to manipulate the content of the MIME wrapper for the SOAP part of the message, as shown in Figure 3-2.

Access to the SOAPEnvelope object

For most practical purposes, the getEnvelope( ) method is the most important feature of SOAPPart:

```
public SOAPEnvelope getEnvelope( ) throws SOAPException;
```

There is no direct way with the SAAJ API to create your own SOAPEnvelope object and use it to replace the one installed when a SOAPMessage is created. However, you can replace the entire content of the SOAPPart, as described next, which has the same effect but is less convenient.

MIME headers

Most of the SOAPPart API is concerned with creating, retrieving, and manipulating MIME headers. These headers, however, are not related to those associated with the SOAPMessage—they are used only when the message has one or more attachments, and become part of the MIME wrapper for the SOAP part of the message. Although you can still use this API for a message that does not have attachments, it will have no practical effect on the message that is finally transmitted.

SOAPPart content replacement

The getContent( ) and setContent( ) methods allow access to and replacement of the content of the SOAPPart in a form that can be manipulated by the JAXP APIs. The setContent( ) method in particular can be used to replace the SOAP envelope with an alternative that is represented by a DOM tree or the content of an input stream encoded in XML. While this might have some practical applications, it would be more useful to be able to import XML in either of these forms into the SOAP body, but there is currently no API that supports this.*

SOAPEnvelope

This object represents the SOAP envelope, which must contain a single SOAPBody object and may contain a SOAPHeader and additional XML elements. If these parts are present, they must appear in the following order: header, body, and additional elements. Like SOAPPart, SOAPEnvelope is of little direct use to most applications, except as a means of accessing the header and body parts.

Access to the SOAP header and body parts

SOAPEnvelope provides methods that allow references to the header and body objects that it contains to be retrieved:

```
public SOAPBody getBody( ) throws SOAPException;
public SOAPHeader getHeader( ) throws SOAPException;
```

The message created by the MessageFactory createMessage( ) method contains empty header and body parts.

Replacement of the SOAP header and body parts

It is possible to create and add a new header or a new body part to a SOAP message. This is useful when modifying the content of a received message in order to forward it or to use it as the basis for the reply to the sender:

```
public SOAPBody addBody( ) throws SOAPException;
public SOAPHeader addHeader( ) throws SOAPException;
```

These methods create, install, and return an empty SOAPBody or SOAPHeader object, respectively. These methods represent the only way to directly create instances of these objects. You can only install a new SOAPHeader or a new SOAPBody if you have already removed the previous one. There are, however, no methods named removeHeader( ) or removeBody( ) that allow you to do this. Instead, you have to rely on the fact that both SOAPBody and SOAPHeader (like SOAPEnvelope) are derived from the javax.xml.soap.Node interface, which provides the detachNode( ) method to allow it to be removed from whatever it is contained in. Here, for example, is how you would remove the SOAPHeader from a SOAPMessage and install a new, empty one:

```
// Remove the message header
SOAPEnvelope envelope = message.getSOAPPart( ).getEnvelope( );
envelope.getHeader( ).detachNode( );
```

---

* The only way to import XML into the SOAP body is to use the SOAPPart getContent( ) method to get access to the content of the SOAPPart, transform it into a DOM tree, import the XML into the DOM tree, and then use setContent( ) to replace the entire SOAP part with the modified content. If you really need to do this, you'll find the necessary code in *Java Web Services*, by David Chappell and Tyler Jewell (O'Reilly).

```
// Add a new header
SOAPHeader header = envelope.addHeader();
```

Nodes are discussed in "Nodes, Elements, and Names," later in this chapter.

Creation of Name *objects*

For reasons of backwards-compatibility with Version 1.0 of JAXM (which contained the API that is now known as SAAJ), SOAPEnvelope includes factory methods that create Name objects for use with XML elements within the envelope. In SAAJ 1.1, the preferred way to create Name objects is by using the SOAPFactory class. Name objects are described in "Nodes, Elements, and Names," later in this chapter.

SOAPHeader

SOAPHeader is a container for headers that determines the way in which the message payload is processed or interpreted. There are standardized uses of SOAP, such as SOAP-RP or ebXML-TRP, that specify the format of certain headers that are of meaning to receivers that implement these standards, but applications are free to define and use their own private headers.* SOAP itself does not specify any standard headers, and therefore the API provided by SOAPHeader is restricted to methods that add a new header entry or allow existing header entries to be accessed. SOAP headers are discussed in "SOAP Headers," later in this chapter.

SOAPBody

SOAPBody is the container that holds the real payload of the SOAP message. Logically, the payload consists of one or more XML document fragments. However, in the SAAJ API, the payload is constructed as a hierarchy of elements and text nodes, represented by the SOAPElement and Node interfaces (described in the next section). The payload is typically included in the body by creating a SOAPBodyElement to represent the root element of each fragment and then adding nested elements and text as necessary:

```
public SOAPBodyElement addBodyElement(Name name) throws SOAPException;
```

The body may also contain a SOAPFault object that reports a failure to properly process either a message header or the message payload itself. SOAPBody provides methods to add a SOAPFault object to the body and to handle one in a message that has been received. This API is covered in "SOAP Fault Handling," later in this chapter.

Nodes, Elements, and Names

The SAAJ interfaces that we have seen so far provide the framework within which SOAP messages can be built, but the actual message content is constructed by

---

* The terminology can get a little confusing when discussing headers. A SOAP message can only contain a single SOAPHeader, but a SOAPHeader may contain any number of XML fragments that represent application-defined headers. When the context does not make it clear whether "header" refers to one such XML fragment or the entire SOAPHeader, we use the term "header entry" instead.

using four more basic interfaces that are described in this section. Here's a brief description of these interfaces, which we'll expand on by reference to an example in the rest of this section:

Name

> In XML terms, a Name object represents a *qualified element name* (or *QName*)— that is, a local name together with an optional namespace prefix and the associated namespace URI. For example, in the case of the XML tag that represents the SOAP envelope:
>
> ```
> <soap-env:Envelope xmlns:soap-env=
>     "http://schemas.xmlsoap.org/soap/envelope/">
> ```
>
> Envelope is the local name of the element, soap-env is the namespace prefix, http://schemas.xmlsoap.org/soap/envelope/ is the URI that uniquely identifies the namespace, and the combination soap-env:Envelope is the qualified element name (qualified because it contains a namespace prefix).

Node

> Node is the base interface for the nodes in the object tree that make up the content of a SOAP message. It provides the methods necessary to link itself to or remove itself from its parent node as well as to allow application code to discover its parent node. However, this interface does not provide a way to add child nodes and therefore represents a leaf in the object tree. SAAJ applications usually do not deal directly with Nodes—instead, they handle objects of the derived types SOAPElement and Text.

Text

> Text is a type of Node that holds a text string. Text is always a leaf node and its content may represent an XML comment.

SOAPElement

> SOAPElement is a subinterface of Node that adds the methods required to attach child nodes, and therefore need not always be a leaf in the object tree.

SOAPElement has a number of subinterfaces that represent entities that can appear within the SOAPPart. These subinterfaces and their relationships to SOAPElement and Node are shown in Figure 3-4.

It is interesting to note that SOAPEnvelope, SOAPBody, and SOAPHeader are all SOAPElements, which implies that you can add content directly to them. This is, of course, true, although we'll see later that both SOAPBody and SOAPHeader have their own specific SOAPElement variants (SOAPBodyElement and SOAPHeaderElement) that are used as their immediate children and take special action when you attempt to add an arbitrary SOAPElement instead. We'll look at how a typical SOAP message is constructed by examining an example application that gets a list of O'Reilly book titles from a server and displays them in list form in a Swing-based user interface. Later in this chapter, we'll extend this example so that it can fetch images of the front covers of these books from the server, as an illustration of the use of non-XML SOAP message attachments.

Before running this example, you need to compile and deploy the service implementation, which is based on SAAJServlet. To do so, start your web server or application server, open a command window and make *chapter3\ bookimageservice* your working directory, and then use the following command to build and deploy the servlet:

```
ant deploy
```

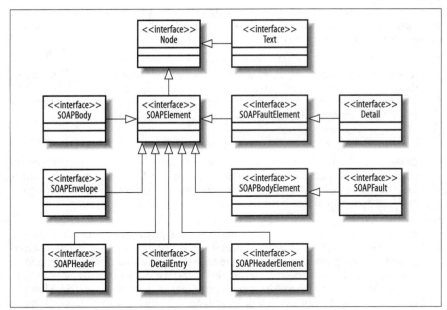

Figure 3-4. SAAJ interfaces used in building SOAP messages

Next, compile and run the client application using the command:

```
ant compile-client run-client
```

Once the client starts, you'll see the list of books that it has obtained from the server, as shown in Figure 3-5.

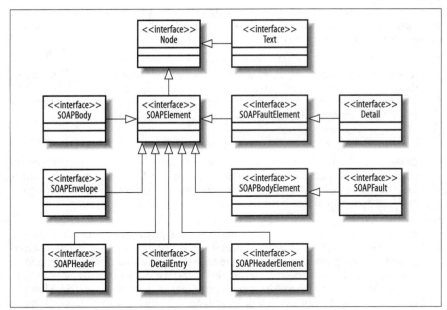

Figure 3-5. SAAJ client showing a list of book titles obtained from a SAAJ server

Constructing the SOAP message to get the book titles

The SOAP message that is sent to get the list of book titles is shown in Example 3-4.

Example 3-4. A SOAP message sent to retrieve book titles from a web service

```
1   <?xml version="1.0" encoding="UTF-8"?>
2   <soap-env:Envelope xmlns:soap-env="http://schemas.xmlsoap.org/soap/envelope/"
3                      xmlns:tns="urn:jwsnut.bookimageservice">
4       <soap-env:Body>
5           <tns:BookList/>
6       </soap-env:Body>
7   </soap-env:Envelope>
```

There are three differences between this message and the empty one shown in Example 3-2:

- The SOAP header part has been removed because headers are not required by this application.
- The addition of a namespace declaration on the Envelope element.
- The SOAP body contains an application-defined element called BookList.

The BookList element is, of course, not defined by the SOAP 1.1 specification—it is a private element that is recognized by the web service as a request to send the list of book titles that it knows about. Since this request does not need any parameters, all that is required is an empty element. However, since the BookList element is private, we define an XML namespace for the web service, assign a prefix to it, and associate the prefix with the element name, so that there is no ambiguity about the meaning of the request.

The namespace itself is defined by the xmlns attribute on the Envelope element, as shown on line 3 of Example 3-4. In order to declare a namespace, we have to assign a prefix and associate it with the namespace's URI. In this case, we chose to use the prefix tns. Although arbitrary, it is quite common to use this particular prefix for the namespace that refers to the service's private elements, since the letters tns serve as a useful mnemonic for "this namespace," as distinct from the namespace used for the elements that are part of the SOAP envelope itself. The namespace URI is, again, arbitrary, although it should be unique, and the same value must be used by both the client and the web service implementation.* Here, we choose to use a URN with a string value that identifies the service as the book image service from this book, but we could have used any other valid URI.

The SOAP 1.1 specification does not actually require elements in the body of the SOAP message to be namespace-qualified, although it recommends that they are. From the point of view of the service implementation, it is just as well to require that the client supplies the namespace so it can unambiguously check that if it receives a BookList element from a client, the element actually represents the BookList request that it provides, rather than a similarly named request for an entirely different service. You'll see shortly how the service implementation makes this check. Incidentally, you don't have to associate a namespace prefix with every

---

* Although the client and the service implementation must use exactly the same URI for the namespace, they do not have to use the same prefix, because the prefix serves only as a shorthand for the URI itself.

SOAP element. You can, if you wish, declare a default namespace on an element, like this:

```
<?xml version="1.0" encoding="UTF-8"?>
<soap-env:Envelope xmlns:soap-env=
    "http://schemas.xmlsoap.org/soap/envelope/"
    xmlns="urn:jwsnut.bookimageservice">
    <soap-env:Body>
        <BookList/>
    </soap-env:Body>
</soap-env:Envelope>
```

An xmlns attribute without an associated namespace prefix specifies the namespace that will be associated with any element, such as BookList, that does not have an explicit namespace prefix. This default is in operation for the scope of the element to which the xmlns attribute is attached.

Now let's look at the code that created the SOAPMessage shown in Example 3-4. This code is shown in Example 3-5.

Example 3-5. Constructing a SOAP message using the SAAJ APIs

```
1     // Build the message
2     SOAPMessage message = messageFactory.createMessage();
3
4     // Remove the message header
5     SOAPEnvelope envelope = message.getSOAPPart().getEnvelope();
6     envelope.getHeader().detachNode();
7
8     // Set up the namespace declaration
9     envelope.addNamespaceDeclaration(SERVICE_PREFIX, SERVICE_URI);
10
11    // Add the element for the book list request
12    SOAPBody soapBody = envelope.getBody();
13    soapBody.addBodyElement(BOOK_LIST_NAME);
```

The first part of this code (lines 2 to 6) creates an empty message, gets a reference to the SOAPEnvelope, and then removes the empty header part, which this application does not use. Line 9 adds the declaration of the private namespace used by this service using the SOAPElement addNamespaceDeclaration() method:

```
public SOAPElement addNamespaceDeclaration(String prefix, String uri)
    throws SOAPException;
```

In this case, the prefix and the URI supplied are declared as static strings within the class definition:

```
// The URI used to qualify elements for this service
private static final String SERVICE_URI = "urn:jwsnut.bookimageservice";

// The namespace prefix used in elements for this service
private static final String SERVICE_PREFIX = "tns";
```

The addNamespaceDeclaration() method can be used to attach a namespace declaration to any SOAPElement. Its effect is scoped to that element and its child elements, and returns a reference to the SOAPElement on which it is invoked. In this case, we apply the declaration to the SOAPEnvelope itself, so that it applies to the entire message.

Lines 12 and 13 are responsible for adding the BookList element to the SOAP body, using the SOAPBody addBodyElement( ) method:

```
public SOAPElement addBodyElement(Name name) throws SOAPException;
```

The Name object passed to this method determines the element name and the namespace within which it is defined. As you'll see later in this chapter, there are several ways to create a Name object. In this case, the Name is created using one of the methods provided by the SOAPFactory class:

```
// The name of the element used to request a book name list
private static Name BOOK_LIST_NAME;

// SOAPFactory for message pieces
private static SOAPFactory soapFactory;

// Create the BookList element
soapFactory = SOAPFactory.newInstance( );
BOOK_LIST_NAME = soapFactory.createName("BookList", SERVICE_PREFIX,
    SERVICE_URI);
```

SOAPFactory is a factory for objects that can be added to SOAP messages, including SOAPElements, Detail objects (which are used in connection SOAP faults), and Names.* A Name object is a representation of a fully qualified element name and therefore requires the following attributes:

- The local name of the element—in this case, BookList
- The URI of the namespace within which the name is defined
- The prefix used to represent the namespace (tns in this example)

It is also possible to have Names that are not namespace-qualified. In these cases, the URI and namespace prefix are both null.

Once the Name is created, the SOAPBody addBodyElement( ) method creates the actual SOAPBodyElement and installs it in the body. Since this element does not have any nested elements, it ends up looking like this:

```
<tns:BookList/>
```

You can see that the namespace prefix and the local name that were used to create the Name object become part of the element.

Handling the BookList request in the service implementation

The book image service is implemented as a servlet derived from SAAJServlet, much of the code for which is shown in Example 3-6.

---

* SOAPFactory is a new class added to SAAJ Version 1.1. The earlier API (JAXM 1.0) used the SOAPEnvelope createName( ) methods, which require access to the SOAPEnvelope object, to create Name objects. In many cases, however, an application will want to construct part of a SOAP message without having to have access to the SOAPEnvelope within which it will eventually be enclosed, so the context-free SOAPFactory class was added to make this possible. SOAPFactory is a generalization of the JAXM 1.0 SOAPElementFactory class, which is deprecated as of SAAJ Version 1.1.

Example 3-6. A servlet that uses SAAJ to provide the book image web service

```java
/**
 * A servlet that uses SAAJ attachments to
 * serve images to a client.
 */
public class BookImageServlet extends SAAJServlet {

    // The XML Schema namespace
    private static final String XMLSCHEMA_URI =
        "http://www.w3.org/2001/XMLSchema";

    // The XML Schema instance namespace
    private static final String XMLSCHEMA_INSTANCE_URI =
        "http://www.w3.org/2001/XMLSchema-instance";

    // Namespace prefix for XML Schema
    private static final String XMLSCHEMA_PREFIX = "xsd";

    // Namespace prefix for XML Schema instance
    private static final String XMLSCHEMA_INSTANCE_PREFIX = "xsi";

    // The namespace prefix used for SOAP encoding
    private static final String SOAP_ENC_PREFIX = "SOAP-ENC";

    // The URI used to qualify elements for this service
    private static final String SERVICE_URI = "urn:jwsnut.bookimageservice";

    // The namespace prefix used in elements for this service
    private static final String SERVICE_PREFIX = "tns";

    // MessageFactory for replies from this service
    private static MessageFactory messageFactory;

    // SOAPFactory for message pieces
    private static SOAPFactory soapFactory;

    // The name of the element used to request a book name list
    private static Name BOOK_LIST_NAME;

    // The name of the element used to reply to a book name list request
    private static Name BOOK_TITLES_NAME;

    // The name of the element used to request a book image
    private static Name BOOK_IMAGE_REQUEST_NAME;

    // The name of the element used to respond to a book image request
    private static Name BOOK_IMAGES_NAME;

    // The name of the attribute used to hold the image encoding
    private static Name IMAGE_TYPE_ATTRIBUTE;

    // The name of the href attribute
    private static Name HREF_ATTRIBUTE;
```

Example 3-6. A servlet that uses SAAJ to provide the book image web service (continued)

```java
/**
 * Handles a received SOAP message.
 */
public SOAPMessage onMessage(SOAPMessage message) throws SOAPException {

    if (messageFactory == null) {
        // Create all static data on first call
        messageFactory = MessageFactory.newInstance( );
        soapFactory = SOAPFactory.newInstance( );
        BOOK_LIST_NAME = soapFactory.createName("BookList", SERVICE_PREFIX,
            SERVICE_URI);
        BOOK_TITLES_NAME = soapFactory.createName("BookTitles",
            SERVICE_PREFIX, SERVICE_URI);
        BOOK_IMAGE_REQUEST_NAME =
                    soapFactory.createName("BookImageRequest",
            SERVICE_PREFIX, SERVICE_URI);
        BOOK_IMAGES_NAME = soapFactory.createName("BookImages",
            SERVICE_PREFIX, SERVICE_URI);
        IMAGE_TYPE_ATTRIBUTE = soapFactory.createName("imageType",
            SERVICE_PREFIX, SERVICE_URI);
        HREF_ATTRIBUTE = soapFactory.createName("href");
    }

    // Create the reply message and define the namespace
    // and encoding for the elements used in the reply.
    SOAPMessage reply = messageFactory.createMessage( );
    SOAPEnvelope replyEnvelope = reply.getSOAPPart( ).getEnvelope( );
    replyEnvelope.getHeader( ).detachNode( );
    replyEnvelope.addNamespaceDeclaration(SERVICE_PREFIX, SERVICE_URI);
    replyEnvelope.addNamespaceDeclaration(SOAP_ENC_PREFIX,
                                    SOAPConstants.URI_NS_SOAP_ENCODING);
    replyEnvelope.addNamespaceDeclaration(XMLSCHEMA_PREFIX, XMLSCHEMA_URI);
    replyEnvelope.addNamespaceDeclaration(XMLSCHEMA_INSTANCE_PREFIX,
                                    XMLSCHEMA_INSTANCE_URI);
    replyEnvelope.setEncodingStyle(SOAPConstants.URI_NS_SOAP_ENCODING);
    SOAPBody replyBody = reply.getSOAPPart().getEnvelope( ).getBody( );

    // There are two requests - one for the list of
    // book titles, the other for the image for a book.
    SOAPBody requestBody = message.getSOAPPart().getEnvelope( ).getBody( );
    Iterator iter = requestBody.getChildElements( );
    if (iter.hasNext( )) {
        // The child element contains the request
        SOAPElement element = (SOAPElement)iter.next( );
        Name elementName = element.getElementName( );
        if (elementName.equals(BOOK_LIST_NAME)) {
            handleBookListRequest(replyBody);
        } else if (elementName.equals(BOOK_IMAGE_REQUEST_NAME)) {
            handleBookImageRequest(element, reply);
        } else {
            // Unrecognized request - this is a fault.
```

```
                    createFault(replyBody, "soap-env:Client.UnknownRequest",
                        "Unrecognized request", SERVICE_URI, elementName.
                        getLocalName( ));
            }
        } else {
            // No request - this is a fault
            createFault(replyBody, "soap-env:Client.MissingRequest",
                "Missing request", SERVICE_URI, "No request found");
        }
        return reply;
    }

    // HELPER METHODS NOT SHOWN...
}
```

The first part of the onMessage( ) method is concerned with creating objects such as Names that will be used to build a reply message the first time the service is used, and then creating the envelope for the reply message, which we'll look at more closely very shortly. Before the reply can be constructed, however, the received message must be examined to identify the client request that it contains. To do this, it is necessary to find the first child element of the SOAP body and extract its element name. Here is the code that does this:

```
SOAPBody requestBody = message.getSOAPPart( ).getEnvelope( )
    .getBody( );
Iterator iter = requestBody.getChildElements( );
if (iter.hasNext( )) {
    // The child element contains the request
    SOAPElement element = (SOAPElement)iter.next( );
```

Although SOAPBody does not provide any methods for accessing its content, the SOAPElement interface from which it is derived does provide this facility. In particular, the getChildElements( ) method returns an Iterator that can be used to step through all of the immediate child elements of the SOAPElement to which it is applied. In this case, we expect to find exactly one child element; if we don't find any, then the message has been constructed incorrectly and the request will not be processed. Instead, a reply message containing a SOAP fault will be returned to the client, as described in "SOAP Fault Handling," later in this chapter.

Assuming that we find a child element, the next step is to find out what it represents. So far, we have only seen the BookList request, but in fact, this servlet can also handle a request for a cover image for a book with a given title, the implementation of which we'll look at when we discuss how to use SOAP attachments. It is therefore necessary to work out which of these two requests has been received:

```
Name elementName = element.getElementName( );
if (elementName.equals(BOOK_LIST_NAME)) {
    handleBookListRequest(replyBody);
} else if (elementName.equals(BOOK_IMAGE_REQUEST_NAME)) {
    handleBookImageRequest(element, reply);
} else {
```

```
        // Unrecognized request - this is a fault.
        createFault(replyBody, "soap-env:Client.UnknownRequest",
          "Unrecognized request", SERVICE_URI, elementName.getLocalName());
    }
```

The SOAPElement getElementName() method returns the Name object that identifies the element, which contains the local element name and the URI for its associated namespace. To determine which request has been received, we compare the element name against two fixed values, BOOK_LIST_NAME and BOOK_IMAGE_REQUEST_ NAME, which are constructed (using the SOAPFactory class) with the appropriate local names and the private URN associated with this service. This is, of course, the same URN (urn:jwsnut.bookimageservice) used by the client. Notice that the comparison is performed using the equals() method, which, for Name objects, returns true if both the local names and the namespace URIs are the same.[*] Depending on the result of the test, the handleBookListRequest() or the handleBookImageRequest() method is called, or, if the element name does not match either of the expected values, a SOAP fault is returned to the client. Here, we are interested only in the handleBookListRequest() method. Before we look at its implementation, however, let's examine the SOAP message that the service sends in reply to the client's BookList request, which is shown in Example 3-7.

Example 3-7. A SOAP message containing a list of book titles

```
<?xml version="1.0" encoding="UTF-8"?>
<soap-env:Envelope xmlns:soap-env="http://schemas.xmlsoap.org/soap/envelope/"
        xmlns:tns="urn:jwsnut.bookimageservice"
        xmlns:SOAP-ENC="http://schemas.xmlsoap.org/soap/encoding/"
        xmlns:xsd="http://www.w3.org/2001/XMLSchema"
        xmlns:xsi="http://www.w3.org/2001/XMLSchema-instance"
        soap-env:encodingStyle="http://schemas.xmlsoap.org/soap/encoding/">
    <soap-env:Body>
        <tns:BookTitles xsi:type="SOAP-ENC:Array"
                        SOAP-ENC:arrayType="xsd:string[]">
            <item>Java in a Nutshell</item>
            <item>J2ME in a Nutshell</item>
            <item>Java 2D Graphics</item>
            <item>Java I/O</item>
            <item>JavaServer Pages</item>
            <item>Java Internationalization</item>
            <item>Java Foundation Classes in a Nutshell</item>
            <item>Java Performance Tuning</item>
            <item>Creating Effective JavaHelp</item>
            <item>Enterprise JavaBeans</item>
            <item>Java Servlet Programming</item>
            <item>Java Swing</item>
        </tns:BookTitles>
    </soap-env:Body>
</soap-env:Envelope>
```

[*] In the case of Names that do not have namespace qualifiers, this test still works because the namespace URI for such a Name is null.

If you compare this to the BookList request message shown in Example 3-4, you'll see that the Envelope of the reply message declares many more namespaces than the request. Each of these namespaces, which are listed in Table 3-2, is added to the SOAPEnvelope object using the addNamespaceDeclaration( ) method that we saw earlier; therefore, they apply to the whole message.

Table 3-2. Namespaces commonly used in SOAP messages

URI	Description
http://schemas.xmlsoap.org/soap/envelope/	Associated with the SOAP message envelope. This namespace is used on all of the standard envelope elements.
http://www.w3.org/2001/XMLSchema	Definitions relating to the W3C XML Schema standard. Typically assigned the prefix xsd and used to indicate built-in datatypes defined by this standard, such as xsd:string.
http://www.w3.org/2001/XMLSchema-instance	Another namespace associated with W3C XML Schema, this is typically assigned the prefix xsi and is attached to attributes such as xsi:type that define the data types of elements in the SOAP message.
http://schemas.xmlsoap.org/soap/encoding/	A namespace that indicates definitions taken from the SOAP section 5 encoding rules.

The implementation shown in Example 3-6 defines constants to represent both the URIs and the prefixes that will be associated with them when constructing SOAP messages. The javax.xml.soap.SOAPConstants interface includes constant values (SOAPConstants.URI_NS_SOAP_ENCODING and SOAPConstants.URI_NS_SOAP_ENVELOPE) for the URIs associated with the SOAP encoding rules and the envelope, but does not define the other URIs, even though they are likely to be used just as often.

The Envelope element also has an attribute that you haven't seen before:

```
soap-env:encodingStyle="http://schemas.xmlsoap.org/soap/encoding/"
```

The value of this attribute is a URI that indicates the encoding rules used to determine the representation of the data within the element to which it is attached. In this case, the message is encoded using SOAP section 5 encoding rules. It is, of course, necessary for both the sender and receiver of the message to understand the encoding rules that are actually used within the message, which is why the SOAP 1.1 specification includes these rules that applications are encouraged (but not absolutely required) to use.

Since the encodingStyle attribute is attached to the Envelope element, it applies to everything within the envelope unless explicitly overridden at the level of a nested element, in which case that element and its child elements can be encoded according to different rules:

```
<OuterElement soap-env:encodingStyle=
    "http://schemas.xmlsoap.org/soap/encoding/">
    <!-- SOAP section 5 encoding rules apply here -->
    <InnerElement soap-env:encodingStyle="urn:MyPrivateStyle">
        <!-- Private encoding rules apply here -->
    </InnerElement>
    <!-- SOAP section 5 encoding rules apply again -->
</OuterElement>
```

Nested encodings such as this might be convenient if the message contains all or part of an XML document that uses a different representation than that used by the parties exchanging SOAP messages and that ultimately will probably be processed by a different application.

The body of the reply message is simply an array of strings, where each string represents the title of a book. In order for the client to understand the reply, it must know how the server will represent an array of strings. Fortunately, the SOAP section 5 encoding rules provide a standard way of representing an array of objects in XML. For simple types such as strings, the canonical form looks like this:

```
<tns:ElementName xsi:type= "SOAP-ENC:Array" SOAP-ENC:arrayType= "arrayType">
    <item>itemValue1</item>
    <item>itemValue2</item>
    <!-- and so on -->
</tns:ElementName>
```

The attribute xsi:type is defined by the W3C XML Schema standard and indicates that the element contains an array as defined by the SOAP encoding rules, since the namespace prefix for the Array attribute is SOAP-ENC, which is mapped, in this example, to the URI for these encoding rules. The arrayType attribute specifies the type of the array. For an array of strings, this will typically have the value:

```
SOAP-ENC:arrayType="xsd:string[]"
```

Here, the value xsd:string is the XML Schema attribute value that defines a string,* and the square brackets obviously indicate an array. In this case, the square brackets are empty, which means that the number of elements in the array should be determined by counting the child elements. It is also possible to specify fixed bounds by composing the attribute like this, to indicate a string array with 12 elements:

```
SOAP-ENC:arrayType="xsd:string[12]"
```

The elements of the array are all represented as nested elements, the names of which (commonly referred to as accessor names) must all be the same but can otherwise be arbitrary. In this example, we use the element name item, but any legal XML name will suffice. In the actual reply message shown in Example 3-7, the array element is actually called BookTitles and, not surprisingly, is qualified with the namespace associated with this web service. Notice, however, that the array elements use an element name (item) that is not namespace-qualified. This is explicitly allowed by the SOAP encoding rules.

Now let's look at the code in the handleBookListRequest() method that creates this representation of a string array, which is shown in Example 3-8.

---

* You can see that xsd:string is an attribute defined by XML Schema because the xsd prefix in this example (represented in Example 3-6 by the constant value XMLSCHEMA_PREFIX) is mapped to the XML Schema URI (represented by the constant value XMLSCHEMA_URI).

Example 3-8. Creating a SOAP message containing an array of book titles

```
/**
 * Handles a request for list of book names.
 */
private void handleBookListRequest(SOAPBody replyBody) throws SOAPException {
    // Create a BookTitles element containing an entry
    // for each book title.
    SOAPBodyElement bodyElement = replyBody.addBodyElement(BOOK_TITLES_NAME);

    // Add 'xsi:type = "SOAP-ENC:Array"'
    bodyElement.addAttribute(
        soapFactory.createName("type", XMLSCHEMA_INSTANCE_PREFIX,
            XMLSCHEMA_INSTANCE_URI), SOAP_ENC_PREFIX + ":Array");

    // Add 'SOAP-ENC:arrayType = "xsd:string[]"
    bodyElement.addAttribute(
        soapFactory.createName("arrayType", SOAP_ENC_PREFIX,
            SOAPConstants.URI_NS_SOAP_ENCODING), XMLSCHEMA_PREFIX +
            ":string[]");

    // Add an array entry for each book
    String[] titles = BookImageServletData.getBookTitles();
    for (int i = 0; i < titles.length; i++) {
        SOAPElement titleElement = bodyElement.addChildElement("item");
        titleElement.addTextNode(titles[i]);
    }
}
```

We're not going to show how the book titles themselves are obtained—the logic for this is hidden in a separate class called BookImageServletData, which provides a method that returns all of the titles in the form of an array of strings. Instead, we're going to concentrate on how to build the SOAP representation of the titles list. The first step is to create the BookTitles element, which is done using the SOAPBody addBodyElement( ) method, using the qualified name of the element as its argument. This is the same way that the client created the BookList request. Next, we need to add to this element the xsi:type and SOAP-ENC:arrayType attributes required by the SOAP-encoding rules to indicate that the element represents an array of strings. To add an attribute to a SOAPElement, the addAttribute( ) method is used:

```
public SOAPElement addAttribute(Name name, String value);
```

name is the qualified name of the attribute, and value is the value to be associated with it. As before, in this example, we use the SOAPFactory class to create Name objects for the attributes, which creates the Name object for the attribute xsi:type, which is then passed to the addAttribute( ) method:

```
// Add 'xsi:type = "SOAP-ENC:Array"'
bodyElement.addAttribute(
            soapFactory.createName("type", XMLSCHEMA_INSTANCE_PREFIX,
                XMLSCHEMA_INSTANCE_URI), SOAP_ENC_PREFIX + ":Array");
```

The addAttribute( ) method returns a reference to the SOAPElement to which the attribute was added, which makes it possible to add multiple attributes by chaining calls:

```
bodyElement.addAttribute(...).addAttribute(...).addAttribute( );
```

Having installed the BookTitles element in the reply body, we now need to add a child element for each book title. The SOAPElement interface provides five methods that allow a nested element to be added. In this case, since the element is part of a SOAP-encoded array definition, its name does not need to be namespace-qualified, so we can use the variant of the addChildElement( ) method that requires a string to specify the local name of the element to be created and returns a reference to the SOAPElement itself:

```
SOAPElement titleElement = bodyElement.addChildElement("item");
```

At this point, we have SAAJ message structures that amount to the following XML:

```
<tns:BookTitles xsi:type="SOAP-ENC:Array" SOAP-
ENC:arrayType="xsd:string[]">
        <item/>
<tns:BookTitles>
```

What is missing here is the book title within the item element. Unlike item itself, the book title should not be represented by an XML element—it is, in fact, just a text string. To add text to a SOAPElement, we need to create and add a Text node, using the SOAPElement addTextNode( ) method:

```
public SOAPElement addTextNode(String text) throws SOAPException;
```

You may be surprised to see that this method is defined to return a SOAPElement instead of an object of type Text, despite its name (especially since Text is not derived from SOAPElement; see Figure 3-4). In fact, this method returns a reference to the SOAPElement on which it was invoked, not the Text object that was created. In most cases, you don't actually need to get access to the Text object itself; the only way to do so is to use the SOAPElement getChildElements( ) method to get an Iterator over all of the element's children and search for the one that implements the Text interface. Adding the following method call:

```
titleElement.addTextNode(titles[i])
```

finally completes the array element for the book title, so that now the message body contains the following:

```
<tns:BookTitles xsi:type="SOAP-ENC:Array" SOAP-ENC:arrayType="xsd:string[]">
        <item>Creating Effecttive JavaHelp</item>
<tns:BookTitles>
```

The rest of the loop in the handleBookListRequest( ) method adds item elements for each of the books that the service knows about. When this method completes, the reply message is completely built and is returned from the servlet's onMessage( ) method, to be sent back to the client.

By now, you have probably realized that implementing a web service using SAAJ involves much more code that deals directly with details such as the exact layouts of SOAP messages than you see if you simply used JAX-RPC. In fact, you might wonder how the author of a client application that needs to connect to a web service implemented by somebody else is supposed to know what message types the service supports and how to build the required element structure. Here, for example, the client application knows how to build the requests for the book image service and how to interpret the replies only because they were both implemented by the same person. In the real world, service providers are supposed to publish the interfaces to their web services in the form of WSDL documents. As you'll see in Chapter 5, WSDL includes XML elements that describe the operations that a web service supports and the formats of the messages required to access them.

Client processing for the reply to the BookList request

The processing performed by the client when it receives the reply to its BookList request is very simple—all it has to do is loop over the SOAP array in the message body and extract the book titles from each nested element. Example 3-9 shows the implementation.

Example 3-9. Handling the server's reply to the BookList request

```
SOAPBody replyBody = reply.getSOAPPart().getEnvelope( ).getBody( );
if (replyBody.hasFault( )) {
    SOAPFault fault = replyBody.getFault( );
    throw new SOAPException("Fault when getting book titles: " +
        fault.getFaultString( ));
}

// The body contains a "BookTitles" element with a nested
// element for each book title.
Iterator iter = replyBody.getChildElements(BOOK_TITLES_NAME);
if (iter.hasNext( )) {
    ArrayList list = new ArrayList( );
    SOAPElement bookTitles = (SOAPElement)iter.next( );
    iter = bookTitles.getChildElements( );
    while (iter.hasNext( )) {
        list.add(((SOAPElement)iter.next( )).getValue( ));
    }
}
```

The first part of this code checks whether the server detected an error with the request by looking for a SOAP fault element in the reply body. SOAPBody provides the convenience methods hasFault( ), which returns true if there is a fault present, and getFault( ), which looks for and returns the SOAPFault element. Since the presence of a fault indicates either an error in the client code that constructed the request or a problem at the server, there is no reasonable recovery possible in this case and a SOAPException is thrown.

If there is no fault, then the body of the reply contains a BookTitles element. Earlier, we saw that SOAPElement has a getChildElements( ) method that returns all of the children of the element that it is invoked on, and which we used previously to get all of the top-level elements in the body of a SOAP message. Here, we use an overloaded variant of that method, which accepts a Name as its argument:

```
public Iterator getChildElements(Name name) throws SOAPException;
```

This method returns only those elements whose name matches the one given. In this case, we get back an Iterator over all of the BookTitles elements in the SOAPBody—there should be exactly one. Once we have a reference to this element, we invoke the getChildElements( ) method on it to gain access to all of the nested array elements. In this case, we use the variant of getChildElements( ) that returns all of the children, both because we know that we need to process all of them and because the name associated with the element is arbitrary (and therefore we cannot construct an appropriate Name object). Finally, we iterate over all of the nested elements and extract the title by using the getValue( ) method, which returns the text associated with a Node, if there is any.

More on SOAPElements

The example that you have just seen shows some of the ways in which a SOAPElement can be created. It also demonstrates some of its API. In this section, we take a closer look at how to create and use SOAPElements.

Creation of SOAPElements

So far, you have seen how to create new SOAPElements and incorporate them into the node tree for a SOAPMessage in a single step. To create a SOAPElement that appears directly in the SOAPBody, in a SOAPHeader, or in a SOAPFault, use convenience methods provided by these classes, of which the one provided by SOAPBody is typical:

```
public SOAPBodyElement addBodyElement(Name name) throws SOAPException;
```

This method returns not a SOAPElement but an instance of SOAPBodyElement, which is derived from SOAPElement. All top-level elements in the SOAP body must be SOAPBodyElements, rather than simply SOAPElements. Similarly, top-level elements inside the SOAPHeader must be of type SOAPHeaderElement, and top-level elements in a SOAPFault will be of type SOAPFaultElement. As far as the SAAJ API is concerned, there is no real difference between a SOAPElement and a SOAPBodyElement or a SOAPHeaderElement, since neither of these interfaces add any methods in addition to those defined by SOAPElement.

Once you have a SOAPElement, you can add child elements to it using one of the five overloaded variants of its addChildElement( ) method, all of which return the newly created SOAPElement:

public SOAPElement addChildElement(Name name)
> This variant adds a new SOAPElement for which the name is obtained by the supplied Name argument. If the Name is a qualified name, then the element as written to the XML output stream has both a local name and an associated namespace prefix; otherwise, it has an unqualified local name.

```
public SOAPElement addChildElement(String localName)
```
Creates a new SOAPElement with the given unqualified name and adds it to the child list of the element on which this method is invoked.

```
public SOAPElement addChildElement(String localName, String prefix,
  String uri)
```
Creates a new SOAPElement with a fully qualified name created from the supplied arguments and adds it to the child list of the element on which this method is invoked. Using this method has the same result as creating a Name using the supplied arguments and then calling the addChildElement(Name name) variant.

```
public SOAPElement addChildElement(String localName, String prefix)
```
This is similar to the previous variant, except that it does not provide the URI for the namespace that the localName argument is associated with. However, if the supplied prefix can be resolved to a namespace URI by examining the SOAPElement on which this method or its ancestors are invoked, then that URI is used when creating the SOAPElement. If this is not possible, then a SOAPException is thrown. For example, consider the following code, where soapBody is a reference to a SOAPBody object:

```
Name name = soapFactory.createName("bodyElement", "tns", "urn:service");
SOAPBodyElement bodyElement = soapBody.addBodyElement(name);
SOAPElement childElement = bodyElement.addChildElement("childElement",
    "tns");
```

Here, the addChildElement() call to create childElement does not specify the namespace URI. However, since the namespace prefix tns supplied as the second argument is defined by the parent node, a mapping to the URN given in that element is inferred and childElement is associated with this URI.

```
public SOAPElement addChildElement(SOAPElement element)
```
Requests that the given SOAPElement be added to the list of children of the element on which it is invoked. Depending on the type of the parent element, however, a different SOAPElement may be added to the parent.

Although the methods all declare the return value to be of type SOAPElement, in reality they may return a subinterface of SOAPElement. In particular, calling addChildElement() on a SOAPBody object (which is possible because SOAPBody is itself a SOAPElement) will always return a SOAPBodyElement. Consider the following code:

```
SOAPElement bodyElement = soapBody.addBodyElement(name);
    // "name" is of type Name
SOAPElement secondElement = soapBody.addChildElement("localName");
```

Here, bodyElement is obviously of type SOAPBodyElement because addBodyElement() is defined to return an object of that type. However, secondElement is also a SOAPBodyElement, since it is a top-level element within a SOAPBody. Similar results are obtained when addChildElement() is invoked on an element of type SOAPHeader or SOAPFault.

Now suppose that element is an existing SOAPElement called TopElement, and then consider the following code, in which soapBody again refers to an object of type SOAPBody:

```
SOAPElement childElement = soapElement.addChildElement("ChildElement");
SOAPBody addedElement = body.addChildElement(element);
```

This attempts to add an existing SOAPElement, complete with a child element of its own, to a SOAPBody. There seems to be a problem here, since the immediate child of a SOAPBody must be a SOAPBodyElement, but the element being added is actually a SOAPElement. What actually happens is that a new SOAPBodyElement is created as a copy of the supplied SOAPElement, added to the SOAPBody instead of it, and returned from the addChildElement( ) method. The copied element also has as its child a copy of the child element associated with the original.

Since all of the SOAPElements that you have seen so far have been created as children of other SOAPElements, you might wonder how we could create the unattached SOAPElement used in the example just shown. To create a freestanding SOAPElement, use one of the following methods of SOAPFactory:

```
public SOAPElement createElement(Name name) throws SOAPException;
public SOAPElement createElement(String localName) throws SOAPException;
public SOAPElement createElement(String localName, String prefix,
    String uri) throws SOAPException;
```

The SOAPElementFactory class also has identical methods to those shown here. However, SOAPElementFactory is deprecated as of SAAJ 1.1 and the SOAPFactory methods (to which those in SOAPElementFactory actually delegate) should be used instead.

These methods can be used, as shown in a small way in the previous example, to build a message fragment as a freestanding entity and then add it to a SOAPMessage, without having to supply a reference to any part of the message to the code that builds the fragment.

Removal of SOAPElements

Although SOAPElement does not provide a method that allows any of its child elements to be removed, the Node interface, from which SOAPElement is derived, has a detachNode( ) method that removes the Node on which it is invoked from its parent. For example, the following code shows how to use this method to remove the first child of a SOAPElement:

```
SOAPElement parent = soapFactory.createElement("Element");
parent.addChildElement("Child1");
parent.addChildElement("Child2");
parent.addChildElement("Child3");
parent.addChildElement("Child4");

// Get the first child and remove it
Iterator iter = parent.getChildElements( );
SOAPElement child = (SOAPElement)iter.next( );
child.detachNode( );
```

Incidentally, it is not possible to remove more than one SOAPElement at a time by using an Iterator in this way, since the next( ) method throws a ConcurrentModificationException when called after removal of the first child element. To remove more than one SOAPElement, use the Iterator remove( ) method instead. The following code shown next, for example, removes all the children of a SOAPElement.

```
Iterator iter = parent.getChildElements( );
while (iter.hasNext( )) {
    iter.remove( );
}
```

SOAP Fault Handling

A SOAP fault is a specific type of XML element placed in the body of a reply message to convey status information or, more usually, to report a fault while processing the original request. SAAJ represents a fault using the SOAPFault interface that, since it must be a top-level element in the SOAP body, is derived from SOAPBodyElement (see Figure 3-4). The SOAP specification requires that there be no more than one SOAP fault in the message body. Faults can be mixed with other top-level elements if necessary.

SOAP faults have three attributes that can be set to provide information about the condition being reported. Each of these attributes has corresponding methods in the SOAPFault interface to allow its value to be set or retrieved:

Attribute	SOAPFault methods	Description
Fault code	getFaultCode( ) setFaultCode( )	A code that indicates the reason for reporting the fault. Applications may define their own private fault codes or use the set of standard values defined by the SOAP 1.1 specification (described later). All fault codes must be namespace-qualified.
Fault string	getFaultString( ) setFaultString( )	A human-readable description of the reason for the fault. The value of this attribute typically is written to a log file or displayed in a user interface.
Fault actor	getFaultActor( ) setFaultActor( )	The URI of the participant in the SOAP message path (referred to in the SOAP specification as an *actor*) that caused the fault element to be generated.

Fault Codes

SOAP defines a small set of fault codes that can be used as appropriate. All of these fault codes belong to the same namespace as the SOAP envelope itself. The SAAJ API does not define constant values for these codes, so the application code must hardcode them.

Fault code	Description
VersionMismatch	This code indicates that a SOAP message was received in which the namespace for the SOAP envelope did not match the version of SOAP that the receiver supports. At the time of this writing, this means that the namespace was something other than *http://schemas.xmlsoap.org/soap/envelope/*.
MustUnderstand	This error is generated when a SOAP actor receives a message containing a header that contains the mustUnderstand attribute with value 1, which it does not know how to process. For further details, see "SOAP Headers," later in this chapter.

Fault code	Description
Client	Indicates that the message was improperly constructed by its originator. It is possible to more closely specify the nature of the problem (albeit in an application-dependent way) by appending one or more qualifiers to the fault code. For example, the book image service uses the fault code `Client.UnknownRequest` if it receives a message in which the top-level element of the body is not one of the requests that it recognizes.
Server	Indicates that a processing error occurred within the server. This might, for example, be because the resources required within the server to handle the message are not currently available. This code should not be used when the cause of the error is related to content or construction of the message. Like the `Client` fault code, it is common to return a more specific error code by appending a qualifier.

Fault Actor

Although in this chapter our examples have involved only a client application and the web service that it is using, in many cases, a SOAP message passes through and is processed by intermediate systems before reaching its final destination. These intermediate systems, referred to as actors, usually perform message validation or processing based on the content of SOAP headers attached to the message. If an error is detected during header processing, the actor may return a fault to the message originator, and must identify itself as the source of the report by using the fault actor attribute, which is technically a URI, but is typically the URL of the system concerned.

When an error is detected at the system that is the ultimate destination of the message, the fault actor attribute need not be set. Note, however, that the SAAJ API does not allow you to set this attribute to null—instead, you need to use an empty string to indicate that the fault actor is not specified.

Fault Details

In addition to the three attributes just described, a SOAP fault also requires a detail element to be present if the fault relates to the content of the message body. No detail element is permitted if the fault relates to header processing. The content of the detail element is application-dependent, but the top-level element must be namespace-qualified.

Creating Fault Elements

The book image web service generates a fault in response to a number of conditions. Later in this chapter, you'll see how the client application and the web service use SOAP attachments to transfer the cover image for one or more books, given a request containing the book titles. If the web service is asked for the image of a book whose title it does not recognize, then it generates a fault. To see an example of this, start the client using the command line:

```
ant run-client-debug
```

Now select No Such Book in the book title list and press the "Fetch" button. The client requests the book cover for a book whose title the web service does not know. In the command window from the start of this example, you'll see the server's reply message, which contains a SOAP fault entry in the body:

```
<?xml version="1.0" encoding="UTF-8"?>
<soap-env:Envelope xmlns:soap-env="http://schemas.xmlsoap.org/soap/
    envelope/"
```

```
        xmlns:tns="urn:jwsnut.bookimageservice"
        xmlns:SOAP-ENC="http://schemas.xmlsoap.org/soap/encoding/"
        xmlns:xsd="http://www.w3.org/2001/XMLSchema"
        xmlns:xsi="http://www.w3.org/2001/XMLSchema-instance"
        soap-env:encodingStyle="http://schemas.xmlsoap.org/soap/encoding/">
    <soap-env:Body>
        <soap-env:Fault>
            <faultcode>soap-env:Client.Title</faultcode>
            <faultstring>Unknown title</faultstring>
            <faultactor>urn:jwsnut.bookimageservice</faultactor>
            <detail>
                <tns:BookFaultDetail>No Such Book</tns:BookFaultDetail>
            </detail>
        </soap-env:Fault>
    </soap-env:Body>
</soap-env:Envelope>
```

As you can see, the Fault element (which is qualified with the SOAP envelope namespace) contains child elements for the fault code, a fault string, the fault actor, and the fault detail:

Fault code

Since the error in this case results from an invalid book title in the received request, the web service uses a fault code from the soap-env:Client set, and qualifies it with the word "Title" to indicate that the error was with the book title. Obviously, for this to be of any use, the client and the service both need to be aware of the possible error codes and their meanings.

Fault string

This is simply a text message that describes the error, for the purposes of logging.

Fault actor

In this case, the fault was detected by the ultimate destination of the message, so it was not mandatory to specify the fault actor. The value supplied here is the URN of the web service.

Detail

The detail element contains an application-defined child element called BookFaultDetail that provides further information regarding the error. This element must be namespace-qualified, and it is appropriate here to qualify it with the URN of the web service. Child elements (if there are any) of the BookFaultDetail element do not need to be namespace-qualified. Applications are free to include any kind of private content in the detail part.

The code used to generate this fault is shown in Example 3-10.

Example 3-10. Creating a SOAP fault element

```
/**
 * Creates a fault in the reply body.
 */
private void createFault(SOAPBody replyBody, String faultCode,
    String faultString, String faultActor, String detailString)
    throws SOAPException {
```

Example 3-10. Creating a SOAP fault element (continued)

```
SOAPFault fault = replyBody.addFault( );
fault.setFaultCode(faultCode);
fault.setFaultString(faultString);
fault.setFaultActor(faultActor);
if (detailString != null) {
    Name detailName = soapFactory.createName("BookFaultDetail",
      SERVICE_PREFIX, SERVICE_URI);
    Detail detail = fault.addDetail( );
    DetailEntry detailEntry = detail.addDetailEntry(detailName);
    detailEntry.addTextNode(detailString);
}
}
```

The Fault element itself is created using the SOAPBody addFault( ) method:

```
public SOAPFault addFault( ) throws SOAPException;
```

Three setter methods are used to set the fault code, fault string, and fault actor. If this method is used to report a fault during header processing, it is not permissible to include a detail element; therefore, the detailString argument is null. In this case, however, the problem is with the message body, so a detail entry is mandatory. To create a detail entry and add it to the SOAPFault object, the SOAPFault addDetail( ) method is used:

```
public Detail addDetail( ) throws SOAPException;
```

Alternatively, a Detail object can be obtained from SOAPFactory, in which case it must be explicitly added to the SOAPFault object:

```
Detail detail = soapFactory.createDetail( );
fault.addChildElement(detail);
```

Finally, to add a top-level element to the Detail object, use its addDetailEntry( ) method, passing it the fully qualified element name (in this case, tns:BookFaultDetail):

```
public DetailEntry addDetailEntry(Name name) throws SOAPException;
```

DetailEntry is a SOAPElement; therefore, further elements can be nested inside it (and need not be namespace-qualified), or text can be added, as shown in Example 3-10.

It is also permissible to add other application-defined elements directly to the SOAPFault, rather than inside the Detail element. These elements can be created using the addChildElement( ) methods that SOAPFault inherits from SOAPElement (see Figure 3-4 for the inheritance hierarchy of SOAPFault) or using the SOAPFactory class in the usual way. All elements added to the SOAPFault element are of type SOAPFaultElement (from which Detail is derived) and must be namespace-qualified.

> The SOAP specification requires that a SOAP reply message containing a Fault element must, when sent over HTTP, have the HTTP response code 500, which indicates an internal server error. SAAJServlet fulfills this requirement by inspecting the message returned by the onMessage( ) method and setting the appropriate response code if the body contains a fault—see Example 3-1.

To make it simple to handle SOAP faults, the SOAPBody interface provides two convenience methods:

```
public boolean hasFault( );
public SOAPFault getFault( );
```

These methods remove the need for application code to search the body looking for a SOAPFault element, which may not be the first element in the SOAP body.

SOAP Messages and MIME Headers

When a SOAP message is wrapped for transmission in HTTP (or another protocol, such as SMTP), suitable MIME headers must be created. At minimum, the wrapper must include the Content-Type and Content-Length headers along with the SOAPAction header that was described in "Receiving a SOAP Message," earlier in this chapter. Similarly, when a message is received, any MIME headers that accompany it must be extracted from the protocol-specific wrapper and be made part of the created SOAPMessage. The MIME headers associated with a SOAPMessage are held in an object of type javax.xml.soap.MimeHeaders.

In terms of the structure of an encapsulated SOAP message, the MIME headers logically appear outside the envelope (as shown in Figure 3-1), where they form the protocol-specific wrapper. In the case of a SOAP message with attachments, in addition to the headers in the outer wrapper, the SOAP message part and each of the attachment parts have their own collection of MIME headers that are distinct from those of the wrapper, as shown in Figure 3-2.

The MimeHeader and MimeHeaders Classes

MimeHeader and MimeHeaders are two of four concrete classes in the java.xml.soap package. The MimeHeader class represents a single MIME header and contains the header name and its associated value, which are set at construction time and cannot subsequently be changed.

MimeHeaders is a collection of MimeHeader objects. When it is created, a MimeHeaders object is empty; headers can be added using one of the following methods:

public void addHeader(String headerName, String headerValue)
: Creates a MimeHeader object with the given header name and value, and adds it to the collection of headers.

public void setHeader(String headerName, String headerValue)
: If the MimeHeaders object does not contain a header with the given name, this method behaves in the same way as addHeader( ). Otherwise, the value for the first header in the collection that has the given name is replaced with the given value, and all other MimeHeader entries with the same name are removed.

As implied by the description of the setHeader( ) method, it is possible to have more than one header with the same name in a MimeHeaders object. The following code results in two header entries, both with the name HeaderName:

```
MimeHeaders headers = new MimeHeaders( );
headers.addHeader("HeaderName", "Value1");
headers.addHeader("HeaderName", "Value2");
```

Calling setHeader( ) method results in exactly one header with the supplied name being present in the collection, no matter how many there were before the call was made. The following line:

```
headers.setHeader("HeaderName", "NewValue");
```

replaces the MimeHeader with name HeaderName; it replaces value Value1 with the value NewValue; and it removes the MimeHeader for the entry with value Value2. Note that this method, like all of the methods of MimeHeaders, uses case-insensitive comparison when searching for headers by name, so that the names HeaderName and HEADERNAME are equivalent.

There are a number of methods that can be used to query the content of a MimeHeaders object:

public Iterator getAllHeaders( )
> Gets an Iterator over all of the headers in the collection. Each item returned by the Iterator is of type MimeHeader.

public String[] getHeader(String headerName)
> Gets all of the values associated with headers whose names match the given name. Using the MimeHeaders object just constructed as an example, the method call getHeaders("HeaderName") would return an array of two strings containing the values Value1 and Value2.

public Iterator getMatchingHeaders(String[] headerNames)
> Gets an Iterator that returns all of the MimeHeader objects that have a name that matches those in the given array.

public Iterator getNonMatchingHeaders(String[] headerNames)
> Gets an Iterator that returns all of the MimeHeader objects that have a name that does *not* match those in the given array.

Finally, there are two methods that remove entries from the collection:

public void removeAllHeaders( )
> Removes all of the MimeHeader objects, leaving an empty collection.

public void removeHeader(String headerName)
> Removes all MimeHeader objects whose name matches the supplied argument.

Setting MIME Headers When a SOAP Message Is Transmitted

When a SOAPMessage is created using the no-argument createMessage( ) method of MessageFactory, it has an empty MimeHeaders object associated with it. You can add headers at any time by retrieving this object from the SOAPMessage and using the addHeader( ) or setHeader( ) method:

```
message.getMimeHeaders().addHeader("Header1", "Value1");
```

The protocol-specific wrapper for a protocol such as HTTP requires that the Content-Length, Content-Type, and SOAPAction headers be included. These headers can be generated automatically by calling the SOAPMessage saveChanges( ) or writeTo( ) methods. The SOAPAction method can be explicitly set by application code and is not overwritten if it already has a value; the other two headers are always set by the saveChanges( ) and writeTo( ) methods. The SOAPMessage class also has a convenience method called `setContentDescription( )` that allows the optional `Content-Description` method to be set. The content description is treated as comment only.

If a SOAP message is transmitted using the `call( )` method of `SOAPConnection`, the `saveChanges( )` method is automatically called to create the appropriate headers, and the content of the resulting `MimeHeaders` object is copied to the outgoing HTTP message, as shown in Figure 3-6.

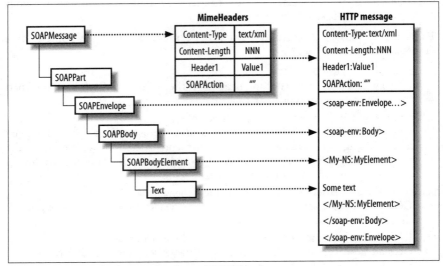

Figure 3-6. Mapping of MIME headers to HTTP headers

On the other hand, if you are implementing a server in a servlet environment and sending a reply message, you won't have a `SOAPConnection`, and therefore you cannot use its `call( )` method to wrap the `SOAPMessage` in the HTTP reply. In this case, you have to manually insert the MIME headers in the HTTP reply and then write the content of the `SOAPMessage` to the servlet's output stream. Much of the code to handle this was shown in the `doPost( )` method in Example 3-1. Note that it is first necessary to ensure that the `MimeHeaders` object is actually populated before copying the headers to the HTTP reply, by calling the `saveChanges( )` method. Once this is done, it is a simple matter to install the headers in the reply. The code for the `SAAJServlet` `setHttpHeaders( )` method is shown in Example 3-11. This method is invoked as follows:

```
// Copy the MIME headers to the HTTP response
setHttpHeaders(reply.getMimeHeaders( ), response);
```

where `response` is the `HttpServletResponse` object passed to the `doPost( )` method.

Example 3-11. Copying MIME headers to an HTTP message

```
private void setHttpHeaders(MimeHeaders mimeHeaders,
    HttpServletResponse response) {
    Iterator iter = mimeHeaders.getAllHeaders( );
    while (iter.hasNext( )) {
```

Example 3-11. Copying MIME headers to an HTTP message (continued)

```
        MimeHeader mimeHeader = (MimeHeader)iter.next( );
        String headerName = mimeHeader.getName( );
        String[] headerValues = mimeHeaders.getHeader(headerName);

        int count = headerValues.length;
        StringBuffer buffer = new StringBuffer( );
        for (int i = 0; i < count; i++) {
            if (i != 0) {
                buffer.append(',');
            }
            buffer.append(headerValues[i]);
        }
        response.setHeader(headerName, buffer.toString( ));
    }
}
```

This method uses the SOAPMessage getAllHeaders( ) method to get an Iterator over all of the MimeHeader objects in the set of headers that is passed, and it uses the HttpServletResponse setHeader( ) method to install the header name and value corresponding to each MimeHeader. As a space optimization, if there is more than one header with the same name, this method gathers all of their values together and writes a single header in which all of the values are comma-separated. This is so that, for example, if a header with name HeaderName appears twice with values Value1 and Value2, the result is a single HTTP header that looks like this:

```
    HeaderName: Value1,Value2
```

Obtaining MIME Headers When a SOAP Message Is Received

When a SOAPMessage is created from an HTTP request received by a servlet, the MessageFactory createMessage( ) method is used, as shown in Example 3-1. This method requires two arguments:

```
    public SOAPMessage createMessage(MimeHeaders headers, InputStream
        inputStream);
```

The MimeHeaders argument supplies the headers to be installed in the SOAPMessage, while the InputStream is used to read the XML that makes up the SOAP envelope and, in the case of a message with attachments, the attachments themselves. The createMessage( ) method associates the supplied MimeHeaders object with the SOAPMessage so that it can be retrieved later by calling the getMimeHeaders( ) method. The Content-Type header from the collection is also used by createMessage( ) to determine whether the SOAP message is in the format shown in Figure 3-1 (where the content type is text/xml) or has attachments as shown in Figure 3-2 (and content type Multipart/Related).

The servlet has to create an appropriate MimeHeaders object from the HTTP wrapper before it can call createMessage( ). The code used by SAAJServlet to do this is shown in Example 3-12.

Example 3-12. Creating a MIMEHeaders object from an HTTP message

```
private MimeHeaders getMIMEHeaders(HttpServletRequest request) {
    MimeHeaders mimeHeaders = new MimeHeaders( );
```

```
Enumeration enum = request.getHeaderNames( );
while (enum.hasMoreElements( )) {
    String headerName = (String)enum.nextElement( );
    String headerValue = request.getHeader(headerName);
    StringTokenizer st = new StringTokenizer(headerValue, ",");
    while (st.hasMoreTokens( )) {
        mimeHeaders.addHeader(headerName, st.nextToken( ).trim( ));
    }
}
return mimeHeaders;
}
```

In this code, the HTTP headers are obtained from the HttpServletRequest object. In most cases, one MimeHeader will be created from each header in the HTTP message. However, if a header contains multiple comma-separated values, such as:

```
HeaderName: Value1,Value2
```

then a separate MimeHeader will be added for each of the values.

SOAP with Attachments

A SOAP message constructed according to the SOAP 1.1 specification can only contain data encoded as XML. The SOAP with attachments specification defines an extension of the SOAP that allows additional data items—which may or may not be XML—to be transferred along with a SOAP message. SAAJ supports SOAP with attachments and provides a simple API that allows the transfer of arbitrary data. However, as we'll see, at the detailed level this interface is not quite as easy to use as it could be.

An Example SOAP with Attachments Application

As a demonstration of the use of attachments, the book image web service uses the SAAJ API to return the cover images for one or more of the books that it knows about. To see how this works, start the client using the following command:

```
ant run-client-debug
```

When the list of book titles appears, select one or more of them by clicking on them with the mouse (hold down the Control key to select more than one), then press the "Fetch" button. The selected images will appear in the user interface, as shown in Figure 3-7, and the message used to deliver them will be written to the command window. Since the message contains the binary data for the images, you'll see some strange characters in the output window. Leaving out the image data itself, a typical message used to transfer three cover images is shown in Figure 3-8.

Before we look at the SOAP with attachments message, let's briefly look at the request message that the client sends. This message (which does not have any attachments) contains an element called BookImageRequest that represents an array

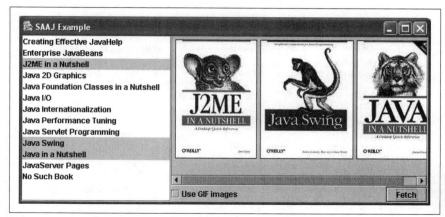

Figure 3-7. Using SOAP with attachments to transfer images

of strings, where each string is the title of a book. Here is what the body of the SOAP request looks like when requesting the cover images for three books:

```
<tns:BookImageRequest
        xsi:type="SOAP-ENC:Array" SOAP-ENC:arrayType="xsd:string[]"
        tns:imageType="image/jpeg">
    <item>J2ME in a Nutshell</item>
    <item>Java Swing</item>
    <item>Java in a Nutshell</item>
</tns:BookImageRequest>
```

As you can see, the BookImageRequest element contains the standard xsi:type and SOAP-ENC:arrayType attributes that indicate that it is a string array encoded using the SOAP section 5 encoding rules. It also includes another attribute defined in the book image web service's own namespace, which specifies the format in which the image should be returned:

```
tns:imageType="image/jpeg"
```

The server supports both JPEG and GIF images, and you can select the type required using the "Use GIF Images" checkbox on the user interface.

Now let's examine the reply message shown in Figure 3-8. As you can see, it is broken down into several parts that map directly to those shown in Figure 3-2. The first part consists of the HTTP headers that wrap the entire SOAP message. These headers are generated when the message is constructed using the saveChanges() method, and include a Content-Type header that indicates that the message is constructed according to the rules for a MIME Multipart/Related message. Any additional MIME headers added by application code to the MimeHeaders object obtained from the getMimeHeaders() method of SOAPMessage appear here.

The boundaries between the message parts are indicated using a text string that is automatically generated when the message is constructed and are supplied as the value of the boundary attribute of the Content-Type header, which in this case is:

```
------=_Part_11_4712040.1027772369874
```

```
HTTP/1.1 200 OK
Content-Type:multipart/related;type="text/xml";
boundary="----=_Part_11_4712040.1027772369874"          MIME headers from SOAPMessage
SOAPAction:""
Date:Sat,27 Jul 2002 12:19:29 GMT
Server:Apache Coyote HTTP/1.1 Connector [1.0 ]


------=_Part_11_4712040.1027772369874
Content-Type:text/xml

<?xml version="1.0"encoding="UTF-8"?>
<soap-env:Envelope
xmlns:soap-env="http://schemas.xmlsoap.org/soap/envelope/"
    xmlns:tns="urn:jwsnut.bookimageservice"
    xmlns:SOAP-ENC="http://schemas.xmlsoap.org/soap/encoding/"
    xmlns:xsd="http://www.w3.org/2001/XMLSchema"            SOAPPart
    xmlns:xsi="http://www.w3.org/2001/XMLSchema-instance"
    soap-env:encodingStyle="http://schemas.xmlsoap.org/soap/encoding/">
  <soap-env:Body>
    <tns:BookImages
xsi:type="SOAP-ENC:Array"SOAP-ENC:arrayType="xsd:anyType []"
      <item href="cid:ID0"/>
      <item href="cid:ID1"/>
      <item href="cid:ID2"/>
    </tns:BookImages>
  </soap-env:Body>
</soap-env:Envelope>
------=_Part_11_4712040.1027772369874
Content-Type:image/jpeg
Content-Id:ID0                                               First attachment

[ Image data not shown ]
------=_Part_11_4712040.1027772369874
Content-Type:image/jpeg
Content-Id:ID1                                               Second attachment

[ Image data not shown ]
------=_Part_11_4712040.1027772369874
Content-Type:image/jpeg
Content-Id:ID2                                               Third attachment

[ Image data not shown ]
------=_Part_11_4712040.1027772369874
```

Figure 3-8. A SOAP with attachments message containing three attachments

You can find a complete description of the format of these messages in RFC 2045 and RFC 2387, both of which can be downloaded from *http://www.ietf.org*.

The second part corresponds to the part of the message represented by the SOAPPart object and includes the SOAP message body. As you can see, this portion of the message also has MIME headers, one of which is the Content-Type header that describes the content as being text/xml. Since the SOAP body is always XML-encoded, this is the only legal value that could appear here. The SOAPPart object has a group of methods that allow application code to set or query the MIME headers that it contains, which are closely related to the methods of the MimeHeaders object described in the previous section of this chapter. These headers are distinct from those associated with the SOAPMessage object and are used only when the message includes attachments.

Following the SOAPPart are the three attachments. Again, each attachment has its own collection of MIME headers that, at minimum, must include a Content-Type header that describes the type of data that the attachment contains. In this case, the header is image/jpeg because all three attachments represent a book cover image encoded in JPEG format. Each attachment also has an additional header that looks like this:

```
Content-Id: ID0
```

This header is added by the book image servlet and acts as a label that is used to refer to the attachment from within the XML part of the message, which is shown in Example 3-13.

Example 3-13. The array of images returned by the book image service

```
<tns:BookImages xsi:type="SOAP-ENC:Array" SOAP-ENC:arrayType="xsd:anyType[]">
    <item href="cid:ID0"/>
    <item href="cid:ID1"/>
    <item href="cid:ID2"/>
</tns:BookImages>
```

By now, you should recognize this as a SOAP-encoded array. In this case, though, the array type is given as xsd:anyType[]. This particular specifier indicates that the element content could be any type—the application needs to examine each element to work out its actual type. This construct is essentially the same as declaring an array of Java Objects.

Another difference between this array and those that you have already seen is the actual element content is not inline with the array itself. Since the data in this case is not XML, it cannot be included directly in the message part, so we have to provide a reference that will allow the receiving application to locate the data. In this case, we choose to do so by using the href attribute, the value of which maps directly to the Content-Id of the attachment part that contains the image data apart from the inclusion of the cid:, which indicates that the value is a Content-Id. This distinguishes this representation from an alternative choice, available only for XML content, which places the value in the body of the message itself and for which the reference uses a # symbol instead of cid:, as shown here:

```
<item href="#ID0"/>
```

Here is a typical example where this style of reference is used:[*]

```
<?xml version="1.0" encoding="UTF-8"?>
<env:Envelope xmlns:env="http://schemas.xmlsoap.org/soap/envelope/"
        xmlns:xsd="http://www.w3.org/2001/XMLSchema"
        xmlns:xsi="http://www.w3.org/2001/XMLSchema-instance"
        xmlns:enc="http://schemas.xmlsoap.org/soap/encoding/"
        xmlns:ns0="urn:jwsnut.chapter2.bookservice/types"
        env:encodingStyle="http://schemas.xmlsoap.org/soap/encoding/">
```

---

[*] Another point to note is that you could try to avoid the use of href and id attributes by simply adopting the convention that the image data for the first book is in the first attachment, the data for the second is in the second attachment, and so on. However, this might not be a good idea, since although the SAAJ API includes a method that gets all the attachments for a message, its definition does not state that they are returned in the same order in which they appear in the message.

```
<env:Body>
    <ans1:getBookInfoResponse xmlns:ans1=
      "urn:jwsnut.chapter2.bookservice/wsdl">
        <result href="#ID1"/>
    </ans1:getBookInfoResponse>
    <ns0:ArrayOfBookInfo id="ID1" xsi:type="enc:Array"
                         enc:arrayType="ns0:BookInfo[12]">
        <item href="#ID2"/>
        <!-- Additional item elements not shown -->
    </ns0:ArrayOfBookInfo>
    <ns0:BookInfo id="ID2" xsi:type="ns0:BookInfo">
        <editor xsi:type="xsd:string">Paula Ferguson, Robert Eckstein
        </editor>
        <author xsi:type="xsd:string">David Flanagan</author>
        <price xsi:type="xsd:double">39.95</price>
        <title xsi:type="xsd:string">Java in a Nutshell</title>
    </ns0:BookInfo>
    <!-- More elements not shown -->
</env:Body>
</env:Envelope>
```

This SOAP message is actually created by JAX-RPC, and the data represents an array of BookInfo objects, which were used in the previous chapter. The result element uses the attribute href="#ID1" to reference the data for the array of BookInfo objects that make up the result of the request, and the element that contains the data, called ArrayOfBookInfo, has an id attribute, the value of which is the referenced identifier. The same technique is used to refer to the array content from within the array.

It is important to note that there is nothing automatic about the use of href and id attributes to cross-reference one part of the message from the other: the references must be included by the application, and the receiver must use the id provided by the href attribute to find the referenced data, either in the SOAP message body as just shown or in an attachment.

Creating and Managing SOAP Attachments

The SAAJ API represents SOAP attachments using an instance of the javax.xml.soap.AttachmentPart class. SOAPMessage provides three methods to create attachments:

public AttachmentPart createAttachmentPart( )
    Creates an AttachmentPart with no associated content. To add some data to the attachment, use one of the methods described in the later section "Attachment Headers and Content."

public AttachmentPart createAttachmentPart(Object content,
  String contentType)
    Creates an AttachmentPart with the given content and with the Content-Type header set from the second argument. SAAJ makes some assumptions about the data type of the content object passed to it based on the supplied content type, as described in the next section.

```
public AttachmentPart createAttachmentPart(DataHandler dataHandler)
```
Creates an `AttachmentPart` where the data for the attachment is supplied by the given `DataHandler`. See the next section for a discussion of this method.

These methods do not connect the `AttachmentPart` to the message. To do this, use the `addAttachmentPart( )` method:

```
public void addAttachmentPart(AttachmentPart part);
```

The number of attachments associated with a `SOAPMessage` can be obtained by calling the `countAttachments( )` method, whereas an `Iterator` that returns some or all of the attachments can be obtained using the following methods:

```
public Iterator getAttachments( )
public Iterator getAttachments(MimeHeaders headers)
```

The `Iterator` returned by the first of these methods will visit all of the attachments, whereas the one returned by the second method returns only those for which the MIME headers include all of those in the given `MimeHeaders` object. For example, to get all of the attachments whose data content is a JPEG image, use the following code:

```
MimeHeaders headers = new MimeHeaders( );
headers.addHeader("Content-Type", "image/jpeg");
Iterator iter = soapMessage.getAttachments(headers);
```

The SAAJ specification does not explicitly require that the order in which the attachments are returned by the `Iterator` matches the order in which they appear in the message.

The `Iterator` returned by these methods can also be used to remove selected attachments from the message. The following code removes all attachments containing JPEG images:

```
MimeHeaders headers = new MimeHeaders( );
headers.addHeader("Content-Type", "image/jpeg");
Iterator iter = soapMessage.getAttachments(headers);
while (iter.hasNext( )) {
    iter.remove( );
}
```

A quicker way to remove all attachments is to use the `removeAllAttachments( )` method.

Attachment Headers and Content

An attachment contains a collection of MIME headers and some data content. This section looks at the API that SAAJ provides for manipulating both of these parts, using the book image web service for illustration purposes.

MIME headers

Like the `SOAPMessage` and the `SOAPPart`, an `AttachmentPart` has associated MIME headers. `AttachmentPart` provides the same API for manipulating these headers (as discussed earlier in "The MimeHeader and MimeHeaders Classes"). An `AttachmentPart` always has a `Content-Type` header that reflects the data type of the object that it contains, which is set when the `AttachmentPart` is created, when content is associated with it using one of the methods that we'll cover shortly, or when explicitly using the `setContentType( )` method. If the latter is used, then the value supplied must match the actual type of the data in the attachment.

`AttachmentPart` also supplies convenience methods for setting two specific MIME headers:

```
public void setContentId(String contentId);
public void setContentLocation(String contentLocation);
```

Both of these headers are usually used to refer to the attachment from elsewhere using an element with an `href` attribute. The difference between these two types of identifier is as follows:

- `Content-Id` is typically associated with an identifier that has only local scope and is guaranteed to be unique only within the message that contains the attachment. Applications commonly use values such as ID0, ID1, etc.

- The value associated with a `Content-Location` is a URI (often a URL), which is more likely to be globally meaningful. If a message with an `AttachmentPart` containing a `Content-Location` header is received, it can more easily be removed and attached to another message than if `Content-Ids` is used, since the `Content-Id` in the `AttachmentPart` might clash with another already attached to the message.

Refer to RFC 2557 (at *http://www.ietf.org/rfc/rfc2557.txt*) for a complete discussion of the use of these identifier types. For an example that uses `Content-Ids` to locate attachments, see "Processing Received Attachments," later in this chapter.

It is important to realize that setting the `Content-Id` or the `Content-Location` header has no actual effect on the data in the `AttachmentPart` other than attaching a label to it.

Associating data with an AttachmentPart

There are four ways to install the data for an `AttachmentPart`:

- Use the `createAttachmentPart(Object content, String contentType)` method of `SOAPMessage`.
- Use the `setContent(Object content, String contentType)` method of `AttachmentPart`.
- Use the `createAttachmentPart(DataHandler handler)` method of `SOAPMessage`.
- Use the `setDataHandler(DataHandler handler)` method of `AttachmentPart`.

The first two are equivalent, as are the second two, so we'll discuss these two different mechanisms separately.

Specifying a value and a content type

This is the easiest way to install content in an attachment. For example, the following code installs a string value in a newly created attachment:

```
AttachmentPart part = soapMessage.createAttachment( );
part.setContent("This is in the attachment", "text/plain");
soapMessage.addAttachmentPart(part);
```

You can achieve the same result using an overloaded variant of the createAttachmentPart( ) method:

```
AttachmentPart part = soapMessage.createAttachment("This is in the
attachment", "text/plain");
soapMessage.addAttachmentPart(part);
```

However, this mechanism is not always as convenient as it may seem, because SAAJ places some requirements on the type of the content object, depending on the Content-Type that you supply. If these requirements are not met, then a SOAPException is thrown.

The content types that the SAAJ specification requires all implementations to recognize and the expected type of the Java object that must be supplied when creating the attachment are listed in Table 3-3. When the attachment contains a string, it is simple enough to make use of this API, since the content can be supplied as a java.lang.String object. Of course, this is probably among the least likely of data types to find in an attachment, and in all the other cases the developer has to work a little harder.

Table 3-3. Mapping between content type and object type for SOAP attachments

Content type	Required object type
text/plain	java.lang.String
text/xml	javax.xml.transform.stream.StreamSource
image/gif	java.awt.Image
image/jpeg	java.awt.Image

To attach XML, you can't simply read the XML into a string and pass the string value—in other words, the following does not work:

```
soapMessage.createAttachmentPart("<AnElement>Content</AnElement>",
    "text/xml");
```

Instead, you have to construct a StreamSource object:

```
soapMessage.createAttachmentPart(
        new StreamSource(new StringReader(
            "<AnElement>Content</AnElement>")), "text/xml");
```

Although this is not so convenient when you have the XML in the form of a String, it does make the task of including XML from a file or an InputStream very simple:

```
soapMessage.createAttachmentPart(new StreamSource(new File(
    "c:\\fileName.xml")), "text/xml");
```

As far as images are concerned, in order to attach one to a message, you need to have it in the form of a java.awt.Image object. While this might not seem too onerous a requirement, it probably is not the best design choice for the following reasons:

- Using the java.awt.Image class implies the use of user interface classes. This is really not a good idea in a server environment, where it should not be necessary to load and initialize any user interface classes.

- Typically, in order to get the required Image object, you will open a file containing the image encoded in byte form in either GIF or JPEG format, and then load the file content using methods provided by java.awt.Component together with a java.awt.MediaTracker. This is all unnecessary overhead, since the Image is then converted back to a byte stream when the SOAP message is transmitted.

- Finally, you cannot use this mechanism to attach an image in GIF format to a message, since the process of converting from an Image to a byte stream requires a GIF encoder, which is not supplied as part of the standard Java platform at the time of this writing (although, of course, it is possible to decode a byte stream in GIF format).

For all these reasons, if you want to include an image as an attachment, you need to use a DataHandler, as described in the next section.

Using a DataHandler

The javax.activation.DataHandler class is part of the JavaBeans Activation Framework (JAF). It is most commonly used in conjunction with JavaMail to encapsulate access to attachments sent and received with Internet mail, which is essentially the same as handling SOAP message attachments. Whenever you create an AttachmentPart while building an outgoing message, or when an AttachmentPart is created to represent part of a received SOAP message, it has an associated DataHandler.

When a SOAP message is being converted from its internal representation to the byte stream that is ultimately transmitted, the DataHandler is responsible for creating a byte stream representation of the data in the attachment. The way in which this is done depends on the type of data to convert, so the DataHandler uses objects called DataContentHandlers, each of which can perform this conversion for a specific data type. DataContentHandlers are created by an object implementing the DataContentHandlerFactory interface, which returns an appropriate DataContentHandler for a given MIME type, if it has one. The SAAJ reference implementation installs a DataContentHandlerFactory that provides handlers for the data types listed in Table 3-3. Unfortunately, the handlers created by this factory for image/jpeg, image/gif, and text/xml work only when they are asked to convert objects of the types listed in the second column of Table 3-3. When the data you need to attach is already in the form of a byte array, simply using the AttachmentPart setContent( ) method in the obvious way:

```
attachmentPart.setContent(imageData, "image/jpeg");
```

cannot be done without also changing the DataContentHandler used to handle objects with this MIME type. The only way to do this is to write and install your own DataContentHandlerFactory. (This is done by using the DataHandler setDataContentHandlerFactory( ) method), but this requires you to imprememt handlers for *all* MIME types that you need to support, since there can only be one factory active at any given time and there is no way to get a reference to the existing factory so that you can delegate to it.

Fortunately, there is a simpler way to solve this problem. A DataHandler can work directly with an object that implements the javax.activation.DataSource interface. A DataSource is used when you have access to the object in a form from which it is simple to create an InputStream and an OutputStream. When you associate a DataSource with a DataHandler, it uses the DataSource to access the underlying data instead of looking for a DataContentHandler. When you have a GIF or JPEG image in the form of an array of bytes, it is natural to use a DataSource instead of a DataContentHandler, because no further data conversion is required. To describe how this can be done, the code that attaches the book cover images to the SOAP reply for the book image service is shown in Example 3-14.

Example 3-14. Attaching images to a SOAP message

```
private void handleBookImageRequest(SOAPElement element, SOAPMessage reply)
                                throws SOAPException {
  // The request element contains an attribute that holds the
  // type of image requested and a nested string for each title.
  // The reply body has a BookImages element and a nested item with
  // a reference to the image which is sent as an attachment
    SOAPBody replyBody = reply.getSOAPPart().getEnvelope().getBody();

    // Determine whether to use JPEG or GIF images
    String imageType = element.getAttributeValue(IMAGE_TYPE_ATTRIBUTE);
    boolean gif = imageType.equalsIgnoreCase("image/gif");

    // Build the BookImages element containing all of the replies
    SOAPBodyElement bodyElement = replyBody.addBodyElement(BOOK_IMAGES_NAME);
    bodyElement.addAttribute(
        soapFactory.createName("type", XMLSCHEMA_INSTANCE_PREFIX,
            XMLSCHEMA_INSTANCE_URI), SOAP_ENC_PREFIX + ":Array");
    bodyElement.addAttribute(
        soapFactory.createName("arrayType", SOAP_ENC_PREFIX,
            SOAPConstants.URI_NS_SOAP_ENCODING), XMLSCHEMA_PREFIX + ":anyType[]");

    // Index of the next attachment to use
    int index = 0;

    // Handle each nested element.
    Iterator iter = element.getChildElements();
    while (iter.hasNext()) {
        // Get the next child element from the request message
        SOAPElement childElement = (SOAPElement)iter.next();

        // Get the book title
        String title = childElement.getValue();

        // Get the image data
        byte[] imageData = BookImageServletData.getBookImage(title, gif);
        if (imageData != null) {
            // Got the data - attach it.
            AttachmentPart attach = reply.createAttachmentPart();
            attach.setDataHandler(new DataHandler(
                            new ByteArrayDataSource("Image Data",
                                imageData,
                                gif ? "image/gif" : "image/jpeg")));
            attach.setContentId("ID" + index);
            reply.addAttachmentPart(attach);
```

Example 3-14. Attaching images to a SOAP message (continued)

```
                // Add an element in the reply pointing to the attachment
                bodyElement.addChildElement("item").addAttribute(HREF_ATTRIBUTE,
                  "cid:ID" + index);

                // Increment the index
                index++;
        } else {
                // No data - this is a fault.
                // Clear the reply and install the fault
                reply.removeAllAttachments();
                bodyElement.detachNode();
                createFault(replyBody, "soap-env:Client.Title", "Unknown title",
                                SERVICE_URI, title);

                return;
        }
    }
}
```

This code loops over all of the book titles in the client request message and adds an element to the body of the reply that points to a corresponding attachment, using an href attribute with the Content-Id of the attachment as the reference value, as shown in Example 3-13. It uses a separate class (BookImageServletData, not shown here) to get the data for a book with a given title in the form of an array of bytes that is encoded in either GIF or JPEG form. The section of this code that is relevant to this discussion is highlighted in bold. The first step is to create the AttachmentPart:

```
    AttachmentPart attach = reply.createAttachmentPart();
```

To associate the image data with the attachment, we need to replace the default DataHandler with one that uses a DataSource that takes its content from the image data. Unfortunately, there is no DataSource implementation that accepts a byte array as its input, but it is simple enough to create one, as shown in Example 3-15.

Example 3-15. A DataSource that encapsulates access to data in a byte array

```
class ByteArrayDataSource implements DataSource {

    private String contentType;

    private byte[] data;

    private String name;

    ByteArrayDataSource(String name, byte[] data, String contentType) {
        this.name = name;
        this.data = data;
        this.contentType = contentType;
    }

    public String getContentType() {
```

Example 3-15. A DataSource that encapsulates access to data in a byte array (continued)

```
        return contentType;
    }

    public InputStream getInputStream( ) throws IOException {
        return new ByteArrayInputStream(data);
    }

    public String getName( ) {
        return name;
    }

    public OutputStream getOutputStream( ) throws IOException {
        throw new IOException(
            "ByteArrayDataSource cannot support getOutputStream( )");
    }
}
```

SAAJ

From the point of view of this example, the DataSource is only required to implement the getContentType( ) method (to return the MIME type of the data that it provides) and the getInputStream( ) method (which needs to return an InputStream to provide access to the data passed to it at construction time). This is easily achieved by wrapping the byte array containing the data in a ByteArrayInputStream. It would be simple to generalize this to also allow the data to be modified by implementing the getOutputStream( ) method, but that is not required here.

Given this DataSource, the image data can be associated with the attachment and then added to the SOAP reply message as follows:

```
            attach.setDataHandler(new DataHandler(
                            new ByteArrayDataSource("Image Data",
                                imageData,
                                gif ? "image/gif" : "image/jpeg")));
            attach.setContentId("ID" + index);
            reply.addAttachmentPart(attach);
```

When the completed reply message is being converted into a byte stream for transmission, the content of the attachments are always read from their DataHandlers. Since we constructed the DataHandler for each attachment with a DataSource, instead of trying to find a DataContentHandler for the attachment's associated MIME type, the data is obtained directly from the input stream returned by the getInputStream( ) method of the ByteArrayDataSource. Not only is this more convenient than converting the data into an Image, it is also much more efficient, and better still, it allows GIF images to be supported. Since there is no need for a GIF encoder to be present, the encoding has already taken place when the image data was created. This web service can now support any type of image, since it simply treats the image data as an opaque byte stream. Whether this is useful depends on the capabilities available to the client to decode the data and display it—obviously, it is not useful to send an image in PNG format to a client that cannot decode PNG images.

This same technique could be used for any type of data for which you have a byte stream representation, for content types that are not listed in Table 3-3, and for which, therefore, the `AttachmentPart` `setContent()` method will not work. If, for example, you have an array of bytes that represents an audio clip in *.wav* format (a format that is not directly supported in the reference implementation), you can associate it with an attachment as follows:

```
byte[] audioData = ......; // Load sound bytes (not shown)
attach.setDataHandler(new DataHandler(
                        new ByteArrayDataSource("Audio Data",
                        audioData, "audio/wav")));
```

As well as installing your own `DataHandler` to make use of a custom `DataSource`, you can also use its other two constructors to attach data to a SOAP message:

```
public DataHandler(Object object, String mimeType);
public DataHandler(URL url);
```

The first constructor is of little use because it is equivalent to using the `AttachmentPart` `setContent()` method. The second constructor can be used to import data from a given URL, where it is assumed that the `URL` `getContent()` method returns an object whose type is consistent with the content types listed in Table 3-3.

Processing Received Attachments

When a SOAP message containing one or more attachments is received, the `SOAPMessage` object will have one `AttachmentPart` per attachment. The interpretation placed on these attachments and the way in which they relate to the XML in the body of the message is, of course, application-dependent. In the case of the book image service, as we saw in Example 3-13, each image returned in response to a `BookImageRequest` has its own entry in the `BookImages` array that appears in the body of the SOAP message sent by the web service to the client. The array entry is bound to the attachment containing the image data by an `href` attribute that contains the value of the `Content-Id` MIME header of the appropriate attachment:

```
<item href="cid:ID0"/>
```

To extract all of the images, the book image client loops over all of the elements in the array, extracts the `href` attribute for each, and finds the `AttachmentPart` that has the corresponding `Content-Id`, as shown in Example 3-16.

Example 3-16. Handling attachments in a SOAP message

```
SOAPBody replyBody = reply.getSOAPPart().getEnvelope().getBody();
if (replyBody.hasFault()) {
    SOAPFault fault = replyBody.getFault();
    throw new SOAPException("Fault when getting book images: " +
            fault.getFaultString() +
            ", actor is [" + fault.getFaultActor() + "]");
}

// The body contains a "BookImages" element with a nested
// element for each book title.
```

Example 3-16. Handling attachments in a SOAP message (continued)

```
Iterator iter = replyBody.getChildElements(BOOK_IMAGES_NAME);
if (iter.hasNext()) {
    ArrayList list = new ArrayList();
    MimeHeaders headers = new MimeHeaders();
    SOAPElement bookImages = (SOAPElement)iter.next();
    iter = bookImages.getChildElements();
    while (iter.hasNext()) {
        SOAPElement element = (SOAPElement)iter.next();
        String imageRef = element.getAttributeValue(HREF_ATTRIBUTE);
        if (imageRef != null) {
            // Get the attachment using the Content-Id, having
            // first removed the "cid:" prefix
            imageRef = imageRef.substring(4);
            headers.setHeader("Content-Id", imageRef);
            Iterator attachIter = reply.getAttachments(headers);
            if (attachIter.hasNext()) {
                AttachmentPart attach = (AttachmentPart)attachIter.next();
                Object content = attach.getContent();
                if (content instanceof Image) {
                    list.add(content);
                }
            }
        }
    }
    int size = list.size();
    Image[] images = new Image[size];
    list.toArray(images);
    return images;
} else {
    // No BookTitles element was found
    throw new SOAPException("No BookImages element in returned message");
}
```

As each child element of the array is found, its href attribute is obtained. Since this is actually in the form cid:ID0, it is necessary to first strip away the leading cid: to obtain the value that is used for the Content-Id header:

```
String imageRef = element.getAttributeValue(HREF_ATTRIBUTE);
if (imageRef != null) {
    // Get the attachment using the Content-Id, having
    // first removed the "cid:" prefix
    imageRef = imageRef.substring(4);
```

As noted earlier, the SAAJ API provides two SOAPMessage methods that return the attachments for the message:

```
public Iterator getAttachments()
public Iterator getAttachments(MimeHeaders headers)
```

There is no direct way to find a single attachment given a content id string. Instead, the second getAttachments() method provides a general facility that returns all attachments that have a given set of MIME headers. Here, we use it to locate the correct `AttachmentPart` by looking for the attachment in which the `Content-Id` header has the value extracted from the message body:

```
MimeHeaders headers = new MimeHeaders();
headers.setHeader("Content-Id", imageRef);
Iterator attachIter = reply.getAttachments(headers);
if (attachIter.hasNext()) {
    AttachmentPart attach = (AttachmentPart)attachIter.next();
```

Given the way that this message is constructed, we expect there to be only one `AttachmentPart` per element in the message body, but this isn't necessarily the case: it is possible to attach more then one object with the same `Content-Id`, perhaps to supply the image and an associated sound file containing some marketing information for the book. The two objects would, of course, be distinguished by the content types, which can be obtained from the `AttachmentPart` using its `getContentType()` method.

Once you have the `AttachmentPart`, you can get its content using the following method:

```
public Object getContent();
```

The actual type of the returned object is determined by the attachment's content type and the `DataContentHandlers` that are installed. In the case of the reference implementation, the mapping from content type to Java object type is as shown in Table 3-3, which means that, in this example, the `getContent()` method should return a `java.awt.Image` containing the image data extracted from the attachment.

Content types for which a `DataContentHandler` is not found are returned as an `InputStream` from which the raw byte data can be read. In the case of the reference implementation, for example, a sound file sent with type `audio/wav` or a byte stream of type `application/octet-stream` is returned in this way.

Another way to extract the data from an attachment is to use the `DataHandler` that is created for each `AttachmentPart`. Using the `DataHandler`, you can bypass the `DataContentHandlerFactory` and get direct access to the raw attachment data, even if the content type is recognized by the SAAJ implementation that you are using. Here, for example, is some code that will create an `Image` object from any of the image types recognized by the JRE that you are using, even if the SAAJ implementation does not provide a `DataContentHandler` for it. At the time of this writing, this code works for PNG images as well as those in GIF or JPEG format:

```
if (attach.getContentType().startsWith("image/")) {
    javax.activation.DataHandler handler = attach.getDataHandler();
    InputStream is = handler.getInputStream();
    int count = is.available();
    byte[] buffer = new byte[count];
    is.read(buffer, 0, count);
    Image img = java.awt.Toolkit.getDefaultToolkit().createImage(buffer);
}
```

Notice that we use the `available()` method of `InputStream` to find out how much data there is in the attachment, even though `AttachmentPart` has a `getSize()` method. The reason for this is the `AttachmentPart` method always seems to return a number that is larger than the actual size of the data.

SOAP Headers

So far, we have only concerned ourselves with the body of a SOAP message and its attachments, both of which are intended solely for the ultimate destination of the message. A message can also include headers, which contain information that is related to the routing or processing of the message, but which are not part of the payload itself. SOAP itself does not define any standard headers, but there are specific uses of SOAP that do, some of which are discussed in Chapter 4. In this section, we'll look in a generic way at the facilities provided by SAAJ for creating and handling headers, and defer detailed discussion of real-world uses of this facility until Chapter 4.

SOAP Actors and the mustUnderstand Attribute

Although the examples that we have shown so far involve only a client and a web service to which the client sends a SOAP message, in practice, a SOAP message may pass through one or more intermediate systems before reaching its ultimate destination. For the purposes of this discussion, an intermediate system is not like a network router, which is concerned only with passing a transport-level packet from node to node until it reaches a destination, but an application-level entity that receives a SOAP message, examines it, and either handles it or forwards it to another SOAP receiver for further processing.

As an example of the use of an intermediate system, suppose that a business wants to make it possible for other businesses to place stock orders by building a SOAP message that contains a purchase order, in response to which it expects confirmation of the order and payment details. Before the order is processed, it might be necessary to check that the initiator is known to the company and has a purchase account to which the transaction can be billed. In order to implement this, the business might separate the handling of the account check from the handling of the purchase order, as follows:

1. When the client sends the purchase order, it is required to include a header that identifies it in a way that is determined by the business providing the service. In practice, this would probably involve the use of some secure mechanism, such as public key cryptography and the inclusion of a certificate to identify the client.

2. The system to which the purchase order is sent looks for this header, extracts the required information, and verifies it. If it is not valid, a fault is returned to the originator. Otherwise, the header is removed and perhaps replaced with one that provides information about the initiator that is in a form that is more useful to the business itself, such as account details.

3. The message is now forwarded to an internal system that handles the purchase order and ultimately returns a response to the order itself.

In the SAAJ API, each SOAPMessage can have a single SOAPHeader element. By default, this element is empty. Headers are created by adding XML elements to the SOAPHeader. Each such header element must be namespace-qualified and may contain an attribute that identifies the system that is intended to process it, known as the *actor* attribute. The value of this attribute is defined to be a URI and, in practice, it is often a URL, although it need not be. There are three cases to consider:

The actor attribute is missing
> When there is no actor attribute, the header is deemed to be intended for the ultimate recipient of the message.

The actor attribute has the distinguished value http://schemas.xmlsoap.org/soap/ actor/next
> A header containing an actor attribute with this value (which a SAAJ application can conveniently refer to by using the constant value SOAPConstants.URI_ SOAP_ACTOR_NEXT) is intended for the first system that receives it.

The actor attribute has some other value
> In this case, the header is intended for the system whose URI matches the value of the attribute.

When a SOAP message is received, the headers must be checked for any that are intended for the recipient. If there are any, the following rules apply:

- The header must be removed from the message.
- If the receiver understands the header, then it may process the header and act upon it. As a result, it may add one or more new headers to the message (which may be identical to the received header). If the header contains the mustUnderstand attribute from the SOAP envelope namespace, and the value of this attribute is 1, the receiver must process the header—or else return a fault to the originator if it chooses not to do so or cannot do so for some reason.
- If the receiver does not understand a header that is addressed to it, it may choose to silently ignore it, unless the mustUnderstand attribute is present and has the value 1, in which case it must return a fault to the originator.

If a fault is returned as a result of the mustUnderstand attribute, then the fault code must have the value soap-env:MustUnderstand and the fault actor must be set to the URI of the system that generated the fault. A system that processes a header may also generate a fault for reasons that are related to the content of the header. In all cases, a fault that arises from header processing may *not* include a detail element.

Creating Header Elements

Header elements are created using the SOAPHeader addHeaderElement( ) method, which requires a Name object from which the element name and its namespace are determined. The SOAP specification requires that header elements are namespaced-qualified. The addHeaderElement( ) method returns a newly created SOAPHeaderElement, which was added as a direct child of the SOAPHeader. Example 3-17 shows how to add a header that contains child elements for a username and a password.

Example 3-17. Adding a header entry to a SOAP message

```
SOAPHeader header = message.getSOAPPart().getEnvelope().getHeader();
SOAPHeaderElement headerElement = header.addHeaderElement(
    soapFactory.createName("AuthInfo"));
```

Example 3-17. Adding a header entry to a SOAP message (continued)

```
headerElement.addNamespaceDeclaration(null, "urn:headerDemo");
headerElement.setMustUnderstand(true);
headerElement.addChildElement("UserName").addTextNode("JWSUserName");
headerElement.addChildElement("Password").addTextNode("JWSPassword");
```

The header element is called `AuthInfo` and its namespace is `urn:headerDemo`, which is an arbitrarily chosen URN. The following method call:

```
headerElement.addNamespaceDeclaration(null, "urn:headerDemo");
```

makes this namespace the default for this element and its subelements, so that the element names will appear without a namespace prefix. The use of the default namespace in this way is a convenience and not a requirement.

The `SOAPHeaderElement` interface has four methods that provide easy access to the SOAP actor and `mustUnderstand` attributes:

```
public void setActor(String actorURI);
public String getActor();
public void setMustUnderstand(boolean cond);
public boolean getMustUnderstand();
```

The code in Example 3-17 sets the `mustUnderstand` attribute to 1 (by virtue of the fact that its argument has the value true), but does not set the actor attribute at all, which implies that the header is to be processed by the ultimate recipient of the message, and must be understood and properly actioned or a fault returned. Here is what a SOAP message produced by this code looks like:

```
<soap-env:Envelope xmlns:soap-env=
    "http://schemas.xmlsoap.org/soap/envelope/">
    <soap-env:Header>
        <AuthInfo xmlns="urn:headerDemo" soap-env:mustUnderstand="1">
            <UserName>JWSUserName</UserName>
            <Password>JWSPasswordJWSPassword</Password>
        </AuthInfo>
    </soap-env:Header>
    <soap-env:Body/>
</soap-env:Envelope>
```

The default value of the `mustUnderstand` attribute is 0, which means that the header can be removed without being processed by its target.

Processing Header Elements

When a SOAP message is received, there are three ways to handle the header entries that it contains once a reference to the `SOAPHeader` has been obtained:

- Get an iterator over all of the child elements of the `SOAPHeader`. This returns all of the `SOAPHeaderElement` objects in the message.
- Get an iterator over all of the headers intended for a given actor. This returns a subset of the `SOAPHeaderElement` objects in the message.
- Get an iterator over all of the headers intended for a given actor and also remove them from the message.

SAAJ

A message recipient must process all headers for which the actor attribute is set to next or to its own URI, and must remove them once they have been processed. The SOAPHeader interface provides two methods that locate the headers intended for a given actor URI:

```
public Iterator examineHeaderElements(String actorURI);
public Iterator extractHeaderElements(String actorURI);
```

The difference between these two methods is that the second removes all of the headers that appear in the Iterator from the message, whereas the first does not. Calling either of these methods with the argument SOAPConstants.URI_SOAP_ACTOR_NEXT returns all of the headers that have the actor attribute set to next and all of those that do not have an actor attribute.* As an alternative to these two methods, you can get an Iterator over all of the header entries without removing any of the them, using the getChildElements() method that SOAPHeader inherits from SOAPElement:

```
// Gets all the SOAPHeaderElements
Iterator  iter = soapHeader.getChildElements();
```

Using SAAJ with Secure Connections

The web service examples used so far in this book have not attempted to provide any security measures to ensure that they can only be accessed by authorized users, or to provide some level of assurance to the client that the server to which it might be about to pass sensitive information is the one to which it thinks it is connected. At the time of this writing, security for web services is the subject of several in-progress JSRs, such as JSR 105 (XML Digital Signature APIs; see *http://jcp.org/jsr/detail/105.jsp*) and JSR 106 (XML Digital Encryption APIs; see *http://jcp.org/jsr/detail/106.jsp*). Until these JSRs are completed and their implementations become part of the Java platform, you can still make use of the authentication mechanisms already provided for HTTP to add a level of security to your service. In this section, you'll see how to configure the client and server parts of the service to use both HTTP basic authentication, which is relatively weak, and HTTPS, which is much more robust but is slightly more difficult to set up.

Using Basic Authentication

HTTP basic authentication is a simple mechanism that requires the client to supply a username and password to gain access to a service. The authentication information is encoded and sent in an HTTP header to the server, which can then verify whether the user should have access to the service at the URL specified in the request. Although it is easy to configure basic authentication, it is a very weak mechanism because the data exchanged by the client and server is not encrypted and there is no protection against unauthorized modification. Furthermore, the algorithm used to encode the username and password is trivial, thus making it a

---

* It is not clear from the SAAJ specification whether this is the intended behavior or just a bug. In my opinion, it would be better if this call returned only those headers with the actor attribute set to next.

simple matter for a snooper to discover what they are. Nevertheless, in an internal corporate network, basic authentication may be sufficient.*

To demonstrate how to use basic authentication, we'll add it to the book image web service. Configuring basic authentication requires three steps:

1. Define the role or roles that are allowed access to some or all of the web service and the set of users that belong to those roles.

2. Define the URLs within the web service that require protection, and specify which roles should be able to use them.

3. Configure the web service client to send the appropriate authentication information when accessing the service.

Adding roles and users to the web container

The first step involves setting up authentication information for the web container that hosts the web service. The details of this process for the J2EE 1.4 reference implementation and the Tomcat web container in the JWSDP are covered in Chapter 1, where we added a role called JWSGroup together with a couple of users allowed to access that role.

Adding URL-based protection

Defining a new role does not add any protection. To achieve this, it is necessary to include authorization information in the *web.xml* file for the web service. The authorization information defines which of the web service's URLs are to be protected and which role or roles are to be allowed to access those URLs. Allowing a role to access a URL has the effect of making it possible for all of the users in that role to access the URL, provided that they can authenticate themselves to the web container by supplying the correct password.

The book image web service can be accessed without requiring authentication at almost any URL that starts with *http://localhost:8000/BookImageService*. In order to illustrate basic authentication, the *web.xml* file for this service is also configured so that only users in the bookimageservice role can acccess the protected URL *http://localhost:8000/BookImageService/basicAuth*. The portion of the *web.xml* file that specifies this restriction is shown in bold in Example 3-18.†

Example 3-18. Adding protected URLs to a web service

```
<?xml version="1.0" encoding="UTF-8" ?>
<!DOCTYPE web-app
```

---

* Basic authentication is what is happening when you log onto a web site for which you preregister for access to member-only areas. The dialog box that pops up to get your username and password is the browser's way to get the information required for the authentication header in the HTTP request.

† The result of this configuration is rather unusual because the web service now has both protected and unprotected URLs, all of which provide access to the same service. In reality, you are most likely to protect all access to the web service by precisely defining which URLs it responds to and mapping them all to the appropriate roles. Here, both a protected and an unprotected service are provided so that we can use it to illustrate the SAAJ APIs without having to first introduce basic authentication.

Example 3-18. Adding protected URLs to a web service (continued)

```
PUBLIC "-//Sun Microsystems, Inc.//DTD Web Application 2.3//EN"
"http://java.sun.com/j2ee/dtds/web-app_2_3.dtd">


<web-app>
    <display-name>SAAJ Book Image Service</display-name>
    <description>SAAJ Book Image Service</description>

    <servlet>
        <servlet-name>BookImageService</servlet-name>
        <display-name>Servlet for the SAAJ book Image Service</display-name>
        <servlet-class>ora.jwsnut.chapter3.bookimageservice.BookImageServlet
        </servlet-class>
    </servlet>

    <servlet-mapping>
        <servlet-name>BookImageService</servlet-name>
        <url-pattern>/*</url-pattern>
    </servlet-mapping>

    <security-constraint>
        <web-resource-collection>
            <web-resource-name>SAAJ Book Image Service</web-resource-name>
            <url-pattern>/basicAuth/*</url-pattern>
        </web-resource-collection>
        <auth-constraint>
            <role-name>JWSGroup</role-name>
        </auth-constraint>
    </security-constraint>

    <login-config>
        <auth-method>BASIC</auth-method>
        <realm-name>Book Image Service</realm-name>
    </login-config>

</web-app>
```

The security-constraint element specifies which URLs are to be protected (using
the url-pattern element) and the role or roles allowed access to them (in the
auth-constraint element). It is also necessary to specify how the identity of the
caller is to be determined. This is achieved by the login-config element, which
requires the use of basic authentication.

You can verify that this constraint is active by attempting to access the service
with your web browser. With the J2EE 1.4 server running, point your browser at
the URL *http://localhost:8000/BookImageService*. You should see an error page
resulting from the fact that the service does not support access using the HTTP
GET method. If, however, you use the URL *http://localhost:8000/
BookImageService/basicAuth*, you are instead prompted to enter a username and
password. Only after you correctly enter these do you see the same error page. If
you are using the JWSDP with the Tomcat web server, use port number 8080
instead of 8000 in these URLs.

Setting up the client

When it is run using the Ant target run-client, the Java client for the book image service that we used earlier in this chapter uses the URL *http://localhost:8000/ BookImageService* to access the web service; therefore, it does not need to supply a username and password. The client gets the URL from its command line, so it is possible to arrange for it to access the protected URL *http://localhost:8000/ BookImageService/basicAuth* instead. If you do this, however, you get an exception, since the web server expects to receive a username and a password to validate access to this URL, and refuses access if it does not get them (or if they are incorrect). SAAJ uses a slightly different URL syntax to allow the username and password to be included with the URL, which looks like this:

> *http://username:password@host:port/path*

In the case of the book image service, for a user called JWSUserName with the password JWSPassword, the appropriate URL is:

> *http://JWSUserName:JWSPassword@localhost:8000/BookImageService/ basicAuth*

The Ant project file for this example includes a target that can be used to run the client with this URL. To try it out, open a command window, make *chapter3\ bookimageservice* (relative to the installation directory of the book's example source code) your working directory, and type the command:

```
ant run-basicauth-client
```

Since JWSUserName has access to the role JWSGroup, the web container allows the client access to the service, based on the auth-constraint element in the *web.xml* file. To prove that access by unauthorized users will be refused, change the value of the USERNAME property in the *jwsnutExamples.properties* file in your home directory so that it does not correspond to a valid user, and then run the example again.

Using HTTPS

If you need more security than basic authentication can provide (as you almost certainly will if you intend to publish your web service on the Internet), you can arrange for it to be accessible over HTTPS instead of HTTP. By using HTTPS, you ensure that all the data exchanged between the client and the server is encrypted and protected against unauthorized modification. The client can also be sure that the server it is actually connected to is the one that it thinks it is connected to, and that the server itself can be trusted. This assurance is possible because the SSL protocol used by HTTPS delivers the server's certificate to the client. This certificate can be verified against a set of trusted certificates held by the client. The certificate also contains information, such as the server's hostname, which can be checked to ensure that the certificate belongs to the server that sent it.

In order to use HTTPS, you need to have the Java Secure Sockets Extension (JSSE) installed on both the client and server systems. If you are using Java 2 Version 1.4, JSSE is part of the core distribution so you do not need to take any extra steps. Otherwise, you should download and install the latest version of the JSSE from *http://java.sun.com* before proceeding.

When performing the following configuration steps, it is important to remember that the client and server will, in general, run on different hosts, although for testing purposes they might reside on the same system. In the descriptions that follow, we will use the names *serverhost* and *clienthost* to distinguish these two different hosts. You should, of course, substitute the names of your machines wherever these terms are used.

Enabling HTTPS in the web server

The means by which you enable HTTPS support in your web server is vendor-dependent. In this section, we describe how to do this for the Tomcat web server distributed with the JWSDP. If you are using a third-party web server, you need to consult your vendor's documentation for the appropriate procedure. In particular, if you are using the J2EE 1.4 reference implementation instead of the JWSDP Tomcat web server, then you can skip this section because it has HTTPS enabled by default.

In the following descriptions, we use the shorthand *${EXAMPLES_ROOT}* to refer to the directory in which you installed the example source code for this book, and we use *${JAVA_HOME}* for the installation directory of J2SE. The first step is to create the certificate that the web server sends to any client that connects to it over HTTPS. To create this certificate, open a command window on *serverhost*, make *${EXAMPLES_ROOT}* your working directory, and type the following command (all on one line):

```
keytool -genkey -alias server -keyalg RSA -keypass changeit
-storepass changeit -keystore server.keystore  -dname "CN=serverhost"
```

The certificate is created in a new keystore whose name is given by the *-keystore* argument, which in this case is stored in the installation directory of the example source code for the sake of convenience. The *-storepass* argument supplies the password used to access the keystore. Here, we use the default JRE keystore password. You can choose a different one, as long as you supply the same password when configuring the server to access the keystore, as described shortly.

The *-dname* argument can be used to supply a set of attributes that identify the certificate and its owning organization. Here, we set only the *CN* attribute, which specifies the name of the host to which the certificate belongs. It is important that you use the correct hostname because the client may extract this attribute and check that it matches the name of the host to which it thinks it is connected.*

The *keytool* command creates a self-signed certificate, which is, strictly speaking, appropriate only for development and testing purposes. In the real world, you should instead apply to a certificate authority for a properly signed server certificate, and then import it into the keystore using the *keytool -import* argument. For further details on the use of the *-import* argument (and on the *keytool* command in general), see *Java in a Nutshell*, by David Flanagan (O'Reilly).

---

* Obviously, in a real-world environment, it is not a good idea to use CN=localhost, but this might be appropriate for testing purposes.

The second step required to activate HTTPS is to enable it in the Tomcat web server by editing the *server.xml* file, which you'll find in its *conf* directory. Open this file in an editor and add the lines shown in bold in the following code section, substituting the pathname of the example source code installation directory in the value of the keyStoreFile attribute:

```
<Service className="org.apache.catalina.core.StandardService" debug="0"
        name="Java Web Services Developer Pack">
  <Connector className="org.apache.coyote.tomcat4.CoyoteConnector"
acceptCount="10" ........>
    <Factory className="org.apache.catalina.net.DefaultServerSocketFactory"
/>
  </Connector>

  <!-- Added for SSL -->
  <Connector className="org.apache.catalina.connector.http.HttpConnector"
        port="8443" minProcessors="5" maxProcessors="75"
        enableLookups="false"
        acceptCount="10" connectionTimeout="60000" debug="0"
        scheme="https" secure="true">
    <Factory className="org.apache.catalina.net.SSLServerSocketFactory"
        keystoreFile="${EXAMPLES_ROOT}\server.keystore"
        keystorePass="changeit"
        clientAuth="false" protocol="TLS"/>
  </Connector>
  <!-- End of SSL section -->
```

Note the following:

- SSL is enabled by adding a second Connector element to the Service element for "Java Web Services Developer Pack." There is also another Service element in this file for internal services—make sure you modify the correct Service element.

- The filename supplied using the keystoreFile attribute must be the name of the keystore in which the certificate was created (or imported) by *keytool*. Similarly, the correct keystore password must be supplied using the keystorePass attribute.

- HTTPS is enabled on port 8443, rather than port 8080. This is one of the two port numbers used by convention for HTTPS; the other is 443 (which, on Unix-based systems, is accessible only to privileged processes).

Having completed these steps, you can check that all is well by restarting the Tomcat web server and pointing your browser at the URL *https://serverhost:8443* (note that the protocol is *https* instead of *http* and the port number is 8443). Your browser will probably ask you to confirm that you accept the server's certificate and will then display the web server's home page. If you have not obtained and installed a certificate from a certificate authority, you will probably be warned that the certificate is from a company that you have chosen not to trust. There is no need to be concerned about this—it is the result of using a self-signed certificate, which relies upon itself for its trust (and therefore cannot be trusted at all).

Setting up the client system

Now let's move to the client system. In order to use the book image web service client with HTTPS, you have to give it the appropriate URL. If you want to use basic authentication together with HTTPS, use the following URL:

https://JWSUserName:JWSPassword@serverhost:7000/BookImageService/ basicAuth

To use HTTPS on its own, use:

https://serverhost:7000/BookImageService

Port number 7000 is used because this is the port on which the J2EE reference implementations listen for HTTPS connections. If you are using the JWSDP with the Tomcat web server, then the port number is 8443 instead of 7000.

When you use either of these URLs, the client connects over HTTPS and expects to receive the server's certificate and validate it. How does the validation work? The complete process is complex and not of any great interest from a web service development viewpoint. However, one of the following two conditions must hold:

- The server's certificate must be installed in a keystore on the client machine to which the client application has access.
- The server's certificate must be issued by a trusted authority whose certificate is installed in the client machine's keystore. In this case, the certificate itself does not need to be in the client's keystore.

In the first case, the certificate for the issuing authority is almost certainly found in the certificate store that is supplied with the JRE, which can be found at *${JAVA_HOME}\jre\lib\security\cacerts*; therefore, there is not any further work to do on the client system. If you created your own self-signed certificate, then you need to import it into a keystore that is accessible to the client.

Although you could import certificates directly into the JRE keystore, we will instead create and use a private keystore in order to demonstrate how simple it is to do this. This also has the advantage that you can experiment with certificates without the possibility of damaging your JRE. On the client machine, copy the *cacerts* file from the JRE to the installation directory of this book's source code and rename it *client.keystore*:

```
copy  ${JAVA_HOME}\jre\lib\security\cacerts
      ${EXAMPLES_ROOT}\client.keystore
```

Next, if you are using a self-signed certificate, you need to get a copy of it and import it into the newly created keystore; you can skip this step if the server is using a certificate issued by a trusted authority. To get the certificate, go to the server machine and proceed as follows:

- If you are using the JWSDP Tomcat web server, go to the directory containing the keystore (*server.keystore*) created in the previous section and type the command:
  ```
  keytool -export -alias server -storepass changeit -keystore server.
      keystore  -file server.cer
  ```

- If you are using the J2EE reference implementation, go to the directory *lib\
security* below the J2EE installation directory and type the command:

```
keytool -export -alias server -storepass changeit -keystore keystore.jks
    -file server.cer
```

Copy the newly created file *server.cer* from the server machine to the
${EXAMPLES_ROOT} directory on the client machine and import it there using
the following command:

```
keytool -import -v -trustcacerts -alias JWSNutshell -storepass changeit
    -keystore client.keystore -file server.cer
```

Reply when asked if you want to trust this certificate. Note that you can use any
valid name for the alias, as long as it does not clash with one already in use in the
keystore. The fact that you do not have to import a server certificate obtained
from a trusted certification authority in this way is a great advantage, of course,
because it means that clients that want to connect to your service do not need to
get a copy of your certificate in advance.

In order to run the client application with HTTPS, it is necessary to supply the
correct URL and arrange for it to use the keystore that has just been created to
look for certificates. To point the application at the correct keystore, the two
system properties listed in Table 3-4 need to be set.

Table 3-4. System properties used by JSSE to access a keystore

Property	Description
javax.net.ssl.trustStore	The pathname of the keystore. In this case, this is *${EXAMPLES_ROOT}\client.keystore.*
javax.net.ssl.trustStorePassword	The password needed to access the keystore. By default, this password is changeit.

A target that runs the web service over HTTPS using basic authentication by
setting the appropriate values for both of these properties has been included in the
Ant buildfile for this example:

```
<target name="run-httpsserver-client" if="client.present"
        depends="init">
    <java classname="${CLIENT_CLASS_NAME}" fork="yes">
        <sysproperty key="javax.net.ssl.trustStore"
                     value="${EXAMPLES_ROOT}/client.keystore"/>
        <sysproperty key="javax.net.ssl.trustStorePassword"
                     value="changeit"/>
        <arg line="${CLIENT_HTTPS_SERVER_AUTH_ARGS}"/>
        <classpath refid="run.path"/>
    </java>
</target>
```

The property CLIENT_HTTPS_SERVER_AUTH_ARGS is set using properties in the
jwsnutExamples.properties file to the appropriate URL for the service, which in
this case is:

*https://JWSUserName:JWSPassword@serverhost:8443/BookImageService/
basicAuth*

(or port 7000 if you are using the J2EE reference implementation).

To use this target, open a command window, make *chapter3\bookimageservice* (relative to the installation directory of the book's example source code) your working directory, and then type the command:

```
ant run-httpsserver-client
```

You should see the application start up and run as usual, although there will probably be a slight delay because of the additional overhead required to set up an HTTPS connection. If you'd like to see the details of the setup process, use the target run-httpsserver-client-debug instead.

4

JAXM

SAAJ is a convenient API that allows applications to exchange SOAP messages containing information encoded in XML, together with arbitrary data held in message attachments. Although it is useful on its own, SAAJ is also the basis for JAX-RPC and for the Java API for XML Messaging (JAXM). This chapter looks at the features that JAXM adds to SAAJ and describes how to configure and use the JAXM reference implementation.

 Although JAXM is part of the Java Web Services Developers Pack, it is not one of the APIs that was selected for inclusion in Version 1.4 of the J2EE platform. The examples in this chapter can therefore only be used with the JWSDP. JAXM may be integrated into a future release of J2EE, but at the time of this writing, there is no commitment on Sun's part to do this.

JAXM Overview

SAAJ allows you to construct SOAP messages and send them directly and synchronously to a web service. JAXM builds on SAAJ to provide a higher-level API with the following additional features:

Messaging profiles
> The SOAP messages returned by the SAAJ `MessageFactory` consist of an empty body and an empty header. However, there are established uses of SOAP that make use of message headers to convey information from the message sender to the receiver, or to intermediate nodes that the message might traverse along its delivery path. JAXM provides the concept of *messaging profiles*, where a profile represents a specific and standardized way of constructing a SOAP message, such as the ebXML Message Service. A JAXM messaging profile is represented by a profile-specific `MessageFactory` that can build SOAP messages according to the rules applicable to the profile.

Asynchronous messaging

Using SAAJ, you can only send a message directly to a service and then wait for the service to send a reply. This mode of operation is well-suited to RPC-style interaction, in which the server is able to reply almost immediately to an incoming message. In many cases, however, it is not possible to operate in this way. If a client submits a purchase order to a company's online business web service, for example, it may not be possible to respond immediately with an order confirmation or an invoice for payment. In these circumstances, it is useful to be able to simply send a message and be prepared to receive a reply at a later time. JAXM supports this by providing several asynchronous messaging modes, described in "JAXM Message Delivery Modes" next.

More robust message delivery

SAAJ requires both the sender and receiver of a message to be active at the same time and works only if it is possible to make a direct connection between the two (although transparent hops—i.e., proxies—are supported in the same way as they are by the generic HTTP support in the JRE). JAXM removes both of these restrictions by providing an intermediary messaging provider that is responsible for the handling of all messages. A *messaging provider* delivers a message by forwarding it, not to the intended recipient, but to another messaging provider, which may or may not be directly connected to the message destination. If delivery to the next provider fails, perhaps because it is not active or because of a temporary lack of network connectivity, the sending provider can be configured to retransmit the message a specified number of times. If a provider receives a message for a recipient that is not currently active, it can store it until the recipient becomes active.

JAXM Message Delivery Modes

The JAXM specification (available at *http://jcp.org/jsr/detail/67.jsp*) requires support for three asynchronous message delivery modes in addition to the synchronous reply/response mode supported by SAAJ.*

Asynchronous inquiry

In an asynchronous inquiry, shown in Figure 4-1, the sender constructs a request (such as a purchase order) and sends it to the web service, then continues with other processing.

When the target web service receives the request, it may or may not process it immediately. Either way—possibly days after the request was received—it creates a reply message (perhaps containing an order confirmation) and returns it to the sender of the request.

---

* In fact, the JAXM specification describes five message delivery modes. In addition to the three listed here, the other two are *synchronous inquiry* and *synchronous update*, both of which result in the sender blocking until a reply to its request is received. In the first case, the reply message contains some useful information, while in the second case, it is an acknowledgment that the request was received. These two cases are not covered here, because they are provided by SAAJ, not JAXM.

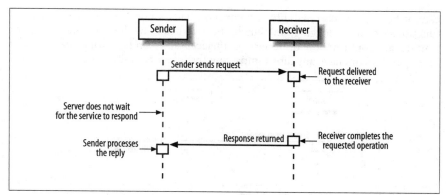

Figure 4-1. Message flow for an asynchronous inquiry

When asynchronous messaging is used, it is necessary for the sender to be able to match each reply to the original request message. JAXM does not concern itself with how this is done, assuming that it is part of the application-level protocol. The SOAP-RP profile, for example, defines a SOAP header that allows a message reference to be included with a request and a matching cross-reference to be sent with the response. See "The SOAP-RP Profile" later in this chapter for details.

Asynchronous update

From the messaging viewpoint, an asynchronous update (shown in Figure 4-2) is identical to an asynchronous inquiry. At the application level, however, there is a difference: the reply to an update is simply an acknowledgement that the request was received, which may or may not imply that the request has been successfully actioned. The exact semantics of the acknowledgement are application-dependent.

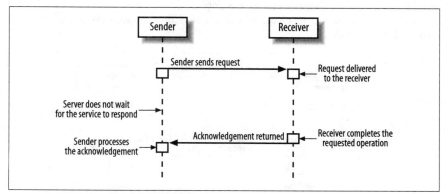

Figure 4-2. Message flow for an asynchronous update

Fire-and-forget

Fire-and-forget, shown in Figure 4-3, simply involves sending a message to a receiver. Since the sender does not receive any acknowledgement from the receiver, it cannot rely on the safe delivery of the message; therefore, this mode cannot be used when reliability is a concern. This mode is suited to noncritical functions, such as logging, in which the overhead involved in generating or waiting for confirmation of receipt is unacceptable, and in which the loss of messages does not have any direct impact on the integrity of the business process.

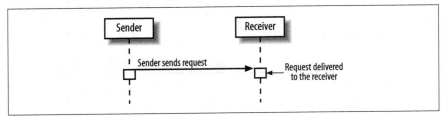

Figure 4-3. Message flow for fire-and-forget

Providers and Asynchronous Messaging

The asynchronous messaging and reliable delivery features of JAXM are implemented by a messaging provider. The specification itself says very little about the provider, other than to describe the API needed to access it, leaving the details to be determined by implementations. In practice, application code is almost unaffected by the presence of a provider, but it is very important to understand how to configure the provider and how to deploy the application with the appropriate settings required to access it. In this section, we look at the API that application code uses to work with the provider, and at how to configure the provider included with the JAXM reference implementation.

Provider Message Path

When a message provider is in use, the *logical* flow of a message is still directly from the sender to the receiver, but the *actual* flow is somewhat different, as shown in Figure 4-4.

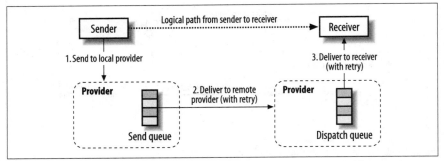

Figure 4-4. Logical and actual message flow when using a messaging provider

In order to send messages, the sender first connects to the local provider and determines whether it supports the messaging profile that it wants to use; if so, it obtains a MessageFactory for that profile. Each message is then handled as follows:

1. The sender creates a SOAP message using the SAAJ API with the MessageFactory for the selected messaging profile.

2. The message is sent to the local provider. This operation returns control to the caller as soon as the provider receives the message, and the sender is free to continue with other processing.

3. The provider stores the message in its outgoing queue.

4. A separate thread handles queued messages, dispatching each of them in turn to the receiving provider. If the receiving provider is not accessible, the message is left in the queue and retried later.

5. The remote provider (eventually) receives the message and stores it in its dispatching queue.

6. If the message receiver is active, the message is delivered to it. Otherwise, it is held in the dispatching queue until it can be delivered, or until the retry count has expired.

7. The receiver processes the message.

It is important to note that the message flow is entirely asynchronous to the sender: once the message is delivered to the local provider, its eventual transmission is scheduled separately (and, in the reference implementation, in a separate thread). Similarly, when the message is received by the remote provider, it is simply written to a queue and dispatched at a later time to the intended recipient. The asynchronous nature of the message flow and the fact that it involves intermediaries is in sharp contrast to the direct connection used by SAAJ applications. The message flow is strictly *unidirectional*: there is no provision (and no possibility) for a reply message, and therefore this flow models the fire-and-forget message mode described earlier in this chapter. If the application-level protocol requires a reply or an acknowledgement, then a separate (asynchronous) message is sent by the receiver to the original sender, using the reverse message path to that shown in Figure 4-4.

You will notice that the diagrams in this chapter use the terms "sender" and "receiver" instead of "client" and "service," since we are focusing on the messaging aspects rather than on the roles of the sender and receiver in the web service. It is important to keep these separate. Although the client is the sender and the service is the receiver when the service is first invoked, the roles are reversed when the service eventually sends a reply to the client. Unlike the synchronous programming model used by SAAJ, in which the service receives a message in its onMessage( ) method and simply returns a SOAPMessage to be sent back to the client (almost as a side effect), the service has to explicitly send the reply via its local messaging provider. In this chapter, we will use the term "JAXM client" to refer to either the sender or the receiver, since we consider both to be clients of the messaging provider.

The arrangement shown in Figure 4-4 is fine when both the sender and the receiver are implemented using JAXM, but this is not the most general case. In the real world, one party may not be associated with a messaging provider, an obvious example of which is a JAXM client accessing a web service running on the Microsoft .NET platform or vice versa. As far as the client or service implementation is concerned, this makes no difference—only the configuration details need to change, as we'll see later in this chapter. The only configuration that does not work is an asynchronous JAXM client connecting to a web service that expects to reply synchronously using the same underlying transport connection as the one on which it received the request. For an explanation of why this does not work, see "Why Synchronous Messaging Does Not Work with a Provider," later in this chapter.

The JAXM Execution Environment

In Chapter 3, you saw an example SAAJ application in which the service was implemented as a servlet in the Tomcat web container and the client was a free-standing Java application. Both JAX-RPC and SAAJ allow the client either to be an application or to reside in a container. However, *all* JAXM applications (including the part you would naturally think of as the "client") must be hosted in a web container or an EJB container. At the time of this writing, the JAXM reference implementation supports only deployment of JAXM applications as servlets within a web container, so the examples used in this chapter are all hosted by servlets. In the future, it is expected that JAXM will also be supported by EJB containers in the form of Message Driven Beans.

 The JAXM 1.1 specification uses the term "JAXM client" to refer either to a client that uses a messaging provider or to one that makes a direct connection to a web service; therefore, it sometimes talks about "freestanding JAXM clients." In this book, we make a sharp distinction between the following two cases:

- A client that connects directly to a service without using a messaging provider is considered to be a SAAJ client. Such a client needs only to use the API provided by the javax.xml. soap package, and can only use a synchronous request/ response model. SAAJ clients can be freestanding J2SE applications, or they may reside in a container.

- A client that uses a messaging provider is a JAXM client. These clients use the javax.xml.soap package to construct their messages, and use the javax.xml.messaging package to interact with the provider. Only JAXM clients can use the asynchronous messaging features of the provider, and they must be hosted by a web container (or an EJB container in the future).

The API provided by JAXM resides in the javax.xml.messaging package. In order to compile a JAXM client, you need to have the JAR files jaxm-api.jar and jaxm-runtime.jar on your CLASSPATH, together with saaj-api.jar for access to the javax.xml.soap package. At runtime, you additionally need access to all of the JAR files listed in Table 3-1. Inclusion of these JAR files is usually automatic, however, since the client is actually deployed in a web container in which JAXM and SAAJ should already have been installed.

The messaging provider that is provided with the JAXM reference implementation is implemented as a servlet that resides at the URL *http://localhost:8081/jaxm-provider* in the default deployment. There is also a web application at the URL *http://localhost:8081/jaxm-provideradmin* that can be used to configure the provider. Further information on the provider and its configuration are found later in this chapter.

Note that these services reside at port 8081, not port 8080. This becomes important when you configure the provider, as you'll see later.

An Example JAXM Application

In order to demonstrate the JAXM APIs and show you how to set up the JAXM provider configuration, we'll look at the implementation of a very simple web service that simply accepts a message and returns it to its sender, having added an XML element containing the date and time at which the message was processed. The process of returning the message requires the receiver to explicitly address the message to its originator and send it back via its own local provider. In other words, each time this service is used, two asynchronous messages are sent, one in each direction.

Since this is a JAXM example, both the sender and the receiver are implemented as servlets in a web container. Both of them need to be able to receive SOAP messages and dispatch them to application code. In Chapter 3, we used a private class called SAAJServlet as the base class for our example web service, but in this chapter, we are going to use the class javax.xml.messaging.JAXMServlet instead. These two servlets are virtually identical—the only real difference between them is that JAXMServlet is included as part of the JAXM API and should therefore be available in all JAXM implementations, whereas SAAJServlet is a private class developed from example code in the JWSDP distribution. We could, of course, have used JAXMServlet in Chapter 3 instead of creating SAAJServlet, but to do so would have introduced a dependency on JAXM, which we wanted to avoid. Like SAAJServlet, JAXMServlet delivers received SOAP messages via the onMessage( ) method, where the application will implement its message handling.

In previous examples, in which the message sender was a freestanding application, we could run it by simply starting the application from the command line. When the message sender is implemented as a servlet, however, we have to take a different approach. We'll implement the servlet's doGet( ) method so that it sends a message to the receiver whenever it is invoked. This allows us to run the example by pointing a web browser at the appropriate URL; this also gives us somewhere to display the message that the receiver returns to us. We don't have a similar issue with the message receiver, which is also deployed as a servlet derived from JAXMServlet, since its task is only to respond to messages when they are delivered to it.

Before we look at the example code, we'll deploy both the sending and receiving servlets. To do this, make sure that the Tomcat web server is running and open a command window. To deploy the receiver, change your current directory to *chapter4\soaprpecho* relative to the installation directory of the example code for this book and type the command:

```
ant deploy
```

This command compiles the code for the receiver and deploys it on the web server. Next, to compile and deploy the sender, change your working directory to *chapter4\soaprpsender* and type the following command to complete the process:

```
ant deploy
```

Although most of the examples in this book need only to be compiled and deployed in order for you to use them, this is not the case here. This example won't work until you have taken some extra steps to configure the JAXM provider, which is covered in "JAXM Configuration," later in this chapter.

Implementing the Sending Servlet for the JAXM Echo Service

Now let's look at how the servlet that provides the functionality of the message sender is implemented. The code for this servlet is shown in Example 4-1.

Example 4-1. The JAXM client for the echo web service

```
package ora.jwsnut.chapter4.soaprpsender;

import java.io.IOException;
import java.io.OutputStream;
import javax.servlet.ServletConfig;
import javax.servlet.ServletException;
import javax.servlet.http.HttpServletRequest;
import javax.servlet.http.HttpServletResponse;
import javax.xml.messaging.Endpoint;
import javax.xml.messaging.JAXMServlet;
import javax.xml.messaging.OnewayListener;
import javax.xml.messaging.ProviderConnection;
import javax.xml.messaging.ProviderConnectionFactory;
import javax.xml.messaging.ProviderMetaData;
import javax.xml.soap.MessageFactory;
import javax.xml.soap.SOAPElement;
import javax.xml.soap.SOAPFactory;
import javax.xml.soap.SOAPMessage;
import com.sun.xml.messaging.jaxm.soaprp.SOAPRPMessageFactoryImpl;
import com.sun.xml.messaging.jaxm.soaprp.SOAPRPMessageImpl;

/**
 * A servlet that creates a SOAP-RP message on demand and sends
 * it to a remote echo service.
 */
public class SOAPRPSenderServlet extends JAXMServlet implements OnewayListener {

    /**
     * Message returned by the echo service.
     */
    private SOAPMessage replyMessage;

    /**
     * Factory used to create parts of SOAP messages
     */
    private SOAPFactory soapFactory;
```

Example 4-1. The JAXM client for the echo web service (continued)

```java
/**
 * ProviderConnection used to send reply messages
 */
private ProviderConnection conn;

/**
 * Factory used to create messages
 */
private MessageFactory msgFactory;

/**
 * Initialize by installing the appropriate MessageFactory
 */
public void init(ServletConfig servletConfig) throws ServletException {
    super.init(servletConfig);
    try {
        // Create the connection to the provider
        conn = ProviderConnectionFactory.newInstance().createConnection();
        soapFactory = SOAPFactory.newInstance();

        // Check that the soaprp profile is supported
        ProviderMetaData metaData = conn.getMetaData();
        String[] profiles = metaData.getSupportedProfiles();
        boolean found = false;
        for (int i = 0; i < profiles.length; i++) {
            if (profiles[i].equals("soaprp")) {
                found = true;
                break;
            }
        }

        if (!found) {
            // No SOAPRP profile
            log("soaprp profile not supported");
            throw new ServletException("soaprp profile not supported");
        }

        // Get the message factory and build the message
        msgFactory = conn.createMessageFactory("soaprp");

        // Install the factory to use when receiving messages
        setMessageFactory(msgFactory);
    }catch (Exception e) {
        e.printStackTrace();
        throw new ServletException(
            "Failed to initialize SOAPRP sender servlet " +
            e.getMessage());
    }
}

/**
 * Handles a request from a client to send a message.
 */
```

Example 4-1. The JAXM client for the echo web service (continued)

```java
public void doGet(HttpServletRequest req, HttpServletResponse resp)
                                throws IOException, ServletException {

    // Only allow gets on the "request" handler
    String path = req.getServletPath( );
    if (!path.equals("/request")) {
        resp.sendError(HttpServletResponse.SC_METHOD_NOT_ALLOWED,
                        "Cannot use get on this URL");
        return;
    }

    // Build and send a message
    boolean sent = sendMessage( );

    // Wait until the echo service has replied,
    // for a maximum of 30 seconds
    if (sent) {
        synchronized (this) {
            replyMessage = null;
            try {
                if (replyMessage == null) {
                    wait(30000L);
                }
            } catch (InterruptedException ex) {
            }
        }
    }

    // Now send the reply to the caller.
    try {
        if (replyMessage == null) {
            resp.sendError(HttpServletResponse.SC_SERVICE_UNAVAILABLE,
                "No reply received");
            return;
        }

        OutputStream os = resp.getOutputStream( );
        resp.setContentType("text/html");
        resp.setStatus(HttpServletResponse.SC_OK);
        os.write("<html><P><XMP>".getBytes( ));
        replyMessage.writeTo(os);
        os.write("</XMP></html>".getBytes( ));
        os.flush( );
    } catch (Exception ex) {
        log("Exception in doGet", ex);
        resp.sendError(HttpServletResponse.SC_SERVICE_UNAVAILABLE,
                        "Exception: " + ex.getMessage( ));
    }

    replyMessage = null;
}
```

Example 4-1. The JAXM client for the echo web service (continued)

```
/**
 * Handles a POST either from a client or as a
 * callback from the provider.
 */
public void doPost(HttpServletRequest req, HttpServletResponse resp)
                                    throws IOException, ServletException {
    // Only allow posts to the "message" handler
    String path = req.getServletPath();
    if (path.equals("/message")) {
        // This is allowed
        super.doPost(req, resp);
    } else {
        // Cannot post to the request path
        resp.sendError(HttpServletResponse.SC_METHOD_NOT_ALLOWED,
            "Cannot post to this URL");
    }
}

/* -- Useful functionality starts here -- */
/**
 * Builds a message and sends it to the service
 */
private boolean sendMessage() {
    try {
        // Build the SOAP-RP message
        SOAPRPMessageImpl message =
            (SOAPRPMessageImpl)msgFactory.createMessage();
        message.setTo(new Endpoint("urn:SOAPRPEcho"));
        message.setFrom(new Endpoint("urn:SOAPRPSender"));
        SOAPElement element =
            message.getSOAPPart().getEnvelope().getBody().addBodyElement(
            soapFactory.createName("Sent", "tns", "urn:SOAPRPSender"));
        element.addTextNode("This is the content");

        // Send the message to the echo service
        conn.send(message);

        // Return indicating that the message was sent.
        return true;
    } catch (Exception ex) {
        log("Failed when sending message", ex);
    }

    return false;
}

/**
 * Handles a received SOAP message - this is the
 * asynchronous reply from the echo service.
 */
public void onMessage(SOAPMessage message) {
    try {
        synchronized (this) {
```

Example 4-1. The JAXM client for the echo web service (continued)

```
                // Save the message for the benefit
                // of the client.
                replyMessage = message;

                // Wake up the client
                notify( );
            }
        } catch (Exception ex) {
            log("Exception", ex);
        }
    }

    public void destroy( ) {
        try {
            if (conn != null) {
                conn.close( );
            }
        } catch (Exception ex) {
            // Don't log this - the provider may already have closed
        }
    }
}
```

Since there is rather a lot of code here, we'll break it down into smaller pieces and examine each of them in turn.

Servlet configuration

The sending servlet will receive inputs from two different sources:

- An HTTP GET request from a browser that we'll use to initiate the sending of a message.
- An HTTP POST request containing received SOAP messages, sent by the web service and delivered by the local JAXM provider.

We can easily distinguish these two different cases because the former will be handled by the doGet( ) method and the latter by doPost( ), but in order to make the distinction between these two different aspects of the servlet clearer, we choose to assign them to different URLs in the *web.xml* file that is shown in Example 4-2.

Example 4-2. The web.xml file for the echo example sending servlet

```
<?xml version="1.0" encoding="UTF-8" ?>

<!DOCTYPE web-app
    PUBLIC "-//Sun Microsystems, Inc.//DTD Web Application 2.3//EN"
    "http://java.sun.com/j2ee/dtds/web-app_2_3.dtd">


<web-app>
    <display-name>SOAP-RP Message Sender</display-name>
    <description>SOAP-RP Message Sender</description>
```

Example 4-2. The web.xml file for the echo example sending servlet (continued)

```
<servlet>
    <servlet-name>SOAPRPSender</servlet-name>
    <display-name>Servlet for the SOAP-RP Message Sender Example
    </display-name>
    <servlet-class>ora.jwsnut.chapter4.soaprpsender.SOAPRPSenderServlet
    </servlet-class>
</servlet>

<servlet-mapping>
    <servlet-name>SOAPRPSender</servlet-name>
    <url-pattern>/request</url-pattern>
</servlet-mapping>
<servlet-mapping>
    <servlet-name>SOAPRPSender</servlet-name>
    <url-pattern>/message</url-pattern>
</servlet-mapping>

</web-app>
```

The servlet will be deployed with the context path SOAPRPSender, so the URLs that correspond to it are as follows (assuming deployment on localhost):

URL	Description
http://localhost:8080/SOAPRPSender/request	Used by a web browser to initiate the sending of a message
http://localhost:8080/SOAPRPSender/message	Used by the JAXM provider to deliver SOAP messages addressed to the sender

Accessing the provider and creating the MessageFactory

When we used SAAJ to send a message, we had to use a factory to create a SOAPConnection, get a MessageFactory to create an empty message, and populate it. We then used the SOAPConnection send( ) method to transmit it and wait for the reply. Here, for example, is the code that we used in the last chapter to obtain SOAPConnection and MessageFactory objects:

```
// Get a SOAPConnection
SOAPConnectionFactory connFactory = SOAPConnectionFactory.newInstance( );
SOAPConnection conn = connFactory.createConnection( );
MessageFactory messageFactory = MessageFactory.newInstance( );
```

When using a messaging provider, the code is almost identical:

```
ProviderConnectionFactory factory = ProviderConnectionFactory.newInstance( );
ProviderConnection conn = factory.createConnection( );
MessageFactory messageFactory = conn.createMessageFactory("soaprp");
```

The most obvious difference between these two code extracts is that we now use javax.xml.messaging.ProviderConnectionFactory and javax.xml.messaging. ProviderConnection instead of SOAPConnectionFactory and SOAPConnection. These methods (at least notionally) create a connection to the local provider and then use that connection to obtain a MessageFactory for messages to be sent using that provider. Simple and logical though this code might appear, it raises an obvious question: how does the createConnection( ) method know where to find the provider that it is creating a connection to? If you refer back to Figure 4-4, you'll see that the provider is a separate entity. In fact, in the JAXM reference implementation, it is a separate web application that may (or may not) reside on the same host as the JAXM client itself. Yet the JAXM client does not need to provide the URL of the provider in order to connect to it. This is because the URL of the provider is part of the configuration information required to deploy a JAXM client, which we'll look at in "JAXM Configuration," later in this chapter. The fact that you don't need to hardwire it or write code to obtain the URL at runtime simplifies the task of writing the client, and also enhances its portability between different JAXM implementations, since the way in which providers are configured is not covered by the JAXM specification, and is therefore a matter for JAXM vendors that can be addressed at deployment time without the need to modify code.

In the future, should JAXM be more tightly integrated into web or J2EE containers, the `ProviderConnectionFactory` will probably become a managed object that is configured into the JNDI naming context of the servlet (or message-driven bean) hosting the JAXM client, which would then follow the usual coding pattern to get a reference to it:

```
InitialContext ctx = new InitialContext( );
ProviderConnectionFactory factory = (ProviderConnectionFactory)ctx.
lookup("key");
```

In the reference implementation, the `createConnection( )` method does not actually cause a connection to be made to the provider, despite its name. A real connection is not established until an attempt is made to send a message, or until the `getMetaData( )` method is called.

Another difference between the code shown here and that used in the previous chapter is the way in which the `MessageFactory` is obtained. When you use a provider, you have to get the `MessageFactory` using the following `ProviderConnection` method:

```
public MessageFactory createMessageFactory(String profile)
        throws JAXMException;
```

where `profile` is a string that represents the message profile to be used when constructing SOAP messages. The reference implementation recognizes two values for this argument, which are described in Table 4-1.

Table 4-1. Messaging profiles supported by the JAXM reference implementation

Profile string	Description
soaprp	Returns a `MessageFactory` that can be used to create messages with preconfigured headers as defined by the SOAP WS-Routing protocol. WS-Routing (which stands for Web Services Routing) was formerly known as the SOAP Routing Protocol, or SOAP-RP (hence the name of the profile—we'll refer to it throughout this chapter as SOAP-RP or soaprp for consistency with the implementation). It allows the route by which a SOAP message reaches its ultimate destination to be recorded in the message header, and for a suitable reverse path to be created as the message is forwarded through intermediary systems. The section "The SOAP-RP Profile," later in this chapter, looks at the support for this profile in the JAXM reference implementation.
ebxml	Returns a `MessageFactory` for messages with headers that conform to the ebXML Message Service specification. See "The ebXML Profile," later in this chapter, for further information on this profile.

JAXM clients that use a messaging provider must use one of the profiles that it supports—it is not possible to create a plain SOAP message using the default MessageFactory (returned by its static newInstance( ) method) and then try to transmit this via a provider.

 The consequence of this restriction is that you cannot get the benefits of using a messaging provider unless you use a messaging profile. You can, on the other hand, create a profiled message and use the SOAPConnection call( ) method to send it without using a provider—in fact, you have to do this if you want to use synchronous messaging with a profiled message.

In practice, this is not really a constraint, since applications will typically be written specifically for a particular messaging profile. As you'll see, the code for this example needs to know that it is using a SOAP-RP message and would not work at all with the ebXML profile. For this reason, most clients will obtain the MessageFactory for their profile by directly requesting it by name, as shown earlier:

```
MessageFactory messageFactory = conn.createMessageFactory("soaprp");
```

If the provider does not support the requested profile, this method throws a JAXMException. You can discover the set of profiles that a messaging provider supports by obtaining its ProviderMetaData object using the following ProviderConnection method:

```
public ProviderMetaData  getMetaData( ) throws JAXMException;
```

and then calling the getSupportedProfiles( ) method, which returns the profile names in the form of a string array. Here's how the example source code uses this method to check whether the SOAP-RP profile is supported, as an alternative to catching a JAXMException from the createMessageFactory( ) method:

```
// Check that the soaprp profile is supported
ProviderMetaData metaData = conn.getMetaData( );
String[] profiles = metaData.getSupportedProfiles( );
boolean found = false;
for (int i = 0; i < profiles.length; i++) {
    if (profiles[i].equals("soaprp")) {
        found = true;
        break;
    }
}

if (!found) {
    // No SOAPRP profile
    log("soaprp profile not supported");
     throw new ServletException("soaprp profile not supported");
}
```

If you refer to Example 4-1, you'll notice that the code that handles the connection to the messaging provider and the obtaining of a MessageFactory is all executed in the servlet's init( ) method. This is appropriate because a single instance of all of these objects can be shared among all users of the servlet; therefore, they need only to be created once, when the servlet is first loaded.

Handling requests from the browser

Having initialized the servlet by connecting to the provider and getting a MessageFactory, there is nothing further to do until the user visits its request URL (*http://localhost:8080/SOAPRPSender/request*), at which time the servlet's doGet() method is called. At this point, we want to do the following:*

1. Construct a SOAP message.
2. Send it to the web service.
3. Wait for the reply message.
4. Send an HTTP response to the browser containing a copy of the SOAP message returned by the web service.

We'll cover the details of the construction of the outgoing message and the handling of the reply later. The important point to deal with here is that the response to the browser has to be sent *before* the doGet() method completes, which means that doGet() has to receive and process the web service's reply.

The problem with this is that when we use a provider, the method that sends a message does not block until the reply arrives—it returns control as soon as the message is handed to the provider. The reply message arrives at some time in the future—or perhaps not at all. Hence, the doGet() method needs to arrange to block until it is notified that the web service's reply message has been received. We achieve this by using an instance variable that is initially set to null, but which is used to store a reference to the reply message when it arrives. The doGet() method uses the Object wait() method to pause for up to 30 seconds. When it resumes, it is either because the reply was received (in which case it prepares a reply containing the message content) or because the time limit expired (when it sends a response containing an error status).

Constructing and sending the message

The message that we're going to send to the web service is obtained using the createMessage() method of the SOAP-RP profile's MessageFactory:

```
// Build the SOAP-RP message
SOAPRPMessageImpl message = (SOAPRPMessageImpl)msgFactory.createMessage();
message.setTo(new Endpoint("urn:SOAPRPEcho"));
message.setFrom(new Endpoint("urn:SOAPRPSender"));
SOAPElement element = message.getSOAPPart().getEnvelope().getBody().
addBodyElement(

soapFactory.createName("Sent", "tns", "urn:SOAPRPSender"));
element.addTextNode("This is the content");
```

---

* Note that the doGet() method would also be called if the browser were incorrectly given the URL *http://localhost:8080/SOAPRPSender/message*, which is intended to be used for delivery of the response message from the web service. In order to exclude this case, the doGet() method uses the HttpServletRequest getServletPath() method to determine the URL used to call it, and returns an error if appropriate.

The first thing to note about this code is that the object returned from the createMessage( ) method—although it is a SOAPMessage—is cast to a reference of type SOAPRPMessageImpl. The SOAPRPMessageImpl class, which resides in the com. sun.xml.messaging.jaxm.soaprp package, is the reference implementation's representation of a SOAP-RP message, and provides convenience methods that allow you to set and retrieve the content of XML elements that form the header entry that SOAP-RP defines without needing to understand the way in which the element structure is built. This class, which is not covered by the JAXM specification, is described in more detail in "The SOAP-RP Profile," later in this chapter.

 Both of the profiles supported by the reference implementation use message classes that are defined in packages that are not covered by the JAXM specification. Unfortunately, due to the fact that you have to use a profiled message with a message provider, you have no choice but to use these classes despite the fact that their API is not formally defined, and hence might be subject to change in the future.

SOAP-RP defines two particular header fields that hold the source and ultimate destination addresses of the message. Both are defined as URIs. The SOAPRPMessageImpl class allows you to set these fields using the setFrom( ) and setTo( ) methods, both of which accept an argument of type javax.xml. messaging.Endpoint. Endpoint is the most general form of address recognized by JAXM. It simply encapsulates a string, the interpretation of which depends entirely on the profile used to create the message and the messaging provider. In this case, the to and from addresses, which are *urn:SOAPRPEcho* and *urn:SOAPRPSender* respectively, are URNs rather than URLs. As we'll see later in the section "JAXM Configuration," these values are simply tokens that are mapped to URLs by the messaging provider.

Using tokens instead of absolute addresses has the obvious advantage that the code is completely independent of the actual addresses that are eventually used. The only requirement is that the sending provider has a mapping for the token that represents the destination address, and the receiving provider has a mapping for the sender's token if it is necessary to send a reply. It is, of course, possible to use the real URLs as the tokens, but it is still necessary to create a trivial identity mapping in the provider configuration.

 Endpoint has a subclass called URLEndpoint that explicitly indicates that the address is supplied in the form of a string that represents a URL. This class does not really add anything more than cosmetic value, because there is no validity checking applied to the address, and it is not possible to use it in conjunction with a real java.net. URL object. It is really just a convenience for SAAJ applications that need to deal directly with URLs (because they do not have a messaging provider to map from a URI), and is largely redundant as of SAAJ 1.1 because the SOAPConnection send( ) method accepts a string argument such as http://localhost:8080/BookImageService as well as the more complex new URLEndpoint("http://localhost:8080/BookImageService"). Note, however, that you cannot simply pass a string to the setTo( ) and setFrom( ) methods of SOAPRPMessageImpl, and that all address handling inside the messaging provider uses Endpoint objects.

Having addressed the message and added a simple XML node containing some text, the last step is to transmit it, which is achieved using the ProviderConnection send() method:

```
public void send(SOAPMessage message) throws JAXMException;
```

Note the two very important differences between this method and the SOAPConnection call() method used in Chapter 3:

- It does not return a value. This, of course, is because send() just sends the message without waiting for a response.

- It doesn't provide an argument that specifies the destination address of the message. The destination is assumed either to be part of the message or to be implicitly known to the provider, depending on the profile in use. We'll see later in "JAXM Configuration" exactly how the addressing works in the case of the SOAP-RP profile.

Handling the response message

At some point after the message is transmitted, the receiving servlet (the code for which will be shown shortly) returns a modified version of it to our local messaging provider, which then uses an HTTP POST request to deliver it to our sending servlet's doPost() method.[*] Since SOAPRPSenderServlet is derived from JAXMServlet, its doPost() method decodes the HTTP POST request and converts its content into a SOAPMessage, using code that is very much like that shown in Example 3-1 in Chapter 3. The SOAPMessage is then delivered to our onMessage() method. In order to decode the content of the HTTP request, JAXMServlet needs an appropriate MessageFactory, so that it can call its createMessage() method in the same way as SAAJServlet does in Example 3-1. For a SAAJ application, the default MessageFactory can be used, but when using a messaging provider, it is necessary to install the factory for the messaging profile in use by using the JAXMServlet setMessageFactory() method. This is typically done in the servlet's init() method, once the ProviderConnection and MessageFactory have been obtained:

```
// Get the message factory
msgFactory = conn.createMessageFactory("soaprp");

// Install the factory to use when receiving messages
setMessageFactory(msgFactory);
```

---

[*] You are probably wondering exactly how the messages manage to find their way from the sending servlet to the receiver and back again when all that we have supplied is a pair of seemingly meaningless URNs. We'll show exactly how this works in "JAXM Configuration," later in this chapter. For now, we're looking only at how the messages themselves are created and handled, which is the only thing that affects the code that you actually write. I am deliberately remaining silent on configuration, which is a deployment issue, to avoid presenting too complex a picture.

If you don't install a MessageFactory in the servlet's init( ) method, JAXMServlet uses the default MessageFactory to decode the messages that it receives. This won't cause any problems with the process of creating the internalized form of the message, but all the messages will be of type SOAPMessage and not the profile-specific subclass that you are probably expecting, the likely result of which is a ClassCastException.

In most cases, then, if you use JAXMServlet as the base class for your JAXM client, you need only to override onMessage( ) to be able to handle messages directed at your client, and there is no need to override doPost( ) yourself. In this example, however, since our servlet is mapped to two URLs, we would like to ensure that only POST requests sent to the URL that ends with */SOAPRPSender/message* are treated as SOAP messages. To do this, we override doPost( ) to inspect the URL to which the POST was directed, and invoke the JAXMServlet doPost( ) method only if the correct URL was used:

```
public void doPost(HttpServletRequest req, HttpServletResponse resp)
                throws IOException, ServletException {
    // Only allow posts to the "message" handler
    String path = req.getServletPath( );
    if (path.equals("/message")) {
        // This is allowed
        super.doPost(req, resp);
    } else {
        // Cannot post to the request path
        resp.sendError(HttpServletResponse.SC_METHOD_NOT_ALLOWED,
            "Cannot post to this URL");
    }
}
```

Once the message is handed to the onMessage( ) method, all we need to do is store a reference to it in the replyMessage instance variable and use the notify( ) method to wake up the thread that handled the original request from the browser that is blocked in the doGet( ) method.

When you derive your servlet class from JAXMServlet, you have to provide an onMessage( ) method to receive SOAP messages. There are two different ways to use the JAXMServlet onMessage( ) method:

- To receive a SOAP message and return another one that will be sent back to the originator of the message that was received. In this mode, if the message was delivered using an HTTP POST request (which will always be the case in the reference implementation), the reply is sent back in the HTTP response. When used in this way, JAXMServlet behaves in the same manner as SAAJServlet, which is used in Chapter 3.

- To receive a SOAP message without returning a reply in the HTTP response. This mode is appropriate for asynchronous messaging, and is the only one that can be used in conjunction with a messaging provider (discussed in "Why Synchronous Messaging Does Not Work with a Provider," later in this chapter). If a reply message is subsequently generated, it must be sent via the messaging provider in the usual way.

JAXMServlet distinguishes these two cases based on which of two interfaces your servlet subclass implements. If it implements the javax.xml.messaging. ReqRespListener interface, the onMessage( ) method must have the following signature:

```
public SOAPMessage onMessage(SOAPMessage message);
```

This interface should only be used as an alternative to using SAAJServlet. Servlets that work with a messaging provider (including the ones shown in this chapter) must implement the javax.xml.messaging.OnewayListener interface, in which the onMessage( ) method does not return a SOAPMessage:

```
public void onMessage(SOAPMessage message);
```

If your servlet does not declare that it implements one or the other of these interfaces, then the doPost( ) method throws a ServletException when it receives a SOAP message.

Implementing the Receiving Servlet for the JAXM Echo Service

The servlet that implements the web service itself and that receives the messages sent by SOAPRPSenderServlet is also derived from JAXMServlet and implements the OnewayListener interface. Unlike SOAPRPSenderServlet, however, it has only one source of message (its local messaging provider). Therefore, it needs only to be mapped to a single URL in its *web.xml* file, which is shown in Example 4-3.

Example 4-3. The web.xml file for the echo example receiving servlet

```
<?xml version="1.0" encoding="UTF-8" ?>

<!DOCTYPE web-app
    PUBLIC "-//Sun Microsystems, Inc.//DTD Web Application 2.3//EN"
    "http://java.sun.com/j2ee/dtds/web-app_2_3.dtd">


<web-app>
    <display-name>SOAP-RP Echo Service</display-name>
    <description>SOAP-RP Echo Service</description>

    <servlet>
        <servlet-name>SOAPRPEcho</servlet-name>
        <display-name>Servlet for the SOAP-RP Message Echo Service</display-name>
        <servlet-class>ora.jwsnut.chapter4.soaprpecho.SOAPRPEchoServlet
        </servlet-class>
        <load-on-startup>1000</load-on-startup>
    </servlet>

    <servlet-mapping>
        <servlet-name>SOAPRPEcho</servlet-name>
        <url-pattern>/message</url-pattern>
    </servlet-mapping>
</web-app>
```

Given that this servlet is deployed with the context path SOAPRPEcho, the URL used to deliver SOAP messages to it would be *http://localhost:8080/SOAPRPEcho/message*.

An important point to note about this *web.xml* file is that it contains the following line:

```
<load-on-startup>1000</load-on-startup>
```

This causes the servlet to be initialized when it is deployed and when the web container starts up, without waiting for it to be invoked as a result of an HTTP request. This is essential for this servlet, but the reason is impossible to describe until we discuss how the provider communicates with the servlet in "JAXM Configuration," later in this chapter. It is not necessary to load the sending servlet at startup, because it is not required until it is asked to send a message as a result of a browser making an HTTP GET request to its */request* URL.

Like the sending servlet, SOAPRPEchoServlet overrides the JAXMServlet init() method to obtain a connection to the messaging provider and install a MessageFactory. The code is almost identical to that shown earlier, but there are some interesting differences. The implementation is shown in Example 4-4.

Example 4-4. The init() method of the receiving servlet

```
public void init(ServletConfig servletConfig) throws ServletException {
    super.init(servletConfig);

    // Workaround for hang when deploying in J2EE container.
    // Do not connect to the provider here - defer to another thread.
    new Thread(new Runnable() {
        public void run() {
            try {
                // Create the connection to the provider
                conn = ProviderConnectionFactory.newInstance()
                    .createConnection();

                // Work around for a JAXM bug
                conn.getMetaData();

                // Install the message factory for the SOAP-RP profile
                setMessageFactory(conn.createMessageFactory("soaprp"));
            } catch (Exception e) {
                log("Exception when initializing", e);
            }
        }
    }).start();
}
```

The ProviderConnection getMetaData() method is called for no apparent reason—the value that it returns is ignored. In JWSDP Version 1.1, this is a workaround for a problem that we'll explain later in "JAXM Configuration." If you don't do this, the provider will be unable to deliver messages to the servlet.

The onMessage() method handles each message that it receives by creating a copy in which the to and from addresses are reversed, and adding an element that contains the date and time at which the message was processed. The new message is then sent to the provider, which delivers it to the original sender (or, more precisely, whatever the from address points to). An extract from this method showing the most interesting lines of code is shown in Example 4-5.

Example 4-5. Handling a SOAP message and returning an asynchronous reply

```java
public void onMessage(SOAPMessage message) {

    try {

        // Create a copy of the message with the same body
        // and with the to and from addresses exchanged.
        SOAPRPMessageImpl soapMsg = (SOAPRPMessageImpl)message;
        MessageFactory factory = soapMsg.getMessageFactory();

        // Create a reply message
        SOAPRPMessageImpl replyMsg = (SOAPRPMessageImpl)factory.createMessage();

        // Move the body content from the received message to the source.
        SOAPBody body = soapMsg.getSOAPPart().getEnvelope().getBody();
        SOAPBody replyBody = replyMsg.getSOAPPart().getEnvelope().getBody();
        Iterator iter = body.getChildElements();
        while (iter.hasNext()) {
            SOAPElement element = (SOAPElement)iter.next();
            replyBody.addChildElement(element);
        }

        // Add an element after the body that contains the date.
        SOAPElement element =
                replyMsg.getSOAPPart().getEnvelope().addChildElement(
                    "Date", "tns", "urn:SOAPRPEcho");
        element.addTextNode(new Date().toString());

        // Copy any attachments
        iter = soapMsg.getAttachments();
        while (iter.hasNext()) {
            replyMsg.addAttachmentPart((AttachmentPart)iter.next());
        }

        // Get the SOAP message ID and install it as the "relates-to" value
        replyMsg.setRelatesTo(soapMsg.getSOAPRPMessageId());

        // Get the the "To" address and install it as the "From" address
        replyMsg.setFrom(soapMsg.getTo());

        // Get the "From" address an install it as the "To" address
        replyMsg.setTo(soapMsg.getFrom());

        // [ CODE HERE NOT SHOWN]

        // Send the reply message
        conn.send(replyMsg);
    } catch (Exception ex) {
```

```
        log("Exception", ex);
    }
}
```

First, the received message is cast to the SOAPRPMessageImpl object so that we can use the convenience methods that it provides to get access to the SOAP-RP fields of the header that we need, especially the to and from addresses. This works because we installed the appropriate MessageFactory in the servlet's init( ) method (and, of course, because we are receiving SOAP-RP messages!). Next, we create an empty message and copy the content of the received message's body and its attachments (if there are any) into it. Although we could use the MessageFactory created in the init( ) method to create the copy, we take the opportunity to demonstrate the SOAPRPMessageImpl getMessageFactory( ) method, which returns a reference to the MessageFactory that was used to create the received message, and use the same one to build the reply.

Next, we add an element to the new message that contains the current date and time:

```
// Add an element after the body that contains the date.
SOAPElement element =
    replyMsg.getSOAPPart( ).getEnvelope( )
    .addChildElement("Date", "tns", "urn:SOAPRPEcho");
element.addTextNode(new Date( ).toString( ));
```

You'll notice that we add this element directly to the SOAP envelope, which means that it appears after the body element rather than inside the body. There is no special reason for this, other than to demonstrate that this is allowed both by the SOAP specification and the SAAJ API.

Finally, we swap the to and from addresses using the SOAPRPMessageImpl convenience methods that provide easy access to these fields. Then, we use the ProviderConnection send( ) method to send the copied and modified message back to the original sender:

```
// Get the the "To" address and install it as the "From" address
replyMsg.setFrom(soapMsg.getTo( ));

// Get the "From" address an install it as the "To" address
replyMsg.setTo(soapMsg.getFrom( ));

// Send the reply message
conn.send(replyMsg);
```

Why Synchronous Messaging Does Not Work with a Provider

When you use a messaging provider, you have no choice but to send your message asynchronously. Furthermore, in the example that we have been looking at in this section, the message receiver is a subclass of JAXMServlet that implements OnewayListener, and returns its reply using another asynchronous call to its local provider. The obvious question to ask is, since the receiver in this case can process the message and generate its reply immediately, why can't it implement the ReqRespListener interface and return the reply message for the provider to send straight back? Although this might seem simpler (and nothing stops you from trying it), it won't actually work—your message will not be delivered.

To understand why you can't implement a synchronous receiver to respond to an asynchronous message, look at the sequence of events that happens when the original message is transmitted:

1. The sender delivers its outgoing message to its local provider.

2. The provider puts the message in its outgoing queue.

3. Some time later, the local provider delivers the message to the receiver's provider.

4. Some time later, the receiver's provider delivers the message to the receiving servlet.

The last step in this process is the critical one. The message is delivered to the servlet by the receiver's provider using an HTTP POST request. If the receiving servlet implemented ReqRespListener, it could return a SOAPMessage and JAXMServlet would place it in the HTTP response. However, the receiving provider is simply not expecting this behavior—it does not examine the content of the HTTP response, so the message is lost.

JAXM Configuration

You have now seen and deployed all of the code for both the sender and receiver parts of the JAXM message echo example. If, however, you were to start your web browser and point it at *http://localhost:8080/SOAPRPSender/request*, which is the URL that causes the sender servlet to transmit a message, you would find that after about 30 seconds, the sender would give up waiting for a reply from the receiver and an error page would be displayed by the browser. Although all of the code is in place, the proper JAXM configuration has not been set up to allow the providers to exchange messages. In this section, we look at how to configure the JAXM reference implementation.

Configuring JAXM Clients

A message traveling from the sending servlet to the receiver has to make three hops:

1. From the sender to the local provider

2. From the local provider to the remote provider

3. From the remote provider to the receiving servlet

We saw earlier that a JAXM client logically connects to its local provider using the ProviderConnectionFactory createConnection( ) method, but we didn't see how the provider itself is located. This information is held in a file called *client.xml*, which must be located in the CLASSPATH of the JAXM client. Since both the sender and the receiver servlets in this example are deployed as web applications, their *client.xml* files should be placed in the *WEB-INF/classes* directory of their WAR files, as shown in the following listing of the files that make up the web archive for the SOAPRPSender servlet:

```
META-INF/MANIFEST.MF
WEB-INF/classes/ora/jwsnut/chapter4/soaprpsender/SOAPRPSenderServlet.class
WEB-INF/classes/client.xml
WEB-INF/web.xml
```

A full description of the *client.xml* file will be found in Chapter 8. The content of the *client.xml* file used by the SOAPRPSender servlet is shown in Example 4-6, in which the line numbers on the left have been added for ease of reference only.

Example 4-6. The client.xml file for the sending servlet

```
1    <?xml version="1.0" encoding="ISO-8859-1"?>
2
3    <!DOCTYPE ClientConfig
4        PUBLIC "-//Sun Microsystems, Inc.//DTD JAXM Client//EN"
5        "http://java.sun.com/xml/dtds/jaxm_client_1_0.dtd">
6    <ClientConfig>
7        <Endpoint>
8            urn:SOAPRPSender
9        </Endpoint>
10       <CallbackURL>
11           http://localhost:8080/SOAPRPSender/message
12       </CallbackURL>
13
14       <Provider>
15           <URI>http://java.sun.com/xml/jaxm/provider</URI>
16           <URL>http://localhost:8081/jaxm-provider/sender</URL>
17       </Provider>
18   </ClientConfig>
```

The lines shown in bold relate to the configuration of the sending servlet; the other lines are fixed content that are the same in all *client.xml* files. The Provider element at the end of the file is used when the client connects to the messaging provider. The two child elements are used as follows:

URI

The URI value identifies the provider in use. For the JAXM reference implementation, you must use the value *http://java.sun.com/xml/jaxm/provider*. The JAXM code that implements the ProviderConnection interface and the provider itself communicate by adding private header entries to the messages sent by JAXM clients. This URI is used as the namespace for the XML elements in these header entries; it is also used to set their actor attribute. When the provider receives a message from a JAXM client, it removes and actions all headers for which the actor attribute has this fixed value.

URL

The URL is where messages from the JAXM client to the provider are actually sent. For the reference implementation in the JWSDP, the provider is a Tomcat service called jaxm-provider, accessible at port 8081. The provider is not required to be on the same host as the JAXM client. If the provider is not co-located with the client, then the name of the provider's host should be used instead of localhost.

Figure 4-5 shows how the URL field of the Provider element is used to locate the JAXM client's local provider.

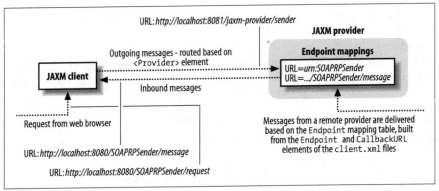

Figure 4-5. JAXM client configuration

When a provider receives a message for delivery to a client, it needs to be able to match the destination address of the message to the client that provides service at that address. As we saw earlier, the destination address that is placed in a SOAP-RP header is a URI that identifies the target of the message—it need not be a URL. Therefore, the provider maintains a list of mappings from the Endpoint URI to the URL of the client that should receive messages destined for that URI. In the *client.xml* file, the Endpoint element declares the URI that corresponds to the client, and the CallbackURL element specifies the URL to which messages for that URI should be delivered. In terms of the example that we are using in this chapter, the sending servlet advertises its URI as *urn:SOAPRPSender*. Since the sending servlet expects to receive messages on the URL *http://localhost:8080/SOAPRPSender/message*, this is the URL to which the sending servlet's URI should be mapped.* Hence, the appropriate Endpoint and CallbackURL entries in the *client.xml* file for the sending servlet would be:

```
<Endpoint>
    urn:SOAPRPSender
</Endpoint>

<CallbackURL>
    http://localhost:8080/SOAPRPSender/message
</CallbackURL>
```

In the case of the receiving servlet (which as a JAXM client also requires its own *client.xml* file), these entries would look like this:

```
<Endpoint>
    urn:SOAPRPEcho
</Endpoint>

<CallbackURL>
    http://localhost:8080/SOAPRPEcho/message
</CallbackURL>
```

* This URL comes from the sending servlet's *web.xml* file, which was shown in Example 4-2.

The receiving servlet also needs a `Provider` element containing the URL of its local provider that, if you deploy both the sending and receiving servlets on the same host, is the same provider used by the sending servlet and therefore requires the same URL.

Configuring the JAXM Provider

The *client.xml* file solves the problem of how to route messages between clients and a provider, but there remains the issue of how the providers route messages among themselves. In the case of the example used in this chapter, the provider needs to deliver messages addressed to the URIs *urn:SOAPRPEcho* and *urn:SOAPRPSender*, by passing them to whichever provider the clients owning these endpoints are connected.* In order to make this possible, providers are configured with URI-to-URL mappings that are similar to those created by the `Endpoint` and `CallbackURL` elements used in the *client.xml* file. Each provider must be configured with a mapping for each remote URI to which messages from its local clients might be addressed, specifying the URL of the provider to which messages carrying that URI as a destination address must be delivered (and not the URL of the receiving client).

In the reference implementation, these mappings are stored in a file called *provider.xml*, which resides in the */WEB_INF* directory of the `jaxm-provider` service, details of which you'll find in Chapter 8. Fortunately, you don't need to deal with this file directly—instead, you can view and change the mappings using the JAXM provider administration service, which can be accessed using a web browser.

The provider administration tool is a web application that provides a user interface that lets you configure the JAXM provider without having to manually edit its *provider.xml* file. Once you understand the content of this file (details of which are provided in Chapter 8), you'll find it very easy to use the administration tool, so we're not going to describe it in great detail. Here, we need to use it to add endpoint mappings for the URIs *urn:SOAPRPEcho* and *urn:SOAPRPSender*. Assuming that this service is running on the same host as your browser, the URL that you need to use to access it is *http://localhost:8081/jaxm-provideradmin*. When you attempt to connect to this service, you are prompted to supply a username and password. When you installed the JWSDP, you were prompted to supply a username and a password, and you should use the same username and password to access the configuration service. If you can't remember them, you can find them in the *tomcat-users.xml* file, which is held in the *conf* directory of the web server. Here is what this file typically looks like, with the important lines highlighted in bold:

```
<?xml version='1.0'?>
<tomcat-users>
```

---

* In general, when there are two JAXM clients on separate machines, there are two providers involved. However, if both the sender and receiver are deployed on the same machine, the likelihood is that they will use the same provider (although you could arrange to run two providers on the same machine). Even though this is the case, the configuration still has to be created in the same way as if there were two providers. The description here is consistent with that.

```
<role rolename="admin"/>
<role rolename="manager"/>
<role rolename="provider"/>
<user username="JWSUserName" password="JWSPassword"
    roles="admin,manager,provider"/>
</tomcat-users>
```

In this case, supply the username JWSUserName and the password JWSPassword. These values can also be found in the *jwsnutExamples.properties* file in your home directory, assuming you created it as described in Chapter 1.

Once you reach the configuration service's home page, expand the tree view that you'll see on the left, and select the entry for http below the SOAPRP profile. You should see a screen like that shown in Figure 4-6.

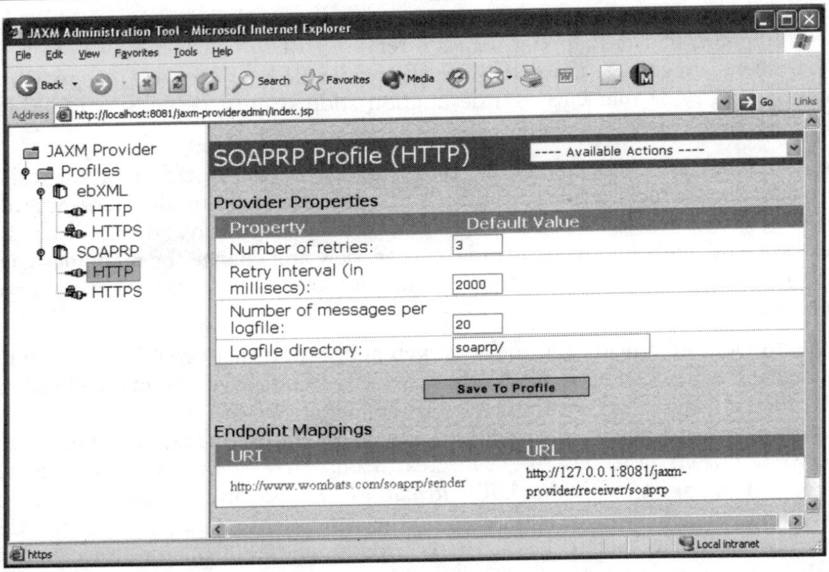

Figure 4-6. The JAXM provider administration screen

This screen contains, among other things, the endpoint mappings for messages being sent by the provider for the SOAP-RP profile using HTTP as the underlying communications protocol. The URL associated with the URI *urn:SOAPRPEcho* needs to be the one required to access the provider to which the receiving servlet is attached, whereas the URL for the URI *urn:SOAPRPSender* should be that of the provider for the sending servlet. A provider has three available URLs; for the case of the JWSDP reference implementation running in the Tomcat web server, these URLs are listed in Table 4-2, where it is assumed that the provider and the clients are all running on the same machine.

Table 4-2. URLs for the JAXM provider in the reference implementation

URL	Description
http://localhost:8081/jaxm-provider/sender	Address to which JAXM clients send outgoing messages. This URL is configured in the client's *client.xml* file and is not part of the provider configuration.
http://localhost:8081/jaxm-provider/receiver/soaprp	Address to which messages using the SOAP-RP profile should be sent.
http://localhost:8081/jaxm-provider/receiver/ebxml	Address to which messages using the ebXML profile should be sent.

If the target provider is on a different machine, substitute the hostname of that machine for localhost in these URLs.

Since the messages in the example used in this chapter use the SOAP-RP profile, both of the JAXM client URIs should be mapped to the URL for the SOAP-RP receiving URL of the target provider, which will be *http://localhost:8081/jaxm-provider/receiver/soaprp*. To add these mappings, select "Create New Endpoint Mapping" from the combo box at the top right of the screen. You are presented with a form that allows you to enter a URI along with its corresponding URL, as shown in Figure 4-7, where the mapping for *urn:SOAPRPEcho* has been entered.

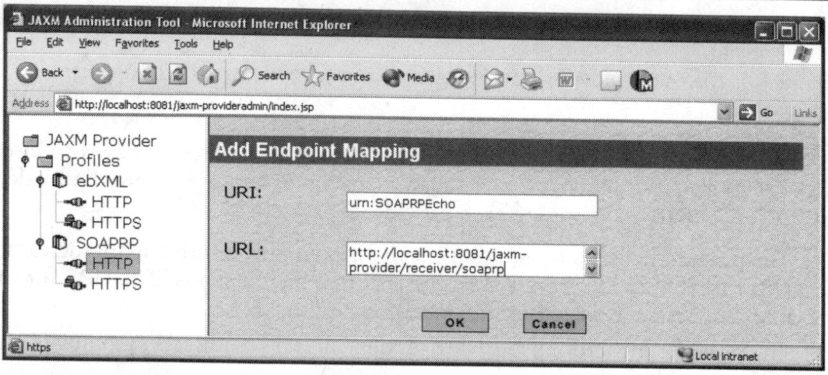

Figure 4-7. Configuring a URI-to-URL mapping

The mappings that you need to enter are shown in Table 4-3.

Table 4-3. URI mappings for the JAXM SOAP-RP profile example

URI	Target URL
urn:SOAPEcho	http://localhost:8081/jaxm-provider/receiver/soaprp
urn:SOAPSender	http://localhost:8081/jaxm-provider/receiver/soaprp

Once both mappings are set up, they should appear on the main screen as shown in Figure 4-8. Select "Save to Profile" to save these mappings.

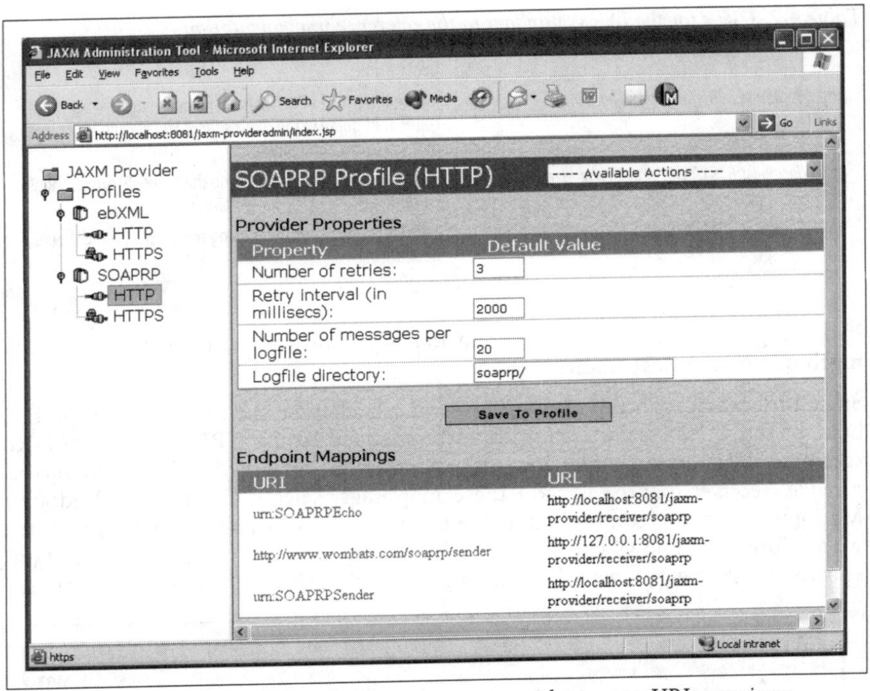

Figure 4-8. The JAXM provider administration screen with two new URI mappings
configured

At this point, the provider is properly configured to forward messages to either
URI. Of course, if the clients are on separate machines and use different providers,
it is then necessary to configure each provider separately:

- The provider local to the sending servlet is configured with a mapping for the
  URI *urn:SOAPRPEcho*—that is, the URI to which it sends. The URL for this
  mapping refers to the other provider.

- The provider local to the receiving servlet similarly requires a mapping for the
  URI *urn:SOAPRPSender*.

You can now finally run the example that we have been using throughout this
chapter. To do so, simply enter the URL *http://localhost:8080/SOAPRPSender/
request* into your browser. After a short delay, you should see the SOAP message
that was sent by the sending servlet and returned by the receiver, an example of
which is shown in Example 4-7. This message has been reformatted for the sake of
readability.

Example 4-7. A SOAP-RP message sent via a messaging provider

```
<?xml version="1.0" encoding="UTF-8"?>
<soap-env:Envelope xmlns:soap-env="http://schemas.xmlsoap.org/soap/envelope/">
    <soap-env:Header>
        <m:path xmlns:m="http://schemas.xmlsoap.org/rp">
            <m:from>urn:SOAPRPEcho</m:from>
```

Example 4-7. A SOAP-RP message sent via a messaging provider (continued)

```
            <m:to>urn:SOAPRPSender</m:to>
            <m:id>9a85b633-2c8f-4d2e-84a5-ff6b21c05f61</m:id>
            <m:relatesTo>3166c06a-e38c-466e-b43e-d55a37f3d3fc</m:relatesTo>
            <m:fwd/>
            <m:rev/>
        </m:path>
    </soap-env:Header>
    <soap-env:Body>
        <tns:Sent xmlns:tns="urn:SOAPRPSender">This is the content</tns:Sent>
    </soap-env:Body>
    <tns:Date xmlns:tns="urn:SOAPRPEcho">Thu Aug 08 15:58:53 BST 2002</tns:Date>
</soap-env:Envelope>
```

The elements in the message header are defined by the SOAP-RP protocol, further information on which can be found later in this chapter. Note the to and from elements, which contain the URIs for the sending and receiving servlets, and the Date element, which follows the SOAP body and contains the date and time at which the message was processed by the receiver.

How a Message Is Sent and Delivered

As a summary of how messaging providers use the JAXM configuration information, the following is a step-by-step account of the way in which a SOAP-RP message is sent from a JAXM client to its destination. The return path would obviously be identical, but with the addresses reversed.

1. The receiving servlet initializes. As it does so, it uses the ProviderConnectionFactory and the ProviderConnection interface to establish a connection to its local provider, as well as calls the ProviderConnection getMetaData( ) method. In order to contact the provider to obtain the metadata, the JAXM code in the client accesses the receiving servlet's *client.xml* file to locate the provider's URL from the Provider element—in this case, *http://localhost:8081/jaxm-provider/sender*. It also passes to the provider the information in the Endpoint and CallbackURL elements so that the provider knows that messages intended for the URI *urn:SOAPRPEcho* should be delivered to the URL *http://localhost:8080/SOAPRPEcho/message*.

2. The sending servlet uses the ProviderConnectionFactory and the ProviderConnection interface to establish a connection to its local provider. It also obtains a MessageFactory for the soaprp profile and constructs a message, setting the from address to *urn:SOAPRPSender* and the to address to *urn:SOAPRPEcho*.

3. The client uses the ProviderConnection send( ) method to transmit the message. The JAXM code in the client accesses the sending servlet's *client. xml* file and uses the URI and URL in the Provider element to find the URL of the provider—in this case, *http://localhost:8081/jaxm-provider/sender*. Also, if it has not already done so, it passes to the provider the information in the Endpoint and CallbackURL elements so that it can map the sending servlet's URI (*urn:SOAPRPSender*) to its message callback URL (*http://localhost:8080/SOAPRPSender/message*). The message is then delivered to the provider at the URL *http://localhost:8081/jaxm-provider/sender*.

4. When the provider receives the message, it stores it in its outgoing message queue. There is a separate set of message queues for each profile that the provider supports, which the reference implementation keeps in a directory hierarchy in temporary storage provided by its host container. If you are running the JWSDP in the Tomcat web server, you'll find the messages that the provider sends and receives held below the directory *work\Services Engine\jwsdp-services\jaxm-provider*, relative to the JWSDP installation directory.

5. When the message is to be transmitted from the outgoing message queue, the provider extracts its destination address. In order to do this, the provider needs to understand where it will find this address, which is profile-dependent. The provider can do this because the class com.sun.xml.messaging.soaprp. SOAPRPMessageImpl that represents a SOAP-RP message is derived from com. sun.xml.messaging.jaxm.util.ProfileMessage (which has abstract methods that extract to to and from addresses from the message). SOAPRPMessageImpl implements these methods so that they extract the correct parts of the SOAP-RP header. The message class for the ebXML profile similarly implements them to extract the Party object from the message (see "The ebXML Profile" later in this chapter, for further information on this). The fact that the provider has to be able to get the destination address from within a SOAP message explains why nonprofiled messages that do not contain a destination address (i.e., SAAJ messages created using the default MessageFactory) cannot be sent using a provider.

6. The provider uses the destination address to check its URI-to-URL mapping, set up using the JAXM provider administration tool, to find the URL of the provider to which the message should be sent. In this case, the destination address is *urn:SOAPRPEcho*, which maps to the URL *http://localhost:8081/ jaxm-provider/receiver/soaprp*. This happens to be a URL belonging to the same provider, of course, but this does not matter. The local provider delivers the message to its peer using an HTTP POST request to this URL. If delivery fails, the provider retries on the assumption that the remote provider is not yet started or there is a problem with network connectivity.

7. When the peer provider receives the incoming SOAP-RP message, it stores it in its received message queue. Subsequently, an attempt is made to deliver this message to the correct JAXM client. Delivery is performed by extracting the destination address from the message, in the same way as the sending provider did when transmitting the message, and using it to access the Endpoint mapping table built from the *client.xml* files of the clients connected to the provider (see Figure 4-5). Here, the destination address *urn:SOAPRPEcho* has been registered by the receiving servlet and mapped to its delivery URL *http://localhost:8080/SOAPRPEcho/message* (see Step 1). The provider delivers the message using an HTTP POST request to that URL. If delivery fails, or if there is no entry for the destination URI in the provider's mapping table, the provider will retry delivery later, on the assumption that the client has not yet been started but will register later.

Servlet Loading Issue

The final point to mention in our discussion of JAXM configuration discusses the reason for including the load-on-startup element in the *web.xml* file of the receiving servlet in our example so that it is loaded when the web container initializes. As we said earlier in the section "Configuring JAXM Clients," a provider uses the Endpoint elements from the *client.xml* files of the JAXM clients that are connected to it to determine where to route the messages it receives. A provider cannot directly read these files—instead, they are read and a representation of their content is passed (in a private SOAP message header) when a client connects to the provider.* The sending servlet, which is not marked to be loaded at startup, initializes and connects to the provider when the request from the browser sent to the URL *http://localhost:8080/SOAPRPSender/request* is received by the web container; therefore, it is registered with the provider before a message addressed to it needs to be dispatched. However, since the receiving servlet's URL is only referenced when the provider tries to deliver a message to it based on an entry in the provider's client URI-to-URL mapping table, if the receiving servlet were not marked to be loaded at startup, it would not have initialized and connected to the provider, and therefore its URL would not be registered in this mapping table.

The SOAP-RP Profile

The SOAP-RP profile is an implementation of the SOAP WS-Routing specification (formerly known as the SOAP Routing Protocol), which can be downloaded from *http://msdn.microsoft.com/ws/2001/10/Routing*. Although a full discussion of the specification is outside the scope of this book, this section contains a brief overview and a description of the API that JAXM provides to allow the construction of messages that conform to the specification.

SOAP-RP Overview

SOAP-RP defines a SOAP header and a set of rules to be followed that enable a SOAP message to be routed from a sender, through zero or more intermediate systems to its final destination. The SOAP-RP header, which is called path, contains child elements from the set listed in Table 4-4.

Table 4-4. SOAP-RP header elements

Element	Description
to	Contains the URI of the ultimate destination of the message. This element is added by the sender and cannot be changed as the message passes through intermediate systems.
from	Contains a URI that identifies the sender of the message.

---

* Exactly when this happens is, of course, implementation-dependent. At the time of this writing, the reference implementation does this the first time the client requests ProviderMetaData, or when the ProviderConnection send() method is called for the first time. The fact that this is left so late also explains why a client that simply listens passively for messages, such as the receiving servlet in the example in this chapter, must call getMetaData( ) as shown in Example 4-4, even though it doesn't make use of the ProviderMetaData. The purpose of the call is simply to register the receiver's Endpoint with the provider so that it can receive messages.

Table 4-4. SOAP-RP header elements (continued)

Element	Description
fwd	If present, this tag contains zero or more URIs that define a list of intermediate systems that must be visited before the message is delivered to its final recipient. All of the systems in this list must be visited in the order in which they appear. If this is not possible, the message is discarded and a fault is returned (see the fault element).
	Each URI is enclosed in a child element called via. As each intermediate system is traversed, it removes its own via entry, which must be at the front of the list. Intermediate systems can add new via entries to the path as necessary, before forwarding.
rev	If present, this tag allows a reverse path to be created as the message traverses the route from sender to receiver. Each intermediate system that handles the message typically inserts its own URI as the first child of this element, in the form of a via tag, although it may insert the URI of some other system if that system would be a more appropriate hop in the return path.
	The final recipient of a SOAP message that contains a reverse path usually extracts it and stores it as the fwd element of the message that it sends in reply.
	The rev tag is inserted by the initial sender. If it is not present, it cannot be added by an intermediate system, and therefore a reverse path cannot be constructed.
action	Contains a URI that defines the intent of the message. Its meaning is private to the application and therefore there is no well-known set of permitted action values. This element must be set by the sender and cannot be modified by intermediate systems.
id	Contains a URI that uniquely identifies the message in which it is contained. The identifier is used to link a reply or a fault to the original message that caused it to be sent.
relatesTo	Contains the value of the id element for the message to which it is related. This element is used when returning a fault, or in an application-level reply to a message sent earlier.
fault	Used to report an error condition detected when trying to route or handle a SOAP-RP message. fault must be used in conjunction with relatesTo to indicate the message to which the fault applies.
	The reason for a fault is described by two child elements that must always be present. The code element contains a numeric code defined by the WS-Routing specification and is intended for application use. The reason element contains a textual description intended for logging or display. Depending on the fault code, other child elements may be present. Refer to the WS-Routing specification for details.

The path element and all of its child elements are defined in the namespace associated with the URI *http://schemas.xmlsoap.org/rp*.

In outline, here is how the SOAP-RP path header is used when routing a message:

1. The message originator constructs a path containing an id element to uniquely identify the message and an action element that specifies what the receiver should do with the message. It may also include a to element, a fwd element, a from element, and a rev element. If it is present, the to element indicates the URI of the intended recipient. The fwd element may contain an ordered set of URIs that determine the route to be taken to reach the recipient. If the header does not contain a to element, then the last entry in the fwd element must be the URI of the target system. A rev element is included only if a reverse path is to be created and would normally be empty.

2. The message originator sends the message to the first intermediary system.

3. The intermediate system looks for a via element in the fwd element of the path header of the received message. If such an element exists, it must contain the intermediate system's own URI; if it does not, a fault is generated and returned to the sender. Assuming that the via entry is valid, it is removed.

4. If the header contains a `fwd` entry, the intermediate system may introduce additional `via` entries in the message path if appropriate. This allows routing to proceed even if the message sender does not know the complete route to the destination when sending the message.

5. If the path header contains a `rev` element, the intermediate system may add a URI as its first child element to indicate a node on the reverse path for the message.

6. The intermediate system uses the first `via` entry of the `fwd` element as the URI for the next hop of the path. If there are no remaining `via` entries, the URI in the `to` element is used instead. If there is no `to` element, a fault is generated and returned to the sender.

7. When the message reaches its intended recipient, it should validate that its own URI is either in the `to` element or in the only remaining `via` entry of the `fwd` element. Failing this, a fault should be generated.

Should the receiver need to send a message back to the originator, it again includes a `path` header with `id` and `action` elements, together with a `relatesTo` element whose value is the URI from the `id` element of the original message. The `to`, `fwd`, `from`, and `rev` elements may also be included and are used as just described. If the original message contains a `rev` element, then its content *may* be used to create the `fwd` element of this message, but this is not mandatory.

For a definitive description of the message routing process, refer to the WS-Routing specification.

The JAXM SOAP-RP Message API

In order to create SOAP-RP messages, you need a `MessageFactory` that implements the SOAP-RP profile. As described earlier, once you have a `ProviderConnection` for a provider that supports this profile, you can obtain a suitable factory using the `createMessageFactory( )` method:

```
// Get a message factory for the SOAP-RP profile
MessageFactory msgFactory = conn.createMessageFactory("soaprp");
```

To arrange for the correct factory to be used when receiving SOAP-RP messages in the `onMessage( )` method of `JAXMServlet`, you must override its `init( )` method to install the same `MessageFactory`, as shown in Example 4-4.

All SOAP messages created using this factory are of type `com.sun.xml.messaging.soaprp.SOAPRPMessageImpl`. They have a minimal path header populated only with empty `fwd` and `rev` elements.* To include other elements or to add entries to the forward and reverse paths, you need to use convenience methods provided by the `SOAPRPMessageImpl` class, definitions of which you will find in the reference section of this book. A typical SOAP-RP message header is shown in Example 4-7, earlier in this chapter. The following sections cover some of the more important aspects of this API.

---

* In fact, this is not a good default. Ideally, `fwd` and `rev` elements are added only when specifically requested, since the absence of the `rev` element has a specific meaning. With the current implementation, it is not possible to create a path header without a `rev` element. This may change in the future, of course.

Getting and setting the message ID

The SOAP-RP specification requires that each message has a unique identifier that can be used to correlate it with either a fault or a reply. Fortunately, you don't have to generate these identifiers for yourself, since one is automatically created each time the factory returns a new SOAP-RP message. The getSOAPRPMessageId( ) method can be used to retrieve the identifier for a message. The most likely reason for calling this method is to use its return value to set the value of the relatesTo element when building a fault or reply message:

```
reply.setRelatesTo(request.getSOAPRPMessageId( ));
```

The API includes a method called newMessageId( ) that lets you set a new identifier for a message, but it is unlikely that you will need to use this because it is called for you when a SOAP-RP message is created.

Getting and updating the forward and reverse message paths

The forward and reverse message paths are held as Vectors containing Endpoint objects. You can retrieve the complete path and modify it directly using the getSOAPRPFwdMessagePath( ) and getSOAPRPRevMessagePath( ) methods. There are also slightly more abstract methods that let you update a path without having to fetch a complete copy of it:

```
public void updateFwdMessagePath(Endpoint uri, int position);
public void updateRevMessagePath(Endpoint uri);
```

The updateFwdMessagePath( ) method requires both the URI to be added and the position in the path at which it is to be inserted, where the value 0 indicates that the entry should be added at the front of the list. The updateRevMessagePath( ) method does not require a position index, since new elements in the reverse path are always added at the start of the list.

If you need to create a reply or generate a fault for a message, you might want to use the reverse path from the message as the forward path for the reply or the fault. To do this, use the getSOAPRPRevMessagePath( ) and updateFwdMessagePath( ) methods together:

```
Vector revPath = soapMsg.getSOAPRPRevMessagePath( );
int count = revPath.size( );
for (int i = 0; i < count; i++) {
    replyMsg.updateFwdMessagePath((Endpoint)revPath.get(i), i);
}
```

 At the time of this writing, there is a problem with the reference implementation of the SOAP-RP profile that causes the forward path to be ignored. The specification requires that the to element of the SOAP-RP header contains the URI of the final destination and that the first via child of the fwd element indicates the URI of the first intermediate system. Unfortunately, the reference implementation currently *always* sends the message to the system whose URI is in the to element, rather than using the forward path, if there is one.

Fault handling

Fault information is included using the `fault` element, which is a direct child of the path header. Unfortunately, the reference implementation does not provide any API for accessing this information or creating it if it is not already present. Therefore, if you want to add fault information to a new message or extract it from a message that you have received, you must do so by directly accessing the path header, and using the usual SAAJ APIs to add or locate the `fault` element. Here's how you might locate the path header for a message:

```
final String SOAPRP_URI = "http://schemas.xmlsoap.org/rp";
message.addHeaders();
SOAPHeader header = message.getSOAPPart().getEnvelope().getHeader();
Iterator iter = header.getChildElements();
while (iter.hasNext()) {
    SOAPElement elem = (SOAPElement)iter.next();
    Name name = elem.getElementName();

    // Compare both the local name and the namespace URI
    if (name.getLocalName().equalsIgnoreCase("path") &&
            name.getURI().equals(SOAPRP_URI)) {
        // "elem" is the path header element.

    }
}
```

When adding fault information to a newly created message, you should call the `addHeaders()` method as shown in this code extract before searching for the path element, since the header is not actually created until this method is invoked. This is not necessary in the case of a message received in the `onMessage()` method of a servlet, since the headers are created automatically as part of the process of converting the received XML to a `SOAPMessage`.

The ebXML Profile

The ebXML initiative aims to create a framework for applications that allow organizations to carry out electronic business by exchanging XML-based messages. The ebXML Transport, Routing, and Packaging (ebXML-TRP) specification (lcoated at *http://www.ebxml.org/specs/ebMS.pdf*) defines the packaging model for ebXML messages, which is based on SOAP with attachments and is therefore compatible with both SAAJ and JAXM. This section briefly describes the ebXML packaging model and looks at how it is supported by the JAXM ebXML profile. The ebXML profile implements Version 1.0 of the ebXML-TRP specification.

Overview of the ebXML Packaging Model

Like WS-Routing, ebXML-TRP uses SOAP headers to carry protocol information. Unlike WS-Routing, however, ebXML-TRP also defines elements that may be added to the SOAP message body. Many of the features described in the ebXML-TRP specification are optional, so we'll restrict ourselves to briefly discussing just the mandatory parts of the specification, which are the only parts actually provided in the JAXM reference implementation. For a definitive description, refer to the ebXML-TRP specification itself.

ebXML-TRP considers a SOAP message to be made up of two separate parts:

The header container
> Despite its name, the header container corresponds to the entire SOAP part of the message and therefore consists of both the SOAP header and the SOAP body. The specification defines six elements that may appear in the header, and four that can be used in the message body. The JAXM ebXML profile supports only one header element and one body element, since the others are optional.

Payload containers
> An ebXML-TRP message may have zero or more payload containers that carry information that supplements the XML in the header container. Each payload container is realized as a SOAP message attachment; therefore, it can carry data of any type that has a MIME representation, such as an image or an XML document. Since SAAJ already provides the ability to add attachments to a message, no additional API is required in the ebXML profile to handle payload containers. However, the application must ensure that each payload container in the message has a corresponding reference in the ebXML-TRP `Manifest` element in the body of the header container, as described shortly.

All ebXML-TRP elements and attributes are in the namespace identified by the URI *http://www.ebxml.org/namespaces/messageHeader*.

The MessageHeader Element

The `MessageHeader` element must appear in the header container of every ebXML-TRP message. The specification defines 10 child elements for this header, of which only the 7 listed in Table 4-5 are supported by the ebXML profile.

Table 4-5. MessageHeader elements supported by the ebXML profile

Element	Description
CPAId	A string that identifies in some way that is known to the application the terms of the agreement entered into between the parties to the message exchange. ebXML defines the concept of a *Collaboration Profile Agreement* (CPA) that encompasses these terms. The CPAId is typically a URI that refers to such a CPA.
ConversationId	A unique, application-defined identifier that is attached to each of the messages that make up a single conversation. What consititutes a conversation is, of course, application-dependent.
Service	Specifies the service supplied by the message receiver that should act upon the message. A service is identified by a combination of a type and a value, in which the type defaults to URI to indicate that the value is itself a URI. Other types may be defined for private use by applications. A typical service description, encoded as a URI, might be *urn:services:OrderProcessing*.

Element	Description
`Action`	Qualifies the service description by specifying the action to be performed by the target service on receipt of the message. This element is simply a string defined by the service, such as `PlaceOrder`.
`To`	Identifies the intended recipient of the message. A message may have multiple recipients, each of which has a corresponding child element of type `Party`. The value of the `Party` element is the recipient's address, which is typically a URI, but may be a different style of address by prior agreement between the sender and the receiver. If the address is not a URI, then its actual type must be specified using the `type` attribute of the `Party` element.
`From`	Identifies the message sender. As with the `To` element, the sender's address is supplied in the form of a `Party` element.
`MessageData`	Contains child elements that allow an individual message to be uniquely identified. The reference implementation supports only the following three child elements: • `MessageId`, which provides a unique identifier for the message, chosen by the sender. This is similar to the `id` element of a SOAP-RP header. • `Timestamp`, which records the time at which the message was constructed. • `RefToMessageId`, which is used to correlate this message to one sent earlier by specifying the value of its `MessageId` element. This is similar to the `relatesTo` element of a SOAP-RP header. The `TimeToLive` element is not supported.

The optional `SequenceNumber`, `Description`, and `QualityOfServiceInfo` elements of `MessageHeader` are not implemented in the ebXML profile; neither are the `TraceHeaderList`, `ErrorList`, `Signature`, `Acknowledgement`, and `Via` header elements.

The Manifest Element

The `Manifest` element appears in the body of the SOAP message. It consists of one or more child elements of type `Reference` that describe payload objects that appear in the body of the message in a payload container or as external resources, such as documents on the Internet.* A `Manifest` element is required only if there is payload to be referenced.

A typical `Manifest` element looks like the following, in which the namespace prefix eb is assumed to be mapped to the ebXML-TRP namespace URI:

```
<eb:Manifest eb:id="payload01"
        xlink:type="simple"
        xlink:href="cid:attachment-01"
        xlink:role="urn:purchaseOrder">
```

The attributes are used as described in Table 4-6.

---

* Although the SOAP body *may* contain payload elements, the specification recommends that this not be done.

Table 4-6. Attributes used with the Manifest element

Attribute	Description
eb:id	This is a standard id attribute that can be used to refer to the element from elsewhere in the message. This attribute is optional.
xlink:type and xlink:href	These attributes together constitute a simple link to the payload content, as described by the XML XLink specification (a description of which can be found in *XML in a Nutshell*, by Elliotte Rusty Harold and W. Scott Means (O'Reilly). The xlink:type attribute always has the value simple, which means that the xlink:href attribute is a URI. There are three cases to be distinguished: • If the payload is contained within the header container (possible, but not recommended), the href attribute refers to the id attribute of the top-level XML element that represents the payload. A typical example is xlink:href="#ID1". • If the payload is in the payload container (i.e., it is in a SOAP attachment), then the href attribute must reference the Content-Id MIME header of the payload attachment, in the same way as described in connection with the SAAJ SOAP with Attachments API in Chapter 3. A typical example of this is xlink:href="cid:attachment-01", which refers to an attachment for which the Content-Id header has the value attachment-01. • The payload may also be an external resource that is not included in the message. In this case, the href is a URI that points to that resource, an example of which is xlink:href="http://www.ora.com".
xlink:role	An optional attribute that identifies the type or use of the payload in some way that has meaning to the application. Like href, this must be a valid URI formed according to the XML XLink specification.

A Reference element may also have the following child elements:

- A Schema element that refers to a schema document (typically an XML-Schema document) that describes the content of the payload. This element is required only for structured content (such as XML) that can be described in this way, and is not included for images or other binary payloads.

- Zero or more Description elements that contain a textual description of the payload. This element has an attribute called lang that specifies the language in which the text is written. If more than one Description element is present, typically to provide the same information in more than one language, then each should have a lang attribute with an appropriate value.

An Example ebXML-TRP Message

The sample code for this book includes a pair of web services that send and echo an ebXML-TRP message in the same way as the SOAP-RP message echoing example that was described earlier in this chapter. In order to run these examples, start the Tomcat web server and deploy them both as follows:

1. Change your working directory to *chapter4\ebXMLecho* relative to the installation directory of the example source code.

2. Type the command ant deploy.

3. Change your working directory to *chapter4\ebXMLsender* relative to the installation directory of the example source code.

4. Type the command ant deploy.

Next, you need to configure the JAXM provider so that it knows how to route messages to these web services. Using a browser, connect to the JAXM provider administration web page (at *http://localhost:8081/jaxm-provideradmin*), select the HTTP protocol under the ebXML profile, add the mappings shown in Table 4-7, and press "Save to Profile".

Table 4-7. URI mappings for the JAXM ebXML profile example

URI	Target URL
urn:ebXMLEcho	http://localhost:8081/jaxm-provider/receiver/ebxml
urn:ebXMLSender	http://localhost:8081/jaxm-provider/receiver/ebxml

Note that the last component of these URLs is *ebxml* rather than *soaprp*, since the messages need to be directed to the provider's received message queues for ebXML messages.

To run the example, point your web browser at the URL *http://localhost:8080/ ebXMLSender/request*. After a short delay, you should see the message that was transmitted by and returned to the sender, which is shown in Example 4-8.

Example 4-8. An ebXML message created using the JAXM ebXML profile

```
<?xml version="1.0" encoding="UTF-8"?>
<soap-env:Envelope xmlns:soap-env="http://schemas.xmlsoap.org/soap/envelope/">
    <soap-env:Header>
        <eb:MessageHeader xmlns:eb=
            "http://www.ebxml.org/namespaces/messageHeader" eb:version="1.0"
            soap-env:mustUnderstand="1">
            <eb:From>
                <eb:PartyId eb:type="URI">urn:ebXMLEcho</eb:PartyId>
            </eb:From>
            <eb:To>
                <eb:PartyId eb:type="URI">urn:ebXMLSender</eb:PartyId>
            </eb:To>
            <eb:CPAId>urn:EchoCollaborationAgreement</eb:CPAId>
            <eb:ConversationId>1</eb:ConversationId>
            <eb:Service eb:type="URI">urn:ECHOSERVICE</eb:Service>
            <eb:Action>ECHO</eb:Action>
            <eb:MessageData>
                <eb:MessageId>7b683c87-3d44-4135-b397-ef436d1437aa</eb:MessageId>
                <eb:RefToMessageId>0c3e1841-29bb-4c6c-bc3f-d4b419846b26
                </eb:RefToMessageId>
                <eb:Timestamp>1030880701373</eb:Timestamp>
            </eb:MessageData>
        </eb:MessageHeader>
    </soap-env:Header>
    <soap-env:Body>
        <tns:Sent xmlns:tns="urn:ebXMLSender">This is the content</tns:Sent>
        <eb:Manifest xmlns:eb="http://www.ebxml.org/namespaces/messageHeader"
                                     eb:id="ID1" eb:version="1.0">
            <eb:Reference eb:id="ID2" xmlns:xlink="http://www.w3.org/1999/xlink"
                                     xlink:href="http://www.ora.com">
                <eb:Description xml:lang="en">O'Reilly Home Page</eb:Description>
            </eb:Reference>
            <eb:Reference eb:id="ID3" xmlns:xlink="http://www.w3.org/1999/xlink"
                    xlink:href="http://www.amazon.com">
                <eb:Description xml:lang="en">Online bookstore</eb:Description>
            </eb:Reference>
        </eb:Manifest>
    </soap-env:Body>
```

Example 4-8. An ebXML message created using the JAXM ebXML profile (continued)

```
    <tns:Date xmlns:tns="urn:ebXMLEcho">Sun Sep 01 12:45:01 BST 2002</tns:Date>
</soap-env:Envelope>
```

The code that was used to create this message will be shown in the next section. For now, note the content of the `MessageHeader` element in the SOAP header and the `Manifest` element in the body, which refers to two payloads that are Internet resources and are therefore not included as part of the message itself.

The JAXM ebXML Message API

To use the ebXML profile, you first need to get a `MessageFactory` that can create ebXML messages. Having done this, you can then call the `createMessage()` method to get such a message. The code that creates the message just shown can be found in Example 4-9.

Example 4-9. Using the JAXM API to create an ebXML message

```
MessageFactory msgFactory = conn.createMessageFactory("ebxml");
EbXMLMessageImpl message = (EbXMLMessageImpl)msgFactory.createMessage();

// Set attributes held in the MessageHeader
message.setAction("ECHO");
message.setService(new Service("urn:ECHOSERVICE", "URI"));
message.setCPAId("urn:EchoCollaborationAgreement");
message.setConversationId("1");

// Set the sending and receiving parties.
message.setReceiver(new Party("urn:ebXMLEcho"));
message.setSender(new Party("urn:ebXMLSender"));

// Add a Manifest with two references to external locations
Manifest manifest = new Manifest("ID1", "1.0");
Reference ref = new Reference("ID2", "http://www.ora.com", null);
Description desc = new Description("en");
desc.setText("O'Reilly Home Page");
ref.setDescription(desc);
manifest.addReference(ref);

ref = new Reference("ID3", "http://www.amazon.com", null);
desc = new Description("en");
desc.setText("Online bookstore");
ref.setDescription(desc);
manifest.addReference(ref);

message.setManifest(manifest);
```

The message that the `createMessage()` method returns is of type `com.sun.xml.messaging.jaxm.ebxml.EbXMLMessageImpl`.[*] To use the convenience methods provided by the API, cast the method's return value to this type.

---

[*] Note the spelling of the last component of this name—the second character is a lowercase "b".

The ebXML MessageHeader element

The first section of code sets the values of child elements that appear in the ebXML MessageHeader element, which will be created in the SOAP message header. This element is mandatory and therefore it is always present. The specification requires that all of the child elements listed in Table 4-5 must appear in an ebXML message; it is your responsibility to ensure that valid values are supplied for them. Elements for which you do not supply values will not be included in the MessageHeader, which may cause the receiver to reject the message. Table 4-8 briefly describes the values that need to be supplied as arguments to the EbXMLMessageImpl methods that install these elements. In some cases, the arguments are instances of other classes that are also part of the com.sun.xml. messaging.jaxm.ebxml package. Documentation for these simple classes can be found in the reference section of this book.

Table 4-8. Arguments supplied to convenience methods for the ebXML MessageHeader element

Method	Argument
setAction( )	A string, the value of which is defined by the target service.
setService( )	A Service object. This object has two attributes: a type and an identifier, which are both supplied as strings. By default, the type attribute is assumed to be URI. However, you should explicitly set this value because the reference implementation transmits the type as an empty string if you do not, which may cause interoperability problems. The target service defines the set of type and identifier values that it understands.
setCPAId( )	A string value, determined (in advance) by agreement between the sender and receiver.
setConversationId( )	A string value that uniquely identifies a related set of messages.
setSender( ) and setReceiver( )	These methods set to To and From elements, respectively. They each require an argument of type Party, which, like Service, has both a type and an identifier. The default for the type attribute is URI; in this case, the reference implementation handles this default properly; therefore, there is no need to supply it explicitly. In the example used in this chapter, the identifier is the URI of the message sender or receiver, and is the key used by the provider to route the message.

There are a couple of points to note regarding the handling of the To and From elements in the reference implementation:

1. While the specification allows either of these elements to contain one or more nested Party elements, at the time of this writing the implementation supports only one. Therefore, you cannot address a message to more than one recipient.

2. Despite the fact that the elements are called To and From, the methods that set them are setReceiver( ) and setSender( ), respectively. This is because the superclass of EbXMLMessageImpl defines the setTo( ) and setFrom( ) methods to have arguments of type Endpoint, while application code more naturally deals with objects of type Party. When transmitting a message, the provider needs an Endpoint and therefore uses the getTo( ) method to obtain the target address. This method gets the Party object set by setReceiver( ), extracts the identifier part, and then uses it to create the corresponding Endpoint object.

You'll note that the code in Example 4-9 does not explicitly set any values for the MessageData element. Nevertheless, this element appears in the message because the timestamp and a unique message identifier are installed automatically by the MessageFactory. In the case of a reply message, the RefToMessageId element must be set to the unique identifier of the message to which it relates. This is not done automatically, but you can set it using the same technique used for the SOAP-RP relatesTo element:

```
// Get the message ID and install it as the "RefToMessageId" value
replyMsg.setRefToMessageId(soapMsg.getMessageId());
```

The ebXML Manifest element

If an ebXML message has any kind of payload, its body must include a Manifest element with one Reference element for each item of payload. These elements are represented in the ebXML message API by the Manifest and Reference classes, respectively.

Manifest is a simple class that is constructed with an XML ID (used to refer to it from elsewhere in the message, if required) and a version number, which must be the version number of the ebXML-TRP specification to which the overall message conforms (in this case, "1.0"). The specification requires that a valid XML ID be provided. The implementation, however, does not prevent the use of null for this attribute, which would result in the creation of a message that is technically not valid. Once you have a Manifest object, you can use its addReference() method to add any number of payload references. The code shown in Example 4-9 installs two references, both to external data that is not actually part of the message itself.

To construct a Reference object, you need to supply an XML ID and appropriate values for its role and href attributes. In order to construct a valid message, an appropriate id and href must be supplied, but the role attribute may be null if appropriate. Following construction, you can associate a Schema and/or a Description with the Reference object using the setSchema() and setDescription() methods, respectively. There are two items to note regarding these methods:

- The setSchema() method requires an argument of type Schema. Schema is a simple container class that is constructed from the URI that defines the schema and the schema version number.

- The setDescription() method uses an argument of type Description. The constructor of the Description class requires a string that specifies the language for the associated text (such as en, en_US, en_GB, etc.), whereas the text itself is added using the setText() method. Although the ebXML-TRP specification allows a Reference element to be associated with any number of descriptions, the reference implementation allows only zero or one.

5

WSDL

In Chapter 2, you saw how simple it is to create a web service using JAX-RPC by starting with a service definition in the form of a Java interface. Given such definitions and a configuration file, the wscompile and wsdeploy utilities can generate the Java code necessary to link both the client and server implementations to the underlying JAX-RPC infrastructure that ultimately creates or consumes SOAP messages. Although this is convenient for Java developers, it is not really acceptable to describe web services—which are supposed to be platform- and language-independent—using the type definition system of a programming language. The JAX-RPC book service created in Chapter 2, for example, uses a command-line client written in Java. In the real world, the client might instead need to be written in VB.NET, C#, or C++, or somebody might want to take the service definition and create an alternative server-side implementation on a different platform, such as Microsoft's .NET. In both of these cases, having the service defined in terms of Java interfaces is not particularly helpful.

The Web Service Description Language (WSDL) is an XML vocabulary that can be used to describe web services in both a platform- and programming language–neutral fashion. Web services defined by WSDL documents are published in a registry. Programmers can then either create their own implementations of these services, or develop clients to consume them by obtaining the WSDL definition and interpreting it in terms of the programming language of their choice. This task is made easier by the availability of tools that can parse WSDL and automatically generate the code necessary to build and decode the SOAP messages used by a web service, thereby freeing developers to concentrate on the business rules of the application instead of the network-level plumbing. In this chapter, we take a brief look at the structure of a WSDL document, and in Chapter 6, you'll see how to use JAX-RPC to implement a web service given a WSDL definition.

This chapter covers WSDL Version 1.1, the specification for which can be downloaded from *http://www.w3.org/TR/wsdl*. WSDL 1.1 was submitted by IBM,

Microsoft, and Ariba and is widely used, but it is not a W3C standard. At the time of the writing, W3C is defining a new version of WSDL that will eventually become the endorsed standard.

WSDL Overview

A WSDL document describes a web service in terms of the operations that it provides and the data types that each operation requires as inputs and can return in the form of results. It is important to note that WSDL itself does not make any assumptions about the way in which the service is provided at the protocol level. Instead, the service is first defined in abstract terms and then mapped onto one or more specific protocols by the use of bindings. A *binding* specifies how each of the inputs and outputs for each operation are mapped onto a protocol (such as SOAP). A WSDL file may also contain a set of addresses at which a bound service can be accessed.

The logical structure of a WSDL file is shown in Example 5-1.

Example 5-1. Logical structure of a WSDL file

```
<wsdl:definitions ....>

    <!-- Import definitions from external sources -->
    <wsdl:import ..../>

    <!-- Definitions of types used only in this WSDL file -->
    <wsdl:types ..../>

    <!-- Definitions of messages for this web service -->
    <wsdl:message .../>

    <!-- Definitions of the interfaces and operations provided by the service -->
    <wsdl:portType .../>

    <!-- Concrete bindings of interfaces and operations to protocols -->
    <wsdl:binding ..../>

    <!-- Defines the service as a collection of interfaces and supplies the
         protocol address -->
    <wsdl:service ..../>

</wsdl:definitions>
```

The order of child elements shown here is a natural one that reflects a progression from most abstract at the beginning to most concrete at the end. It also approximately matches the order in which we discuss the elements in this chapter and is the only order strictly permitted by the schema document for WSDL, which can be obtained from *http://schemas.xmlsoap.org/wsdl*, a URL that also defines the namespace for WSDL elements.

Any WSDL element can contain a single documentation element with arbitrary content that can be used to add descriptive text to it for the benefit of implementors of the service itself or of clients that will use the service. The use of documentation elements is preferred over XML comments because XML parsers are not required to pass XML comments to application code.[*] Here's a trivial example of the use of a documentation element:

```
<wsdl:types>
    <wsdl:documentation>
        This section defines the data types used by this service.
    </wsdl:documentation>
    <!-- Type definitions would be added here -->
</wsdl:types>
```

Each element can also contain any number of other elements that are not defined by the generic part of the WSDL specification. This feature allows the use of *extensibility elements*, which contain information relevant to particular bindings of a service to an underlying protocol. For example, the binding section is typically composed of extensibility elements that describe how to map the service onto SOAP messages. There are also extensibility elements that can be used to map a simple web service onto HTTP GET and POST messages, and another set of elements that describe web service messages that contain data that is represented using a MIME encoding. Each of these sets of elements is defined by its own XML schema, which is also used as the namespace for those elements, as shown in Table 5-1.

Table 5-1. Schemas and namespaces commonly used in WSDL documents

Element type	Schema location and namespace URI
Generic WSDL elements	*http://schemas.xmlsoap.org/wsdl*
Elements for the SOAP binding	*http://schemas.xmlsoap.org/wsdl/soap*
Elements for the HTTP binding	*http://schemas.xmlsoap.org/wsdl/http*
Elements for the MIME binding	*http://schemas.xmlsoap.org/wsdl/mime*

Aside from documentation, the top-level elements that may appear in a WSDL file are as follows:

import

> Allows parts of a web service definition to be spread over multiple files and then imported as required. Use of this technique is recommended, in order to allow different web services to share the same data types or to separate the definition of a web service and its protocol bindings from the elements that provide the address of a server that offers the service. See "Using the import Element" at the end of this chapter for some examples of this.

types

> Defines the data types used by the web service. See "Type Definitions" later in this chapter for details.

---

[*] At the time of this writing, application code that needs to parse or manipulate WSDL must do so by using a DOM or SAX parser or a third-party class library. However, a standardized Java API called JWSDL that provides a higher-level interface to a WSDL document is currently being developed by the JSR 110 expert group. See *http://jcp.org/jsr/detail/110.jsp* for details.

message
> These elements describe the data that is exchanged between the web service and its clients in terms of the data types defined within the type elements. In concrete terms, each message defined here corresponds to a SOAP message when SOAP is used as the underlying communications mechanism.

portType
> Defines the operations that a web service provides. A port type is the WSDL equivalent of a service endpoint interface, as described in Chapter 2.

binding
> Describes how the operations and messages defined by the message and portType elements are mapped onto their concrete representations when a specific transport mechanism is used. WSDL defines extensions that allow the description of bindings to SOAP with attachments and to HTTP.

port
> Gives the address at which a binding of a portType can be found. Port addresses are used by clients to connect to the web service.

service
> Groups related ports together and thereby represents an entire web service.

WSDL Elements

In this section, we take a closer look at each of the WSDL elements. To illustrate the discussion, we'll use examples from the WSDL document that describe the JAX-RPC book service that you saw in Chapter 2. That particular web service was developed by starting with Java interface definitions, rather than from a WSDL file. If you already have a distributed application written in Java (perhaps using RMI) that you need to convert to a web service, this is the natural path to follow. However, in order to make the service generally available, you must create and publish a WSDL document. Fortunately, the wsdeploy utility provided with the JAX-RPC reference implementation generates a WSDL file from the information provided in its *jaxrpc-ri.xml* file together with the class files for the Java interfaces, thus saving you the trouble of trying to build one manually.

 As described in Chapter 2, the wsdeploy utility creates the WSDL document for a web service while constructing a deployable web archive from a portable WAR file. If you just want to see what the WSDL document corresponding to a Java interface definition looks like, you can use the wscompile utility to generate it without having to first create a portable WAR file. See Chapter 8 for a description of how this can be done.

The WSDL file for the JAX-RPC book service, which is called *BookQuery.wsdl*, can be found in the web archive at *chapter2\bookservice\Books.war* relative to the installation directory for this book's example source code. If this file is missing, you can recreate it by making *chapter2\bookservice* your working directory and typing the command:

```
ant web-package
```

Throughout this chapter, we'll show extracts from this file, slightly reformatted for better readability. A complete listing can be found in the Appendix.

Although it is very likely that the majority of WSDL files will be both created and consumed by software tools, it is still extremely useful to be able to read and understand a WSDL document so that you can see the operations provided by a web service that you need to interact with before using the stub and tie code (created by tools like `wscompile` and `wsdeploy`) to create a client for the service or to create your own implementation of it.

The WSDL definitions Element

The root element of every WSDL file must be a `definitions` element, which has two attributes:

name
> The WSDL specification describes this attribute as lightweight documentation for the content of the file. It is typically not used by software that parses WSDL files with the intent of generating code. In particular, this attribute does not provide the name of the web service, which is obtained instead from the `service` element.

targetNamespace
> The value of this attribute is a URI that becomes the XML namespace for the elements used to describe the services, ports, messages, and bindings defined in the file. It is not necessary (or possible) to explicitly state the namespace when declaring these objects, because they will automatically be associated with the target namespace.

As a typical example, the `definitions` element from the WSDL file generated for the book service is shown in Example 5-2.

Example 5-2. A typical WSDL definitions element

```
<?xml version="1.0" encoding="UTF-8"?>

<definitions name="BookService"
        targetNamespace="urn:jwsnut.chapter2.bookservice/wsdl/BookQuery"
        xmlns:tns="urn:jwsnut.chapter2.bookservice/wsdl/BookQuery"
        xmlns="http://schemas.xmlsoap.org/wsdl/"
        xmlns:soap="http://schemas.xmlsoap.org/wsdl/soap/"
        xmlns:xsd="http://www.w3.org/2001/XMLSchema"
        xmlns:ns2="urn:jwsnut.chapter2.bookservice/types/BookQuery"
        xmlns:ns3="http://java.sun.com/jax-rpc-ri/internal">

  <!-- All nested elements omitted -->

</definitions>
```

Here, the target namespace is urn:jwsnut.chapter.bookservice/wsdl/BookQuery, which is also associated with the namespace prefix tns so that it can be conveniently referred to throughout the file. In the case of a WSDL file generated by `wsdeploy`, the URL from this namespace is obtained by combining the typeNamespaceBase attribute of the webServices element in the *jaxrpc-ri.xml* file, and the name attribute of the endpoint element for the service in the same file, as described in "JWSDP configuration files and XML namespaces" in Chapter 2. Prefixes for other namespaces that will be referenced are also typically defined within this element. The default namespace in this example, as in most WSDL files, is the namespace associated with WSDL itself rather than the target namespace, since most of the elements in the document will be WSDL elements.

Type Definitions

The data types that are used in the messages exchanged by a web service and its clients are defined using the WSDL types element, and are referenced from the message elements that will be described later in this chapter.* The schema document for WSDL allows this element to contain arbitrary content, although in practice it will contain type definitions described using a schema language, plus an optional documentation element. The WSDL specification recommends the use of XML schema as the preferred schema language, and existing software tools that parse WSDL, including wscompile, currently expect to find XML schema elements here.

If you intend to manually build WSDL documents, you need a good understanding of XML schema to create the content of the types element. XML schema is a large and complex subject that is well beyond the scope of this book but is fully covered in Eric van der Vlist's book, *XML Schema* (O'Reilly). Fortunately, XML schemas are slightly easier to read than they are to write, as you can see from Example 5-3, which shows the types element in the WSDL document generated by wsdeploy for the book web service.

Example 5-3. Type definitions from the book service WSDL file

```
<types>
    <schema targetNamespace="urn:jwsnut.chapter2.bookservice/types/BookQuery"
            xmlns:xsi="http://www.w3.org/2001/XMLSchema-instance"
            xmlns:tns="urn:jwsnut.chapter2.bookservice/types/BookQuery"
            xmlns:soap-enc="http://schemas.xmlsoap.org/soap/encoding/"
            xmlns:wsdl="http://schemas.xmlsoap.org/wsdl/"
            xmlns="http://www.w3.org/2001/XMLSchema">
        <complexType name="ArrayOfBookInfo">
          <complexContent>
            <restriction base="soap-enc:Array">
              <attribute ref="soap-enc:arrayType" wsdl:arrayType="tns:BookInfo[]"/>
            </restriction>
          </complexContent>
        </complexType>
        <complexType name="BookInfo">
          <sequence>
            <element name="editor" type="string"/>
```

---

* It is possible to use type definitions found in external schema documents instead of (or as well as) defining types within the WSDL document itself. See "Using the import Element" at the end of this chapter for details.

```
        <element name="author" type="string"/>
        <element name="price" type="double"/>
        <element name="title" type="string"/>
      </sequence>
    </complexType>
    <complexType name="BookServiceException">
      <sequence>
        <element name="message" type="string"/>
      </sequence>
    </complexType>
  </schema>

  <schema targetNamespace="http://java.sun.com/jax-rpc-ri/internal"
        xmlns:xsi="http://www.w3.org/2001/XMLSchema-instance"
        xmlns:tns="http://java.sun.com/jax-rpc-ri/internal"
        xmlns:soap-enc="http://schemas.xmlsoap.org/soap/encoding/"
        xmlns:wsdl="http://schemas.xmlsoap.org/wsdl/"
        xmlns="http://www.w3.org/2001/XMLSchema">
    <complexType name="hashMap">
      <complexContent>
        <extension base="tns:map">
          <sequence/>
        </extension>
      </complexContent>
    </complexType>
    <complexType name="map">
      <complexContent>
        <restriction base="soap-enc:Array">
          <attribute ref="soap-enc:arrayType" wsdl:arrayType="tns:mapEntry[]"/>
        </restriction>
      </complexContent>
    </complexType>
    <complexType name="mapEntry">
      <sequence>
        <element name="key" type="anyType"/>
        <element name="value" type="anyType"/>
      </sequence>
    </complexType>
  </schema>
</types>
```

The first thing to note is that there are two XML schema declarations here. This is necessary because they are declaring types within different namespaces (as defined by the targetNamespace attribute), and a single schema element can only refer to one namespace. The first schema contains the data types that appear in the Java interface definitions for the book web service, whereas the second is added by wsdeploy to allow the use of HashMap as a method return value.

The namespace for the first schema is obtained by combining the typeNamespaceBase attribute of the webServices element in the *jaxrpc-ri.xml* file supplied to wsdeploy with the name attribute of the endpoint element in the same file. It is good practice to use separate namespaces for the type definitions and the

WSDL

definitions of the messages, port types, etc. that also appear in the WSDL document, which you can achieve by supplying different values for the typeNamespaceBase and targetNamespaceBase attributes of the webServices element. It is permissible, as shown here, to have more than one namespace within the type element.

For reference, here is the definition of the remote interface supported by the book web service, from which the WSDL document was generated:

```
public interface BookQuery extends Remote {
    public abstract int getBookCount( ) throws RemoteException;
    public abstract String getAuthor(String name) throws RemoteException;
    public abstract String getEditor(String name) throws RemoteException;
    public abstract double getPrice(String name)
        throws BookServiceException,RemoteException;
    public abstract BookInfo[] getBookInfo( ) throws RemoteException;
    public abstract HashMap getBookMap( ) throws RemoteException;
}
```

Most of the methods in this interface have arguments and return values that are either Java primitives or of type String. These types do not require definitions in the type section, because they can be represented directly by predefined XML schema elements such as xsd:int and xsd:string. Therefore, the schema section for the book web service declares a type for the BookServiceException class, the BookInfo class, and another that represents an array of BookInfo objects.* Data types can be defined as abstract types, using the XML schema complexType and simpleType elements, or they can be defined as elements that are either instances of predefined types or custom types, possibly with restrictions or extensions added. We'll examine these two possibilities separately.

Use of XML schema complexType and simpleType elements

Without delving too deeply into XML schema, it should be obvious that the following extract from the schema definitions shown in Example 5-3 declares a type called BookInfo that has four fields, three that contain strings and another that holds a double:

```
<complexType name="BookInfo">
  <sequence>
    <element name="editor" type="string"/>
    <element name="author" type="string"/>
    <element name="price" type="double"/>
    <element name="title" type="string"/>
  </sequence>
</complexType>
```

The name used to declare a type, in this case BookInfo, cannot be explicitly namespace-qualified. It is automatically assigned to the targetNamespace of the enclosing schema element, which is urn:jwsnut.chapter2.bookservice/types/BookQuery. The attributes of the schema element also associate this namespace with

---

* The schema section does not include a declaration for HashMap, since this type is not defined by the book web service—it is provided by the JAX-RPC reference implementation and is actually defined in the second schema section in the WSDL file.

the prefix tns (see Example 5-3) so that the fully qualified name of the BookInfo type can be used in the schema definition for an array of BookInfo objects:

```
<complexType name="ArrayOfBookInfo">
  <complexContent>
    <restriction base="soap-enc:Array">
      <attribute ref="soap-enc:arrayType"
                 wsdl:arrayType="tns:BookInfo[]"/>
    </restriction>
  </complexContent>
</complexType>
```

Without the explicit namespace qualifier, BookInfo would be incorrectly taken as a name in the XML schema namespace.

A type that represents an array of objects of type Foo is usually given the name ArrayOfFoo. This convention is suggested in the WSDL specification and is honored by wsdeploy. In the rather terse definition just shown, the restriction element together with its base attribute specify that an ArrayOfBookInfo type is an Array, as defined by the SOAP specification (and described in Chapter 3), in which the arrayType attribute has the value tns:BookInfo[]. In other words, the array may contain an unspecified number of BookInfo objects.

The type declarations in a WSDL document describe the data only in abstract terms, so it does not follow that the actual representation of this array within a message sent or received by participants in the book web service will necessarily be as a SOAP Array element. The mapping from the abstract description to a concrete representation for each message appears in the bindings section, which is described later in this chapter. Of course, when the service is bound to SOAP messaging, it is natural for the bindings to require the use of SOAP section 5 encoding rules and result in an object of type ArrayOfBookInfo being encoded as a SOAP Array element.

The second schema element in Example 5-3 is generated as a result of the use of a HashMap as the return value of the getBookMap( ) method in the BookQuery interface. The schema essentially defines a new type called hashMap, which extends a private type called map and consists of an array of key/value pairs in which both the key and the value are described by the XML schema type anyType. This type should be used wherever an object of any kind is valid—in other words, wherever you would use java.lang.Object in a Java method definition. Both hashMap and map appear in the private namespace *http://java.sun.com/jax-rpc-ri/internal,* which is not likely to be understood by non-JAX-RPC implementations; therefore, the use of HashMap (or any of the Java collection classes) may lead to interoperability issues with web service platforms that are not based on the JAX-RPC reference implementation.[*]

---

[*] As a side issue, it might have been better if the namespace *http://java.sun.com/jax-rpc-ri/internal* contained schema definitions for the Java collection classes so that this extra schema element did not need to be added to the WSDL file by wsdeploy. This would not, of course, remove the interoperability problem, but it would simplify the WSDL document a little.

The complexType element is used to define a type that can contain other objects, such as the BookInfo object or the ArrayOfBookInfo array. A simpleType element, by contrast, declares a type that does not contain any other objects, such as integers and strings. It is not necessary to define new types in cases where the object can be represented directly using an XML schema primitive type. However, the simpleType element can be used to qualify the use of another simple type by applying restrictions to it. For example, consider the following:

```
<simpleType name="BookType">
    <restriction base="string">
        <enumeration value="paperback"/>
        <enumeration value="hardback"/>
    </restriction>
</simpleType>
```

This schema extract defines a simple type called BookType that must have a string value that is either "paperback" or "hardback". Note, however, that while this constraint is useful as documentation for a human reader, it is not guaranteed that automatically generated code will check that BookType values received in messages actually satisfy the constraint.

For further information on the XML scheme complexType and simpleType elements, see *XML Schema*, by Eric van der Vlist.

Use of XML schema element element

The complexType and simpleType elements define data types, not actual data elements. The distinction between these two is analogous to the difference between a class and an instance of that class. Put another way, given the definitions shown in the schema in Example 5-3, you would not expect to find a BookInfo element in a message sent by the book web service, but you could define an element with the characteristics of the BookInfo type by using an XML schema element called (appropriately enough) element, referring to the BookInfo type:

```
<element name="BookInfoElement" type= "BookInfo"/>
```

With this definition in place, an item of book information could be encoded like this:

```
<BookInfoElement>
    <editor>Robert Eckstein</editor>
    <author>Kim Topley</author>
    <price>29.95</price>
    <title>J2ME in a Nutshell</title>
</BookInfoElement>
```

An element can also simply be a redefinition of a simple type, as in:

```
<element name="author" type="xsd:string"/>
```

or it can have an associated but anonymous type declaration:

```
<element name="BookTypeElement">
    <simpleType>
        <restriction base="string">
            <enumeration value="paperback"/>
```

```
            <enumeration value="hardback"/>
        </restriction>
    </simpleType>
</element>
```

Defining Messages

Having defined the types that a web service will use, the next step is to describe the messages that the service expects to receive or send to its clients. Each message is represented by a message element, which may contain any number of part elements. Example 5-4 shows some of the message elements generated for the book web service.

Example 5-4. Message elements for the book web service

```
<message name="BookQuery_getAuthor">
    <part name="String_1" type="xsd:string"/>
</message>
<message name="BookQuery_getAuthorResponse">
    <part name="result" type="xsd:string"/>
</message>
<message name="BookQuery_getBookInfo"/>
<message name="BookQuery_getBookInfoResponse">
    <part name="result" type="ns2:ArrayOfBookInfo"/>
</message>
<message name="BookQuery_getBookMap"/>
<message name="BookQuery_getBookMapResponse">
    <part name="result" type="ns3:hashMap"/>
</message>
<message name="BookServiceException">
    <part name="BookServiceException" type="xsd:string"/>
</message>
```

You'll notice that the message elements are paired—for example, BookQuery_getAuthor is matched with BookQuery_getAuthorResponse. Based on their name attributes, you would probably guess that these messages represent the set of arguments passed to a JAX-RPC method call and the values to be returned from that call, respectively. This is correct, although the only way to be sure that this is actually the case is to check the operation elements that actually associate the messages with the service's method calls.

Message names

The value of a message element's name attribute must be unique within the WSDL document. Apart from this constraint, there is no requirement to follow any specific pattern when choosing a name, although tools that generate WSDL from programming language code are likely to use a convention similar to the one defined by JAX-RPC and illustrated in Example 5-4:

- The name of the message that supplies the arguments for a JAX-RPC method call is formed from the name of the service endpoint interface (such as BookQuery) and the method name (such as getBookInfo).

- The name of the message that represents the return values from a method call is the name of the corresponding request message with the word Response appended.

- The name of a message that represents the content of an exception thrown in response to a method call is the same as the name of the exception itself.

In the case of an overloaded method name, a number is appended in order to create a unique value for the name attribute so that, for example, if the getBookInfo( ) method had a second variant that required an argument, then the request message for this method is assigned the name BookQuery_getBookInfo2 and the response message is called BookQuery_getBookInfo2Response. Again, this is a convention used by the JAX-RPC reference implementation that may not be followed by other tools that generate WSDL.

The value of the name attribute is used to refer to the element from the operation element or elements that use it, as described next.

Message parts

The part elements represent an item of data that is part of the message. Since a message element provides only an abstract description of the data that it is associated with, the order of part elements does not in any way determine how that data is represented within the message at runtime. That information is provided using binding elements, as described later in this chapter. That said, however, in practice it is quite common for there to be a direct relationship between part elements and the fields in the XML message that will be constructed when a method call is made or a response is to be returned.

JAX-RPC uses a single part element for each method call parameter or return value. The BookQuery_getAuthor message, for example, supplies a string value that is actually the title of the book for which the author name is required. Methods that do not require any arguments, such as BookQuery_getBookInfo, are represented as message elements with no parts. The name attribute of a part element must be unique within its surrounding message but is otherwise arbitrary.[*] By convention, the part that corresponds to the return value of a JAX-RPC method call uses the name result.

For web services that are not RPC-based (i.e., document-based web services, such as the book image service created in Chapter 3 using the SAAJ APIs), message elements are used in the same way as they are for an RPC service to represent the logical content of the messages exchanged by the client and server. For document-based services, however, there are no naming conventions to be concerned with, since there is no mapping to the elements of a programming language. SAAJ, being a low-level API, is not WSDL-aware; therefore, there are no tools to create WSDL from the SAAJ code used to construct a SOAP message and vice versa. However, as will be shown in Chapter 6, you can use JAX-RPC instead of SAAJ to build a document-based web service from an existing WSDL description.

---

[*] For an RPC-style web service in which a part element represents a method argument, it is natural to use the name of the argument to name the element itself. Tools that create WSDL documents from programming language definitions may not always be able to follow this convention, however. In particular, since argument names are not preserved in Java class files, wsdeploy uses the Java type of the argument (followed by a numeric value to make it unique) rather than its name when creating the corresponding part object, as illustrated by the part name String_1 in Example 5-4.

The data type associated with a part is declared using either a type or an element attribute, only one of which may be specified. When the type attribute is used, several examples of which are shown in Example 5-4, its value is the namespace-qualified name of the type that describes the item. This could be a standard type defined by a schema language (such as xsd:anyType, xsd:string, or xsd:int), a user-defined type to be found in the types section of the WSDL document (such as ns2:ArrayOfBookInfo), or could be imported into it from an external source, as described in "Using the import Element," later in this chapter. If the element attribute is used instead, then it must refer to an element element in the types section (see "Use of XML schema element element" earlier in this chapter for details) or in an imported schema document.

 The reference implementation of JAX-RPC does not generate WSDL files that use the element attribute and, at least at the time of this writing, it also does not accept such files, despite the fact that the specification states that it should.

Port Types and Operations

The operations that a web service provides are represented, not surprisingly, by operation elements. These operations are grouped together as child elements of a portType element. You can think of a portType as corresponding to the service endpoint interface, and therefore to the Java interface when the service is implemented in Java. An operation is equivalent to a Java method within that interface.

The portType and operation elements generated for the BookQuery endpoint interface in the book web service are shown in Example 5-5.

Example 5-5. WSDL portType and operation elements

```
<portType name="BookQuery">
  <operation name="getAuthor" parameterOrder="String_1">
    <input message="tns:BookQuery_getAuthor"/>
    <output message="tns:BookQuery_getAuthorResponse"/>
  </operation>
  <operation name="getBookCount" parameterOrder="">
    <input message="tns:BookQuery_getBookCount"/>
    <output message="tns:BookQuery_getBookCountResponse"/>
  </operation>
  <operation name="getBookInfo" parameterOrder="">
    <input message="tns:BookQuery_getBookInfo"/>
    <output message="tns:BookQuery_getBookInfoResponse"/>
  </operation>
  <operation name="getEditor" parameterOrder="String_1">
    <input message="tns:BookQuery_getEditor"/>
    <output message="tns:BookQuery_getEditorResponse"/>
  </operation>
  <operation name="getPrice" parameterOrder="String_1">
    <input message="tns:BookQuery_getPrice"/>
    <output message="tns:BookQuery_getPriceResponse"/>
    <fault name="BookServiceException" message="tns:BookServiceException"/>
  </operation>
```

Example 5-5. WSDL portType and operation elements (continued)

```
<operation name="getBookMap" parameterOrder="">
  <input message="tns:BookQuery_getBookMap"/>
  <output message="tns:BookQuery_getBookMapResponse"/>
</operation>
</portType>
```

The portType element

The portType element must supply a name attribute whose value is unique over all of the portTypes in the WSDL document. The wsdeploy command in the JAX-RPC reference implementation uses the Java interface name for the value of this attribute when creating a WSDL file. In Example 5-5, therefore, the portType element is assigned the name BookQuery.

Operation elements

Each operation element within a portType has a required name attribute, the value of which is required to be unique within its enclosing portType. Since an operation element maps to a Java method in an RPC-style web service, it would be natural to use the name of the method as the value of the name attribute. In the case of an overloaded method name, as with the message element, wsdeploy generates a unique name by appending a numeric value for the operation elements generated for the second and subsequent methods. When manually creating a WSDL file for such a case, any approach can be used to ensure a unique name.

A web service operation, whether it is RPC- or document-based, requires some or all of the following:

- A message containing input values
- A message containing output values
- A message containing error information, in the event that the operation did not complete properly

The messages associated with a given operation are listed as nested elements of type input, output, and fault, respectively. Each of these elements refers to a message element defined elsewhere in the WSDL document. Each operation element may have zero or one input element, zero or one output elements, and any number of fault elements (including none). Which of these elements is present, and the order in which they occur, depends on the type of the operation, as shown in Table 5-2.

Table 5-2. Web service operation types

Type	Elements and ordering	Description
One-way	input	The client sends a message to the server, to which there is no reply. This maps to the asynchronous mode supported by JAXM. One-way calls can also be made by JAX-RPC clients using the dynamic invocation mechanism that will be covered in Chapter 6.

Table 5-2. Web service operation types (continued)

Type	Elements and ordering	Description
Request-response	input output Zero or more fault elements, as required	The operation consists of a message sent from the client to the server, followed by either a response message from the server or a message that reports one of several possible error conditions. If SOAP is used as the underlying messaging system, the fault elements used to link to the definitions of the message sent as a result of error condition are normally mapped to SOAP fault elements. Request-response operations are directly supported by both JAX-RPC and SAAJ.
Solicit-response	output input Zero or more fault elements, as required	The same as request-response, except that the first message is sent by the server to the client, thus reversing their roles. These operations are not supported by either JAX-RPC or SAAJ.
Notification	output	A notification is a message sent from the server to the client, to which there is no reply. Such an operation might be used to report an event within the server that the client might need to be aware of. This is not supported by either JAX-RPC or SAAJ. These operations can be supported by using the asynchronous facilities provided by JAXM, as described in Chapter 4.

Note that although you can construct an operation element that describes a solicit-response or a notification operation, the concrete bindings described in the WSDL 1.1 specification do not provide a way to map these operations onto existing network protocols. Therefore, in practice, only one-way and request-response operations can be used.

In Example 5-5, the getAuthor operation corresponds to the getAuthor( ) method in the BookQuery interface, which is defined as follows:

```
public String getAuthor(String name) throws RemoteException;
```

This is obviously a request-response operation, and the operation element reflects this through the presence and ordering of both input and output elements:

```
<operation name="getAuthor" parameterOrder="String_1">
  <input message="tns:BookQuery_getAuthor"/>
  <output message="tns:BookQuery_getAuthorResponse"/>
</operation>
```

Although the getAuthor( ) method can throw a RemoteException, no fault element is required, since this exception is generated by the underlying communication layers rather than as a result of an error message to be returned by the server.

The input and output elements refer to message definitions using the message attribute, the value of which is the name assigned to the message using its own name attribute, qualified by its namespace. The input and output messages for this operation are defined as follows:

```
<message name="BookQuery_getAuthor">
  <part name="String_1" type="xsd:string"/>
</message>
<message name="BookQuery_getAuthorResponse">
  <part name="result" type="xsd:string"/>
</message>
```

These definitions state that the message sent to the server consists of a single string, which will represent the method argument. The reply message also contains a string. It so happens that the string in the reply message will become the return value of the method call, but you cannot tell this from the message definitions (although the use of the name *result* for the message element is a useful hint). To see how the method arguments and return values are mapped to the values in the input and output messages, you need to refer back to the operation element itself:

```
<operation name="getAuthor" parameterOrder="String_1">
```

RPC method arguments are of three types:

In arguments
> These arguments are sent in the input message but do not change as a result of the method invocation. This is a direct mapping of the pass-by-value semantics of arguments in Java method calls.

Out arguments
> These arguments appear in the method signature, but their value is not sent with the input message. However, a new value for the argument may appear in the response message and, if so, the argument is modified from the returned value. Java method calls do not directly support *out* arguments; instead, JAX-RPC uses holder classes to allow the argument value to be modified, as described in Chapter 2.

In/out arguments
> The value of an *in/out* argument is sent in the input message and is modified from the reply message. An *in/out* argument is therefore both an in and out argument, and is supported by JAX-RPC using holder classes.

Parts that appear in the parameterOrder attribute of the operation element represent method arguments and must reflect the order in which the arguments appear in the original method signature. This attribute and the input and output messages are then used as follows:

1. Parts that appear in the input message but not in the output message represent *in* arguments.

2. Parts that appear in the output message but not in the input message represent *out* arguments.

3. Parts that appear in both the input and output messages are assumed to represent *in/out* arguments.

4. If the output message contains a single part that does not appear in the parameterOrder attribute, then it represents the return value of the method call. If there is no such part, then the method does not return a value (and its Java return type will be void).

In the case of the getAuthor operation, only String_1 appears in the parameterOrder attribute. Since this part is listed in the input message, it must be an *in* argument. The output message contains a single part that is not listed in the parameterOrder attribute. This part must therefore be the return value.

The WSDL specification allows the parameterOrder attribute to be omitted. In this case, the rules just described are still used to identify which message parts represent input and output parameters. However, there is possible doubt over the way in which parts listed in the output message but not in the input message are to be treated—do they represent *out* arguments, or is one of them to be considered the result of the method call? When generating Java code from WSDL, it doesn't really matter, except as a matter of style, which interpretation is chosen, since the calling code will be written with knowledge of the signature of the generated method. JAX-RPC therefore resolves the issue as follows:

- If there is a single part in the output message that is not also in the input message, it is mapped to the return value of the method.

- If there is more than one part in the output message that is not in the input message, they are all mapped as *out* arguments and the return type of the method is void.

Naturally, if all of the parts appear in both the input and output messages, then they all represent *in/out* arguments and the return type of the method is void.

A method that does not have any arguments is described using an input message that has no parts. An example of this is the getBookCount( ) method, which is mapped to the getBookCount operation:

```
<operation name="getBookCount" parameterOrder="">
  <input message="tns:BookQuery_getBookCount"/>
  <output message="tns:BookQuery_getBookCountResponse"/>
</operation>
```

The BookQuery_getBookCount message contains no parts:

```
<message name="BookQuery_getBookCount"/>
```

A Java method that may throw an exception as a result of an error detected by the service implementation is mapped to an operation element containing one fault element for each possible exception. The getPrice( ) method, defined as follows, is an example of this:

```
public abstract double getPrice(String name)
    throws BookServiceException, RemoteException;
```

The operation element for this method looks like this:

```
<operation name="getPrice" parameterOrder="String_1">
  <input message="tns:BookQuery_getPrice"/>
  <output message="tns:BookQuery_getPriceResponse"/>
  <fault name="BookServiceException" message="tns:BookServiceException"/>
</operation>
```

Note that only the service-defined exception is listed as a fault element. The message that describes the fault contains the information to be made available through accessor methods of the Java exception class. In this case, the exception provides only a string that describes the error that was detected. The BookServiceException method therefore consists of a part that contains a simple XML schema type:

```
<message name="BookServiceException">
  <part name="BookServiceException" type="xsd:string"/>
</message>
```

In the case of an exception with more than one associated data element, wsdeploy creates a complexType in the types section that has a field for each data element for which the exception has a public accessor method, and it uses the type attribute of the part element to refer to it. For example, suppose we define BookServiceException so that it supplies an extra Boolean value that indicates a transient error, in order for the client to retry the failed operation later. To map this, wsdeploy generates the following complexType in the types section:

```
<complexType name="BookServiceException">
  <sequence>
    <element name="message" type="string"/>
    <element name="retry" type="boolean"/>
  </sequence>
</complexType>
```

The message element now looks like this:

```
<message name="BookServiceException">
  <part name="BookServiceException" type="ns2:BookServiceException"/>
</message>
```

The fault element is, of course, unaffected by this change.

The input, output, and fault elements must all have a name, unique within the enclosing portType element, that can be used to link them to their associated bindings (described in the next section). The name is declared using the name attribute, as the fault element in the definition of the getPrice operation shows:

```
<operation name="getPrice" parameterOrder="String_1">
  <input message="tns:BookQuery_getPrice"/>
  <output message="tns:BookQuery_getPriceResponse"/>
  <fault name="BookServiceException" message="tns:BookServiceException"/>
</operation>
```

Notice that in this example, the input and output elements do not provide a value for this attribute. This is possible because the WSDL specification allows the name attribute to be defaulted, with the default value being inferred according to the following rules:

- For a one-way or notification message, the name attribute has the same value as the name attribute of the operation itself.

- For a request-response operation, the name attribute of the input element is defaulted to XXXRequest, and the name attribute of the output element is defaulted to XXXResponse, where XXX is the value of the name attribute of the operation.

- For a solicit-response operation, the name attribute of the ouput element is defaulted to XXXSolicit, and the name attribute of the input element is defaulted to XXXResponse, where XXX is the value of the name attribute of the operation.

Given these rules, the definition of the getPrice operation just shown is equivalent to the following:

```
<operation name="getPrice" parameterOrder="String_1">
  <input name="getPriceRequest" message="tns:BookQuery_getPrice"/>
  <output name="getPriceResponse"
```

```
                  message="tns:BookQuery_getPriceResponse"/>
    <fault name="BookServiceException" message="tns:BookServiceException"/>
  </operation>
```

The name attribute for a fault element cannot be defaulted.

Concrete Bindings

The elements that you have seen so far create an abstract definition of a web service that tells you the operations that it provides, and what information each of them requires as input and returns as output. At this point, though, you don't know which protocols can be used to access the service or how the inputs and outputs are mapped to real protocol messages. The binding elements provide this information.

Each binding element describes the protocol binding for a *single* portType to a *single* protocol. To map a web service to more than one protocol, create a separate set of bindings for each protocol. The overall structure of a binding element is shown in Example 5-6.

Example 5-6. Structure of the WSDL binding element

```
<binding name="bindingName" type= "portTypeName">
  <!-- Binding-specific information for the portType goes here -->
  <operation name="operationName">  <!-- One of these per operation -->
    <!-- Binding-specific information for this operation goes here -->
    <input name="messageName"> <!-- 0 or 1 of these -->
      <!-- Binding-specific information for this message goes here -->
    </input>
    <output name="messageName"> <!-- 0 or 1 of these -->
      <!-- Binding-specific information for this message goes here -->
    </output>
    <fault name="messageName"> <!-- 0 or 1 for each fault -->
      <!-- Binding-specific information for this message goes here -->
    </fault>
  </operation>
</binding>
```

A binding element contains an operation element for each operation in its associated portType, and each input, output, and fault element in the portType operation also has a corresponding input, output, or fault element here. The core WSDL specification defines only the binding, operation, input, output, and fault elements—the additional elements necessary to provide the actual binding information are defined by individual per-protocol bindings. These elements are inserted at the points indicated by the comments in Example 5-6. Since SOAP is the most commonly used binding for web services, the WSDL specification describes a set of elements that can be used to specify a SOAP binding, but recognizes that it may need to be extended to meet future requirements. The specification also defines elements that can be used to bind a web service onto HTTP, but in this chapter, we deal only with bindings in which the underlying protocol is SOAP 1.1.

WSDL

The SOAP Binding

The purpose of the SOAP binding is to define the following:

- The transport protocol used to carry the SOAP messages.
- The value of the SOAPAction header needed to access the service.
- Whether each operation is RPC-style or document-style.
- For each part of the input, output, and fault messages associated with the operation, whether the corresponding elements appear within the SOAP header or the body and how they are encoded. If there are any parts that appear in an attachment, then the MIME binding described later in this chapter is used in conjunction with the SOAP binding to describe the structure of the message.

A typical example of a SOAP binding is shown in Example 5-7, which contains part of the binding element generated for the BookQuery interface of the book web service. For the sake of clarity, only two of the operations are included here. The bindings for the other operations follow the same pattern as those shown and do not use any additional constructs. The elements that relate to the SOAP binding, which are highlighted, all have the prefix soap. This prefix is mapped to the namespace URI for the SOAP binding—*http://schemas.xmlsoap.org/wsdl/soap*.[*]

Example 5-7. SOAP bindings for the book web service

```
<binding name="BookQueryBinding" type="tns:BookQuery">
  <soap:binding transport="http://schemas.xmlsoap.org/soap/http" style="rpc"/>
  <operation name="getAuthor">
    <soap:operation soapAction=""/>
    <input>
      <soap:body encodingStyle="http://schemas.xmlsoap.org/soap/encoding/"
          use="encoded" namespace="urn:jwsnut.chapter2.bookservice/wsdl/
BookQuery"/>
    </input>
    <output>
      <soap:body encodingStyle="http://schemas.xmlsoap.org/soap/encoding/"
          use="encoded" namespace="urn:jwsnut.chapter2.bookservice/wsdl/
BookQuery"/>
    </output>
  </operation>
  <operation name="getPrice">
    <soap:operation soapAction=""/>
    <input>
      <soap:body encodingStyle="http://schemas.xmlsoap.org/soap/encoding/"
          use="encoded" namespace="urn:jwsnut.chapter2.bookservice/wsdl/
BookQuery"/>
    </input>
    <output>
      <soap:body encodingStyle="http://schemas.xmlsoap.org/soap/encoding/"
          use="encoded" namespace="urn:jwsnut.chapter2.bookservice/wsdl/
BookQuery"/>
```

---

[*] A full description of the SOAP binding, together with the HTTP and MIME bindings, can be found in the WSDL 1.1 specification.

Example 5-7. SOAP bindings for the book web service (continued)

```
  </output>
  <fault name="BookServiceException">
    <soap:fault encodingStyle="http://schemas.xmlsoap.org/soap/encoding/"
        use="encoded" namespace="urn:jwsnut.chapter2.bookservice/wsdl/
BookQuery"/>
  </fault>
    </operation>
</binding>
```

The WSDL binding element specifies that this is a binding for the BookQuery portType and assigns it the name BookQueryBinding. This name is used later in a port element to associate a protocol address with this binding (see the later section, "Ports and Services"). Within the binding, each operation from the portType has a corresponding operation element, linked to the operation using the name element. Here, the bindings for the getAuthor and getPrice operations (which are shown in Example 5-5) are defined.

Each abstract operation in a WSDL document is defined in terms of its input, output, and error messages. In the binding for the same operation, the concrete representation of each of these messages is specified. The linkage between the input and output elements in the binding and the corresponding elements in the portType operation element is implicit, since there cannot be more than one instance of each of these elements for any given operation. For example, the input element for the getAuthor operation describes the SOAP binding of the BookQuery_ getAuthor message, since this is the message associated with the input element of the getAuthor operation in Example 5-5. By contrast, there may be more than one fault element for a given operation; therefore, the name attribute should be used to link the binding for each fault to its definition in the portType operation element, as shown in the binding for the getPrice operation in Example 5-7.

The soap:binding and soap:operation elements

Each binding element has a corresponding soap:binding element that provides information that is applicable to all of the operations for the portType to which it relates. The soap:binding element for the BookQuery portType looks like this:

```
<soap:binding  transport="http://schemas.xmlsoap.org/soap/http"
    style="rpc"/>
```

The presence of this element makes it clear that the binding that it is part of uses SOAP messaging. It has two attributes:

transport
> Although HTTP is currently the protocol most commonly used to carry SOAP messages, other protocols such as SMTP or even FTP could also be used. Different conventions might be used to wrap a SOAP message in each protocol—for example, SOAP messages carried by HTTP make use of HTTP headers and, if there are attachments, MIME headers for each attachment are also added. The transport attribute indirectly specifies the conventions to be applied by supplying a URI that identifies the underlying transport protocol. Implementations that use a binding for a particular protocol are assumed to know how SOAP messages are wrapped for that protocol. For HTTP, this URI is *http://schemas.xmlsoap.org/soap/http*.

WSDL

style

> This attribute is a default that specifies whether the operations in this binding are RPC-style or document-style. It takes the value rpc or document, as appropriate. Each operation can override this default if necessary. If this attribute is omitted, then the style of each operation is taken to be document unless otherwise stated in the soap:operation element.

The attributes of the soap:binding element just shown tell us that it relates to a mapping of SOAP messages to the HTTP protocol and that its operations are RPC-style by default. Most web services created using JAX-RPC will use this style, whereas those built with SAAJ (or JAXM) are more likely to use document-style interactions. However, as you'll see in Chapter 6, it is also possible to use JAX-RPC to create a web service that uses document-style operations.

Each operation element within a binding normally contains a soap:operation element that specifies SOAP-related information relating to that operation. This element has two attributes.

soapAction

> The value of this attribute is a URI that becomes the value of the SOAPAction header for the operation. SOAP over HTTP requires that this header be present, even if the service implementation does not use it (as is the case with JAX-RPC). If the service does not make use of SOAPAction, then the value should be supplied as an empty string, as shown for both operations in Example 5-7. For other protocols, this attribute should not be supplied at all.

style

> The style attribute allows each operation to override the default style specified by the soap:binding element. If neither the soap:operation element nor the soap:binding element provides a value for this attribute, then the operation has document style.

Message construction elements

The remaining SOAP binding elements specify how the parts in the messages referred to from the input, output, and fault elements of the portType operation element are used to construct a SOAP message. The soap:body and soap:header elements are used to assign parts to the message body and header, respectively, whereas soap:fault and soap:headerfault create fault information either in the body or the header. The general form of soap:body looks like this:

```
<soap:body parts= "partslist" use= "literal  | encoded"
    encodingStyle= "uriList" namespace="uri"/>
```

The parts attribute lists those parts from the list associated with the message element that will appear in the SOAP message body with these attributes. It is permissible to use more than one soap:body element if some parts need to be included with, for example, a different encoding. If the parts attribute is omitted (which is probably the most common case), then all parts of the message are included.

The required use attribute and the optional encodingStyle attribute specify how the types listed for the message parts are to be serialized into the message. If use has the value literal, then the associated data is serialized according to its schema in the types section of the WSDL document. The value encoded specifies that an encoding scheme or series of encoding schemes, whose URIs are given by the encodingStyle parameter, are used to serialize the data. Although these attributes partly determine the way in which the parts are represented within the SOAP message, the operation style also affects the final encoding. We'll see examples that demonstrate exactly how this works in Chapter 6.

The namespace attribute supplies the URI for the namespace to be applied to XML elements created from this part that do not have an explicit namespace assigned as a result of the encoding in use. It may be omitted if not required.

The input and output elements for the getAuthor operation in Example 5-7 contain a typical soap:body element:

```
<soap:body encodingStyle="http://schemas.xmlsoap.org/soap/encoding/"
        use="encoded" namespace="urn:jwsnut.chapter2.bookservice/wsdl/
BookQuery"/>
```

This element specifies that all parts of the input message will appear in the body (all parts appear because the parts attribute is omitted). The namespace for any elements that do not have a namespace explicitly assigned in the serialization schema will be *urn:jwsnut.chapter2.bookservice/wsdl/BookQuery*. The data will be encoded using the standard SOAP section 5 encoding rules (described in Chapter 3).

The soap:fault element has the same attributes as soap:body and results in the content that it describes being added as a Detail element inside a SOAP Fault element in the message body. As an example of the use of this element, the getPrice operation has a fault element that is bound as follows:

```
<soap:fault encodingStyle="http://schemas.xmlsoap.org/soap/encoding/"
        use="encoded" namespace="urn:jwsnut.chapter2.bookservice/wsdl/
BookQuery"/>
```

The soap:header and soap:headerfault elements are identical to soap:body and soap:fault, respectively, apart from the fact that they have an extra attribute and their output appears in the SOAP message header instead of the body. The soap:header element looks like this:

```
<soap:header message="message" part="partslist" use= "literal  | encoded"
        encodingStyle= "uriList" namespace="uri"/>
```

The soap:body and soap:fault elements refer implicitly to the message associated with the input, output, or fault element in their surrounding operation element. Both soap:header and soap:headerfault can use parts from a different message by explicitly referencing that message with the message attribute. This allows headers and message bodies to be described separately for convenience. If this attribute is not used, then the parts are obtained from the message that is normally associated with the element.

The MIME Binding

The SOAP binding on its own is sufficient for messages that do not require attachments. The MIME binding can be used when attachments are needed. The WSDL description for a message that contains one or more attachments consists of a set of mime:part elements wrapped in a mime:multipartRelated element, where the namespace prefix `mime` is mapped to the URI *http://schemas.xmlsoap.org/wsdl/ mime*. For example, the parts for an output message for an operation that returns some image data might be declared like this:

```
<message name="imageResult">
  <part name="body" type= "bodyType"/>
  <part name="imageData" type= "ArrayOfHexBinary"/>
</message>
```

where `bodyType` and `ArrayOfHexBinary` are assumed to be defined in the types section. In the binding shown here, the body part is mapped to the SOAP body, while `imageData` appears as an attachment:

```
<output>
  <mime:multipartRelated>
    <mime:part>
      <soap:body parts="body">
    </mime:part>
    <mime:part>
      <mime:content part="imageData" type="image/gif"/>
      <mime:content part="imageData" type="image/jpeg"/>
      <mime:content part="imageData" type="image/png"/>
    </mime:part>
  </mime:multipartRelated>
</output
```

The `mime:multipartRelated` element signals that this binding represents a SOAP with attachments message, where the SOAP envelope and each attachment are represented by a nested `soap:part` element. The first such element contains a `soap:body` element and is therefore mapped to the body part of the SOAP envelope. It is also permissible to use `soap:header`, `soap:fault`, and `soap:headerfault` elements as required.

MIME content within an attachment is described using a `mime:content` element, where the type attribute specifies the MIME type of the data that may appear in the attachment. Where, as in this case, several such elements appear, any of the listed MIME types might be expected to appear in the attachment. Alternate types can also be specified using wildcards, such as:

```
<mime:content part="imageData" type="image/*"/>
```

which allows all types of images, and:

```
<mime:content part="imageData" type="*/*"/>
```

which permits arbitrary MIME-encoded data. In all cases where there are alternatives, the actual type of the data in an attachment must be determined at runtime by examining the MIME headers of the received message.

The MIME binding also provides a way to describe arbitrary XML within an attachment using the `mime:mimeXml` element:

```
<mime:mimeXml part="partName"/>
```

The schema for the XML itself can be inferred from the part based on either the type or the element within the types section (or an imported schema document) that it refers to.

Ports and Services

A binding element describes how the operations within a portType are mapped to SOAP messages or messages in other protocols, but they don't tell you how to locate an instance of the portType. This is the job of the port element, which maps a binding of a portType to a URI that can be used to access it using the protocol associated with the binding. A service element groups together a set of related ports. A WSDL document may contain several service elements, which are distinguished from each other by their name attributes. There is no requirement for a service to contain elements for each port defined in the WSDL document or for all of the ports in a given service element to use the same binding. Example 5-8 shows the service and port elements for the book web service.

Example 5-8. service and port elements for the book web service

```
<service name="BookService">
  <port name="BookQueryPort" binding="tns:BookQueryBinding">
    <soap:address location="http://localhost:8000/Books/BookQuery"/>
  </port>
</service>
```

A port is associated with a binding via its binding attribute. The actual address is specified using an element that is specific to the binding's protocol. Here, the soap:address element from the SOAP binding is used to provide the URL at which the service endpoint interface for the port can be accessed.

Using the import Element

So far in this chapter, we have described a WSDL document as if it were a single file. In the real world, however, it would be more useful to be able to break down a WSDL definition into smaller pieces and place each of them in a separate file, so that a set of common definitions can be shared by several web services without having to replicate them in each WSDL document. This can be achieved by using either or both of the WSDL import and XML schema import elements. The following sections show how you might use these elements to distribute the definitions for the book web service over several files.

Importing types from an XML schema definition

One obvious way to improve reusability of WSDL definitions is to extract those data type definitions that might be of general use and place them in a separate XML schema document, which could then be imported into any number of WSDL documents. As noted in "Type Definitions" and shown in Example 5-3 earlier in this chapter, the generated WSDL file for the book service contains two sets of type definitions:

- Definitions of types that are part of the book service itself, such as the BookInfo value type

- Definitions that are introduced by JAX-RPC to describe data types that it provides internally, such as HashMap

These definitions belong to different namespaces and are contained in two separate schema elements within the type element of the generated WSDL file. Since an XML schema document can only contain a single schema element (and since the definitions, being in different namespaces, cannot be merged together), it is necessary to create two XML schema documents to extract them from the WSDL file, which we'll call *bookTypes.xsd* (the content of which is shown in Example 5-9) and *baseTypes.xsd* (shown in Example 5-10).

Example 5-9. Schema document containing service-related type definitions for the book service

```xml
<?xml version="1.0" encoding="UTF-8"?>
<schema targetNamespace="urn:jwsnut.chapter2.bookservice/types/BookQuery"
        xmlns:tns="urn:jwsnut.chapter2.bookservice/types/BookQuery"
        xmlns:soap-enc="http://schemas.xmlsoap.org/soap/encoding/"
        xmlns:wsdl="http://schemas.xmlsoap.org/wsdl/"
        xmlns="http://www.w3.org/2001/XMLSchema">
  <complexType name="ArrayOfBookInfo">
    <complexContent>
      <restriction base="soap-enc:Array">
        <attribute ref="soap-enc:arrayType" wsdl:arrayType="tns:BookInfo[]"/>
      </restriction>
    </complexContent>
  </complexType>
  <complexType name="BookInfo">
    <sequence>
      <element name="editor" type="string"/>
      <element name="author" type="string"/>
      <element name="price" type="double"/>
      <element name="title" type="string"/>
    </sequence>
    </complexType>
    <complexType name="BookServiceException">
      <sequence>
        <element name="message" type="string"/>
      </sequence>
    </complexType>
</schema>
```

Example 5-10. Schema document containing JAX-RPC-specific type definitions

```xml
<?xml version="1.0" encoding="UTF-8"?>
<schema targetNamespace="http://java.sun.com/jax-rpc-ri/internal"
        xmlns:tns="http://java.sun.com/jax-rpc-ri/internal"
        xmlns:soap-enc="http://schemas.xmlsoap.org/soap/encoding/"
        xmlns:wsdl="http://schemas.xmlsoap.org/wsdl/"
        xmlns="http://www.w3.org/2001/XMLSchema">
  <complexType name="hashMap">
    <complexContent>
      <extension base="tns:map">
        <sequence/>
      </extension>
    </complexContent>
  </complexType>
```

```
<complexType name="map">
  <complexContent>
    <restriction base="soap-enc:Array">
      <attribute ref="soap-enc:arrayType" wsdl:arrayType="tns:mapEntry[]"/>
    </restriction>
  </complexContent>
</complexType>
<complexType name="mapEntry">
  <sequence>
    <element name="key" type="anyType"/>
    <element name="value" type="anyType"/>
  </sequence>
</complexType>
</schema>
```

Notice that these are completely freestanding XML schema documents. Therefore, each has its own schema element that declares the target namespace for its definitions, together with any other namespaces that the enclosed elements and attributes reference. Notice also that the target namespaces are different—*bookTypes.xsd* defines its elements in the namespace assigned to types associated with the book service, while *baseTypes.xsd* uses a private namespace belonging to the JAX-RPC reference implementation. In the case of *bookTypes.xsd*, if the types that it declares are to be used in other web services, then it might be appropriate to assign them to another namespace whose name implies a wider scope than simply the book service itself.

Having separated out the type definitions, it is now necessary to import them into the WSDL document for the book service, using the WSDL import element. Example 5-11 shows how this is done.

Example 5-11. Importing definitions into a WSDL document

```
<?xml version="1.0" encoding="UTF-8"?>
<definitions name="BookService"
        targetNamespace="urn:jwsnut.chapter2.bookservice/wsdl/BookQuery"
        xmlns:tns="urn:jwsnut.chapter2.bookservice/wsdl/BookQuery"
        xmlns="http://schemas.xmlsoap.org/wsdl/"
        xmlns:soap="http://schemas.xmlsoap.org/wsdl/soap/"
        xmlns:xsd="http://www.w3.org/2001/XMLSchema"
        xmlns:ns2="urn:jwsnut.chapter2.bookservice/types/BookQuery"
        xmlns:ns3="http://java.sun.com/jax-rpc-ri/internal">

    <import namespace="urn:jwsnut.chapter2.bookservice/types/BookQuery"
            location="bookTypes.xsd"/>
    <import namespace="http://java.sun.com/jax-rpc-ri/internal"
            location="baseTypes.xsd"/>

    <message name="BookQuery_getAuthor">
      <part name="String_1" type="xsd:string"/>
    </message>

    <!-- Rest of the file unchanged -->
</definitions>
```

The WSDL `import` element has two attributes, both of which must be present:

`namespace`
> The namespace into which the definitions from the included file are to be imported. The value of this attribute *must* match the target namespace defined in the imported schema document.

`location`
> A URI that indicates where the imported definitions will be found. This is usually an absolute URL. In the example shown here, a relative filename is used. While this works if the WSDL file is simply used as input to the `wscompile` command, it would not be acceptable if it were published in a registry. For this reason, the specification requires that published WSDL documents use absolute URIs.

Note that imported types are not wrapped within a `types` element like those declared within the WSDL file. It is, however, possible to mix the use of imported and inline declaration within the same WSDL document by using both the `import` and `types` elements:

```
<!-- Import common types -->
<import namespace="urn:jwsnut.chapter2.bookservice/types/BookQuery"
location="bookTypes.xsd"/>
<import namespace="http://java.sun.com/jax-rpc-ri/internal"
location="baseTypes.xsd"/>
<types>
    <schema targetNamespace= ". . .">
        <!-- Add local declarations here -->
    </schema>
</types>
```

The `import` element can be used to include schema definitions from any schema, not simply those that you might create specifically to define the types for your own web services. XML schema also has its own `import` element that can be used to reference one schema from within another. Using this element, the *bookTypes.xsd* file could be changed to reference the definitions in *baseTypes.xsd*, as shown in Example 5-12.[*]

Example 5-12. Using the XML schema import element to provide nested inclusion of types

```
<?xml version="1.0" encoding="UTF-8"?>
<schema targetNamespace="urn:jwsnut.chapter2.bookservice/types/BookQuery"
        xmlns:tns="urn:jwsnut.chapter2.bookservice/types/BookQuery"
        xmlns:soap-enc="http://schemas.xmlsoap.org/soap/encoding/"
        xmlns:wsdl="http://schemas.xmlsoap.org/wsdl/"
        xmlns="http://www.w3.org/2001/XMLSchema">

  <import namespace="http://java.sun.com/jax-rpc-ri/internal"
schemaLocation="baseTypes.xsd"/>

  <!-- Rest of the file left unchanged -->
</schema>
```

---

[*] While this illustrates how to nest schema imports, it is not particularly advantageous to actually do this for the book service, because the types defined in *bookTypes.xsd* do not depend on those in *baseTypes.xsd*.

Following this change, only a single WSDL import element is required in the WSDL file, as shown in Example 5-13.

Example 5-13. WSDL document utilizing a schema with nested imports

```
<?xml version="1.0" encoding="UTF-8"?>
<definitions name="BookService"
        targetNamespace="urn:jwsnut.chapter2.bookservice/wsdl/BookQuery"
        xmlns:tns="urn:jwsnut.chapter2.bookservice/wsdl/BookQuery"
        xmlns="http://schemas.xmlsoap.org/wsdl/"
        xmlns:soap="http://schemas.xmlsoap.org/wsdl/soap/"
        xmlns:xsd="http://www.w3.org/2001/XMLSchema"
        xmlns:ns2="urn:jwsnut.chapter2.bookservice/types/BookQuery"
        xmlns:ns3="http://java.sun.com/jax-rpc-ri/internal">

    <import namespace="urn:jwsnut.chapter2.bookservice/types/BookQuery"
        location="bookTypes.xsd"/>

    <message name="BookQuery_getAuthor">
      <part name="String_1" type="xsd:string"/>
    </message>

    <!-- Rest of the file left unchanged -->
</definitions>
```

Notice that the XML schema import element shown in Example 5-12 imports definitions from a different namespace than the target namespace for its parent schema element. This is perfectly valid. However, the namespace attribute on the import element in the WSDL file still declares only the namespace of the schema that it directly refers to.

 Keep in mind that there are two different import elements being used here. You can tell which is which because they belong to different XML namespaces. The import element in Example 5-12 is an XML schema element because the default namespace declared by its parent schema element is *http://www.w3.org/2001/XMLSchema*, whereas the default namespace for the schema element in Example 5-13 implies that the import element used there is a WSDL element.

Separating WSDL definitions into separate files

The WSDL import element can be used to include all types of definitions that may appear in a WSDL document—it is not limited to schema types. You can use this feature to separate out as much of a service definition as you like into smaller files, the primary motivation for this being reuse.

One particularly useful application of this feature is to separate the generic definition of a web service interface and its bindings from the service element that contains the addresses at which the service can be located. This allows you to use a single service definition to describe several different instances of the service that are hosted on different servers. You might, for example, decide that the demand for the book service is so great that you want to create mirror sites around the world, and allow users to make use of the mirror that gives them the fastest service by publishing the WSDL document in several registries, each with a different service element. Instead of copying and propagating the entire WSDL file, you would install only the part that contains the service element itself in the registry and import the rest of the definition by reference to its single location using an absolute URL (or other URI).

Achieving this separation for the book service is extremely simple. The first step is to remove the service elements from the *BookService.wsdl* file, leaving only generic definitions, as shown in Example 5-14.

Example 5-14. Converting the BookService.wsdl file to a generic service definition

```
<?xml version="1.0" encoding="UTF-8"?>
<definitions name="BookService"
        targetNamespace="urn:jwsnut.chapter2.bookservice/wsdl/BookQuery"
        xmlns:tns="urn:jwsnut.chapter2.bookservice/wsdl/BookQuery"
        xmlns="http://schemas.xmlsoap.org/wsdl/"
        xmlns:soap="http://schemas.xmlsoap.org/wsdl/soap/"
        xmlns:xsd="http://www.w3.org/2001/XMLSchema"
        xmlns:ns2="urn:jwsnut.chapter2.bookservice/types/BookQuery"
        xmlns:ns3="http://java.sun.com/jax-rpc-ri/internal">

  <import namespace="urn:jwsnut.chapter2.bookservice/types/BookQuery"
location="bookTypes.xsd"/>
  <import namespace="http://java.sun.com/jax-rpc-ri/internal"
location="baseTypes.xsd"/>

  <message name="BookQuery_getAuthor">
    <part name="String_1" type="xsd:string"/>
  </message>
  <!-- OTHER FILE CONTENT NOT SHOWN -->
  <binding name="BookQueryBinding" type="tns:BookQuery">
    <!-- Binding content not shown -->
  </binding>

  <!-- The <service> element that was here has been removed from this file -->

</definitions>
```

Each instance of the service is realized by creating a WSDL document that imports the generic service definition and supplies the appropriate URI for its ports within the service element. Example 5-15 shows how this technique is used to declare an instance of the book service running at port 8000 of a host called targethost.

Example 5-15. Importing generic service definitions into a WSDL document

```
<?xml version="1.0" encoding="UTF-8"?>
<definitions name="BookServiceInstance"
        targetNamespace="urn:jwsnut.chapter2.bookservice/wsdl/BookQuery"
        xmlns:tns="urn:jwsnut.chapter2.bookservice/wsdl/BookQuery"
```

```
        xmlns="http://schemas.xmlsoap.org/wsdl/"
        xmlns:soap="http://schemas.xmlsoap.org/wsdl/soap/" >

<!-- Import the common definitions for the generic service -->
<import namespace="urn:jwsnut.chapter2.bookservice/wsdl/BookQuery"
        location="BookService.wsdl"/>

<!-- Define the location of this instance of the service -->
<service name="BookService">
  <port name="BookQueryPort" binding="tns:BookQueryBinding">
    <soap:address location="http://targethost:8000/Books/BookQuery"/>
  </port>
</service>
</definitions>
```

Note that since both files are WSDL documents, they both need to have definitions as their root element, and they both declare a target namespace. Although the namespaces match in this example, this is not a requirement.

It might be difficult to see why this technique is useful for a JAX-RPC service, since, so far, you have only seen how to create a JAX-RPC client using stubs supplied by wscompile based on Java interface definitions, and then connected it to the server by supplying the URL yourself. In the next chapter, however, you'll see how to use a WSDL document as the basis for your client and how to build a dynamic method call that makes use of the port address in a WSDL file.

WSDL

6

Advanced JAX-RPC

Chapter 2 introduced the concepts behind JAX-RPC and demonstrated how to create simple JAX-RPC applications starting with a service endpoint defined in the form of a Java interface. This chapter builds on the discussion of SOAP messaging in Chapter 3 and of WSDL in Chapter 5 to show you how to do much more with JAX-RPC. This is quite a long chapter, which introduces many features of the JAX-RPC API and the wscompile and wsdeploy utilities that were not covered in Chapter 2. While reading this chapter, you will probably find it useful to refer to the detailed API coverage in the reference section of this book and to Chapter 8, which contains more information on the command-line tools and their associated configuration files.

Using WSDL with JAX-RPC

The book web service example that was used in Chapter 2 demonstrates how to create a web service client application when you have access to a description of the service interface in the form of a Java interface definition. Although this approach is convenient, it is unlikely that you will be able to use it when writing a client for a third-party web service. Web services are not always implemented in Java and, even for those that are, the public definition of the service interface is almost always provided in the form of a WSDL document rather than Java class files.

One way to create a web service client from a WSDL file is to start by pointing the wscompile tool at the WSDL document. To do this, you change the content of the *config.xml* file so that it contains a wsdl element instead of the configuration element shown in Example 2-9. To see how this works, imagine that the book web service from Chapter 2 had been created by a third party so that you don't have access to Java class files for the BookQuery interface or the BookInfo class that is used by the methods in that interface. You can, however, obtain a WSDL file

234

that describes the service because, as noted in "Special handling for the HTTP GET request" in Chapter 2, when a service is deployed using the JAX-RPC reference implementation, you can append the query string ?WSDL to a URL that references the service in order to fetch the WSDL definition of that service. For other implementations, the URL may be different, and in some cases, you may have to download the WSDL document from a registry.

Example 6-1 shows the content of a *config.xml* file that can be used with wscompile to generate client-side artifacts from a WSDL document.

Example 6-1. A config.xml file referencing a WSDL document

```
<?xml version="1.0" encoding="UTF-8" ?>

<configuration xmlns="http://java.sun.com/xml/ns/jax-rpc/ri/config">
    <wsdl location="http://localhost:8000/Books/BookQuery?WSDL"
        packageName="ora.jwsnut.chapter6.wsdlbookservice"/>
</configuration>
```

The wsdl element has two attributes:

location
> A URI that gives the location of the WSDL document. In most cases, this is a URL. Here, it is the URL of the WSDL file generated for the book web service developed in Chapter 2 and deployed in the Tomcat or J2EE web container. The wscompile utility also accepts a filename so that you can reference a WSDL document held locally, such as one downloaded from a registry.

packageName
> The name of the Java package into which all of the generated classes are placed. If the WSDL document contains definitions in more than one namespace, it is possible to arrange for the Java classes that correspond to these definitions to be placed in different packages based on their owning namespaces. For details, see "wscompile—JAX-RPC Stub and Tie Generation Utility" in Chapter 8.

The command line used to generate client-side artifacts from WSDL is the same as that required when you supply Java interface definitions, since wscompile distinguishes the two cases based only on the content of *config.xml*:

```
wscompile -gen:client -keep -s generated/client -d output/client
    -classpath classpath config.xml
```

To see what this generates for the WSDL document corresponding to the book web service, you must first start the web container and deploy the book web service as described in Chapter 2.

If you are using the beta release of J2EE 1.4 to run the examples for this book, you need to work around a bug that prevents clients generated from WSDL documents from working. If you go to the directory *repository\applications\Books* beneath the installation directory of the J2EE reference implementation, you will find a file whose name will be something like *JAX-RPC Book Service25695.wsdl* (the numeric part will probably be different on your system). Open this file with an editor and go to the last line, which should contain a `<soap:address>` tag. You'll see that this tag has an attribute called `location`, which contains the URL of the deployed book service—something like *http://localhost:8000//Books/BookQuery*. The fact that there are two "/" characters before Books causes the client to fail when it connects to the service. To fix this problem, just replace the "//" pair with one slash, thus making the address *http://localhost:8000/Books/BookQuery*. This problem will hopefully be fixed in the FCS release of J2EE 1.4.

Open a command window, make your working directory *chapter6\wsdlbookservice* relative to the example source code for this book, and type the command:

```
ant generate-client
```

This buildfile target runs the `wscompile` command line shown above, the output from which is written to the following directories:

Name	Directory
Java source code	*chapter6\wsdlbookservice\generated\client\ora\jwsnut\chapter6\wsdlbookservice*
Compiled class files	*chapter6\wsdlbookservice\output\client\ora\jwsnut\chapter6\wsdlbookservice*

where the *ora\jwsnut\chapter6\wsdlbookservice* suffix is determined by the value of the `packageName` attribute of the `wsdl` element, as shown in Example 6-1. Table 6-1 lists some of the Java source files that are created by this command.

Table 6-1. A subset of the client-side source files generated by wscompile from a WSDL document

Source	Generated files
Service	*BookService.java*
	BookService_Impl.java
	BookService_SerializerRegistry.java
Exception	*BookServiceException.java*
	BookServiceException_SOAPSerializer.java
	BookServiceException_SOAPBuilder.java
Value type	*BookInfo.java*
	BookInfo_SOAPSerializer.java
	BookInfo_SOAPBuilder.java

Table 6-1. *A subset of the client-side source files generated by wscompile from a WSDL document (continued)*

Source	Generated files
BookQuery interface	*BookQuery.java*
	BookQuery_Stub.java
	BookQuery_getAuthor_RequestStruct.java
	BookQuery_getAuthor_ResponseStruct.java
	BookQuery_getAuthor_RequestStruct_SOAPBuilder.java
	BookQuery_getAuthor_ResponseStruct_SOAPBuilder.java
	BookQuery_getAuthor_RequestStruct_SOAPSerializer.java
	BookQuery_getAuthor_ResponseStruct_SOAPSerializer.java
	BookQuery_getBookCount_RequestStruct.java
	BookQuery_getBookCount_ResponseStruct.java
	BookQuery_getBookCount_RequestStruct_SOAPSerializer.java
	BookQuery_getBookCount_ResponseStruct_SOAPSerializer.java

It is interesting to compare this list of source files with the content of Table 2-5 in Chapter 2, which shows what is generated when you start from a Java interface definition. You'll see that you get essentially the same set of files, whether you start from a Java interface definition or the corresponding WSDL document. In the latter case, of course, wscompile generates the class for the BookQuery interface, together with BookInfo and BookServiceException, whereas in Chapter 2, these are the files that we started with. In general, in order to write a client for a web service for which you have only a WSDL definition, you need to create the corresponding Java interface definition (i.e., the equivalent of the BookQuery and BookInfo classes in this example). Here, we obtain those files by using the -gen:client option of wscompile, which also generates the client-side stubs. If you just want to generate the interface files (perhaps because you intend to use one of the methods of accessing the web service described later that do not require client-side stubs), you can use the -import option of wscompile instead, as described in "JAX-RPC and J2EE 1.4 Application Clients," later in this chapter.

By using the WSDL document generated from the Java service definitions for the book web service as the input to wscompile, we have performed a round-trip from Java source code to WSDL and back again. However, the source code that we end up with does not exactly match what we started with—for one thing, if you compare the content of the generated *BookInfo.java* file with that created manually in Chapter 2, you'll notice that the parameter order for the constructor is different. The JAX-RPC specification does not require implementations to create exactly the same source code as the result of a round-trip such as this, and, in the real world, you are unlikely to ever need to do this.

Another difference that is not apparent from the source code—but is nevertheless very important—is that when you get the stub for the BookQuery interface using a BookService object generated from a WSDL file, its target endpoint address may already have been set. To illustrate this, here is the code that we used in Chapter 2 to get a list of books from the web service:

```
// Get a reference to the stub and set the service address
BookService_Impl  service = new BookService_Impl();
```

```
BookQuery  bookQuery = (BookQuery)service.getBookQueryPort( );
((Stub)bookQuery)._setProperty(Stub.ENDPOINT_ADDRESS_PROPERTY, args[0]);

BookInfo[] books = bookQuery.getBookInfo( );
```

The code required to get the same list of books using the classes generated from the WSDL for this service, which you can find in the file *chapter6\wsdlbookservice\ client\ora\jwsnut\chapter6\client\WSDLBookServiceClient.java*, is slightly different:

```
BookService_Impl service = new BookService_Impl( );
BookQuery  bookQuery = (BookQuery)service.getBookQueryPort( );

BookInfo[] books = bookQuery.getBookInfo( );
```

The new code does not explicitly reference the stub class and does not set its ENDPOINT_ADDRESS_PROPERTY. There is no need to set the web service address because the stub that you obtain from the getBookQueryPort( ) method is *preconfig-ured* with this information, which is obtained from the soap:address element within the port element corresponding to the BookQuery portType in the WSDL file, if one exists. You can find the relevant portion of the WSDL document by pointing your web browser at the URL *http://localhost:8000/Books/BookQuery?WSDL*:

```
<service name="BookService">
  <port name="BookQueryPort" binding="tns:BookQueryBinding">
    <soap:address xmlns:wsdl="http://schemas.xmlsoap.org/wsdl/"
        location="http://localhost:8000/Books/BookQuery"/>
  </port>
</service>
```

Note, however, that not all WSDL documents need contain a port element. As noted in "Separating WSDL definitions into separate files" in Chapter 5, it is useful to create a WSDL document that describes a generic service (such as an electronic book store) without specifying its actual location. Service providers can then create and advertise their own WSDL documents to import the generic defi-nition and additionally supply the location information for their implementation of that service. If you generate the client-side artifacts from the generic WSDL document (for any conforming electronic book store), then there will be no addressing information with which to preconfigure the stubs.

You can compile and run this example using the commands:

```
ant compile-client
ant run-client
```

As a result, you should see the same list of books as that returned by the original client developed in Chapter 2.

 If, instead, you get the error message "Missing port information" and you are using J2EE 1.4 beta, you need to fix the problem described in the note earlier in this section.

To get the editor, author, or price of a specific book instead of the complete list, you can use the CLIENT_ARGS property to supply the required command-line argu-ments. Here are two examples:

```
ant -DCLIENT_ARGS="author Java Swing" run-client
ant -DCLIENT_ARGS="editor J2ME in a Nutshell" run-client
```

Notice that, since the deployed WSDL file for this service contains the service address, this version of the client does not require the address to be given as a command-line argument.

Stubs and One-Way Operations

Because the JAX-RPC specification requires only stubs to support request-response operations (as defined in Table 5-2), if you import a WSDL file for a service that contains a one-way operation, you'll need to add an empty output message to the operation element and pass your modified copy of the WSDL document to wscompile. This has the effect of making the operation appear to use the request-response pattern, in which no valid reply is expected.

For example, suppose a service defines a one-way operation to make a log entry, requiring a single string argument. The input message for this operation might be defined like this:

```
<message name="LogRequest">
  <part name="String_1" type="xsd:string"/>
</message>
```

The operation might be defined as follows:

```
<operation name="makeLogEntry" parameterOrder="String_1">
  <input message="tns:LogRequest"/>
</operation>
```

To convert this to a form acceptable to wscompile, you need to add an empty message:

```
<message name="LogEmptyResponse"/>
```

and then reference it from the operation element:

```
<operation name="makeLogEntry" parameterOrder="String_1">
  <input message="tns:LogRequest"/>
  <output message="tns:LogEmptyResponse"/>
</operation>
```

ServiceFactory and the Service Interface

In Chapter 2, you saw that in order to get a stub for a web service endpoint interface, it was first necessary to obtain a reference to a Service object, using code like this:

```
BookService_Impl  service = new BookService_Impl( );
BookQuery bookQuery = (BookQuery)service.getBookQueryPort( );

BookInfo[] books = bookQuery.getBookInfo( );
```

where BookService_Impl is a class generated by wscompile that implements the javax.xml.rpc.Service interface. As noted in Chapter 2, there is no standard naming convention for this generated class (although the JAX-RPC specification recommends one); therefore, making use of the class name in this way introduces a dependency in your code on a specific JAX-RPC implementation. Although there is nothing that you can do about this if your client application uses the stubs generated by wscompile, it is possible to make your code more portable if you use *dynamic proxies* or the *dynamic invocation interface* instead of static stubs, or if you build a *J2EE application client* instead of a standalone J2SE client. In order to see how this can be done, it is necessary first to look in more detail at the Service interface and the ServiceFactory class to which it is related.

The ServiceFactory Class

ServiceFactory is an abstract class that can be used to create Service objects in a portable manner. The public methods of ServiceFactory are shown in Example 6-2.

Example 6-2. The ServiceFactory class

```
public abstract class ServiceFactory {
    public static ServiceFactory newInstance();
    public abstract Service createService(URL wsdlLocation, QName serviceName);
    public abstract Service createService(QName serviceName);
}
```

The static newInstance( ) method returns an implementation-dependent instance of the ServiceFactory class:

```
ServiceFactory factory = ServiceFactory.newInstance( );
```

Although it is unlikely that you would ever need to do so, you can change the ServiceFactory implementation class by setting the system property ServiceFactory.SERVICEFACTORY_PROPERTY to the name of the class to be used.[*]

The two createService( ) methods return instances of an implementation-dependent class that implements the Service interface. The first variant returns a Service object that has access to the ports of a service described in a WSDL document whose URL is supplied as its first argument. The name of the required service is supplied in the form of a QName object. QName represents an XML namespace-qualified name and is therefore composed of a namespace part and a local part. Here is how to create a QName object that refers to the book service developed in Chapter 2:

```
QName serviceName = new QName("urn:jwsnut.chapter2.bookservice/wsdl/
BookQuery", "BookService");
```

The constructor requires the namespace and local parts of the name, in that order. The namespace part is determined by the targetNamespace attribute of the definitions element in the WSDL definition of the service, while the local name comes from the name attribute of the service element. Refer to Appendix A for a complete listing of the WSDL document for this service. The following code obtains the actual Service object for this service:

```
URL wsdlURL = new URL("http://localhost:8000/Books/BookQuery?WSDL");
Service service = factory.createService(wsdlURL, serviceName);
```

---

[*] Properties such as this are used not by developers, but by third-party vendors that provide their own implementations of JAX-RPC. By setting an appropriate value, they cause their own classes to be instantiated instead of the default classes provided by the reference implementation.

The second variant of createService( ) requires only a QName argument. A Service object returned by this method can only be used in conjunction with the dynamic invocation interface, which is described later in this chapter.

ServiceFactory is intended to be used by standalone J2SE clients in the case where the target service is defined in a WSDL document. However, for container-resident clients (such as J2EE application clients), you should use the technique covered in "JAX-RPC and J2EE 1.4 Application Clients" later in this chapter to get a reference to a Service object instead of using ServiceFactory.

The Service Interface

An object that implements the Service interface provides the *client-side* view of a web service (despite the name that might lead you to think that this is a server-side interface). Logically, it maps to the entity represented by the service element in a WSDL document. The methods that make up the Service interface are shown in Example 6-3.

Example 6-3. The javax.xml.rpc.Service interface

```
public interface Service {
    // Accessors
    public HandlerRegistry getHandlerRegistry( );
    public TypeMappingRegistry getTypeMappingRegistry( );
    public QName getServiceName( )
    public URL getWSDLDocumentLocation( );

    // Access to ports
    public Iterator getPorts( ) throws ServiceException;
    public Remote getPort(Class endpointInterface) throws ServiceException;
    public Remote getPort(QName portName, Class endpointInterface)
        throws ServiceException;

    // DII-related methods
    public Call createCall( ) throws ServiceException;
    public Call createCall(QName portName) throws ServiceException;
    public Call createCall(QName portName, QName operationName)
        throws ServiceException;
    public Call createCall(QName portName, String operationName)
        throws ServiceException;
    public Call[] getCalls(QName portName);
}
```

When you use wscompile to create stubs from a Java interface definition or from a WSDL file, one of the files that is generated is a class that implements the Service interface. The generated Service class includes a method that can be used to get a client-side stub for the service endpoint interface. In the book service example used in Chapter 2, for example, the following method is generated:

```
public BookQuery getBookQueryPort( )
```

This method is not, of course, part of the Service interface and it is obviously not, therefore, available from a Service object returned by the ServiceFactory createCall( ) method. If you use a ServiceFactory to create your Service object instead of directly instantiating a generated Service class, you will need to use one of the getPort( ) methods listed in Example 6-3 to get access to an object that can be used to invoke the service endpoint's methods. These methods may, according to the JAX-RPC specification, return an instance of a precompiled stub, just as the getBookQueryPort( ) method would. It may also return an object called a dynamic proxy that is created on-the-fly. The use of the getPort( ) methods is discussed later.

The various createCall( ) methods return a Call object that can be used to invoke an operation that belongs to the web service's endpoint interface without requiring the generation and compilation of a stub. The Call object is the core class for the JAX-RPC dynamic invocation interface (DII), which provides lower-level access than either generated stubs or dynamic proxies, at the expense of additional coding. Clients that use the DII can make one-way calls, whereas those that use the other mechanisms are restricted to request-response operations. DII is covered in "The Dynamic Invocation Interface," later in this chapter.

The remaining four Service methods can be used to access various items of state:

public String getServiceName( )
> Returns the name of the service.

public URL getWSDLDocumentLocation( )
> Gets the URL for the WSDL document for the service. This is null if the WSDL document location is not known—that is, if the Service object was generated by wscompile starting from a Java interface definition, or if it was returned by the variant of the ServiceFactory createService( ) method that does not require a WSDL document URL as one of its arguments.

public HandlerRegistry getHandlerRegistry( )
> Returns a reference to the configured SOAP handlers for this service. A client can install handlers to perform processing on a SOAP message created as a result of a JAX-RPC call before it is transmitted, or on a response message when it is received and before its content is used to generate the results of the JAX-RPC call. The HandlerRegistry is described in "SOAP Header Processing," later in this chapter.

public TypeMappingRegistry getTypeMappingRegistry( )
> Returns a reference to the TypeMappingRegistry for this service. This registry contains the serializers and deserializers that are used to convert between Java primitive types and objects and their XML representation in SOAP messages. See "Serialization and Type Mappings," later in this chapter, for a discussion of this registry and how its contents are determined.

Using the getPort( ) Methods of a Generated Service Object

Although a Service object (such as BookService_Impl) generated by wscompile has a method (like getBookQueryPort( )) that can be used to get a client-side stub, it is still possible to call the getPort( ) method of such an object instead. This method has two variants, the first of which requires a QName object that identifies the port and a reference to a class object for the service endpoint interface:

```
public Remote getPort(QName portName, Class endpointInterface);
```

The port name is formed by combining a namespace with the local name of the port. The way in which you obtain these names depends on whether wscompile generated the Service object from Java interface definitions (as was the case in Chapter 2) or from a WSDL file:

- For a Service generated from a Java interface definition, the namespace value is taken from the targetNamespace attribute of the configuration element in the *config.xml* file, while the local name is the name of the Java interface itself with the string Port appended to it. Therefore, in Example 2-9, you can see that the namespace value for the BookQuery port of the book web service should be *urn:jwsnut.chapter2.bookservice/wsdl/BookQuery*, while the local part of the name is BookQueryPort, since BookQuery is the name of the interface defined in Example 2-3.

- For a Service created from WSDL, the namespace is the one that applies to the port as defined in the WSDL document, which is determined by the targetNamespace attribute of the definitions element enclosing the port element. The local part of the name is taken from the name attribute of the port element itself. In the case of the book web service, the namespace is therefore *urn:jwsnut.chapter2.bookservice/wsdl/BookQuery* (see Example 5-2) and the local name is BookQueryPort (see Example 5-8).

In both cases, then, an appropriate QName object for the service endpoint interface of the book web service can be created as follows:

```
QName portName = new QName("urn:jwsnut.chapter2.bookservice/wsdl/BookQuery",
                "BookQueryPort");
```

The following code sequence can therefore be used to get an object that can be used to invoke the methods of this interface:

```
BookService_Impl service = new BookService_Impl();
QName portName = new QName("urn:jwsnut.chapter2.bookservice/wsdl/BookQuery",
                "BookQueryPort");
BookQuery bookQuery =  (BookQuery)service.getPort(portName,
                                        BookQuery.class);
```

The second variant of getPort() requires only the Class object for the Java interface:

```
BookService_Impl service = new BookService_Impl();
BookQuery bookQuery = (BookQuery)service.getPort(BookQuery.class);
```

Because the getPort() method is defined to return only a class that implements the Remote interface, it is necessary to explicitly cast the returned value to the actual interface type before it can be used to invoke the methods of the web service's endpoint interface.

When used with a generated Service object, these two variants of the getPort() method are equivalent. Therefore, there is no advantage to using the variant that requires a QName to describe the port in addition to the service interface Class object. In fact, in the reference implementation, both of these methods return the same generated stub object that would be returned by the getBookQueryPort() method, so there is little reason to use getPort() when you are dealing with a generated Service object.

Using getPort( ) with a Service Object from a ServiceFactory

When you obtain your Service object from a ServiceFactory, you can't use a method like getBookQueryPort( ) to get a client-side stub. Therefore, you have to use the getPort( ) methods (or use DII, which is considerably more complex). Consider the code shown in Example 6-4.

Example 6-4. Using the getPort() method with a Service object created by a ServiceFactory

```
ServiceFactory factory = ServiceFactory.newInstance();
QName serviceName = new QName("urn:jwsnut.chapter2.bookservice/wsdl/BookQuery",
                             "BookService");
URL wsdlURL = new URL("http://localhost:8000/Books/BookQuery?WSDL");
Service service = factory.createService(wsdlURL, serviceName);

QName portName = new QName("urn:jwsnut.chapter2.bookservice/wsdl/BookQuery",
                           "BookQueryPort");
BookQuery bookQuery = (BookQuery)service.getPort(portName, BookQuery.class)
```

This code uses a ServiceFactory to obtain a Service object for a web service defined in a WSDL document and then calls its getPort( ) method to get an object that refers to the service's endpoint interface. As you can see, there is no dependency on any client-side artifacts of the type created by wscompile (and in particular, no reliance on knowledge of the class names used for such artifacts). The only things that this code uses that might differ from service to service are the location of the WSDL document and the name of the service within it for which a Service object is required. The fact that you can access a web service in this way without having to pregenerate either a Service object or the client-side stubs seems to greatly simplify the process of building web service clients. Moreover, it appears that this code is completely independent of any particular client-side JAX-RPC implementation, whereas applications that use generated Service objects are not, since they need to use the name of the Service class, which is not defined by the JAX-RPC specification. However, there are a few points to bear in mind when choosing this approach:

- The ServiceFactory createService( ) method needs to read and parse the WSDL document at runtime in order to determine the services and ports that it defines. Apart from the parsing overhead that this incurs, there may be a noticeable delay if the WSDL document resides on a host that is accessed over the Internet. By contrast, when you use wscompile to pregenerate the Service object and the client-side stubs, this overhead is incurred only while the client application is being built.

- Even though the WSDL document is read at runtime, you still need to have prefetched it in order to determine the fully qualified name of the service, which the createService( ) method requires.

- Although using the ServiceFactory class allows you to avoid using precompiled client-side stubs, you still have to create a Java interface for the service endpoint itself. In this case, this means generating and compiling the class file for the BookQuery interface. The easiest way to do this is, of course, to use wscompile.

- When you use wscompile to generate client-side stubs, the getBookQueryPort( ) and getPort( ) methods simply have to create and return an instance of the stub class. However, when you use the getPort( ) method of a Service object returned from a ServiceFactory, there is no stub class available. Instead, getPort( ) constructs and returns an object, called a *dynamic proxy*,[*] that implements the methods of the service endpoint interface (BookQuery), as well as implementing the javax.xml.rpc.Stub interface so that it functions properly as a client-side stub. The process of creating this object involves runtime overhead that will probably be greater than simply instantiating an existing class.

Once you have a Service object obtained from a ServiceFactory, you can use either of its two getPort( ) methods to get a reference to a service endpoint interface. It is probably better to use the variant that supplies both the port name and the service endpoint interface class, as shown in Example 6-4. If you use the variant that supplies only the service endpoint interface class, the required endpoint is located by searching the WSDL document for a portType that has operation elements that map to the methods defined in the service endpoint interface class. This is potentially a very time-consuming process and therefore should be avoided wherever possible.

You can try out an example that uses dynamic proxies by opening a command window, making your working directory *chapter6\proxybookservice* relative to the installation directory of the example source code for this book, and then typing the commands:

```
ant generate-client
ant compile-client
ant run-client
```

As with the previous example in this chapter, this provides a client for the book web service developed in Chapter 2 by importing its WSDL definition. Therefore, you must have already started the web container and deployed the book web service before typing these commands, so that the WSDL definition can be obtained from the web container.

The generate-client target uses wscompile to access the WSDL file and generate the definitions of the BookQuery interface and the BookInfo object that it relies on, using the -import option of wscompile (see "JAX-RPC and J2EE 1.4 Application Clients," later in this chapter, or Chapter 8 for a description of this option). The same *config.xml* file is shown in "Using WSDL with JAX-RPC" earlier in this chapter. The run-client target uses a client application to invoke the getBookCount( ) method of the book web service and then prints the result. The output from this command should look like this:

```
run-client:
     [java] Book count = 12
```

---

[*] Dynamic proxies were introduced in J2SE Version 1.3. You don't need to understand how dynamic proxies work in order to use the one returned by the getPort( ) method, but if you are curious, refer to the descriptions of java.lang.reflect.Proxy and java.lang.reflect.InvocationHandler in the J2SE documentation bundle or in *Java in a Nutshell*, by David Flanagan (O'Reilly).

If you see the error message "Missing port information" instead of the output shown above and you are running the beta version of J2EE 1.4, you need to apply a workaround to a bug that affects clients generated from WSDL documents in that release. Refer to the note in "Using WSDL with JAX-RPC," earlier in this chapter, for details of the problem and the workaround.

The important point to note about this example is that, as the following code extract shows, once the BookQuery object is obtained, the fact that it happens to be a dynamic proxy is not of any concern to the application, which invokes its methods in the same way as it would invoke those of a generated stub:

```
ServiceFactory factory = ServiceFactory.newInstance();
QName serviceName = new QName(
    "urn:jwsnut.chapter2.bookservice/wsdl/BookQuery", "BookService");
Service service = factory.createService(wsdlURL, serviceName);
QName portName = new QName("urn:jwsnut.chapter2.bookservice/wsdl/BookQuery",
                           "BookQueryPort");
BookQuery bookQuery = (BookQuery)service.getPort(portName,
                                                 BookQuery.class);
int bookCount = bookQuery.getBookCount();
```

Notice also that, because the BookQuery object was created from information in a WSDL document, there is no need to cast it to the type javax.xml.rpc.Stub and use the _setProperty() method to set the endpoint address. You could, however, perform this cast to set any of the stub properties listed in Table 2-6 if this is required, since the dynamic proxy returned by getPort() implements the Stub interface as well as BookQuery.

The full command line for this example application provides options that allow you to use the other methods of the service endpoint interface. The general form of the command line is as follows:

```
ProxyBookServiceClient wsdlURL [args]
```

Here, wsdlURL is the URL to be used to obtain the WSDL document for the service, and args is the additional argument that indicates which method is to be invoked and supplies any required parameters. The run-client target does not supply any additional arguments, the result of which is the getBookCount() method being called. Other legal argument combinations are as follows:

Arguments	Description
author title	Gets the name of the author of the book with the given title, using the getAuthor( ) method
editor title	Gets the name of the book's editor, using the getEditor( ) method
price title	Gets the book's price, using the getTitle( ) method
list	Gets a list of all books, using the getBookInfo( ) method

You can use the CLIENT_ARGS property to set the arguments to be passed to the application. For example, the following command line calls the getEditor() method to get the name of the editor of the book *Java Swing*:

```
ant -DCLIENT_ARGS="http://locahost:8000/Books/BookQuery?WSDL
    editor Java Swing" run-client
```

The result is:

```
run-client:
    [java] NAME = [Java Swing]
    [java] Mike Loukides
```

The Dynamic Invocation Interface

A JAX-RPC implementation typically implements dynamic proxies by using the more primitive dynamic invocation interface (or DII for short). As well as being used internally in this way, the DII is a public API that provides another way for application code to access a web service without needing to generate stub classes. Creating an application that uses the DII involves more coding effort than using either dynamic proxies or precompiled stubs. However, the DII makes it potentially possible to write clients that can work with web services that are not discovered until runtime, in much the same way as the Java reflection feature allows software tools to call methods on classes that it does not know about at compile time.

The steps required to use the dynamic invocation interface are as follows:

1. A client application gets a Service object for a web service.

2. Using the Service object, the application creates a Call object that is used to invoke the service's operations. Call is the central class of the DII.

3. Methods of the Call interface are used to specify which operation is to be called, and to discover and list the Java and XML types of the operation's arguments and its return types.

4. The application invokes the operation by calling the invoke( ) method of the Call object, which provides the result of the operation as its return value.

The Service interface provides five methods that can be used to obtain Call objects:

public Call createCall( ) throws ServiceException
> This method returns a generic Call object that is not associated with any port or operation. It must be configured by application code before it can be used.

public Call createCall(QName portName) throws ServiceException
> Returns a Call object that can be used to call any method of the named port. The setOperationName( ) method must be used to specify the operation to be invoked.

public Call createCall(QName portName, QName operationName) throws
ServiceException
> Returns a Call object associated with the specified operation of the given port.

public Call createCall(QName portName, String operationName) throws
ServiceException
> This method is the same as the previous one, except that the operation name is supplied as a string instead of a QName. The name must be the local part of the operation name; the namespace is implicitly taken to be the same as the one associated with the port.

```java
public Call[] getCalls(QName portName)
```
Returns an array of Call objects, each of which is preconfigured to invoke one of the methods of the given port. The getOperationName( ) method can be used to discover which operation a given Call object from the returned array is associated with. This method works only if the Service object was obtained using the variant of the ServiceFactory createService( ) method that accepts a WSDL document location.

To demonstrate how to use the dynamic invocation interface, we'll use a simplified version of the book web service that we've used for earlier examples in this chapter and in Chapter 2. The endpoint interface for this web service is shown in Example 6-5.

Example 6-5. A small web service used to demonstrate
the dynamic invocation interface

```java
package ora.jwsnut.chapter6.smallbookservice;

import java.rmi.Remote;
import java.rmi.RemoteException;
import javax.xml.rpc.holders.StringHolder;

/**
 * The interface definition for the small
 * book web service.
 */
public interface SmallBookQuery extends Remote {

    /**
     * Gets the number of books known to the service
     * @return the number of books known to the service.
     */
    public abstract int getBookCount( ) throws RemoteException;

    /**
     * Gets the title of a given book.
     * @param index the index of the book whose title is required
     * @return the title of the given book, or <code>null</code> if
     * the index is not valid.
     */
    public abstract String getBookTitle(int index) throws RemoteException;

    /**
     * Gets the author for a books with a given title
     * @param title the titles of the book
     * @param author an output parameter that will be set to the author of the
     * given book
     * @throws SmallBookServiceException if the book title is unknown
     */
    public abstract void getBookAuthor(String title, StringHolder author)
            throws SmallBookServiceException, RemoteException;

    /**
```

*Example 6-5. A small web service used to demonstrate
the dynamic invocation interface (continued)*

```
* Makes a log entry.
* @param value the value to be logged.
*/
public abstract void log(String value) throws RemoteException;
}
```

In order to run the example code used in this section, you should first deploy the service by opening a command window, making *chapter6\smallbookservice* your working directory, and typing the command:

```
ant deploy
```

Exactly how you use a Call object to invoke a web service method depends on whether the Service object from which it was created has an associated WSDL description of the service. We'll look first at the case where there *is* a WSDL definition. Later, you'll see how to call services for which you do not have such a definition, which requires a little more work.

As noted earlier in this chapter, if you are using the beta release of J2EE 1.4 to run the examples for this book, you need to work around a bug that prevents clients generated from WSDL documents from working. If you go to the directory *repository\applications\SmallBooks* beneath the installation directory of the J2EE reference implementation, you will find a file whose name is something like *JAX-RPC Small Book Service54134.wsdl* (the numeric part will probably be different on your system). Open this file with an editor and go to the last line, which should contain a <soap:address> tag. You'll see that this tag has an attribute called location, which contains the URL of the deployed book service—something like *http://localhost:8000//SmallBooks/SmallBookQuery*. The fact that there are two "/" characters before SmallBooks causes the client to fail when it connects to the service. To fix this problem, just replace the "//" pair with one slash, thus making the address *http://localhost:8000/SmallBooks/SmallBookQuery*.

Dynamic Invocation of a Service Defined by WSDL

If you have access to a WSDL definition of a service, then it is very simple to invoke its methods using the DII. This is because the WSDL definition lists all of the available operations, together with the number and types of the arguments that each operation requires and the type of its return value, if there is one. As you'll see in the next section, in the absence of a WSDL document, you need to use the addParameter( ) and setReturnType( ) methods to supply this information yourself.

The first step when using DII is to obtain a Service object for the web service that you want to access. When the web service provides a WSDL description, you can obtain a Service object associated with the service definition that it contains from a ServiceFactory, in the usual way:

```
QName serviceName = new QName(SERVICE_URI, "SmallBookService");
ServiceFactory factory = ServiceFactory.newInstance( );
Service service = factory.createService(new URL(args[0]), serviceName);
```

This code is intended to be used to connect to a service that implements the SmallBookQuery endpoint interface shown in Example 6-5, where the actual location of the WSDL definition is supplied as a command-line argument to the application. The WSDL document for the implementation of this service can be found at the URL *http://localhost:8000/SmallBooks/SmallBookQuery?WSDL*; if you examine it, you'll find that the service that it defines is called SmallBookService. The namespace associated with this name is the target namespace of the WSDL document, which, in this case, is *urn:jwsnut.chapter6. smallbookservice/wsdl/SmallBookQuery*. For the sake of convenience, this URI is shown as SERVICE_URI throughout this section. This service name and namespace URI are used in the previous code to create the QName passed to the ServiceFactory createService( ) method to get the Service object for the service.

The next step is to use the Service object get a Call object for the operation that you want to invoke. The most direct way to achieve this is to use the Service createCall( ) method that accepts both a port name and an operation name as arguments. To get a Call object for the getBookCount( ) method, for example, use the following code:

```
QName portName = new QName(SERVICE_URI, "SmallBookQueryPort");
Call call = service.createCall(portName, new QName(SERVICE_URI,
                                "getBookCount"));
```

Both the port name (SmallBookQueryPort) and the operation name (getBookCount) can be obtained from the WSDL document itself. Note that, as with the service description, both of these names are provided in QName form and therefore include both the simple name and the WSDL namespace value. There is, however, another variant of createCall( ) that allows you to supply the operation name as a simple string, allowing its namespace to be defaulted to that of the port:

```
Call call = service.createCall(portName, "getBookCount");
```

Whichever variant you use, both the port and the operation must be defined in the WSDL document passed to the ServiceFactory createService( ) method, and the operation must be valid for the given port. If these conditions are not met, a ServiceException is thrown.

The other variants of the createCall( ) method can be used to obtain Call objects that are not associated with a specific operation and port. Before attempting to invoke an operation using such an object, however, you need to fully specify both the port to be used and the operation to be performed. For example, the following code creates a Call object for the port SmallBookQueryPort and then calls the setOperationName( ) method to select from that port the operation that will be invoked:

```
Call call = service.createCall(new QName(SERVICE_URI,
    "SmallBookQueryPort"));
call.setOperationName(new QName(SERVICE_URI, "getBookCount"));
```

To use a Call object returned by the zero-argument variant of createCall( ), you need to specify the required port and operation. Unfortunately, the current Call API does not include a method that allows the port to be set programmatically. It does, however, include a method called setPortType( ), which appears to set an attribute that is never used. It appears that this is an oversight in the definition of the API that renders the zero-argument createCall( ) method useless for application code.

You can use the setOperationName( ) method to change the operation that a Call object is associated with. For example, the following sequence is valid:

```
Call call = service.createCall(new QName(SERVICE_URI,
    "SmallBookQueryPort"));
call.setOperationName(new QName(SERVICE_URI, "getBookCount"));

// Use Call object to invoke the getBookCount( ) method (code not shown)

call.setOperationName(new QName(SERVICE_URI, "getBookAuthor"));
// Use Call object to invoke the getBookAuthor( ) method (code not shown)
```

This feature allows you to conserve resources by creating only one Call object instead of one Call object per operation invocation.

It appears that, at the time of this writing, there is a bug in the reference implementation that devalues this technique if you associate a Call object with an operation, invoke that operation, then select another operation. Under some circumstances, an attempt to invoke the second operation fails, due to an apparent mismatch between the number of parameters supplied and the number that is expected.

Once you have a fully configured Call object, you can use the setProperty( ) method to set optional properties that might affect the call, such as authentication information. The properties that you can set are described in "Call Object Properties," later in this chapter. Finally, call the remote method using the invoke( ) method:

```
public Object invoke(Object[] inputParams) throws RemoteException;
```

The inputParams array contains the values to be used as method arguments, in the order in which they appear in the definition of the method in the original Java interface definition (if there is one), or in the operation element of the WSDL document. If the method does not require any arguments, then you can set the inputParams argument to null. Here, for example, is how you invoke the getBookCount( ) method shown in Example 6-5, which does not require any arguments:

```
QName portName = new QName(SERVICE_URI, "SmallBookQueryPort");
Call call = service.createCall(portName, new QName(SERVICE_URI,
    "getBookCount"));
Object result = call.invoke(null);
```

In cases in which the remote method returns a Java primitive type, the invoke( ) method returns an instance of the Java wrapper class for that primitive type. In the case of the getBookCount( ) method, which returns an int, the actual return value from invoke( ) is an object of type java.lang.Integer:

```
Object result = call.invoke(null);
int bookCount = ((Integer)result).intValue( );
```

Similarly, to supply the value for an argument that is a Java primitive type, you should pass an instance of the corresponding wrapper class. To illustrate this, the following code invokes the getBookTitle( ) method, which requires an integer argument in the range of 0 to one less than the number of books returned by getBookCount( ):

```
Call call = service.createCall(portName, new QName(SERVICE_URI,
    "getBookTitle"));
// Get title for book with index = 3
Object result = call.invoke(new Object[] { new Integer(3) });
String title = (String)result;
```

The getBookAuthor( ) method demonstrates a different approach to returning a value from a web service. Here is its definition:

```
public void getBookAuthor(String title, StringHolder author)
    throws SmallBookServiceException;
```

The intent of this method is that the caller supplies the title of a book as the first argument, while the service returns the book's author in the StringHolder given as the second argument. Recall from Chapter 2 that Holder classes make it possible to have parameters whose values change as the result of a method call (i.e., output parameters), a feature that Java does not directly support. The specification of the invoke( ) method states that its Object[] argument should contain only those parameters that supply input values. Since author is a return value, the proper way to call this method using the DII is as follows:

```
Call call = service.createCall(portName, new QName(SERVICE_URI,
    "getBookAuthor"));
String title = "J2ME in a Nutshell";
call.invoke(new Object[] { title });
```

However, this code would not work if the WSDL definition that the Call object is associated with was originally created from a Java interface definition. The reason for this is that without additional information, it is not possible for the tool that generates the WSDL definition (wscompile) to tell whether the author argument is just an output parameter or whether it both supplies an input value and receives an output value. As a result, it assumes the latter and generates the WSDL shown in Example 6-6.

Example 6-6. The WSDL definitions for the getBookAuthor() method

```
<message name="SmallBookQuery_getBookAuthor">
  <part name="String_1" type="xsd:string"/>
  <part name="String_2" type="xsd:string"/>
</message>
<message name="SmallBookQuery_getBookAuthorResponse">
  <part name="String_2" type="xsd:string"/>
</message>
<portType name="SmallBookQuery">
  <!-- Some operation elements not shown -->
  <operation name="getBookAuthor" parameterOrder="String_1 String_2">
    <input message="tns:SmallBookQuery_getBookAuthor"/>
    <output message="tns:SmallBookQuery_getBookAuthorResponse"/>
    <fault name="SmallBookServiceException"
        message="tns:SmallBookServiceException"/>
  </operation>
</portType>
```

This WSDL extract shows that the input message for the getBookAuthor operation (called SmallBookQuery_getBookAuthor) requires *two* string parameters, while the reply message (called SmallBookQuery_getBookAuthorResponse) returns a single string value. Since the WSDL specifies two string parameters, the DII invoke( ) call for this operation has to look like this:

```
call.invoke(new Object[] { title, null });
```

where null is supplied as the input value for the author parameter, since there is no meaningful value that could possibly be used here.

The fact that you have to supply a value for an argument that is not actually used by the service is unfortunate but is not something that you are likely to encounter in practice, since the WSDL definition for a real web service will almost certainly have been created (or adjusted) so that it does not require inputs for arguments that are output-only. In fact, if you were to edit the WSDL file generated by wsdeploy and change the specification of the SmallBookQuery_getBookAuthor message to the following:

```
<message name="SmallBookQuery_getBookAuthor">
  <part name="String_1" type="xsd:string"/>
</message>
```

then you could, indeed, pass only the single book title argument to the invoke( ) method.

As you saw earlier, the value returned by the invoke( ) method is the value returned by the RPC call itself, if any. So how are the values of any output parameters obtained (as opposed to the method return value)? There are two Call methods that can be used to get the output values:

```
public List getOutputValues( );
public Map getOutputParams( );
```

The java.util.List returned by the getOutputValues( ) method contains a single entry for each input-output or output-only parameter, the order of which reflects the ordering in the Java method signature (or the ordering implied by the parameterOrder attribute of the operation element in the WSDL definition). For the getBookAuthor( ) method, the following code illustrates one way to get the returned author name:

```
Call call = service.createCall(portName, new QName(SERVICE_URI,
    "getBookAuthor"));
String title = "J2ME in a Nutshell";
call.invoke(new Object[] { title });
List results = call.getOutputValues( );
String author = (String)result.get(0);
```

Alternatively, the getOutputParams( ) method returns a java.util.Map in which the key for each entry is the parameter name, and the associated value is the value returned by the web service. Note, however, that to determine the correct parameter name, you need to inspect the WSDL definition rather than rely on the original Java interface definition (if there is one). In particular, the following code does not work with the JAX-RPC reference implementation:

```
Map map = call.getOutputParams( );
author = (String)map.get(new QName("author"));
```

This is because the author parameter from the original method definition actually becomes String_2 in the WSDL definition. Instead, you need to use the following code:

```
Map map = call.getOutputParams( );
author = (String)map.get(new QName("String_2"));
```

 According to the JAX-RPC specification, the keys for the Map returned by the getOutputParams( ) method should be of type java.lang.String. Therefore, to get the value assigned to the parameter mapped to the name String_2, the following code should be used:

```
Map map = call.getOutputParams( );
author = (String)map.get("String_2"));
```

In the JAX-RPC reference implementation, however, the keys are of type QName rather than String—hence, the use of QName objects in place of simple strings in the code shown previously. Given that the implementation does not match the specification, expect one or the other to change at some point. It is also likely that vendor implementations will follow the specification and require a string argument.

It might seem a little strange at first that, despite the fact that the getBookAuthor( ) method defines the author argument as type StringHolder, the value retrieved by getOutputValues( ) or getOutputParams( ) is actually a String. In fact, StringHolder is just a convenience class that appears in the Java definition of the web service and does not survive as far as the WSDL description, which instead describes the parameter as a string. When using the DII, you have to work with the actual parameter types that appear in the WSDL description of the service. The service implementation class, however, receives a StringHolder, and, if you used wscompile to generate client-side stubs for the SmallBookQuery interface, the stub for the getBookAuthor( ) method also expects the calling client application to supply a StringHolder object. At runtime, the stub gets the string value returned by the service and installs it in the StringHolder passed by the caller, from where it could be retrieved on completion of the method call. In general, when working with the DII, refer to the WSDL definition for the service at all times.

The example source code for this book contains a client application that uses the code shown in this section to invoke the methods of the SmallBookQuery interface by importing its WSDL definition. You can try it out by making *chapter6\dynamicclients* your working directory and typing the following commands:

```
ant compile-client
ant run-first-client
```

The output from this client shows the total number of books as well as the title and author of each book, obtained by using the DII to call the getBookTitle( ) and getBookAuthor( ) methods, respectively. The complete source code for this client application can be found in the file *chapter6\dynamicclients\client\ora\jwsnut\ chapter6\client\FirstDynamicClient.java*.

Note that it has not been necessary to specify the URI of the web service before calling the invoke( ) method, because the selection of a port defined in a WSDL document automatically determines the URI. If you use a Call object that is not associated with a WSDL document (as described in the next section), or if you want to use a target address that is not the same as the one in the WSDL, you can set an explicit address using the setTargetEndpointAddress( ) method of the Call object.

Dynamic Invocation of a Service Not Defined by WSDL

Using the dynamic invocation interface for a service defined in a WSDL document is very convenient for the programmer, since the Call objects are automatically initialized with the number and runtime types of the input and output parameters and with the return value for each available operation. All you have to do is select the port and operation that you want to use, supply the input parameter values, and then invoke the operation. This convenience is obtained at the expense of the runtime cost of the time taken to read and parse the WSDL document when the Service object is obtained. If you don't want to incur this expense, or if you won't have access to the WSDL definition at runtime for any reason, you can programmatically configure the Call objects with the same information. This is, however, very complex, as you'll see.

As before, the first step is to obtain a Service object. In this case, since you don't have a WSDL document, you need to use the single argument createService( ) method and supply only the service name:

```
QName serviceName = new QName(SERVICE_URI, "SmallBookService");
ServiceFactory factory = ServiceFactory.newInstance( );
Service service = factory.createService(serviceName);
```

Next, you get a Call object for the method that you want to invoke, such as getBookCount( ):

```
Call call = service.createCall(portName, new QName(SERVICE_URI,
    "getBookCount"));
```

This code is unchanged from the case in which we used a WSDL definition. One important difference, however, is that, in the absence of a WSDL definition, there is no way for the JAX-RPC runtime to check that the port and operation name that you supply are valid. Therefore, any errors made here are not detected until you attempt to invoke the method.

The next step is to configure the Call object with the information that would previously have been obtained from the WSDL document. The attributes that you most commonly need to set are listed in Table 6-2.

Table 6-2. Attributes of the Call object that should be set before invoking an operation

Property	Comment
Parameter definitions	Set using the addParameter( ) method
Return type	Set using the setReturnType( ) method
Service URI	Set using the setTargetEndpointAddress( ) method
Encoding style	Set using the setProperty( ) method
Operation style	Set using the setProperty( ) method

In the case of the getBookCount( ) method, there are no parameters and the return value is an integer. Here is how you would tailor the Call object to match this specification before invoking this method:

```
call.setReturnType(XMLType.XSD_INT, java.lang.Integer.class);
call.setProperty(Call.ENCODINGSTYLE_URI_PROPERTY,
    SOAPConstants.URI_NS_SOAP_ENCODING);
call.setTargetEndpointAddress(args[0]);
```

The setReturnType( ) method requires that the data type of the return value be described both as an XML type and as a Java type. The correct Java type is obviously java.lang.Integer, but what about the XML type? If you didn't already know that the XML Schema type that represents an integer is xsd:int, the quickest way to find out the correct value to supply is to look at the WSDL definition for the getBookCount operation, the relevant parts of which are shown in Example 6-7.

Example 6-7. WSDL definitions for the getBookCount operation

```
<message name="SmallBookQuery_getBookCountResponse">
  <part name="result" type="xsd:int"/>
</message>
<portType name="SmallBookQuery">
  <!-- Not all operations are shown here -->
  <operation name="getBookCount" parameterOrder="">
    <input message="tns:SmallBookQuery_getBookCount"/>
    <output message="tns:SmallBookQuery_getBookCountResponse"/>
  </operation>
</portType>
```

The operation element specifies that the return value is defined in the SmallBookQuery_getBookCountResponse message, which defines the type of the result as xsd:int. Instead of hardcoding this constant value (as a QName), we make use of the javax.xml.rpc.encoding.XMLType class, which defines constant values for many of the data types defined by the XML Schema specification. In this case, XMLType.XSD_INT is actually a QName constructed from the namespace URI for the XML Schema data types and the local name int. See the reference materials at the back of this book for a list of the other values defined by the XMLType class.

The next line uses the setProperty( ) method to set the encoding style to be used when creating the SOAP message for this operation. Unless you are going to use your own private encoding scheme (which also involves writing custom serializers and deserializers), you should always specify the use of the default SOAP encoding rules by setting the ENCODINGSTYLE_URI_PROPERTY property of the Call object. For more information on these properties, see "Call Object Properties," later in this chapter.

Another property of the Call object determines whether the call uses rpc or document semantics. In this case, there is no need to explicitly set the property because the default, rpc, is appropriate here. See "RPC-Style and Document-Style JAX-RPC," later in this chapter, for a discussion of these two different operation styles.

Finally, the setTargetEndpointAddress( ) method is called to set the URI of the web service to be called. In this case, we get the address from the command line, which amounts to the following:

```
call.setTargetAddress("http://localhost:8000/SmallBooks/SmallBookQuery");
```

Once the Call object is configured, invoke the getBookCount( ) method and get the results in the same way as shown earlier:

```
Object result = call.invoke(null);
int bookCount = ((Integer)result).intValue( );
```

Invoking the getBookTitle( ) method involves an extra line of code because it requires an integer argument:

```
Call bookTitleCall = service.createCall(portName,
    new QName(SERVICE_URI, "getBookTitle"));
bookTitleCall.addParameter("int_1", XMLType.XSD_INT,

java.lang.Integer.class, ParameterMode.IN);
bookTitleCall.setReturnType(XMLType.XSD_STRING, java.lang.String.class);
bookTitleCall.setProperty(Call.ENCODINGSTYLE_URI_PROPERTY,
                        SOAPConstants.URI_NS_SOAP_ENCODING);
bookTitleCall.setTargetEndpointAddress(args[0]);
```

Specify the types of the method call arguments by calling addParameter( ) once for each of them. The first argument supplies the name of the parameter being configured, which must be obtained from the WSDL definition rather than the original Java interface definition. The WSDL definition for the getBookTitle operation is shown in Example 6-8, where you can see that the part that corresponds to the method argument is called "int_1".

Example 6-8. The WSDL definitions for the getBookTitle operation

```
<message name="SmallBookQuery_getBookTitle">
  <part name="int_1" type="xsd:int"/>
</message>
<message name="SmallBookQuery_getBookTitleResponse">
  <part name="result" type="xsd:string"/>
</message>
<portType name="SmallBookQuery">
  <operation name="getBookTitle" parameterOrder="int_1">
    <input message="tns:SmallBookQuery_getBookTitle"/>
    <output message="tns:SmallBookQuery_getBookTitleResponse"/>
  </operation>
</portType>
```

The next two arguments supply the XML and Java types of the parameter value, which are determined in the same way as they are for setReturnType( ). In this case, since the argument is an integer, the appropriate values are XMLType.XSD_INT and java.lang.Integer.class, respectively. The final argument specifies whether the parameter is an input, output, or input-output value using constant values defined by the javax.xml.rpc.ParameterMode class. In this case, since the parameter is an input-only value, the appropriate value for this argument is ParameterMode.IN. The other properties are set in the same way as they were for the getBookCount operation, except that the return value in this case is a String rather than an integer.

Now that the Call object has been fully configured, you can use it in the usual way:

```
result = bookTitleCall.invoke(new Object[] { new Integer(3) });
String title = (String)result;
```

 The addParameter( ), setReturnType( ), and removeAllParameters( ) methods (the latter of which is not described here) can only be used with a Call object created from a Service object that is *not* associated with a WSDL definition. If you attempt to use these methods in violation of this rule, a JAXRPCException is thrown. This is reasonable, since the argument and return types for methods defined in a WSDL file are already known and should not be changed.

You can programmatically determine whether a Call object will allow its parameters and return type to be set by calling the isParameterAndReturnSpecRequired( ) method. If this method returns true, you must use addParameter( ) and setReturnType( ) to configure the Call object. If it returns false, you must *not* call these methods.

Lastly, let's look at how to configure a Call object to invoke the getBookAuthor( ) method. Recall from the previous section that this method does not have a return value. Instead, it uses an output parameter to return the name of the author of the book whose title is supplied as its first argument. Here's how to create and tailor a Call object for this case (the important lines are highlighted):

```
Call bookAuthorCall = service.createCall(portName, new QName(SERVICE_URI,
                                        "getBookAuthor"));
bookAuthorCall.addParameter("String_1", XMLType.XSD_STRING,
                            java.lang.String.class, ParameterMode.IN);
bookAuthorCall.addParameter("String_2", XMLType.XSD_STRING,
                            java.lang.String.class, ParameterMode.OUT);
bookAuthorCall.setReturnType(null);
bookAuthorCall.setProperty(Call.ENCODINGSTYLE_URI_PROPERTY,
                            SOAPConstants.URI_NS_SOAP_ENCODING);
bookAuthorCall.setTargetEndpointAddress(args[0]);
```

Looking at the WSDL definition for this operation (in Example 6-6 earlier in this chapter), you can see that the actual names to be used for the arguments are String_1 and String_2, respectively. We know that the first argument (String_1) is an input-only value and therefore its parameter mode should be ParameterMode. IN. The second argument, however, does not require a valid value when the method is called—instead, the value is supplied by the reply message. The appropriate mode for this argument is, therefore, ParameterMode.OUT.

The Java return type of this method is void; therefore, the setReturnType( ) method is called with argument null to indicate this. The variant of setReturnType( ) used previously requires a QName that describes the XML return type, but does not require the corresponding Java data type, which is inferred based on the XML type. Hence, the following calls are equivalent:

```
call.setReturnType(XMLType.XSD_INT);
call.setReturnType(XMLType.XSD_INT, java.lang.Integer.class);
```

To invoke the getBookAuthor( ) method and extract the result, the following code is used:

```
bookAuthorCall.invoke(new Object[] { title });
List list = bookAuthorCall.getOutputValues( );
String author = (String)list.get(0);
```

Note that, since the second parameter has been defined with mode ParameterMode.OUT, you should not supply a value for it in the argument list passed to the invoke( ) method. If it was defined with mode ParameterMode.INOUT, however, then a valid input value would have been required.

You can find the source code for the client application shown in this section in the file *chapter6\dynamicclients\client\ora\jwsnut\chapter6\client\SecondDynamicClient. java*. To run this example, which produces the same result as the earlier version that used a WSDL definition to configure its Call objects, make *chapter6\ dynamicclients* your working directory and type the following commands:

```
ant compile-client
ant run-second-client
```

DII and Exceptions

Some of the methods in the SmallBookQuery interface are defined to throw service-specific exceptions to report error conditions to the caller. For example, the getBookAuthor( ) method throws a SmallBookServiceException when asked for the author of a book whose title it does not recognize:

```
public abstract void getBookAuthor(String title, StringHolder author)
    throws SmallBookServiceException, RemoteException;
```

If you use wscompile to generate client-side stubs, and then use those stubs to call this method with an invalid book title, a SmallBookServiceException is thrown from the client's method call, provided that the exception class is defined in such a way that it obeys the rules for properly formed service-specific exceptions, as listed in "Defining the service interface" in Chapter 2.

The current version of the JAX-RPC specification does *not* require that this behavior be preserved for methods that are invoked using the dynamic invocation interface. In fact, in the reference implementation, when the invoke( ) method is called in circumstances that should result in a SmallBookServiceException, application code actually receives a java.rmi.ServerException, for which the associated message is the name of the service-specific exception thrown by the service implementation—in this case, ora.jwsnut.chapter6.smallbookservice.SmallBookServiceException. This is not particularly helpful, and, hopefully, a future version of the JAX-RPC specification will require the original exception to be propagated to the caller of the invoke( ) method.

One-Way Calls

When you use the invoke( ) method, the JAX-RPC runtime builds a SOAP message, sends it to the server, and blocks until a response is received, thus giving the same effect as a method invocation using a precompiled client-side stub or a dynamic proxy. In some cases, however, it is useful to be able to call a method and not block until the server completes it. The JAX-RPC specification requires that all implementations support this nonblocking mode, which it describes as a *one-way call* (a sequence diagram for which can be found in Figure 2-6 in Chapter 2).

To perform a one-way call, obtain and configure (if necessary) a Call object in the usual way, and then use the invokeOneWay( ) method instead of invoke( ). The client applications used in this section both make such a call to record logging information:

```
Call logCall = service.createCall(portName, new QName(SERVICE_URI, "log"));
logCall.addParameter("String_1", XMLType.XSD_STRING, java.lang.String.class,
                     ParameterMode.IN);
logCall.setReturnType(null);
logCall.setProperty(Call.ENCODINGSTYLE_URI_PROPERTY,
                    SOAPConstants.URI_NS_SOAP_ENCODING);
logCall.setTargetEndpointAddress(args[0]);
logCall.invokeOneWay(new Object[] { "Successful completion." });
```

This code makes a one-way call to a method called log( ) that requires a single string argument and does not return anything. Logging is a good candidate for implementation as a nonblocking operation because the client cares only that something is logged, but doesn't want to wait until the log entry is written. One-way operations cannot return a value (for obvious reasons), and they also cannot throw exceptions to report errors encountered in the service implementation.

It is important to note that the extent to which the invokeOneWay( ) method lives up to its claim of being a nonblocking operation is implementation-dependent. Some implementations might choose to provide true nonblocking semantics by using a separate thread to make the method call, so that the invokeOneWay( ) method returns to the caller even before the SOAP message is sent. At the other extreme, invokeOneWay( ) might construct and send the message before it returns control—therefore, it will probably be only slightly faster than using the invoke( ) method (or perhaps not any faster at all).

Call Object Properties

The Call object provides several standard properties that you can use to customize the way in which a method invocation is performed. The set of properties defined by the JAX-RPC specification is shown in Table 6-3. Note that some of these properties are the same as those defined for use with the Stub interface and listed in Table 2-6.

Table 6-3. Properties associated with the Call object

Property name	Description
Call.USERNAME_PROPERTY Call.PASSWORD_PROPERTY	The username and password to be supplied to the server when basic authentication is in use. See "JAX-RPC Authentication" later in this chapter for a discussion of authentication in the context of JAX-RPC.
Stub.ENDPOINT_ADDRESS_PROPERTY	The URI of the target endpoint. This property is usually set using the convenience method setTargetEndpoint-Address( ), and is set automatically when the Call object is associated with a WSDL definition.

Table 6-3. Properties associated with the Call object (continued)

Property name	Description
Call.ENCODINGSTYLE_URI_PROPERTY	Specifies the encoding rules to be used when building SOAP messages. Under normal circumstances, you would use SOAP section 5 encoding, which can be selected by setting this property to the value SOAPConstants.URI_NS_SOAP_ENCODING. This property is set automatically when the Call object is associated with a WSDL definition.
Call.OPERATION_STYLE_PROPERTY	Specifies whether the operation is RPC- or document-style. For typical RPC operations, this attribute should be set to rpc, which is its default value. See "RPC-Style and Document-Style JAX-RPC" later in this chapter for more information on operation styles. Support for this property is optional.
Call.SESSION_MAINTAIN_PROPERTY	A java.lang.Boolean value that determines whether the server should enter into an HTTP session with this client when HTTP is the underlying transport mechanism. This property is false by default. The use of sessions as a means of retaining context between method calls is discussed in "Client and Server Context Handling," later in this chapter.
Call.SOAPACTION_URI_PROPERTY	The URI to be used for the SOAPAction header when making the call. This URI is used only when the SOAPACTION_USE_ PROPERTY has the value true. Since JAX-RPC–hosted services do not use SOAPAction, this attribute need not be set when calling such a service. An appropriate value should be used when calling a non-JAX-RPC implementation. This property is set from the WSDL definition of an operation when the Call object is created from a Service that is associated with a WSDL document.
Call.SOAPACTION_USE_PROPERTY	A java.lang.Boolean value that indicates whether a SOAPAction header should be included. If this property has the value true, then the URI given by SOAPACTION_URI_ PROPERTY is used if it is set, or "" (an empty string) is used if it is not set.

You can set the value of a property by calling the setProperty( ) method, supplying the property name as the first argument:

```
public void setProperty(String name, Object value) throws JAXRPCException;
```

An exception is thrown if the property name is not recognized, if it is an optional property that the implementation does not support, or if the supplied value is invalid. You can find out which properties a particular implementation supports by calling the getPropertyNames( ) method, which returns an Iterator in which each entry is a String representing the name of a supported property.

The value of a given property can be obtained using the getProperty( ) method:

```
Boolean useSession = (Boolean)call.getProperty(Call.SESSION_MAINTAIN_
PROPERTY);
```

You can remove a property (thereby making its value undefined) using the removeProperty( ) method.

JAX-RPC and J2EE 1.4 Application Clients

So far, you have seen two different ways for a client to get a reference to the Service object that it needs before it can invoke the methods of a web service:

- Direct instantiation of the Service implementation class. This is the technique used in Chapter 2. Although this works, it requires the application to know the name of the generated Service class, which makes it dependent on a particular JAX-RPC implementation.

- Using a ServiceFactory to create a Service object, as shown earlier in this chapter. While this frees your code from dependency on the JAX-RPC implementation, the object you get back implements only the Service interface, not the actual interface defined by the web service (such as BookService). Therefore, it doesn't have methods such as getBookQueryPort( ) that directly return references to the service endpoint interface.

If you are writing a J2SE application client, these are the only choices available to you. However, J2EE 1.4 allows container-resident clients to retrieve references to Service objects defined in their JNDI environment. Furthermore, these Service objects can be instances of generated classes such as BookService. By using this facility, you can write code that is vendor-independent (in the sense that it does not rely on the actual name of the generated Service class), while still having the convenience of using methods such as getBookQueryPort( ). This section shows how to make use of this feature by demonstrating how to create a J2EE application client that works with the book web service developed in Chapter 2.

Unlike J2SE clients, J2EE application clients run inside a client container provided by the vendor of the application server in which the service is deployed. In order to build a J2EE application client, you need to package it into a JAR file, use the application server's deployment tools to deploy it to the target server, and finally run it under the control of the client container. Although very little in this process depends on whether you are writing a client for a web service, for the sake of completeness, I'll show you everything that is necessary to create and deploy a web service client for the J2EE 1.4 reference implementation. If you are using a different application server, the details of the deployment might change but the same application code should work, since the APIs and even some of the deployment descriptors are part of the J2EE 1.4 platform specification.

Adding a Web Service Reference to the JNDI Environment

The application client that you are going to see in this section uses the book web service developed in Chapter 2. J2EE 1.4 allows a container-based client to get a reference to the Service object for a deployed service from an entry in its JNDI environment. You create such an entry for an application client by including a file called *webservicesclient.xml* in the *META-INF* directory of its JAR file (which will be referred to here as the *client JAR file*). Example 6-9 shows the content of this file for a client that needs to access the book web service.

Example 6-9. A webservicesclient.xml file for a client of the book web service

```
<?xml version="1.0" encoding="UTF-8"?>
<!DOCTYPE webservicesclient PUBLIC
```

Example 6-9. A webservicesclient.xml file for a client of the book web service (continued)

```
"-//IBM Corporation, Inc.//DTD J2EE Web services client 1.0//EN"
"http://www.ibm.com/standards/xml/webservices/j2ee/j2ee_web_services_client_1_
0.dtd">
<webservicesclient>
    <service-ref>
        <description>Book Service Reference</description>
        <service-ref-name>service/BookService</service-ref-name>
        <service-interface>ora.jwsnut.chapter2.bookservice.BookService
        </service-interface>
        <wsdl-file>BookService.wsdl</wsdl-file>
        <jaxrpc-mapping-file>META-INF/model</jaxrpc-mapping-file>
    </service-ref>
</webservicesclient>
```

The `service-ref` element defines a reference to a web service that is deployed somewhere on an application server. The meanings of the elements nested inside `service-ref` are as follows:

`service-ref-name`

> The `service-ref-name` child element determines where the reference to the service appears in the JNDI environment, relative to `java:comp/env`. In this case, the reference appears at `java:comp/env/service/BookService`, a name that was chosen to be consistent with the recommendation in the J2EE specification that all web service references should appear under `java:comp/env/service`.

`service-interface`

> The fully qualified name of the generated `Service` class for the book web service. It is also possible to use the value `javax.xml.rpc.Service` here, in which case the reference bound in the JNDI environment is an instance of `Service` rather than `BookService`, and the application code needs to use one of the `getPort( )` methods rather than `getBookQueryPort( )` to gain access to the service endpoint.

`wsdl-file`

> The WSDL definition for the service. The value of this element gives the location of the WSDL file relative to the root of the JAR file that contains the client application.

`jaxrpc-mapping-file`

> The J2EE 1.4 mapping file that describes how to map from the WSDL definition to the corresponding Java service endpoint interface. This path is also relative to the root of the JAR file containing the application. As noted in Chapter 2, the reference implementation of J2EE 1.4 allows you to use a `wscompile` model file instead of a mapping file.

The information in this file is processed by the deployment tools, and results in the generation of a class that implements the `Service` interface, together with the client-side stubs that the application will need to call the service itself. Unlike previous examples, code generation takes place when the client is deployed, rather than as part of the process of writing the application itself.

Advanced JAX-RPC

Writing the J2EE Application Client

As far as using the service endpoint interface of the book web service is concerned, it does not matter whether you implement the client as a J2SE application, a J2EE client, or as part of an EJB or a servlet—you still invoke the same methods with the same arguments. The difference lies in the way that container-resident clients obtain a Service object. The J2SE client in Chapter 2 was obliged to know the name of the Service implementation class:

```
BookService_Impl service = new BookService_Impl( );
BookQuery bookQuery = (BookQuery)service.getBookQueryPort( );
((Stub)bookQuery)._setProperty(Stub.ENDPOINT_ADDRESS_PROPERTY, args[0]);
```

A container-resident client that includes a service-ref element in its *webservicesclient.xml* file can, instead, obtain a Service object from its JNDI environment. Here's how such a client would access the Service object declared in Example 6-9:

```
InitialContext ctx = new InitialContext( );
BookService service = (BookService)PortableRemoteObject.narrow(
    ctx.lookup("java:comp/env/service/BookService"),
    BookService.class);
BookQuery bookQuery = (BookQuery)service.getBookQueryPort( );
((Stub)bookQuery)._setProperty(Stub.ENDPOINT_ADDRESS_PROPERTY, args[0]);
```

Notice that this code deals only with the implementation-independent BookService and BookQuery interfaces; it is up to the deployment tools to provide suitable implemention classes and make them available to the application at runtime. Not only does this lack of dependence on concrete implementation classes make the code more portable, it also removes the need for these classes to be generated while the application is being developed. In fact, the only information that the developer needs about the service is contained in its WSDL definition, from which the only classes needed to create the application (i.e., the service endpoint interface and the other classes that it uses) can be generated by using the -import option of the wscompile utility:

```
wscompile -import -f:norpcstructures  -d output/interface config.xml
```

The -import option requires a *config.xml* file that specifies the location of the WSDL definition. Used on its own, this option results in the generation of the service endpoint interface and additional classes that know how to build the SOAP requests for the interface methods. Since we don't want the SOAP message creation classes, we use the -f:norpcstructures option, so that only the implementation-independent service endpoint interface classes (BookQuery, BookInfo, and BookServiceException) are generated.

Packaging and Deploying the Application Client

Unlike a J2SE client, a J2EE application client needs to be packaged and deployed to an application server. The purpose of the deployment is not to make the client available for remote access—rather, it is to give the deployment tools the opportunity to create the appropriate server-dependent client-side stubs as well as other information that will be needed to run the application from a client machine.

To deploy the application, you need to create a client JAR file that contains the files shown in Table 6-4.

Table 6-4. Files required for the book web service application client JAR file

File type	Filename
Service endpoint interface	*ora.jwsnut.chapter2.bookservice.BookQuery*
	ora.jwsnut.chapter2.bookservice.BookInfo
	ora.jwsnut.chapter2.bookservice.BookServiceException
Service interface	*ora.jwsnut.chapter2.bookservice.BookService*
Application implementation	*ora.jwsnut.chapter6.client.BookServiceAppClient*
WSDL file	*BookService.wsdl*
Deployment descriptors	*META-INF/application-client.xml*
	META-INF/mapping.xml or META-INF/model
	META-INF/webservicesclient.xml
Manifest file	*META-INF/MANIFEST.MF*

The client JAR file is actually used in two ways:

- For deployment to the server in order to create the stubs
- As the source for the class files for the application client at runtime

The WSDL file and the deployment descriptors are required at deployment time, whereas the class files and the manifest file are needed when the application is started on the client system. You've already seen the *webservicesclient.xml* file and the *mapping.xml* file (or the wscompile model file, which may be substituted for it in the case of the J2EE 1.4 reference implementation) as well as what they contain. These files are specific to the J2EE 1.4 web service implementation. The other deployment file, *application-client.xml*, is a generic file that is used to describe a J2EE application client and does not contain anything related to web services.

Having created the client JAR file, you can either deploy it directly or wrap it in an EAR file and deploy that instead. Whichever choice you make, you need to arrange for the file containing the generated client stubs to be returned and stored on the client system so that they can be used when the application is executed. You can build and deploy the client JAR file for this example by making *chapter6\ appclient* your working directory and typing the command:

```
ant appclient-deploy
```

Having built the client JAR file (called *appclient.jar*) and packaged it inside an Enterprise Archive file (called *appclient.ear*), the appclient-deploy target of the Ant buildfile deploys it to the server using the following command:

```
deploytool -deployModule -id BooksAppClient appclient.ear stubs.jar
```

Following successful deployment, the generated stubs are written to a file called *stubs.jar*. The JAR also contains a file called *sun-j2ee-ri.xml* that contains information generated by the deployment tools intended for the application container within which the client is executed. The content of this file, which is specific to the J2EE 1.4 reference implementation, is shown in Example 6-10.*

Example 6-10. The sun-j2ee-ri.xml file generated for the book web service application client

```xml
<?xml version="1.0" encoding="UTF-8"?>
<!DOCTYPE j2ee-ri-specific-information
    PUBLIC "-//Sun Microsystems Inc.//DTD J2EE Reference Implementation 1.4//EN"
    "http://localhost:8000/sun-j2ee-ri_1_4.dtd">
<j2ee-ri-specific-information>
  <rolemapping/>
  <app-client>
    <module-name>appclient.jar</module-name>
    <service-ref>
      <service-ref-name>service/BookService</service-ref-name>
      <service-impl-class>ora.jwsnut.chapter2.bookservice.BookService_Impl
      </service-impl-class>
      <service-qname>
        <namespaceURI>urn:jwsnut.chapter2.bookservice/wsdl/BookQuery
        </namespaceURI>
        <localpart>BookService</localpart>
      </service-qname>
    </service-ref>
  </app-client>
</j2ee-ri-specific-information>
```

The most interesting part of this file is highlighted in bold; these two lines instruct the application container to bind an instance of the class `ora.jwsnut.chapter2.bookservice.BookService_Impl` into the application's JNDI environment at `java:comp/env/service/BookService`. The JNDI location was obtained by the deployment tools from the service-ref element in the *webservicesclient.xml* file shown in Example 6-9. The class name, however, was not specified in that file—it is dependent on the JAX-RPC implementation and corresponds to one of the generated artifacts in the *stubs.jar* file. In fact, the *stubs.jar* file contains compiled versions of all of the implementation-dependent files listed in Table 6-1. The difference between this case and the discussion earlier in this chapter is that these classes were compiled and generated by the deployment tools rather than as part of the development of the client-side application itself.

---

* Actually, deployment of the application client is only one way to generate the required stubs. Since the JAR file for an application client can be included in the same EAR as the WAR file or EJB JAR file containing a web service implementation, it is often convenient to use deploytool as shown here to create the stubs when the service itself is deployed. If you want to keep the application separate, however, you could choose to use the j2eec command instead, which can also generate the stubs and the *sun-j2ee-ri.xml* file, and does not require access to the target application server. Of course, like deploytool, j2eec works only with the J2EE reference implementation. To create stubs for a third-party application server, you need to use the vendor's equivalent of j2eec. The j2eec command is described in Chapter 8.

Running the Application Client

Although creating a J2EE application client has the benefit of removing vendor-specific dependencies from the code, there are two important points that are worth bearing in mind:

- This technique works only when the application can be deployed into a J2EE application server so that the appropriate stubs can be generated. This is not as limiting as it may appear, however, as it doesn't necessarily mean that you use only the resulting combination of client and stubs to talk to the container in which the application was deployed. On the contrary, since the stubs simply generate SOAP messages, it should be possible to use them to connect to any implementation of the same web service, whether it is hosted by a J2EE-based application server or in a .NET environment.

- You can't just run the application client using a simple java command. Instead, you need to run it under the control of an application client container. Furthermore, because the stubs file contains information that is currently not part of the J2EE platform specification, you will almost certainly have to use the client container provided by your application server vendor.

You can run the application client for the book web service by typing the command:

```
ant appclient-run
```

This command uses the J2EE command-line utility runclient, which invokes the reference implementation's client container. Here is the actual command that gets executed by this Ant buildfile target:

```
runclient -client appclient.jar  -stubs stubs.jar
    http://localhost:8000/Books/BookQuery
```

The *appclient.jar* file is, of course, the client JAR file containing only the vendor-independent application implementation (the content of which was listed in Table 6-4), while *stubs.jar* contains all of the files that depend on the target application server. By using these two JAR files together, it should be possible to supply the address of any implementation of the book web service and successfully interwork with it, provided that the underlying JAX-RPC implementation is capable of interworking with the server that it is directed to connect to. In case you were wondering how the runclient utility knows which class in the client JAR contains the main() method of the application itself, this information is provided by a Main-Class entry in the *MANIFEST.MF* file of the client JAR:

```
Main-Class: ora.jwsnut.chapter6.client.BooksAppClient
```

Although in this example the client JAR was deployed to the application server in order for the stubs to be generated, the deployed module is not used further. In fact, you can undeploy it from the application server and still run the application. To prove this, use the following commands:

```
ant appclient-undeploy
ant appclient-run
```

You'll see that the application continues to work even after being "undeployed."

Web Service References for Servlets and EJBs

It is worth noting that J2EE 1.4 allows both EJBs and servlets to act as clients of web services that may reside in the same application server or, more likely, at a remote location. This facility makes it possible for a server-side component to satisfy some or all of a client request by delegating it to an external web service, without the client needing to be aware that this is the case.

The deployment information for EJBs and web applications that need to communicate with web services must include a `service-ref` element that describes the service endpoint interface and points to its WSDL definition. This element appears in the *web.xml* file in the case of a servlet or in the *ejb-jar.xml* file for an EJB. As with the `service-ref` element in the *webservicesclient.xml* file (which is not used for servlets or EJBs), this element results in an appropriate Service object being bound into the component's JNDI environment at runtime. A servlet or EJB uses the same techniques as the application client just shown to access the Service object and invoke web service methods.

Using Attachments

In Chapter 3, you saw that SOAP messages can carry information either in the body part or in separate attachments. Typically, you would use an attachment when you need to include data of a type that cannot be placed in the SOAP body, which is restricted to valid XML. You might also use an attachment to carry plain text or an XML document or document fragment in cases where it would be difficult or inconvenient to embed it within the body part itself. Whereas SAAJ requires the use of a specific API to create SOAP messages with attachments, JAX-RPC transparently places the values of method arguments and return values with any of the following Java types into SOAP attachments:

- `java.awt.Image`
- `javax.activation.DataHandler`
- `javax.mail.internet.MimeMultipart`
- `javax.xml.transform.Source`

Arguments and return types that are arrays of these data types are handled by creating one attachment for each array entry.

Since JAX-RPC handles the creation of attachments transparently, neither the client nor the service implementation needs to be aware that some of the data they are exchanging may be carried in an attachment. This is far more convenient than the lower-level API provided by SAAJ, which requires the programmer to explicitly manage each attachment and to create references from the message body to any associated data in an attachment if necessary.

 At the time of this writing, the reference implementation's handling of attachments is such that it generates nonstandard SOAP messages that probably will not be properly understood by third-party products. This is, however, only a shortcoming of the reference implementation. Commercial products will almost certainly use the standard MIME binding described in Chapter 5 in order to ensure full interoperability.

In order to illustrate the use of attachments, the example source code for this book includes a JAX-RPC web service that is similar to the book image web service implemented in Chapter 3 using the SAAJ API. The endpoint interface definition for this service, which you can find in the file *chapter6\extendedbookservice\interface\ora\ jwsnut\chapter6\extendedbookservice\EBookQuery.java*, is shown in Example 6-11.

Example 6-11. A JAX-RPC web service that uses data types encoded in attachments

```
package ora.jwsnut.chapter6.extendedbookservice;

import java.awt.Image;
import java.rmi.Remote;
import java.rmi.RemoteException;
import javax.activation.DataHandler;
import javax.mail.internet.MimeMultipart;
import javax.xml.transform.Source;

public interface EBookQuery extends Remote {

    //Gets the number of books known to the service
    public abstract int getBookCount() throws RemoteException;

    // Gets the set of book titles.
    public abstract String[] getBookTitles() throws RemoteException;

    // Gets the images for books with given titles
    public abstract Image[] getImages(String[] titles, boolean gif)
        throws EBookServiceException, RemoteException;

    // Gets book images in the form of a DataHandler
    public abstract DataHandler[] getImageHandlers(String[] titles, boolean gif)
        throws EBookServiceException, RemoteException;

    // Gets the book images in MimeMultipart form
    public abstract MimeMultipart getAllImages()
        throws EBookServiceException, RemoteException;

    // Gets XML details for a given list of books.
    public abstract Source[] getBookDetails(String[] titles)
        throws EBookServiceException, RemoteException;
}
```

The service implementation has a list of books, keyed by book title, for each of which it holds a cover image in both GIF and JPEG form as well as an XML document fragment that contains details of the book. The methods of the EBookQuery interface allow a client application to get the complete list of book titles and then to retrieve the cover images and the XML information for any number of them. You can build and install the web service for this example by opening a command window, making *chapter6\extendedbookservice* your working directory and then typing the following:

```
ant deploy
```

The client application is a variant of the Swing GUI client that was used in Chapter 3. To compile and run it, type the following commands:

```
ant compile-client
ant run-client
```

When the user interface appears, you will see that it contains a list of the book titles that the web service knows about, together with a blank area in which the cover images will be displayed and a set of checkboxes that determine which of the service methods will be used to retrieve them, as shown in Figure 6-1.

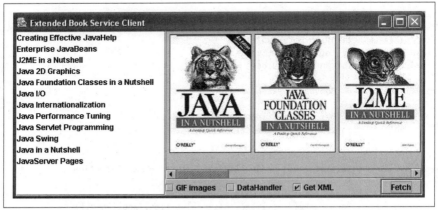

Figure 6-1. A client that uses JAX-RPC to retrieve images and XML documents

The following sections use the client and server implementations for this example to illustrate how to exchange the various different types of data that JAX-RPC places into attachments. Although the methods of the EBookQuery interface are defined in such a way that the attachments are all associated with method return values, it is perfectly possible for an attachment to be sent from the client to the server. For example, a method defined like this:

```
public void addImage(String title, Image image);
```

results in the image data being placed in an attachment in the SOAP request message sent to the server.

Image Attachments

You can exchange images that are encoded using formats supported by the JRE by declaring a java.awt.Image object as a method argument or return value. Having done this, the sender simply has to create the Image object, and the receiver uses the copy that it receives in the normal way. Neither the sender nor the receiver has to be concerned about how the image is encoded in the SOAP message.

Example 6-12 shows the server-side implementation of the getImages() method from the EBookQuery interface. The helper class EBookServiceServantData holds book cover image data in the form of two byte arrays for each book—one encoded in GIF format, and the other in JPEG format. The method arguments specify the titles of the books for which the cover images are required and whether the GIF or JPEG encoding should be returned.* The code in Example 6-12 gets the correct set of image data from the helper class, converts each item of the set into an Image object, and returns an array containing an entry for each of them. None of this code uses any JAX-RPC API, but it is fairly typical of code that handles images.

Example 6-12. Server implementation of a method that returns Image objects

```java
public Image[] getImages(String[] titles, boolean gif) throws
EBookServiceException {
    int length = titles.length;
    Image[] images = new Image[length];
    for (int i = 0; i < length; i++) {
        byte[] imageData = EBookServiceServantData.getImageData(titles[i], gif);
        if (imageData == null) {
            throw new EBookServiceException("Unknown title: [" +
                                        titles[i] + "]");
        }
        if (tracker == null) {
            tracker = new MediaTracker(new Component() {});
        }
        Image image = Toolkit.getDefaultToolkit().createImage(imageData);
        tracker.addImage(image, 0);
        images[i] = image;
    }
    try {
        tracker.waitForAll();
        for (int i = 0; i < length; i++) {
            tracker.removeImage(images[i]);
        }
    } catch (InterruptedException ex) {
    }

    return images;
}
```

The client code that uses this method, shown in Example 6-13, is also very straightforward—the Image objects that are returned are used to create Swing ImageIcons that are then displayed in the user interface using JLabels. Once again, as you might expect, there is no JAX-RPC–specific code involved.

Example 6-13. Client code that uses a JAX-RPC method returning Image objects

```java
Image[] images = bookQuery.getImages(selectedTitles, isGif.isSelected());
for (int i = 0; i < images.length; i++) {
    imagePanel.add(new JLabel(new ImageIcon(images[i])));
}
```

---

* As of Java 2 Version 1.3, PNG images are also supported. In Java 2 Version 1.4, it is also possible to plug in encoders and decoders for other image formats. For simplicity, this example uses only GIF and JPEG images.

To trigger this code, start the Swing client, select one or more book titles from the list on the lefthand side of the window, make sure that the "DataHandler" checkbox is *not* selected, then press the button labeled "Fetch." After a short delay, you should see the cover images for the books that you selected displayed in the righthand side of the window.

Although this seems very straightforward, this code probably does not behave in quite the way you might expect, although you're unlikely to notice the problem simply by looking at the results. The issue revolves around the way in which the image is transferred from the web service. The second argument of the getImages( ) method in Example 6-12 specifies whether to use the GIF- or JPEG-encoded version of the image data. The value that is used depends on whether the "GIF images" checkbox in the user interface is selected. This value is correctly conveyed to the server, which will build Image objects from the appropriately encoded image data. Once the server's getImage( ) method returns the Image objects, the JAX-RPC runtime has to encode them in byte form for inclusion in an attachment.* However, as noted during the discussion of attachments in Chapter 3, the JRE includes an encoder for JPEG images but not for GIF images. As a result, the JAX-RPC runtime included in the reference implementation cannot produce a GIF-encoded byte stream for an image. It actually always creates an attachment in which the content type is image/jpeg. Therefore, although you might request a GIF image, and the service implementation class might return an Image object created from GIF-encoded data, the client nevertheless receives an Image object created from a JPEG-encoding of that image. The same is true for PNG images, or any other type of image that the server might support. In practice, this is not really very important, since the Image class does not provide a means of finding out how the image was originally encoded and therefore there is no way for the client to be affected by this implementation quirk. There is really only a problem if the JRE used a JPEG encoding algorithm that noticably reduced the quality of the image.

DataHandler Attachments

As you saw in Chapter 3, the DataHandler class, which is part of the JavaBeans Activation Framework, can be used to encapsulate any kind of data that has a MIME encoding. It therefore represents an extremely flexible way to transport data—such as images, sound files, movies, and so on—from a web service to an application client. Since the programming interface is independent of the encapsulated data, the client does not need to be specifically coded to handle a specific set of possible data types, but can instead deal only with a DataHandler object and use its getContentType( ) method to determine the type of data that it has received. Processing could then be delegated to an appropriate helper, which is most likely configured and selected based on the content type.

In the case of the EBookQuery interface, the getImageHandlers( ) method is provided as an alternative to getImages( ), to return a DataHandler for each book's cover image instead of an Image. The server-side implementation of this method is shown in Example 6-14.

---

* This is, of course, rather counter-productive, since we already had the image data in byte form and then converted it to an Image object for the sake of the method call. As you'll see in the next section, there is a more efficient way to return image data to the client.

Example 6-14. Server implementation of a method that returns DataHandler objects

```java
public DataHandler[] getImageHandlers(String[] titles, boolean gif) throws
EBookServiceException {
    int length = titles.length;
    DataHandler[] handlers = new DataHandler[length];
    for (int i = 0; i < length; i++) {
        byte[] imageData = EBookServiceServantData.getImageData(titles[i], gif);
        if (imageData == null) {
            throw new EBookServiceException("Unknown title: [" +
                                           titles[i] + "]");
        }
        handlers[i] = new DataHandler(new ByteArrayDataSource("Image Data",
                                      imageData,
                                      gif ? "image/gif" : "image/jpeg"));
    }
    return handlers;
}
```

As you can see, this code is much simpler than that of the getImage( ) method in Example 6-12. All that is necessary is to get the encoded image data and then create a DataHandler to encapsulate it. A DataHandler typically is created from a Java object representing the data itself and a string that represents the content type of the data (such as image/jpeg). However, in this case, we associate the DataHandler with the data through a custom DataSource class called ByteArrayDataSource. The rationale for doing this, together with the implementation of the ByteArrayDataSource class, is covered in detail in "Using a DataHandler" in Chapter 3 (which you should read before proceeding, if you have not already done so).

On the client side, an application that calls the getImageHandlers( ) method can use the DataHandler getContent( ) method to get a Java object that represents the encapsulated data. The code in the Swing GUI client that uses this method is shown in Example 6-15.

Example 6-15. Client code that uses a JAX-RPC method returning DataHandler objects

```java
DataHandler[] handlers = bookQuery.getImageHandlers(selectedTitles,
                                                    isGif.isSelected( ));
for (int i = 0; i < handlers.length; i++) {
    imagePanel.add(new JLabel(new ImageIcon((Image)handlers[i].getContent( ))));
}
```

This code uses the getContent( ) method to extract the data from each returned DataHandler in object form, which it expects to be an Image object. This assumption is justified because the JAX-RPC specification requires that implementations of the getContent( ) method return objects of specific types based on the content type of the data, which can itself be obtained by calling the DataHandler getContentType( ) method. Table 6-5 shows the mapping from MIME type to Java types required by the specification.

Table 6-5. Mapping of MIME types to Java types for the DataHandler getContent()
method

MIME type	Java data type
image/gif	`java.awt.Image`
image/jpeg	`java.awt.Image`
text/plain	`java.lang.String`
text/xml	`javax.xml.transform.Source`
application/xml	`javax.xml.transform.Source`
multipart/*	`javax.mail.internet.MimeMultipart`

In the case of this example, since the data always has content type `image/gif` or `image/jpeg`, the object obtained from the `getContent()` method can be assumed to be of type `Image`. To return objects of the other types, the server implementation creates a `DataHandler` in which the content type is set appropriately. For example, to convey plain text in an attachment, the server does the following:

```
DataHandler handler = new DataHandler("Some plain text", "text/plain");
```

while XML can be incorporated by supplying a `javax.xml.transform.Source` object and setting the content type to text/xml:

```
Source source = new javax.xml.transform.stream.StreamSource(
    new StringReader("<detail><name>Fred</name></detail>"));
DataHandler handler = new DataHandler(source, "text/xml");
```

`MimeMultipart` and XML data can also be explicitly passed via method arguments and the return value, as will be described in the sections "MimeMultipart Attachments" and "XML Attachments," later in this chapter. For content types that are not listed in Table 6-5, the `DataHandler` `getContent()` method may return an appropriate Java object, or an instance of `java.io.InputStream` that can be used to access the byte stream representation of the object. For all content types, you can use the `DataHandler` `getInputStream()` method to get an `InputStream` instead of a Java object representation, should you need to do so.

The example client calls the `getImageHandlers()` method when you select one or more book titles and check the "DataHandler" checkbox. Select or unselect the "GIF images" checkbox to request GIF or JPEG images.

Leaving aside the fact that the intent is slightly less clear, there are two main advantages to be gained by using a `DataHandler` in preference to `Image` objects when defining remote method signatures:

- As shown in Example 6-14, the server needs only to keep the image in byte form, exactly as it would be read from a file. This avoids the use of `Image` objects, which are more appropriate to a client application than a server, and take up memory resources as well as the time required to create them.

- When a `DataHandler` is used, the JAX-RPC runtime does not need to perform the time-consuming process of converting the content of an `Image` back to a byte stream, almost certainly reversing the process used by the service implementation to create the `Image` object in the first place. The fact that no conversion is involved also means that images handled using a `DataHandler` are encoded in SOAP message attachments using their correct MIME type—in other words, GIF (and PNG) images are not converted to JPEG form first.

MimeMultipart Attachments

A `javax.mail.internet.MimeMultipart` object is a convenient wrapper that can be used to move one or more items of MIME-encoded data between the client and the server. Although there is no requirement for the data encapsulated within the `MimeMultipart` object to be all of the same MIME type, the `getAllImages()` method of the `EBookQuery` interface always returns a `MimeMultipart` in which each part is a JPEG image. The implementation of this method is shown in Example 6-16.

Example 6-16. Server implementation of a method that returns a MimeMultipart object

```
public MimeMultipart getAllImages() throws EBookServiceException {
    String[] titles = EBookServiceServantData.getBookTitles();
    Image[] images = getImages(titles, false);

    try {
        MimeMultipart mp = new MimeMultipart();
        for (int i = 0; i < images.length; i++) {
            MimeBodyPart mbp = new MimeBodyPart();
            mbp.setContent(images[i], "image/jpeg");
            mbp.addHeader("Content-Type", "image/jpeg");
            mp.addBodyPart(mbp);
        }
        return mp;
    } catch (MessagingException ex) {
        throw new EBookServiceException("Failed building MimeMultipart: " +
                                    ex.getMessage());
    }
}
```

To add an item to a `MimeMultipart` object, first create a `MimeBodyPart`, then associate it with the data by calling its `setContent()` method, which also specifies the MIME data.* In this case, the data is the `Image` object for a book cover image. Alternatively, the data can be supplied in the form of a `DataHandler` using the `setDataHandler()` method. This technique could be used to reimplement the `getAllImages()` method using code similar to that shown in Example 6-14, thereby avoiding the need to use intermediate `Image` objects.

A `MimeBodyPart` is incorporated in the `MimeMultipart` using the `addBodyPart()` method. Once the `MimeBodyPart` for each image is added, `getAllImages()` returns the image to the JAX-RPC runtime.

The client code that uses a `MimeMultipart` object is essentially the reverse of the server implementation, as shown in Example 6-17. The example application executes this code when you press the "Fetch" button when there are no book

---

* It is also necessary to use the `MimeBodyPart` `addHeader()` method to add a MIME header for the content type. This seems a little strange given that the content type has already been specified by the `setContent()` method, but, at least in Sun's implementation, if you fail to call `addHeader()`, the part of the `MimeMultipart` attachment that contains the data does not have a MIME `Content-Type` header. This typically results in the data being interpreted as if it had type `text/plain`.

titles selected in the list on the lefthand side of Figure 6-1. This results in the cover images for all of the books being obtained in JPEG form, ignoring the settings of the "GIF images" and "DataHandler" checkboxes.

Example 6-17. Client code that uses a JAX-RPC method returning a MimeMultipart object

```
MimeMultipart mp = bookQuery.getAllImages();
count = mp.getCount();
for (int i = 0; i < count; i++) {
    BodyPart bp = mp.getBodyPart(i);
    Image img = (Image)bp.getContent();
    imagePanel.add(new JLabel(new ImageIcon(img)));
}
```

To handle the images, each `BodyPart` is obtained by calling the `MimeMultipart` `getBodyPart()` method.* The simplest way to get the encapsulated image data is, as shown here, to use the `BodyPart` `getContent()` method, which returns a Java object whose type is determined by the MIME type of the data, as listed in Table 6-5. In this case, the returned object is an `Image`. Alternatively, you can access the data by calling the `getDataHandler()` method to retrieve a `DataHandler`, from which you can then either obtain an `InputStream` or the same Java object that is returned by the `BodyPart` `getContent()` method.

XML Attachments

You can use an XML document (or an array of them) in a JAX-RPC method by defining the argument or return type to be of type `javax.xml.transform.Source`. The `EBookQuery` interface uses this facility to allow a client application to retrieve an XML fragment that describes one or more books:

```
public abstract Source[] getBookDetails(String[] titles)
        throws EBookServiceException,  RemoteException;
```

A `Source` object can contain XML in the form of a DOM model, a SAX event stream, or an input stream. On receiving an attachment for which the content type is text/xml (or application/xml), the JAX-RPC runtime creates a `Source` object of one of these types (i.e., `DOMSource`, `SAXSource`, or `StreamSource`), where the choice is implementation-dependent. The implementation of this method in the example web service is shown in Example 6-18.

Example 6-18. Server implementation of a method that returns Source objects

```
public Source[] getBookDetails(String[] titles) throws EBookServiceException {
    int length = titles.length;
    Source[] sources = new Source[length];

    for (int i = 0; i < length; i++) {
        String data = EBookServiceServantData.getXMLDetails(titles[i]);
```

---

* BodyPart is an abstract base class from which MimeBodyPart is derived. The server needs to explicitly use a MimeBodyPart when creating the MimeMultipart object, but the client does not need to be aware exactly which subclass of BodyPart has been used and therefore is not required to cast the return value of the getBodyPart() method.

```
        if (data == null) {
            throw new EBookServiceException("Unknown title: [" +
                                            titles[i] + "]");
        }
        try {
            data = "<?xml version=\"1.0\" encoding=\"UTF-8\"?>\n" + data;
            sources[i] = new StreamSource(new ByteArrayInputStream(
                                          data.getBytes("utf-8")));
        } catch (UnsupportedEncodingException ex) {
            ex.printStackTrace( );
        }
    }

    return sources;
}
```

This method gets the XML data for a specific book based on its title, in the form of a String, then wraps it in a StreamSource object—which implements the Source interface—by interposing a ByteArrayInputStream (since the StreamSource constructors do not directly accept XML in the form of a String). If you have an XML document in the form of a DOM model, you can use a similar pattern to include some or all of it as an attachment by using a DOMSource instead of a StreamSource:

```
Document doc = ....... ; // Get XML document as a DOM model
Element rootElement = doc.getDocumentElement( );

// Using the "rootSource" object would result in the entire
// document being included in the attachment.
DOMSource rootSource = new DOMSource(rootElement);

// Using the "firstChild" object would result in only that
// part of the document at and below the first child element
// being included in the attachment
Node firstChild = rootElement.getFirstChild( );
DOMSource childSource = new DOMSource(firstChild);
```

The example client requests XML data when you check the "Get XML" checkbox and then press the "Fetch" button. Once it retrieves all of the image data, it calls the getBookDetails( ) method to get the XML details for the same set of books, and writes the result to its standard output. Here is a typical result:

```
<?xml version="1.0" encoding="UTF-8"?>
<detail><author>Kim Topley</author><editor>Robert Eckstein</editor><price>
29.95</price></detail>
------------------------
<?xml version="1.0" encoding="UTF-8"?>
<detail><author>Robert Eckstein et al</author><editor>Mike Loukides</editor>
<price>44.95</price></detail>
------------------------
```

The client code that calls the getBookDetails( ) method is shown in Example 6-19.

Example 6-19. Client code that uses a JAX-RPC method returning a Source object

```
Source[] sources = bookQuery.getBookDetails(selectedTitles);
if (transformer == null) {
    transformer = TransformerFactory.newInstance().newTransformer();
    streamResult = new StreamResult(System.out);
}
for (int i = 0; i < sources.length; i++) {
    transformer.transform(sources[i], streamResult);
    System.out.println("\n-----------------------");
}
```

Most of this code is concerned with getting a Transformer object that will extract the XML from the Source objects returned by the server and write it in a readable form to the standard output stream. Even though the server provided the XML to the JAX-RPC runtime in the form of an array of StreamSource objects, you cannot assume that the client will receive a StreamSource object with the data extracted from the received attachment, since the choice between DOMSource, SAXSource, and StreamSource depends on the implementation of the client-side JAX-RPC runtime. You can, of course, use a Transformer to convert whatever you get into whichever type you want. For example, the following code gets a DOM model from any kind of Source object:

```
// Convert the source to a DOM model
DOMResult domResult = new DOMResult();
transformer.transform(sources[i], domResult);

// Get the root node of the DOM model
Node node = domResult.getNode();
```

RPC-Style and Document-Style JAX-RPC

In "The SOAP Binding" in Chapter 5, it was noted that the SOAP binding for an individual operation or for all operations defined within a portType element can have a style attribute that takes either of the values rpc or document. However, not much was said about the actual differences between these two styles. This section looks at how RPC- and document-style operations are represented in SOAP messages as well as at the support that JAX-RPC provides for each.

RPC-Style Operations

Perhaps not surprisingly, when you create client-side stubs and server-side ties for a web service for which the definition is supplied in the form of a Java interface, each method in the interface is mapped to an RPC-style operation. The distinguishing feature of an RPC-style operation is the way in which it is represented as a SOAP message, which is specified in section 7 of the SOAP 1.1 specification. For example, Figure 6-2 shows the message that is sent as a result of invoking the following method from the BookQuery interface from the book web service created in Chapter 2:

```
public String getAuthor(String name) throws RemoteException;
```

As you can see, the SOAP body contains a single element that is named for the operation being invoked. This element is in the namespace associated with the web service, which is provided in the *config.xml* file supplied to wscompile, as shown in Example 2-9. The arguments required for the method call are nested as child elements. In this case, a single element containing the name of the book for which the author name is required is added to the getAuthor element. In the case of a method that requires more than one argument, each has a corresponding child element (commonly referred to as an "accessor"), the order of which is the same as that of the arguments that they represent in the method signature.

```
<env:Envelope
    xmlns:env="http://schemas.xmlsoap.org/soap/envelope/"
    xmlns:xsd="http://www.w3.org/2001/XMLSchema"
    xmlns:xsi="http://www.w3.org/2001/XMLSchema-instance"
    xmlns:enc="http://schemas.xmlsoap.org/soap/encoding/"
    xmlns:ns0="urn:jwsnut.chapter2.bookservice/types/BookQuery"
    xmlns:ns1="http://java.sun.com/jax-rpc-ri/internal"
    env:encodingStyle="http://schemas.xmlsoap.org/soap/encoding/
">
    <env:Body>
        <ans1:getAuthor ◄─────────────────────────────────── Operation Name
            xmlns:ans1="urn:jwsnut.chapter2.bookservice/wsdl/BookQuery">
            <String_1 xsi:type="xsd:string">Java Swing</String_1> ◄──── Argument
        </ans1:getAuthor> Operation Name Argument
```

Figure 6-2. SOAP representation of an RPC-style operation

The SOAP specification states that each accessor should be named for its corresponding argument. It is clear, however, that JAX-RPC does not strictly follow this rule, since the accessor for the title argument in Figure 6-2 has been given the name String_1. The practical reason for the use of this rather strange name is that wscompile sees only the compiled class file for the BookQuery interface. Since class files do not contain information about the names used in the source code for method arguments, the best wscompile can do is to use the argument type (String) together with a numeric suffix to create a unique accessor name. Since the name assigned to the part element that describes this argument (which is shown in Example 6-20) in the WSDL description of the service created at the same time as the client stubs will be the same as that used in the SOAP message, it really doesn't matter that it doesn't happen to be the same as the name that the developer used in the Java method signature.*

Example 6-20. WSDL elements relating to the getAuthor() method

```
<!-- Extracts from the message elements: -->
<message name="BookQuery_getAuthor">
  <part name="String_1" type="xsd:string"/>
</message>
<message name="BookQuery_getAuthorResponse">
```

---

* This situation exists only when wscompile is supplied with a Java interface definition as its starting point. When a WSDL description of a service is used to create a Java interface definition and client-side stubs, the argument names that wscompile generates match the part names used in the WSDL document.

Example 6-20. WSDL elements relating to the getAuthor() method (continued)

```
    <part name="result" type="xsd:string"/>
</message>
<!-- Extracts from the portType element: -->
<operation name="getAuthor" parameterOrder="String_1">
  <input message="tns:BookQuery_getAuthor"/>
  <output message="tns:BookQuery_getAuthorResponse"/>
</operation>
```

It is clear from the WSDL extracts shown in Example 6-20 that the presence of the getAuthor element is actually part of the RPC binding for this operation, because the generic WSDL definition of the getAuthor operation indicates only that it requires a message labeled BookQuery_getAuthor that consists of a single part called String_1. As you'll see in the next section, *wrapper elements* such as getAuthor are a characteristic of the SOAP section 7 representation of RPC-style operations, and are not used for document-style operations.

The result of the method call is returned in a response message that is constructed according to similar rules. A typical response message resulting from an invocation of the getAuthor operation is shown in Figure 6-3.

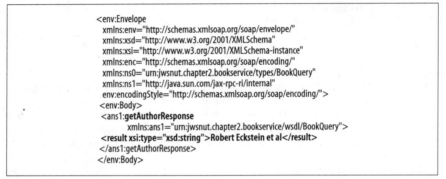

```
<env:Envelope
  xmlns:env="http://schemas.xmlsoap.org/soap/envelope/"
  xmlns:xsd="http://www.w3.org/2001/XMLSchema"
  xmlns:xsi="http://www.w3.org/2001/XMLSchema-instance"
  xmlns:enc="http://schemas.xmlsoap.org/soap/encoding/"
  xmlns:ns0="urn:jwsnut.chapter2.bookservice/types/BookQuery"
  xmlns:ns1="http://java.sun.com/jax-rpc-ri/internal"
  env:encodingStyle="http://schemas.xmlsoap.org/soap/encoding/">
  <env:Body>
  <ans1:getAuthorResponse
        xmlns:ans1="urn:jwsnut.chapter2.bookservice/wsdl/BookQuery">
  <result xsi:type="xsd:string">Robert Eckstein et al</result>
  </ans1:getAuthorResponse>
  </env:Body>
```

Figure 6-3. A SOAP response message for an RPC-style operation

In this case, the SOAP body contains a single element whose name is formed by appending Response to the name of the operation from the original request message. Although this convention is commonly used, it is not mandatory—in fact, any name could be used, since the response message is implicitly associated with the preceding request. Like the getAuthor element shown in Figure 6-2, getAuthorResponse is a wrapper element that is required by the SOAP binding for RPC-style operations, and does not appear in the WSDL description of the response message. The SOAP section 7 rules require the wrapper element to contain an accessor for the value that will become the return value of the method call, followed by accessors that provide the values for any output parameters, if there are any. In this case, since the getAuthor method does not have any output parameters, only the method call result accessor is present. By convention, this accessor is called result, but this is not a requirement. If the return type of the method is void, then the wrapper element contains only accessors for the output parameters. The wrapper for a method that has no return value and no output parameters therefore has no child elements.

In some cases, the wrapper element that represents the operation will be followed by other elements that contain data referenced from one or more of the accessors. For example, consider the getBookInfo( ) method from the book web service:

```
public abstract BookInfo[] getBookInfo( ) throws RemoteException;
```

A reference to the array of returned BookInfo elements is encoded as an accessor within a wrapper element called getBookInfo, but the array itself and the individual BookInfo objects that it contains are placed in the SOAP message body, as shown in Figure 6-4.

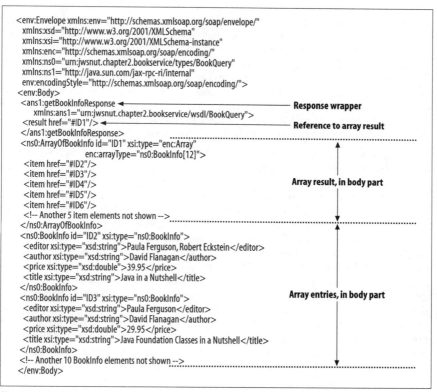

Figure 6-4. An RPC response message with data following the wrapper element

The discussion of the WSDL soap:body element in Chapter 5 mentioned the related attributes use and encodingStyle. The use attribute specifies whether the data types associated with the parts of a SOAP message are encoded according to some set of encoding rules specified by the encodingStyle attribute or whether they are included literally. In most cases, RPC-style operations specify use="encoded" and supply the URI *http://schemas.xmlsoap.org/soap/encoding/* as the value of the encodingStyle attribute to indicate that the message content is encoded according to the SOAP section 5 encoding rules that were outlined in Chapter 3. WSDL also allows the use of literal encoding with RPC-style operations, but JAX-RPC implementations are not required to support it. All WSDL files created by `wscompile` from Java interface definitions contain only RPC-style operations encoded using SOAP section 5 rules. Literal encoding is most often used with document-style operations, which are covered next.

Document-Style Operations

Although RPC-style operations are very common, some web services are defined in terms of the XML documents that the client and server exchange rather than in terms of programming-language operations. An operation defined in this way is referred to as a *document-style* operation. As an example of a web service using document-style operations, a company that allows clients to place orders over the Internet might create an XML Schema that defines a type to represent a purchase order and another to represent an order confirmation. A client application is expected to build a purchase order document and send it to the server, which, following validation, stock checks, credit checks, and so on, then builds and returns an order confirmation document. By contrast, an RPC-style version of this service represents each field in the purchase order as an input method parameter, and each field of the order confirmation as an output parameter or return value. Of course, this can quickly become unmanagable if the number of required arguments is large.

In Chapter 3, the SAAJ API was used to build a book image web service, which required a client to create a SOAP message with a particular set of elements in the body part that would specify a list of books for which it required the cover images. The service implementation used the SAAJ APIs to examine the XML document in the SOAP body part, extract the book titles, and construct a reply message containing the required images. The operations provided by the book image web service are all examples of document-style operations. In order to demonstrate the SOAP encoding rules, all of the data types used by its operations were encoded using the SOAP section 5 rules. However, document-style web services are not required to use any particular encoding rules. Also, since such services are usually defined by an XML Schema that explicitly specifies the data type of each message part, it is more usual for document-style operations to use the so-called *literal encoding*. In the literal encoding, the XML elements that make up a SOAP message do not carry explicit type qualification. For an example of the difference between encoded and literal use, an element that contains floating-point content looks like the following when encoded using the SOAP section 5 encoding rules:

```
<price xsi:type="xsd:double">29.95</price>
```

whereas a literal encoding would omit the typing attribute:

```
<price>29.95</price>
```

The use of literal encoding relies on the XML Schema document for the service containing a definition such as the following:

```
<element name="price" type= "xsd:double"/>
```

This makes typing information in the message itself redundant.

JAX-RPC support for document-style operations

As you saw in Chapter 3, creating web services with SAAJ requires quite a lot of low-level coding. Fortunately, JAX-RPC developers can avoid this work because

JAX-RPC includes support for document-style operations that allows you to delegate to the runtime the hard work of constructing and interpreting the SOAP messages. However, this support works only if the messages in the WSDL definition of the service are constructed in such a way that they look very much like those that are generated for RPC-style operations. The easiest way to explain how document-style operations are supported is to look at an example—in this case, yet another version of the book service that we have been using throughout this chapter.

Since wscompile always maps the methods of a Java interface definition to RPC-style operations, the only way to create a web service that contains document-style operations is to start by putting together a WSDL definition (or importing one in the case of an existing service) from which the Java interface definition can be generated.[*] Since WSDL files are quite verbose, we'll show only short extracts of the file that contains the definitions for the document-style book web service. You can find a complete listing in the Appendix. It is important to bear in mind throughout the following discussion that the WSDL has been carefully constructed so that it satisfies certain criteria that make it possible for the JAX-RPC runtime to generate and consume the messages that correspond to the SOAP bindings that it contains. You'll see what these criteria are as the discussion proceeds.

Let's start by looking at the portType element, which defines the operations that the service provides, and the binding element for one of those operations. The relevant extracts from the WSDL document are shown in Example 6-21.

Example 6-21. A WSDL extract showing a document-style operation

```
<portType name="DocBookQuery">
  <operation name="getBookCount" parameterOrder="">
    <input message="tns:DocBookQuery_getBookCount"/>
    <output message="tns:DocBookQuery_getBookCountResponse"/>
  </operation>
  <operation name="getBookTitle" parameterOrder="index">
    <input message="tns:DocBookQuery_getBookTitle"/>
    <output message="tns:DocBookQuery_getBookTitleResponse"/>
  </operation>
  <operation name="getBookAuthor" parameterOrder="title author">
    <input message="tns:DocBookQuery_getBookAuthor"/>
    <output message="tns:DocBookQuery_getBookAuthorResponse"/>
  </operation>
  <operation name="getBookInfo" parameterOrder="title result">
    <input message="tns:DocBookQuery_getBookInfo"/>
    <output message="tns:DocBookQuery_getBookInfoResponse"/>
  </operation>
  <operation name="getStockInfo" parameterOrder="title">
    <input message="tns:DocBookQuery_getStockInfo"/>
    <output message="tns:DocBookQuery_getStockInfoResponse"/>
```

---

[*] This is true at the time of this writing. However, a future version of JAX-RPC is likely to contain an enhancement that allows document-style messages to be created for a service endpoint defined in terms of a Java interface.

```
    </operation>
  </portType>
  <binding name="DocBookQueryBinding" type="tns:DocBookQuery">
    <soap:binding transport="http://schemas.xmlsoap.org/soap/http"
                  style="document"/>
    <operation name="getBookCount">
      <soap:operation soapAction=""/>
      <input>
        <soap:body use="literal"
             namespace="urn:jwsnut.chapter6.docbookservice/wsdl/DocBookQuery"/>
      </input>
      <output>
        <soap:body use="literal"
             namespace="urn:jwsnut.chapter6.docbookservice/wsdl/DocBookQuery"/>
      </output>
    </operation>
    <!-- Additional operation bindings not shown -->
  </binding>
```

Looking first at the soap:binding element, you can see that the style attribute has the value document. This indicates that any operation that does not explicitly state otherwise is a document-style operation. Since none of the soap:operation elements in this file have their own style attribute, it follows that all of the operations of this web service use the document style. Next, look at the soap:body elements for both operations. In both cases, the use attribute of these elements has the value literal. Since all of the soap:body elements in this file are the same as the ones shown here, every operation provided by this service is document-style with literal encoding.

Now let's look specifically at the getBookTitle operation. The definitions of the input and output messages for this operation are shown in Example 6-22.

Example 6-22. Message definitions for the getBookTitle operation

```
<message name="DocBookQuery_getBookTitlet">
  <part name="body" element="typesns:BookTitleRequest"/>
</message>
<message name="DocBookQuery_getBookTitleResponse">
  <part name="result" element="typesns:BookTitleResponse"/>
</message>
```

The input message consists of a single part called body that represents an element of type BookTitleRequest. As noted in Chapter 5, a part element can refer to either an element or a type definition that may be either in the types section of the WSDL document or in an imported schema (see "Using the import Element" in Chapter 5 for information on how to import external schema information into a WSDL document). In this case, the part element refers to a concrete element definition via the element attribute, rather than using a type attribute to reference an abstract type. Although either is acceptable, according to both the WSDL and JAX-RPC specifications, at the time of this writing, the JAX-RPC reference implementation does not allow the use of the type attribute for a message part associated with a document-style operation.

The next step is to look at the definition of the `BookTitleRequest` element. Before doing this, however, it is useful to review the way in which message parts are defined for RPC-style operations by looking at the WSDL definition for the `getAuthor` operation in the RPC-based book web service shown in Example 6-20. The input message for that operation looks like this:

```
<message name="BookQuery_getAuthor">
  <part name="String_1" type="xsd:string"/>
</message>
```

which resulted in the body of the SOAP message being constructed as follows:

```
<env:Body>
  <ans1:getAuthor
    xmlns:ans1="urn:jwsnut.chapter2.bookservice/wsdl/BookQuery">
    <String_1 xsi:type="xsd:string">Java Swing</String_1>
  </ans1:getAuthor>
</env:Body>
```

Since the operation in this case was RPC-style, the element for the `String_1` part was not placed directly in the SOAP body but inside a wrapper element named for the operation itself. For document-style RPC, however, this does *not* happen. Instead, the element that corresponds to each part of the input or output message is added directly to the SOAP body, with *no* wrapper element. The problem with this is that the JAX-RPC runtime always expects to receive an outer wrapper element that corresponds to the requested operation, with nested accessors that provide the values of the operation arguments. This remains true even for document-style web services. Since this wrapper is not added automatically when the SOAP message is built, for a document-style operation it must be included as part of the schema definition of the element itself. Bearing this in mind, suitable definitions for the `BookTitleRequest` and `BookTitleResponse` elements are shown in Example 6-23

Example 6-23. The BookTitleRequest and BookTitleResponse elements for the document web service

```
<element name="BookTitleRequest">
  <complexType>
    <sequence>
      <element name="index" type="xsd:int"/>
    </sequence>
  </complexType>
</element>
<element name="BookTitleResponse">
  <complexType>
    <sequence>
      <element name="result" type="xsd:string"/>
    </sequence>
  </complexType>
</element>
```

Advanced JAX - RPC

The XML Schema definition for the `BookTitleRequest` element states that it is a compound type that contains a single nested child element called `index`, whose associated value must be an integer. Similarly, the `BookTitleResponse` element must contain a string-valued child element called result. Since the WSDL extract in Example 6-22 indicates that the BookTitleRequest and BookTitleResponse elements are placed directly in the SOAP body, the body part for a typical request message for the getBookTitle operation constructed from these definitions would look like this:

```
<env:Body>
  <ns:BookTitleRequest env:encodingStyle="">
    <index>11</index>
  </ns:BookTitleRequest>
</env:Body>
```

The prefix ns corresponds to the namespace within which the types used in the WSDL document are defined. As you can see, this looks very much like an RPC-style request message for an operation called BookTitleRequest that requires a single argument called index with the value 11. The data type of the index argument is not explicitly specified in the index element, since the encoding style is literal and therefore SOAP encoding rules do not apply.

 Note that we chose to use the name BookTitleRequest instead of getBookTitle for the element referred to from the input message for the getBookTitle operation, and chose to use BookTitleResponse instead of getBookTitleResponse for the output message, so that these names did not appear both as part names and as operation names. This choice was made simply so that it would be obvious that the name of the element placed directly in the SOAP body is that of the element referred to by the message part, rather than the name of the operation itself. You could, if you wish, use the name getBookTitle instead of BookTitleRequest, and use getBookTitleResponse in place of BookTitleResponse. While this would change the content of the SOAP messages so the elements in the body part are named after the operations in the WSDL definition, it would not have any effect on the client and server implementations, as long as the stubs and ties (or their equivalents in the case of a non-JAX-RPC platform) are both generated from the same WSDL document.

Summarizing this discussion, in order for a document-style web service to be compatible with JAX-RPC, it must satisfy the following criteria:

- The input and output messages must each define only a single part, so that only one element is placed directly in the SOAP body. This restriction is placed by the JAX-RPC reference implementation and does not appear in the specification. Therefore, it may not apply to other implementations and may disappear in future revisions of the reference implementation.

- The part element must use the element attribute rather than the type attribute. This is also a restriction that is present in the reference implementation but not in the specification; therefore, it may be lifted in later releases.

- The element referenced by the part must be a complexType constructed as a sequence that contains one nested element for each parameter that the operation requires.

It is entirely possible that you will come across third-party service definitions that do not meet these criteria. In this case, it may not be possible for you to use JAX-RPC to create a client for such a service and you will need to use SAAJ instead.

JAX-RPC interface to document-style operations

To proceed with the implementation after creating a WSDL definition for your web service, you need to generate the corresponding Java interface definition. You can do this by using wscompile with the -import argument in the usual way. The example source code for this book contains an implementation of this web service, which you can use by opening a command window and making *chapter6\ docbookservice* your working directory. To generate the Java interface definition, type the command:

```
ant generate-interface
```

This command runs wscompile with the appropriate command-line arguments, and places the following generated files in the directory *chapter6\docbookservice\ generated\interface\ora\jwsnut\chapter6\docbookservice*:

- *BookAuthorRequest.java*
- *BookAuthorResponse.java*
- *BookCountRequest.java*
- *BookCountResponse.java*
- *BookInfo.java*
- *BookInfoRequest.java*
- *BookTitleRequest.java*
- *BookTitleResponse.java*
- *DocBookQuery.java*
- *StockInfoRequest.java*
- *StockInfoResponse.java*

The file *DocBookQuery.java* contains the Java interface definition corresponding to the DocBookQuery portType. The other files contain the Java source code for the complex types, such as BookTitleRequest and BookTitleResponse, that represent the parts of the input and output messages used by the document-style operations defined by this service. The generated Java interface is shown in Example 6-24.

Example 6-24. The Java interface definition for a web service containing document-style operations

```
public interface DocBookQuery extends java.rmi.Remote {
    public int getBookCount( ) throws  java.rmi.RemoteException;
    public java.lang.String getBookTitle(int index)
        throws  java.rmi.RemoteException;
    public java.lang.String getBookAuthor(java.lang.String title)
        throws  java.rmi.RemoteException;
    public ora.jwsnut.chapter6.docbookservice.BookInfo
        getBookInfo(java.lang.String title) throws java.rmi.RemoteException;
    public javax.xml.soap.SOAPElement getStockInfo(java.lang.String title)
        throws  java.rmi.RemoteException;
}
```

Taking the getBookTitle( ) method as a typical example, it is interesting to note that even though the definition in the WSDL document for the operation that corresponds to this method used the complex types BookTitleRequest and BookTitleResponse to describe the content of its input and output messages, the Java classes that correspond to these complex types do not appear in the method definition. An inspection of the WSDL extracts shown in Example 6-22 and Example 6-23, which contain the definitions relevant to the getBookTitle operation, would lead you to expect that the generated getBookTitle( ) method would look like this:

```
public BookTitleResponse getBookTitle(.BookTitleRequest request)
    throws RemoteException
```

The method signature that is actually generated is as follows:

```
public String getBookTitle(int index) throws RemoteException;
```

This is, of course, a much better reflection of the intent of the operation, and is identical to the hand-created definition used by the original RPC-based version of this service shown earlier in this chapter. On the other hand, the declaration of the getBookInfo( ) method *does* include a class generated from the complex type that appears in the definition of the output message for its corresponding operation:

```
public BookInfo getBookInfo(String title) throws RemoteException;
```

So how is the actual method call signature determined? Let's discuss how the JAX-RPC reference implementation works.

In the case of the method arguments, the complex type associated with the input message is examined and an argument is added for each field within it, for which JAX-RPC defines a standard mapping to XML. In the case of the getBookTitle operation, for example, the BookTitleRequest type (the definition of which is shown in Example 6-23 earlier in this chapter) contains only a single field of type xsd:int. Since JAX-RPC maps xsd:int to the Java primitive type int, the generated method will have a single argument of type int, the name of which is taken from the name attribute of its element definition.

For a method that has a return value, the method definition depends on the complex type that represents the output message of the operation. In the case of the getBookTitle operation, the BookTitleResponse type (also shown in Example 6-23) has only a single child element of type xsd:String; the generated method therefore returns a String value. The output message for the getBookInfo operation, however, consists of a part that references the element definition shown in Example 6-25.

Example 6-25. The BookInfo type declared as the output
from the getBookInfo operation

```
<element name="BookInfo">
  <complexType>
    <sequence>
      <element name="title" type="xsd:string"/>
      <element name="author" type="xsd:string"/>
      <element name="editor" type="xsd:string"/>
      <element name="price" type="xsd:double"/>
      <element name="stock" type="xsd:int"/>
```

```
    </sequence>
   </complexType>
</element>
```

In cases such as this, in which there is more than one field in the output message, the Java method returns an instance of the value type class generated from the BookInfo element, which acts as a convenient holder for all five return values. An alternative approach is to generate a Holder class for the BookInfo item and use the following method signature:

```
public void getBookInfo(String title, BookInfoHolder holder) throws
RemoteException;
```

This is a more general solution, since it continues to work even if the output message for the operation contains more than one part. However, at the time of this writing—since the reference implementation allows only messages associated with document-style operations to have a single part—this generality is not required and method signatures utilizing Holder classes in this way are not generated.

The last method in the generated DocBookQuery interface is a little different from the others:

```
public javax.xml.soap.SOAPElement getStockInfo(java.lang.String title)
    throws RemoteException;
```

This method returns the number of copies of a given book that are in stock. The return value should, therefore, be an integer, and you might expect the generated method to look like this:

```
public int getStockInfo() throws RemoteException;
```

Instead of returning a Java primitive int, however, this method is defined to return an object of type javax.xml.soap.SOAPElement, which is a class defined by the SAAJ API (and described in Chapter 3) that represents an XML element in a SOAP message. To see why this return value is used instead of int, it is necessary to look at the parts of the WSDL document that define the output message for the getStockInfo operation, which are shown in Example 6-26.

Example 6-26. WSDL definitions for the getStockInfo operation

```
<element name="StockInfoResponse">
  <complexType>
    <sequence>
      <element name="stock" type="xsd:nonNegativeInteger"/>
    </sequence>
  </complexType>
</element>

<message name="DocBookQuery_getStockInfoResponse">
  <part name="result" element="typesns:StockInfoResponse"/>
</message>

<!-- Operation definition (from portType) -->
<operation name="getStockInfo" parameterOrder="title">
  <input message="tns:DocBookQuery_getStockInfo"/>
```

Example 6-26. WSDL definitions for the getStockInfo operation (continued)

```
    <output message="tns:DocBookQuery_getStockInfoResponse"/>
</operation>
```

These definitions amount to a statement that says the output message contains an element called stock with XML Schema type xsd:nonNegativeInteger. Perhaps surprisingly, although JAX-RPC maps xsd:int to a Java primitive int, it does not have a standard mapping to a Java type for xsd:nonNegativeInteger. When, as here, there is no mapping for an element in literal mode, JAX-RPC uses a SOAPElement to represent it in the generated Java interface. As a result, you'll need to use SAAJ APIs in your client application or service implementation code to provide or extract the return value of the getStockInfo( ) method, as you'll see later in this section.

The schema type for this return value was chosen deliberately in order to demonstrate the way in which JAX-RPC handles types for which it does not have a mapping. The same stock information is also available in the BookInfo object returned from the getBookInfo( ) method, the XML schema definition for which was shown in Example 6-25. In this case, however, for the sake of simplicity, the data type of the stock quantity was defined as xsd:int. Had it instead been declared as xsd:nonNegativeInteger, then the stock field of the generated BookInfo class would have been of type SOAPElement rather then int, as shown in the following code extract (the differences from the actual generated code are highlighted):

```
// How the BookInfo class would have looked had "stock"
// been defined with schema type xsd:nonNegativeInteger
// (code not affected by this change is not shown)
public class BookInfo {
    private java.lang.String title;
    private java.lang.String author;
    private java.lang.String editor;
    private double price;
    private SOAPElement stock;

    public BookInfo( ) {
    }

    public BookInfo(java.lang.String title, java.lang.String author,
                    java.lang.String editor,
                    double price, SOAPElement stock) {
        this.title = title;
        this.author = author;
        this.editor = editor;
        this.price = price;
        this.stock = stock;
    }

    public SOAPElement getStock( ) {
        return stock;
    }

    public void setStock(SOAPElement stock) {
        this.stock = stock;
    }
}
```

Implementing a service containing a document-style operation

As with our earlier examples, in order to provide the service described in the WSDL document, you have to create a class that implements the DocBookQuery interface. The fact that the SOAP messages that are exchanged between the service and client applications are document-style messages and do not use the SOAP section 5 encoding rules is taken care of by the generated stub and tie classes, and is therefore not visible either to the service or to code in the client application. Most of the code that implements the service is very similar to that shown earlier in this chapter and in Chapter 2, and can be found in the directory *chapter6\docbookservice\server\ora\jwsnut\chapter6*. Nevertheless, there are some differences in the implementation and packaging of the service that you need to be aware of.

As far as the implementation is concerned, the only method of the service interface that is affected by the fact that the operation that it corresponds to is a document-style operation using literal encoding is getStockInfo( ). This gets the quantity of a given book that is currently in stock, which must return a SOAPElement instead of the int that is required for an RPC-style operation. The implementation details of this method are shown in Example 6-27.

Example 6-27. Implementation of the getStockInfo() method

```
public SOAPElement getStockInfo(String title) {
    BookInfo book = findBook(title);
    SOAPElement element = null;
    if (book != null) {
        try {
            if (factory == null) {
                factory = SOAPFactory.newInstance( );
            }
            element = factory.createElement("stock");
            element.addTextNode(String.valueOf(book.getStock( )));
        } catch (SOAPException ex) {
            // Just return null in this case
            element = null;
        }
    }
    return element;
}
```

As you can see, this method uses the SAAJ SOAPFactory class, described in Chapter 3, to create the SOAPElement that will become its return value. For the sake of efficiency, a single SOAPFactory instance is created when this method is first called. The SOAPElement's name must be taken from the value of the name attribute for the corresponding element in the WSDL document. As you can see from Example 6-26, this means that the element must be called stock. Once the SOAPElement is created, the actual stock quantity value is included by adding a text node with the quantity as its value. The SOAPElement that this code creates corresponds to XML that looks like this:

```
<stock>10</stock>
```

The client code that would use the value returned from this method is also slightly more complicated than it would be for an RPC-style operation, since it needs to use the SOAPElement getValue( ) method to access the content of the text node that it contains:

```
SOAPElement element = bookQuery.getStockInfo(title);
int stock = Integer.parseInt(element.getValue( ));
```

The only other point of interest in the construction of the service is the way in which it is packaged for deployment. Recall from Chapter 2 that packaging is a two-step process:

1. A portable WAR file is created, containing the implementation-independent classes that contain the code for the service itself, together with any other classes and resources that it requires.

2. The content of the portable WAR file is used by wsdeploy or j2eec to generate a deployable WAR file that contains implementation-dependent server-side ties and serializers, as well as the developer-supplied classes and resources from the portable WAR file.

In principle, this process should not be any different for a service that contains document/literal operations than it is for any of the other examples that you have seen so far, which contained only RPC-style operations. However, there is one small part of the process for creating the WAR file for JWSDP deployment (but not for J2EE 1.4 deployment) that is a little different in this case.

In order for the wsdeploy utility to create a deployable archive, it reads the *jaxrpc-ri.xml* file from the portable archive, and uses the information that it contains to generate server-side ties and serializer classes that know how to convert between the data types used in the Java interface definition and their XML representation in SOAP messages. In order to create the serializers and tie classes, wsdeploy uses Java reflection to introspect on the methods and arguments of the Java interface definition indicated by the interface attribute of the endpoint element. The problem with this, of course, is that there is nothing in the class file to indicate whether any of the methods of the Java interface correspond to document-style operations. In the absence of this information, wsdeploy assumes that they are all RPC-style. This causes it to create a WSDL document, ties, and serializers that are suitable for an RPC-style service using the SOAP encoding. These classes will not work properly for document-style operations.

To avoid this potential problem, it is necessary to indicate explicitly to wsdeploy which operations have document-style semantics and which are RPC-style. One way to do this is to have it parse the WSDL document, since this shows clearly the semantics of each operation. Unfortunately, wsdeploy does not parse WSDL documents, but it will accept a model file as an alternative source of information in place of a Java interface definition. As noted in Chapter 2, a model file contains a binary representation of a service, its ports, port types, operations, messages, and types built by wscompile while parsing the WSDL document. It is therefore equivalent to the WSDL definition. You can refer wsdeploy to the model file for an endpoint by setting the model attribute of the endpoint element in the *jaxrpc-ri.xml* file.

You can see a plain-text version of the model file for the book web service from Chapter 2 by pointing your web browser at the URL *http://localhost:8000/Books/BookQuery?model* and opening the *model.gz* file that is returned. Although it is interesting to see what is in this file, there is no real point in spending too much time trying to decode it, since it is specific to the JAX-RPC reference implementation and you won't need to do anything with it apart from create it and supply it to wsdeploy.

Assuming that you have a model file, you simply need to place it in the portable web archive and include a line in the *jaxrpc-ri.xml* file indicating where it can be found, as shown in Example 6-28. Whenever an endpoint element in a *jaxrpc-ri.xml* file contains a model attribute, the model file that it refers to is used in preference to the Java interface class as a source of information regarding the web service to be deployed. It is still necessary to supply the interface attribute, however, because the class file that it refers to is used by JAXRPCServlet at runtime.

Example 6-28. The final version of the jaxrpc-ri.xml file for the document-based book web service

```
<?xml version="1.0" encoding="UTF-8"?>
<webServices
    xmlns="http://java.sun.com/xml/ns/jax-rpc/ri/dd"
    version="1.0"
    targetNamespaceBase="urn:jwsnut.chapter6.docbookservice/wsdl/"
    typeNamespaceBase="urn:jwsnut.chapter6.docbookservice/types/">

    <endpoint
        name="DocBookQuery"
        displayName="DocBookQuery Port"
        description="Document-style Book Query Port"
        model="/WEB-INF/model"
        interface="ora.jwsnut.chapter6.docbookservice.DocBookQuery"
        implementation=
            "ora.jwsnut.chapter6.docbookservice.DocBookServiceServant"/>

    <endpointMapping
        endpointName="DocBookQuery"
        urlPattern="/DocBookQuery"/>
</webServices>
```

Advanced JAX - RPC

Note that the model file is placed in the *WEB-INF* directory of the portable web archive. This is an appropriate place for it because it will then appear in the *WEB-INF* directory of the deployed web service, where it is protected from direct access from HTTP clients.

The remaining point to clear up is how the model file is created. Fortunately, this is very simple—all you need to do is use the -model argument when running the wscompile utility. In the Ant buildfile for this example, this can be done when running wscompile to generate the Java interface definition from the WSDL document:

```
wscompile -gen:server -model output/interface/model -s generated/interface
-d output/interface config.xml
```

All of this does not apply when deploying a service to a J2EE 1.4 application server because, as mentioned in Chapter 2, the deployable WAR archive for J2EE 1.4 includes a WSDL definition of the service along with a mapping file that allows you to define the way in which the WSDL definition is mapped to Java interfaces. Unlike *jaxrpc-ri.xml*, these files clearly indicate whether each operation is RPC- or document-style, and whether it uses literal or RPC-style encoding.

In fact, all of the JAX-RPC examples in this book are packaged with a model file. This is not strictly necessary in most cases, since the information that wsdeploy can obtain by reflecting on the endpoint interface classes is usually sufficient. The model file is actually included in every case so that the same example source code can be used whether you choose to run the examples with the JWSDP or on the J2EE 1.4 platform (in which the model file can be used in lieu of the J2EE 1.4 XML mapping file). In the text that accompanies the example, we'll point out where including the model file would have been a requirement even if it wasn't for this compatibility issue.

To build and deploy this web service, with *chapter6\docbookservice* as your working directory, type the command:

```
ant deploy
```

The example source code also contains a simple application client that uses this service, which you can run using the following commands:

```
ant compile-client
ant run-client
```

Suppressing the mapping of message content to method arguments

If you supply the -f:nodatabinding option to wscompile, it generates a Java interface in which the SOAP-level interface of a document-style operation is exposed directly, instead of attempting to map the content of the SOAP messages to method arguments and return values. In the case of the example used in this section, the Java interface resulting from the use of this option would be as shown in Example 6-29, which you should compare to Example 6-24.

Example 6-29. Java interface generated for document/literal operations with data binding disabled

```
public interface DocBookQuery extends java.rmi.Remote {
    public javax.xml.soap.SOAPElement
        getBookCount(javax.xml.soap.SOAPElement body) throws RemoteException;
    public javax.xml.soap.SOAPElement
        getBookTitle(javax.xml.soap.SOAPElement body) throws RemoteException;
    public javax.xml.soap.SOAPElement
        getBookAuthor(javax.xml.soap.SOAPElement title) throws RemoteException;
    public javax.xml.soap.SOAPElement
        getBookInfo(javax.xml.soap.SOAPElement title) throws RemoteException;
    public javax.xml.soap.SOAPElement
        getStockInfo(javax.xml.soap.SOAPElement title) throws RemoteException;
}
```

Turning off data binding in this way requires you to both create the SOAP elements to be included in the outgoing messages, and decode the responses using low-level code written using the SAAJ API. Therefore, this is not for the faint-hearted!

Client and Server Context Handling

All of the JAX-RPC examples that you have seen so far have treated the client application and the service implementation as independent entities that communicate only by passing information as method arguments and return values. In reality, however, it is often useful for the server to have access to additional context information that is supplied by the environment in which it operates or is propagated from the client on each method call. This section looks at the various types of context information that the JAX-RPC runtime makes available to web service implementations.

The web service implementation classes discussed so far have been self-contained and have confined themselves to implementing the methods of the service endpoint interface. Resources that might be required, such as the list of books known to a book service or the cover images for those books, have been bundled into the WAR file along with the implementation class, and accessed at runtime using the Class getResource( ) and getResourceAsStream( ) methods. This technique is acceptable when all of the resources and configuration information for a web service are known when the service is packaged, but it does not allow for configuration to be performed at deployment time. Web containers typically provide some mechanism that allows configuration of this type to be performed, and the servlet environment includes APIs that allow access to this information at runtime. However, there is a problem. How does the service implementation class get access to the environment of its hosting servlet? The JAX-RPC server-side API includes an interface (javax.xml.rpc.server.ServiceLifecycle) that a service class can implement that makes this possible.

 As discussed in Chapter 2, J2EE Version 1.4 allows a web service to be hosted in a servlet environment or implemented as a stateless session bean. The discussion in this section relates only to the former case. A web service implemented as a session bean can use the lifecycle methods of the bean itself to perform initialization and cleanup, while runtime context information is provided by the SessionContext object passed to its setSessionContext( ) method. Therefore, the ServiceLifecycle interface is not applicable to a web service implemented as a session bean.

The ServiceLifecycle Interface

The definition of the ServiceLifecycle interface is shown in Example 6-30.

Example 6-30. The ServiceLifecycle interface

```
public interface ServiceLifecylce {
    public void init(Object context) throws ServiceException;
    public void destroy( );
}
```

When JAXRPCServlet (or an implementation-specific equivalent) receives requests that require the invocation of a method of a web service, it creates one or more instances of the servant class that provides that service. If (and only if) the service class implements the ServiceLifecylce interface, then following execution of its constructor and before any of the methods that implement the service endpoint interface are invoked, JAXRPCServlet calls its init( ) method. A servant class normally uses the init( ) method to perform resource allocation, and may throw a ServiceException if it encounters any errors that would prevent it from providing its service. If JAXRPCServlet can determine that it no longer requires an instance of a servant class, then when its hosting web container is being closed down, it typically calls the servant class's destroy( ) method to allow it to release resources. JAX-RPC implementations that create a pool of instances of a servant class call the destroy( ) method of an instance when removing it from the pool, following which no further web service method calls will be delegated to it.

When the init( ) method of the servant class is called, it is passed an instance of an object that provides runtime context information. In order to allow web services to be hosted in different environments, the init( ) method signature simply declares this argument to be of type Object. However, for the servlet environment, the actual runtime type of this object is javax.xml.rpc.server. ServletEndpointContext. This object remains valid throughout the lifetime of the service instance (that is, until the destroy( ) method is completed), and a reference to it may therefore be stored for use within the methods that implement the service endpoint interface.

The ServletEndpointContext Interface

The ServletEndpointContext object provides access to the runtime environment in which a servant class hosted by a servlet is executing. The methods defined by this interface are shown in Example 6-31.

Example 6-31. The ServletEndpointContext interface

```
public interface ServletEndpointContext {
    public ServletContext getServletContext( );
    public Principal getUserPrincipal( );
    public HttpSession getHttpSession( );
    public MessageContext getMessageContext( );
}
```

These methods are typically used as follows:

- The getServletContext( ) method retrieves the ServletContext object for the web application hosting the web service implementation. This is the only attribute of the ServletEndpointContext that is valid during the execution of the init( ) method. Among other things, the ServletContext gives you access to the servlet's initialization parameters, which are set when the web service is packaged and may be overridden at deployment time. You can therefore use the *web.xml* file for the web application in which the service is deployed to supply configuration information intended for the web service itself. An example of this is shown later.

- The getUserPrincipal( ) method, which can be called only from within a method implementing the service endpoint interface, returns a java.security. Principal object for the user that invoked the endpoint interface method. The value returned from this method is null unless the hosting servlet is configured so that the web container performs authentication for the URL used to access the service. When authentication is enabled, the client application is required to supply authentication information. Requests that fail to do so, or that supply invalid credentials, will be rejected by the web container before the web service method is called. See "JAX-RPC Authentication" later in this chapter for an example of the use of web service authentication.

- The getHttpSession( ) method returns the javax.servlet.http.HttpSession object for the HTTP session within which the web service method is invoked (if there is one). If the client application does not explicitly enable the use of HTTP sessions, then this method returns null. See the later section "Session Management" for an example of the use of an HTTP session.

- The getMessageContext( ) method returns a MessageContext object that can be used to acccess the SOAP message that caused the currently executing service endpoint interface method to be called. The same MessageContext object is shared by any message handlers configured for the endpoint; therefore, it can also be used to store state information that needs to be shared between message handlers or between message handlers and the web service implementation itself. See "SOAP Header Processing" later in this chapter for further information on the MessageContext object.

In addition to the state available from the ServletEndpointContext, a web service implementation class can access information stored in the JNDI environment of its hosting servlet.

Multithreaded Access to the ServletEndpointContext Object

Even though a single instance of the ServletEndpointContext interface is passed to a servant's init( ) method, the values of each of the attributes of this object, apart from the ServletContext, depend on the context of a specific web service method and are therefore valid only when that method is being executed. However, as discussed in Chapter 2, a single servant instance may be used to service any number of web service method invocations, which may or may not be serialized relative to each other. In other words, it is possible that there may be more than one thread simultaneously executing the servant's methods at any given time.

This situation might seem to cause a problem with the use of the ServletEndpointContext object, since it needs to return the attributes applicable to one client application in one thread and those for a different application (and probably a different user) in another thread. Fortunately, there is no conflict between simultaneous uses of the ServletEndpointContext object in different threads, since the request-specific information that it makes available is held in thread-local variables. Each thread, therefore, has its own private copy of the state relating to the client application request that it is handling, which is returned by the methods of the ServletEndpointContext when invoked from that thread.

An Example Web Service Using ServletEndpointContext

To illustrate the use of the ServiceLifecycle and ServletEndpointContext inter-faces, we'll use an extended version of the SmallBookService that was shown earlier in this chapter. The definition of the service interface for this example is shown in Example 6-32.

Example 6-32. The ContextBookQuery service endpoint interface

```
public interface ContextBookQuery extends Remote {
    public abstract void setUpperCase(boolean cond) throws RemoteException;
    public abstract boolean isUpperCase() throws RemoteException;
    public abstract int getBookCount() throws RemoteException;
    public abstract String getBookTitle(int index) throws RemoteException;
    public abstract void getBookAuthor(String title, StringHolder author)
            throws ContextBookServiceException, RemoteException;
    public abstract void log(String value) throws RemoteException;
}
```

The only difference between this interface and the SmallBookQuery interface is the addition of the setUpperCase() and isUpperCase() methods, which are included for the sake of demonstrating the use of HTTP sessions in the next section. From the point of view of this section, the most interesting aspect of this example is the servant implementation class, extracts from which are shown in Example 6-33.

Example 6-33. Extract from the implementation class
for the ContextBookQuery interface

```
public class ContextBookServiceServant implements ContextBookQuery,
ServiceLifecycle {

    // ServletEndpointContext object
    private ServletEndpointContext endpointContext;

    // Name of an authorized user.
    private String userName;

    // Records whether book names should be sorted
    private boolean sorted;

    /* -- Implementation of the ServiceLifeCycle interface -- */
    public void init(Object context) throws ServiceException {
        endpointContext = (ServletEndpointContext)context;

        // Get the authorized user name from the init parameters
        ServletContext servletContext = endpointContext.getServletContext();
        userName = servletContext.getInitParameter("UserName");

        // Get alphabetic sorting flag from JNDI
        try {
            InitialContext namingCtx = new InitialContext();
            Object value = namingCtx.lookup("java:comp/env/sorted");
```

```
        sorted = value instanceof Boolean ? ((Boolean)value).booleanValue( )
                                          : false;
        ContextBookServiceServantData.setSorted(sorted);
    } catch (NamingException ex) {
        servletContext.log("Exception while accessing naming context", ex);
    }
}

/**
 * Called when the service instance is no longer required.
 */
public void destroy( ) {
    // Nothing to do
}

// Service endpoint interface implementation methods not shown
}
```

Since this class implements the ServiceLifecycle interface, it is obliged to provide
the init( ) and destroy( ) methods, although in the case of the latter, there is
nothing to do for this particular service. The init( ) method begins by casting the
object that is passed to the type ServletEndpointContext, and storing it for later
use in the web service implementation methods. The remaining code in this
method illustrates two ways for the servant class to get configuration information:

- Servlet initialization parameters can be obtained by calling the
  getInitParameter( ) method of ServletContext. The ServletContext for the
  hosting servlet is obtained by calling the getServletContext( ) method of
  ServletEndpointContext. In this case, the init( ) method gets the value of an
  initialization parameter called UserName, which it stores for later use. This
  value is used in the second part of Example 6-33, and is described later in
  "JAX-RPC Authentication."

- The values associated with entries in the hosting servlet's JNDI namespace
  can be obtained by creating an InitialContext object and then using the
  lookup( ) method with an appropriate key. Here, the value of a Boolean setting held under the key java:comp/env/sorted is retrieved. Service implementation classes are permitted to access the JNDI context in their web service
  implementation methods, as is init( ).

The initialization parameter and the value of the sorted entry in the JNDI environment can be set by including appropriate tags in the *web.xml* file that is included
in the portable WAR. The *web.xml* file for this example, with the tags needed to
declare the parameters used in this example highlighted, is shown in
Example 6-34.*

---

* The *web.xml* file also contains a security constraint that ensures that only users in the JWSGroup role
can access this web service. You'll see how a JAX-RPC client identifies itself to the web container
in order to satisfy this constraint in the section "JAX-RPC Authentication," later in this chapter.

Example 6-34. The web.xml file for the ContextBookQuery web service

```
<!DOCTYPE web-app
    PUBLIC "-//Sun Microsystems, Inc.//DTD Web Application 2.3//EN"
    "http://java.sun.com/j2ee/dtds/web-app_2_3.dtd">

<web-app>
    <display-name>Context-handling JAX-RPC Book Service</display-name>
    <description>Context-handling Book Service Web Application using JAX-RPC
        </description>

    <context-param>
        <param-name>UserName</param-name>
        <param-value>JWSUserName</param-value>
    </context-param>

    <security-constraint>
        <web-resource-collection>
            <web-resource-name>ContextBookService</web-resource-name>
            <url-pattern>/*</url-pattern>
        </web-resource-collection>
        <auth-constraint>
            <role-name>JWSGroup</role-name>
        </auth-constraint>
    </security-constraint>
    <login-config>
        <auth-method>BASIC</auth-method>
        <realm-name>Context Book Service</realm-name>
    </login-config>

    <env-entry>
        <env-entry-name>sorted</env-entry-name>
        <env-entry-value>true</env-entry-value>
        <env-entry-type>java.lang.Boolean</env-entry-type>
    </env-entry>
</web-app>
```

As well as providing access to initialization parameters, having a reference to the ServletContext allows the servant class to make entries in the web container's log file. The log( ) method in the service endpoint interface exploits this fact to improve on the original implementation described in "One-Way Calls" earlier in this chapter, which wrote the logging information to System.out:

```
public void log(String value) {
    if (checkAccess()) {  // checkAccess( ) is described later in this
    section
        endpointContext.getServletContext( ).log(new Date() + ": " + value);
    }
}
```

To run this example, make *chapter6\contextbookservice* your working directory and type the command:

```
ant deploy
```

This command compiles, packages, and deploys the service implementation. The client application for this example calls the getBookCount( ) method of the service endpoint interface to get the number of books, then loops to get the author and title of each, printing the results in the command window. You can run this client using the commands:

```
ant compile-client
ant run-client
```

When you run these commands, you'll notice that the book titles appear in alphabetical order. This happens because the ContextBookServiceServantData class, which provides the book data to the servant class for this example, uses the value of the Boolean variable obtained from the JNDI value java:comp/env/sorted, as shown in Example 6-33, to determine whether to return sorted data. As you can see from the *web.xml* file in Example 6-34, this variable is set to true and therefore the book titles are sorted.

Session Management

For reasons discussed in "Server-side architecture" in Chapter 2, servant classes cannot store state information relating to individual client applications. As a result, the methods in the service endpoint interface are almost always self-describing in the sense that all required inputs to the operation are provided as arguments. However, a web service that is hosted by a servlet *can* store client-related information if it makes use of the HTTP session support provided by the web container.

The servant class gets access to the session information by calling the getHttpSession( ) method of the ServletEndpointContext object passed to its init( ) method, and then uses the HttpSession setAttribute( ) method to store values that can be retrieved in subsequent invocations of the endpoint interface methods. For an example of how this might be used, consider the setUpperCase( ) and isUpperCase( ) methods in the ContextBookQuery interface shown in Example 6-32. The intent of the setUpperCase( ) method is to allow the client to specify whether the book titles returned by the getBookTitle( ) method should be all in their natural case or in uppercase. A client should be able to invoke this method once and then be able to get the title of any book without having to respecify the required case setting with each method call. The isUpperCase( ) method should return the value set by the most recent invocation of setUpperCase( ) by the same client, or else return a default value if the client has never called it. The state set by the setUpperCase( ) method needs to be stored on a per-client basis.

In order to provide this functionality, the servant class needs to keep the value set by the setUpperCase( ) method in the HTTP session associated with the client that invokes it, from which it can be retrieved later when it is required. The implementation of the setUpperCase( ) and isUpperCase( ) methods is shown in Example 6-35.

Example 6-35. Using an HTTP session to store client-related state

```
public void setUpperCase(boolean cond) {
    HttpSession session = endpointContext.getHttpSession( );
    if (session != null) {
```

```
    session.setAttribute(UPPER_CASE, cond ? Boolean.TRUE : Boolean.FALSE);
    }
}

public boolean isUpperCase() {
    HttpSession session = endpointContext.getHttpSession();
    if (session != null) {
        Boolean upperCase = (Boolean)session.getAttribute(UPPER_CASE);
        return upperCase == null ? false : upperCase.booleanValue();
    }

    // No session - upper case mode not allowed
    return false;
}
```

As you can see, both methods check whether the value returned by getHttpSession() is null before attempting to access or store a value. This step is necessary because the client application might not have enabled the use of HTTP sessions or the web container might not support them. In order to enable HTTP sessions, the client must explicitly set a property on the JAX-RPC client stub:

```
// Get the endpoint interface
ContextBookService_Impl service = new ContextBookService_Impl();
ContextBookQuery bookQuery = service.getContextBookQueryPort();
Stub stub = (Stub)bookQuery;
stub._setProperty(Stub.ENDPOINT_ADDRESS_PROPERTY, args[0]);

// Enable session maintenance so that the setUpperCase() method works.
stub._setProperty(Stub.SESSION_MAINTAIN_PROPERTY, Boolean.TRUE);
```

The same technique is required for a dynamic proxy Stub obtained using one of the Service getPort() methods. If you are using the dynamic invocation interface, then the Call.SESSION_MAINTAIN_PROPERTY of the Call object should be set to Boolean.TRUE:

```
Call call = service.createCall(...);
call.setProperty(Call.SESSION_MAINTAIN_PROPERTY, Boolean.TRUE);
```

The client application for this example uses a command-line parameter to determine the argument passed to the setUpperCase() method, which it calls before invoking any other web service method. The example also retrieves the value to demonstrate that the setting is persistent, and therefore constitutes a client-specific state retained between invocations of the web service's endpoint interface methods:

```
boolean upperCase = args.length > 1 && args[1].
equalsIgnoreCase("uppercase");
bookQuery.setUpperCase(upperCase);
System.out.println("Upper case? " + bookQuery.isUpperCase());
```

You can run the example with the appropriate command line by using the command:

```
ant run-client-uppercase
```

As a result, you should see the usual list of books, with all of the titles in uppercase.

JAX-RPC Authentication

JAX-RPC does not have any authentication mechanisms of its own. However, you can make use of the generic facilities provided by the hosting web container to provide the same level of security to your web services as are available to other web applications. Both HTTP connections with basic authentication and HTTPS connections (with or without authentication) can be used to carry JAX-RPC traffic, provided that you properly configure the web container and the servlet, and then use the appropriate URL when accessing the service. The topic of web containers and authentication has already been fully discussed in "Using SAAJ with Secure Connections" in Chapter 3, and, as far as the service implementation is concerned, the setup details for a JAX-RPC service are the same as they are for SAAJ.

In the case of the ContextBookQuery web service, the *web.xml* file shown in Example 6-34 contains security-constraint and login-config tags that enforce the use of basic authentication and allow access only to users in the contextbookservice role. The roles referred to in the *web.xml* file, and the users that belong to that role, must be configured with the web container. For the J2EE 1.4 reference implementation, this is done using the realmtool command-line utility, whereas for Tomcat, you need to edit the *tomcat-users.xml* file. For both of these cases, the details can be found in Chapter 1. If you are using a different application server, you should consult the application server's documentation to find out how to add to its authentication database.

With this protection in place, any attempt to access the URLs provided by this service are rejected unless the client provides the correct authentication information. A JAX-RPC client using either a statically generated stub or a dynamic proxy returned by the Service getPort( ) method can supply the username and password required for HTTP basic authentication by setting two Stub properties:

```
String userName = System.getProperty("ContextBooks.user");
String password = System.getProperty("ContextBooks.password");
if (userName != null && password != null) {
    stub._setProperty(Stub.USERNAME_PROPERTY, userName);
    stub._setProperty(Stub.PASSWORD_PROPERTY, password);
}
```

A client using the dynamic invocation interface associates the username and password with the Call object instead:

```
Call call = service.createCall(.....);
call.setProperty(Call.USERNAME_PROPERTY, userName);
call.setProperty(Call.PASSWORD_PROPERTY, password);
```

Using container authentication in this way allows a web service to delegate the verification of the identify of the client to the container rather than having to be coded to perform this task itself. In many cases, this check provides all the security that the web service requires. If necessary, however, the service can add its own explicit security checks to those performed by the container. Each time a properly authenticated request is made to a servlet, the container creates a java. security.Principal object containing the name of the authenticated user. The implementation methods of a servlet-hosted web service can get access to this object by calling the getUserPrincipal( ) method of its ServletEnpointContext. A web service implemented as a session bean can get the same information from the getCallerPrincipal( ) method of its SessionContext, which is supplied to it during its initialization. The ContextBookQuery web service uses this information to allow only a single user access to the information that it provides. The name of the authorized user is obtained from the initialization parameters of its hosting servlet (see the context-param element in Example 6-34), and the access check is made by the code shown in Example 6-36.

Example 6-36. Using the getUserPrincipal() method to get authentication information

```
private boolean checkAccess( ) {
    boolean allowed = true;
    if (userName != null) {
        // Authentication is configured.
        Principal principal = endpointContext.getUserPrincipal( );
        allowed = principal != null && userName.equals(principal.getName( ));
    }
    return allowed;
}
```

This check is performed at the start of each method that implements the service endpoint interface. If the calling user is not the one named in the initialization parameters, then the web service implementation method returns a zero count or a null string, depending on the required return type.

The client application for this example obtains the username and password that it should use from properties set on its command line, which in turn come from the *jwsnutExamples.properties* file in your home directory, as does the name of the authorized user in the servlet initialization parameters. When you run this example, the client application supplies the same username as the one in the *web.xml* file. Therefore, it passes the web service's authorization check and you get back the complete list of books. If you change the values of the USERNAME and PASSWORD properties in the *jwsnutExamples.properties* file to those of the other user in the JWSGroup role—i.e., AnotherUser and Pwd—then the web container allows the client application to invoke the methods of the web service, since the username and password are valid and correspond to a user in the role JWSGroup. However, because the username is not the same as the one in the *web.xml* file, the service's checkAccess( ) method returns false. As a result, no book information is returned. If you choose a user that is not in the JWSGroup role, or if you supply an incorrect password, the web container rejects the request before it reaches the web service itself.

SOAP Header Processing

In the section "RPC-Style and Document-Style JAX-RPC," earlier in this chapter, you saw that for both RPC- and document-style operations JAX-RPC method call arguments and return values are placed in the SOAP message body. However, SOAP extensions and higher-level business frameworks based on SOAP messaging, such as WS-Routing and ebXML, typically add elements to the SOAP header as well as or instead of using the message body. The WS-Security extension, for example, provides a framework to include in the SOAP header authentication information, and provides security tokens (such as X.509 certificates) that can be used to verify the identity of the message sender or protect against modification of the message while it is in transit. Applications built using the SAAJ API have direct access to the SOAP header and can therefore add any necessary elements to it before a message is transmitted as well as process header blocks when a message is received. A JAX-RPC application can also access the SOAP header using one (or both) of two techniques that are the subject of this section—mapping header content to method arguments or creating a SOAP message handler.

Mapping Header Content to Method Arguments

Mapping header content to method arguments is a natural and convenient way for a JAX-RPC application to access the header because it is consistent with the JAX-RPC programming model and avoids the need for application code to have any direct dependency on the structure of the underlying messages. You can use this technique provided that the following conditions are satisfied:

- The service is described by a WSDL document rather than a Java interface definition.

- The message parts that are to be included in the SOAP header are described using soap:header elements in the binding section of the WSDL document.

To illustrate the mapping of header blocks to method arguments, we'll create a web service based on the one used to demonstrate the dynamic invocation interface earlier in this chapter (the definition of which you'll find in Example 6-5). However, we'll add to it a header element that contains authentication information for the user invoking the service. The authentication information will be inserted by the client application and extracted and interpreted by the web service implementation. This example provides a very simplistic demonstration of how you can use the JAX-RPC APIs to provide application-level security instead of relying on the web container to authenticate the calling user, as shown in the previous section. The element that will be added to the header is shown in Example 6-37.

Example 6-37. Authentication information to be included in a SOAP message header

```
<auth>
    <UserName>JWSUserName</UserName>
    <Password>JWSPassword</Password>
</auth>
```

In a real application, you would want to encrypt some or all of this information to protect it from unauthorized disclosure, and you would also need to include some kind of security token that would guarantee that the authentication information belongs to and was provided by the message sender. In order to keep this example simple, we're not going to attempt either of these things. If you'd like to investigate how this might be done, the WS-Security specification, originated by IBM, Microsoft, and Verisign, defines SOAP header elements and procedures that make it possible to securely incorporate authentication details and other sensitive information in a SOAP message. The specification can be downloaded from *http://www.verisign/wss/wss.pdf.*

Adding header parts to a service definition

In order to handle header information through JAX-RPC–generated method calls, you need to have a WSDL definition of the service. Such a definition was created during the deployment of the service whose original Java interface definition is shown in Example 6-5. For the purposes of this example, we'll take a copy of the WSDL document for that service and add to it the elements required to send authentication information to the server whenever the client application invokes any of the service endpoint interface methods. We'll also arrange for an element containing the date and time at which the service processed the request to be returned to the client to be included.

The first step is to add to the WSDL file a definition to the types section for the authentication information, as shown in Example 6-38.

Example 6-38. XML Schema definition for a simple authentication element

```
<types>
  <schema xmlns="http://www.w3.org/2001/XMLSchema"
          xmlns:xsi="http://www.w3.org/2001/XMLSchema-instance"
          xmlns:soap-enc="http://schemas.xmlsoap.org/soap/encoding/"
          xmlns:wsdl="http://schemas.xmlsoap.org/wsdl/"
          targetNamespace=
            "urn:jwsnut.chapter6.headerbookservice/types/HeaderBookQuery">
    <!-- Header element for user name and password -->
    <complexType name="Authentication">
      <sequence>
        <element name="UserName" type="xsd:string"/>
        <element name="Password" type="xsd:string"/>
      </sequence>
    </complexType>
  </schema>
</types>
```

Next, you need to arrange for an instance of this type to be included in the header of the SOAP messages generated for each operation defined by this service. Recall from Chapter 5 that the WSDL definition for a web service describes the content of the SOAP message sent by the client application for a particular operation as follows:

- In the portType section, the operation element for the operation specifies an input message made up of zero or more parts, whose types are defined in the types section or imported from an external schema.

- Within the binding section, there is a corresponding operation element that maps these parts to the SOAP message body, to the header, or to an attachment, as appropriate.

Here, for example, are the relevant parts of the WSDL definition for the getBookTitle operation, which requires an integer argument:

```
<!-- Input message definition -->
<message name="SmallBookQuery_getBookTitle">
  <part name="int_1" type="xsd:int"/>
</message>
```

```
<!-- Subset of complete portType definition -->
<portType name="SmallBookQuery">
  <operation name="getBookTitle" parameterOrder="int_1">
    <input message="tns:SmallBookQuery_getBookTitle"/>
    <output message="tns:SmallBookQuery_getBookTitleResponse"/>
  </operation>
</portType>

<!-- Subset of complete binding definition -->
<binding name="SmallBookQueryBinding" type="tns:SmallBookQuery">
  <operation name="getBookTitle">
    <soap:operation soapAction=""/>
    <input>
      <soap:body encodingStyle="http://schemas.xmlsoap.org/soap/encoding/"
          use="encoded" namespace="urn:jwsnut.chapter6.smallbookservice/wsdl/
              SmallBookQuery"/>
    </input>
    <output>
      <soap:body encodingStyle="http://schemas.xmlsoap.org/soap/encoding/"
          use="encoded" namespace="urn:jwsnut.chapter6.smallbookservice/wsdl/
              SmallBookQuery"/>
    </output>
  </operation>
</binding>
```

The result of this definition is that the integer argument defined by the part labeled int_1 is placed in the body of the SOAP message, wrapped in the usual way with an element named for the operation. In order to arrange for an additional element to be added to the header, you need to define that element as a part and then reference it from a soap:header element within the operation definition in the binding section. Since the same header information is going to be included in each SOAP request message, instead of adding the part to each individual message element, we create a new message element containing only this part, and use the message attribute of the soap:header element to cause it to be included in the SOAP message header.* We'll use the same technique to define the part that contains the time at which the server processed the SOAP message, which is placed in the SOAP header of the reply message.

In this case, since the same additional information is to be carried in the SOAP headers for all request and reply messages, it is obviously more convenient to define the parts in a separate message rather than include them in the existing message elements for each operation in the WSDL document. At the time of this writing, however, if you attempt to add these elements to the existing messages, you'll find that the version of wscompile in the reference implementation refuses to process the resulting WSDL document. Since there is nothing in the WSDL specification that prohibits the mapping of elements from the original message into the SOAP header, this is probably just an implementation error that will be fixed at some point.

---

* Refer to "Message construction elements" in Chapter 5 for a description of the soap:header element.

The WSDL document that results from these changes can be found in the file *chapter6\headerbookservice\Input_HeaderBookQuery.wsdl* relative to the example source code for this book. This document defines a new web service containing a service endpoint interface called HeaderBookQuery, whose operations are the same as those of SmallBookQuery, apart from the addition of authentication and time-stamp information. Here's how the additional message elements that contain the authentication information and the timestamp are defined:

```
<message name="HeaderBookQuery_Auth">
  <part name="auth" type="typesns:Authentication"/>
</message>
  <message name="HeaderBookQuery_Time">
    <part name="time" type="xsd:dateTime"/>
  </message>
```

Note that the time element uses a built-in XML Schema type and therefore does not require a new type to be defined in the types section.

Each operation in the binding section is modified to include soap:header elements that refer to these message parts. For example, the modified definition for the getBookTitle operation looks like this:

```
<operation name="getBookTitle">
  <soap:operation soapAction=""/>
  <input>
    <soap:header message="tns:HeaderBookQuery_Auth" part="auth"
                 encodingStyle="http://schemas.xmlsoap.org/soap/encoding/"
                 use="encoded"
                 namespace=
                   "urn:jwsnut.chapter6.headerbookservice/wsdl/
                      HeaderBookQuery"/>
    <soap:body encodingStyle="http://schemas.xmlsoap.org/soap/encoding/"
               use="encoded"
               namespace="urn:jwsnut.chapter6.headerbookservice/wsdl/
               HeaderBookQuery"/>
  </input>
  <output>
    <soap:header message="tns:HeaderBookQuery_Time" part="time"
                 encodingStyle="http://schemas.xmlsoap.org/soap/encoding/"
                 use="encoded"
                 namespace=
                   "urn:jwsnut.chapter6.headerbookservice/wsdl/
                      HeaderBookQuery"/>
    <soap:body encodingStyle="http://schemas.xmlsoap.org/soap/encoding/"
               use="encoded" namespace="urn:jwsnut.chapter6.
               headerbookservice/wsdl/HeaderBookQuery"/>
  </output>
</operation>
```

The input message element now includes a soap:header element that specifies that an instance of the auth part from the HeaderBookQuery_Auth message must be bound to the SOAP message header when the request message is sent. Similarly, the SOAP header for the reply message must contain a time element, as defined by the message element called HeaderBookQuery_Time. The JAX-RPC runtime is responsible for obtaining the value to be used to construct the auth element in the outgoing message and for making the returned timestamp available to the client application when the response is received. These values are conveyed via the arguments of the methods in the Java interface that are created from these WSDL definitions.

Generating the Java interface and client-side stubs

Having completed the WSDL definition, before you can write either the service implementation or an application client, you need the corresponding Java interface. As you saw earlier in this chapter, this is generated from the WSDL definition using the wscompile utility by giving it a *config.xml* file containing a wsdl element. You can create and compile the Java interface definition by opening a command window, making *chapter6\headerbookservice* your working directory, and typing the command:

```
ant generate-interface
```

The wscompile utility does not automatically include method call arguments for parts that are mapped to the SOAP header. To force it to do so, you need to use the -f:explicitcontext option.* Here is the command line used by the generate-interface target:

```
wscompile -gen:server -f:explicitcontext -keep
          -model generated/interface/model
          -s generated/interface
          -d output/interface config.xml
```

The generated files are placed in the directory *generated/interface/ora/jwsnut/chapter6/headerbookservice*. The type defined in Example 6-38 to hold the authentication information becomes a simple value type called Authentication with attributes that hold a username and password. This value type is used in the signatures of all of the methods in the generated service endpoint interface, which is shown in Example 6-39.

Example 6-39. A Java interface definition containing arguments that access the SOAP header

```
public interface HeaderBookQuery extends java.rmi.Remote {
      public void log(java.lang.String string_1, Authentication auth,
              javax.xml.rpc.holders.CalendarHolder time)
throws java.rmi.RemoteException;
              public int getBookCount(Authentication auth,
                      javax.xml.rpc.holders.CalendarHolder time)
throws java.rmi.RemoteException;
              public java.lang.String getBookTitle(int int_1,
      Authentication auth,
                      javax.xml.rpc.holders.CalendarHolder time)
```

---

* The name explicitcontext is used because when this option is specified, the elements carried in the SOAP header, which typically represent context for the request or response in the body (and here carry security context information) are *explicitly* exposed in the method signatures of the service endpoint interface. This contrasts with *implicit* context information—such as the authenticated Principal available from the ServletEndpointContext or the SessionContext—which does not manifest itself in the programming interface of the web service.

Example 6-39. A Java interface definition containing arguments
that access the SOAP header (continued)

```
throws java.rmi.RemoteException;
                public void getBookAuthor(java.lang.String string_1,
                           javax.xml.rpc.holders.StringHolder string_2,
                           Authentication auth, javax.xml.rpc.holders.
CalendarHolder time)
    throws HeaderBookServiceException, java.rmi.RemoteException;
}
```

Notice that the arguments that represent the explicit context, which are highlighted, have been added *after* the regular method arguments. Note also that the time value that will be returned in the SOAP header of every response message is represented by a CalendarHolder object because it is an output parameter. This, of course, is a special case, since the data type of this value is one of those directly supported by JAX-RPC and for which a predefined Holder object exists. If you define your own type (such as the Authentication type) and assign it as a value to be returned in a response message, then a suitable Holder class is generated by wscompile and included in the method signature.

Invoking the service

The most convenient aspect of using explicit context is that application code simply passes the value or values required for the SOAP header as method arguments and does not need to be aware that they are actually being carried in the header. Similarly, values received in a SOAP header become associated with Holder arguments in the usual way. Example 6-40 shows an extract from the example client application for this service.

Example 6-40. Invoking service methods that contain explicit context

```
// Get a reference to the stub.
HeaderBookService_Impl service = new HeaderBookService_Impl();
HeaderBookQuery bookQuery = (HeaderBookQuery)service.getHeaderBookQueryPort();

// Create the required authentication information
String userName = System.getProperty("HeaderBooks.user");
String password = System.getProperty("HeaderBooks.password");
Authentication auth = new Authentication(userName, password);

// Get info for each book.
StringHolder stringHolder = new StringHolder();
CalendarHolder calendarHolder = new CalendarHolder();

int count = bookQuery.getBookCount(auth, calendarHolder);
Calendar calendar = (Calendar)calendarHolder.value;
System.out.println("Book count = " + count);
System.out.println("Processed at: " + calendar.getTime());
```

As you can see, the username and password are obtained from system properties (which are actually set on the command line using values in your *jwsnutExamples. properties* file) and then used to construct the Authentication object. This object and a `CalendarHolder` are passed as arguments to the `getBookCount()` method, and the timestamp returned by the service implementation is extracted and printed in the normal way.

The service implementation

The service implementation consists of a servant class that implements the generated `HeaderBookQuery` interface shown in Example 6-39. Given that the values that represent the explicit context are presented as method arguments, the servant class can retrieve the authentication information that is supplied for each method call from the `Authentication` argument, as well as return the invocation time in the `CalenderHolder` supplied to it by the JAX-RPC runtime system. This makes the servant class as transparent to the fact that these values are carried in the SOAP header as the client application is. The implementation of the `getBookCount()` method, for example, is shown in Example 6-41, together with the `checkAccess()` method that it uses to verify the username and password supplied to it. The correct username and password values are obtained from servlet initialization parameters, using the same code as that shown in Example 6-33.

Example 6-41. Implementation of a service method that uses explicit content

```
public int getBookCount(Authentication auth, CalendarHolder calendarHolder) {
    calendarHolder.value = new GregorianCalendar();
    String[] titles = HeaderBookServiceServantData.getBookTitles();
    return titles == null || !checkAccess(auth) ? 0 : titles.length;
}

/**
 * Check whether the calling user is authenticated.
 */
private boolean checkAccess(Authentication auth) {
    boolean allowed = false;
    if (userName != null && password != null && auth != null) {
        // Authentication is configured.
        return userName.equals(auth.getUserName()) &&
                password.equals(auth.getPassword());
    }
    return allowed;
}
```

In order to make this work with the JWSDP, however, you need to be careful when packaging the service implementation. Recall that the ties for the service implementation are generated when you run `wsdeploy`, which bases its actions on the endpoint definitions in the *jaxrpc-ri.xml* file. Ordinarily, the ties are generated by introspecting the methods of the Java interface definition in the `HeaderBookQuery` class, which is passed to it by the `interface` attribute of the endpoint element. However, without additional information, there is no way to tell which of the method arguments map to body content and which map to the SOAP header. This information was originally supplied in the WSDL document, which cannot be supplied to `wsdeploy`. In the absence of any information to the contrary, `wsdeploy` generates ties that expect all of the method arguments to correspond to elements in the SOAP message body, which leads to incorrect behavior in this case.

The solution to this problem is the same one we used in the section "JAX-RPC interface to document-style operations," earlier in this chapter, where we had to ensure that wsdeploy knew that the methods of a Java endpoint interface should map to document-style operations—we generate a model file and reference it from the endpoint element in the *jaxrpc-ri.xml* file. This, then is another case in which we genuinely need to include the model file. The model file provides the same information to either j2eec or deploytool, if you are using the J2EE 1.4 reference implementation.

To verify that this example works, you can package and deploy the service by making *chapter6\headerbookservice* your working directory and typing the command:

```
ant deploy
```

Then, build and run the client application by typing:

```
ant compile
ant run-client
```

The client prints the number of books returned by the getBookCount( ) method followed by the time at which the server performed the operation, as returned in the SOAP header of the reply message. It then prints the title and author of all of the books that the server knows about. This works because when you build and deploy the service implementation, its *web.xml* file is initialized with the username and password from your *jwsnutExamples.properties* file as the credentials for the user to be allowed to access the service. When you run the client, it extracts the same values and uses them to populate the Authentication object. If you temporarily change the username or password in your *jwsnutExamples.properties* file and run the client again (without redeploying the service), the values in the Authentication object sent by the client do not match the username and password known to the server. As a result, the getBookCount( ) method returns 0 and you do not see any books listed.

SOAP Message Handlers

Mapping SOAP header content to method arguments is a simple and convenient way to expose that content without introducing the complexities of SOAP message handling into application-level code. It is, therefore, a useful technique to use in cases where information that forms part of the service endpoint interface definition happens to be carried in the SOAP header. It is, however, not the only means available to the JAX-RPC developer for getting at header content, although it is by far the easiest to use.

Another way to process headers is to access the underlying SOAP message directly. This option is open to any service implementation class that implements the ServiceLifecycle interface, or to a web service implemented as a stateless session bean. It requires the service to use the MessageContext object that can be obtained by calling the getMessageContext( ) method of the ServletEndpoint-Context in the case of a servlet-hosted web service, or by calling the getMessageContext( ) method of SessionContext for a session bean. In the case of

SOAP messaging, the MessageContext is actually an instance of the derived interface javax.xml.rpc.handler.soap.SOAPMessageContext, which provides a method that returns the SOAP message currently being handled:

```
public SOAPMessage getMessage()
```

This method can be called whenever the SOAPMessageContext is valid—that is, from within any of the methods of the servant that implement the service endpoint interface. Once you have a reference to the message, you can use the SAAJ API to access any part of it. To process headers, for example, you might use code like this:

```
SOAPMessageContext ctx = (SOAPMessageContext)endpointContext.
getMessageContext();
SOAPMessage message = ctx.getMessage();
SOAPHeader header = message.getSOAPPart().getEnvelope().getHeader();
if (header != null) {
    // Process the header...
}
```

This technique is very useful, but it has at least two drawbacks:

- It can only be used within the web service implementation class. There is nothing corresponding to ServletEndpointContext that would allow a client application to process the SOAP message received as the reply to its request.

- It results in low-level logic appearing in what should really be application-level code.

One possible way to make use of message-level access is to compute a digital signature for some or all of the content of a request message, and then place it into a SOAP header before it is transmitted from the client. The header is extracted when the message is received by the server and the signature is verified. Using a digital signature in this way ensures that the part of the message to which the signature applies is not modified while in transit. Obviously, as an application developer, you wouldn't want to be concerned with the details of digital signature algorithms, and you certainly wouldn't want to have to introduce code that intercepts SOAP messages and handles digital signatures into what should really be business logic. Instead, it is more convenient to be able to implement this code separately, outside of the application itself, and have it operate on the messages that the JAX-RPC runtime creates in response to method calls on the service endpoint interface. This capability is provided by JAX-RPC *message handlers*.

Message-handling architecture

A message handler is a class that can receive and possibly act upon a SOAP message. Depending on what the handler is supposed to do, it might modify the message, log its content somewhere, ignore it, or deem it to be invalid and initiate some form of error handling, such as the generation of a SOAP fault. Message handlers are grouped into a handler chain, which may be inserted into the processing path for a specific service endpoint on the client side, the server side, or both. Figure 6-5 shows a handler chain installed on the client side of a web service.

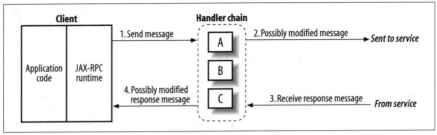

Figure 6-5. Client-side message-handling architecture

The chain in this instance consists of three handlers labeled A, B, and C. As indicated in the diagram, the chain is in the message-processing path for both outgoing and incoming messages. When there is a handler chain associated with a service endpoint, SOAP messages are processed as follows:

1. The client application invokes a method of the service endpoint interface using a generated stub, a dynamic proxy, or the dynamic invocation interface.

2. The JAX-RPC runtime uses the method argument values to create a SOAP request message.

3. The request message is passed to the handler chain.

4. The handler chain passes the request message to each handler in turn. The handler may modify the message, perhaps by adding a header, or may indicate that processing of the message is to be terminated.

5. If a handler wishes to stop the processing of a message as a result of detecting an error, it must replace that message with another containing a suitable Fault element. A handler may also stop message processing because it can generate the appropriate reply without needing to transmit the message to the server, perhaps because the handler acts as a cache mapping previous requests to received responses. If such a caching handler recognized a request that it had already sent, it might be able to supply a copy of the response that it received to the original request. Whether the handler generates a fault message or supplies a different message, that message is treated in the same way as if it were a reply received from the server, as described starting at Step 8. This situation is illustrated in Figure 6-6.

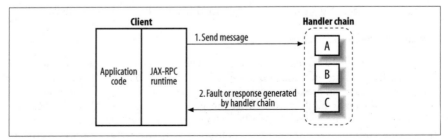

Figure 6-6. A handler intercepting an outgoing message

6. A handler that detects an error may also throw an exception. In this case, no further processing takes place and the exception is thrown back to application code.

7. If the message successfully reaches the end of the handler chain, it is sent to the server.

8. When a reply message or a fault message is received (or the processing of an outgoing message is terminated by a handler and a substitute message provided), it is delivered to the same handler chain. The handler chain first verifies that the handler chain can successfully process all of the headers intended for the receiving node that have their mustUnderstand attribute set to "1". If it cannot, then the message is not processed and a SOAPFaultException is thrown to application code. More details on the handling of the mustUnderstand attribute are provided later in this section.

9. Next, every handler is given the opportunity to process and modify the response message. This may result in headers being removed, content being modified, or a completely different message being substituted before the next handler is invoked. If a handler throws an exception, that exception is thrown back to application code and the message is not processed further. If a handler indicates (without throwing an exception) that handler processing of the message should end, then no more handlers in the chain are invoked. It does not, however, prevent Step 10 from being performed.

10. Assuming that no exception has been thrown during processing of the response, the JAX-RPC runtime extracts the values of any output parameters and the return value from the (possibly modified) message, and arranges for them to be returned to the caller of the service endpoint interface method.

The JAX-RPC specification allows the order in which handlers within a chain are invoked to be implementation-dependent. However, the following is likely to be typical behavior:

- An outgoing message is passed to handlers in a specific order. In terms of Figure 6-5, this order might be A, B, C.

- When a response message or a fault message is received from the server, the handlers are invoked in the reverse order. That is, in Figure 6-5, the processing order for the response would be C, B, A.

- If processing for an outgoing message is blocked by a handler, the substituted fault or response message is processed by the same handlers that have already handled the outgoing message, but not by those that have not. For example, if handlers A and B in Figure 6-5 process a message and handler B blocks further processing of that request, then the fault or reply message supplied by handler B and shown in Figure 6-6 is processed by handler B and then handler A, but not by handler C (since it did not see the outgoing message).

In general, handlers in a chain operate independently and therefore do not rely on the presence of other handlers in the chain or the order in which they are invoked.

A handler chain may also be installed on the server side of a web service, as shown in Figure 6-7.

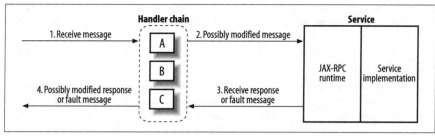

Figure 6-7. Server-side message handling architecture

The processing of messages on the server side is similar to that performed for the client:

1. A SOAP message is received from the underlying transport and passed to the generated tie class for the service endpoint interface.

2. If a handler chain is configured, the message is given to the handler chain. Otherwise, processing resumes at Step 5.

3. The handler chain first verifies that its handlers can successfully process all of the headers intended for the receiving node that have their mustUnderstand attribute set to "1". If it cannot, then a fault message is created and processing resumes at Step 8. More details on the handling of the mustUnderstand attribute are provided later in this section.

4. The handlers in the chain are given the opportunity to process the message in some way. If any handler throws an exception other than a SOAPFaultException, a fault message is created and processing resumes at Step 8. If a handler detects an error that should result in a Fault being returned to the client, it must replace the original message with one containing the appropriate fault details and throw a SOAPFaultException, which causes processing to resume at Step 6. If a handler indicates that processing of the request message should not continue (but does not throw an exception), no further handlers in the chain are invoked and processing continues at step 7. This is the server-side equivalent of the situation shown in Figure 6-6. In this case, the target method of the service endpoint implementation class is not invoked and the handler must install an appropriate reply message before returning control.

5. If there is no handler chain or the handler chain was completed traversed, the (possibly modified) message is decoded and the appropriate method of the service endpoint implementation class is invoked. If an exception occurs either while the message is being decoded or during the execution of the service endpoint method, then a fault message is generated. Otherwise, the return value and output values from the method call are used to build an appropriate response message.

6. If a fault message has been created, then the handler chain is given the opportunity to handle it. If any handler throws an exception while processing the fault message, the chain terminates and a new fault message reporting the exception is created instead. If a handler requests that chain processing is complete, then no further handlers are invoked.

7. Similarly, if a response message is generated, it is passed to the handler chain. Again, if any handler throws an exception while processing the reply, the chain terminates and a fault message reporting the exception is created instead. If a handler requests that chain processing is complete, then no further handlers are invoked.

8. Finally, the (possibly modified) response or fault message is transmitted to the client.

Message handler classes and interfaces

The classes and interfaces used in connection with message handling belong to the javax.xml.rpc.handler and javax.xml.rpc.handler.soap packages. To implement a handler, you need to create a class that implements the Handler interface shown in Example 6-42.

Example 6-42. The javax.xml.rpc.handler.Handler interface

```
public interface Handler {
    public void init(HandlerInfo config);
    public void destroy();
    public QName[] getHeaders();
    public boolean handleRequest(MessageContext ctx);
    public boolean handleResponse(MessageContext ctx);
    public boolean handleFault(MessageContext ctx);
}
```

For convenience, the javax.xml.rpc.handler package contains an abstract class called GenericHandler that provides default implementations of the methods of the Handler interface, with the exception of getHeaders(). You can use GenericHandler as the base class for your own handlers to avoid having to include empty methods where no specific behavior is required.

Handlers are stateless objects that may be pooled by a JAX-RPC implementation and must provide a public, no-argument constructor. When a handler is created, its init() method is called and passed an object of type HandlerInfo that contains configuration information that it may use to initialize itself or customize its behavior. If the JAX-RPC runtime decides that it no longer needs a specific instance of a handler, it calls its destroy() method to allow it to release any resources it may have allocated at construction time or during the execution of the init() method.

The HandlerInfo object passed to a handler's init() method contains information supplied when the handler is configured using the API described in "Message handler configuration," later in this chapter. The most useful HandlerInfo method is getHandlerConfig():

```
public java.util.Map getHandlerConfig();
```

The Map returned by this method contains properties that can be set at configuration time and used by the handler to customize its behavior. The example handlers shown later in this chapter use this facility to determine whether to print debugging information.

The getHeaders() method is required to return the names of the header elements that the handler processes, if any. Each value in the returned array must be a QName object representing the fully qualified name of the top-level element of any such header. Handlers that process only the body of the message or provide other functionality that is not related to a specific SOAP header should return an empty array from this method.

The handleRequest(), handleResponse(), and handleFault() methods are where the real work of the handler is done. These methods are invoked when the handler chain is processing a SOAP request message, a response message, or a fault message, respectively. As a request message is being processed, the handler chain invokes the handleRequest() method of each handler in turn. If this method returns true, then the chain continues processing with the next handler. If it returns false, chain processing terminates and response or fault processing may begin, as described earlier in the section "Message-handling architecture." These methods may throw runtime exceptions as well. These also result in chain processing being terminated, with consequences that differ depending on whether the handler chain is associated with the client or server side of the web service, as described in the previous section.

When a message is being processed on either the client or server side, it is associated with an instance of an object that implements the javax.xml.rpc.handler.MessageContext interface. On the client side, a MessageContext object is associated with the handler chain when the request message is created, and the same instance of that object is passed to each handler in the handler chain. When the response message or a fault message is received, the same MessageContext object is then passed to each handler as it processes the inbound message. On the server side, when a request is received, all handlers that process that request are passed the same MessageContext instance. This MessageContext object is available to the servant class that implements the web service, provided that it implements the ServiceLifecycle interface, from the getMessageContext() method of ServletEndpointContext and to a session bean implementation via the getMessageContext() method of its SessionContext. The MessageContext is also passed to the handlers in the handler chain when the outgoing response or fault message is being processed.

The methods of the MessageContext interface are shown in Example 6-43.

Example 6-43. The javax.xml.rpc.handler.MessageContext interface

```
public interface MessageContext {
    public boolean containsProperty(String name);
    public Iterator getPropertyNames();
    public Object getProperty(String name);
    public void setProperty(String name, Object value);
    public void removeProperty(String name);
}
```

As you can see, MessageContext is essentially a container for property values.* Since the same instance of MessageContext is shared between all of the handlers in a chain (and also, on the server side, with the servant class), it can be used to share state between handlers or between one or more handlers and the web service implementation itself. You'll see how this technique can be used in "A message handler example," later in this chapter.

For SOAP messaging (which is the only form of messaging currently supported by JAX-RPC), the MessageContext object passed to the handlers and the web service itself are actually instances of a SOAP-specific derived interface called javax.xml. rpc.handler.soap.SOAPMessageContext. This method contains a small number of additional methods that are shown in Example 6-44.

Example 6-44. The javax.xml.rpc.handler.soap.SOAPMessageContext interface

```
public interface SOAPMessageContext extends MessageContext {
    public SOAPMessage getMessage();
    public void setMessage(SOAPMessage message);
    public String[] getRoles();
}
```

When a SOAP message is received, a reference to it is stored in the SOAPMessageContext by calling the setMessage() method. Handlers can then get access to the message by casting their MessageContext argument to SOAPMessageContext and calling the getMessage() method. In some cases, a handler may wish to replace the received message with another one, and may call the setMessage() method to achieve this. The replacement message is then the one that is processed by the other handlers in then chain and, on the server side, by the web service implementation if the substitution occurs during request processing.

A complete handler chain is managed by an implementation-supplied object that implements the javax.xml.rpc.handler.HandlerChain interface. A HandlerChain is responsible for invoking the handleRequest(), handleResponse(), and handleFault() methods of each of the handlers that it contains when its own methods of the same name are called, and is responsible for terminating execution of the chain when a handler throws an exception or returns the value false. Since handler chains are managed internally by the JAX-RPC runtime, you don't need to deal with them directly, despite the fact that the HandlerChain interface itself is public. For a description of the HandlerChain interface, refer to the reference section of this book.

Message handler configuration

Handler chains are associated with service endpoints. For each service endpoint, there may be zero or one handler chain configured on the client side and zero or one handler chain on the server side. Configure a handler chain by adding a handlerChains element to the *config.xml* file used by wscompile on the client side. The format of the handlerChains element is shown in Example 6-45.

---

* In the reference implementation, the implementation of this interface simply delegates its behavior to a HashMap.

Example 6-45. the handlerChains element, used to configure a message handler chain

```
<handlerChains>
  <chain runAt="client|server" roles="URI list">
  <!-- 0 or 1 with "client" and 0 or 1 with "server" -->
    <handler className="handlerClassName" headers="QName list">
    <!--- Any number permitted -->
    <property name="name" value="value"/>
    <!--- Any number permitted -->
    </handler>
  </chain>
</handlerChains>
```

A handlerChains element can contain zero, one, or two chain elements. The runAt attribute determines whether a client-side or server-side chain is being described. There can be only one of each type within a handlerChains element. The wscompile utility handles chain elements with runAt set to client while generating client-side stubs. The meaning of the optional roles attribute will be described later in this chapter in "Headers, roles, and the mustUnderstand attribute."

A chain element may contain any number of handler elements, each of which configures a single message handler. The set of all handler elements describes the content of the handler chain. The className attribute gives the name of the Java class that implements the handler. As mentioned earlier, this class must have a public, no-argument constructor, and must implement the Handler interface. The headers attribute is optional and is described later in "Headers, roles, and the mustUnderstand attribute."

Each handler element may have an arbitrary number of nested property elements that provide configuration information for the handler. The value of the className and headers attributes of the handler element along with a Map constructed from the property elements are used to initialize the HandlerInfo object that is passed to the message handler's init( ) method. The property values can be obtained by calling the getHandlerConfig( ) method of the HandlerInfo object.

If you are using the JWSDP, on the server side the information used to build the handler chain for an endpoint is obtained from the handlerChains element in the *jaxrpc-ri.xml* file and built into the tie classes generated by wsdeploy. For J2EE 1.4, the handler chain is described in the *webservices.xml* file, as discussed later in this section. The handler chain for each endpoint is constructed when the tie for that endpoint is initialized. There is currently no way for a web service implementation to programmatically access or change the configuration of the handler chain that it is associated with.

On the client side, wscompile gets handler information from the handlerChains element in the *config.xml* file and adds the code necessary to build a handler chain to the generated stub class for each endpoint. This code accesses a registry of handlers that is owned by the generated Service class for that endpoint and initialized in the constructor of that Service class. The registry is an instance of an implementation-dependent class that implements the javax.xml.rpc.handler. HandlerRegistry interface, which is shown in Example 6-46.

Example 6-46. The javax.xml.rpc.handler.HandlerRegistry interface

```
public interface HandlerRegistry {
  public java.util.List getHandlerChain(QName portName);
  public void setHandlerChain(QName portName, java.util.List chain);
}
```

As long as you use only stubs generated by wscompile to access web services, you won't need to concern yourself with the HandlerRegistry. However, if you use a Service object obtained from a ServiceFactory (as you would if you invoke a web service using a dynamic proxy or the dynamic invocation interface), that Service object will not have an initialized HandlerRegistry, since it is not created as a result of code generated by wscompile. To ensure that the proper handler chain is constructed in this case, you need to initialize the HandlerRegistry yourself, before calling the Service getPort( ) or createCall( ) methods. An example that demonstrates how this can be done is shown in "Initializing the HandlerRegistry when using dynamic proxies or dynamic invocation," later in this chapter.

Headers, roles, and the mustUnderstand attribute

Each Handler implements the getHeaders( ) method to return a list of QNames for the headers that it processes if they appear in the messages that are passed to it. When a handler chain is created, the HandlerChain object calls the getHeaders( ) method of each Handler to create a list of the headers that can be handled by the entire chain. This header list is used in conjunction with the role list set, using the roles attribute of the chain element to determine whether the chain can process all of the headers that it needs to be able to handle.

 As you can see from Example 6-45, the handler tag has an optional headers attribute whose value is a set of QName objects. In the reference implementation, the value assigned to this attribute is passed to the handler in the HandlerInfo object that it receives at initialization time. It is not clear why this would be necessary, since a handler must, as a matter of implementation, know which headers it is capable of processing. It is possible that this attribute is intended to allow a restriction to be placed on which headers will actually be processed by a handler in a given configuration. Since the meaning of this attribute is unclear, for the example shown in the next section, I initialized it to the full set of headers that the handler in that example processes.

The roles attribute is initialized using a list of URIs that represent the SOAP actors that the handlers in the chain represent (refer to "SOAP Actors and the mustUnderstand Attribute" in Chapter 3 for a discussion of SOAP actors and the rules for handling SOAP headers that contain an actor attribute). If this list is non-empty, then the HandlerChain takes the following steps before passing a received request message (on the client side) or a response message (on the server side) to the first handler in the chain for processing:

1. Gets a list of the headers from the SOAP message that are intended for one of the actors in the actor list, or that are addressed to the actor next.

2. For each header in this list that has the mustUnderstand attribute set to "1", checks whether the header QName is in the set of QNames for the headers that can be handled by the chain.

3. If the header is not in the list, then there is no handler that can process the header. The SOAP specification requires that a fault be generated in this case, so the HandlerChain does not proceed with processing of the message but creates a fault message instead.

If the chain element does not have a roles attribute, then it is assumed that only headers that are intended for the ultimate recipient of the message are to be processed and this check does not take place.

A message handler example

To demonstrate how you can make use of a SOAP message handler, we'll reimplement the example used earlier in the section "Mapping Header Content to Method Arguments" without mapping the authentication information that appears in the header of the request message, or mapping the timestamp that is placed in the reply message header, to explicit method arguments. Instead, we'll handle these headers entirely in two message handlers—one created for the client side, the other for the server side.

As before, the starting point for this example is the WSDL definition of the service. Since the wire format of the messages will not change from that used in the original implementation, we'll start with a WSDL definition that is exactly the same as that used in the previous version of this example (apart from the fact that the filename is changed, as are the URIs within the file) to reflect the directory structuring of the example source code. Using this WSDL definition, the next step is to create the Java interface definition for the service using wscompile. On this occasion, however, we don't use the -f:explicitcontext option, so that the soap:header elements in the binding section of the WSDL document are ignored. You can generate the interface definitions by opening a command window, making *chapter6\ handlerbookservice* your working directory, and then typing the command:

```
ant generate-interface
```

The output from this command is written to the directory *chapter6\ handlerbookservice\generated\interface\ora\jwsnut\chapter6\handlerbookservice*. If you look at the file *HandlerBookQuery.java* in this directory, you'll see the Java interface definition for this service, which is reproduced here as Example 6-47.

Example 6-47. The service interface definition for HandlerBookQuery service

```
public interface HandlerBookQuery extends java.rmi.Remote {
    public void log(java.lang.String string_1) throws java.rmi.RemoteException;
    public int getBookCount( ) throws java.rmi.RemoteException;
    public java.lang.String getBookTitle(int int_1)
        throws java.rmi.RemoteException;
    public void getBookAuthor(java.lang.String string_1, StringHolder string_2)
        throws HandlerBookServiceException,  java.rmi.RemoteException;
}
```

Comparing this with Example 6-39, you'll see that the method call arguments corresponding to the authentication information and the timestamp are no longer present. In this example, these attributes are handled as follows:

- On the client side, instead of the client application supplying the authentication information with every method call on the service endpoint interface, a message handler inserts the username and password in the SOAP header of every request message. This is beneficial not only because it simplifies the application code, but also because by substituting a different handler (which is a matter of changing the *config.xml* file and the *jaxrpc-ri.xml* or *webservices.xml* file), an alternative authentication mechanism can be used without requiring a change to application code.

- On the server side, the authentication information is extracted from the SOAP message header by a server-side handler that knows the format of the header element that carries it. It is then made available to the web service implementation via the MessageContext object.

- Instead of each service endpoint method recording the time at which it was called, as shown in the implementation of the getBookCount( ) method in Example 6-41, the server-side handler inserts a header element containing this information in each response message that it processes.

Let's look first at the implementation of the handler used on the server side, the source code for which you'll find in the file *chapter6\handlerbookservice\server\ora\jwsnut\chapter6\handlerbookservice\ServiceHandler.java*. The initialization code for this handler is shown in Example 6-48.

Example 6-48. Initialization code for a server-side message handler

```
public class ServiceHandler extends GenericHandler {

    // Namespace for types used by this handler
    private static final String NS_URI =
        "urn:jwsnut.chapter6.handlerbookservice/wsdl/HandlerBookQuery";

    // Namespace prefix used by this handler
    private static final String NS_PREFIX = "tns";

    // Name of the authentication header
    private static final QName authHeader = new QName(NS_URI, "auth");

    // Name of the date/time header
    private static final QName timeHeader = new QName(NS_URI, "time");

    // Formatter for dates
    private static final SimpleDateFormat format =
        new SimpleDateFormat("yyyy-MM-dd'T'HH:mm:ss");

    // SOAPFactory used to create Names
    private static SOAPFactory factory;

    // Name of the authentication header as a Name
    private static Name authHeaderName;
```

Example 6-48. Initialization code for a server-side message handler (continued)

```
// Name of the date/time header as a Name
private static Name timeHeaderName;

// The headers that this handler is associated with
private static QName[] headers;

// Debug flag
private boolean debug;

// Performs initialization
public void init(HandlerInfo info) {

    // Extract the debug setting from the configuration
    Map config = info.getHandlerConfig();
    String value = (String)config.get("debug");
    debug = value == null ? false : Boolean.valueOf(value).booleanValue();

    // Create Names
    try {
        factory = SOAPFactory.newInstance();
        authHeaderName = factory.createName("auth", NS_PREFIX, NS_URI);
        timeHeaderName = factory.createName("time", NS_PREFIX, NS_URI);
        headers = new QName[] { authHeader, timeHeader };
    } catch (SOAPException ex) {
        throw new JAXRPCException("Init failure", ex);
    }

    if (debug) {
        System.out.println("Server-side handler initialized");
    }
}

// Other code not shown here
}
```

Notice first that the handler class is derived from GenericHandler, which contained default implementations for methods of the Handler interface that do not need to provide special behavior for this example.

For the JWSDP, the init( ) method receives a HandlerInfo object whose content is created from the handler configuration information provided in the *jaxrpc-ri.xml* file, which is shown in Example 6-49.

Example 6-49. The jaxrpc-ri.xml file for a JWSDP-hosted web service using a JAX-RPC message handler

```
<?xml version="1.0" encoding="UTF-8"?>
<webServices
    xmlns="http://java.sun.com/xml/ns/jax-rpc/ri/dd"
    version="1.0"
    targetNamespaceBase="urn:jwsnut.chapter6.handlerbookservice/wsdl/"
    typeNamespaceBase="urn:jwsnut.chapter6.handlerbookservice/types/">
```

Example 6-49. The jaxrpc-ri.xml file for a JWSDP-hosted web service using a JAX-RPC message handler (continued)

```
<endpoint
    name="HandlerBookQuery"
    displayName="HandlerBookQuery Port"
    description="Handler Book Query Port"
    model="/WEB-INF/model"
    interface="ora.jwsnut.chapter6.handlerbookservice.HandlerBookQuery"
    implementation=
        "ora.jwsnut.chapter6.handlerbookservice.HandlerBookServiceServant">
  <handlerChains>
    <chain runAt="server"
    xmlns:tns="urn:jwsnut.chapter6.handlerbookservice/wsdl/HandlerBookQuery">
        <handler
          className="ora.jwsnut.chapter6.handlerbookservice.ServiceHandler"
          headers="tns:auth tns:time">
            <property name="debug" value="true"/>
        </handler>
    </chain>
  </handlerChains>
</endpoint>

<endpointMapping
    endpointName="HandlerBookQuery"
    urlPattern="/HandlerBookQuery"/>
</webServices>
```

This configuration specifies that the handler chain associated with this service consists of a single handler implemented in the class ora.jwsnut.chapter6. handlerbookservice.ServiceHandler. Since the chain element does not have a roles attribute, the handler is assumed to handle only headers that are intended for the ultimate recipient of each SOAP message. The headers attribute of the handler element indicates that the handler processes two different headers called auth and time, which are names defined in the XML namespace associated with this example (*urn:jwsnut.chapter6.handlerbookservice/wsdl/HandlerBookQuery*). The property element associated with this handler defines a single property called debug that, in this case, has the value true.

The corresponding server-side configuration for the J2EE 1.4 platform appears in the service's *webservices.xml* file, which is shown in Example 6-50.

Example 6-50. The webservices.xml file for a web service using a message handler

```
<?xml version="1.0" encoding="UTF-8"?>

<!DOCTYPE webservices
    PUBLIC "-//IBM Corporation, Inc.//DTD J2EE Web services 1.0//EN"
    "http://www.ibm.com/standards/xml/webservices/j2ee/j2ee_web_services_1_0.dtd">

<webservices>
  <webservice-description>
    <webservice-description-name>Book Service Web Application with message
      handler using JAX-RPC</webservice-description-name>
```

```
    <wsdl-file>HandlerBookQuery.wsdl</wsdl-file>
    <jaxrpc-mapping-file>WEB-INF/model</jaxrpc-mapping-file>
    <port-component>
        <port-component-name>HandlerBookQueryPort</port-component-name>
        <wsdl-port>
            <namespaceURI>urn:jwsnut.chapter6.handlerbookservice/wsdl/
                HandlerBookQuery</namespaceURI>
            <localpart>HandlerBookQueryPort</localpart>
        </wsdl-port>
        <service-endpoint-interface>ora.jwsnut.chapter6.handlerbookservice.
            HandlerBookQuery</service-endpoint-interface>
        <service-impl-bean>
            <servlet-link>HandlerBookQueryServlet</servlet-link>
        </service-impl-bean>

        <!-- Handler for this port -->
        <handler>
            <handler-name>Service Handler</handler-name>
            <handler-class>ora.jwsnut.chapter6.handlerbookservice.ServiceHandler
            </handler-class>
            <init-param>
              <param-name>debug</param-name>
              <param-value>true</param-value>
            </init-param>
            <soap-header>
              <namespaceURI>
                urn:jwsnut.chapter6.handlerbookservice/wsdl/HandlerBookQuery
              </namespaceURI>
              <localpart>auth</localpart>
            </soap-header>
            <soap-header>
              <namespaceURI>
                urn:jwsnut.chapter6.handlerbookservice/wsdl/HandlerBookQuery
              </namespaceURI>
              <localpart>time</localpart>
            </soap-header>
        </handler>
    </port-component>
  </webservice-description>
</webservices>
```

Here, the headers that the handler will process are described using nested soap-header elements, while the SOAP roles are specified using one or more soap-rule elements. In this case, since there are no soap-role elements, the handlers process only headers intended for the ultimate recipient of each message.

The handler's class name and the header names are made available in the HandlerInfo object passed to its init( ) method, together with the property value, which appears as an entry in the Map that can be retrieved using its getHandlerConfig( ) method. The init( ) method, which is shown in Example 6-48, extracts this value and stores it in an instance variable for later use. This setting determines whether debugging information will be printed. The rest of this method uses the `javax.xml.soap.SOAPFactory` class to create the names of the header elements that this handler will process. These names are used when calling methods from the SAAJ API when the handler is processing SOAP messages. The handler's processing for SOAP request messages is shown in Example 6-51.

Example 6-51. Handling a SOAP request message
in a server-side SOAP message handler

```
public boolean handleRequest(MessageContext ctx) {
    try {
        if (debug) {
            System.out.println("handleRequest called");
        }

        String userName = null;
        String password = null;
        SOAPMessage message = ((SOAPMessageContext)ctx).getMessage();
        SOAPHeader header = message.getSOAPPart().getEnvelope().getHeader();
        if (header != null) {

            // Locate the "auth" header
            Iterator iter = header.getChildElements(authHeaderName);
            if (iter.hasNext()) {
                SOAPElement element = (SOAPElement)iter.next();
                Iterator children = element.getChildElements();
                while (children.hasNext()) {
                    SOAPElement childElement = (SOAPElement)children.next();
                    String localPart = childElement.getElementName()
                                                    .getLocalName();
                    if (localPart.equals("UserName") && userName == null) {
                        userName = childElement.getValue();
                    } else if (localPart.equals("Password") && password == null)
{
                        password = childElement.getValue();
                    }
                }

                // Remove this header
                element.detachNode();
            }

            // Remove any other "auth" headers.
            while (iter.hasNext()) {
                ((SOAPElement)iter.next()).detachNode();
            }

            // Install the user name and password in the MessageContext.
            // This installs null if either attribute was missing.
            ctx.setProperty(HandlerBookServiceConstants.USERNAME_PROPERTY,
                            userName);
            ctx.setProperty(HandlerBookServiceConstants.PASSWORD_PROPERTY,
                            password);

            if (debug) {
```

```
                System.out.println("Got auth: user: [" + userName +
                              "], password: [" + password + "]");
            }
        }
    } catch (SOAPException ex) {
        throw new JAXRPCException("Error in handleRequest", ex);
    }
    return true;
}
```

This code expects to find a header called auth carrying the username and password for the user calling the methods of the web service endpoint on which it is configured. Most of this code is concerned with using the SAAJ APIs described in Chapter 3 to locate this header, the format of which is shown in Example 6-37. If the header is present, the code extracts the values that it contains. The points of relevance to the construction of the message handler itself are the following:

- In order to process the SOAP header, this method needs to be able to access the SOAP message. This is achieved by casting the MessageContext object passed to it to the type SOAPMessageContext and then calling its getMessage( ) method. Almost every handleRequest( ), handleResponse( ), and handleFault( ) method in a message handler will contain code like this.

- Once the auth header is found and its content extracted, it is removed from the SOAP message. This follows the rules for header handling in the SOAP specification (and also described in "SOAP Headers" in Chapter 3).

- Having obtained the username and password, the handler needs to be able to make them available to the methods in the servant class that implement the service endpoint interface. It does this by storing them under well-known names in the MessageContext, which is also available to the service methods. Handlers can also use the MessageContext to pass information to other handlers in the handler chain.

The difference that this handler makes to the service class can be seen by looking at the implementation of the same methods that were shown in Example 6-41, where explicit context was used to convey the information now extracted by the message handler. The new implementations of these methods are shown in Example 6-52.

Example 6-52. Implementing authentication without explicit context

```
public int getBookCount( ) {
    String[] titles = HandlerBookServiceServantData.getBookTitles( );
    return titles == null || !checkAccess( ) ? 0 : titles.length;
}

private boolean checkAccess( ) {
    boolean allowed = false;

    // Get the username and password from the MessageContext
    MessageContext context = endpointContext.getMessageContext( );
```

```
String callingUser = (String)context.getProperty(
                            HandlerBookServiceConstants.USERNAME_PROPERTY);
String callingPwd = (String)context.getProperty(
                            HandlerBookServiceConstants.PASSWORD_PROPERTY);

if (userName != null && password != null) {
    // Authentication is configured.
    return userName.equals(callingUser) &&
            password.equals(callingPwd);
}
    return allowed;
}
```

As you can see, the getBookCount( ) method no longer receives any authentication information. Instead, it simply invokes the helper method checkAccess( ), and relies upon it to obtain the caller's username and password. The checkAccess( ) method gets the user's credentials from the MessageContext (where the message handler stored them), a reference to which it obtains from the ServletEndpointContext object that was passed to the servant's init( ) method.

You'll notice also that the getBookCount( ) method no longer provides the time at which it was invoked. In the new implementation, this information is no longer supplied by the servant class. Instead, it is added to the header of each response message by the handleResponse( ) method of the message handler, which is shown in Example 6-53.

Example 6-53. Handling a SOAP response message in a server-side SOAP message handler

```
public boolean handleResponse(MessageContext ctx) {
    try {
        if (debug) {
            System.out.println("handleResponse called");
        }

        SOAPMessage message = ((SOAPMessageContext)ctx).getMessage( );
        SOAPHeader header = message.getSOAPPart().getEnvelope().getHeader( );
        if (header == null) {
            header = message.getSOAPPart().getEnvelope().addHeader( );
        }
        SOAPElement element = header.addChildElement(timeHeaderName);
        String text = format.format(new Date( ));
        element.addTextNode(text);

        if (debug) {
            System.out.println("Added time header, value " + text);
        }
    } catch (SOAPException ex) {
        throw new JAXRPCException("Error in handleRequest", ex);
    }
    return true;
}
```

The implementation of the handler used on the client side, which you'll find in the file *chapter6\handlerbookservice\client\ora\jwsnut\chapter6\client\ClientHandler.java*, is very similar to that of the server-side handler just shown. Since almost all of the code is concerned with simple header manipulation using the SAAJ APIs covered in Chapter 3, I'm not going to show it here. The handler's init( ) method obtains the username and password to be used from the system properties and stores them for use by the handleRequest( ) method, which places them in an auth element that it adds to the SOAP header of each message that is passed to it. The handleResponse( ) method looks for a time element in the SOAP header of the response messages that it receives and extracts from it the timestamp inserted by the handler on the server side. There is no way, however, for the handler to communicate this value to the client application in a manner that does not require the application to be tied to the handler itself, since there is no client-side API that exposes the MessageContext object in the same way that there is on the server side. This being the case, having extracted the timestamp, the handler simply prints it on the System.out stream.

To activate a client-side handler, include a handlerChains element in the *config.xml* file from which the client-side stubs are generated, as shown in Example 6-54. Note that, in this case, the runAt attribute of the chain element has the value client. It is possible to include a server-side handler chain in the *config.xml* file, but this would only be useful if you intend to use wscompile to generate server-side artifacts.

Example 6-54. Configuring a client-side message handler

```
<?xml version="1.0" encoding="UTF-8" ?>

<configuration
        xmlns="http://java.sun.com/xml/ns/jax-rpc/ri/config">
    <wsdl location=
      "C:\JWSNutshell\draft1\examples\chapter6\handlerbookservice/
      HandlerBookQuery.wsdl"
            packageName="ora.jwsnut.chapter6.handlerbookservice">
      <handlerChains>
        <chain runAt="client"
           xmlns:tns="urn:jwsnut.chapter6.handlerbookservice/wsdl/
HandlerBookQuery">
            <handler className="ora.jwsnut.chapter6.client.ClientHandler"
                      headers="tns:auth tns:time">
                <property name="debug" value="true"/>
            </handler>
        </chain>
      </handlerChains>
    </wsdl>
</configuration>
```

You can run this example by deploying the service implementation using the command:

```
ant deploy
```

To run the client application, use the commands:

```
ant compile-client
ant run-client
```

Since debugging has been enabled by setting the debug property in both the client- and server-side handlers, you'll see messages printed as the handlers' handleRequest() and handleResponse() methods are called. An extract from the client-side output, reformatted for the sake of readability, is shown here:

```
[java] handleRequest called
[java] OUTGOING MESSAGE:
[java] <?xml version="1.0" encoding="UTF-8"?>
[java] <soap-env:Envelope
    xmlns:soap-env="http://schemas.xmlsoap.org/soap/envelope/"
    xmlns:env="http://schemas.xmlsoap.org/soap/envelope/"
    xmlns:xsd="http://www.w3.org/2001/XMLSchema"
    xmlns:xsi="http://www.w3.org/2001/XMLSchema-instance"
    xmlns:enc="http://schemas.xmlsoap.org/soap/encoding/"
    xmlns:ns0="urn:jwsnut.chapter6.handlerbookservice/types/HandlerBookQuery"
    xmlns:ns1="urn:jwsnut.chapter6.handlerbookservice/wsdl/HandlerBookQuery"
    env:encodingStyle="http://schemas.xmlsoap.org/soap/encoding/">
        <soap-env:Header>
        <tns:auth xmlns:tns=
        "urn:jwsnut.chapter6.handlerbookservice/wsdl/HandlerBookQuery">
                <UserName>JWSUserName</UserName>
                <Password>JWSPassword</Password>
        </tns:auth>
        </soap-env:Header>
        <soap-env:Body>
        <ns1:log>
            <String_1 xsi:type="xsd:string">
            HandlerBookServiceClient: success
            </String_1>
        </ns1:log>
        </soap-env:Body>
        </soap-env:Envelope>
[java] handleResponse called
[java] Request processed at: 2002-10-24T21:13:59
```

The client handler's handleRequest() method prints the complete SOAP request message, including the auth header that it adds (highlighted in bold in the previous code listing), while the handleResponse() method displays the timestamp obtained from the time header provided by the server-side handler. Similar output from the server-side handler can be found in the *catalina.out* file in the *logs* directory of the Tomcat web server, or in the file used to capture the System.out stream for the J2EE application server.

Initializing the HandlerRegistry when using dynamic proxies or dynamic invocation

When your client application uses stubs generated by wscompile, the generated Service object contains the code necessary to create a handler chain if one is specified in the *config.xml* file. However, a Service object obtained from a ServiceFactory is generic and therefore cannot create an application-specific handler chain. To use handler chains in conjunction with dynamic proxies or the dynamic invocation interface, you have to add code to your application to install the necessary information in the HandlerRegistry associated with the Service object before using its getPort( ) or createCall( ) methods. Example 6-55 shows an extract from a client application that uses a dynamic proxy to access the book web service that we have been using in this section.

Example 6-55. Dynamically updating the HandlerRegistry for a service endpoint

```
// Form the names of the service and of the port
QName serviceName = new QName(NS_URI, "HandlerBookService");
QName portName = new QName(NS_URI, "HandlerBookQueryPort");

// Get the Service
ServiceFactory factory = ServiceFactory.newInstance( );
Service service = factory.createService(wsdlURL, serviceName);

// Build a handler chain with one handler
QName[] headers = new QName[] {
                    new QName(NS_URI, "auth"),
                    new QName(NS_URI, "time")
                };
HashMap map = new HashMap( );
map.put("debug", "true");
HandlerInfo info = new HandlerInfo(ClientHandler.class, map, headers);
ArrayList handlerList = new ArrayList( );
handlerList.add(info);

// Add the handler chain to the HandlerRegistry
HandlerRegistry handlerRegistry = service.getHandlerRegistry( );
handlerRegistry.setHandlerChain(portName, handlerList);

// Now get the dynamic proxy
HandlerBookQuery bookQuery =
                    (HandlerBookQuery)service.getPort(portName,
                                        HandlerBookQuery.class);
```

This code gets a reference to the HandlerRegistry by calling the getHandlerRegistry( ) method of the Service object obtained from the ServiceFactory. A handler chain is configured for a specific service endpoint using the HandlerRegistry setHandlerChain( ) method:

```
public void setHandlerChain(QName portName, java.util.List handlerChain);
```

The portName argument provides the name of the port for which the handler is to be configured in the form of a QName. The port name can, of course, be obtained from the port element in the WSDL definition of the service:

```
final String NS_URI =
  "urn:jwsnut.chapter6.handlerbookservice/wsdl/HandlerBookQuery";
QName portName = new QName(NS_URI, "HandlerBookQueryPort");
```

The handlerChain argument is a java.util.List object containing an entry of type HandlerInfo containing configuration information for each handler in the chain. In the reference implementation, the order of elements in this list determines the order in which the handlers are invoked during request processing. This behavior however, is implementation-dependent. In this example, the handler chain has only one handler.

The `HandlerInfo` constructor requires three arguments:

```
public HandlerInfo(Class handlerClass, java.util.Map config,
    QName[] headers);
```

The first argument is the `Class` object for the handler implementation class. The second argument is a `Map` containing configuration parameters for the handler. This map should contain the values that you ordinarily supply using property elements in the *config.xml* file. In this case the `Map` is initialized so that the debug property has the value true, which results in the same configuration as that shown in Example 6-54. The final argument lists the header types that the handler chain can process.

Once the list of handlers is constructed, it is installed in the registry:

```
// Add the handler chain the HandlerRegistry
HandlerRegistry handlerRegistry = service.getHandlerRegistry();
handlerRegistry.setHandlerChain(portName, handlerList);
```

With registry initialization complete, it is now possible to use the getPort() method to obtain a dynamic proxy for the target port (or one of the createCall() methods if you intend to use the dynamic invocation interface). The proxy uses the information in the registry to construct the handler chain before the first message is sent to the server. You can verify that this works by running the code using the command:

```
ant run-proxy-client
```

This should produce the same result as the client used in the previous section, which used precompiled stubs to access the web service.

As noted earlier in this chapter, if you are using the beta release of J2EE 1.4 to run the examples for this book, you need to get around a bug that prevents clients generated from WSDL documents from working. If you go to the directory *repository\applications\ HandlerBooks* beneath the installation directory of the J2EE reference implementation, you will find there a file whose name will be something like *Book Service Web Application with message handler using JAX-RPC54173.wsdl* (the numeric part will probably be different on your system). Open this file with an editor and go to the last line, which should contain a `<soap:address>` tag. You'll see that this tag has an attribute called `location`, which contains the URL of the deployed book service—something like *http://localhost:8000// HandlerBooks/HandlerBookQuery*. The fact that there are two "/" characters before `HandlerBooks` causes the client to fail when it connects to the service. To fix this problem, just replace the "//" pair with one slash, thus making the address *http://localhost:8000/ HandlerBooks/HandlerBookQuery*.

Serialization and Type Mappings

In "RPC-Style and Document-Style JAX-RPC," earlier in this chapter, you saw that there are two different sets of encoding rules that are commonly used when creating

SOAP messages—SOAP section 5 encoding, which is typically used for RPC-style operations, and literal encoding, which is the usual choice for a document-style operation. In order to create a SOAP message from the name and parameters of a method call or from its return value and output parameters, the JAX-RPC runtime has to know how to convert the Java primitive types and the Java objects used in the method definition into the corresponding XML representation that will appear in the message. The process of converting a Java type to its XML representation is called *serialization*, and the reverse process is termed *deserialization*. A class that can perform these conversions is called a serializer or a deserializer. In practice, both the serialization and deserialization rules for a specific type are implemented in the same class, which I will refer to simply as a serializer. In this section, we look at how JAX-RPC handles the serialization and deserialization processes. In case you think that you don't really need to know much about this somewhat esoteric issue, in the course of this discussion you'll see that you can't always assume that JAX-RPC will arrange for all of the serializers that you require to be available at runtime. This section shows you how to make sure that they are.

Type Mappings and the Type Mapping Registry

The JAX-RPC runtime stores information relating to serialization in a TypeMappingRegistry. There is a separate TypeMappingRegistry for each service endpoint being used by a client application or hosted by a servlet or session bean. On the client side, the TypeMappingRegistry is associated with the Service object. Client code can obtain a reference to it using the Service getTypeMappingRegistry() method. On the server side, it is owned and initialized by the tie class generated by wsdeploy (JWSDP) or deploytool (J2EE 1.4) and is not accessible to the web service implementation class. The relationship between the Service object, a server-side tie, and the TypeMappingRegistry, together with the objects within the registry, is shown in Figure 6-8.

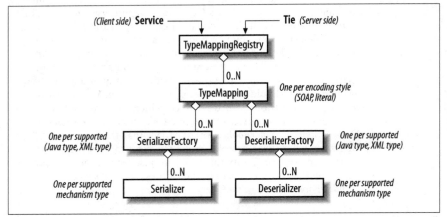

Figure 6-8. JAX-RPC TypeMapping architecture

A TypeMappingRegistry contains zero or more TypeMapping objects, each of which manages the serializers that encapsulate the encoding rules for a particular encoding style. The TypeMapping object for a given encoding style can be obtained by calling the TypeMappingRegistry getTypeMapping( ) method and supplying the URI that uniquely identifies the encoding style, provided that the TypeMappingRegistry has been initialized with a TypeMapping for that URI. The JAX-RPC reference implementation creates registries that are preconfigured with TypeMappings for the SOAP section 5 encoding rules and for literal encoding. Given a Service object, the following code can be used to get the TypeMapping for each of these encoding styles:

```
Service service = ......; // Get Service object
TypeMapping soapMapping = service.getTypeMappingRegistry( ).getTypeMapping(
    javax.xml.rpc.NamespaceConstants.NSURI_SOAP_ENCODING));
TypeMapping literalMapping = service.getTypeMappingRegistry( ).
getTypeMapping("");
```

The serializers and deserializers required for each encoding style are registered with the TypeMapping object using the register( ) method:

```
public void register(Class javaType, QName xmlType, SerializerFactory sf,
                     DeserializerFactory dsf);
```

SerializerFactory and DeserializerFactory are interfaces implemented by classes that can return a serializer or deserializer that can map between the given Java type and XML type. A TypeMapping stores factory references instead of instances of the actual serializers so that the factory can determine when it is appropriate to create serializer instances. In the reference implementation, these factories create only a single instance of each serializer and deserializer, thereby minimizing object creation overhead as well as memory utilization.

When a serializer to map from a given Java type to a given XML type is required, the TypeMapping getSerializer( ) method is called:

```
public SerializerFactory getSerializer(Class javaType, QName xmlType);
```

If there is no factory registered for this combination of types, then null is returned. Once a factory is obtained, the serializer itself can be retrieved using the SerializerFactory getSerializerAs( ) method:

```
public Serializer getSerializerAs(String mechanismType);
```

The mechanismType argument is provided to allow serializers and deserializers to be developed that work with different underlying XML processing mechanisms. A deserializer factory may be able to provide deserializers that work with the input from any or all of a DOM model, a SAX event stream, or a streaming pull parser (i.e., a parser that processes XML elements on request by application code, rather than by delivering events or providing a complete document model). The current version of the JAX-RPC specification does not specify any fixed values for the mechanismType argument, and the reference implementation supports only one mechanism type that corresponds to a streaming pull parser. The same arrangement exists for deserializers.

The javax.xml.rpc.encoding.Serializer and javax.xml.rpc.encoding. Deserializer interface must be implemented by all serializers and deserializers, respectively. They are defined as follows:

```
public interface Serializer {
    public String getMechanismType( );
```

```
    }

    public interface Deserializer {
        public String getMechanismType( );
    }
```

The getMechanismType( ) method returns the identifier for the XML processing mechanism that the serializer or deserializer supports. Surprisingly, these interfaces do not include methods that actually perform any serialization or deserialization! The reason for this is that the current version of the JAX-RPC specification provides only a framework within which serializers and deserializers can be registered and located on demand. It does not specify how these objects are to be implemented nor how they are called, leaving these details to be determined by JAX-RPC vendors. In the future, the JAX-RPC specification is likely to be extended to allow developers to create serializers and deserializers that are portable between different vendors' JAX-RPC implementations.

For an example of the effect of the encoding style on the content of a SOAP message, consider how a date might be mapped to XML. The standard JAX-RPC mapping for the Java Date class (and also for Calendar) is to map to the XML Schema type xsd:dateTime. The standard serializer that maps from Date to xsd:dateTime included in the TypeMapping object for the SOAP section 5 encoding rules creates XML that looks like this:

```
    <ns1:time xsi:type="xsd:dateTime">2002-10-25T19:53:53.250+01:00</ns1:time>
```

In this case, time is a type defined in the WSDL specification of a service to contain a value of type xsd:dateTime. If literal encoding is used, the XML is slightly different:

```
    <ns1:time>2002-10-25T19:53:53.250+01:00</ns1:time>
```

Since these are relatively cumbersome representations, if you implement a web service intended for use in a closed environment, you might agree with the users of your service that dates could be encoded in a more lightweight form, perhaps as the number of milliseconds since January 1, 1970:

```
    <ns1:time>1035657051647</ns1:time>
```

In order to do this, you would introduce a new serializer and deserializer for the Java Date and Calendar classes and plug them into the TypeMapping object for the SOAP-encoding style and/or the literal-encoding style. At the present time, however, it is not possible to write a custom serializer, either to change the way in which a supported type is serialized or to provide serialization for application-specific types, without becoming tied to a specific vendor's product. Therefore, it is best, wherever possible, to create web service interfaces that require only those types for which support is provided by the JAX-RPC specification.[*]

---

[*] The lack of a specification for portable serializers also means that you cannot implement a custom-encoding style without making assumptions about the serialization framework of a particular JAX-RPC implementation, since a new encoding style would require serializers and deserializers that implement the new encoding rules.

Initialization of the TypeMappingRegistry

When the tie class for a server-side web service implementation class is initialized or a client application obtains a Service object for a web service endpoint, the TypeMappingRegistry associated with that endpoint is initialized. The registry content is constructed as follows:

- A standard set of mappings is installed for both the SOAP and literal encodings. All JAX-RPC implementations are required to provide serializers and deserializers for the Java primitive types and the object types listed in "Supported data types" in Chapter 2. The JAX-RPC reference implementation also includes serializers and deserializers for some of the Java collection classes.

- On the server side, the tie class installs serializers and deserializers for arrays and value types used in the service endpoint interface, as well as for the SOAP messages that will exchanged with the client. These serializers and deserializers are generated by wsdeploy and included in the deployable WAR file.

- The same set of serializers is installed on the client side by the Service class generated by wscompile.

For an example of what might be included in the TypeMappingRegistry for a given service endpoint interface, consider the BookQuery interface defined for the book web service used in Chapter 2, which is shown in Example 6-56.

Example 6-56. The BookQuery interface for the book web service

```
public interface BookQuery extends Remote {
    public abstract int getBookCount( ) throws RemoteException;
    public abstract String getAuthor(String name) throws RemoteException;
    public abstract String getEditor(String name) throws RemoteException;
    public abstract double getPrice(String name)
        throws BookServiceException, RemoteException;
    public abstract BookInfo[] getBookInfo( ) throws RemoteException;
    public abstract HashMap getBookMap( ) throws RemoteException;
}
```

The registry will need serializers and deserializers for the SOAP request and response messages for each method call, which will themselves need to use lower-level serializers that can handle the data types used as method call arguments and return values. In the case of this interface, the data types concerned are as follows:

- int
- double
- String
- HashMap
- BookInfo
- BookInfo[]

The first three of these are standard types for which all JAX-RPC implementations are required to provide serializers, whereas HashMap is supported as an extension by the JAX-RPC reference implementation. The serializers and deserializers for these four types therefore appear in the TypeMappingRegistry when it is initialized. The BookInfo class is a value type that contains values that are directly supported by JAX-RPC. A custom serializer is generated for this class by both wscompile and wsdeploy.* Similarly, a serializer for an array of BookInfo objects is generated. These custom serializers are registered by the Service object on the client side and by the tie class on the server side.

Adding Additional Serializers to the Registry

Both wscompile and wsdeploy ensure that the registry contains serializers for all of the types that are used in the Java interface or WSDL document that defines the service endpoint interface for a web service. Sometimes, however, this is not sufficient. Some examples of instances in which these tools cannot generate all of the serializers that are required at runtime, given only the information in the WSDL document or the Java interface, are described in the following list.

Use of collection classes
>The JAX-RPC reference implementation can serialize and deserialize a subset of the Java collection classes from the java.util package. These serializers know how to create XML that represents the structure of the collection, including the pairing of keys with values for collections such as HashMap. However, it is still necessary for the registry to contain specific serializers for the objects that are stored in the collection. This requirement is met if the collection contains only the standard JAX-RPC types such as String, Integer, Date, etc. It is also met for objects that are used elsewhere in the interface or WSDL definition from which the stubs and ties for the service are generated. In the case of the BookQuery interface, for example, the HashMap returned by the getBookMap( ) method contains only Strings (for the entry keys) and BookInfo objects (for the entry values). String is a JAX-RPC supported type, while BookInfo is explicitly referenced elsewhere in the interface definition—therefore, both of these types already have serializers installed. This requirement would not be met if the collection contained an instance of a class that does not appear in the interface definition (even if that class is a value type that could be serialized by JAX-RPC), or if it contained an array of objects of any type—even primitive objects for which serializers are already registered (such as String[ ]).

Methods that use base class or interface arguments
>Suppose that the provider of the web service that uses the BookQuery interface decides to include a new category of books that could be viewed over the Internet by registered subscribers. To accommodate this, a subclass of BookInfo, called ElectronicBookInfo, might be developed that includes the URL at which the book could be found. The methods of the BookQuery interface would continue to refer to BookInfo throughout, since they would need to handle any kind of book. However, since ElectronicBookInfo is not mentioned in the interface definition, there is not a serializer for it.

Put in a more general form, this issue arises when there is a collection class in the interface definition, or when the Java method declarations or the WSDL

---

* Of course, a deserializer for this type is also generated. For the sake of brevity, from this point forward, I'll use the term "serializer" as shorthand for both serializer and deserializer, unless otherwise stated.

document refer to base classes (perhaps abstract base classes) or interfaces, in which the objects that are actually transferred are instances of derived classes or classes that implement the specified interface. If the actual types are not mentioned anywhere in the endpoint interface definition, neither wscompile nor wsdeploy generates serializers for them.

Suppose that we were to extend the book web service from Chapter 2 by adding a URL for those books that can be viewed over the Internet, as previously suggested. We do this using the class ElectronicBookInfo, the definition of which is shown in Example 6-57.

Example 6-57. A subclass of BookInfo with a URL attribute

```java
public class ElectronicBookInfo extends BookInfo {
    private String url;

    /**
     * Constructs an <code>ElectronicBookInfo</code> object.
     * This constructor is used for deserialization.
     */
    public ElectronicBookInfo() {
    }

    /**
     * Constructs an <code>ElectronicBookInfo</code> object initialized
     * with given attributes.
     */
    public ElectronicBookInfo(String title, String author, String editor,
                              double price, String url) {
        super(title, author, editor, price);
        this.url = url;
    }

    public String getURL() {
        return url;
    }

    public void setURL(String url) {
        this.url = url;
    }
}
```

The addition of this subclass does not, of course, result in any changes in the BookQuery interface (which is shown in Example 6-56). As far as the results of calling the methods of this interface are concerned, the introduction of this BookInfo subclass has the following effect:

- The array of BookInfo objects returned by the getBookInfo( ) method will be populated with BookInfo objects for those books that cannot be viewed on the Internet, and with ElectronicBookInfo objects for those that can.

- Similarly, in the HashMap returned by getBookMap( ), in which the keys are the book titles, the value associated with each book is either a BookInfo or an ElectronicBookInfo object.

The client code shown in Example 6-58 could be used to fetch the books from the web service using both methods, and prints the results.

Example 6-58. Getting a list of BookInfo and ElectronicBookInfo objects from the book web service

```
// Get all of the books
BookInfo[] info = bookQuery.getBookInfo( );
System.out.println("Books from getBookInfo( )");
for (int i = 0; i < info.length; i++) {
    boolean eBook = info[i] instanceof ElectronicBookInfo;
    System.out.println("\tTitle: " + info[i].getTitle( ) +
                    (eBook ? "; URL: " +
                    ((ElectronicBookInfo)info[i]).getURL( ) : "; not E-Book"));
}

// Get the books in a HashMap
HashMap map = bookQuery.getBookMap( );
System.out.println("Books from getBookMap( )");
Iterator iter = map.values( ).iterator( );
while (iter.hasNext( )) {
    BookInfo book = (BookInfo)iter.next( );
    boolean eBook = book instanceof ElectronicBookInfo;
    System.out.println("\tTitle: " + book.getTitle( ) +
                    (eBook ? "; URL: " +
                    ((ElectronicBookInfo)book).getURL( ) : "; not E-Book"));
}
```

Notice that after calling each method, the runtime type of each `BookInfo` object is checked to determine whether it is accessible over the Internet. If we modified the servant for the book web service to include a mixture of books that are and are not accessible over the Internet, and then run this client code, we get output like that shown here (some lines have been omitted for the sake of brevity):

```
Books from getBookInfo( )
    Title: Java in a Nutshell; not E-Book
    Title: J2ME in a Nutshell; not E-Book
    Title: Java Swing; not E-Book
            .
            .
            .
    Title: Java Internationalization; not E-Book
Books from getBookMap( )
    Title: Java in a Nutshell; not E-Book
    Title: J2ME in a Nutshell; not E-Book
            .
            .
            .
    Title: Java Internationalization; not E-Book
            .
            .
            .
    Title: Java Swing; not E-Book
```

These results indicate that all of the objects returned were of type `BookInfo`, despite the fact that the server has a mixture of `BookInfo` and `ElectronicBookInfo` objects. This is perhaps not surprising, since neither the client nor the server have a serializer for the ElectronicBookInfo class (which is not explicitly mentioned in the BookQuery interface). As a result, the ElectronicBookInfo objects are all serialized as instances of the base class BookInfo, for which a serializer *is* available.

Adding serializers to the client side

On the client side, you can arrange for wscompile to generate serializers for classes that do not appear in the service endpoint interface definition by including one or more additionalTypes elements in the *config.xml* file. Example 6-59 shows the *config.xml* file for a client that will access a version of the book web service that has been enhanced to return both BookInfo and ElectronicBookInfo objects.

Example 6-59. The additionalTypes element in the config.xml file

```
<?xml version="1.0" encoding="UTF-8" ?>

<configuration
        xmlns="http://java.sun.com/xml/ns/jax-rpc/ri/config">
    <service name="SerializerBookService"
            targetNamespace=
            "urn:jwsnut.chapter6.serializerbookservice/wsdl/SBookQuery"
            typeNamespace=
            "urn:jwsnut.chapter6.serializerbookservice/types/SBookQuery"
            packageName="ora.jwsnut.chapter6.serializerbookservice">

        <interface name="ora.jwsnut.chapter6.serializerbookservice.SBookQuery"/>
        <typeMappingRegistry>
            <additionalTypes>
                <class name=
                "ora.jwsnut.chapter6.serializerbookservice.ElectronicBookInfo"/>
            </additionalTypes>
        </typeMappingRegistry>
    </service>
</configuration>
```

The typeMappingRegistry element shown here has several possible child elements that can be used to specify the content of the TypeMappingRegistry associated with the Service object being configured, all of which are described in Chapter 8. The additionalTypes element lists the classes for which serializers must be generated and added to the registry at runtime. Each such class requires a class element with a name attribute set to its fully qualified name.

Adding serializers to the server side

A serializer for the ElectronicBookInfo class must also be available to the JAX-RPC runtime on the server side. However, the schema definition for the *jaxrpc-ri.xml* file, which wsdeploy uses to determine the tie classes and serializers that it needs to generate, does not include a typeMappingRegistry element. The only way to communicate a requirement for additional serializers to wsdeploy is to generate a model file from the information contained in the *config.xml* file and then include a reference to it in the endpoint element for the service. This is the same technique that we used when it was necessary to arrange for wsdeploy to generate ties for a document-style service endpoint interface in "RPC-Style and Document-Style JAX-RPC," earlier in this chapter. The model file is created by supplying the -model argument to wscompile when creating the client-side artifacts, and is then placed in the *WEB-INF* directory of the portable WAR file used by wsdeploy, along with a suitably modified *jaxrpc-ri.xml* file, as shown in Example 6-60.

Example 6-60. Using a model file to include additional serializers in a server-side deployment

```
<?xml version="1.0" encoding="UTF-8"?>
<webServices
    xmlns="http://java.sun.com/xml/ns/jax-rpc/ri/dd"
    version="1.0"
    targetNamespaceBase="urn:jwsnut.chapter6.serializerbookservice/wsdl/"
    typeNamespaceBase="urn:jwsnut.chapter6.serializerbookservice/types/">

    <endpoint
        name="SBookQuery"
        displayName="SBookQuery Port"
        description="Serializer Book Query Port"
        interface="ora.jwsnut.chapter6.serializerbookservice.SBookQuery"
        model="/WEB-INF/model"
        implementation=
            "ora.jwsnut.chapter6.serializerbookservice.SBookServiceServant"/>

    <endpointMapping
        endpointName="SBookQuery"
        urlPattern="/SBookQuery"/>
</webServices>
```

These changes make serializers for the types listed in the additionalTypes elements of the *config.xml* file available in the TypeMappingRegistry used by the server-side tie classes for this web service, as well as in the registry created by the generated Service object used on the client side. To run this service, make *chapter6\serializerbookservice* your current directory, and deploy it into your web container using the command:

```
ant deploy
```

Next, you need to compile and run the client application, which uses the code shown in Example 6-58, using the following commands:

```
ant compile-client
ant run-client
```

Apart from a few lines left out for the sake of brevity, the output from the client looks like this:

```
Books from getBookInfo()
        Title: Java in a Nutshell; not E-Book
        Title: J2ME in a Nutshell; not E-Book
        Title: Java Swing; not E-Book
                .
                .
                .
        Title: Java Internationalization; not E-Book
```

```
Books from getBookMap( )
    Title: Java in a Nutshell; URL: http://www.ora.com/catalog/javanut
    Title: J2ME in a Nutshell; URL: http://www.ora.com/catalog/j2meanut
        .
        .
        .
    Title: Java Internationalization; not E-Book
    Title: Java Swing; not E-Book
```

It is obvious that the values returned from the getBookInfo( ) method do not match those in the HashMap obtained by calling getBookMap( ). The values in the HashMap are a mixture of ElectronicBookInfo (those where a URL is shown) and BookInfo objects (where there is no URL); these are the "correct" results because they match the values held at the server. However, the array returned by getBookInfo( ) contains only BookInfo objects—even those books that have associated URLs have been serialized and deserialized as BookInfo objects rather than ElectronicBookInfo objects. This difference arises from the way in which the values were serialized. Here are the rules that govern the way in which a serializer is chosen:

- If the runtime type of the object cannot be fully resolved at compilation time, then an appropriate serializer is chosen at serialization time. This is the case when the type is declared to be java.lang.Object, which is an *abstract* type or a Java interface.

- In all other cases, the serializer to be used is determined during the code generation process for the client-side stubs or server-side ties.

In the case of the getBookInfo( ) method, the return value is declared to be an array of BookInfo objects. Since BookInfo is a concrete class, the stubs and ties are generated in such a way that a serializer for BookInfo is used, even though the runtime type of any of the objects in the array could be either BookInfo or its subclass ElectronicBookInfo. By contrast, the values in a HashMap are of type java.lang.Object. Therefore, the serializer is chosen at runtime based on the actual type of each value in the collection. As a result, BookInfo objects are serialized using the BookInfo serializer, and ElectronicBookInfo objects by the ElectronicBookInfo serializer.

Had the getBookInfo( ) method been defined like this:

```
public Object[] getBookInfo( );
```

then the returned array would have contained a mixture of BookInfo and ElectronicBookInfo objects. Of course, replacing BookInfo[] with Object[] in this way is bad programming practice. A better alternative is to make BookInfo an abstract base class and then create two concrete subclasses:

```
public abstract class BookInfo {
    // Same definition as existing BookInfo class
}

public class HardCopyBookInfo extends BookInfo {
    // Nothing added
    public HardCopyInfo( ) {
        // Required default constructor
    }
```

```
    public HardCopyInfo(String title, String author, String editor,
                        double price) {
      super(title, author, editor, price);
    }
}

public class ElectronicBookInfo extends BookInfo {
    // Defined as shown in Example 6-57
}
```

When defining classes—abstract or otherwise—whose names will appear as method arguments or return values, it is essential that they follow the JAX-RPC rules described in "Value types" in Chapter 2. In particular, the HardCopyBookInfo class is required to have a default constructor as shown in the previous example. Also, at least in the JAX-RPC reference implementation, a value type must have at least one attribute (making it impossible to define a "marker" base class containing no methods, and use it in the signature of a JAX-RPC method call), and an interface must contain properly matched getter and setter methods.

Once BookInfo is made abstract, the serialization of the BookInfo array returned by getBookInfo( ) uses serializers chosen at runtime. Naturally, it is also necessary to include HardCopyBookInfo in the additionalTypes list in *config.xml* so that a serializer for HardCopyBookInfo is created.

JAXR

JAX-RPC and SAAJ are enabling technologies that allow companies to create electronic business applications that exchange information using XML and SOAP. WSDL (see Chapter 5) is the means by which a developer finds out about the interface provided by a web service. As you saw in Chapter 6, once you have a WSDL definition for a service, you can quickly create the client-side stubs that an application needs in order to communicate with it using JAX-RPC. The remaining question is, given that your business needs to find a provider for a specific service, how do you go about locating businesses that offer that service, evaluate their offerings, and, if appropriate, fetch the WSDL definition for the service itself? The answer lies in the *XML-based registries* that are currently being established on the Internet.

A *registry* contains information that allows businesses to discover and make use of the services of potential corporate electronic partners. A business might want to deal directly with another party (purchasing components or other services from that company), or perhaps, it may intend to add value to the other party's offerings—for example, by providing a specialized interface to the other's web service, such as the one offered by Amazon.com.

A provider company submits an entry to a registry and categorizes it in various ways that will make it easier to find. The submitting company might include in its registry entries links to technical specifications that describe its service at the level required by a potential implementor of an application client, or it might include marketing information for the consumption of management-level decision makers. The enquiring company searches the registry for information using various criteria, such as name hints (thus treating the registry as a source of White Pages information), categories of interest (a Yellow Pages search), or a geographical location (a Green Pages search). The information that it retrieves can be inspected and compared with what is available from other sources. Finally, if a business agreement is reached, the client company retrieves the WSDL definition for the service that it needs to use, which is typically also available through the registry, and uses that as the basis for creating a SAAJ- or JAX-RPC-based application client.

UDDI and ebXML Registries

There are currently two different XML-based registry standards being developed:

The UDDI Version 2.0 Registry
> The Universal Description, Discovery, and Integration (UDDI) registry standard was originally created by IBM, Microsoft, and Ariba, but the technical committee that is responsible for its ongoing development now has more than 50 members. The UDDI registry is intended primarily for the publication of metadata relating to web services.

The ebXML Registry/Repository
> The ebXML Registry/Repository standard was created by OASIS and is aimed at the e-commerce market. It is currently more feature-rich than UDDI, and also provides a repository, which allows companies to store documents and other data in the registry, as well as links to information that is kept elsewhere.

There is a public production UDDI business registry maintained by IBM, Microsoft, and SAP. Businesses can register with any of these *UDDI operator* companies to enter and update their details. Changes made in one operator company's copy of the registry are automatically propagated to those of the other operators so that they can be seen by users of any of the operators' views and thus give the appearance that there is a single, global registry. The registry offers an interface that allows you to submit queries from your web browser using one of the following URLs:

- *https://uddi.ibm.com/ubr/registry.html*
- *http://uddi.microsoft.com*
- *http://udditest.sap.com*

The business search page provided at the IBM web site is shown in Figure 7-1.

This page allows you to locate business entries based on criteria such as the company name (which can include a wildcard character) or categories that might have been applied by the company to its registry entry, such as a geographical location qualifier. If, for example, you perform a case-insensitive search for businesses whose name starts with the string "amazon," you would probably get two results, as shown in Figure 7-2.

A business may offer one or more services, the descriptions of which can be obtained by clicking the *Services* link. In the case of the entry for Amazon.com, this leads to another page, shown in Figure 7-3. As you can see, Amazon.com provides one web service, which describes itself as a fee-earner for developers that create application clients that are subsequently used to purchase items from the online store. To find out more, you select the link in the *Service Name* column, which fetches the actual service details, as shown in Figure 7-4. Among the information on this page is an *Access URL,* which supplies the location of the service's WSDL definition, from which you can create the stubs required to access the service using JAX-RPC.

This UDDI registry is intended for production use and contains real business information. The UDDI operators also provide test registries that can be used during

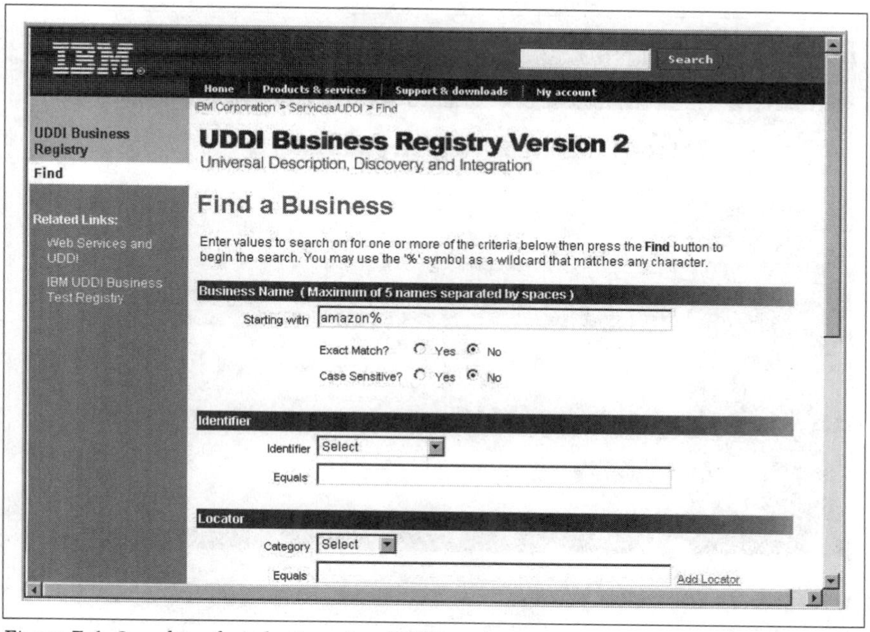

Figure 7-1. Searching for a business in a UDDI registry

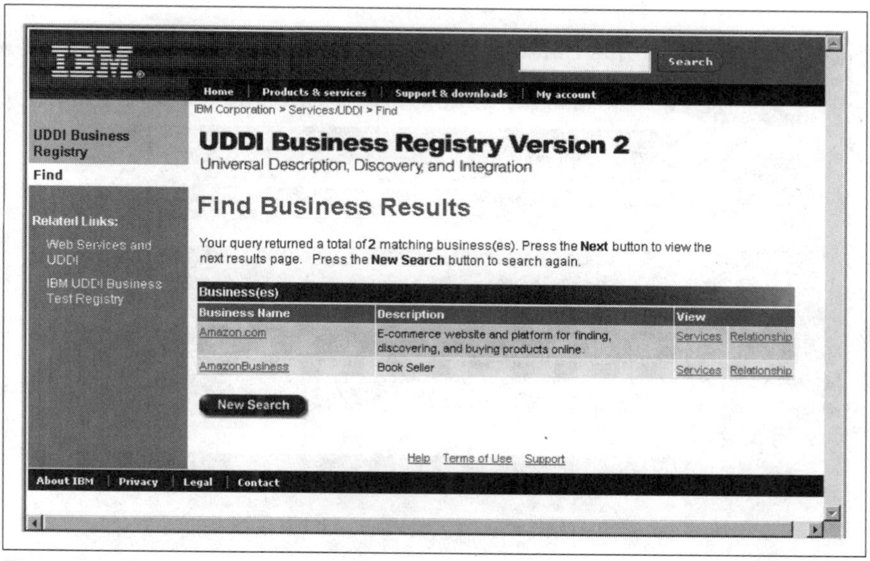

Figure 7-2. The results of a business search in the UDDI registry

development and testing, one of which can be found at *http://uddi.ibm.com/ testregistry/registry.html*. While registry searching can be performed anonymously, you'll typically need to register in order to be able to update a registry.

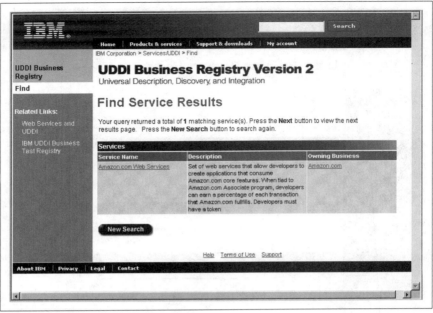

Figure 7-3. Services offered by Amazon.com

Service Details

The details of the selected service are shown below. Please use your browser's **Back** button to return to the previous page OR Press the **New Search** button to search again.

Service Information

Key
BA6D9D56-EA3F-4263-A95A-EEB17E5910DB

Owning Business	Owner Key
Amazon.com	18B7FDE2-D15C-437C-8877-EBEC8216D0F5

Service Name(s)

Name	Language
Amazon.com Web Services	en

Service Description(s)

Description	Language
Set of web services that allow developers to create applications that consume Amazon.com core features. When tied to Amazon.com Associate program, developers can earn a percentage of each transaction that Amazon.com fulfills. Developers must have a token	en

Access Point(s)

Protocol	Address	Description	Actions
http	http://soap.amazon.com/schemas/AmazonWebServices.wsdl	The WSDL file that allows developers to make use of Amazon.com features on their own site.	Details

Figure 7-4. Service details for Amazon.com

There is also a test version of the ebXML registry/repository available for public use at *http://registry.csis.hku.hk:8201/ebxmlrr/registry*. At the time of this writing, this registry does not have a browser-based interface. Instead, you have to download and install a Java client that can be used to access the registry. Details of this client are provided in the next section.

JAXR Architecture

Aside from the fact that they both provide an XML-based interface to application clients (in addition to the browser interface offered by the UDDI public registry), from a developer's point of view, the UDDI and ebXML registries have little in common. In particular, the structure of information within the registry and the programming interface are very different. As a result, applications written to use the native facilities provided by the UDDI registry cannot be used with an ebXML registry and vice versa. The Java API for XML Registries (JAXR) solves this problem by providing a common interface that allows a Java application to access a registry without needing to be aware of its implementation details. Figure 7-5 shows the JAXR software architecture. The JAXR specification was developed under the Java Community Process and can be downloaded from *http://jcp.org/jsr/detail/93.jsp*.

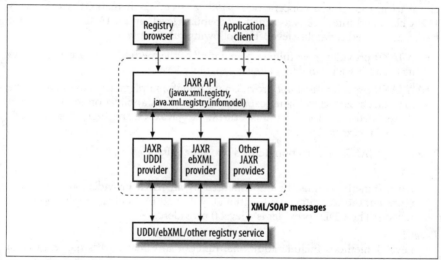

Figure 7-5. JAXR architecture

The first thing to note is that, unlike SAAJ and JAX-RPC, JAXR is a client-side only API—the implementation details of the registry service itself are of no concern, except insofar as the registry service provides the XML-based interface and information model required by its specification. Furthermore, although the internal information models defined for the UDDI and ebXML registries are quite different, a JAXR application can extract business and service information from either of them, since the JAXR API transparently maps them both to its own information model, which happens to be based upon and very similar to that of the ebXML registry.*

A JAXR application client (such as a registry browser, a development tool, or a web services client that needs to fetch registry-based information at runtime) uses the classes and interfaces in the `javax.xml.registry` and `javax.xml.registry.infomodel` packages to make requests of the target registry service. The mapping to the programming interface and information model of a specific registry is performed by a JAXR provider that is specific to a particular type of registry. The JAXR reference implementation includes a UDDI registry provider and a registry server that is useful for development and testing purposes. A free, open source implementation of a JAXR provider for ebXML, together with an ebXML registry/repository, can be downloaded from *http://ebxmlrr.sourceforge.net*. We'll use both of these JAXR implementations in this chapter.

If you leave aside the details, the UDDI and ebXML registries have much in common. These common facilities are mapped by the JAXR provider to the corresponding JAXR API. However, the ebXML registry has some features that do not exist in UDDI and that cannot reasonably be emulated by the UDDI JAXR provider. Rather than opt for a lowest common denominator API, which in this case would have omitted the additional ebXML facilities, the JAXR expert group chose to introduce the concept of *capability levels*. Each method within every JAXR class and interface is assigned a capability level, and a JAXR provider also has an associated capability level. The following rules apply:

- A JAXR provider must fully implement *all* of the methods that are assigned to its capability level *and* to all lower capability levels.

- A JAXR provider must *not* provide a meaningful implementation of any of the methods assigned to higher capability levels. If an application invokes one of these methods, then it must throw a `javax.xml.registry.Unsupported-CapabilityException`.

The current JAXR specification defines two capability levels:

Level 0
> Level 0 methods must be implemented by all JAXR providers and therefore represent the common core functionality that all JAXR client applications can rely on. The UDDI provider is a level 0 provider.

Level 1
> Level 1 methods include additional functionality that covers the features of the ebXML registry/repository that cannot be mapped so that they also appear to work with a UDDI provider. An ebXML provider must be a level 1 provider.

---

* You can obtain the specifications for the UDDI registry from *http://uddi.org* and for the ebXML registry/repository from *http://www.ebxml.org*. Although you don't need to read these specifications in order to use JAXR, it is sometimes useful to know how JAXR operations affect the registry. Also, a knowledge of the internals of the registry may occasionally be helpful when debugging JAXR applications.

It is important to note that the JAXR specification does not officially assign capability levels to classes or interfaces, so that all providers must include an implementation of the whole API. However, in practice, some interfaces are entirely composed of level 1 methods and are therefore effectively level 1–only facilities. The reference documentation in this book for the javax.xml.registry and javax.xml.registry.infomodel packages indicates the capability level of each method.

The capability level of a provider is available at runtime for the benefit of application clients that can tailor their behavior according to the available functionality.

 Although every provider is required to implement JAXR level 0 functionality, unfortunately they cannot all do this to the same degree. As an example of this, the level 0 API includes the ability to define private classification schemes, but, as we'll see later in this chapter, even though this feature exists, an application client cannot *programmatically* construct such a scheme when connected to a UDDI registry.* Instead, the classification scheme has to be defined and supplied to the JAXR provider at initialization time. As a consequence, the classification scheme does not actually appear in the registry itself.

By contrast, the ebXML registry provides everything necessary to allow user-defined classification schemes to be set up dynamically by application clients.

Using the JAXR Examples

In order to use the example source code for this chapter, you need to install and configure the JAXR providers that you intend to use and set a small number of properties that the examples will use to locate and connect to the registry.

Using a UDDI Registry

Since the JAXR reference implementation includes a UDDI provider and a UDDI registry server, it is very simple to use the example source code with this registry type. The following sections describe what you need to do.

Edit the jwsnutJaxrExamples.properties file

The *jwsnutJaxrExamples.properties* file in your home directory (which should have been created according to the instructions given in "Examples Online" in the Preface) specifies the authentication information for the UDDI registry server and the URLs required to access it. In most cases, the default settings in this file, shown here, are appropriate:

```
#
# User name and password for the UDDI JAXR registry server
#
```

---

* Note also that an application client that attempts to define a private classification scheme using the level 0 API for doing so would appear to succeed. However, the classification scheme would not be properly defined in the case of a UDDI registry, and an attempt to use it by another client would fail.

```
JAXR_UDDI_USER = testuser
JAXR_UDDI_PASSWORD = testuser

#
# URLs for the UDDI JAXR registry server
#
JAXR_UDDI_SERVER_QUERY_URL =
    ${WEBURL}/${REGISTRY_SERVER_APP}/RegistryServerServlet
JAXR_UDDI_SERVER_LIFECYCLE_URL =
    ${WEBURL}/${REGISTRY_SERVER_APP}/ RegistryServerServlet
```

The JAXR_UDDI_USER and JAXR_UDDI_PASSWORD properties should be set to the user-name and password required to access the UDDI registry. The settings shown here are appropriate for the user that is already defined in the registry when you install the JWSDP or J2EE 1.4. If you intend to use a different test UDDI registry (such as those provided by the UDDI registry operators), you need to register with them and obtain a username and password.

The JAXR_UDDI_SERVER_QUERY_URL and JAXR_UDDI_SERVER_LIFECYCLE_URL properties are the URLs that should be used to send queries to the registry and to make registry updates, respectively. The values just shown are correct for the reference implemen-tation, which is deployed as a service in the Tomcat web container or, in the case of the J2EE 1.4 platform, as an external service accessed via a connector. If you register with one of the UDDI operators, you should enter the appropriate URLs here. Note that registry queries typically do not require authentication and usually use the HTTP protocol, whereas updates are permitted only to registered users and require HTTPS. The reference implementation is a special case that uses HTTP in both cases (although it does require a valid username and password for updates).

Start the registry server

If you are using the registry in the JAXR reference implementation, you need to ensure that the Tomcat web container is running before attempting to use the example source code. This registry stores its data in an XML-based database called *Xindice*, which is also provided as part of the reference implementation. If you are using J2EE 1.4, you can start the registry server and the database at the same time as the J2EE application server by supplying the -startRegistry argu-ment to its startup script:

```
j2ee -startRegistry
```

If you are using the JWSDP, the registry server is started automatically.

Install the sample registry data

The example source code uses sample registry data that must be installed before any of the examples can be executed. To install the data, open a command window, make *chapter7\setup* (relative to the installation directory of the example source code) your working directory, and type the commands:

```
ant compile
ant run-uddi-install-client
```

The data only needs to be installed once. You can clean up your registry at any time using the `run-uddi-delete-client` target of the Ant buildfile:

```
ant run-uddi-delete-client
```

Using an ebXML Registry

The JWSDP reference implementation does not include either an ebXML JAXR provider or an ebXML registry server. If you intend to run any of the examples that illustrate level 1 JAXR facilities, you need to obtain at least an ebXML JAXR provider. Having done so, you can then make use of a public test ebXML registry. Alternatively (and probably more conveniently), you can install a test registry of your own.

One source for both a provider and a registry server can be found at *http:// ebxmlrr.sourceforge.net*. This site contains source and binary distributions for both components, together with installation and setup instructions. Having installed the software and deployed the registry server in the Tomcat web container using the instructions provided at the web site, follow the instructions shown next to configure the registry and set up the example source code to use it.

The example source code assumes that it is using the ebXML provider and registry from the web site just given. This assumption is necessary because the means by which a registry client authenticates to the registry, which is necessary in order to update its content, is registry-specific. The following instructions are specific to this particular registry implementation—if you plan to use a different implementation, you may have to modify the example source code and perform the setup differently.

Create configuration files for the ebXML registry server

Among the files for the ebXML registry server there is one called *ebxmlrr. properties*. If the machine on which you are running the server is *not* connected to the Internet, you should copy this file to your home directory and edit the copy to look like the lines shown here so that both properties are set to false:

```
#Decide whether to checkURLs in external links or not
#
ebxmlrr.persistence.rdb.ExternalLinkDAO.checkURLs=false
#Decide whether to checkURLs in service bindings or not
#
ebxmlrr.persistence.rdb.ServiceBindingDAO.checkURLs=false
```

You do not need to do this if your registry server will have Internet access.

Start the registry server

The registry server is deployed as a web application on the Tomcat web container; therefore, it is started at the same time as the web container itself. If the web container is currently active, stop and restart it so that the registry server reads the *ebxmlrr.properties* file set up in the previous step.

Create a registry user

The example source code needs to install some test data in the registry. Since only registered users can update the registry, you need to create an identity for yourself. As you'll see in "Registry Security" at the end of this chapter, an ebXML registry requires a client to provide a certificate as proof of identity. Therefore, part of the process of creating a new registry user involves obtaining a suitable certificate. The simplest way to do this is to use the registry browser that is supplied with the registry. Before you can do this, you need to create a file called *.java.login.config* in your home directory and add the following lines to it:

```
JAXRTest {
    com.sun.security.auth.module.KeyStoreLoginModule required debug=true
        keyStoreURL="file://c:/homedir//jaxr-ebxml/security/keystore.jks";
};

jaxr-ebxml-provider {
    com.sun.security.auth.module.KeyStoreLoginModule required debug=true
        keyStoreURL="file://c:/homedir/jaxr-ebxml/security/keystore.jks";
};
```

c:/homedir should be replaced by the path name of your home directory. On a Windows system, this would be something like *c:/Documents and Settings/My Name*. Note that forward slashes are acceptable (since this is a URL) and that the text shown in bold should appear on a single line (even though it is split over two lines here for the sake of readability).

Next, copy the file *jaxr-ebxml.properties* from the ebXML download to your home directory and modify the lines beginning with jaxr-ebxml.security so that they look like this:

```
jaxr-ebxml.security.keystore=security/keystore.jks
jaxr-ebxml.security.storepass=ebXMLStorePassword
jaxr-ebxml.security.keypass=ebXMLKeyPassword
```

These lines are used to create the keystore for the certificate that is used to authenticate you to the registry server. You do not have to use the values for the storepass and keypass keys shown here, but if you change them, you must remember to use the same values when registering yourself with the server.

Now start the registry browser by making the root directory of the registry server download your working directory and typing the command:

```
ant run.browser
```

Select the URL of the registry in the Registry Location field (this is *http://localhost:8080/ebxmlrr/registry/soap* if the web container is running on your local system) and then press the "Show User Registration Wizard" toolbar button (which has an icon showing a person and a small green cross). This displays a dialog that allows you to create your identity within the registry. Many of the fields in this dialog can be left empty. However, you must provide at least a username, and you must complete the following fields that appear at the bottom of the dialog:

Keystore Alias

> This is the name under which the certificate that authenticates you will be held within the keystore. You should remember the value that you enter here, because you will need to use it later. As an example, I'll suppose that you choose the alias ebXMLtestuser.

Keystore Password

This is the password that will be used to protect the keystore. You should use the value assigned to the jaxr-ebxml.security.storepass key in the *jaxr-ebxml.properties* file, which, in the example just shown, is ebXMLStorePassword.

Private Key Password

This is the password that will be used to protect the private key corresponding to your certificate in the keystore. You should use the value assigned to the jaxr-ebxml.security.keypass key in the *jaxr-ebxml.properties* file, which, in the example just shown, is ebXMLKeyPassword.

Once you complete the dialog, press the OK button. You are then presented with another dialog that authenticates you to the registry server using the certificate that has just been created. Enter the same alias and passwords that you supplied to the registration wizard and press OK. If you don't see any errors, then your identity has been successfully registered.

Edit the jwsnutJaxrExamples.properties file

Several properties need to be set in the *jwsnutJaxrExamples.properties* file in your home directory before you can successfully run the example source code with an ebXML registry. Typical settings for these properties are shown here.

```
#
# URLs for the ebXML JAXR registry server, if installed
#
JAXR_EBXML_SERVER_QUERY_URL = ${WEBURL}/ebxmlrr/registry/soap
JAXR_EBXML_SERVER_LIFECYCLE_URL = ${WEBURL}/ebxmlrr/registry/soap

# Location of the lib directory for the ebXML registry
# provider, if it is installed. This should be something
# like c:/ebxmlrr-client/lib.
JAXR_EBXML_PROVIDER=c:/ebxmlrr-client/lib

#
# Authentication for the ebXML JAXR registry server.
#
JAXR_EBXML_KEYSTORE_FILE=${user.home}/jaxr-ebxml/security/keystore.jks
JAXR_EBXML_ALIAS = ebXMLtestuser
JAXR_EBXML_KEY_PASSWORD = ebXMLKeyPassword
JAXR_EBXML_KEYSTORE_PASSWORD = ebXMLStorePassword
```

JAXR_EBXML_SERVER_QUERY_URL and JAXR_EBXML_SERVER_LIFECYCLE_URL are the URLs that map to the registry server's query and update functionality. The values shown here are correct for the default deployment in the Tomcat web container.

The JAXR_EBXML_PROVIDER property is the full pathname of the directory in which the client-side JAR files for the ebXML JAXR provider are located. The correct path depends on where you install the JAXR provider. You can easily locate it by looking for a file called *jaxr-ebxml.jar*.

The remaining properties relate to the keystore for the user that you registered earlier in the section "Create a registry user." The JAXR_EBXML_KEYSTORE_FILE property supplies the full pathname of the keystore itself. You may use the property

${user.home} to refer to your home directory, as shown here. The location of the keystore is always *${user.home}/jaxr-ebxml/*, followed by the value of the jaxr-ebxml.security.keystore property from the file *jaxr-ebxml.properties*; hence, the value shown here is correct if you use the settings shown in "Create a registry user." The JAXR_EBXML_ALIAS, JAXR_EBXML_KEY_PASSWORD, and JAXR_EBXML_KEYSTORE_PASSWORD properties must have the same values as those supplied when completing the user details in the user registration wizard of the registry browser, as the values shown here illustrate.

Install the sample registry data

With all of the configuration details in place, the last step is to install the test data in the registry. Make sure that the Tomcat web server is running, then make *chapter7\setup* (relative to the installation directory of the example source code) your working directory and type the commands:

```
ant compile
ant run-ebxml-install-client
```

The data only needs to be installed once. You can clean up your registry at any time using the run-ebxml-delete-client target of the Ant buildfile:

```
ant run-ebxml-delete-client
```

Note that, since the UDDI and ebXML registries are separate, installing or removing the data for one of them has no effect on the other.

JAXR Registry Model Overview

A JAXR client views the registry as a set of objects whose types are defined in the javax.xml.registry.infomodel package. The information model is based on the one defined by the ebXML registry/repository specification, with some minor differences. A JAXR provider for a particular registry is required to transparently map between the JAXR information model and the real model of the registry itself, so that JAXR clients are not dependent on the details of any particular registry. This section provides an overview of the JAXR registry information model. You'll see more detail when we look at the JAXR registry programming model later in this chapter.

Figure 7-6 shows a small part of the complete JAXR registry model, illustrating the elements that are of greatest importance to most JAXR clients. The first thing to note about this diagram is that it contains only Java interfaces. In fact, ignoring exceptions, the JAXR API contains only one class that is not an interface. The use of interfaces allows a JAXR provider to supply its own implementation classes for each element of the information model without exposing them to application code. From the client application's point of view, this has the effect that objects within the registry cannot be created directly—instead, they are obtained from using factory methods of a class called BusinessLifeCycleManager, which will be described later in this chapter.

A business that submits information to the registry is represented by an Organization object. Associated with each Organization is a distinguished person

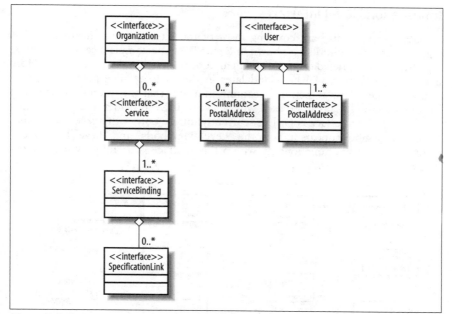

Figure 7-6. Organization- and Service-related registry objects

called the primary contact, represented by a User object. User has several attributes, including two that are shown here: a name and a postal address. As we'll see later, the PostalAddress interface is particularly interesting because there is no commonly agreed way to represent a postal address within a registry, which leads to some complications for the application client. User objects also appear within the *audit trail* (not shown in the diagram) that is maintained by level 1 registries.

An organization usually enters itself into a registry in order to advertise its services. Each such service is represented by a Service object. In the JAXR information model, a Service object is bound to an organization and therefore organizations offering identical services cannot share the same registry entries for those services. Service is actually a simple container object that references one or more ServiceBindings. A ServiceBinding contains the information that a client might need to use a service, including the URI at which the service can be reached, and, optionally, one or more SpecificationLinks that might provide technical information on how the service is to be invoked. In a properly constructed ServiceBinding, one of the SpecificationLinks would point to the WSDL definition for the service.

In the case of a UDDI registry, a WSDL definition for a service is referenced using its URI, whereas an ebXML registry might actually contain a copy of the definition itself. This illustrates an important difference between these two registry types: a UDDI registry is a pure registry and contains only metadata, whereas the ebXML registry is also a repository, allowing the storage of objects as well as metadata. In terms of the JAXR API, the repository functionality is modeled by the ExtrinsicObject interface, which is a level 1 feature described later in this chapter.

Information Model Interfaces

A class hierarchy diagram covering most of the interfaces that form the JAXR registry information model is shown in Figure 7-7. The complete set of interfaces, together with a brief description of their function, is listed in Table 7-1. More detailed descriptions will be found later in this chapter. The presence of a ✓ symbol in the "Level 0 methods" column indicates that the interface includes at least one method that can be used with a level 0 JAXR provider. If this column is empty, then the interface is (at least currently) of use only with a level 1 provider. When a ✓ symbol appears in both the "Level 0 methods" and "Level 1 methods" columns, then some functionality within the interface is useful only in conjunction with a level 1 provider.

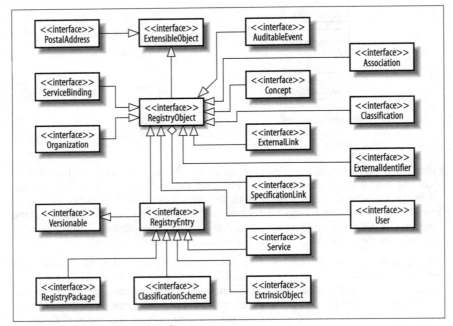

Figure 7-7. Registry object class diagram

Table 7-1. Interfaces in the javax.xml.registry.infomodel package

Interface	Level 0 methods	Level 1 methods	Description
Association	✓		Represents an association between two entities in the registry. An association has a type, which reflects the kind of relationship being described. An example of this is Replaces, which could be used to indicate that one service has been superseded by another. See "Associations" later in this chapter for further information.
AuditableEvent		✓	An entry in the audit trail for an object in the registry. Only level 1 registries provide auditing, which is described in "Auditing," later in this chapter.

Interface	Level 0 methods	Level 1 methods	Description
Classification	✓		Represents a classification that can be applied to a registry object. Applying one or more classifications to an object can make it much easier for clients to locate businesses and services of interest. See "Classification of Registry Objects," later in this chapter.
ClassificationScheme	✓	✓	A scheme used to classify registry objects. See "Classification of Registry Objects" later in this chapter for further information.
Concept	✓		A facet of the JAXR registry model that maps onto several different features of the UDDI and ebXML registries. Concepts are typically used to represent nodes in a classification scheme or elements of an enumerated type.
EmailAddress	✓		Represents an email address associated with a User object. A User may have any number of email addresses.
ExtensibleObject	✓		The base interface for all objects within the registry. ExtensibleObject provides methods that allow arbitrary attributes to be added to a registry object without the need for an additional API. See "Extensible-Object and Slots" later in this chapter for a description of this interface.
ExternalIdentifier	✓		A string value that may be attached to a registry object to provide additional identification information for that object. See "RegistryObject and RegistryEntry" later in this chapter for further information.
ExternalLink	✓		Used to associate a link to additional information with a registry object. The most common use of an external link is to include a reference to the home page of the organization that submitted the registry object.
ExtrinsicObject		✓	Represents stored data that is not of a type that the registry can handle directly, such as a document or an image file. ExtrinsicObjects can only be used with a level 1 registry provider. See "ExtrinsicObjects" later in this chapter for an example of the use of this facility.
InternationalString	✓		Used in the JAXR API where a string that may need to be localized is required. It contains a LocalizedString instance for each locale for which a representation of the string has been supplied.
Key	✓		Each object in the registry is assigned a unique identifier when it is created. The value of this identifier is held within the RegistryObject as a Key object. The key can be used to fetch the object at a later time, or to delete it. See "RegistryObject and RegistryEntry" for further information.
LocalizedString	✓		A localized version of a string, together with its associated locale and character set. LocalizedStrings are wrapped within InternationalStrings.
Organization	✓	✓	Represents a business within the registry. See "Creating Organizations and Users," later in this chapter.
PersonName	✓	✓	Represents the name of a registry user. See "Creating Organizations and Users," later in this chapter.

Interface	Level 0 methods	Level 1 methods	Description
PostalAddress	✓		Represents the address of a user or (for a level 1 registry) an organization. Unfortunately, as described in "Postal Addresses," later in this chapter, this is not as simple a topic as you might expect.
RegistryEntry		✓	A subinterface of RegistryObject from which a small number of objects in the registry information model are derived. See "RegistryObject and Registry-Entry" later in this chapter for more information.
RegistryObject	✓	✓	Defines the attributes and methods that form part of every object stored in the registry. See "RegistryObject and RegistryEntry" later in this chapter for a more complete description.
RegistryPackage		✓	A container class that allows registry objects to be grouped together. Holding a set of objects in a RegistryPackage makes it simple to get a list of them all at a later time, perhaps in order to remove them all. RegistryPackages are supported only by level 1 providers.
Service	✓		Represents a service advertised by an organization. A Service contains one or more ServiceBindings.
ServiceBinding	✓		Contains the information necessary for a client to invoke an instance of a service and may also refer, via SpecificationLinks, to technical information regarding the service. See "Services, ServiceBindings, and SpecificationLinks" later in this chapter for details.
Slot	✓		Used to attach additional attributes to ExtensibleObjects as described in "ExtensibleObject and Slots," later in this chapter.
SpecificationLink	✓		Used to add a reference to a technical description to a ServiceBinding. The link may be a URI or, in the case of a level 1 registry, may refer to an ExtrinsicObject in the repository.
TelephoneNumber	✓	✓	Represents a telephone number for a registry user. See "Creating Organizations and Users" later in this chapter.
URIValidator	✓		An interface implemented by other objects that contain a URI and that may optionally be requested to validate it. For example, when an ExternalLink is created, the registry may check that the URI that it contains points to an accessible object. The methods of URIValidator allow this validation to be turned on or off, as required.
User	✓	✓	Represents a user of the registry. References to User objects also appear in the audit trail maintained by level 1 registries. See "Creating Organizations and Users" and "Auditing" later in this chapter for further details.
Versionable		✓	An interface implemented by objects that might have associated version numbers. All RegistryEntry objects implement this interface.

RegistryObject and RegistryEntry

RegistryObject is the base interface from which almost all of the other interfaces that represent entities stored in the registry are derived. RegistryObject is itself derived from ExtensibleObject, a simple interface that makes it possible to add additional attributes to any object in the registry, as described later in "Extensible-Object and Slots." Only very simple objects that exist as part of other entities in the registry, such as PersonName, EMailAddress, and TelephoneNumber, are not derived from RegistryObject.

Every RegistryObject has a set of basic attributes, which are shown in the class diagram in Figure 7-8 and described in the following paragraphs.

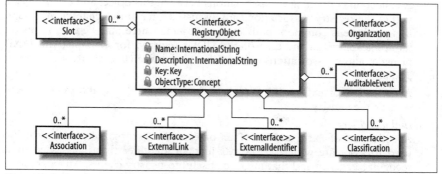

Figure 7-8. Attributes of RegistryObjects

Name

> The name of the RegistryObject is of type InternationalString, reflecting the fact that it might need to be localized. This field typically contains the name of an Organization or the title of a Service. Registry searches can be performed based on the value of this attribute.

Description

> Like the name attribute, the description is also an InternationalString. It is intended to contain localized text that will help a potential client searching the registry to determine whether the corresponding Organization or Service is what he requires.

Key

> Each entry in the registry has a unique identifier that can be used to locate it without requiring a search based on the name or other criteria. The key is assigned by the registry when the entry is created and never changes. Both the ebXML and UDDI registries assign 128-bit DCE unique identifiers (UUIDs) to newly created objects, which the JAXR provider wraps in a Key object. UUIDs are formed using an algorithm that ensures that they are globally unique.* Some well-known registry objects have values that are published in their respective specifications. For example, the registry object that represents

---

* The specification for the UUID generation algorithm is available for purchase or online viewing (following registration) at *http://www.opengroup.org/publications/catalog/c706.htm.*

the NAICS classification scheme (which will be covered later in this chapter) has the UUID C0B9FE13-179F-413D-8A5B-5004DB8E5BB2. Since this is a universal identifier, it is valid and has the same meaning in all registries.

Object type
Identifies the type of the registry object. The values that may appear in this field are `Concepts` defined in a classification scheme called `ObjectType`, which will be described later in "Classification of Registry Objects." This attribute is valid only for `RegistryObjects` in a level 1 registry.

Organization
Identifies the `Organization` that submitted this object to the registry.

Associations
A collection containing the associations between this object and other objects within the registry. Associations are discussed later in this chapter. Although this attribute is common to all `RegistryObjects`, there may be limitations on its applicability. In the case of the UDDI registry, for example, the JAXR provider allows associations to be made only between `Organizations`.

External links
A collection of `ExternalLink` objects containing links to information held outside the registry.

External identifiers
A collection of `ExternalIdentifier` objects. An `ExternalIdentifier` can be used to associate with a `RegistryObject` an identifier that is assigned by a recognized agency and that might be useful to registry clients. An example of this is the nine-digit Dun and Bradstreet D-U-N-S number (see *http://www.dnb.com*) that uniquely identifies a registered company. External identifiers are scoped by a classification scheme that acts as a namespace for the actual value. The D and B numbering scheme, for example, is represented by a classification scheme with a UUID value of 8609C81E-EE1F-4D5A-B202-3EB13AD01823.

Classifications
A collection of `Classification` objects that apply to the `RegistryObject`. Unlike external identifiers that generally uniquely identify something, a classification applies to a class of organizations, services, or other entities that have a common trait, such as the business type or geographical location. A `RegistryObject` can have any number of associated classifications. See "Classification of Registry Objects" later in this chapter for further information.

Auditable events
A collection of `AuditableEvent` objects that record operations performed on the `RegistryObject` that caused changes to its state. Auditing, described later in this chapter, is supported only by level 1 registries.

Slots
Slots are inherited from `ExtensibleObject` and are described in the next section.

Four interfaces in the JAXR information model (`Service`, `ClassificationScheme`, `ExtrinsicObject`, and `RegistryPackage`) are based on a derived interface of `RegistryObject` called `RegistryEntry`. `RegistryEntry` has the following additional attributes that are meaningful only when the object is stored in a level 1–compatible registry (such as an ebXML registry):

Version number

A RegistryEntry has three version-related attributes that can be managed using the methods of the Versionable interface, from which it is derived. The major and minor version numbers are both integers, the initial values for which are set by the registry when the object is first created. The values may be explicitly changed using the methods of the Versionable interface, and may also be changed by the registry if the RegistryEntry is modified in any way. There is also a user version, which is a string value that can be set and read by application code. It is intended to be the version of the object as seen by registry users and is not modified by the registry itself.

Stability

This attribute indicates whether the content of the RegistryEntry may change. The value RegistryEntry.STABILITY_STATIC means that the content will not change; RegistryEntry.STABILITY_DYNAMIC_COMPATIBLE implies that although the content might change, its new value will be backward-compatible with its previous value; and RegistryEntry.STABILITY_DYNAMIC indicates that the content may change in any way at any time.

Expiration

The expiration attribute is a java.util.Date object that indicates the time up to which the value of the stability attribute is valid. If it has the value null, then the stability attribute is valid indefinitely. Otherwise, the stability of the entry is effectively RegistryEntry.STABILITY_DYNAMIC once the expiration time has passed.

Status

This attribute corresponds to the state of the RegistryEntry within its overall life cycle. When initially created, the object has the state RegistryEntry. STATE_SUBMITTED. The state may then change to RegistryEntry.STATE_ APPROVED, RegistryEntry.STATE_WITHDRAWN, or RegistryEntry.STATE_ DEPRECATED. The JAXR API allows a client application to deprecate an object, but there is currently no provision for an object to be approved or withdrawn. Nevertheless, these states may be seen because they may be set in the registry by clients using more capable APIs.

ExtensibleObject and Slots

All RegistryObjects implement the ExtensibleObject interface, which allows arbitrary attributes to be added to any object in the registry without requiring a change to the registry API. Each such attribute is represented by a Slot, which has three properties:

Name

The name property can be used to retrieve a given Slot from its associated ExtensibleObject. There cannot be more than one Slot with the same name attached to an ExtensibleObject. The JAXR specification does not describe what should happen if this rule is ignored. In the reference implementation for the UDDI registry, adding a Slot with the same name as an existing Slot causes the old instance to be replaced by the new one, whereas in the case of the ebXML registry, an exception is thrown when an attempt is made to store the RegistryObject.

Type
> A string that specifies the type of the Slot. There is no predefined set of valid types. This attribute has value null by default.

Values
> A collection of values associated with the Slot. Each value must be a unique String.

Application use of Slots

A registry application can use a Slot to associate additional information with a RegistryObject. The ebXML registry model specification suggests that a submitting organization might use a Slot to mark all of its RegistryObjects with a copyright notice. Obviously, registry applications must have prior knowledge of the existence and meaning of specific Slots in order to make use of them.

The mapping of the JAXR API to the UDDI registry model defined in the JAXR specification does not describe how Slots should be stored in the registry, and, in fact, the reference implementation does not store them at all. Therefore, JAXR applications that need to work with a UDDI registry cannot, in general, create Slots and expect them to be saved in the registry. One specific exception to this rule is the sortCode attribute of the UDDI equivalent of the JAXR PostalAddress object, which can be set by application code using a Slot, as described in "Postal Addresses," later in this chapter.

Registry use of Slots

A registry implementation can attach Slots to a RegistryObject to expose attributes available from the registry itself that are not mapped in the JAXR information model. There are several examples of this in the case of the UDDI registry:

- The operator and authorizedName fields of the registry objects that represent JAXR Organizations and ClassificationSchemes are available in Slots, called Slot.OPERATOR_SLOT and Slot.AUTHORIZED_NAME_SLOT, respectively.
- A slot is defined for use by the PostalAddress object when a mapping to the UDDI postal address scheme has not been defined. See "Postal Addresses" later in this chapter for details.

Classification of Registry Objects

All RegistryObjects have a name that can be used when searching the registry. You can, for example, locate the Organization object for Amazon.com by searching on the full name or by using a wildcard search with a wildcard such as %mazon%. However, when searching for potential business partners, it is more likely that you will know the type of company that you want to deal with, rather than individual company names. You might, for example, want to locate book publishers or book stores. In order to make this type of search possible, a submitting organization can apply one or more *classifications* to any of its registry entries.

Classifications belong to *classification schemes,** which categorize objects according to a specific criterion.

A registry can, in theory, support any number of different classification schemes, and the JAXR specification requires that it be possible to add user-defined schemes to a registry, a topic that is covered in "Creating User-Defined Classification Schemes and Enumerated Types," later in this chapter. It also requires that all registries support at least three standard classification schemes:

NAICS - the North American Industry Classification System
> Classifies organizations according to the type of service that they provide. Examples of classifications from this scheme include "Book Publisher" and "Book, Periodical, and Music Stores." See *http://www.ntis.gov/product/naics.htm* for details.

ISO 3166
> Classifies by geographical location. Organizations can categorize themselves according to location in order to allow potential clients to restrict their search to a specific country or group of countries. Typical classifications from these scheme are US and GB. See *http://www.din.de/gremien/nas/nabd/iso3166ma* for more information on this scheme.

UNSPSC - the Universal Standard Products and Services Classification
> This scheme is intended to provide classifications that are applicable worldwide, unlike NAICS, which is, strictly speaking, biased toward the American marketplace. It is also broader in scope, including product types (such as "Leathers" or "Twill weave cotton fabrics") as well as services. See *http://eccma.org/unspsc* for more information on this classification scheme.

You can inspect the classifications provided by these three schemes by starting the UDDI registry browser provided by the reference implementation (using the *jaxr_browser.bat* or *jaxr_browser.sh* script in the *bin* directory), selecting a registry in the Registry Location field, or entering the URL for a specific registry (such as *http://localhost:8000/RegistryServer* for the test registry server provided by the JWSDP and the reference implementation of the J2EE 1.4 platform)†, and then selecting Classifications in the Find by field. This results in the set of classifications supported by the registry being displayed in a tree control in the bottom left of the browser window. To see the classifications provided by a particular scheme, double-click on its name.

All three of the standard classification schemes are hierarchical. The NAICS scheme, for example, includes a top-level classification called Information, below which is another classification called Publishing Industries. Within this classification, there is Newspaper, Periodical, Book and Database Publishers, and within that, Book Publishers. Assuming that you have installed the test data for this chapter in the registry (as described in "Using the JAXR Examples," earlier in this

* The JAXR specification uses the terms "classification scheme" and "taxonomy" interchangeably. For the sake of clarity and consistency with the JAXR API (which calls the relevant interface ClassificationScheme), I'll use only the term "classification scheme" in this chapter.

† Note that the registry browser was not included in the beta version of J2EE 1.4.

chapter), if you select Book Publishers and then press Search, an entry for O'Reilly & Associates is returned, as shown in Figure 7-9.

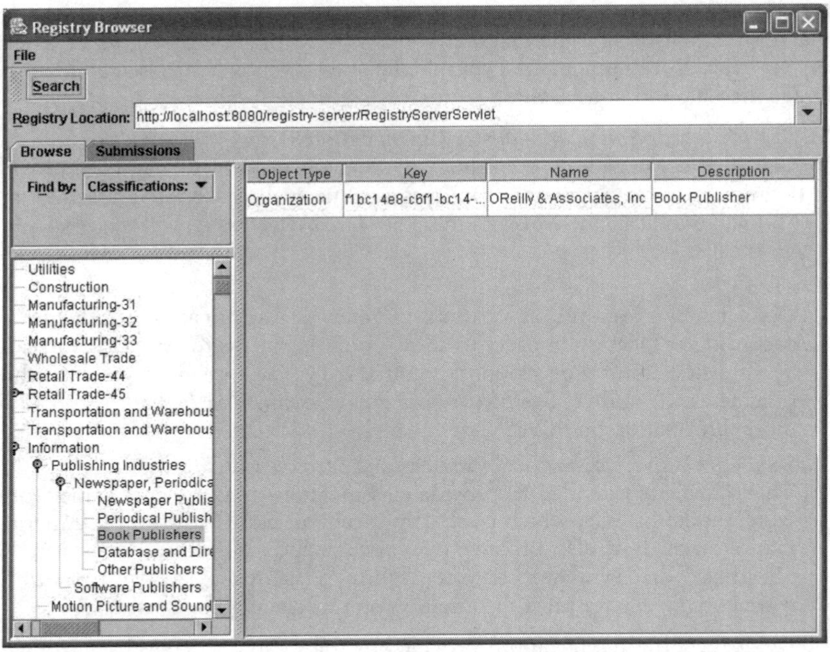

Figure 7-9. Searching the registry by classification

This search works because the Organization object representing O'Reilly & Associates in the registry has the Book Publishers classification from the NAICS classification scheme attached to it. It also has a geographical classification that indicates that it is based in the USA, as you can demonstrate by opening the classification scheme labeled iso-ch:3166:1999, and drilling down through the classification level for North America to United States. Select this classification and press Search again. This time, you see entries for O'Reilly & Associates and Amazon.com. You can search on both criteria together by selecting Book Publishers, then holding the Ctrl key while selecting United States. This search looks for entries that have both selected classifications and therefore return just the single entry for O'Reilly & Associates. You'll see later in this chapter how to add classifications to a RegistryObject and how to search the registry given one or more classifications.

External and internal classification schemes

As previously noted, classification schemes are hierarchical. Figure 7-10 shows a very small portion of the logical hierarchy tree that makes up the standard NAICS classification. The box at the top of the figure represents the classification scheme itself. In terms of the JAXR registry information model, this would be an instance of the javax.xml.registry.infomodel.ClassificationScheme interface. The nodes below this can all be used to categorize other entries in the registry. The relationship between these nodes reflects the granularity of the categorization so that, for example, a Book Publisher is a member of the set of Newspaper, Periodical, Book and Database publishers. Logically speaking, these nodes all represent elements of the classification scheme hierarchy and could therefore be used as possible classification values, but in the JAXR registry model, they would *not* be instances of the `javax.xml.registry.infomodel.Classification` interface. How these nodes map onto the JAXR information model depends on whether the classification scheme is internal or external.

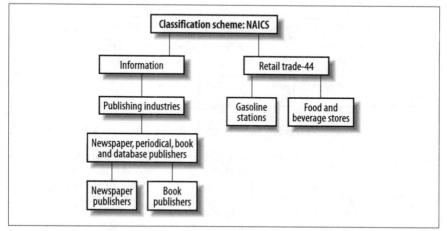

Figure 7-10. A logical view of part of the NAICS classification scheme

A JAXR UDDI provider is required to provide the NAICS, ISO 3166, and UNSPSC schemes as internal classification schemes. In the case of an internal classification scheme, both the root `ClassificationScheme` object and the complete hierarchy of nodes that represent classification scheme elements are known and available within the provider implementation. The nodes themselves are instances of `javax.xml.registry.infomodel.Concept`, an interface that has several different uses within the JAXR API. A `Concept` is a `RegistryObject` that has the following attributes (among others):

- A name (inherited from its parent interface, `RegistryObject`).
- A value, which is of type `String`.
- A `ClassificationScheme` with which it is associated. Not all `Concept`s represent nodes in a classification scheme hierarchy; for those that do not, this attribute has the value `null`.
- A list of child `Concept`s and a reference to a parent `Concept`. These attributes allow `Concept`s to be linked together in the hierarchical structure shown in Figure 7-10.

An internal classification scheme, then, is represented as a linked hierarchy of `Concept`s, rooted at a `ClassificationScheme` object. The actual `Concept` hierarchy for the part of the NAICS classification scheme illustrated in Figure 7-10 is shown in Figure 7-11, where all of the objects apart from the `ClassificationScheme` at the top of the diagram represent `Concept`s.

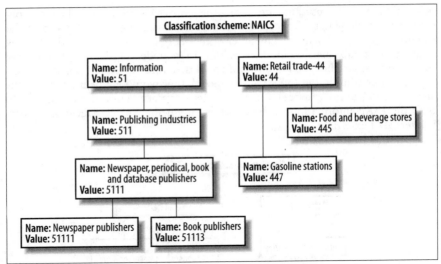

Figure 7-11. Part of the Concept hierarchy for the NAICS classification scheme

Notice that this diagram shows both the name and value attributes for each Concept. The name is used only for display purposes; it is the value attribute that determines which element of the classification scheme hierarchy the Concept represents. In the case of the NAICS classification scheme, the values are all numbers, where the number of digits is an indicator of the position of the value within the overall scheme. For example, the Information node has the value "51." The values associated with all of the nodes located below this point will start with "51," with an extra digit added for each additional level of nesting. Hence, the Concept representing Book Publishers has the value "51113" and is therefore three levels below the Information node, while the Concept for Newspaper Publishers, at the same level, has the value 51111. A complete list of the names and values for all of the Concepts in this classification scheme and the others that the JAXR provider is required to support can be found in the following files, which are in the *jaxr-ri.jar* file in the JAXR reference implementation:

NAICS:	*com/sun/xml/registry/common/tools/resources/naics.xml*
ISO 3166:	*com/sun/xml/registry/common/tools/resources/iso3166.xml*
UNSPSC:	*com/sun/xml/registry/common/tools/resources/unspsc.xml*

An external classification scheme is one for which the element hierarchy is not known to the JAXR registry provider—only the ClassificationScheme node itself is registered. It is obviously easier to create an external classification scheme because there is only one item to install in the registry provider, whereas an internal scheme might require many hundreds of Concepts to completely describe it. However, there are advantages to using an internal scheme:

- Since the JAXR provider has a record of which Concept values exist within the classification scheme, it can check whether a proposed classification is actually valid before applying it to a registry object.

- Application code can use the linkage between Concept nodes to browse the hierarchy of an internal classification scheme to discover (and perhaps offer to the user) valid classification values. In the case of an external scheme, the application must either know all legal values by some external means or trust the user to supply only correct values.

- Using an internal scheme, it is possible to search the registry for objects that are members of groups of classifications. For example, it is possible to search for all registry objects that are categorized as Newspapers, Periodical, Book, and Database Publishers, or any category below that node in the Concept hierarchy (such as Book Publishers). See "Retrieving Objects from the Registry" later in this chapter for an example that shows how this is done.

 It is tempting to think that the node hierarchy for an internal classification scheme is held within the registry itself. However, this is not necessarily the case. The UDDI registry information model, for example, does not provide any reasonable way to represent a hierarchy of Concepts and therefore cannot store an internal classification scheme. A JAXR provider is, however, required to provide a hierarchical view of an internal classification. The means by which this is achieved is implementation-dependent. The JAXR reference implementation achieves this by reading the classification files listed previously and creating a local version of the node hierarchy within the client application. The ebXML registry, by contrast, provides full support for internal classifications, which can, therefore, be stored in the registry itself. The difference between these two approaches becomes important if you want to create your own classification scheme. See "Creating User-Defined Classification Schemes and Enumerated Types" later in this chapter for further discussion on this topic.

In order to add a classification to a RegistryObject, you need an instance of a Classification object. As with classification schemes, there are two types of classification: internal and external.

An *internal classification* is created by referencing a Concept from the node hierarchy of an internal classification scheme. A Classification object for an internal classification representing Book Publisher in the NAICS classification scheme is shown in Figure 7-12.

An internal classification is very easy to create once you have the associated Concept. It is known to be valid since it refers to a node in the validated hierarchy of a classification scheme. Furthermore, given such a Classification object, application (or registry) code can obtain a reference to the underlying Concept and use it to navigate the hierarchy and create related Classifications, if necessary.

An *external* Classification object, by contrast, contains a reference to its parent ClassificationScheme and a name and value that correspond to those of the classification that it represents. An external classification, therefore, may or may not be valid, depending on whether the value part is populated with a legal classification value. External classifications *must* be used if the classification scheme itself is external, but may also be used in conjunction with an internal classification scheme. You can see examples of both cases in "Retrieving Objects from the Registry," later in this chapter.

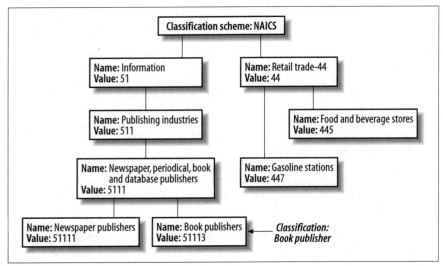

Figure 7-12. An internal classification

Concepts as enumerated types

Another use for Concepts and classification schemes is to provide a means of creating enumerated types that can then be used as arguments to JAXR API method calls. An enumeration is created by defining a ClassificationScheme and attaching a Concept that represents each possible value within the enumeration. There are several such enumerations defined by the JAXR specification that every JAXR provider must recognize. One such enumeration, called ObjectType, contains distinguished values for each type of RegistryObject, plus a few other commonly used object types. This enumeration actually consists of a ClassificationScheme called ObjectType and a set of Concepts, whose value fields are listed here:

```
Association          AuditableEvent        Classification
Concept              ExternalIdentifier    ExternalLink
ExtrinsicObject      Organization          Package
Service              ServiceBinding        User
CPP                  CPA                   Process
WSDL
```

In order to use one of these values when making API calls, it is necessary to get a reference to the Concept that represents it. One way to do this involves using the findConceptByPath( ) method of the javax.xml.registry.BusinessQueryManager interface, which will be discussed in the next section. This method requires a path that specifies the required Concept. In the case of predefined enumerations, this path consists of the ClassificationScheme name (i.e., the enumeration name), followed by the value attribute of the Concept itself. Since the ClassificationScheme in this case is called ObjectType, the following code returns the Concept for the Service value of the enumeration, assuming that the variable bqm is an instance of BusinessQueryManager:

```
Concept service = bqm.findConceptByPath("/ObjectType/Service");
```

As shown in "Creating User-Defined Classification Schemes and Enumerated Types," later in this chapter, it is possible to define your own enumerations.

The use of the ClassificationScheme name as the first part of the path is a special case that the JAXR specification provides for easy access to the Concepts of predefined enumerations. As you'll see in "Searching by Classification," later in this chapter, findConceptByPath( ) usually requires the unique ID of the ClassificationScheme to be supplied as the first component of the path rather than the scheme name.

At the time of this writing, the ebXML registry provider available from *http://ebxmlrr.sourceforge.net* does not support this special case. An alternative way to retrieve the Concepts for an enumerated type can be found in "Associations," later in this chapter.

JAXR Programming

So far in this chapter, you have seen the JAXR registry information model, which is mapped to the javax.xml.registry.infomodel package. This section looks at the API that allows you to search or update a registry, which is defined in the package javax.xml.registry. The examples shown in this section assume that you have installed the sample registry data in either a UDDI or ebXML registry, as described in "Using the JAXR Examples," earlier in this chapter.

Connecting to the Registry

In order to use a registry, you first have to create a connection to it. This process requires two steps:

1. Obtain a ConnectionFactory object and optionally set properties that determine how it will behave.

2. Use the ConnectionFactory object to obtain a Connection or FederatedConnection to the target registry.

There are two ways to get a ConnectionFactory object. In a J2EE environment, the preferred way is to use the JNDI API to look up a preconfigured ConnectionFactory:

```
InitialContext ctx = new InitialContext( );
ConnectionFactory factory = (ConnectionFactory)ctx.lookup("pathToFactory");
```

J2SE-based registry clients that do not have a preconfigured JNDI environment can instead use the static newInstance( ) method:

```
ConnectionFactory factory = ConnectionFactory.newInstance( );
```

ConnectionFactory is an abstract class. The actual class of the object returned by the newInstance( ) method is determined by the property javax.xml.registry. ConnectionFactoryClass, which can be set in either of the following locations (in order of priority):

- As a system property (and therefore accessible by calling System. getProperty("javax.xml.registry.ConnectionFactoryClass")).
- In a file called *jaxr.properties* that is located in the *lib* directory of the installed JRE.

If a value for this property is not found in either of these locations, then a file called *javax.xml.registry.ConnectionFactoryClass* is searched for in a directory called *META-INF/services* within the classpath of the Java VM.[*] If this file exists, its content is expected to be a single line of text that gives the name of the ConnectionFactory class to be loaded. Failing this, a default ConnectionFactory implementation is used. In the case of the JAXR reference implementation, the default factory creates Connection objects that can be used to access a UDDI registry.

The behavior of Connection objects that are obtained from a ConnectionFactory is determined by a set of properties associated with the ConnectionFactory. These properties are set by calling the setProperties( ) method, which requires as its argument a Properties object containing some or all of the standard property values listed in Table 7-2.

Table 7-2. Standard JAXR ConnectionFactory properties

Property name	Description
javax.xml.registry.queryManagerURL	The URL at which the registry query service can be accessed. This property must always be set.
javax.xml.registry.lifeCycleManagerURL	The URL at which the service used to update the registry can be accessed. If not set, the query URL is used.
javax.xml.registry.semanticEquivalences	Allows a mapping to be established in the JAXR provider between pairs of Concepts that are to be regarded as equivalent. This property is most often used in connection with postal addresses held in UDDI registries, and is described in "Postal Addresses," later in this chapter.
javax.xml.registry.security. authenticationMethod	Specifies the way in which the JAXR provider is to authenticate itself to the registry. The client must select an authentication mechanism that is recognized by the registry that it is attempting to use. Authentication is usually required only when updating the registry. See "Registry Security" later in this chapter for further information.

---

[*] This file is typically included in the JAR file containing the implementation of a registry provider. The first such JAR file to be processed, in classpath order, determines which registry implementation is used.

Table 7-2. Standard JAXR ConnectionFactory properties (continued)

Property name	Description
javax.xml.registry.uddi.maxRows	Specifies the maximum number of elements that a registry find query is allowed to return. This value applies only to a UDDI registry and must be a well-formed integer. If this property is not specified, then no limit is placed on the number of rows that will be returned.
javax.xml.registry.PostalAddressScheme	Gives the UUID of the postal address scheme used to map postal address items in the registry to attributes of the JAXR PostalAddress object. This property is currently used only by UDDI registry implementations. See "Postal Addresses" later in this chapter for further information.

JAXR implementations are free to specify additional properties as required to allow customization of their behavior. The UDDI provider in the JAXR reference implementation recognizes the eight additional properties listed in Table 7-3.

Table 7-3. JAXR ConnectionFactory properties recognized by the reference implementation UDDI provider

Property name	Description
com.sun.xml.registry.http.proxyHost	Hostname for an HTTP proxy if a direct connection to the registry is not possible.
com.sun.xml.registry.http.proxyPort	Port number to be used for an HTTP connection to a registry via a proxy host.
com.sun.xml.registry.https.proxyHost	Hostname used when making an HTTPS connection to a proxy host. Some registries require secure connections for registry updates.
com.sun.xml.registry.https.proxyPort	Port name used when making an HTTPS connection to a proxy host.
com.sun.xml.registry.http.proxyUserName	If a proxy is in use and the proxy requires clients to authenticate, this property should be used to set the username expected by the proxy.
com.sun.xml.registry.http.proxyPassword	Sets the password to be used if proxy authentication is required.
com.sun.xml.registry.http.useCache	If this property has the value true, the registry may store objects in a local cache from which it may return them in response to later queries that require the same object. This property is true by default.
com.sun.xml.registry.http.useSOAP	By default, the UDDI JAXR provider uses the SAAJ API to send client requests to the registry server. If this property is set to true, it uses Apache SOAP instead. This property is not likely to be of much practical use in a production environment.

JAXR

A typical piece of code that obtains a connection to a registry is shown in Example 7-1.

Example 7-1. Connecting to a registry

```
Properties props = new Properties( );
props.put("javax.xml.registry.queryManagerURL", queryURL);
```

Example 7-1. Connecting to a registry (continued)

```
props.put("javax.xml.registry.lifeCycleManagerURL", lifecycleURL);

ConnectionFactory cf = ConnectionFactory.newInstance();
cf.setProperties(props);

// Get and initialize the connection
Connection conn = cf.createConnection();
conn.setCredentials(credentials);

// Get the RegistryService and the managers
RegistryService registry = conn.getRegistryService();
BusinessQueryManager bqm = registry.getBusinessQueryManager();
BusinessLifeCycleManager blcm = registry.getBusinessLifeCycleManager();
```

The Properties object created at the start of this example is populated with the URLs required to access the registry's query and update services, and then passed to the ConnectionFactory object, which uses it when creating a Connection. In the case of the JWSDP JAXR reference implementation deployed in a Tomcat web container or in J2EE 1.4, the query and update URLs both have the value *http://localhost:8080/RegistryServer/RegistryServerServlet*, assuming that the client application and the registry are running on the same system.

The ConnectionFactory getConnection() method returns a Connection object that can be used to access a single registry. ConnectionFactory also supports the creation of a FederatedConnection, via the createFederatedConnection() method:

```
public FederatedConnection createFederatedConnection(Collection
    connections);
```

FederatedConnection is an interface derived from Connection that does not add any new methods. Each object in the Collection passed to createFederatedConnection() method must be a Connection representing a connection to a single registry or another FederatedConnection object. The intent of FederatedConnection is to allow queries made via the FederatedConnection to be sent to all of the registries with which it is associated, and for the query results to be merged to create a single result set. Although createFederatedConnection() is a capability level 0 method, it is still considered an optional feature, and therefore may not be implemented by all registry providers. In particular, the UDDI registry provider in the JAXR reference implementation does not support it and throws an UnsupportedCapabilityException if the createFederatedConnection() method is called.

The act of obtaining a Connection object does not actually make a connection to a registry. The provider is free to defer the establishment of a connection until such time as the client makes an API call that actually requires an operation to be performed by the registry. If the registry requires authentication information from a client, then the setCredentials() method should be called after obtaining a Connection object, as shown previously. The argument passed to this method is a java.util.Collection containing one or more credentials, the data type of which depends on the authentication method used by the registry server. Registry authentication is discussed in more detail in "Registry Security" at the end of this chapter.

From the Connection object, a registry client obtains an instance of the interface RegistryService. RegistryService is the central object within a JAXR provider. There is one instance of this object for each registry Connection. From a RegistryObject, a client can discover the capability level of the provider (from the getCapabilityProfile( ) method) and also obtain references to the following interfaces:

BusinessQueryManager

> BusinessQueryManager is an interface that provides the methods necessary to search the registry using crtiteria that are expressed in terms of the JAXR information model. For example, you can use the methods of the BusinessQueryManager to find all Organizations whose names match a given pattern or with given classifications. BusinessQueryManager is described later in "Retrieving Objects from the Registry."

DeclarativeQueryManager

> A DeclarativeQueryManager allows a client to search the registry using expressions written using one or more query languages. DeclarativeQueryManager is supported only by level 1 JAXR providers. Using this interface, a client might be able to search a registry using queries written in SQL-92 syntax or using an OASIS ebXML Registry Filter query. See "Declarative Queries" later in this chapter for more information.

BusinessLifeCycleManager

> The BusinessLifeCycleManager interface contains methods that allow a registry client to create, update, or delete registry content. In most cases, a client must be properly authenticated with the registry in order to make changes to its content. BusinessLifeCycleManager is discussed later in "Modifying the Registry."

Default Postal Scheme

> This represents the ClassificationScheme used by the JAXR provider for handling PostalAddress objects. This may be null if the registry includes native support for postal addresses that is consistent with that required by the JAXR specification (as is the case with the ebXML registry). See "Postal Addresses" later in this chapter for more on this subject.

RegistryObject also provides a method (makeRegistrySpecificRequest( )) that can be used by specialized registry applications to send a request to a registry in the native format used by that registry. Since this method requires an understanding of the message schemes used by specific registries, it will not be further discussed in this book.

Retrieving Objects from the Registry

The BusinessQueryManager and QueryManager interfaces in the javax.xml.registry package provide methods that allow information held in the registry to be retrieved. The methods provided by QueryManager return objects based on object type, object owner, or the unique key assigned to them when they are created. BusinessQueryManager is derived from QueryManager and provides methods that allow the registry to be searched using various business-related criteria, including object name or a list of classifications. A search by name is equivalent to looking up an entry in a White Pages directory, while a classification-based search is analogous to using the Yellow Pages to locate a company or service based on its type (e.g., Book Publisher, Plumber, etc.).

Using QueryManager methods to retrieve registry objects

You can use the methods provided by QueryManager when you know the key assigned to the objects that you want or the type of that object, or you want to fetch all of the objects that you have created in the registry.

When you know the registry key of the object that you want, you can use one of the following methods to retrieve it:

```
public RegistryObject getRegistryObject(String id) throws JAXRException;
public RegistryObject getRegistryObject(String id, String type)
    throws JAXRException;
```

The first of these methods requires only the key, but is supported only by level 1 JAXR providers. A level 0 provider (such as a UDDI V2 registry) requires the type of the object as well as the key generated when it was stored in the registry. The possible values for the object type are available as constants defined by the LifeCycleManager interface. The following code, for example, returns the Organization object corresponding to the ID supplied by the variable key, where bqm is assumed to refer to a QueryManager instance:

```
String key = "f1d13cc1-e0f1-d13c-8671-22c9c07a9a76";
Organization org = (Organization)bqm.getRegistryObject(key,
    LifeCycleManager.ORGANIZATION);
```

The getRegistryObject( ) method throws a JAXRException if the key or the type are invalid, or if the key does not correspond to a RegistryObject of the specified type. JAXRException is actually a base class for the small number of checked exceptions that a JAXR provider can throw, which are shown in Figure 7-13.

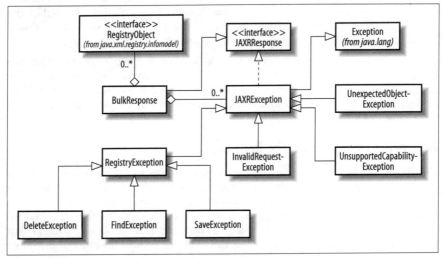

Figure 7-13. Response and exception classes in the JAXR API

There are four getRegistryObjects() methods that fetch different sets of RegistryObjects:

```
public BulkResponse getRegistryObjects() throws JAXRException;
public BulkResponse getRegistryObjects(String type) throws JAXRException;
public BulkResponse getRegistryObjects(Collection keys)
    throws JAXRException;
public BulkResponse getRegistryObjects(Collection keys, String type)
    throws JAXRException;
```

Each of these methods returns an object of type BulkResponse. BulkResponse contains a Collection that holds the RegistryObjects that meet the selection criteria implied by the arguments (if any) supplied to getRegistryObjects(), a reference to which can be obtained by calling the getCollection() method. The following code can be used to iterate over the results of a getRegistryObjects() method call:

```
BulkResponse res = bqm.getRegistryObjects();
Collection coll = res.getCollection();
Iterator iter = coll.iterator();
while (iter.hasNext()) {
    RegistryObject obj = (RegistryObject)iter.next();
}
```

BulkResponse also contains a collection of exceptions that indicate errors that occurred while completing the method call. The getExceptions() method returns a reference to this Collection, or returns null if no exceptions occurred. The exceptions in this collection are all derived from JAXRException and are therefore checked exceptions. The exception hierarchy for the JAXR API is shown in Figure 7-13. Both BulkResponse and JAXRException implement the JAXRResponse interface. JAXRResponse contains methods that are used in conjunction with asynchronous requests to the registry, which are described later in "Asynchronous Queries."

The set of objects returned by each of the getRegistryObjects() methods depends on the arguments supplied, as follows:

getRegistryObjects()
: Returns all of the objects in the registry that are owned by the user making the call.

getRegistryObjects(String type)
: Returns all of the objects in the registry of the supplied type (such as LifeCycleManager.ORGANIZATION) that are owned by the user making the call.

getRegistryObjects(Collection keys)
: Returns the objects from the registry for which the keys are supplied in the Collection passed as the argument. Each element of the collection must be an object of type Key.

getRegistryObjects(Collection keys, String type)
: Returns the objects from the registry of the supplied type, for which the keys are passed in the given Collection. The objects corresponding to the supplied keys must all be of the specified type.

For those methods that return collections of objects owned by the calling user, the user's identity is obtained from the credentials passed to the ConnectionFactory setCredentials() method. If valid credentials have not been set, then a JAXRException is thrown.

Finding registry objects using BusinessQueryManager

The BusinessQueryManager interface provides methods that allow registry searches based on the values of specific attributes of RegistryObjects to be performed. These methods form two groups: those that return an individual RegistryObject given a specification of exact attributes that the object must have, and those that return a BulkResponse containing a collection of RegistryObjects that meet specified criteria. In this section, we look at the methods that fall into the second of these groups.

The methods that return a set of results all require a set of input parameters, some of which are optional, that supply the acceptable values for specific attributes of a particular class of object to be found within the registry. The findOrganizations() method is a typical example that we'll use to demonstrate how these methods work:

```
public BulkResponse getOrganizations(Collection findQualifiers,
    Collection namePatterns, Collection classifications, Collection
    specifications, Collection externalIdentifiers, Collection
    externalLinks);
```

In this case, all of the arguments are Collections. Each Collection is expected to contain objects of a specific type and may be null if it is not required to search on the basis of the corresponding attribute. Supplying null for the external-Identifiers argument, for example, allows Organizations with any associated ExternalIdentifiers (including none) to be included in the response set. In some cases, where there is more than one entry in a Collection, the corresponding attribute of a RegistryObject must have all of the specified values (i.e., there is an implied AND operation), while in other cases, it is required to have only one of the given values (i.e., an implied OR operation). Supplying two values in the externalIdentifiers argument, for example, requires that RegistryObjects have both ExternalIdentifiers in order to be returned. Table 7-4 shows the types of the objects required in each Collection and the way in which multiple entries are handled.

Table 7-4. Arguments used by the BusinessQueryManager find methods

Collection argument	Object in Collection	Combination rule
associationTypes	Concept	OR
classifications	Classification	AND
externalIdentifiers	ExternalIdentifier	AND
externalLinks	ExternalLink	AND
namePatterns	String or LocalizedString	OR
specifications	See the following description	AND

In most cases, the type of object in the Collection can be inferred directly from the name used for the argument in the method signature. There are, however, a few cases that require more description:

associationTypes

An Assocociation is a formal linkage between two RegistryObjects that reflects a specific kind of relationship between them. The different types of relationships that may exist are defined as an enumeration, each element of which is represented within the registry model by a Concept. To select Assocations of various types, include the Concepts representing each of those relationship types in the Collection and call the findAssociations() or findCallerAssociations() method. See "Associations" later in this chapter for more on this topic.

namePatterns

This Collection contains one or more objects of type String or LocalizedString that is used to match against the name attribute of RegistryObjects of the type searched by the method in use. To facilitate wild-card searching, the string may contain the character % to match any number of characters—for example, the string % would match any name, while %a% would match any name that contains at least one letter a. Whether the search is case-sensitive depends on the find qualifiers in use, as described shortly. Note that the JAXR specification states that a name pattern follows the syntax defined for the SQL-92 LIKE clause in a SELECT statement. At the time of this writing, however, the JAXR reference implementation does not support the full syntax of this clause.

specifications

This Collection can contain any object that might be used as the specification object of a SpecificationLink. These objects are most likely to be Concepts in the case of a UDDI registry, and ExtrinsicObjects for an ebXML registry. See "Services, ServiceBindings, and SpecificationLinks" later in this chapter for more on the use of SpecificationLinks.

Many of the search methods (including findOrganizations()) accept a Collection of *find qualifiers* that can be used to control the search or to place requirements on the way in which the return values are organized. Each element in this Collection must be one of the constant values defined by the FindQualifiers interface and described in the reference materials for the javax.xml.registry package in the second part of this book.

Searching by Classification

In order to demonstrate how to locate information in a registry, we'll look at an example that searches for an organization based on its associated classification—in other words, a Yellow Pages search. Specifically, the example searches for organizations that are categorized as Book Publishers in the NAICS classification scheme. Initially, this is a simple task, since the BusinessQueryManager interface provides a method called findOrganizations() that lets you search given various different criteria, including the classifications applied to Organization objects. The interesting part of this example is the way in which the Classification objects that the findOrganizations() method requires are created.

As noted in "Classification of Registry Objects," earlier in this chapter, a JAXR provider is obliged to support the NAICS scheme as an internal classification scheme. This means that we can create either an internal or an external Classification to represent Book Publishers under this scheme. Classifications are created using the createClassification() methods of the BusinessLifeCycleManager interface, which will be covered in detail in "Modifying the Registry," later in this chapter. There are three such methods:

```
public Classification createClassification(ClassificationScheme scheme,
    String name, String value);
public Classification createClassification(ClassificationScheme scheme,
    InternationalString name, String value);
public Classification createClassification(Concept concept);
```

The first two methods can be used with either an internal or an external classification scheme and create an internal classification. The third method creates a Classification corresponding to a Concept in the node hierarchy of an internal classification scheme, as illustrated in Figure 7-12.

The code required to create an external classification is very simple—all that is necessary is to look up the parent ClassificationScheme and then supply the name and value of the classification itself. This is shown in the following code extract, where the variables bqm and blcm refer to instances of BusinessQueryManager and BusinessLifeCycleManager, respectively.

```
ClassificationScheme naics = bqm.findClassificationSchemeByName(null,
    "%naics%");
if (naics == null) {
    naics = bqm.findClassificationSchemeByName(null, "%NAICS%");
    if (naics == null) {
        System.out.println("COULD NOT FIND NAICS CLASSIFICATION SCHEME.");
        System.exit(1);
    }
}

// Create external classification
Classification bookPublishers = blcm.createClassification(naics,
    "Book Publishers", "51113");
```

When creating an external classification, it is important to supply the correct value argument (in this case, "51113"), since this is what actually identifies the classification. The name argument ("Book Publishers") is not so important, because it is not used when comparing the created Classification against those associated with objects in the registry during a search. It should be clear from this code that it is perfectly possible to create an external classification that has no real meaning, simply by supplying an inappropriate value argument:

```
Classification bookPublishers = blcm.createClassification(naics,
    "Book Publishers", "ABCDEF");
```

This code succeeds in creating a Classification object, even though the NAICS scheme does not contain a classification with value "ABCDEF".

It is a little more difficult to create an internal classification, since it is necessary to locate the Concept that represents the node of the hierarchy for which a

Classification object is required. The benefit of doing so, however, is that an internal classification is known to be valid. Recall from Figure 7-12 that the Concept nodes are arranged beneath the ClassificationScheme object with which they are associated, in a hierarchy that reflects the classification scheme itself. In order to create an internal classification that represents Book Publishers, you need first to locate the Concept with the value "51113" shown at the bottom right of Figure 7-12, which can then be passed to the third variant of the createClassification( ) method just shown.

There are two ways to locate the required Concept. The first involves searching for it in the set of Concepts that are descendents of the ClassificationScheme:

```
Concept publisherConcept = null;
Collection concepts = naics.getDescendantConcepts();
Iterator conceptIter = concepts.iterator();
while (conceptIter.hasNext()) {
    Concept concept = (Concept)conceptIter.next();
    String value = concept.getValue();
    if (value != null && value.equals("51113")) {
        publisherConcept = concept;
        break;
    }
}
```

The getDescendentConcepts( ) method returns a Collection containing all of the Concepts associated with the ClassificationScheme. To find the one that is required, it is necessary to iterate over this Collection until a Concept for which the value attribute of "51113" is found. A more elegant solution, however, is to use the findConceptByPath( ) method, which requires that you specify the location of the required Concept by giving its path. The path is formed by specifying first the key of the ClassificationScheme, then appending the values of each Concept on the node tree leading from the ClassificationScheme to the Concept itself, with each part being separated by a "/" character. By referring to Figure 7-12, you can see that the appropriate path for the Concept whose name is "Book Publisher" is therefore given by the expression:

```
"/" + naics.getKey().getId() + "/51/511/5111/51113"
```

Note that the path contains the *value* attribute of each Concept node, not the name. The following code locates the correct Concept and creates the corresponding internal classification object:

```
String path = "/" + naics.getKey().getId() + "/51/511/5111/51113";
Concept publisherConcept = bqm.findConceptByPath(path);
Classification bookPublishers = blcm.createClassification(publisherConcept);
```

Even though the createClassification( ) methods are part of the BusinessLifeCycleManager interface, which is intended to allow registry updates, you don't actually make any changes to the registry itself by calling them; therefore, you don't need to have authenticated with the registry in order to do so.

Once you have a Classification object, you can use the findOrganizations( ) method to carry out the required search, as shown in Example 7-2.

Example 7-2. Searching the registry for an Organization with a given classification

```
ArrayList classifications = new ArrayList();
classifications.add(bookPublishers);
BulkResponse res = bqm.findOrganizations(null, null, classifications,
                                         null, null, null);

// Process results (if any)
Collection coll = res.getCollection();
System.out.println("Internal classification search #2 found " + coll.size());
Iterator iter = coll.iterator();
while (iter.hasNext()) {
    Organization org = (Organization)iter.next();
    System.out.println("\t" + org.getName().getValue());
}
```

The example source code for this chapter includes a client that uses this code to search the registry for book publishers. To run this code, make *chapter7\jaxr* your working directory and type the commands:

```
ant compile
ant run-uddi-classify-client
```

The client uses the three different methods shown above to create the `Classification` object used to perform the search. Each search should return and display the `Organization` object for O'Reilly & Associates. You can use the command:

```
ant run-ebxml-classify-client
```

to use an ebXML registry instead of the UDDI registry in the reference implementation.

Extended Classification searches

When you use the `findOrganizations()` method (or any of the other find methods of `BusinessQueryManager`) to search for a registry object based on its associated classifications, a match is made against the *exact* classifications passed in the method call. This can have some unexpected consequences. For example, suppose you want to find the entries for all organizations that operate under the classification "Newspaper, Periodical, Book, and Database Publishers" in the NAICS classification scheme. If you simply create a `Classification` object for this category and then call `findOrganizations()`, in all probability you won't find anything, since the companies that operate in this marketplace are likely to have categorized themselves using the more specific classifications such as "Book Publisher" and "Newspaper Publishers" that appear below the "Newspaper, Periodical, Book, and Database Publishers" classification in Figure 7-12.

In order to perform a query for an organization that has a given classification or any of the more specific classifications that reside below it in the classification scheme, you need to include all of the individual classifications in the `Collection` supplied to the `findOrganizations()` method. If the classification scheme is external, in order to achieve this you must explicitly create `Classification` objects for all of the descendent classifications by referring to a diagram like a more

---

complete version of Figure 7-12, which shows how the classification scheme is organized. For an internal classification scheme, however, you can make use of the fact that the structure of the scheme is known to the JAXR provider to get all of the Concepts that are descended from "Newspaper, Periodical, Book, and Database Publishers," and then create Classifications for each of them. The advantage of working with an internal classification scheme is that this does not require prior knowledge of the structure of the scheme below the node representing the initial classification.

The code required to find the Concept for the "Newspaper, Periodical, Book and Database Publishers" classification node, and then to create the corresponding Classification, is straightforward:

```
ArrayList classifications = new ArrayList();
String path = "/" + naics.getKey().getId() + "/51/511/5111";
Concept publisherConcept = bqm.findConceptByPath(path);
Classification bookPublishers = blcm.createClassification(publisherConcept);
classifications.add(bookPublishers);
```

Since NAICS is an internal classification scheme, we can use the findConceptByPath() method to find the correct Concept. The path that corresponds to this node begins with the ID of the classification scheme itself, followed by the values of the nodes leading to the one that we require. You can read off the required values from Figure 7-12. Once the correct Concept is found, the createClassification() method is called to create a Classification object, which is then added to an ArrayList that is eventually passed to the findOrganizations() method. The next step is to add to this ArrayList the Classification objects for all of the descendents of the Concept that we just found. To do this, we use the getDescendentConcepts() method, which locates all of the direct descendents of the Concept to which it is applied, and all of the child Concepts of those descendents, and so on:

```
Collection concepts = publisherConcept.getDescendantConcepts();
Iterator conceptIter = concepts.iterator();
while (conceptIter.hasNext()) {
    Concept concept = (Concept)conceptIter.next();
    System.out.println("Adding child: " + concept.getName().getValue());
    classifications.add(blcm.createClassification(concept));
}
```

Each descendent Concept is then wrapped in a Classification object and added to the ArrayList.

Finally, to locate the set of Organizations with any of these classifications, we pass the list of Classifications to the findOrganizations() method:

```
ArrayList findQualifiers = new ArrayList();
findQualifiers.add(FindQualifier.OR_LIKE_KEYS);
BulkResponse res = bqm.findOrganizations(findQualifiers, null,
    classifications, null, null, null);
```

If you refer back to Table 7-4, you'll see that in a find operation that includes more than one Classification, they are combined using an AND operation—in other words, the AND operation looks for objects that have *all* of the specified Classifications. Since we want to retrieve Organizations that have *any* of the

Classifications, we need to convert this to an OR operation. To do this, we need to pass a set of find qualifiers containing `FindQualifier.OR_LIKE_KEYS` as the first argument to the `findOrganizations()` method. You can try out this code by making *chapter7\jaxr* your working directory and typing the command:

```
ant run-extended-uddi-classify-client
```

or:

```
ant run-extended-ebxml-classify-client
```

The output from either of these commands shows the classifications that are being included and the result of the search, which should be the single entry for O'Reilly & Associates.

Declarative Queries

In addition to the search facilities provided by `BusinessQueryManager`, level 1 registries also allow you to retrieve information using queries written in one or more query languages. The query language or languages available may vary from registry to registry, and the JAXR specification does not require any particular query language to be supported. The `javax.xml.registry.Query` interface defines constants for three specific query languages, which are listed in Table 7-5.

Table 7-5. Query languages identified by the Query interface

Constant	Description
QUERY_TYPE_EBXML_FILTER_QUERY	An ebXML filter query, as described in the ebXML Registry Service specification.
QUERY_TYPE_SQL	A query using a subset of SQL-92.
QUERY_TYPE_XPATH	A query using the W3C XPath language.

The rules that govern the use of ebXML filters and SQL as query languages are defined in the ebXML Registry Service specification, which can be downloaded from *http://www.oasis-open.org/committees/regrep/documents/2.1/specs/ebrs.pdf*.

In order to submit a query, you first need to obtain an instance of the `DeclarativeQueryManager` interface from the `RegistryService` object associated with your connection to the registry. You can then use the `DeclarativeQueryManager` object to build a query and submit it to the registry. The code in Example 7-3 illustrates how to retrieve all of the `Organizations` from the registry, using an SQL query.

Example 7-3. Using an SQL query to fetch a set of Organizations from the registry

```
RegistryService registry = conn.getRegistryService();
DeclarativeQueryManager dqm = registry.getDeclarativeQueryManager();
Query query = dqm.createQuery(Query.QUERY_TYPE_SQL,
    "SELECT o.id FROM Organization o");
BulkResponse res = dqm.executeQuery(query);
```

*Example 7-3. Using an SQL query to fetch a set of Organizations
from the registry (continued)*

```
// Process results (if any)
Collection coll = res.getCollection( );
Iterator iter = coll.iterator( );
while (iter.hasNext( )) {
    Organization org = (Organization)iter.next( );
    System.out.println("\t" + org.getName( ).getValue( ));
}
```

The query is represented by a Query object, which is obtained by passing the constant representing the query language to be used and the query itself to the createQuery( ) method of DeclarativeQueryManager. The query is then performed using the executeQuery( ) method, which returns a BulkResponse containing the RegistryObjects that match the query.

Although a registry may support SQL as a query language, it does not necessarily follow from this that the registry is implemented using a relational or object database. Instead, the registry server is required to provide a logical mapping of the registry information model to a set of SQL tables, which can then be the target of SQL queries. The details of this mapping are outside the scope of this book, and can be found in the ebXML Registry Service specification, together with a specification of the subset of the SQL SELECT statement syntax that can be used in conjunction with the executeQuery( ) method. The following is an incomplete summary that covers only the major points:

- The SELECT statement may only return a single column from one registry table. That column must be the id column, which represents the unique identifier assigned to the RegistryObject when it is created. The BulkResponse will contain the RegistryObjects that correspond to the IDs returned by the SELECT statement.*

- Each RegistryObject is mapped to a table that is typically named for its concrete type, such as Organization, ClassificationScheme, etc. There are some exceptions, such as User, which is mapped to a table named User_.

- RegistryObject and RegistryEntry are represented as relational views that include all of the rows from the individual tables that correspond to the concrete types and thus allow queries that are independent of the actual type of an object to be made. Therefore, while SELECT o.id FROM Organization o returns all Organization objects, the query SELECT r.id FROM RegistryObject r produces a result set containing *all* RegistryObjects, including all Organizations.

- Not all attributes of a RegistryObject appear in the table that represents that object. Some attributes, such as the name and description, appear as rows in a separate table that has a column called parent that links it to the RegistryObject that it should be associated with. For example, the query SELECT o.id FROM Organization o, Name nm WHERE o.id = nm.parent AND nm. value LIKE '%ei%' returns all Organizations for which the name contains the characters ei (such as O'Reilly & Associates).

---

* At the time of this writing, the ebXML registry implementation available from sourceforge.net actually requires that the SELECT statement return more than just the ID column. As a workaround for this problem, you can use SELECT * FROM ..... instead of SELECT id FROM.

- Attributes of a RegistryObject that are defined as Collections—such as the set of Classifications, ExternalLinks, etc.—can be obtained by invoking a stored procedure, and passing the ID of the RegistryObject as a parameter. The set of stored procedures that are defined for this purpose can be found in the ebXML Registry Service specification.

The example source code for this book contains a simple example that shows how to submit an SQL query to an ebXML registry. To run this example, make *chapter7\jaxr* your working directory and type the command:

```
ant run-ebxml-query-client
```

This example uses the SQL query shown above to find all Organization objects in the registry for which the name contains the string ei and then fetches the Classifications associated with each of them. The SQL query required to fetch the Classifications demonstrates how to use one of the small number of stored procedures that return attributes defined as Collections, as shown in Example 7-4.

Example 7-4. Using a stored procedure to get the Classifications for a RegistryObject

```
Query classQuery = dqm.createQuery(Query.QUERY_TYPE_SQL,
    "SELECT c.id FROM Classification c WHERE id IN " +
    "(RegistryObject_classifications('" + org.getKey().getId() + "'))");
```

The stored procedure RegistryObject_classifications() requires the ID of the RegistryObject for which the Classifications are required, and returns the ID for each of them. Note that the ID argument must be surrounded by single quotes to satisfy the SQL syntax. The output from this command, when run against an ebXML registry with just the sample data for this chapter installed, looks like this:

```
Query found 1
    OReilly & Associates, Inc
    Book Publishers   United States
```

Asynchronous Queries

It has been implicitly assumed in the examples shown so far in this chapter that when a request is made to the registry, the calling thread blocks until a reply is received. For most applications, this is an acceptable mode of operation, since they have little or nothing else to do until the result of the operation is known. However, applications that do not wish to be blocked awaiting a response can use the Connection setSynchronous() method with the argument false to select an asynchronous mode of operation. Once this mode is selected, queries made via BusinessQueryManager or DeclarativeQueryManager, and registry modifications made using BusinessLifeCycleManager (described shortly), behave as follows:

- The provider allocates a unique identifier to the request and creates a JAXRResponse (which, in practice, is a BulkResponse), with its request identifier attribute set to the value of this identifier and its status set to JAXRResponse.STATUS_UNAVAILABLE. The JAXRResponse is returned to the caller, as usual.

- The provider is responsible for arranging for the request to be performed without blocking the calling thread. A provider typically does this by creating a new thread to handle the request, or by handing it off to an existing thread dedicated to handling asynchronous requests.
- When the request completes, successfully or otherwise, the provider loads any responses or exceptions into the JAXRResponse and sets its status to either STATUS_SUCCESS, STATUS_WARNING, or STATUS_FAILURE.

Application code can treat the BulkResponse returned by the provider in the usual way by immediately calling the getCollections( ) or getExceptions( ) methods to retrieve the results of the call. However, if it does so, it is blocked until the request actually completes. In order to make use of the asynchronous nature of the request, it must instead wait to be notified that the results are available, by inspecting the value returned by the JAXRResponse getStatus( ) method or calling the convenience method isAvailable( ). These methods do not block. The code shown in Example 7-5 illustrates how to asynchronously request the set of all Organizations known to a registry.

Example 7-5. Making an asynchronous registry request

```
ConnectionFactory cf = ConnectionFactory.newInstance( );

// Get and initialize the connection
Connection conn = cf.createConnection( );
conn.setSynchronous(false);

// Get the RegistryService and the BusinessQueryManager
RegistryService registry = conn.getRegistryService( );
bqm = registry.getBusinessQueryManager( );

// Request all organizations
ArrayList namePatterns = new ArrayList( );
namePatterns.add("%");
BulkResponse res = bqm.findOrganizations(null, namePatterns,
    null, null, null, null);

// Wait until the request has completed
System.out.println("Request submitted - id = " + res.getRequestId( ));
while (!res.isAvailable( )) {
    System.out.println("Request status: " + res.getStatus( ));
    try {
        Thread.sleep(1000);
    } catch (InterruptedException ex) {
    }
}
System.out.println("Request completed");

// Process results (if any)
Collection coll = res.getCollection( );
```

You can try this example by making *chapter7\jaxr* your working directory and typing the following command:

```
ant run-uddi-async-client
```

or:

```
ant run-ebxml-async-client
```

 The JAXR specification does not require that support for asynchronous operations be provided to clients that reside in a J2EE container because of the restrictions placed on container-resident code by the programming environment in which it must execute (such as the inability to use threads). Asynchronous operations are therefore limited to J2SE application clients.

Modifying the Registry

Although registries typically allow any client to browse their content, registry updates can only be made by authenticated users. In order to authenticate yourself with the registry, you need to obtain a valid user identity (which might consist of a username and password or an X509 certificate), and then use the Connection setCredentials( ) method to provide your authentication details before calling getRegistryService( ). The section "Registry Security" later in this chapter describes in more detail how to supply authentication information to the JAXR provider.

The methods that allow registry data to be modified are defined by two interfaces: LifeCycleManager and BusinessLifeCycleManager, which is derived from it. Since RegistryService allows only the creation of a BusinessLifeCycleManager object, in the rest of this section I'll discuss the methods of both these interfaces as if they were all defined by BusinessLifeCycleManager.

 It is important to note that you don't need to be authenticated in order to obtain a reference to a BusinessLifeCycleManager object. As we have already seen, it is necessary for unauthenticated clients to be able to create Classification objects using BusinessLife-CycleManager in order to be able to search for RegistryObjects that have specific classifications. Authentication is required only if you intend to use the methods that actually save information in the registry or delete entries from it.

BusinessLifeCycleManager allows you to modify the registry in three different ways:

- Creating new objects
- Modifying existing objects
- Deleting existing objects

In order to enter new data into the registry, first use one or more of the BusinessLifeCycleManager createXXX( ) methods to build an object representation of the information model that you want to create. To add a new organization, for example, you would use the createOrganization( ) method to obtain an object that represents the organization itself, then create and add a Service object for each service that the organization will offer. Within each Service, you would create and add ServiceBindings that provide the information needed to access the service itself. Having built the object representation of the organization, save it to the registry. No changes are made to the registry unless they are explicitly committed using one of the BusinessLifeCycleManager saveXXX( ) methods.

To modify existing data, use a BusinessQueryManager findXXX( ) method or the getRegistryObject( ) method to obtain a memory-resident copy of its current value, make the required changes, and then commit them using the BusinessLifeCycleManager saveXXX( ) methods.

Registry objects can be deleted using one of the BusinessLifeCycleManager deleteXXX( ) methods. In order to delete an object, you need to supply the unique key assigned to it when it was created.

The rest of this section uses extracts from the registry client used to install the test data used for the examples in this chapter to illustrate how new content can be installed in the registry. You can find the source code for this client in the file *chapter7\setup\src\ora\jwsnut\chapter7\setup\RegistrySetup.java* relative to the installation directory of the example source code for this book. For more information on the LifeCycleManager and BusinessLifeCycleManager interfaces, refer to the reference material for the javax.xml.registry package in the second part of this book.

Creating Organizations and Users

An Organization object is created using the BusinessLifeCycleManager createOrganization( ) method, which has two variants:

```
public Organization createOrganization(String name) throws JAXRPCException;
public Organization createOrganization(InternationalString name)
    throws JAXRPCException;
```

Every RegistryObject has a name attribute of type InternationalString, which allows representations of the name to be stored in a form suitable for any number of Locales. Typically, when creating a RegistryObject, you may choose to supply the name either as a String or as an InternationalString. In the former case, the name is actually stored as an InternationalString in which the supplied value is used as the representation for the Locale on which the client application is running.

An InternationalString is a collection of LocalizedString objects, each of which contains a Locale specifier, the character set to be used for that Locale, and a String appropriate to that Locale. Since both InternationalString and LocalizedString are interfaces, you need to use factory methods provided by BusinessLifeCycleManager to create instances of them. Here's an example that shows how to create an Organization, supplying both the name and description attributes as InternationalStrings:

```
InternationalString name = blcm.createInternationalString(
    "OReilly & Associates, Inc");
Organization ora = blcm.createOrganization(name);
ora.setDescription(blcm.createInternationalString("Book Publisher"));
```

An InternationalString is created with values for either zero or one Locales. You can add additonal Locales by creating LocalizedStrings and calling the addLocalizedString( ) or addLocalizedStrings( ) methods:

```
LocalizedString str = blcm.createLocalizedString(Locale.UK, "O'Reilly and
Associates UK");
name.addLocalizedString(str);
```

Further information on both InternationalString and LocalizedString can be found in the reference material in the second part of this book.

Other than its name, an Organization is initially created with an empty set of attributes. An Organization has the following set of attributes, in addition to those inherited from RegistryObject:

Address
> Level 1 registries allow an Organization to have an address attribute of type PostalAddress. If you are using a level 0 registry, the Organization's address is taken to be that of its primary contact. See "Postal Addresses" later in this chapter for a discussion of the way in which level 0 registries store PostalAddress objects, which is not as straightforward a subject as you might expect.

Telephone Numbers
> An Organization can have any number of contact numbers, each of which is of type TelephoneNumber. These objects can be created using the BusinessLifeCycleManager createTelephoneNumber( ) method.

Primary Contact
> A User object containing contact information for the person responsible for the Organization's registry data. In the case of a level 0 registry, the PostalAddress attribute of the primary contact is taken to be the address of the Organization itself.

Users
> A collection of User objects represents users affiliated to the Organization. This list always contains the primary contact; the JAXR provider inserts an entry for the primary contact in this collection if it is not already present.

Services
> A list of Service objects describing the services offered by the Organization. Refer to "Services, ServiceBindings, and SpecificationLinks" later in this chapter for further information.

Parent, Children, and Root Organizations
> Level 1 registries allow the creation of Organization hierarchies. Each Organization in such a hierarchy has a single parent Organization and zero or more child Organizations. A reference to the root Organization for the hierarchy is also available from each Organization. Organization hierarchies are not supported by level 0 registries.

The User object is the registry's representation of a person affiliated to a business. In addition to those that it inherits from RegistryObject, User has the following attributes:

Person Name
> This attribute provides personal identification information for the user in the form of a PersonName object. In a level 0 registry, the PersonName object

provides only the full name of the user, expressed as a single `String`. Level 1 registries additionally allow the user's first, middle, and last name to be supplied as separate `String`s.* Note that the `PersonName` attribute is additional to the name attribute inherited from `RegistryObject`.

Email Addresses

This is a collection of zero or more email addresses for the user, each of which is represented as an object of type `EmailAddress`. An `EmailAddress` object contains the actual email address (e.g., *info@amazon.com*) and a type attribute that allows qualifying information specifying the way in which the address is to be used to be included.

Telephone Numbers

A collection of zero or more contact telephone numbers for the user. Each entry in the collection is a `TelephoneNumber` object that, in a level 0 registry, holds the telephone number in the form of a single, uninterpreted string. Level 1 registries break the telephone number down into its constituent parts, including country code, area code, and so on.

Addresses

A collection of `PostalAddress` objects giving the contact addresses for the user. These are taken as the addresses of the `Organization` itself if the `User` object represents the primary contact in a level 0 registry.

Type

This attribute contains a string whose content is not interpreted by the registry. It is typically used to describe the role that the user plays within the `Organization`, such as "Technical Contact."

URL

A URL that is in some way associated with the user. This attribute is supported only by level 1 registries.

A `User` object is created by calling the `BusinessLifeCycleManager` `createUser( )` method, which initializes all of its attributes to `null`. The code extract in Example 7-6 shows how to create an `Organization`, associate it with a primary contact `User`, and initialize some of the attributes of both objects.

Example 7-6. Creating Organization and User objects in a registry

```
// Create an entry for Amazon.com
Organization amazon = blcm.createOrganization(blcm.
createInternationalString("Amazon.com"));
amazon.setDescription(blcm.createInternationalString(
    "Amazon.com e-commerce web services"));


// Add telephone numbers
TelephoneNumber number = blcm.createTelephoneNumber( );
number.setNumber("206-266-2335");
```

---

* Version 1.0 of the JAXR specification is not clear what should happen if you choose to set the full name of a user for a level 1 registry. In particular, it does not specify whether the supplied value should be broken into several fields and stored as the first, middle, and last names, or whether the full name should be treated as a separate attribute from the first, middle, and last name attributes.

```
ArrayList list = new ArrayList( );
list.add(number);
amazon.setTelephoneNumbers(list);
list.clear( );

// Add a link to the home page
ExternalLink eLink = blcm.createExternalLink("http://www.amazon.com",
    "Amazon.com home page");
eLink.setValidateURI(connected);
list.add(eLink);
amazon.setExternalLinks(list);
list.clear( );

// Create the Amazon submitting user
User user = blcm.createUser( );
personName = blcm.createPersonName("Amazon.com Corporate");
user.setDescription(blcm.createInternationalString(
    "Amazon.com primary contact"));
user.setPersonName(personName);
address = blcm.createPostalAddress("1200", "12th Avenue South", "Seattle",
    "Washington", "US", "98144", "Headquarters");
list.add(address);
user.setPostalAddresses(list);
list.clear( );

list.add(number);
user.setTelephoneNumbers(list);
list.clear( );

EmailAddress email = blcm.createEmailAddress("info@amazon.com");
list.add(email);
user.setEmailAddresses(list);
list.clear( );

// Install the primary contact for Amazon.com
amazon.setPrimaryContact(user);
```

You'll notice that because many of the attributes of both Organization and User can have multiple associated values, in order to set them, you have to create a Collection (in this case, an ArrayList is used), add the value or values to the Collection, and call the appropriate setter method. This is a pattern that you'll find yourself using very often when writing code that installs registry data.

Another point worth noting is that this code associates an ExternalLink with the Organization object for Amazon.com. As mentioned earlier, an ExternalLink points to an arbitrary URL that might contain some information of use to registry clients. In this case, the ExternalLink points to the organization's home page. The registry is free to check the validity of the link by attempting to access it. If this is not convenient, perhaps because the URL is not currently valid or because you are using a private test registry that is not connected to the Internet, you can use the setValidateURI( ) method to disable the check. In this case, the Boolean variable connected is assumed to be true if the client is connected to the Internet, and it is false if the client is not connected.

When the test data for this chapter is installed in the registry, three Organization objects are created for Amazon.com, O'Reilly & Associates, and Keyboard Edge Limited (my consulting company). You can see that the data has been correctly installed by using a registry browser. The JAXR reference implementation is supplied with a browser that works with UDDI registries, which we'll use in this chapter. If you are using the ebXML registry available from *http://ebxmlrr. sourceforge.net*, you'll find that it has a similar tool. To start the registry browser on a Windows platform, go to the *bin* directory of the JWSDP installation and type:

```
jaxr-browser.bat
```

On a Unix/Linux platform, type:

```
jaxr-browser.sh
```

and enter the URL of the registry you want to browse in the Registry Location field. This field has a drop-down box that contains several commonly used URLs, including one that corresponds to the reference implementation's UDDI registry server when run on the local host (*http://localhost:8000/RegistryServer/ RegistryServerServlet*). Having selected a URL, you can enter a name pattern in the Name field and look for Organizations whose names match the pattern. You can also choose to search by Classification, which is a common operation when looking for businesses by business type. In fact, all of the Organizations in the test registry data have associated Classifications. You'll see how these are added later in "Classifying registry objects." Enter the string "%" in the Name field and press the Search button. This string matches all names in the registry; therefore, three entries should be returned, as shown in Figure 7-14.

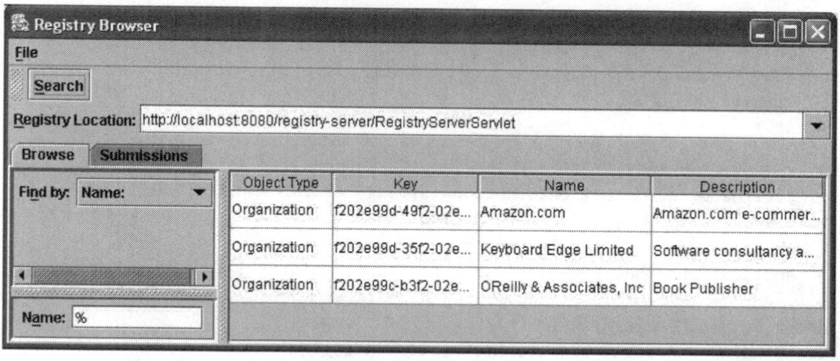

Figure 7-14. Using the registry browser to examine registry data

To take a closer look at the data for a specific Organization, double-click its entry in the table on the righthand side of the window. This opens a dialog box that displays the contact information and classifications for the Organization, and also allows you to examine its associated Service objects, which will be discussed in the next section. Figure 7-15 shows the information returned for Amazon.com. Note that this is test data only and does not necessarily represent the most current information for Amazon.com, which you can find by looking at the public UDDI registries mentioned at the start of this chapter.

Figure 7-15. More detailed registry information for an Organization

Services, ServiceBindings, and SpecificationLinks

As described in "JAXR Registry Model Overview," a service offered by an Organization is represented in the registry by a hierarchy of Service, ServiceBinding, and SpecificationLink objects. Each of these types can be created using factory methods provided by BusinessLifeCycleManager. Typical use of these methods is illustrated in Example 7-7, which shows the code used to add a Service and a ServiceBinding to the Organization entry for Amazon.com when the test data for this chapter is installed.

Example 7-7. Adding a Service and a ServiceBinding to an Organization
in the registry

```
// Create a Service entry
Service service = blcm.createService("Amazon web service");
service.setName(blcm.createInternationalString("Amazon web service"));
service.setDescription(blcm.createInternationalString(
    "Web services that allow developers to create" +
    " applications that consume Amazon.com core features"));

// Add a ServiceBinding
ServiceBinding binding = blcm.createServiceBinding();
binding.setName(blcm.createInternationalString("Amazon service binding"));
binding.setDescription(blcm.createInternationalString(
    "Access to Amazon web services"));
binding.setValidateURI(connected);
binding.setAccessURI("http://soap.amazon.com/onca/soap");

// Add the binding to the service and
// the service to the organization
// "list" is an existing, empty ArrayList
list.add(binding);
```

*Example 7-7. Adding a Service and a ServiceBinding to an Organization
in the registry (continued)*

```
service.addServiceBindings(list);
list.clear( );
amazon.addService(service);
```

A Service object represents a single service of some kind (possibly a web service) that an Organization provides. An Organization may have any number of associated services. Amazon.com provides a web service interface that allows browsing and purchasing of of items in its online store. The Service object just created is intended to encapsulate that service. The information required to access the service is provided by a ServiceBinding nested within the Service object. Each ServiceBinding describes a particular means that can be used to access the service. In the case of Amazon.com, there is one ServiceBinding that advertises SOAP-based access to the service.* Additional access methods, perhaps a user-to-business interface using HTTP to be displayed in a browser, could be advertised by adding additional ServiceBinding objects.

The ServiceBinding includes an attribute called accessURI that associates an address with the binding. There is no fixed meaning for this attribute—it might, for example, be an HTTP or *mailto:* URL to which a SOAP message can be sent. In order to know how to interpret it, you need to read the technical specification for the service binding. As with ExternalLinks, it is possible to use the setValidateURI( ) method (of ServiceBinding) to specify whether this URI should be validated when the registry entry is created.

In some cases, a ServiceBinding does not directly reference the service implementation but is instead redirected to another ServiceBinding. It might be convenient to do this if you are creating several Organization entries that have some service implementations in common, and you want only to specify the binding details once so that they can easily be changed if necessary. To do this, you can use the ServiceBinding setTargetBinding( ) method to install a reference to the ServiceBinding that holds the real access information. It is not legal to have both a target binding and an access URI in the same ServiceBinding object.

A ServiceBinding can have a number of associated SpecificationLinks. A SpecificationLink is intended to provide a link to information that provides the technical details necessary for a developer to access the service using the binding that it is associated with. An organization might, for example, create human-readable documentation that describes the service and/or a formal specification of the service interface such as a WSDL document. Each of these could be associated with the ServiceBinding using separate SpecificationLink objects.

The useful information is included within the SpecificationLink using a specificationObject attribute, which is formally of type RegistryObject. The way in which you might use a SpecificationLink to refer to the WSDL definition for a web service is not formally defined, but there are conventions that are in use within both the ebXML and UDDI registries.

JAXR

---

* You cannot tell from the ServiceBinding that the access being offered is SOAP-based; you have to examine the SpecificationLinks to infer this.

Storing a WSDL document reference in an ebXML registry

Since an ebXML registry has an associated repository, it is possible to actually hold documentation referred to from a SpecificationLink within the repository in the form of an ExtrinsicObject. This means that a registry client can obtain the WSDL document (or any other form of technical specification) directly from the registry rather than having to be redirected to the owning company. An example that shows how to store a WSDL document in an ebXML registry/repository is shown in "ExtrinsicObjects," later in this chapter.

Storing a WSDL document reference in a UDDI registry

The way in which WSDL document references should be stored in a UDDI registry is not mandated by the UDDI registry specifications. Instead, there is a "best practice" document available from the OASIS web site at *http://www.oasis-open.org/committees/uddi-spec/bps.shtml* that recommends a convention to be followed. This document uses terms from the UDDI registry information model to describe how WSDL should be referenced. In this section, you'll see how this recommendation can be mapped to the information model defined by the JAXR specification so that it can be used with the JAXR API.

The simplest way to explain the recommendation is to describe an example JAXR implementation of it, which is shown in Example 7-8.

Example 7-8. Creating a reference to a WSDL document in a UDDI registry

```
// Set up a SpecificationLink
SpecificationLink sLink = blcm.createSpecificationLink( );
sLink.setName(blcm.createInternationalString("WSDL specification"));
sLink.setUsageDescription(blcm.createInternationalString("WSDL specification"));

// Create the specification object
Concept sConcept = blcm.createConcept(null, "AmazonWSDL", "AmazonWSDL");
ExternalLink eLink = blcm.createExternalLink(
    "http://soap.amazon.com/schemas/AmazonWebServices.wsdl",
    "WSDL Specification");
eLink.setValidateURI(connected);
sConcept.addExternalLink(eLink);
ClassificationScheme uddiTypes = bqm.findClassificationSchemeByName(
    null, "uddi-org:types");
Classification wsdlClass = blcm.createClassification(uddiTypes, "wsdlSpec",
    "wsdlSpec");
sConcept.addClassification(wsdlClass);
ArrayList list = new ArrayList( );
list.add(sConcept);
BulkResponse res = blcm.saveConcepts(list);
list.clear( );
Collection coll = res.getCollection( );
sConcept.setKey((Key)coll.iterator( ).next( ));

// Store the specification object
sLink.setSpecificationObject(sConcept);
```

```
// Associate the SpecificationLink with the ServiceBinding
// and set the accessURI
binding.addSpecificationLink(sLink);
binding.setValidateURI(connected);
binding.setAccessURI("http://soap.amazon.com/onca/soap");
```

The first part of this code creates the SpecificationLink object that contains the reference to the WSDL document. Since the UDDI registry does not have a repository, it is not possible for the SpecificationLink to refer directly to the WSDL specification. Instead, the object stored in the SpecificationLink must be a Concept object that has the following properties:

- It has an ExternalLink that points to the WSDL document.
- It has a Classification with value wsdlSpec associated with a ClassificationScheme called uddi-org:types. This ClassificationScheme is defined by the UDDI specification and must be made available by all JAXR providers for UDDI registries.

Having created the Concept and added the appropriate ExternalLink and Classification, the code in Example 7-8 uses the setSpecificationObject() method to install it in the SpecificationLink and then adds the SpecificationLink to the ServiceBinding. Finally, the accessURI attribute of the ServiceBinding is set to point to the actual URL of the web service itself.*

When a registry client locates the Organization entry for Amazon.com and accesses this ServiceBinding, it is able to deduce that the SpecificationLink refers to a WSDL document by virtue of the fact that its specification object (the Concept) has the classification wsdlSpec from the uddi-org:types ClassificationScheme. The WSDL document can then be retrieved from the location specified by the ExternalLink associated with the specification object and used to create the JAX-RPC client-side artifacts or to build a SAAJ client that can access the service.

The final point to note is that, as you saw in Chapter 5, the WSDL document for a service may contain service and port elements that provide the URL at which the service defined by the document may be accessed. That being the case, why is it necessary to also include the service access point address as the accessURI of the ServiceBinding when it could be obtained from the WSDL document? The intent of this apparent duplication of information is to accomodate WSDL documents that *don't* include the service and port information. As described in "Separating WSDL definitions into separate files" in Chapter 5, it is quite reasonable to separate the reusable parts of a WSDL definition (i.e., the type definitions and the service bindings) from the service element, which simply specifies where an instance of the service can be reached and is therefore not reusable. As an example of a case in which this might be useful, suppose that at some future time a group of companies agrees on a common service interface for an online shopping service. This common interface would be expressed as a WSDL definition and placed in a

---

* This last step is also shown in Example 7-7, but is repeated here for the sake of clarity.

central location, probably under the control of the industry body responsible for the specification of the interface. This WSDL document would not, of course, indicate where actual implementations of the service could be found. Instead, the ServiceBinding elements associated with the Organization entries for each online shopping store would refer to the single WSDL document describing the service that they provide from a SpecificationLink, and the URL of its particular implementation of the shopping interface would be provided using the accessURI attribute of the ServiceBinding.

Classifying registry objects

Any registry object can have zero or more associated Classifications. As mentioned earlier in this chapter, Classifications are added to allow registry users to search for businesses or services using criteria such as geographical location or business type. Adding Classifications to an object is simply a matter of creating the appropriate Classification object and calling the RegistryObject addClassification() or addClassifications() method. You have already seen how to create a Classification object to represent a specific element of a classification scheme (see "Searching by Classification," earlier in this chapter.) The code extract shown in Example 7-9 illustrates how the Classifications listed in Figure 7-15 were added to the Organization entry for Amazon.com.

Example 7-9. Adding Classifications to RegistryObjects

```
ClassificationScheme naics = bqm.findClassificationSchemeByName(null, "%naics%");
if (naics == null) {
    naics = bqm.findClassificationSchemeByName(null, "%NAICS%");
    if (naics == null) {
        System.out.println("COULD NOT FIND NAICS CLASSIFICATION SCHEME.");
        System.exit(1);
    }
}
ClassificationScheme isocs = bqm.findClassificationSchemeByName(null, "%iso%");
if (isocs == null) {
    isocs = bqm.findClassificationSchemeByName(null, "%ISO%");
    if (isocs == null) {
        System.out.println("COULD NOT FIND ISO CLASSIFICATION SCHEME.");
        System.exit(1);
    }
}

ArrayList amazonClass = new ArrayList();
amazonClass.add(blcm.createClassification(naics,
    "Book, Periodical, and Music Stores", "4512"));
amazonClass.add(blcm.createClassification(isocs, "United States", "US"));
amazon.addClassifications(amazonClass);
```

Saving content in the registry

Content created using the various createXXX() methods of BusinessLifeCycleManager exists only within the client application until it is

---

explicitly saved. One way to save previously created objects is to use the saveObjects( ) method:

```
public BulkResponse saveObjects(Collection objects) throws JAXRException;
```

The Collection passed to this method contains any number of RegistryObjects that need not all be of the same type. As each object is saved, a unique key is generated for it and entered into the Collection that is returned in the BulkResponse. If any of the objects could not be saved for any reason, then a SaveException is generated and stored in the set of exceptions associated with the BulkResponse.

Note that the key attribute of a RegistryObject held within a client application is not automatically updated as a result of a successful save operation, even though the object is assigned a valid key by the registry. Furthermore, even though the key is returned in the BulkResponse, since Collections are not ordered, there is no way to match each returned key with the RegistryObject that it is associated with, unless only one object is saved in each call. The only way to acquire the key for a RegistryObject is to use a findXXX( ) method to retrieve the object, and to use the getKey( ) method to extract it.

BusinessLifeCycleManager provides additional methods that allow groups of objects of the same type to be saved together:

```
public BulkResponse saveAssociations(Collection associations,
    boolean replace) throws JAXRException;
public BulkResponse saveClassificationSchemes(Collection schemes)
    throws JAXRException;
public BulkResponse saveConcepts(Collection concepts) throws JAXRException;
public BulkResponse saveOrganizations(Collection organizations)
    throws JAXRException;
public BulkReponse saveServiceBindingd(Collection bindings)
    throws JAXRException;
public BulkResponse saveServices(Collection services) throws JAXRException;
```

All of the saveXXX( ) methods either create a new registry object or update an existing one if the object already exists in the registry. An update occurs if the object being saved contains a valid key. A perhaps unexpected consequence of this is that it is possible to create any number of RegistryObjects of the same type with the same name, simply by calling methods like createOrganization( ) and then saving the objects that are returned. To avoid this, it is advisable to check before adding new registry content whether the objects that it contains already exist in the registry.

When a memory-resident RegistryObject is saved (or updated), the provider is required to traverse all of the objects that it references and create or update their registry counterparts as well. As a result of this, in order to create registry entries for a set of Organizations together with their associated links, services, and service bindings, it is only necessary to create a Collection containing the Organization objects and use the saveOrganizations( ) method to save the content of this Collection:

```
ArrayList orgs = new ArrayList( );
orgs.add(ora);
orgs.add(kbedge);
orgs.add(amazon);
BulkResponse res = blcm.saveOrganizations(orgs);
```

Associations

It is sometimes useful to be able to reflect the existence of a relationship of some kind between two objects within the registry. A business, for example, might want to indicate that it makes use of the services of another organization whose details can be found in the same registry. Relationships of this type can be recorded in the registry by creating an *association* between a pair of RegistryObjects, which is represented by an object of type javax.xml.registry.infomodel.Association. An Association has three major attributes, which are illustrated in diagram form in Figure 7-16.

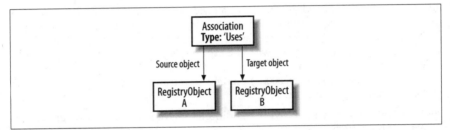

Figure 7-16. An Association object

Source *object*
> The object to which the Association is applied.

Target *object*
> The object that is to be considered to be associated with the source object.

Association *type*
> Describes the nature of the association.

The JAXR specification defines 15 different association types, which are listed here:

Contains	EquivalentTo	Extends	ExternallyLinks
HasChild	HasMember	HasParent	Implements
InstanceOf	RelatedTo	Replaces	ResponsibleFor
SubmitterOf	Supersedes	Uses	

Notice that each of these association types is clearly directional. To reflect this fact, the two RegistryObjects involved are labeled as the source and target of the association. The example shown in Figure 7-16 expresses the fact that RegistryObject "A" uses RegistryObject "B". Here, the association type is "Uses", the source object is "A", and the target object is "B".

> Although an Association can theoretically be applied to any pair of RegistryObjects, limitations may be imposed by specific registry types. In particular, the UDDI registry in the JAXR reference implementation permits Associations to be made only between Organizations.

There are two distinct Association types: *intramural* and *extramural*. An intramural Association is one in which the source and target objects, and the Association itself, are all submitted by the same user. An extramural Association is one in which at least one of the objects does not have the same owner (i.e., was submitted to the registry by a different user) as the Association itself.

In order to be considered trustworthy, an extramural Association must be confirmed by the owner of both objects involved. A registry user confirms an Association by using the confirmAssociation() method of BusinessLifeCycleManager, and may unconfirm it at any point using the unConfirmAssocation() method. The isConfirmed(), isConfirmedBySourceOwner(), and isConfirmedByTargetOwner() methods of Association can be used to retrieve the current confirmation status. Extramural Associations are not visible to registry owners that are not a party to the Association until they have been confirmed.

An intramural Association is always considered to be confirmed, since the three objects involved are all owned by the same registry user.

An Association is created using the createAssociation() method of LifeCycleManager:

```
public Association createAssociation(RegistryObject target, Concept type)
    throws JAXRException;
```

The association type required by this method is a Concept from an enumerated type under a ClassificationScheme called AssociationType. The code extract in Example 7-10 shows how to create and apply a "Uses" Association between two Organizations.

Example 7-10. Creating an Association between two Organizations

```
// Find the source organization
ArrayList list = new ArrayList();
list.add("%Reilly%");
BulkResponse res = bqm.findOrganizations(null, list, null, null, null, null);
Collection coll = res.getCollection();
Iterator iter = coll.iterator();
if (!iter.hasNext()) {
    System.out.println("Please load sample data into the registry");
    System.exit(1);
}
Organization ora = (Organization)iter.next();
list.clear();

// Find the target organization
list.add("%Keyboard%");
res = bqm.findOrganizations(null, list, null, null, null, null);
coll = res.getCollection();
iter = coll.iterator();
if (!iter.hasNext()) {
    System.out.println("Please load sample data into the registry");
    System.exit(1);
}
Organization kbedge = (Organization)iter.next();
```

Example 7-10. Creating an Association between two Organizations (continued)

```
list.clear();

// Get the concept for the association type
ClassificationScheme types = bqm.findClassificationSchemeByName(null,
    "AssociationType");
if (types == null) {
    System.out.println("Cannot find AssociationTypes scheme");
    System.exit(1);
}
String path = "/" + types.getKey().getId() + "/Uses";
Concept uses = bqm.findConceptByPath(path);
if (uses == null) {
    System.out.println("Cannot find 'Uses' concept");
    System.exit(1);
}

// Create the association
Association a = blcm.createAssociation(kbedge, uses);
ora.addAssociation(a);

// Save the association
list.add(a);
res = blcm.saveAssociations(list, false);
if (res.getExceptions() != null) {
    System.out.println("Failed to save association");
    iter = res.getExceptions().iterator();
    while (iter.hasNext()) {
        System.out.println(iter.next());
    }
    System.exit(1);
}
list.clear();
```

The first part of this code uses the findOrganizations() method of BusinessQueryManager to obtain references to the source and target Organizations, which are O'Reilly & Associates and Keyboard Edge Limited, respectively. The next step is to obtain the Concept for the type of Association to be created, which in this case is a "Uses" Association. Since the association types are predefined enumerations, the JAXR specification allows the path /AssociationType/Uses to be passed to findConceptByPath() to get a reference to this Concept. However, as noted in "Concepts as enumerated types," earlier in this chapter, this path is a special case that is not supported by all providers. The code shown here does not rely on the availability of the special case, because it retrieves the ClassificationScheme object for the enumeration and builds the path using its unique identifier, as described earlier in "Searching by Classification."

The Association is created by supplying the target object and the type to the LifeCycleManager createAssociation() method:

```
Association a = blcm.createAssociation(kbedge, uses);
```

Note that the source object is not supplied—instead, it is implied by calling the
addAssociation( ) method of the source object itself, which is the Organization
object for O'Reilly & Associates:

```
ora.addAssociation(a);
```

Finally, the Association is made effective by storing it in the registry:

```
list.add(a);
res = blcm.saveAssociations(list, false);
```

The saveAssocations( ) method requires a Collection of Assocations and a
Boolean argument that, if true, replaces all existing Associations owned by the
caller with those in the supplied Collection. This argument is usually false, which
has the effect of adding the supplied Associations to those already in existence.
There is no need to save the affected Organization objects because they are automatically updated.

Since the two Organizations and the Association are all owned by the same user,
this will be an intramural Association, and therefore there is no need for it to be
explicitly confirmed.

You can obtain the list of Associations for a RegistryObject by calling its
getAssociations( ) method. You can also use the findAssociations( ) and
findCallerAssociations( ) methods of BusinessQueryManager to search for
Associations using appropriate criteria.

Creating User-Defined Classification Schemes and Enumerated Types

It is sometimes useful to be able to add your own classification scheme or enumerated type to the registry. Since an enumerated type is just a classification scheme
with only a single hierarchy level, the same technique can be used to create either.
Unfortunately, this is one of the few cases in which you have to use different
approaches depending on the actual type of the registry that is being used. In this
section, you'll see how to add an enumerated type called TestEnum that has the
distinguished values 1, 2, 3, and 4 with both the UDDI and ebXML providers.

Adding classification schemes to an ebXML provider

An ebXML registry provides the internal mechanisms necessary to install a new
ClassificationScheme and its associated Concept hierarchy within the registry
itself. The code required to do this is very simple and is shown in Example 7-11.

Example 7-11. Creating a custom classification scheme in an ebXML registry

```
ClassificationScheme scheme = blcm.createClassificationScheme("TestEnum",
    "Custom Enumeration");
scheme.setValueType(ClassificationScheme.VALUE_TYPE_UNIQUE);
ArrayList list = new ArrayList();
list.add(blcm.createConcept(scheme, "Value 1", "1"));
list.add(blcm.createConcept(scheme, "Value 2", "2"));
list.add(blcm.createConcept(scheme, "Value 3", "3"));
list.add(blcm.createConcept(scheme, "Value 4", "4"));
```

```
scheme.addChildConcepts(list);
blcm.saveConcepts(list);
list.clear();

list.add(scheme);
blcm.saveClassificationSchemes(list);
```

The first line creates the ClassificationScheme itself, supplying the name TestEnum under which it can be found by other registry clients. The *value type* of the scheme is then set to VALUE_TYPE_UNIQUE, which is one of three possible values that describe the constraint that will apply to the values of the Concepts within this ClassificationScheme:[*]

VALUE_TYPE_UNIQUE

Each Concept has a unique value (obtainable by calling its getValue( ) method).

VALUE_TYPE_NON_UNIQUE

The same value may be associated with more then one Concept in the hierarchy.

VALUE_TYPE_EMBEDDED_PATH

The value associated with each Concept is the complete path from the ClassificationScheme to the Concept itself. The developer is responsible for arranging that each Concept has the correct value. Obviously, this implies VALUE_TYPE_UNIQUE.

Next, the individual Concepts are created using the createConcept( ) method of LifeCycleManager, of which there are two variants that differ according to whether the name is suppled as a String or an InternationalString:

```
public Concept createConcept(RegistryObject parent, String name, String
value) throws JAXRException;
public Concept createConcept(RegistryObject parent, InternationalString
name, String value)

throws JAXRException;
```

In this case, the parent argument is supplied as a reference to the ClassificationScheme to which the Concepts will belong, since there is only a single hierarchy level. In the case of a more complex hierarchy, a Concept might be created with another Concept as its parent.

The name argument supplies the display name for the Concept. The value argument is the one that really matters—it is the one that is considered to be the distinguished value in the case of an enumerated type. It is also the value that must appear in the path used to locate the Concept when using the getConceptByPath( ) method.

---

[*] Note that the value type attribute can be used only with a level 1 JAXR provider.

Having created the ClassificationScheme and all of the Concepts, the final step is to commit them all to the registry using the saveConcepts() and saveClassificationSchemes() methods. Once this is done, the scheme becomes visible to all registry clients.

Adding classification schemes to a UDDI provider

Unfortunately, UDDI registries currently do not support the storage within the registry of user-defined classification schemes that have Concept hierarchies.* However, a JAXR provider is required to provide a means whereby such a scheme can be made available to registry clients. How this is achieved is implementation-dependent. Here, we'll look at the mechanism provided by the JAXR reference implementation.

In the reference implementation, user-defined classification schemes are loaded by the JAXR provider from one or more files whose locations are provided by a system property called com.sun.xml.registry.userTaxonomyFilenames. This property consists of a list of files, separated by vertical bar (|) characters. Note that, at least at the time of this writing, the filenames are not allowed to have any embedded spaces. This may be inconvenient for Windows users, since users' home directories very frequently have pathnames that contain spaces. At some point during the execution of a JAXR client application, the provider reads this property, extracts the filenames that it contains, and attempts to load the contents of each named file as a Concept hierarchy for a ClassificationScheme.

 Note that com.sun.xml.registry.userTaxonomyFilenames is a *system* property, and not one of the properties set on the ConnectionFactory object.

The steps that a developer must take to create a custom ClassificationScheme are as follows:

1. Define the ClassificationScheme itself in the registry using the createClassificationScheme() method, then save it.

2. Get the UUID assigned to the ClassificationScheme.

3. Create the file that contains the definition of the Concept hierarchy. In order to create this file, you need the scheme's UUID.

4. In JAXR client applications, include the full pathname of the file in the com.sun.xml.registry.userTaxonomyFilenames system property.

Once these steps are completed, you can treat the ClassificationScheme in the same way as if it had been installed into the registry. In particular, you can use findConceptByPath() to locate the Concept objects within the hierarchy, and then use them to create internal Classifications.

---

* In fact, you can create ClassificationSchemes and Concepts within a UDDI registry, but it is not possible to link them in a hierarchal fashion. You can actually run the code shown in Example 7-11 against a UDDI registry and it will appear to work. However, although the ClassificationScheme and Concepts are created, you won't be able to locate any of the Concepts by calling findConceptByPath() or by trying to access them as children of the ClassificationScheme object.

The installation process for the example registry data for this book includes the creation of a ClassificationScheme called TestEnum, which we will use to illustrate how to populate a custom enumeration (which is actually a single-level ClassificationScheme). By installing the test registry data, therefore, you completed the first of the steps listed previously.* To get the UUID, make *chapter7\jaxr* your working directory, and type the command:

```
ant run-uddi-enum-client-step1
```

This command retrieves the UUID of the ClassificationScheme from the registry and displays it. Make sure to note the UUID, which will look something like this:

```
uuid:f1ef390d-08f1-ef39-3f48-e3438b38f908
```

You'll need this value for the second part of this example. The next step is to define the hierarchy of Concepts within the ClassificationScheme. The example source code for this chapter includes a file that defines the same Concept hierarchy as that created programmatically within the ebXML registry in the previous section. The content of this file (which is called *chapter7\jaxr\CustomScheme.xml. template*) is shown in Example 7-12.

Example 7-12. Template for a definition of a custom ClassificationScheme

```
<PredefinedConcepts>
   <JAXRClassificationScheme id="@@" name="TestEnum">
      <JAXRConcept id="@@/1" name="Value 1" parent="@@" code="1"></JAXRConcept>
      <JAXRConcept id="@@/2" name="Value 2" parent="@@" code="2"></JAXRConcept>
      <JAXRConcept id="@@/3" name="Value 3" parent="@@" code="3"></JAXRConcept>
      <JAXRConcept id="@@/4" name="Value 4" parent="@@" code="4"></JAXRConcept>
   </JAXRClassificationScheme>
</PredefinedConcepts>
```

Within this file, the token @@ represents the places at which the UUID of the ClassificationScheme itself should be inserted to convert this template into a valid definition. Looking at the structure of this XML file, the elements are used as follows:

PredefinedConcepts
   The root element of the file and must always be present.

JAXRClassificationScheme
   Wraps the definition of a new ClassificationScheme. Any number of these elements may appear within the PredefinedConcepts element.

   The id attribute supplies the UUID of the ClassificationScheme in the registry for which this element defines the Concept hierarchy, while the name attribute fairly obviously gives the scheme's name.

---

* Refer to "Using the JAXR Examples" earlier in this chapter for the procedure for installing the test data in the registry, if you have not already done so.

JAXRConcept

Defines a Concept at some level within the ClassificationScheme. The id attribute supplies a unique ID for the Concept. It is typically formed by appending a unique value to the UUID of the scheme itself.

The name attribute supplies the name of the Concept.

The code attribute gives the actual value of the Concept, which is returned by its getValue( ) method.

The parent attribute is the id of the Concept that resides immediately above this Concept in the hierarchy, or of the ClassificationScheme itself in the case of a top-level Concept.

The Ant buildfile in the *chapter7\jaxr* directory contains a target that replaces the @@ token in the template file with the UUID of the ClassificationScheme, and writes the result to a given location in the filesystem. To use this target, you need to add the following two properties to the *jwsnutJaxrExamples.properties* file in your home directory:

```
CUSTOM_ENUM_UUID = uuid:f1ef390d-08f1-ef39-3f48-e3438b38f908
CUSTOM_ENUM_FILE = c:\\temp\\CustomSchemes.xml
```

The value of the CUSTOM_ENUM_UUID property *must* be the UUID of the ClassificationScheme that was obtained by running the first part of this example, *not* the value just shown. The CUSTOM_ENUM_FILE property gives the name of the file to be created by the editing process, which you are free to choose, subject to the following important constraints that apply to the filename:

- It cannot contain spaces.
- For Windows users, the "\" separator must be represented as "\\", since a single "\" is taken as an escape character.

The editing process can be carried out using the command:

```
ant build-enum-file
```

The result of performing this operation on the template from Example 7-12 is shown in Example 7-13.

Example 7-13. Edited ClassificationScheme definition file

```
<PredefinedConcepts>
  <JAXRClassificationScheme id="uuid:f1ef390d-08f1-ef39-3f48-e3438b38f908"
      name="TestEnum">
  <JAXRConcept id="uuid:f1ef390d-08f1-ef39-3f48-e3438b38f908/1" name="Value 1"
      parent="uuid:f1ef390d-08f1-ef39-3f48-e3438b38f908" code="1"/>
  <JAXRConcept id="uuid:f1ef390d-08f1-ef39-3f48-e3438b38f908/2" name="Value 2"
      parent="uuid:f1ef390d-08f1-ef39-3f48-e3438b38f908" code="2"/>
  <JAXRConcept id="uuid:f1ef390d-08f1-ef39-3f48-e3438b38f908/3" name="Value 3"
      parent="uuid:f1ef390d-08f1-ef39-3f48-e3438b38f908" code="3"/>
  <JAXRConcept id="uuid:f1ef390d-08f1-ef39-3f48-e3438b38f908/4" name="Value 4"
      parent="uuid:f1ef390d-08f1-ef39-3f48-e3438b38f908" code="4"/>
  </JAXRClassificationScheme>
</PredefinedConcepts>
```

In order to use this file, a JAXR client application must contain the following line of code, which results in the definition of the custom classification being loaded from the file given by the value of the com.sun.xml.registry. userTaxonomyFilenames property:

```
System.setProperty("com.sun.xml.registry.userTaxonomyFilenames",
    "c:\\temp\\CustomScheme.xml");
```

The following command:

```
ant run-uddi-enum-client-step2
```

runs an example that sets the com.sun.xml.registry.userTaxonomyFilenames property as shown previously and uses the ClassificationScheme getDescendentConcepts() method to demonstrate that the four Concepts with values 1, 2, 3 and 4 listed in Example 7-13 have been created. It also uses the findConceptByPath() method to access one of the Concepts, as shown in Example 7-14.

Example 7-14. Using the getDescendentConcepts() and getConceptByPath() methods

```
// First find the classification scheme
ClassificationScheme scheme = bqm.findClassificationSchemeByName(null,
    "TestEnum");
if (scheme == null) {
    System.out.println("Please install the registry test data");
    System.exit(1);
}
System.out.println("Scheme id is " + scheme.getKey().getId());

// Now look for the Concepts
Collection coll = scheme.getDescendantConcepts();
System.out.print("Enumeration values: ");
Iterator iter = coll.iterator();
while (iter.hasNext()) {
    Concept c = (Concept)iter.next();
    System.out.print(c.getValue() + "  ");
}
System.out.println();

// Locate by path
String path = "/" + scheme.getKey().getId() + "/1";
Concept c = bqm.findConceptByPath(path);
if (c != null) {
    System.out.println("Located concept by path: value = " + c.getValue());
} else {
    System.out.println("Failed to locate concept by path");
}
```

The result of running this command should be:

```
Scheme id is uuid:f1ef390d-08f1-ef39-3f48-e3438b38f908
Enumeration values: 1  2  3  4
Located concept by path: value = 1
```

None of the code used in Example 7-14 is specific to the UDDI registry, and you can actually run the same example against the ebXML registry to demonstrate that the technique used in the previous section to programmatically create the same ClassificationScheme produces an identical result. You can try this using the command:

```
ant run-ebxml-enum-client.
```

Although this example creates a ClassificationScheme with a single hierarchy level, it is equally simple to produce one with more than one level by making appropriate use of the parent attribute of the JAXRConcept element. For example, Example 7-15 demonstrates how to add a Concept with the value 41 immediately below the one with the value 4.

Example 7-15. Adding an additional level to a ClassificationScheme

```
<PredefinedConcepts>
  <JAXRClassificationScheme id="uuid:f1ef390d-08f1-ef39-3f48-e3438b38f908"
    name="TestEnum">
    <JAXRConcept id="uuid:f1ef390d-08f1-ef39-3f48-e3438b38f908/1" name="Value 1"
      parent="uuid:f1ef390d-08f1-ef39-3f48-e3438b38f908" code="1"/>
    <JAXRConcept id="uuid:f1ef390d-08f1-ef39-3f48-e3438b38f908/2" name="Value 2"
      parent="uuid:f1ef390d-08f1-ef39-3f48-e3438b38f908" code="2"/>
    <JAXRConcept id="uuid:f1ef390d-08f1-ef39-3f48-e3438b38f908/3" name="Value 3"
      parent="uuid:f1ef390d-08f1-ef39-3f48-e3438b38f908" code="3"/>
    <JAXRConcept id="uuid:f1ef390d-08f1-ef39-3f48-e3438b38f908/4" name="Value 4"
      parent="uuid:f1ef390d-08f1-ef39-3f48-e3438b38f908" code="4"/>
    <JAXRConcept
      id="uuid:f1ef390d-08f1-ef39-3f48-e3438b38f908/41" name="Value 41"
      parent="uuid:f1ef390d-08f1-ef39-3f48-e3438b38f908/4" code="41"/>
  </JAXRClassificationScheme>
</PredefinedConcepts>
```

Note the following with regard to the line that has been added:

- The code attribute is set to 41, which is the required value for the new Concept.

- The parent attribute is set to the ID value of the Concept 4, which indicates that the new Concept should be a child of that Concept.

- The id attribute for the new Concept ends in /41 rather than /4/41. This is actually a matter of choice, and either would be valid. The IDs are not required to reflect the actual hierarchy, since that job is done by the parent attribute.

You can see more examples of the use of these XML elements by looking at the definition files that the JAXR provider for UDDI uses to create the NAICS, ISO-3166, and UNSPSC classification schemes. These can be found in the *jaxr-ri.jar* file for the JAXR reference implementation, at the following locations:

NAICS	*com\sun\xml\registry\common\tools\resources\naics.xml*
ISO 3166	*com\sun\xml\registry\common\tools\resources\iso3166.xml*
UNSPSC	*com\sun\xml\registry\common\tools\resources\unspsc.xml*

Postal Addresses

The JAXR API represents address information using the PostalAddress interface, which has attributes that map to the various parts of the address, such as street number, street name, and so on. Mapping this structure to an ebXML registry is simple, since its information model represents an address in exactly the same way. However, the UDDI registry does not have such a well-defined address structure. The UDDI information model stores address information in an address element, which may contain any number of nested addressLine elements. The information model specification does not define how individual addressLines are to be interpreted as street number, street, city, and so on. It does, however, allow two attributes to be associated with each addressLine that can be used to provide linkage between its content and the part of the original address to which it corresponds. The values that these attributes may take are, however, not defined within the specification. Instead, they are given meaning by an address scheme, which is itself referred to from the parent address element. Registries can therefore define their own (essentially arbitrary) address schemes, and as a result, it is not possible for a JAXR provider to implement a fixed mapping between the attributes of a PostalAddress object and the addressLines of the registry's address structure.

Example 7-16 shows an example of an address stored in a UDDI registry. Note that each address line has a keyName and a keyValue attribute. These attributes indicate what role the addressLine plays in the original address. To interpret each addressLine, you need to look at the address scheme referred to by the tModelKey attribute of the surrounding address element. In fact, the representation shown here is the default provided by a JAXR provider for UDDI, and the tModelKey attribute refers to a ClassificationScheme called PostalAddressAttributes that is defined within the provider itself.* You can think of this as the "reference" layout for addresses, as recognized by the JAXR provider in the reference implementation.

Example 7-16. A PostalAddress stored in a UDDI registry using the default JAXR address scheme

```
<address sortCode="" tModelKey="PostalAddressAttributes" useType="Headquarters">
    <addressLine keyName="StreetNumber" keyValue="StreetNumber">1005
        </addressLine>
    <addressLine keyName="Street" keyValue="Street">Gravenstein Highway North
        </addressLine>
    <addressLine keyName="City" keyValue="City">Sebastopol</addressLine>
    <addressLine keyName="State" keyValue="State">CA</addressLine>
    <addressLine keyName="PostalCode" keyValue="PostalCode">95472</addressLine>
    <addressLine keyName="Country" keyValue="Country">USA</addressLine>
</address>
```

---

* This ClassificationScheme is defined using the technique shown in "Creating User-Defined Classification Schemes and Enumerated Types," earlier in this chapter. You can find its definition in the file *jaxrconcepts.xml*, which is in the *com\sun\xml\registry\common\tools\resources* directory of the *jaxr-ri.jar* file.

The JAXR reference implementation also includes a definition for a second address ClassificationScheme called IBMDefaultPostalAddressAttributes. Using this scheme, the same address would be represented slightly differently, as shown in Example 7-17.

Example 7-17. A PostalAddress stored using the IBM postal address scheme

```
<address sortCode=""
    tModelKey="uuid:6EAF4B50-4196-11D6-9E2B-000629DC0A2B" useType="Headquarters">
    <addressLine keyName="StreetAddressNumber" keyValue="StreetAddressNumber">
1005</addressLine>
    <addressLine keyName="StreetAddress" keyValue="StreetAddress">
        Gravenstein Highway North</addressLine>
    <addressLine keyName="City" keyValue="City">Sebastopol</addressLine>
    <addressLine keyName="State" keyValue="State">CA</addressLine>
    <addressLine keyName="ZipCode" keyValue="ZipCode">95472</addressLine>
    <addressLine keyName="Country" keyValue="Country">USA</addressLine>
</address>
```

Note first that the tModelKey of the address element is different: the value shown in Example 7-17 is the UUID assigned to the IBMDefaultPostalAddressAttributes scheme within the registry. This indicates immediately that the addressLines within this element are not going to be encoded in the same way as they would be in the default JAXR representation, and, as you can see, there are some differences. For example, the addressLines that represent the street address and postal code attributes of the PostalAddress object have their keyValue attributes set to StreetAddress and ZipCode in this case, whereas in Example 7-16, the values Street and PostalCode are used.

Creating a representation of a registry addressing scheme

There are two problems for the JAXR provider: how to map the attributes of a given PostalAddress attribute to the proper set of addressLines for the UDDI registry that it is connected to, and, when reading an address from the registry, how to determine which PostalAddress attribute each addressLine corresponds to. The solution is to require the registry client to provide the information required to perform this mapping. Here's what the client is required to do:

1. Define the address scheme for the registry as a ClassificationScheme with one concept corresponding to each of the PostalAddress attributes that is stored by the registry's addressLine elements. The name and value attributes for each Concept are taken from the keyName and keyValue attributes of the addressLine element to which it corresponds.

2. Specify the mapping from the Concepts of the new address scheme to those of the default JAXR addressing scheme (which is a predefined Classification-Scheme called PostalAddressAttributes).

3. Include the UUID of the address ClassificationScheme as well as a representation of the Concept mapping in the Properties object supplied to the ConnectionFactory used to create the Connection to the registry.

The mapping that is created for a typical addressing scheme (in this case the IBM scheme used in Example 7-17) is shown in Figure 7-17. The blocks at the top of the diagram represent the ClassificationScheme and Concepts for the default JAXR addressing scheme. These are all predefined within the provider and cannot be renamed. The lower part of the diagram shows the ClassificationScheme and Concepts for the IBM addressing scheme, which is also predefined within the JAXR reference implementation. To create a mapping for a third-party addressing scheme, use the technique described earlier in "Creating User-Defined Classification Schemes and Enumerated Types" to define the ClassificationScheme hierarchy to the JAXR provider. The Concept names and values must be taken from the keyName and keyValue attributes that appear in the addressLine elements within the registry. In this case, you can see by reference to Example 7-17 that these should be StreetAddressNumber, StreetAddress, and so on. The arrows represent the relationship between these Concepts and those defined within the default JAXR addressing scheme.

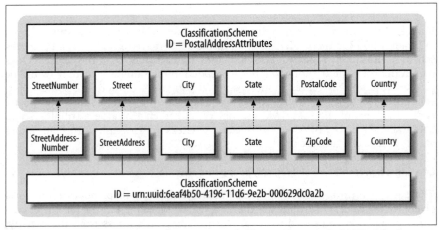

Figure 7-17. Creating a mapping from a registry address scheme to the JAXR default scheme

In order to activate this mapping, you need to set the following two properties in the Properties object passed to the ConnectionFactory:

javax.xml.registry.postalAddress
> Specifies the ID of the ClassificationScheme that represents the postal address scheme to be used for the registry.

javax.xml.registry.semanticEquivalences
> Specifies the mapping from the Concepts defined for the registry address scheme and the JAXR default postal addressing scheme. The format of this property is shown later in "Using the JAXR default PostalAddress scheme."

To see how the mapping information is used, consider what happens if the JAXR provider needs to create a PostalAddress object from the registry information shown in Example 7-17. First of all, notice that the tModelKey attribute of the address element contains the ID assigned to the IBM addressing scheme, as shown in the lower part of Figure 7-17. If this ID is supplied to the provider via the `javax.xml.registry.postalAddress` property, then it knows that it can use the mapping in the `javax.xml.registry.semanticEquivalences` property to map from the `keyName` and `keyValue` attributes in the `addressLine` elements to the `Concepts` that make up the standard JAXR addressing scheme.

For the example shown in Example 7-17, the first `addressLine` has `keyValue` `StreetAddressNumber`. Referring to Figure 7-17, you can see that this `Concept` corresponds to `StreetNumber` in the JAXR addressing scheme. (In reality, this match is made using the `javax.xml.registry.semanticEquivalences` property, as you'll see shortly.) The provider knows that the `StreetNumber` `Concept` corresponds to the `StreetNumber` attribute of the `PostalAddress` object, so it uses the value 1005 to set this attribute. The next `addressLine` has `keyValue` `StreetAddress`. This is mapped to the `Street` `Concept` of the JAXR addressing scheme; therefore, the value `Gravenstein Highway North` is assigned to the `Street` attribute of the `PostalAddress` object. The same procedure is used to map all of the `addressLines` to `PostalAddress` attributes, and is used in reverse when storing the content of a `PostalAddress` into the registry.

In summary, the way in which address information in the UDDI registry is translated into `PostalAddress` objects (and vice versa) depends on the settings of the `javax.xml.registry.postalAddressScheme` and `javax.xml.registry.semantic-Equivalences` properties in the `Properties` object associated with the `ConnectionFactory` at the time that the `Connection` object for the registry is created. The following sections show in more detail—and with specific examples—how the values of these properties affect the translation process, both when a `PostalAddress` is stored in the registry and when one is created as a result of loading an object from the registry. The explanations that follow make use of a client application supplied with the example source code for this book that stores a `PostalAddress` in the UDDI registry using the IBM addressing scheme. Before proceeding, you should make *chapter7\jaxr* your working directory and install the new `PostalAddress` using the following command:

```
ant run-postal-install-client
```

The address is stored by creating another `Organization` and including it as the address of its primary contact. The result of storing the address is shown in Example 7-18.

Example 7-18. A PostalAddress stored in a UDDI registry using an IBM registry address scheme

```
<address sortCode="1234"
    tModelKey="uuid:6EAF4B50-4196-11D6-9E2B-000629DC0A2B" useType="Headquarters">
    <addressLine keyName="StreetAddressNumber" keyValue="StreetAddressNumber">
        1005</addressLine>
    <addressLine keyName="StreetAddress" keyValue="StreetAddress">Gravenstein
        Highway North</addressLine>
    <addressLine keyName="City" keyValue="City">Sebastopol</addressLine>
    <addressLine keyName="State" keyValue="State">CA</addressLine>
    <addressLine keyName="ZipCode" keyValue="ZipCode">95472</addressLine>
    <addressLine keyName="Country" keyValue="Country">USA</addressLine>
</address>
```

As a result of installing this address, the registry now contains two copies of the address for O'Reilly & Associates. One is stored using the default JAXR addressing scheme, and the other is stored with the IBM scheme. There are two differences between the IBM representation of the address shown in Example 7-18 and the default JAXR representation in Example 7-16:

- The addressLine elements are different, since a different addressing scheme is used.
- The address element in Example 7-18 has the value 1234 associated with its sortCode attribute, while in Example 7-16, this attribute is empty. The sortCode attribute is part of the UDDI information model for addresses, but it is not mapped as an attribute in the JAXR PostalAddress interface. You can, however, supply a sortCode value by attaching a Slot to the PostalAddress, using the following code (which is used when creating the PostalAddress in Example 7-18). This is independent of the addressing scheme in use and could also have been done when the address in Example 7-16 was stored.

```
address.addSlot(blcm.createSlot(Slot.SORT_CODE_SLOT, "1234", null));
// Attach sortCode value
```

Mapping without a PostalAddress scheme

When the javax.xml.registry.postalAddressScheme property has not been set, the JAXR provider does not know how addresses are mapped within the registry. In this case, when populating a PostalAddress object with registry data, it makes no attempt to guess which addressLines might correspond to the various attributes of the PostalAddress object. Instead, it adds a Slot called Slot.ADDRESS_LINES_SLOT and stores the text from the addressLine elements as the Slot value (which, as described in "ExtensibleObject and Slots," earlier in this chapter, is a Collection). To try this out, use the command:

```
ant run-postal-none-client
```

Part of the output of this command is shown in Example 7-19.

Example 7-19. Retrieving a PostalAddress with no postal scheme installed

```
POSTAL ADDRESS for OReilly & Associates, Inc
    Street number:
    Street:
    City:
    State:
    Postcode:
    Country:

SLOTS:
    sortCode: ;
    addressLines: 1005; Gravenstein Highway North; Sebastopol; CA; 95472; USA;
```

As you can see, the PostalAddress attributes are all empty and the information retrieved from the registry is stored in its addressLines slot.

Storing a PostalAddress in a registry when no value has been set for the javax. xml.registry.postalAddressScheme property is slightly different. There are two cases to consider:

- A PostalAddress may have its own postal address scheme that overrides the default, which may be set using the PostalAddress setPostalScheme( ) method. If this is not null, then the address is stored according to that scheme.

- Otherwise, the PostalAddress is stored as if the JAXR default postal address scheme were in use. As a result, the address is mapped to the registry as shown in Example 7-16.

Using the JAXR default PostalAddress scheme

You can specify use of the default JAXR postal address scheme by setting the javax. xml.registry.postalAddressScheme and javax.xml.registry.semanticEquivalences properties as shown in Example 7-20.

Example 7-20. Specifying use of the default JAXR postal scheme

```
props.setProperty("javax.xml.registry.postalAddressScheme",
    "PostalAddressAttributes")
props.setProperty("javax.xml.registry.semanticEquivalences",
  "urn:uuid:PostalAddressAttributes/StreetNumber," +
  "urn:uuid:PostalAddressAttributes/StreetNumber|" +
  "urn:uuid:PostalAddressAttributes/Street," +
  "urn:uuid:PostalAddressAttributes/Street|" +
  "urn:uuid:PostalAddressAttributes/City," +
  "urn:uuid:PostalAddressAttributes/City|" +
  "urn:uuid:PostalAddressAttributes/State," +
  "urn:uuid:PostalAddressAttributes/State|" +
  "urn:uuid:PostalAddressAttributes/PostalCode," +
  "urn:uuid:PostalAddressAttributes/PostalCode|" +
  "urn:uuid:PostalAddressAttributes/Country," +
  "urn:uuid:PostalAddressAttributes/Country");
```

The value PostalAddressAttributes assigned to the javax.xml.registry. postalAddressScheme property selects the default addressing scheme. The value assigned to the other property simply sets up a direct equivalence between the default scheme and itself. It really should not be necessary to do this but, at least at the time of this writing, the JAXR reference implementation requires it. The format of the value assigned to this property will be described in the next section.

When this scheme is selected, all PostalAddress objects saved to the registry use the default JAXR mapping shown in Example 7-16.

When the provider receives address information from the registry, it inspects the tModelKey attribute of the address element. If it has the value PostalAddressAttributes, then the addressLines should have keyValue attributes that are consistent with the default postal address scheme—that is, they should be the same as those shown in Example 7-16. The content of the addressLines with keyValue attributes that are valid are mapped to the corresponding attributes of the PostalAddress object (that is, the value of the addressLine element with the keyValue attribute set to StreetNumber is mapped to the StreetNumber attribute, and so on). If the set of addressLines should, for some reason, contain one or more elements that have keyValue attributes that do not match the values of the Concepts in the PostalAddressAttributes classification scheme, then they are grouped together in a Collection and stored as the value of a Slot.ADDRESS_LINES_ SLOT slot that is added to the PostalAddress.

If you type the command:

```
ant run-postal-default-client
```

you'll see the results of loading two addresses from the registry with the default classification scheme selected. You'll notice that the PostalAddress object for O'Reilly & Associates is properly populated, since it was stored when the default scheme was selected. However, the other address was written to the registry using the IBM postal address scheme. Therefore, when it is retrieved, all of its addressLines are stored in the Slot.ADDRESS_LINES_SLOT slot, as shown in Example 7-21.

Example 7-21. Result of retrieving an address whose postal does not match the selected scheme

```
POSTAL ADDRESS for Another Organization
    Street number:
    Street:
    City:
    State:
    Postcode:
    Country:

SLOTS:
    sortCode: 1234;
    addressLines: 1005; Gravenstein Highway North; Sebastopol; CA; 95472; USA;
```

This output is actually the same as that shown in Example 7-19, which illustrates that the result of loading an address that uses a different postal address scheme from the one in use by the JAXR provider is the same as if a postal address scheme had not been selected at all. Even though this scheme has several addressLines that have keyValues that are valid for the default JAXR address scheme (such as City and Country), the values still do not appear in the PostalAddress object.

Using a different PostalAddress scheme

In order to select a nondefault postal address scheme, you need to properly initialize the same two properties. Example 7-22 shows how you would select the IBM postal address scheme.

Example 7-22. Specifying the use of the IBM postal address scheme

```
props.setProperty("javax.xml.registry.postalAddressScheme",
    "uuid:6EAF4B50-4196-11D6-9E2B-000629DC0A2B")
props.setProperty("javax.xml.registry.semanticEquivalences",
    "urn:uuid:PostalAddressAttributes/StreetNumber," +
```

```
"urn:uuid:6EAF4B50-4196-11D6-9E2B-000629DC0A2B/StreetAddressNumber|" +
"urn:uuid:PostalAddressAttributes/Street," +
"urn:uuid:6EAF4B50-4196-11D6-9E2B-000629DC0A2B/StreetAddress|" +
"urn:uuid:PostalAddressAttributes/City," +
"urn:uuid:6EAF4B50-4196-11D6-9E2B-000629DC0A2B/City|" +
"urn:uuid:PostalAddressAttributes/State," +
"urn:uuid:6EAF4B50-4196-11D6-9E2B-000629DC0A2B/State|" +
"urn:uuid:PostalAddressAttributes/PostalCode," +
"urn:uuid:6EAF4B50-4196-11D6-9E2B-000629DC0A2B/ZipCode|" +
"urn:uuid:PostalAddressAttributes/Country," +
"urn:uuid:6EAF4B50-4196-11D6-9E2B-000629DC0A2B/Country");
```

As before, the value of the javax.xml.registry.postalAddressScheme property must be the ID of the postal address scheme to be used; the value shown here is the UUID assigned to the IBM postal address scheme. The javax.xml.registry. semanticEquivalences property describes the mapping between the Concepts of the default JAXR postal address scheme and the one to be used. Its task is to describe the mapping shown diagrammatically in Figure 7-17. It is made up of a set of Concept pairs, in which each pair is separated from the other pairs by a vertical bar (|) character. Each pair is made up of two identifiers separated by a comma, where the first identifier is the path for the Concept in the default JAXR postal address scheme, and the second identifier is for the corresponding Concept in the target postal address scheme. For example, the following extract:

```
"urn:uuid:PostalAddressAttributes/StreetNumber," +
"urn:uuid:6EAF4B50-4196-11D6-9E2B-000629DC0A2B/StreetAddressNumber|" +
"urn:uuid:PostalAddressAttributes/Street," +
"urn:uuid:6EAF4B50-4196-11D6-9E2B-000629DC0A2B/StreetAddress|" +
```

maps the StreetAddressNumber Concept in the IBM address scheme to the StreetNumber Concept in the JAXR address scheme, and maps the IBM scheme's StreetAddress Concept to the JAXR scheme's Street concept.

If there are Concepts in the target address scheme that do not map to any of those in the default scheme, then they cannot be included. As a result, the corresponding addressLine is mapped to the Slot.ADDRESS_LINES_SLOT slot instead. As an example of this, if the target scheme includes an addressLine with a keyValue of District, which cannot be mapped to one of the standard Concepts, then it will not appear in the javax.xml.registry.semanticEquivalences property and its value will be stored in the slot (although the keyValue is lost). Similarly, if there is no addressLine in the target scheme that can be mapped to one or more of the standard Concepts (e.g., because the target scheme does not have a PostalCode equivalent), the entry for that Concept in the javax.xml.registry. semanticEquivalences property should be omitted, and the corresponding attribute in a PostalAddress object created from registry data will be empty.

When a nondefault scheme is active, all PostalAddress objects saved to the registry are mapped using the addressLines defined by that scheme, an example of which is shown in Example 7-18 in which the IBM postal address scheme is active. The results of loading a PostalAddress from the registry mirror those described in the last section.

- Addresses whose tModelKey attribute matches the ID of the selected postal address ClassificationScheme are mapped to PostalAddress attributes as described in the previous section.
- All other addresses are mapped directly to the Slot.ADDRESS_LINES_SLOT slot of an otherwise empty PostalAddress object.

The command:

```
ant run-postal-ibm-client
```

retrieves the same two addresses used in the previous section, but this time with the IBM address scheme selected. This time, the O'Reilly & Associates address, which was stored using the JAXR default address scheme, is unloaded into the Slot.ADDRESS_LINES_SLOT slot. The other address is decoded properly, since it was stored using the IBM postal address scheme.

Deleting Registry Objects

Objects in the registry can be deleted using one of the deleteObjects( ) methods provided by BusinessLifeCycleManager:

```
public BulkResponse deleteObjects(Collection keys) throws JAXRException;
public BulkResponse deleteObjects(Collection keys, String objectType) throws
JAXRException;
```

These methods remove the objects whose keys are supplied by the Collection argument. The first variant, which allows the deletion of an arbitrary set of objects, is supported only by level 1 providers. If you are using a level 0 provider, you need to use the second variant, which allows the removal of only a single type of object with each call. The type is supplied as the second argument, using one of the constants defined in the LifeCycleManager interface:

```
BulkResponse res = blcm.deleteObjects(keys, LifeCycleManager.ORGANIZATION);
```

BusinessLifeCycleManager also includes convenience methods that delete objects of specific types:

```
public BulkResponse deleteAssociations(Collection associationKeys)
    throws JAXRException;
public BulkResponse deleteClassificationSchemes(Collection schemeKeys)
    throws JAXRException;
public BulkResponse deleteConcepts(Collection conceptKeys)
    throws JAXRException;
public BulkResponse deleteOrganizations(Collection organizationKeys)
    throws JAXRException;
public BulkResponse deleteServiceBindings(Collection bindingKeys)
    throws JAXRException;
public BulkResponse deleteServices(Collection serviceKeys)
    throws JAXRException;
```

The BulkResponse returned by all of the deleteXXX( ) methods contains the keys for those objects that were successfully removed and a DeleteException for any that were not. An attempt to delete an object that is referenced by another object in the registry may succeed or may result in an InvalidRequestException, depending on the level of checking performed by the registry. Since the JAXR specification does not specify whether deletion of an object automatically results in the deletion of any related objects that are no longer referenced, it may be necessary (depending on the registry implementation) for application code to manually delete all Services attached to an Organization being deleted as well as all ServiceBindings for those Services, and so on.

It is important to note that the Collections passed to the deleteXXX( ) methods must contain the keys for the objects to be deleted, not the objects themselves. Some JAXR provider implementations (including the UDDI provider in the reference implementation) silently ignore elements of the Collection that are not of type Key, with the result that no objects are deleted and there is no error reported.

Level 1 Registry Features

Level 1 providers, such as those used with ebXML registries, provide additional functionality that can be used by client applications that do not need to be portable to all registry types. This section describes the most important of these additional features. Since the motivation for this functionality comes from ebXML, additional information can be found in the ebXML Registry Service specification, which can be obtained from the OASIS web site at *http://www.oasis-open.org*.

ExtrinsicObjects

ExtrinsicObjects are RegistryObjects that have associated data that is not of a type that is normally handled by the registry and is therefore stored in the repository rather than the registry itself. When creating an ExtrinsicObject, it is necessary to supply the data to be stored and the MIME type of that data. BusinessLifeCycleManager provides a method that allows an ExtrinscObject to be created:

```
public ExtrinsicObject createExtrinsicObject(DataHandler data)
    throws JAXRException;
```

The javax.activation.DataHandler passed to this method encapsulates both the data and its MIME type. As discussed in "Using a DataHandler" in Chapter 3, there are several ways to create a DataHandler, one of which uses a URL to point to the associated data. In this case, the MIME type of the data is obtained from the data source (e.g., an HTTP server) if it is available, or inferred from the data content or URL if possible. Once an ExtrinsicObject is created, the MIME type can be changed if necessary by calling the setMimeType( ) method, and new data can be installed by calling setRepositoryItem( ), passing a new DataHandler instance. If the data is not in a form in which it can be directly read by the registry (or application clients), perhaps because it is encrypted, the setOpaque( ) method should be called with the argument true to indicate this.

ExtrinsicObjects are often used in conjuction with SpecificationLinks to include service-related documentation in the repository, to be retrieved by users who locate the parent ServiceBinding. The following code extract shows how you might create an ExtrinsicObject to store a WSDL definition for a web service (in this case, the one offered by Amazon.com) in an ebXML registry and associate with it with a SpecificationLink:

```
ExtrinsicObject eObj = blcm.createExtrinsicObject(
    new DataHandler(new URL(
    "http://soap.amazon.com/schemas/AmazonWebServices.wsdl")));
SpecificationLink sLink = blcm.createSpecificationLink();
sLink.setName(blcm.createInternationalString("WSDL specification"));
sLink.setUsageDescription(sLink.getName());
sLink.setSpecificationObject(eObj);
```

RegistryPackages

A RegistryPackage is a container that allows arbitrary groupings of RegistryObjects to be created. Since a RegistryPackage is a RegistryObject, a RegistryPackage may contain another RegistryPackage. BusinessLifeCycleManager provides two methods that allow the creation of an empty RegistryPackage:

```
public RegistryPackage createRegistryPackage(String name)
    throws JAXRException;
public RegistryPackage createRegistryPackage(InternationalString name)
    throws JAXRException;
```

Objects can be added to and removed from the package either individually or in groups by using methods provided by the RegistryPackage interface. The getRegistryObjects() method returns a Collection containing all of the objects in the package. One possible use for a RegistryPackage is to group together all of the objects relating to an Organization so that they can be easily deleted:

```
BulkResponse res = package.getRegistryObjects();
ArrayList keys = new ArrayList();
Iterator iter = res.getCollection().iterator();
while (iter.hasNext()) {
    keys.add(((RegistryObject)iter.next()).getKey());
}
```

Object deprecation

The life cycle for RegistryObjects in a level 1 registry includes a *deprecated* state. In this state, the object continues to exist, but cannot be made the target of new links from other objects. An attempt to create a new link results in a JAXRException. Objects can be deprecated and undeprecated using the following LifeCycleManager methods:

```
public BulkResponse deprecateObjects(Collection keys) throws JAXRException;
public BulkResponse unDeprecateObjects(Collection keys)
    throws JAXRException;
```

Note that the Collections passed to these methods contain the keys for the objects whose state is to be changed, not the objects themselves.

Even though deprecation applies at the `RegistryObject` level, there is no way for a registry client to determine in advance whether a given object is deprecated, except in the case that the object is a `RegistryEntry`. To determine whether a `RegistryEntry` is deprecated, use the `getStatus()` method and test for the return value `RegistryEntry.STATUS_DEPRECATED`.

Auditing

The registry contains an audit trail that keeps a record of the following events relating to `RegistryObjects`:

- Creation
- Deletion
- Deprecation
- Undeprecation
- Updates, other than classification, being made the target of an `Assocation` or being added to or removed from a `RegistryPackage`
- Changes to the version numbers

The audit trail for a `RegistryObject` can be obtained by calling its `getAuditTrail()` method, which returns a `Collection` of objects of type `AuditableEvent`, each of which records the following information:

- The event type, as defined in the `AuditableEvent` interface. Object creation is recorded with type `AuditableEvent.EVENT_TYPE_CREATED`.
- The time at which the event occurred, which is available in the form of a `java.util.Date` object.
- The `RegistryObject` to which the event relates.
- The `User` object for the user that caused the event.

The code extract shown in Example 7-23 obtains and processes the complete audit trail for each `Organization` in the registry.

Example 7-23. Getting and processing the registry audit trail for an object

```
// Get the Organization entries
ArrayList namePatterns = new ArrayList();
namePatterns.add("%");
BulkResponse res = bqm.findOrganizations(null, namePatterns, null, null, null,
null);

// Process the results
Collection coll = res.getCollection();
if (!coll.isEmpty()) {
    Iterator iter = coll.iterator();
    while (iter.hasNext()) {
        Organization org = (Organization)iter.next();
        coll = org.getAuditTrail();
        System.out.println("Events for " + org.getName().getValue() +
            ": " + coll.size());
        Iterator aIter = coll.iterator();
```

Example 7-23. Getting and processing the registry audit trail for an object (continued)

```
        while (aIter.hasNext()) {
            AuditableEvent evt = (AuditableEvent)aItet.next();
            // Do something with "evt"
        }
    }
}
```

Since you cannot get a RegistryObject for an object that has been deleted, you cannot see the AuditableEvent that records the deletion by using the getAuditTrail() method. An alternate way to retrieve AuditableEvents is to exploit the fact that they are RegistryObjects and use the BusinessQueryManager getRegistryObjects() method, as shown in Example 7-24.

Example 7-24. Getting all AuditableEvents caused by the current user

```
BulkResponse    res = bqm.getRegistryObjects(LifeCycleManager.AUDITABLE_EVENT);
if (res != null) {
    coll = res.getCollection();
    System.out.println("Events for current user: " + coll.size());
    Iterator aIter = coll.iterator();
    while (aIter.hasNext()) {
        AuditableEvent evt = (AuditableEvent)aIter.next();
        // Do something with "evt"
    }
}
```

Since getRegistryObjects() returns only objects belonging to the authenticated user, you must have set valid credentials on the Connection object used to establish a connection to the registry. This code returns all AuditableEvents caused by the actions of the authenticated user, which will include those for object deletion.

Registry Security

Since a registry contains business-related information, it is important that its integrity is protected and that mechanisms are provided to ensure that only the legitimate owner of registry data is allowed to modify it. From the developer's viewpoint, the registry security model provided by the JAXR API is a particularly simple one that requires the provider and the registry itself to be responsible for providing and interpreting security tokens when necessary. The only obligations placed on the application developer are to choose an authentication method and to supply credentials that are acceptable to the target registry before obtaining the RegistryService object. This section briefly looks at the security features that may be offered by a registry and how the developer can make use of them.

Authorization

The rules regarding who can access and modify registry data are very simple:

- Any user is allowed to submit queries to the registry, and therefore read-only access requires no authorization checks to be made. It follows that there is no need for a client who does not intend to modify registry data to supply any kind of identifying information before accessing the registry.

- Operations that modify registry data can be performed only by properly authenticated users. Furthermore, with the possible exception of "super users" who might be required for administration purposes by some registries, registry objects can only be modified or deleted by the user that originally created them. In order to enforce these restrictions, write access to the registry requires that clients provide authentication information that link them to a predefined registry User. Objects created in the registry are associated with the User object of their creator; attempts to change or delete them are valid only if they are made from a client authenticated as the same User.

The way in which users are registered with a registry is registry-dependent. The public UDDI registries, for example, provide a web-based interface that allows you to sign up and obtain a username and password that enables you to enter registry data. In the case of an ebXML registry, the procedure is likely to be more complex because these registries use stronger, certificate-based authentication. The way in which a JAXR client supplies identification information to a registry is described later in "User authentication."

Confidentiality

While it might be acceptable for the results of registry query operations to be transmitted in-clear over public networks, it is less desirable for messages that contain usernames and passwords to be easily readable. In order to provide confidentiality, registries may require the use of HTTPS when write access to the registry is required. Since the JAXR API recognizes both a query URL and an update URL for any given registry, it is possible for a registry to provide an unauthenticated query service over HTTP, together with an authenticated and confidential update service that uses HTTPS as the transport mechanism. Since HTTPS encrypts messages in transit and includes a mechanism that can detect modification en route, it not only protects the integrity of the data being installed in the registry, but also ensures that the credentials supplied to authenticate the client are not readable by third parties.

From the point of view of a JAXR client developer, there is very little that you need to do in order to support the use of HTTPS connections to a registry. Most importantly, you need to ensure that the Java Secure Sockets Extension (JSSE) is installed on the client system. If you are using J2SE Version 1.4 or higher, then this requirement is already satisfied because JSSE is included. If not, then you need to download and install the JSSE extension from *http://java.sun.com*.

HTTPS uses public key certificates. During connection establishment, the registry server sends a certificate identifying itself. In order for the certificate to be recognized, either the certificate itself or that of its issuing Certificate Authority (CA) must already be installed in a trust store on the client system. Since the most commonly used CA certificates are included with the J2SE distribution, in most cases you will probably find that this requirement is automatically satisfied. If not, then you need to obtain and install in a local trust store the appropriate CA certificate. If the trust store you intend to use is not the default provided by J2SE, then you may need to set the javax.net.ssl.trustStore and javax.net.ssl.trustStorePassword system properties to those appropriate for your trust store. Information on installing certificates and setting up these properties can be found in "Using HTTPS" in Chapter 3.

User authentication

Different registries use different authentication mechanisms. A JAXR client is required to select an authentication method and set the javax.xml.registry.security.authenticationMethod property in the Properties object passed to the ConnectionFactory setProperties( ) method accordingly. The literal strings shown in the lefthand column of Table 7-6 are to be used to indicate the most common authentication methods. Note that the current JAXR specification does not define constant values to represent these strings.

Table 7-6. JAXR registry authentication mechanisms

Value	Meaning
UDDI_GET_AUTHTOKEN	An authentication scheme defined in the UDDI specification. The client supplies a username and password and obtains in return a token that is included by the client in each subsequent request that requires user credentials. Naturally, in order for this mechanism to offer any kind of security, it must be safeguarded against tampering. Therefore, HTTPS should be used as the underlying transport protocol.
HTTP_BASIC	The standard HTTP basic authentication scheme. The client supplies a username and password when challenged by the server. This type of authentication is carried out by the HTTP server itself. The registry server can obtain a Principal object for the validated user when handling a request that requires the caller's identity to be known.
CLIENT_CERTIFICATE	Uses a public key certificate as proof of identity. This is a much stronger security mechanism than those listed previously. It is used by ebXML registries.
MS_PASSPORT	Microsoft Passport authentication mechanism.

Providers are not required to implement all of these authentication mechanisms. In fact, it is only required to support the mechanism or mechanisms used by the registry type for which it is designed. At the time of this writing, the UDDI provider in the JAXR reference implementation supports only UDDI_GET_AUTHTOKEN, while the ebXML provider available from *http://ebxmlrr.sourceforge.net* recognizes only CLIENT_CERTIFICATE. If an unsupported authentication method is requested, the ConnectionFactory createConnection( ) method throws an UnsupportedCapabilityException.

Having selected an authentication method, the JAXR client must also supply appropriate credentials using the Connection setCredentials( ) method:

```
public void setCredentials(Collection credentials) throws JAXRException;
```

This call should be made before a RegistryService object is obtained. Changing credentials has no effect on any existing RegistryService object.

The argument passed to this method is a Collection that may contain objects of any kind. A provider is required to search the Collection to find objects that supply authentication information in a form that is consistent with the authentication method that has been selected by the javax.xml.registry.security.authenticationMethod property, and ignore all other content. This makes it possible for a JAXR client to create a Collection that contains credentials suitable for several different authentication methods. The JAXR specification specifies the form that the credentials supplied by the JAXR client must take for the UDDI_GET_AUTHTOKEN, HTTP_BASIC, and CLIENT_CERTIFICATE cases as described in the following paragraphs.

For the simple cases in which a username and password are required (i.e., UDDI_ GET_AUTHTOKEN and HTTP_BASIC), the credentials are supplied in the form of a java. net.PasswordAuthentication object. An object of this type can be created very easily, since the constructor requires only the username and password:

```
String user = "testuser";
String password = "testuserpassword";
PasswordAuthentication auth = new PasswordAuthentication(user,
    password.toCharArray( ));
```

In the CLIENT_CERTIFICATE case, an object of type javax.security.auth.x500. X500PrivateCredential must be provided. This object combines an X.509 public certificate with the corresponding private key as well as the alias used to retrieve it from a keystore. The code shown in Example 7-25 illustrates how to create such an object.*

Example 7-25. Creating an X500PrivateCredential object for certificate-based authentication

```
public static X500PrivateCredential getCredentials(String file, String alias,

String keyPassword, String storePassword) throws Throwable {
    KeyStore ks = KeyStore.getInstance("JKS");
    ks.load(new FileInputStream(file), storePassword.toCharArray( ));
    X509Certificate cert = (X509Certificate)ks.getCertificate(alias);
    PrivateKey key = (PrivateKey)ks.getKey(alias, keyPassword.toCharArray( ));
    return new X500PrivateCredential(cert, key, alias);
}
```

Supplying the certificate and private key is sometimes not sufficient. For example, at the time of this writing, the ebXML provider available from *http://ebxmlrr.sourceforge.net* also requires access to the keystore from which the certificate was obtained in order to obtain the complete certificate chain. Since the X500PrivateCredential object does not point to the keystore itself, its location is obtained from a property held in a configuration file that must be installed in your home directory. See "Using an ebXML Registry" earlier in this chapter for further information.

The arguments to be supplied to this method are as follows:

file

The full pathname of the keystore file in which the certificate and private key are found. If you create a self-signed certificate for testing purposes using the J2SE keytool command as described in "Using HTTPS" in Chapter 3, the value of this argument should be the full path to the file named with the -keystore command-line argument to keytool.

---

* This code can be found in the file *chapter7\util\src\ora\jwsnut\chapter7\util\Util.java* in the example source code for this book.

alias
> The alias under which the certificate is stored in the keystore. This is the same as the value of the -alias argument of the keytool utility.

keyPassword
> The password assigned to the private key. When creating a self-signed certificate, the private key is generated and stored in the keystore at the same time. The private key password required here is the same value as that supplied to keytool using its -keypass command-line argument.

storePassword
> The password required to access the keystore. This is the same value supplied to keytool using its -storepass argument.

8

Web Service Tools and Configuration Files

The Java Web Services Developer Pack and the J2EE platform include a number of command-line tools that can be used to create, configure, and administer web services. This chapter provides reference information for these tools and the configuration files that they use. In some cases, it is useful to refer to examples in order to illustrate how these tools are intended to be used. When this is the case, references are made to examples shown in earlier chapters of this book.

wscompile — JAX-RPC Stub and Tie Generation Utility

Availability

J2EE 1.4 reference implementation and Java Web Services Developer's Pack.

Synopsis

```
wscompile [options] config-file
```

Description

The wscompile utility is a tool supplied by the JAX-RPC reference implementation. It is driven by a configuration file (the format of which is shown in Examples 8-1 through 8-5) and a set of command-line options.

The basic function of wscompile is to generate and compile artifacts that are required to link a JAX-RPC client application or web service implementation to a particular JAX-RPC runtime. Like wscompile itself, these artifacts are implementation-dependent. Providing a tool that creates them removes the need for developers to concern themselves with the way in which these artifacts are constructed, and allows much of the complexity of the JAX-RPC infrastructure to be hidden.

Depending on the content of the configuration file and the command-line options supplied, wscompile may generate some or all of the following:

- A Java interface containing methods that correspond to the operations provided by the web service.

- A Web Service Description Language (WSDL) file that contains a definition of a web service expressed in a portable language- and platform-independent manner. A WSDL file is an XML document that may be imported into various development environments (such as Microsoft Visual Studio .NET) as a starting point for the generation of code that implements or interfaces with the service that it describes.

- A model file that provides a binary representation of the service in a form that can be used more efficiently by tools such as wscompile or wsdeploy than either a WSDL file or a Java interface definition.

- Client-side stub classes that act as proxies for the methods in the web service's interface definition.

- Server-side tie classes that mediate between a servlet and a web service implementation class.

- RPC structures that collect method call arguments and return values together. These are used internally by the JAX-RPC runtime to hold all of the information for a SOAP request or response message.

- Serializers and deserializers that convert between Java primitive and object types and their corresponding XML representations.

Although wscompile is capable of creating both client- and server-side artifacts, in most cases, it is used in connection with a web service client application. Artifact generation for the server side is usually performed as part of the preparation of a deployable web archive, using the wsdeploy utility or the J2EE 1.4 deploytool command.

Options

The operation of the wscompile utility is determined in part by its command-line options, of which exactly one of -gen, -define, and -import must appear. The behavior of this command is also partly determined by which of three elements (service, modelfile, and wsdl) appear in the configuration file. These elements are described in detail in the later section "Configuration File." The presence or absence of one of these elements may have an effect on the validity or meaning of the command-line options. When this is the case, it is noted along with the description of the options concerned.

-classpath *path*
-cp *path*
> Synonymous options that specify a semicolon- (Windows) or colon-separated (Unix) list of directories, as well as JAR and ZIP files that contain classes that are required in order to compile the client- or server-side artifacts created by wscompile. This option is typically used to supply the location of the compiled Java class files that represent the service endpoint interface when the configuration file contains a service element (see the later section "Configuration File"). It is not necessary to include the JAR files that contain the class files for the JAX-RPC reference implementation.

-d *directory*

The pathname of a directory below which compiled class files are placed (unless subject to the -nd option described later in this list). The specified directory must already exist. If this option is omitted, the working directory is used instead.

-define

This option may only be used when the configuration file contains a service element. It causes wscompile to construct its internal model of the service based on a Java interface definition, and writes a WSDL file describing the service to the directory indicated by the -nd option (see later in this list). This option can also be used together with -model as a way to create a model file without also generating stubs and/or tie classes.

-f:*featurelist*
-features:*featurelist*

Specifies a comma-separated list of suboptions that should be turned on. The available features are described later in the section "Features."

-g

Includes debugging information when compiling the generated Java source files.

-gen
-gen:client
-gen:server
-gen:both

Specifies whether artifacts for the client-side, server-side, or both are to be generated. The option -gen is equivalent to -gen:client. See "Generated Artifacts" later in this chapter for a description of what is generated in each case.

-httpproxy:*host[:port]*

Provides the host and port information for the HTTP proxy to be used when accessing external resources such as a WSDL definition or a schema document that it refers to. This option is not required when a direct connection can be made. The port, if not specified, defaults to 8080.

-import

Imports a service definition in the form of a WSDL document and generates the files listed later in the section "Generated Artifacts." This option can only be used when the configuration file contains a wsdl element.

-keep

Causes generated Java source files to be retained after compilation. By default, these files are deleted. If a WSDL file is generated, it is not deleted, even if the -keep option is not used.

-model *file*

Writes a copy of the internal representation of the web service—created from a Java interface definition or a WSDL document—to the given file. This file is in binary format and is typically created so that it can be supplied to wsdeploy via the *jaxrpc-ri.xml* file. A human-readable version of this file can be obtained by using the -Xdebugmodel option.

-nd *directory*

> Specifies the directory in which files that are not Java source files or compiled Java class files should be placed. This directory must already exist. By default, these files are placed in the directory specified using the -d option, or else in the working directory if that option is also not specified. Currently, only the generated WSDL file is placed in this directory.

-O

> Causes generated code to optimize when compiled.

-s *directory*

> Specifies the directory in which generated source files should be placed. This directory must already exist. If this option is not specified, these files are placed in the directory given by the -d option, or in the working directory if that option is also omitted. Generated source files are deleted once they are compiled unless the -keep option is used.

-verbose

> Prints extra messages that indicate what wscompile is doing.

-version

> Displays the version number of the wscompile utility in use and exits. Any other arguments are ignored.

-Xdebugmodel:*file*

> Writes a human-readable version of the model file for the service to the given file.

-Xprintstacktrace

> Causes stack traces to be printed for all exceptions encountered during execution of wscompile.

Configuration File

The wscompile utility uses an XML configuration file, typically called *config.xml*, to indicate where the definition of a web service may be found, and to provide additional information that may be required while generating and compiling the requested artifacts. A typical example of a configuration file is shown in Example 2-9 in Chapter 2.

The top-most element of the file is always a configuration element. This element may contain exactly one child element, which determines both the location of the web service definition and the form in which it is held. This element must be one of the following:

service

> Specifies that the service is defined by a Java interface

wsdl

> Specifies a service defined by a WSDL document

modelfile

> Specifies a service defined in a JAX-RPC model file

Each of these elements has its own set of attributes and child elements that can be used to control the actions taken by wscompile. All of the elements in the configuration file are defined in the XML namespace associated with the URI *http://java. sun.com/xml/ns/jax-rpc/ri/config*, which is usually assigned to be the default namespace.

The service element

This element is used when the web service endpoint interface is defined as a Java interface. The attributes and child elements permitted with the service element are shown in Example 8-1. Values must be supplied for all of these attributes.

Example 8-1. The service element in the wscompile configuration file

```
<service name="name" targetNamespace="URI" typeNamespace="URI"
        packageName="name">
  <interface name="name" servantName="className"
          soapAction="string" soapActionBase="string">
      <!-- Any number allowed -->
    <handlerChains>          <!-- 0 or 1 allowed -->
      <!-- handlerChains content shown later -->
    </handlerChains>
  </interface>
  <typeMappingRegistry>      <!-- 0 or 1 allowed -->
    <!-- typeMappingRegistry content shown later -->
  </typeMappingRegistry>
  <handlerChains>            <!-- 0 or 1 allowed -->
    <!-- handlerChains content shown later -->
  </handlerChains>
  <namespaceMappingRegistry> <!-- 0 or 1 allowed -->
    <!-- namespaceMappingRegistry content shown later -->
  </namespaceMappingRegistry>
</service>
```

The name attribute provides the name that is used when generating the Service interface and implementation class for this service. If this attribute has the value BookService, for example, then the generated interface is called BookService and the implementation class is called BookService_Impl. These classes, along with all of the others generated by wscompile, is placed in the package whose name is supplied by the packageName attribute.

The targetNamespace and typeNamespace attributes are used when constructing the logical WSDL definition for this service. Elements of the WSDL definition that would reside in the schema part (such as XML schema complex types created from value types included in the interface definition) are assigned the namespace given by the typeNamespace attribute, while those that would appear elsewhere (e.g., port names, operation names, message definitions, etc.) have the namespace given by the targetNamespace attribute.

Within the service element, there can be any number of interface elements, each of which maps a Java interface definition to a portType of the corresponding WSDL definition. Although it is possible to include more than one interface element in a service definition, the effects of doing so when the server-side artifacts are created are perhaps not what you would expect. Although the client-side artifacts correctly represent each interface element as a separate portType within the service, and the generated Service object has a method (such as getBookQueryPort( )) that returns an instance of the stub object for each interface, on the server side, each interface is effectively mapped as a separate service, in the sense that it has its own WSDL definition.

Of the attributes of the interface element, only name is mandatory, supplying the fully qualified name of the compiled Java interface that defines the endpoint methods. The servantName attribute supplies the name of the server-side implementation class for this interface. This attribute was meaningful during the early releases of the JWSDP when both the client-side and server-side artifacts were generated from one configuration file by a utility called xrpcc. In later releases, however, the server-side generation was taken over by the wsdeploy utility, which expects the servant name to be specified in the *jaxrpc-ri.xml* file. Therefore, this attribute is no longer used.

The optional soapAction and soapActionBase attributes can be used to determine the value of the SOAPAction header for the SOAP messages generated when the methods of this interface are invoked. There are three cases to consider:

- When neither of these attributes is specified, the SOAPAction header has the value " " (i.e., an empty string). This is the appropriate setting for a service that is also implemented using JAX-RPC, since JAX-RPC does not rely on the use of SOAPAction for message routing.

- If the soapAction attribute is set, then its value is used as the value of the SOAPAction header, and the value of the soapActionBase attribute is ignored.

- If the soapActionBase attribute is defined but soapAction is not, then the value of the SOAPAction header is formed by appending the operation name to the value of this attribute. For example, if this attribute has the value urn:actionBase/ and an interface method called getValue( ) is invoked, then the SOAPAction header of the request message for that method has the value urn:actionBase/getValue.

Each interface may have one nested handlerChains element. This element configures one or more SOAP message handlers that are activated whenever a request, response, or fault message is processed for any of the methods in the interface. The syntax of this element is described later in the section "The handlerChains element."

Following the interface elements, the schema definition allows a typeMappingRegistry element, a handlerChains element, and a namespaceMappingRegistry element. Only one instance of each of these elements is permitted. Although allowed by the schema definition, the namespaceMappingRegistry element is ignored, as is the handlerChains element. Handler chains should instead be configured by nesting the handlerChains element inside the interface element. The syntax and meaning of each of these elements are described later in this section.

The wsdl element

The wsdl element is used in place of service when the service definition is contained in a WSDL document rather than framed in terms of Java classes. You are likely to use this element when constructing clients for web services implemented by third parties. The syntax of this element is shown in Example 8-2.

Example 8-2. The wsdl element in the wscompile configuration file

```
<wsdl location="URI" packageName= "name">
  <typeMappingRegistry>          <!-- 0 or 1 allowed -->
    <!-- typeMappingRegistry content shown later -->
  </typeMappingRegistry>
  <handlerChains>                <!-- 0 or 1 allowed -->
    <!-- handlerChains content shown later -->
  </handlerChains>
  <namespaceMappingRegistry>  <!-- 0 or 1 allowed -->
    <!-- namespaceMappingRegistry content shown later -->
  </namespaceMappingRegistry>
</wsdl>
```

The location attribute is usually a URL that can be used to fetch the WSDL document, but may also be the pathname of a file. The packageName attribute supplies the name of the Java package in which the generated artifacts are placed by default. It is possible to arrange for code to be placed in different packages based on the XML namespace of the item from which it is generated by using the namespaceMappingRegistry element, which is described later in this section. The typeMappingRegistry and handlerChains elements can be used to modify the type mapping registry and the set of SOAP handlers associated with the endpoints generated from the WSDL document, as described later in the sections "The typeMappingRegistry element" and "The handlerChains element."

The modelfile element

This element is used when the service definition resides in a model file created by a previous invocation of wscompile. The modelfile element has a single (mandatory) attribute and may not have any child elements:

```
<modelfile location="URI"/>
```

The URI specifies the location of the model file and may be either a URL or the pathname of a file.

The handlerChains element

A handlerChains element configures a chain of SOAP message handlers for either or both of the client and server side of a web service endpoint. It may be used in both the *config.xml* file and the *jaxrpc-ri.xml* file, which is discussed in conjunction with the wsdeploy utility, later in this chapter. The syntax of this element is shown is Example 8-3.

Example 8-3. The handerChains element

```
<handlerChains>
  <chain runAt="client|server" roles="URI list">    <!-- 0, 1 or 2 allowed -->
    <handler className="name" headers= "QName list"> <!-- Any number allowed -->
      <property name="name" value= "value"/>         <!-- Any number allowed -->
    </handler>
  </chain>
</handlerChains>
```

A handlerChain element may contain up to two nested chain elements, in which one must have the runAt element set to the value client, and the other set to the value server. The wscompile utility processes the appropriate entry depending on whether it is generating client- or server-side artifacts.

The roles attribute of the chain element contains a space-separated list of URIs representing the SOAP actors on behalf of which the SOAP message handlers (see "SOAP Header Processing" in Chapter 6) in the chain can act. If this attribute is omitted, it is assumed that the chain acts on behalf of the SOAP actor next and the ultimate recipient of the message. SOAP message handlers have complete access to a SOAP request message before it is transmitted, as well as to SOAP response and fault messages before they are processed as method call replies. A message handler typically adds or removes and processes SOAP header blocks, but may also inspect or modify the message body.

The SOAP message handlers in a chain are added as children of the chain element. Each handler element has a mandatory className attribute that supplies the name of the Java class that contains the handler implementation. This class must provide a public, no-argument constructor and implement the javax.xml.rpc.handler. Handler interface. The optional headers attribute is a space-separated list of QNames for the headers that the handler can process. Each QName consists of a namespace prefix and a local element part, such as tns:SecurityHeader. The namespace prefix must be defined and associated with a URI on this element or on one of its parents. If this attribute is omitted, the handler makes no statement about the set of headers it can handle. For a description of the way in which this attribute is used, refer to "Headers, roles, and the mustUnderstand attribute" in Chapter 6.

Configuration information may be passed to a handler using one or more nested property elements. The values configured here are made available to the handler implementation class when it is initialized in the form of a java.util.Map.

The typeMappingRegistry element

The typeMappingRegistry element is used to add serializers and deserializers to the type mapping registry associated with each service endpoint interface. This element may contain up to three child elements that modify the type mapping registry in different ways. The syntax of this element is shown in Example 8-4.

Example 8-4. The typeMappingRegistry element

```
<typeMappingRegistry>
  <import> <!-- 0 or 1allowed -->
    <schema namespace="URI" location="URI"/> <!-- Any number allowed -->
  </import>
  <typeMapping encodingStyle="URI">          <!-- Any number allowed -->
    <entry schemaType="QName" javaType="type"
                serializerFactory="className" deserializerFactory=
                        "className"/>        <!-- Any number allowed -->
  </typeMapping>
  <additionalTypes> <!-- 0 or 1 allowed -->
    <class name="className"/>                <!-- Any number allowed -->
  </additionalTypes>
</typeMappingRegistry>
```

The import element can be used to import types from one or more external schema documents, the location of which is provided by the location attribute. The types are imported into the namespace given by the namespace attribute, which should match the targetNamespace attribute of the schema element in the document itself, but may not be the same as either the targetNamespace or typeNamespace of the service element within which this element is nested.

The typeMapping element is used to install (probably custom) explicitly named serializers and deserializers to be used when encoding and decoding SOAP elements with the encoding style specified using the encodingStyle attribute. Typical values for this attribute are *http://schemas.xmlsoap.org/soap/encoding/*, which represents SOAP section 5 encoding rules, and " ", which represents literal encoding. The nested entry elements each create a mapping between a Java type given by the javaType attribute and a corresponding XML schema type specified by the schemaType attribute. The mapping indicates the factories to be used to get serializer and deserializer classes that are to perform the conversion between the Java type and the XML representation given by the schema type, or vice versa. Since there is currently no way to write portable serializers and deserializers (and the API for creating these objects in the reference implementation is not public), it is unlikely that this element will be frequently used.

The additionalTypes element is used to arrange for serializers and deserializers for specified Java types to be generated and included in the type mapping registry. Each nested class element causes an additional serializer/deserializer pair to be included. For example, the following extract arranges for serializers for one- and two-dimensional arrays of strings to be added to the registry:

```
<additionalTypes>
    <class name="java.lang.String[ ]"/>
    <class name="java.lang.String[ ][ ]"/>
</additionalTypes>
```

It is not necessary to use this element to include serializers and deserializers for types that are explicitly referred to in the service endpoint interface (i.e., appear as method parameters or return types). For a discussion of this subject, refer to "Serialization and Type Mappings" in Chapter 6.

This element is permitted with both the service and wsdl elements, but is ignored when used with the wsdl element.

The namespaceMappingRegistry element

The namespaceMappingRegistry element can be used to create a set of mappings from XML namespaces to Java packages. The format of this element is shown in Example 8-5.

Example 8-5. The namespaceMappingRegistry element

```
<namespaceMappingRegistry>
  <namespaceMapping namespace="URI" packageName= "name"/>
      <!-- Any number allowed -->
</namespaceMappingRegistry>
```

Although the schema allows this element to appear within either a service or wsdl element, it is actioned only when used with a wsdl element. By default, the packageName attribute of the wsdl element determines where all generated classes are placed in the package hierarchy. Using the namespaceMapping element, you can individually assign generated artifacts to packages based on their owning namespace. This is particularly useful if your WSDL document imports one or more XML schemas and you would like to logically separate the implementation classes for the types obtained from these schemas from each other and/or from your own schema types.

As an example of the use of this element, consider the following *config.xml* file:

```
<configuration
    xmlns="http://java.sun.com/xml/ns/jax-rpc/ri/config">
    <wsdl location="http://localhost:8080/Books/BookQuery?WSDL"
          packageName="ora.jwsnut.chapter6.wsdlbookservice">

        <namespaceMappingRegistry>
            <namespaceMapping namespace=
                "urn:jwsnut.chapter2.bookservice/types/BookQuery"
                packageName="ora.jwsnut.chapter2.bookserviceTypes"/>
        </namespaceMappingRegistry>
    </wsdl>
</configuration>
```

The WSDL document imported in this case has a targetNamespace of urn:jwsnut. chapter2.bookservice/wsdl/BookQuery, while its nested schema element uses the namespace urn:jwsnut.chapter2.bookservice/types/BookQuery. The effect of this mapping is to place all classes generated from the targetNamespace of the WSDL document into the package ora.jwsnut.chapter6.wsdlbookservice, and all of those whose namespace is taken from the nested schema into the package ora. jwsnut.chapter2.bookserviceTypes. Without the mapping, all of the generated classes would have been placed in the package ora.jwsnut.chapter6. wsdlbookservice.

Generated Artifacts

The artifacts generated by wscompile depend on its command-line arguments and the content of the configuration file. Table 8-1 summarizes what might be created based on whether wscompile is being run to create client-side or server-side artifacts or to import a WSDL service definition. If the -gen:both option is used, then the artifacts listed in both the -gen:client and -gen:server columns are created.

Table 8-1. Artifacts generated by the wscompile utility

Artifact	-gen:client	-gen:server	-import
Stubs	✓		
Service interface	✓		
Service implementation class	✓		
Ties		✓	
WSDL document[a]		✓	

Table 8-1. Artifacts generated by the wscompile utility (continued)

Artifact	-gen:client	-gen:server	-import
Serializers/deserializers	✓	✓	
Java service endpoint interface[b]	✓	✓	✓
Java service endpoint interface template class[c]			✓
Custom classes	✓	✓	✓
RPC structures[d]	✓	✓	✓

[a] A WSDL document is not generated if the configuration file contains a `wsdl` element.
[b] The Java interface is not generated if the configuration file contains a `service` element.
[c] This is a class that provides dummy implementations of each method in the service endpoint interface. It is intended to be used as a starting point for an actual implementation.
[d] Creation of these files can be suppressed by using the `-f:norpcstructures` option.

Naturally, wscompile does not output copies of files that are supplied as input. Hence, no WSDL document is generated when the configuration file contains a wsdl element, and a Java interface is not required when one is supplied by an interface element.

When Java classes are generated, the source code is placed below the directory supplied by the -s option, but is deleted following compilation if the -keep option is not used. Compiled Java class files appear below the directory indicated by the -d argument. The WSDL document is placed in the same directory, but may be redirected to another location using the -nd option.

All serializers/deserializers appear in the same location as the objects that they serialize or deserialize. This includes the serializers/deserializers for SOAP messages, which are placed together with the stub or tie class implementations that they correspond to.

Features

Certain wscompile features can be enabled or disabled using the -f argument, which requires a comma-separated list of items from those listed in the following list. For example:

```
wscompile -f:datahandleronly,explicitcontext ......
```

This enables explicit binding of SOAP message headers to method arguments, and suppresses the mapping of attachments to specific Java classes.

datahandleronly
    Causes the content of attachments to be mapped to a method argument of type DataHandler. When this feature is not turned on, certain attachment types are mapped to Java types such as Image or javax.xml.transform.Source. See "Using Attachments" in Chapter 6 for a list of these special types.

explicitcontext
    Causes message parts assigned to the SOAP message header to appear as additional method arguments in the Java service endpoint interface generated from a WSDL document. See "Mapping Header Content to Method Arguments" in Chapter 6 for further details.

Tools and Configuration

`infix=<name>`

> Specifies a string to be included in the name of generated serializers. For example, if the option `-f:infix=value` is used, then the name of the serializer class for a value type called `BookInfo` is `BookInfo_value_SOAPSerializer` instead of `BookInfo_SOAPSerializer`.

`nodatabinding`

> Requests that the binding of message content to method arguments and return values that is performed for document/literal operations be suppressed. If you use this option, you will need to use the SAAJ API to construct a `SOAPElement` containing the XML to be placed in the body of each request message and decode the response, which will be returned as a `SOAPElement`. See "Suppressing the mapping of message content to method arguments" in Chapter 6 for an example of the use of this feature.

`noencodedtypes`

> This feature causes the `xsi:type` attribute that appears by default in the SOAP encoding of arrays and value types to be suppressed. The SOAP section 5 encoding rules allow this attribute to be omitted if the type of the enclosed data can be discovered by reference to a schema. As an example of the difference that this makes, a value type that is encoded like this by default:

```
<ns0:BookInfo id="ID1" xsi:type="ns0:BookInfo">
    <editor xsi:type="xsd:string">Paula Ferguson, Robert Eckstein</editor>
    <author xsi:type="xsd:string">David Flanagan</author>
    <price xsi:type="xsd:double">39.95</price>
    <title xsi:type="xsd:string">Java in a Nutshell</title>
</ns0:BookInfo>
```

> looks like this when `noencodedtypes` is specified:

```
<ns0:BookInfo id="ID2">
    <editor xsi:type="xsd:string">Paula Ferguson, Robert Eckstein</editor>
    <author xsi:type="xsd:string">David Flanagan</author>
    <price xsi:type="xsd:double">39.95</price>
    <title xsi:type="xsd:string">Java in a Nutshell</title>
</ns0:BookInfo>
```

> Note that the `xsi:type` attribute still appears in the encoding of the basic XML schema data types that make up this object.

`nomultirefs`

> Certain values (such as arrays) are encoded into a SOAP message as multireference values—that is, the value is serialized as an independent entity with an associated identifier, which is then referenced from within the message using an element with an `href` attribute whose value matches the value's identifier. If the same value is used more than once within a message, the use of space is reduced by serializing only one copy and including only a reference to it wherever it should appear. When the `nomultirefs` feature is enabled, all types appearing in the message body are serialized inline instead of using references.

`norpcstructures`

> Switches off the output of Java classes that are used to group together parameters and return values for the methods of the service endpoint interface. These classes are used internally by the JAX-RPC runtime. Typically, you

would use this option in conjunction with -import to obtain from a WSDL file only the Java classes that define the service endpoint interface—without also creating the RPC structures, which are not part of the service interface.

novalidation

Switches off validation of the WSDL document when the wsdl element is used. Using this feature can reduce the execution time of wscompile when the WSDL document is already known to be valid.

searchschema

Causes wscompile to generate serializers/deserializers and Java classes for *all* types that appear in the schema associated with a WSDL document, whether or not they are explicitly referenced as parts in the message definitions within the document. This feature should be used when creating client-side artifacts from a WSDL definition if there are messages that are defined in terms of abstract types, but where instances of derived types are actually used as inputs or outputs, which are not themselves explicitly named in the message definitions.

serializeinterfaces

At the time of this writing, use of this feature has no effect.

wsdeploy — JAX-RPC Deployable Web Archive Generation Utility

Availability

Java Web Services Developer's Pack. The nearest equivalents for the J2EE 1.4 platform are the deploytool and j2eec utilities described later in this chapter.

Synopsis

```
wsdeploy [options] sourceWarFile
```

Description

The wsdeploy utility is a command-line tool supplied by the JAX-RPC reference implementation in the JWSDP. Its purpose is to create a web archive (WAR) file that can be deployed into a web container (in which the server-side components of the reference implementation are already installed) from a WAR file that contains implementation-independent components together with configuration information. The location of the source WAR file is provided as a command-line argument. This file must contain the following:

- The Java classes that define the service endpoint interface (or interfaces) for the web service. These classes typically appear in the */WEB-INF/classes* directory of the archive.

- The classes that provide the server-side implementation of the service endpoint interfaces, together with any other classes and resources (e.g., images, sound files, text files) that they depend upon. These classes and resources are placed in the */WEB-INF/classes* directory of the archive, or in the */WEB-INF/ lib* directory if they are packaged in JAR files.

- A partial *web.xml* file for the web application that hosts the web service. This file must appear in the */WEB-INF* directory.

- A configuration file (called *jaxrpc-ri.xml*) from which `wsdeploy` obtains the information necessary to create the deployable WAR file. This file must appear in the */WEB-INF* directory.

- Optionally, a model file created by `wscompile` that provides additional information to `wsdeploy`.

Separating the process of creating the runtime artifacts required by a specific JAX-RPC server-side implementation from the process of implementing the web service makes it possible for developers to create a single WAR file that can then be processed by different vendor tools to create a deployable archive for any number of target environments. In practice, each such tool is likely to require vendor-specific information to complete the deployment. In the case of `wsdeploy`, this information is provided in the *jaxrpc-ri.xml* file, which must be placed in the */WEB-INF* directory of the source WAR file and optionally by a model file, the location of which is specified within the *jaxrpc-ri.xml* file. A portable WAR file that is capable of being processed by more than one vendor's deployment tools would need to supply vendor-dependent information for each tool.

The `wsdeploy` utility is part of the JWSDP. It is not included in the reference implementation of J2EE 1.4, which uses the J2EE `deploytool` utility to deploy web services instead.

Note that, despite what its name might imply, `wsdeploy` does not actually deploy the WAR file that it creates. This step must be performed using the deployment tools provided by the target application server or web container.

Options

The behavior of the `wsdeploy` utility can be controlled to a limited extent using command-line options. Use of the -o option to specify the full pathname of the deployable WAR file is mandatory; all of the other options are truly optional.

-classpath *path*
-cp *path*

> Synonymous options that specify a semicolon- (Windows) or colon-separated (Unix) list of directories, JAR, and ZIP files that contain classes that are required in order to compile the artifacts created by `wsdeploy`. It is not necessary to include the JAR files that contain the class files for the JAX-RPC reference implementation.

-keep

> Causes temporary files generated by `wsdeploy` to be retained. By default, these files are deleted. Temporary files are placed in a system-dependent location, or in the directory given by the -tmpdir option, which is typically used in conjunction with -keep.

-o *targetWarFile*

> Supplies the full pathname of the deployable WAR file that `wsdeploy` creates. If this file already exists, it is overwritten. The directory in which the WAR file is placed must already exist. This option must be supplied.

-tmpdir *dirName*
> Causes wsdeploy to use the given directory, which must already exist, as the location for its temporary files. If this option is not used, a system-dependent temporary directory is chosen instead. This option is commonly used with -keep in order to retain temporary files for inspection once wsdeploy exits.

-verbose
> Prints extra messages that indicate what wsdeploy is doing.

-version
> Displays the version number of the wsdeploy utility in use and exits. Any other arguments are ignored.

Configuration File

The wsdeploy utility uses a configuration file called *jaxrpc-ri.xml*, which must be placed in the */WEB-INF* directory of the source archive, to obtain information about the service endpoints of the web service for which it will create a deployable web archive file. All of the elements in the *jaxrpc-ri.xml* file are defined in the XML namespace associated with the URI *http://java.sun.com/xml/ns/jax-rpc/ri/dd*, which is usually assigned to be the default namespace.

The general form of the *jaxrpc-ri.xml* file is shown in Example 8-6 and a typical example will be found in Example 2-15 in Chapter 2.

Example 8-6. The jaxrpc-ri.xml file

```
<webServices version="1.0"
             targetNamespaceBase="URI"
             typeNamespaceBase="URI"
             urlPatternBase= "/base">
    <!-- Nested endpoint elements -- shown later -->
    <!-- Nested endpointMapping elements -- shown later -->
</webServices>
```

The webServices element is always the top-level element in the *jaxrpc-ri.xml* file. The version attribute is required and, at the time of this writing, must have the value "1.0".

The targetNamespaceBase and typeNamespaceBase attributes supply URIs from which the namespaces for the elements and types associated with the web services in the WAR file are generated. The namespaces for a specific endpoint are formed by appending the endpoint name to the corresponding base name. For example, if the targetNamespaceBase attribute is set to *urn:jwsnut.chapter2.bookservice/wsdl/*, then the actual target namespace for a nested endpoint called BookQuery is *urn:jwsnut.chapter2.bookservice/wsdl/BookQuery*. This *must* match the targetNamespace attribute assigned in the configuration file supplied to wscompile when creating the client-side artifacts. However, if the endpoint element contains a model attribute (see later in this chapter), both the targetNamespace and typeNamespace are taken from the model file rather than by derivation from the attributes of the webServices element, thus ensuring that the client and server agree.

The typeNamespaceBase and targetNamespaceBase attributes may be omitted if each endpoint element in the file has a valid model attribute.

The urlPatternBase attribute is a partial URI used to create the servlet path for those endpoints defined in the *jaxrpc-ri.xml* file that do not have a corresponding endpoint mapping. See "The endpointMapping element" later in this chapter for further information. This attribute may be omitted if each endpoint element has a matching endpointMapping element.

The endpoint element

The endpoint element defines a single service endpoint interface within a web service. Each endpoint therefore corresponds to a single Java interface. A webServices element may contain more than one endpoint element, in which case each is effectively treated as a separate web service, in the sense that each has its own WSDL definition that defines a service containing that endpoint as its only port. All of the endpoints are, however, managed by the same servlet.

The format of the endpoint element is shown in Example 8-7.

Example 8-7. The endpoint element in the jaxrpc-ri.xml file

```
<endpoint name= "name"
          displayName= "name"
          description= "text"
          imp;lementation= "className"
          interface="className"
          model= "modelFile">
    <!-- Optional nested handlerChains element -->
</endpoint>
```

The required name attribute supplies the endpoint name, which should be unique within the file. This name may be used in conjunction with the urlPatternBase attribute of the webServices element to generate the URL used to access the endpoint, or as a key to obtain the URL from the corresponding endpointMapping element if there is one (as described shortly). The optional displayName and description elements supply text that describe the endpoint. At the time of this writing, this information does not appear to be used.

The required implementation attribute supplies the fully qualified name of the web service implementation class (or *servant* class). This class must implement the methods of the service endpoint interface and must be present in the portable WAR file supplied to wsdeploy.

The required interface attribute supplies the fully qualified name of the Java class that defines the web service endpoint interface. This class must also be present in the portable WAR file.

The optional model attribute can be used to pass a model file created by wscompile to wsdeploy. The model file can reside anywhere in the portable WAR file, but is typically placed in the */WEB-INF* directory. The value of this attribute gives the location of the model file relative to the archive. A typical value would, therefore, be */WEB-INF/model*. If this attribute is omitted, wsdeploy builds a model file based on the service endpoint interface definition referred to by the interface attribute.

If a model file is not supplied, wsdeploy introspects the Java service endpoint interface definition to discover its methods and the types of its parameters in order to generate the necessary server-side ties and any necessary serializers and deserializers. When a model file is used, this information is obtained directly from the model file. Circumstances under which you would need to supply a model file include the following:

- The endpoint interface was originally derived from a WSDL document and you want to preserve the method argument names in the generated code rather than use the type-based names (such as String_1) obtained by introspecting the Java interface definition.

- The endpoint interface was originally derived from a WSDL document and contains document-style operations. See "RPC-Style and Document-Style JAX-RPC" in Chapter 6 for an example.

- The type information that can be deduced from the Java interface definition is not sufficient to generate all of the necessary serializers. A typical example of this is the use of abstract types or interfaces in method definitions. In such cases, you use a typeMappingRegistry element containing one or more additionalTypes elements in the wscompile configuration file when creating the client-side artifacts. Since the *jaxrpc-ri.xml* file does not provide a typesMappingRegistry element, this information must be obtained from the model file created by wscompile. See "Serialization and Type Mappings" in Chapter 6 for an example.

An endpoint element may contain a nested handlerChains element that configures a server-side chain of SOAP message handlers for the endpoint. The format and use of this element are described in "The handlerChains element" in the description of the wscompile utility, earlier in this chapter.

The endpointMapping element

This optional element specifies the URL mapping for an endpoint configured using an endpoint element. Its format is shown in Example 8-8.

Example 8-8. The endpointMapping element in the jaxrpc-ri.xml file

```
<endpointMapping endpointName="name" urlPattern="pattern"/>
```

The endpointName attribute matches with the value of the name attribute of the endpoint element for which it supplies the URL mapping. The value of the urlPattern attribute is appended to the context URL for the hosting web application to give the full URL for the endpoint to which this element relates. For example, in a web application deployed at the URL *http://localhost:8080/Books*, the following mapping:

```
<endpointMapping endpointName= "BookQuery" urlPattern= "/MyBookQuery"/>
```

makes the BookQuery endpoint interface available at the URL *http://localhost:8080/Books/MyBookQuery*. If an endpoint element does not have a corresponding endpointMapping, the URL is formed as follows:

```
context-URL + "/" + urlPatternBase + "/" + endpointName
```

For example, for an endpoint called BookQuery defined within a webServices element for which the urlPatternBase attribute has the value /base, the endpoint URL is *http://localhost:8080/Books/base/BookQuery*.

Target Web Archive File Content

The web archive created by wsdeploy contains the items described in the following sections.

Original class files and resources

The class files, resource files, and JAR files that appear in the original WAR file are copied unchanged into the deployable WAR file.

Tie and serializer/deserializer classes

The wsdeploy utility creates a tie class for each endpoint and the appropriate serializer/deserializer classes for each value type defined in the endpoint interface and for the SOAP request and response messages that will be used. For a discussion of the function of tie classes, see "Server-side architecture" in Chapter 2.

These classes are all placed in the same package as the Java interface definition for the corresponding endpoint. Following compilation, they appear below the */WEB-INF/classes* directory of the web archive.

Model file

If the endpoint element in the *jaxrpc-ri.xml* file contains a model attribute, then the referenced model file is copied into the deployable web archive. Otherwise, a model file is created based on introspection of the Java interface definition and placed in the */WEB-INF* directory. The model file is called *name_model.xml.gz*, where *name* is the value of the name attribute of the endpoint element.

WSDL document

A WSDL definition describing each endpoint is created and placed in a file called *name.wsdl* in the */WEB-INF* directory, where *name* is the value of the name attribute of the endpoint element. Note that a service with multiple endpoints will have the same number of generated WSDL documents, each describing a service with a single port.

Deployment descriptors

Two files containing deployment information are placed in the */WEB-INF* directory of the output WAR file: *web.xml* and *jaxrpc-ri-runtime.xml*.

The *web.xml* file is derived from the skeleton version of the file included in the portable WAR file. Certain elements of the input file are preserved, while others are added (or replaced if they were originally specified).

The principal reason why wsdeploy utility modifies the *web.xml* file is to create the appropriate URL mappings for each web service endpoint, and to associate the

---

hosting web application with JAXRPCServlet, which is the servlet provided by the reference implementation that handles the dispatching of received SOAP messages to the appropriate tie classes. The original *web.xml* file is not required to contain the elements that accomplish these tasks, because the association with JAXRPCServlet is implementation-dependent. When deploying the web service in another vendor's server implementation, a different servlet might be used and additional information might need to be included.

For example, Example 8-9 shows a typical set of elements added to the *web.xml* file during the deployment of a web service with a single endpoint called HandlerBookQuery.

Example 8-9. Elements added by wsdeploy to the web.xml file

```
<listener>
    <listener-class>com.sun.xml.rpc.server.http.JAXRPCContextListener
    </listener-class>
</listener>
<servlet>
    <servlet-name>HandlerBookQuery</servlet-name>
    <display-name>HandlerBookQuery</display-name>
    <description>JAX-RPC endpoint - HandlerBookQuery</description>
    <servlet-class>com.sun.xml.rpc.server.http.JAXRPCServlet</servlet-class>
    <load-on-startup>1</load-on-startup>
</servlet>
<servlet-mapping>
    <servlet-name>HandlerBookQuery</servlet-name>
    <url-pattern>/HandlerBookQuery</url-pattern>
</servlet-mapping>
```

The URL mapping defined by the servlet-mapping element is derived from the endpointMapping element in the *jaxrpc-ri.xml* file—or, if there is no such element, from the endpoint name together with the urlPatternBase attribute of the webServices element.

 Note the presence of a listener element in the *web.xml* file. Since this element was introduced in Version 2.3 of the Java Servlet Specification, it follows that the JWSDP requires a web container that conforms to Java Servlets Version 2.3 or later.

Other elements present in the *web.xml* file (including context parameters, environment entries, and so on) are preserved unchanged by wsdeploy. A copy of the original file is placed in the */WEB-INF* directory under the name *web-before.xml*.

The other deployment-related file placed in the */WEB-INF* directory is called *jaxrpc-ri-runtime.xml*. This file contains deployment information derived from the *jaxrpc-ri.xml* file; since it is only intended for internal use, its content is not discussed here. The original *jaxrpc-ri.xml* file can be found in */WEB-INF/jaxrpc-ri-before.xml*.

J2EEC — Utility for Creating Stubs and Ties for a JAX-RPC Web Service

Availability

J2EE 1.4 reference implementation.

Synopsis

```
j2eec [-keep | -keepgenerated ] [-o output] module
```

Description

j2eec is a command-line utility that is part of the J2EE reference implementation. It accepts a deployable J2EE module and creates a JAR file containing some or all of the following:

- Client-side stubs for EJBs that have a remote interface
- Client-side stubs for web services
- Server-side ties for web services
- A *sun-j2ee-ri.xml* file containing information that can be used by containers into which the original module is deployed

The newly created JAR file can be used as follows:

- To deploy the original module to a J2EE RI application server using the -deployGeneratedModule option of the deploytool command (discussed later), without incurring the overhead of stub and tie generation. This technique may be useful if you need to deploy the same module to more than one server.
- As the stubs file when running a J2EE application client using the runclient utility, as described in "JAX-RPC and J2EE 1.4 Application Clients" in Chapter 6. If the client JAR file contains service-ref elements referring to web services deployed in the server, the *sun-j2ee-ri.xml* file contains the information that the client container needs to bind a generated Service object that can be used to access the service in the application's JNDI environment at runtime.

Options

The behavior of the j2eec command is determined primarily by the deployment descriptors provided in the J2EE module supplied on its command line, which may be an EJB JAR file, a web archive, a J2EE client application archive, or an EAR file containing any combination of the other module types. In the latter case, the generated file includes all of the stubs, ties, and other information required for each of the modules that it contains. The following command-line options are also available:

`-keep`
`-keepgenerated`

Synonymous options that cause the Java source files for the stubs and ties and other files generated by j2eec to be retained. By default, these files are deleted. Temporary files are placed in a system-dependent location. For Windows 2000 and Windows XP, for example, you'll find these files in a directory beneath *%HOME%\Local Settings\Temp*, where *%HOME%* represents your home directory. The actual location is displayed on standard output when the command is executed.

`-o` *filename*

Specifies the name of the JAR file to which j2eec should write its output. If this argument is not supplied, output is written to a file called *generated.jar* in the caller's working directory.

J2EE Deploytool — Utility for Deploying Modules and Enterprise Applications

Availability

J2EE 1.4 reference implementation.

Synopsis

```
deploytool [-server name[:port]] -deployModule [-id moduleID]
    module [client_JAR]
deploytool [-server name[:port]] -deployGeneratedModule [-id moduleID]
module generated_JAR
deploytool [-server name[:port]] -listModules type
deploytool [-server name[:port]] -undeploy moduleID
```

Description

The deploytool utility provided with the J2EE 1.4 reference implementation provides both a command-line and a graphical user interface that allow you to create and deploy J2EE modules to the J2EE RI application server. You can also use the same utility to deploy an existing module. The GUI interface is used when no command-line arguments are supplied. This section covers only those command-line features of the deploytool utility that are relevant to web services.

Options

Most forms of the deploytool command include an optional module ID, which is used to uniquely identify a deployed module within the application server. If an explicit module ID is not supplied, then one is created by taking the display name of the module and replacing all spaces by underscore characters. The display name is obtained from the display-name element of the module's deployment descriptor (i.e., *META-INF/ejb-jar.xml* for an EJB JAR file, *WEB-INF/web.xml* for a web archive, *META_INF/application-client.xml* for a client archive, *META-INF/ra.xml* for a Connector resource archive, or *META-INF/application.xml* for an Enterprise Archive).

```
-server name[:port]
```
Specifies that hostname, and optionally, the port number, for the target application server. If this option is not used, the server is assumed to be accessible at port 8000 on localhost.

```
-deployModule [-id moduleID] module [client_JAR]
```
Deploys a J2EE module to the application server. If a module with the same name is already deployed, it is removed and the new version is deployed in its place. The module argument must be the path name of an EJB JAR, a web archive, a client application archive, a resource archive, or an Enterprise Archive. The deployment process may include the generation of stub and tie classes and other information of use to client programs or to a J2EE client application container. This information, which is the same as that created by the j2eec utility described earlier in this chapter, may optionally be returned by the server and stored in the file given by the client_JAR argument. It may be used in conjunction with the -deployGeneratedModule option or when running a J2EE application client, as described in "JAX-RPC and J2EE 1.4 Application Clients" in Chapter 6.

```
-deployGeneratedModule [-id moduleID] module generated_JAR
```
This option is the same as -deployModule, except that the stub generation step is omitted. The stubs are assumed to have already been created by an earlier invocation of this command using the -deployModule option or by the j2eec utility, and must be supplied using the generated_JAR argument.

```
-listModules type
```
Lists all deployed modules of the specified type, which must be one of car (client archive), ear (Enterprise Archive), ejb (EJB JAR), rar (Connector resource archive), or war (web archive).

```
-undeployModule moduleId
```
Undeploys the module identified by the given module ID.

JAXM Client and Provider Configuration

Availability

Java Web Services Developer's Pack. There is no equivalent for the J2EE 1.4 platform, since JAXM is not included.

Description

The Java API for XML Messaging (JAXM) provides a means to send and receive SOAP messages via a provider instead of using a direct connection from the sender to the receiver. The benefits of this arrangement, as discussed in Chapter 4, are:

Asynchronous operation
Clients deliver outgoing messages to their provider. The provider then has responsibility for arranging the delivery of each message to the provider local to the intended recipient. If the receiving provider is not active or not reachable, it will be necessary to retry delivery until it succeeds or a preconfigured limit is reached.

Persistence

Messages can be received for a client that is not active and stored within the provider for delivery later.

Location transparency

Whereas SAAJ applications need to know the address of the recipient of each message they send, a JAXM client can use an address token that is independent of the real address of the receiving application. The mapping from an address token to an actual address is configured in the provider, where it can be more easily changed if necessary.

In order to provide these features, two levels of configuration are required. First, the provider has to be configured with the details of the token-to-address mappings that provide location transparency for applications and with other information, such as how many times to retry a failed message delivery. Secondly, the client application needs to be configured with information required by its provider. This section covers the configuration details for the JAXM reference implementation.

Provider Configuration

Provider configuration information is held in a file called *provider.xml*, which is located in the */WEB-INF* directory of the deployed JAXM provider. The format of the file content is shown in Example 8-10.

Example 8-10. The JAXM provider.xml file

```
<ProviderConfig>
  <Profile profileId="profile">          <!-- 1 or more -->
    <Transport> <!-- 1 or more -->
      <Protocol>protocol</Protocol>
      <!-- Endpoint mappings for this protocol -->
      <Endpoint type="uri | urn">        <!-- 1 or more -->
        <URI>token</URI>
        <URL>targetAddress</URL>
      </Endpoint>

      <ErrorHandling>                     <!-- 0 or 1 --->
        <Retry>
          <MaxRetries>N</MaxRetries>
          <RetryInterval>M</RetryInterval>
        </Retry>
      </ErrorHandling>

      <Persistence>                       <!-- 0 or 1 -->
        <Directory>path</Directory>
        <RecordsPerFile>N</RecordsPerFile>
      </Persistence>
    </Transport>

    <ErrorHandling>                       <!-- 0 or 1 -->
      <Retry>
        <MaxRetries>N</MaxRetries>
```

Example 8-10. The JAXM provider.xml file (continued)

```
        <RetryInterval>M</RetryInterval>
      </Retry>
    </ErrorHandling>

    <Persistence>                           <!-- 0 or 1 -->
      <Directory>path</Directory>
      <RecordsPerFile>N</RecordsPerFile>
    </Persistence>
  </Profile>
</ProviderConfig>
```

Nested within the top-level `ProviderConfig` element, the *provider.xml* file contains a separate `Profile` element for each message profile that it supports, where the `profileId` attribute identifies the profile. Valid values for `profileId` in the reference implementation are `soaprp` and `ebxml`; therefore, there are typically two `Profile` elements, each of which configures the address mapping and other policy details for its particular profile.

A profile may operate over one or more transport mechanisms, each of which requires a nested `Transport` element whose first child element supplies the name of the protocol. The reference implementation recognizes the values `http` and `https` as valid protocol identifiers. The remaining child elements of the `Transport` element configure endpoint mappings, error handling, and local storage for the provider when using the profile given by the containing `Profile` element over the specified transport protocol.

The `ProviderConfig` element may also have nested `ErrorHandling` and `Persistence` elements that configure default settings for all transports. These elements can appear within any `Transport` element if it is necessary to override the defaults for a specific transport type. Only one instance of each element can appear within the `ProviderConfig` element and within each `Transport` element.

Endpoint mappings

The `Endpoint` elements map the address tokens used by JAXM client programs to the transport addresses to which messages using those tokens are to be sent. Here is typical example of an `Endpoint` element configured for the soaprp profile:

```
        <Endpoint>
          <URI>urn:SOAPRPEcho</URI>
          <URL>http://localhost:8081/jaxm-provider/receiver/soaprp</URL>
        </Endpoint>
```

This element causes SOAP-RP messages in which the to address has the value *urn:SOAPRPEcho* to be sent to the URL *http://localhost:8081/jaxm-provider/ receiver/soaprp*. The destination address in the URL element should always be that of a JAXM provider and is formed as follows:

- The first part of the URL—in this case, *http://localhost:8081/jaxm-provider*— corresponds to the URL of the JAXM provider web application that should receive the message. In this case, the target provider is on the same machine as the sender, but this is not usually the case in the real world. Port number 8081 is correct for the default installation of the JWSDP when running in the Tomcat web container.

- The second part of the URL is *receiver/soaprp* if the receiver at the receiving endpoint expects messages to be built using the SOAP-RP profile and *receiver/ebxml* for ebXML profile messages. The client application must, of course, be coded to use the same profile. If more profiles are added in the future, then each will need its own unique URL for receiving messages.

The address token given by the URI element can be any URI that is considered to be a valid address for the profile being configured. In this example, it happens to be a URN, but it could also be a URL. In practice, the provider does not attempt to interpret this token other than to match it against the destination address of a message being sent by a client.*

Error handling

The ErrorHandling element determines the actions that the provider takes when it is unable to deliver a message immediately. There are two conditions that trigger error recovery:

- A provider attempts to send a message to a remote provider and fails to do so because the provider is not active or is not currently accessible for some other reason. In this case, the message is held in the outgoing queue for retransmission.

- A provider receives a message and attempts to deliver it to a local client whose endpoint is not currently active. In this case, the message is held in the receiver queue in the expectation that the client will shortly connect to the provider.

A typical ErrorHandling element looks like this:

```
<ErrorHandling>
  <Retry>
    <MaxRetries>3</MaxRetries>
    <RetryInterval>2000</RetryInterval>
  </Retry>
</ErrorHandling>
```

The MaxRetries element determines how many times the provider will retry an attempt to deliver the message (this does not count the initial attempt). The RetryInterval element gives the time between successive attempts to deliver a message, in milliseconds. In the example shown here, a total of four attempts will be made to deliver a message, with one attempt being made approximately every two seconds.

If the ErrorHandling element appears within a Transport element, its values apply only to that transport type. This element may also appear directly beneath the ProviderConfig element, in which case it supplies default values that apply to all transports that do not have a nested instance. In the case where a Transport

---

* The URI element has an optional type attribute that, according to its DTD, can have the value uri or urn. These values are curious—it seems more logical to require url or urn. In any case, there is no need to supply a value for this attribute, and, at least at the time of this writing, any value that is supplied is ignored.

element does not provide its own error-handling values and there is no default ErrorHandling element, then the provider attempts 10 retries separated by approximately 2 seconds (these being hardcoded values).

Message persistence

The Persistence element specifies the directory within which the provider implements its outgoing and received message queues as well as the way in which messages are mapped to temporary storage files in that directory.

The Directory element gives the relative pathname of a directory for a set of queues. In the current implementation, this directory is created in the location reserved by the hosting container for a web application's temporary files. Beneath this directory, the provider creates four subdirectories, each of which represents a separate queue and is described here:

received
> Contains messages that have been received and successfully delivered to the local client that they were intended for

sent
> Contains messages that have been successfully sent to the appropriate remote provider

toBeSent
> Contains messages that have not yet been successfully delivered to a remote provider

toBeDispatched
> Contains messages received for local clients that have not yet been successfully delivered

Within a queue, the messages are written to files. The order of messages in the queue is reflected by the creation date of each file and by the order of the messages within each file—that is, the messages in the oldest file come first, and so on. As messages are successfully transmitted, they are removed from their containing file and, when the file is empty, it is deleted. The maximum number of messages that are placed in each individual file is given by the RecordsPerFile element.

According to the DTD for the *provider.xml* file, the Persistence element may appear either as a child element of a Transport element or as a direct child of the ProviderConfig element. In the former case, it is intended to configure the queues for a particular profile when operating over a specific transport mechanism. In the latter case, presumably, it provides a single queue location for those transports that do not have their own configuration. At the time of this writing, however, each Transport element is required to contain its own Persistence element, and a Persistence element appearing below the ProviderConfig element is ignored.

Client Application Configuration

JAXM client applications are always associated with a provider. However, the application code itself does not explicitly provide the address of that provider. Instead, this information is provided in a configuration file called *client.xml* that must appear in the application's `CLASSPATH`. A JAXM client that uses the provider only as a means of building profile-specific messages and uses the synchronous message delivery mechanism provided by SAAJ may be implemented as a stand-alone J2SE-based application. All other JAXM clients must be container-based. At the present time, this means that such clients must be hosted by a servlet.

The layout of the *client.xml* file is shown in Example 8-11.

Example 8-11. The JAXM client.xml file

```
<ClientConfig>
  <Endpoint>URI</Endpoint>
  <CallbackURL>URL</CallbackURL>
  <Proxy>     <!-- Any number (including none) allowed
   <Host>hostname</Host>
   <Port>portNumber</Port>
  </Proxy>
  <Provider>
    <URI>providerURI</URI>
    <URL>providerURL</URL>
  </Provider>
</ClientConfig>
```

The `Endpoint` element supplies the URI associated with the client itself. This is the URI that appears as the from address in all messages sent from this client (if the profile in use carries that information), and is the destination address to which messages sent to this client should be addressed. It may be a real URL, but is more likely to be a logical address. Providers that need to deliver messages to the client at this URI must be configured to send them to the client's local provider by including an `Endpoint` mapping in their *provider.xml* file, where the value associated with its `URI` child element matches the value of this `URI` element. Refer to "How a Message Is Sent and Delivered" in Chapter 4 for a full description of the message delivery path and the way in which the values assigned to these elements are used.

The `CallbackURL` element is used when the provider receives a message addressed to the endpoint. As just noted, JAXM clients that receive asynchronous messages from a provider must be hosted in a servlet environment. This is most easily achieved by implementing the client as a subclass of `JAXMServlet`, which is part of the JAXM reference implementation. The value of the `CallbackURL` is the URL that corresponds to the instance of this servlet containing the JAXM client. See "An Example JAXM Application" in Chapter 4 for a complete example of a JAXM client hosted by `JAXMServlet`. In the case of a JAXM client hosted by a J2SE application, this value is unused.

The optional `Proxy` element can be used to configure the host and port number for an HTTP proxy that resides between the client application and its provider, if there is one. This element should not be included if the client can directly access the provider. Although the DTD for the *client.xml* file indicates that there can be any number of `Proxy` elements, at the time of this writing, only the first such element found is used.

The Provider element is used to locate the provider with which the client is associated. The URI child element contains a unique URI that identifies the provider implementation. For the JAXM provider supplied with the reference implementation, this must have the value *http://java.sun.com/xml/jaxm/provider*. The URL child element contains the URL for the outgoing message queue of the provider, which is constructed as follows:

1. The leading part of the URL is *http://host:8081/jaxm-provider*.
2. The final part of the URL is always *sender*, which selects the outgoing message queue.

A typical Provider element therefore looks like this:

```
<Provider>
  <URI>http://java.sun.com/xml/jaxm/provider</URI>
  <URL>http://localhost:8081/jaxm-provider/sender</URL>
</Provider>
```

J2EE 1.4 Web Services Configuration File

Availability

All J2EE 1.4 platforms.

Description

All J2EE modules that contain a web service are required to provide information that allows deployment tools to locate the classes that implement the service, the WSDL document describing its service interface, and a mapping file that describes how that interface should be mapped to elements of the Java programming language. The location of this file depends on the archive in which it resides:

- For a web service hosted by a servlet, the file belongs to the hosting web application and must be called *WEB-INF/webservices.xml*.
- For an EJB-hosted web service, the file is placed in the same EJB JAR file as the implementing bean and is called *META-INF/webservices.xml*.

The content of this file is defined by an XML Schema document that can be downloaded from *http://www.ibm.com/webservices/xsd/j2ee_web_services_1_1.xsd*. An outline of the content of this file is shown in Example 8-12.

Example 8-12. The webservices.xml file

```
<webservices>
  <webservice-description>            <!-- One or more -->
    <description>text</description>         <!-- Optional -->
    <display-name>text</display-name>       <!-- Optional -->
    <icon> <!-- Optional -->
      <small-icon>name</small-icon>         <!-- Optional -->
      <large-icon>name</large-icon>         <!-- Optional -->
    </icon>
    <web-service-description-name>name</web-service-description-name>
```

Example 8-12. The webservices.xml file (continued)

```
<wsdl-file>file-location</wsdl-file>
<jaxrpc-mapping-file>file-location</jaxrpc-mapping-file>
<port-component>                          <!-- One or more -->
   <description>text</description>        <!-- Optional -->
   <display-name>text</display-name>      <!-- Optional -->
   <icon>                                 <!-- Optional -->
      <small-icon>name</small-icon>       <!-- Optional -->
      <large-icon>name</large-icon>       <!-- Optional -->
   </icon>
   <port-component-name>name</port-component-name>
   <wsdl-port/>                           <!-- See text -->
   <service-endpoint-interface>class name</service-endpoint-interface>
   <service-impl-bean>                    <!-- See text -->
   <handler/>                             <!-- Zero or more. See text -->
</port-component>
  </webservice-description>
</webservices>
```

Each web service defined in the module requires its own `webservice-description` element, in which the `web-service-description-name` has a value that is unique within the module. The `wsdl-file` and `jaxrpc-mapping-file` elements specify the locations of the WSDL file and the JAX-RPC mapping file that apply to the service, relative to the root of the module. Either absolute or relative paths may be used and are interpreted in the same way—that is, the tags shown here:

```
<wsdl-file>BookService.wsdl</wsdl-file>
```

and the tags shown here:

```
<wsdl-file>/BookService.wsdl</wsdl-file>
```

refer to the same location. The `jaxrpc-mapping-file` specifies the mapping from the elements of the WSDL file to Java programming language elements and is described in "J2EE 1.4 JAX-RPC Mapping File," later in this chapter.

Each `webservice-description` element contains one or more `port-component` elements, each of which describes a single port within the service. The `port-component-name` element provides a name for the port that must be unique within the module, whereas the `service-endpoint-interface` element gives the fully qualified name of the Java class that implements the service endpoint interface. A `port-component` is linked to a port element from the associated WSDL file using the `wsdl-port` element, which is structured as follows:

```
<wsdl-port>
   <namespaceURI>urn:jwsnut.chapter2.bookservice/wsdl/BookQuery
   </namespaceURI>
   <localpart>BookQueryPort</localpart>
</wsdl-port>
```

The `namespaceURI` element must match the namespace within which the port is defined, which is the same as the value of the `targetNamespace` attribute of the `definitions` element in the WSDL definition file. The `localpart` is the value of the name attribute of the port element in the WSDL file. The values shown previously correspond to the following parts of the WSDL definition for the book web service created in Chapter 2.

```
<definitions name="BookService"
             targetNamespace="urn:jwsnut.chapter2.bookservice/wsdl
                 /BookQuery"
             xmlns:tns="urn:jwsnut.chapter2.bookservice/wsdl/
                 BookQuery" .... >
    .....
    <service name="BookService">
        <port name="BookQueryPort" binding="tns:BookQueryBinding">
         <soap:address location="http://localhost:8000/Books/BookQueryPort"/>
        </port>
    </service>
</definitions>
```

The service implementation class is linked to by the service-impl-bean element, which may be either a servlet or an EJB. Servlets are referred to using the servlet-link element:

```
<service-impl-bean>
   <servlet-link>BookQueryServlet</servlet-link>
</service-impl-bean>
```

where, in this case, BookQueryServlet must be the value of a servlet-name element in the *web.xml* file located in the same module as the *webservices.xml* file. A web service implemented as an EJB requires an ejb-link element instead:

```
<service-impl-bean>
   <ejb-link>BookQueryBean</ejb-link>
</service-impl-bean>
```

The target of the link must be the value of the ejb-name element of a stateless session bean declared in the *ejb-jar.xml* file in the same module.

An optional set of SOAP message handlers (see "SOAP Message Handlers" in Chapter 6) can be configured using one or more handler elements, which is structured as shown in Example 8-13.

Example 8-13. The handler element in the webservices.xml file

```
<handler>
  <handler-name>name</handler-name>
  <handler-class>class name</handler-class>
  <init-param>                          <!-- Zero or more -->
    <description>text</description>      <!-- Optional -->
    <param-name>name</param-name>
    <param-value>value</param-value>
  </init-param>
  <soap-header>                          <!-- Zero or more -->
    <namespaceURI>URI</namespaceURI>
    <localpart>name</localpart>
  <soap-header>
  <soap-role>rolename</soap-role>        <!-- Zero or more -->
</handler>
```

The Java class that implements the handler is named by the handler-class element. This class must implement the javax.xml.rpc.handler.Handler interface. Optional initialization parameters may be passed to the handler's init( ) method by including one or more init-param elements.

The soap-header and soap-role elements specify respectively the header or headers that the message handler can process and the SOAP roles that apply to the message handler. See "Headers, roles, and the mustUnderstand attribute" in Chapter 6 for a full description of message headers and SOAP roles. The soap-header element requires the specification of both the namespace URI and the local part of the name:

```
<soap-header>
    <namespaceURI>urn:jwsnut.chapter6.handlerbookservice/wsdl/
HandlerBookQuery</namespaceURI>
    <localpart>auth</localpart>
</soap-header>
```

J2EE 1.4 JAX-RPC Mapping File

Availability

All J2EE 1.4 platforms.

Description

Every web service deployed on the J2EE 1.4 platform must have an associated mapping that describes how the namespaces, port types, operations, exceptions, and data types defined in the WSDL definition of the service are to be mapped to Java language packages, interfaces, methods, exception classes, and primitive or object types. In the simplest cases, it is permissible to specify only the namespace to package mapping, allowing everything else to be defaulted according to built-in rules for the WSDL to JAX-RPC mapping described in the JAX-RPC specification.

The JAX-RPC mapping file does not have a fixed name. Instead, its location is given by the wsdl-file element in the *webservices.xml* file in the same J2EE module. The J2EE 1.4 reference implementation allows a model file to be used instead of a mapping file. This is extremely convenient because the model file can be created automatically from a WSDL definition. Since the mapping file is complex, it is likely that other vendors will provide tool-based support for creating it.

The content of the JAX-RPC mapping file is defined by an XML Schema document that can be downloaded from *http://www.ibm.com/webservices/xsd/j2ee_jaxrpc_mapping_1_1.xsd*. Example 8-14 shows the elements that appear at the two outer-most nesting levels of this document.

Example 8-14. The JAX-RPC mapping file

```
<java-wsdl-mapping>
    <package-mapping/>          <!-- One or more  - see text -->
    <java-xml-type-mapping/>     <!-- Zero or more - see text -->
```

Example 8-14. The JAX-RPC mapping file (continued)

```
<exception-mapping/>              <!-- Zero or more - see text -->

<!-- Any number of the next two elements may appear -->
<service-interface-mapping>       <! -- Zero or one may appear - see text -->
<service-endpoint-interface-mapping> <!-- One or more -- see text -->
</java-wsdl-mapping>
```

At the time of this writing, the beta release of J2EE Version 1.4 supports only the package-mapping element of this file; therefore, this section covers only that element. Note that, in most cases, this is the only part of the file that you need to supply. Following the FCS release of J2EE 1.4, updated information on this file will be posted on the web page for this book at O'Reilly's web site (*http://www. oreilly.com/catalog/javawsian*).

Package mappings

The package-mapping element describes the correspondence between namespaces used in the WSDL file and the Java packages in which the classes for the objects in those namespaces should be generated. The structure of the package-mapping element is shown in Example 8-15.

Example 8-15. The package-mapping element in the JAX-RPC mapping file

```
<package-mapping>
    <package-type>Java package</package-type>
    <namespaceURI>namespace</namespaceURI>
</package-mapping>
```

There should be one package-mapping element for each namespace from which Java objects will be generated. The most common case would require an element that maps the namespace given by the targetNamespace attribute of the definitions element in the WSDL file. If the types defined or imported by the WSDL file have a different targetNamespace, and those types require the generation of Java classes, then a mapping should also be included for each such namespace. In the case of the book web service from Chapter 2, for example, the types element uses a different namespace from that of the definitions themselves:

```
<definitions name="BookService"
              targetNamespace="urn:jwsnut.chapter2.bookservice/wsdl/
              BookQuery" ... >
    <types>
      <schema targetNamespace=
        "urn:jwsnut.chapter2.bookservice/types/BookQuery" ...>
```

Since there are two different namespaces, to create a Java implementation of this web service and deploy it on the J2EE 1.4 platform, you need to include a JAX-RPC mapping file with two package-mapping elements:

```
<package-mapping>
    <package-type>ora.jwsnut.chapter2.bookservice</package-type>
    <namespaceURI>urn:jwsnut.chapter2.bookservice/wsdl/BookQuery</
namespaceURI>
```

```
</package-mapping>
<package-mapping>
    <package-type>ora.jwsnut.chapter2.bookservice</package-type>
    <namespaceURI>urn:jwsnut.chapter2.bookservice/types/BookQuery</
namespaceURI>
</package-mapping>
```

The extract shown here defines a mapping in which Java objects from both namespaces are created in a package called ora.jwsnut.chapter2.bookservice. It is permissible, however, to use a different Java package for each namespace if you wish to.

II

API Quick Reference

Part II is the real heart of this book: quick-reference material for the J2EE web services APIs. Please read the following section, *How to Use This Quick Reference*, to learn how to get the most out of this material.

How to Use This Quick Reference

The quick-reference section that follows packs a lot of information into a small space. This introduction explains how to get the most out of that information. It describes how the quick reference is organized and how to read the individual quick-reference entries.

Finding a Quick-Reference Entry

The quick reference is organized into chapters, each of which documents a single package of the Java platform or a group of related packages. Packages are listed alphabetically within and between chapters, so you never really need to know which chapter documents which package—you can simply search alphabetically, as you might do in a dictionary. The documentation for each package begins with a quick-reference entry for the package itself. This entry includes a short overview of the package and a listing of the classes and interfaces included in the package. In this listing of package contents, classes and interfaces are first grouped by general category (interfaces, classes, and exceptions, for example). Within each category, they are grouped by class hierarchy, with indentation to indicate the level of the hierarchy. Finally, classes and interfaces at the same hierarchy level are listed alphabetically.

Each package overview is followed by individual quick-reference entries for the classes and interfaces defined in the package. All of the entries in this reference are organized alphabetically by class *and* package name, so related classes are grouped near each other. This means that to look up a quick-reference entry for a particular class, you must also know the name of the package that contains that class. Usually, the package name is obvious from the context, and you should have no trouble looking up the quick-reference entry you want. Use the tabs on the outside edge of the book and the dictionary-style headers on the upper corner of each page to help you quickly find the package and class you need.

Occasionally, you may need to look up a class for which you do not already know the package. In this case, refer to the Class Index. This index allows you to look up a class by class name and find out what package it is part of.

Reading a Quick-Reference Entry

The quick-reference entries for classes and interfaces contain quite a bit of information. The sections that follow describe the structure of a quick-reference entry, explaining what information is available, where it is found, and what it means. While reading the descriptions that follow, you may find it helpful to flip through the reference section itself to find examples of the features being described.

Class Name, Package Name, Availability, and Flags

Each quick-reference entry begins with a four-part title that specifies the name, package name, and availability of the class, and may also specify various additional flags that describe the class. The class name appears in bold at the upper left of the title. The package name appears, in smaller print, in the lower left, below the class name.

The upper-right portion of the title indicates the availability of the class; it specifies the earliest release that contained the class. If a class was introduced in Java 1.1, for example, this portion of the title reads "Java 1.1". The availability section of the title is also used to indicate whether a class has been deprecated, and, if so, in what release. For example, it might read "Java 1.1; Deprecated in Java 1.2".

In the lower-right corner of the title you may find a list of flags that describe the class. The possible flags and their meanings are as follows:

checked
> The class is a checked exception, which means that it extends java.lang. Exception, but not java.lang.RuntimeException. In other words, it must be declared in the throws clause of any method that may throw it.

cloneable
> The class, or a superclass, implements java.lang.Cloneable.

collection
> The class, or a superclass, implements java.util.Collection or java.util. Map.

comparable
> The class, or a superclass, implements java.lang.Comparable.

error
> The class extends java.lang.Error.

event
> The class extends java.util.EventObject.

event adapter
> The class, or a superclass, implements java.util.EventListener, and the class name ends with "Adapter".

event listener

>The class, or a superclass, implements `java.util.EventListener`.

runnable

>The class, or a superclass, implements `java.lang.Runnable`.

unchecked

>The class is an unchecked exception, which means it extends `java.lang.RuntimeException` and therefore does not need to be declared in the throws clause of a method that may throw it.

Description

The title of each quick-reference entry is followed by a short description of the most important features of the class or interface. This description may be anywhere from a couple of sentences to several paragraphs long.

Hierarchy

If a class or interface has a nontrivial class hierarchy, the "Description" section is followed by a figure that illustrates the hierarchy and helps you understand the class in the context of that hierarchy. The name of each class or interface in the diagram appears in a box; classes appear in rectangles (except for abstract classes, which appear in skewed rectangles or parallelograms). Interfaces appear in rounded rectangles, in which the corners have been replaced by arcs. The current class—the one that is the subject of the diagram—appears in a box that is bolder than the others. The boxes are connected by lines: solid lines indicate an "extends" relationship, and dotted lines indicate an "implements" relationship. The superclass-to-subclass hierarchy reads from left to right in the top row (or only row) of boxes in the figure. Interfaces are usually positioned beneath the classes that implement them, although in simple cases, an interface is sometimes positioned on the same line as the class that implements it, resulting in a more compact figure. Note that the hierarchy figure shows only the superclasses of a class. If a class has subclasses, those are listed in the cross-reference section at the end of the quick-reference entry for the class.

Synopsis

The most important part of every quick-reference entry is the class synopsis, which follows the title and description. The synopsis for a class looks a lot like the source code for the class, except that the method bodies are omitted and some additional annotations are added. If you know Java syntax, you know how to read the class synopsis.

The first line of the synopsis contains information about the class itself. It begins with a list of class modifiers, such as `public`, `abstract`, or `final`. These modifiers are followed by the `class` or `interface` keyword and then by the name of the class. The class name may be followed by an extends clause that specifies the superclass and an implements clause that specifies any interfaces the class implements.

The class definition line is followed by a list of the fields and methods that the class defines. Once again, if you understand basic Java syntax, you should have no

How to Use

trouble making sense of these lines. The listing for each member includes the modifiers, type, and name of the member. For methods, the synopsis also includes the type and name of each method parameter and an optional throws clause that lists the exceptions the method can throw. The member names are in boldface, so it is easy to scan the list of members looking for the one you want. The names of method parameters are in italics to indicate that they are not to be used literally. The member listings are printed on alternating gray and white backgrounds to keep them visually separate.

Member availability and flags

Each member listing is a single line that defines the API for that member. These listings use Java syntax, so their meaning is immediately clear to any Java programmer. There is some auxiliary information associated with each member synopsis, however, that requires explanation.

Recall that each quick-reference entry begins with a title section that includes the release in which the class was first defined. When a member is introduced into a class after the initial release of the class, the version in which the member was introduced appears, in small print, to the left of the member synopsis. For example, if a class was first introduced in Java 1.1, but had a new method added in Java 1.2, the title contains the string "Java 1.1", and the listing for the new member is preceded by the number "1.2". Furthermore, if a member has been deprecated, that fact is indicated with a hash mark (#) to the left of the member synopsis.

The area to the right of the member synopsis is used to display a variety of flags that provide additional information about the member. Some of these flags indicate additional specification details that do not appear in the member API itself. Other flags contain implementation-specific information. This information can be quite useful in understanding the class and in debugging your code, but be aware that it may differ between implementations. The implementation-specific flags displayed in this book are based on Sun's Linux implementation of Java.

The following flags may be displayed to the right of a member synopsis:

native
    An implementation-specific flag that indicates that a method is implemented in native code. Although native is a Java keyword and can appear in method signatures, it is part of the method implementation, not part of its specification. Therefore, this information is included with the member flags, rather than as part of the member listing. This flag is useful as a hint about the expected performance of a method.

synchronized
    An implementation-specific flag that indicates that a method implementation is declared synchronized, meaning that it obtains a lock on the object or class before executing. Like the native keyword, the synchronized keyword is part of the method implementation, not part of the specification, so it appears as a flag, not in the method synopsis itself. This flag is a useful hint that the method is probably implemented in a thread-safe manner.

Whether a method is thread-safe is part of the method specification, and this information *should* appear (although it often does not) in the method documentation. There are a number of different ways to make a method thread-safe, however, and declaring the method with the synchronized keyword is only one possible implementation. In other words, a method that does not bear the synchronized flag can still be thread-safe.

Overrides:

This flag indicates that a method overrides a method in one of its superclasses. The flag is followed by the name of the superclass that the method overrides. This is a specification detail, not an implementation detail. As we'll see in the next section, overriding methods are usually grouped together in their own section of the class synopsis. The Overrides: flag is only used when an overriding method is not grouped in that way.

Implements:

This flag indicates that a method implements a method in an interface. The flag is followed by the name of the interface that is implemented. This is a specification detail, not an implementation detail. As we'll see in the next section, methods that implement an interface are usually grouped into a special section of the class synopsis. The Implements: flag is only used for methods that are not grouped in this way.

empty

This flag indicates that the implementation of the method has an empty body. This can be a hint to the programmer that the method may need to be overridden in a subclass.

constant

An implementation-specific flag that indicates that a method has a trivial implementation. Only methods with a void return type can be truly empty. Any method declared to return a value must have at least a return statement. The constant flag indicates that the method implementation is empty except for a return statement that returns a constant value. Such a method might have a body like return null; or return false;. Like the empty flag, this flag may indicate that a method needs to be overridden.

default:

This flag is used with property accessor methods that read the value of a property (i.e., methods whose names begins with "get" and take no arguments). The flag is followed by the default value of the property. Strictly speaking, default property values are a specification detail. In practice, however, these defaults are not always documented, and care should be taken because the default values may change between implementations.

Not all property accessors have a default: flag. A default value is determined by dynamically loading the class in question, instantiating it using a no-argument constructor, and then calling the method to find out what it returns. This technique can be used only on classes that can be dynamically loaded and instantiated and that have no-argument constructors, so default values are shown for those classes only. Furthermore, when a class is instantiated using a different constructor, the default values for its properties may be different.

For static final fields, this flag is followed by the constant value of the field. Only constants of primitive and String types and constants with the value null are displayed. Some constant values are specification details, while others are implementation details. The reason that symbolic constants are defined, however, is so you can write code that does not rely directly upon the constant value. Use this flag to help you understand the class, but do not rely upon the constant values in your own programs.

In Chapters 11 and 12, which deal with the JAXR API, each method has the designator "L0" or "L1." These designators indicate whether the method is part of the Level 0 API (which must be supported by every JAXR provider), or the Level 1 API (which is available only from more capable providers). Broadly speaking, Level 0 features are provided by UDDI registries, while features in Level 1 represent the additional functionality provided by the ebXML registry/repository. Refer to Chapter 7 for further information.

Functional grouping of members

Within a class synopsis, the members are not listed in strict alphabetical order. Instead, they are broken down into functional groups and listed alphabetically within each group. Constructors, methods, fields, and inner classes are all listed separately. Instance methods are kept separate from static (class) methods. Constants are separated from nonconstant fields. Public members are listed separately from protected members. Grouping members by category breaks a class down into smaller, more comprehensible segments, making the class easier to understand. This grouping also makes it easier for you to find a desired member.

Functional groups are separated from each other in a class synopsis with Java comments, such as // Public Constructors, // Inner Classes, and // Methods Implementing DataInput. The various functional categories are as follows (in the order in which they appear in a class synopsis):

Constructors
> Displays the constructors for the class. Public constructors and protected constructors are displayed separately in subgroupings. If a class does not define a constructor, the Java compiler adds a default no-argument constructor that is displayed here. If a class defines only private constructors, it cannot be instantiated, so a special, empty grouping entitled "No Constructor" indicates this fact. Constructors are listed first because the first thing you do with most classes is instantiate them by calling a constructor.

Constants
> Displays all of the constants (i.e., fields that are declared static and final) defined by the class. Public and protected constants are displayed in separate subgroups. Constants are listed here, near the top of the class synopsis, because constant values are often used throughout the class as legal values for method parameters and return values.

Inner classes
> Groups all of the inner classes and interfaces defined by the class or interface. For each inner class, there is a single-line synopsis. Each inner class also has its own quick-reference entry that includes a full class synopsis for the

inner class. Like constants, inner classes are listed near the top of the class synopsis because they are often used by a number of other members of the class.

Static methods

Lists the static methods (class methods) of the class, broken down into subgroups for public static methods and protected static methods.

Event listener registration methods

Lists the public instance methods that register and deregister event listener objects with the class. The names of these methods begin with the words "add" and "remove" and end in "Listener". These methods are always passed a java.util.EventListener object. The methods are typically defined in pairs, so the pairs are listed together. The methods are listed alphabetically by event name rather than by method name.

Property accessor methods

Lists the public instance methods that set or query the value of a property or attribute of the class. The names of these methods begin with the words "set", "get", and "is", and their signatures follow the patterns set out in the JavaBeans specification. Although the naming conventions and method signature patterns are defined for JavaBeans, classes and interfaces throughout the Java platform define property accessor methods that follow these conventions and patterns. Looking at a class in terms of the properties it defines can be a powerful tool for understanding the class, so property methods are grouped together in this section. Property accessor methods are listed alphabetically by property name, not by method name. This means that the "set", "get", and "is" methods for a property all appear together.

Public instance methods

Contains all of the public instance methods that are not grouped elsewhere.

Implementing methods

Groups the methods that implement the same interface. There is one subgroup for each interface implemented by the class. Methods that are defined by the same interface are almost always related to each other, so this is a useful functional grouping of methods.

If an interface method is also an event registration method or a property accessor method, it is listed both in this group and in the event or property group. This situation does not arise often, but when it does, all of the functional groupings are important and useful enough to warrant the duplicate listing. When an interface method is listed in the event or property group, it displays an Implements: flag that specifies the name of the interface of which it is part.

Overriding methods

Groups the methods that override methods of a superclass, broken down into subgroups by superclass. This is typically a useful grouping, because it helps to make it clear how a class modifies the default behavior of its superclasses. In practice, it is also often true that methods that override the same superclass are functionally related to each other.

Sometimes a method that overrides a superclass is also a property accessor method or (more rarely) an event registration method. When this happens, the method is grouped with the property or event methods and displays a flag that indicates which superclass it overrides. The method is not listed with other overriding methods, however. This is different from interface methods, which, since they are more strongly functionally related, may have duplicate listings in both groups.

Protected instance methods
Contains all of the protected instance methods that are not grouped elsewhere.

Fields
Lists all of the nonconstant fields of the class, breaking them down into subgroups for public and protected static fields and public and protected instance fields. Many classes do not define any publicly accessible fields. For those that do, many object-oriented programmers prefer not to use those fields directly, but instead to use accessor methods when such methods are available.

Deprecated members
Deprecated methods and deprecated fields are grouped at the very bottom of the class synopsis. Use of these members is strongly discouraged.

Cross-References

The synopsis section of a quick-reference entry is followed by a number of optional cross-reference sections that indicate other, related classes and methods that may be of interest. These sections are the following:

Subclasses
This section lists the subclasses of this class, if there are any.

Implementations
This section lists classes that implement this interface.

Passed To
This section lists all of the methods and constructors that are passed an object of this type as an argument. This is useful when you have an object of a given type and want to figure out what you can do with it.

Returned By
This section lists all of the methods (but not constructors) that return an object of this type. This is useful when you know that you want to work with an object of this type, but don't know how to obtain one.

Thrown By
For checked exception classes, this section lists all of the methods and constructors that throw exceptions of this type. This material helps you figure out when a given exception or error may be thrown. Note, however, that this section is based on the exception types listed in the throws clauses of methods and constructors. Subclasses of RuntimeException and Error do not have to be listed in throws clauses, so it is not possible to generate a complete cross-reference of methods that throw these types of unchecked exceptions.

Type Of
This section lists all of the fields and constants that are of this type, which can help you figure out how to obtain an object of this type.

A Note About Class Names

Throughout the quick reference, you'll notice that classes are sometimes referred to by class name alone and at other times referred to by class name and package name. If package names were always used, the class synopses would become long and hard to read. On the other hand, if package names were never used, it would sometimes be difficult to know what class was being referred to. The rules for including or omitting the package name are complex. They can be summarized approximately as follows, however:

- If the class name alone is ambiguous, the package name is always used.
- If the class is part of the `java.lang` package or is a very commonly used class, the package name is omitted.
- If the class being referred to is part of the current package (and has a quick-reference entry in the current chapter), the package name is omitted.

How to Use

9

The javax.xml.messaging Package

Package javax.xml.messaging

JAXM 1.1; JWSDP 1.0

The javax.xml.messaging package contains the classes and interfaces that make up the Java API for XML-based Messaging (JAXM). JAXM is a software layer above SAAJ that provides the same access to the low-level features of SOAP messaging and adds the following features:

Asynchronous message transmission
Whereas a SAAJ client blocks after sending a message until the server sends a response, JAXM clients resume execution shortly after the message is sent. In fact, JAXM does not recognize the concept of request-response messaging, viewing these instead as the transmission and receipt of two independent messages.

More reliable delivery
If the intended recipient of a SOAP message is not active or not reachable when a SAAJ client transmits it, the message is not delivered and the application is responsible for error recovery. By contrast, messages sent by JAXM clients are resent a configurable number of times before being considered undeliverable. As a consequence of this, a JAXM receiver may receive messages that were sent to it while it was inactive.

Profiles
JAXM implementations may support one or more industry-standard profiles that represent agreed ways to construct SOAP messages. Application code is required to specify the profile to be used and supply the values to be included in the message, but the JAXM implementation is responsible for ensuring that the message is constructed as required by the profile.

JAXM provides these features by interposing message providers between the JAXM sender and the JAXM receiver. Instead of addressing and sending a SOAP message directly to its ultimate recipient, the sender instead delivers it to a local messaging provider. The destination address in the message is typically not that of the receiver, but a URI (actually an instance of the Endpoint class) that the provider will map to a real address using internal configuration information. The resolved address will actually be that of another JAXM provider that is local to receiver. Having chosen the destination, the sending provider transmits the message one or more times until it is successfully delivered to the peer JAXM provider or a configurable retry limit is reached. Since the call made by the JAXM client to send the message returns before it is known whether the message will be successfully delivered, no reporting of errors to the client is possible when using JAXM.

When a JAXM provider receives a message, it maps the destination address to a local endpoint and looks for a receiver willing to receive messages for that endpoint. If such a receiver exists, the message is delivered to it. If not, the provider retains the message for a configurable period, waiting for a receiver to register to receive messages addressed to that endpoint. If no such client registers within the time-out period, the message is discarded.

The asynchronous nature of the message delivery path means that a provider must be able to deliver a message to a receiver at any time. Since all communication takes place over HTTP, this means that the message receiver must be prepared to accept an HTTP connection. Since J2SE does not provide a server-side implementation of HTTP, the practical implication of this is that all JAXM clients that wish to receive messages must be container-resident.

The configuration information required to allow a JAXM provider to map between logical Endpoint addresses and real network addresses, and the mechanism used by a receiver to specify the Endpoint address or addresses on which it is prepared to listen are implementation-dependent. Refer to Chapter 4 for a description of the mechanism used by the JAXM reference implementation.

JAXM providers typically support only profiled messages. The reference implementation provides basic support for the WS-Routing profile (formerly known as SOAP-RP) and the ebXML TRP profile. The API required for these profiles is not part of the JAXM specification and cannot, therefore, be considered portable. No coverage of these APIs is provided in this chapter, although there is some discussion of both profiles in Chapter 4.

Since JAXM senders and receivers always communicate directly with a provider rather than with each other, they are both in the client role relative to the provider, even though one of them may play the server role in respect of their (indirect) interaction with each other. Throughout this section, the term "JAXM client" will be used to refer to both a JAXM sender or a receiver.

Unlike SAAJ, JAXM was not incorporated in the J2EE 1.4 platform. There is, however, an implementation available in the JWSDP, although its applicability is clearly going to be limited for the time being unless the J2EE vendors provide their own implementations.

Interfaces

public interface **OnewayListener**;
public interface **ProviderConnection**;
public interface **ProviderMetaData**;
public interface **ReqRespListener**;

Classes

public class **Endpoint**;
public class **URLEndpoint** extends Endpoint;
public abstract class **JAXMServlet** extends javax.servlet.http.HttpServlet;
public abstract class **ProviderConnectionFactory**;

Exceptions

public class **JAXMException** extends javax.xml.soap.SOAPException;

JAXM 1.1; JWSDP 1.0

```
public class Endpoint {
// Public Constructors
    public Endpoint( String uri);
// Public Methods Overriding Object
    public String toString( );
// Protected Instance Fields
    protected String id;
}
```

The Endpoint class encapsulates the concept of a JAXM endpoint, which is the point of communication between a JAXM application client and its local messaging provider. A JAXM client typically builds a SOAP message containing source and destination Endpoint addresses, and delivers it to its local provider, which is responsible for delivering it. Similarly, a JAXM receiver will register with its local provider and supply the Endpoint for which it wishes to receive inbound messages.

An Endpoint is constructed from a URI, which is essentially an arbitrary string that represents a message destination. Here's an example of the construction of an Endpoint:

```
    Endpoint endpoint = new Endpoint("urn:SOAPRPecho");
```

When a message addressed to this endpoint is sent, the messaging provider is expected to convert the logical address urn:SOAPRPecho to the real address of the receiving JAXM messaging provider using configuration information supplied in an implementation-dependent manner. The actual endpoint address is typically carried in the message as part of a SOAP message header so that it can be interpreted by the receiving provider and used to locate the intended recipient. Both the WS-Routing and ebXML profiles include headers that carry this information.

Subclasses   URLEndpoint

JAXM 1.1; JWSDP 1.0   serializable checked

```
public class JAXMException extends javax.xml.soap.SOAPException {
// Public Constructors
    public JAXMException( );
    public JAXMException( Throwable cause);
    public JAXMException( String reason);
    public JAXMException( String reason, Throwable cause);
}
```

JAXMException is a checked exception (derived from javax.xml.soap.SOAPException) that is used to report errors encountered during the execution of methods of the JAXM API.

A JAXMException typically includes a text string giving a human-readable description of the error and, in some cases, may have an associated Throwable that represents the root cause of the problem. The four constructors allow a JAXMException to be created with any combination of text message and Throwable, which may subsequently be retrieved using the getMessage( ) and getCause( ) methods. Note that the Throwable attribute can be set either at construction time or by using the initCause( ) method. However, a java.lang.IllegalStateException is thrown if this method is called when the Throwable attribute has already been set.

Thrown By ProviderConnection.{close( ), createMessageFactory( ), getMetaData( ), send( )}, ProviderConnectionFactory.{createConnection( ), newInstance( )}

JAXMServlet

JAXM 1.1; JWSDP 1.0   serializable

```
public abstract class JAXMServlet extends javax.servlet.http.HttpServlet {
// Public Constructors
    public JAXMServlet( );
// Protected Class Methods
    protected static javax.xml.soap.MimeHeaders getHeaders(javax.servlet.http.HttpServletRequest req);
    protected static void putHeaders(javax.xml.soap.MimeHeaders headers, javax.servlet.http.HttpServletResponse res);
// Public Instance Methods
    public void setMessageFactory(javax.xml.soap.MessageFactory msgFactory);
// Public Methods Overriding HttpServlet
    public void doPost(javax.servlet.http.HttpServletRequest req, javax.servlet.http.HttpServletResponse resp)
        throws javax.servlet.ServletExceptionjava.io.IOException;
// Public Methods Overriding GenericServlet
    public void init(javax.servlet.ServletConfig servletConfig)
        throws javax.servlet.ServletException;
// Protected Instance Fields
    protected javax.xml.soap.MessageFactory msgFactory;
}
```

JAXMServlet is a skeleton servlet that can be subclassed to create a container-resident JAXM client. The subclass must do the following:

- Declare that it implements either the OnewayListener or ReqRespListener interface
- Install a suitable MessageFactory in the init( ) method
- Provide an implementation of the onMessage( ) method

A SOAP message is delivered to the servlet as an HTTP POST request and is therefore handled in the servlet's doPost( ) method, which converts the body of the request to a javax.xml.soap.SOAPMessage object. This object is then passed to the onMessage( ) method, which the JAXM client is required to implement.

A client should implement the OnewayListener interface if it does not intend to return a reply immediately. In this case, the onMessage( ) method has the following signature:

```
public void onMessage(SOAPMessage message);
```

The ReqRespListener interface is intended for clients that create a synchronous reply—that is, the reply method is sent back as the body of the HTTP response message. This interface, therefore, has a variant of onMessage( ) that requires the client to construct and return a reply message:

```
public SOAPMessage onMessage(SOAPMessage message);
```

In the JAXM reference implementation, it is not possible to construct a working JAXM client that implements the ReqRespListener interface, since the message returned by onMessage( ) is ignored by the JAXM provider. All JAXM clients must, therefore, be asynchronous. It is possible, however, to use JAXMServlet as the base class for a SOAP message receiver that uses the SAAJ API and implements the ReqRespListener interface rather than a JAXM client (although this option is not available for the J2EE 1.4 platform, which does not include JAXM).

The conversion between the representation of a SOAP message in the body of an HTML request or response and the corresponding SOAPMessage is performed by a javax.xml.soap.MessageFactory. A suitable factory must be installed by overriding the init() method, calling super.init(), and then using the setMessageFactory() method. By default, JAXMServlet installs a factory that does not perform processing specific to any of the JAXM profiles. A client that wishes to handle profiled messages (e.g., for WS-Routing or ebXML TRP) must instead supply the message factory provided by that profile. These classes are implementation-dependent, but you can get one in a portable fashion by using the createMessageFactory() method of the ProviderConnection class, as the following code snippet shows:

```
ProviderConnection conn = ProviderConnectionFactory.newInstance( )
                               .createConnection( );
setMessageFactory(conn.createMessageFactory("soaprp"));
```

OnewayListener   javax.xml.messaging

JAXM 1.1; JWSDP 1.0

```
public interface OnewayListener {
// Public Instance Methods
    public abstract void onMessage(javax.xml.soap.SOAPMessage message);
}
```

The OnewayListener interface is implemented by a JAXMServlet subclass that receives a SOAP message but does not wish to return an immediate response. The onMessage() method is called whenever a message is received and is provided with a SOAPMessage object created from that message as its only argument. The implementation may handle the message immediately or defer its processing to a more convenient time.

A JAXM client that implements this interface and wishes to return a reply message must create the message using the MessageFactory of the JAXM profile that it is using, set the destination address using a profile-specific method, and then call the ProviderConnection send() method. See the description of the JAXMServlet for information on obtaining an appropriate MessageFactory.

ProviderConnection   javax.xml.messaging

JAXM 1.1; JWSDP 1.0

```
public interface ProviderConnection {
// Public Instance Methods
    public abstract void close( ) throws JAXMException;
    public abstract javax.xml.soap.MessageFactory createMessageFactory(String profile) throws JAXMException;
    public abstract ProviderMetaData getMetaData( ) throws JAXMException;
    public abstract void send(javax.xml.soap.SOAPMessage message) throws JAXMException;
}
```

A ProviderConnection object represents a connection path between a JAXM client and a JAXM provider. An instance of this class can be obtained using the createConnection()

method of **ProviderConnectionFactory**, as described in the reference section for that class. Here's a typical example:

```
ProviderConnectionFactory pcf = ProviderConnectionFactory.newInstance( );
ProviderConnection conn = pcf.createConnection( );
```

All JAXM clients work with a JAXM message profile, which constructs SOAP messages according to agreed rules. A JAXM client can use the **getMetaData( )** method to obtain a **ProviderMetaData** object that can be used to get the names of the profiles that the provider supports. In practice, however, a JAXM client has to be written with knowledge of the classes that implement a particular profile; therefore, this mechanism will probably only be used to verify that the required profile is available.

The **createMessageFactory( )** method returns an object that can create messages formed according to the rules of the profile whose name is provided as its argument. The set of profiles supported by a provider and the names by which they are known are implementation-dependent. The reference implementation recognizes the names **soaprp** and **ebxml**. The following code returns a message factory that knows how to build SOAP messages according to the rules in the WS-Routing (formerly SOAP-RP) specification:

```
MessageFactory factory = conn.createMessageFactory("soaprp");
```

A **JAXMException** is thrown if the provider does not support the requested profile. Refer to the reference section for the **javax.xml.soap** package for a description of the **MessageFactory** class.

Having constructed a SOAP message, a client forwards it to its local provider using the **send( )** method, which requires only the message itself as an argument. Unlike the **send( )** method of the SAAJ **SOAPConnection** class, this method does not have an explicit destination address argument. Instead, the message is expected to specify the intended recipient using an address element that is specific to the profile according to which it was constructed. Furthermore, the address is usually not a fixed transport address (such as a URL). More likely, it is a URI that is used as a key to a configuration table in the provider where the URL of the JAXM provider local to the message recipient is held.

The **close( )** method is used to release the **ProviderConnection** object when it is no longer required.

Returned By   ProviderConnectionFactory.createConnection( )

ProviderConnectionFactory   javax.xml.messaging

JAXM 1.1; JWSDP 1.0

```
public abstract class ProviderConnectionFactory {
// Public Constructors
    public ProviderConnectionFactory( );
// Public Class Methods
    public static ProviderConnectionFactory newInstance( ) throws JAXMException;
// Public Instance Methods
    public abstract ProviderConnection createConnection( ) throws JAXMException;
}
```

ProviderConnectionFactory is an abstract class that can be used to create **ProviderConnection** objects for the purpose of obtaining a connection to a JAXM provider. In a container-based environment, a JAXM client uses a JNDI lookup to obtain a preconfigured

ProviderConnectionFactory that results in the message that it subsequently created being sent to a JAXM provider chosen by an administrator.

An alternative way to obtain an instance of this class is to call the static newInstance() method. This method locates a concrete implementation of ProviderConnectionFactory as follows, stopping when a suitable class is found:

1. Looks in the system properties for a property called javax.xml.messaging.ProviderConnectionFactory. If this property is defined, its value is assumed to be the class name of a concrete implementation of ProviderConnectionFactory.

2. Looks for the same property in a file called ${JAVA_HOME}/lib/jaxm.properties. If the property is found, its value is assumed to be the required class name.

3. Looks for a resource called META-INF/services/javax.xml.messaging.ProviderConnectionFactory in the classpath. If such a resource exists, it is opened and a single line is read from it. If the line is not empty, it is used as the required class name.

4. Finally, an implementation-dependent default class is used. In the case of the reference implementation, this class is called com.sun.xml.messaging.jaxm.client.remote. ProviderConnectionFactoryImpl.

The createConnection() method returns a ProviderConnection object that allows a client to communicate with a JAXM provider. The means by which the provider is located is implementation-dependent. In the case of the reference implementation, the provider's address is configured in a file called *client.xml*, which must be accessible as a resource in the classpath of the client. For a description of the content of this file, refer to Chapter 4.

Returned By   ProviderConnectionFactory.newInstance()

ProviderMetaData   javax.xml.messaging

JAXM 1.1; JWSDP 1.0

```
public interface ProviderMetaData {
// Public Instance Methods
  public abstract int getMajorVersion();
  public abstract int getMinorVersion();
  public abstract String getName();
  public abstract String[] getSupportedProfiles();
}
```

ProviderMetaData provides information about a JAXM provider. An instance of this object can be obtained by calling the getMetaData() method of a ProviderConnection object.

The getName() method can be used to obtain an identifier for the JAXM provider to which the client is connected, while getMajorVersion() and getMinorVersion() return version information. These methods may be useful for logging purposes. The getSupportedProfiles() method returns the names of the SOAP profiles that the provider supports. The names themselves are provider-specific and can be passed to the ProviderConnection createMessageFactory() method to obtain a factory that can create messages built according to the rules of the named profile.

Returned By   ProviderConnection.getMetaData()

JAXM 1.1; JWSDP 1.0

```
public interface ReqRespListener {
// Public Instance Methods
   public abstract javax.xml.soap.SOAPMessage onMessage( javax.xml.soap.SOAPMessage message);
}
```

The ReqRespListener interface is implemented by a JAXMServlet subclass that receives a SOAP message to which it immediately creates a response. The onMessage() method is called whenever a message is received and is provided with a SOAPMessage object created from that message as its only argument. The return value from this method may be either null or a SOAPMessage that is returned to the originator of the request message.

For reasons mentioned in the description of the JAXMServlet class, a JAXM client that implements this interface may not behave as expected in the JAXM reference implementation. Specifically, the reply message returned from the onMessage() method is not delivered.

URLEndpoint

javax.xml.messaging

JAXM 1.1; JWSDP 1.0

```
public class URLEndpoint extends Endpoint {
// Public Constructors
   public URLEndpoint( String url);
// Public Instance Methods
   public String getURL( );
}
```

URLEndpoint is a subclass of Endpoint in which the URI that represents the endpoint address is expected to be a valid URL.

This class is used internally within the JAXM reference implementation to represent the addresses to which a URI used by a JAXM clients is mapped within the JAXM provider, since each such address must be the URL of the provider that will receive a message with that URI. From the viewpoint of a JAXM client, however, the URLEndpoint class is of no practical use, at least in the reference implementation, since neither of the profiles that it supports will accept a message destination that is a URL.

A URLEndpoint can be used by a SAAJ client in conjunction with the SOAPConnection send( ) method. However, it is simpler to use a string version of the URL instead.

10

The javax.xml.namespace Package

Package javax.xml.namespace

This package contains only a single class, QName, that represents a namespace-qualified XML element name. Theoretically, many of the XML APIs, including those that are not directly related to web services, could make use of this class. At the present time, however, it is used only by the packages that form the JAX-RPC API.

Classes

public class **QName** implements Serializable;

QName   javax.xml.namespace

JAX-RPC 1.0; JWSDP 1.0, J2EE 1.4   serializable

```
public class QName implements java.io.Serializable {
// Public Constructors
    public QName( String localPart);
    public QName( String namespaceURI, String localPart);
// Public Class Methods
    public static QName valueOf( String s);
// Public Instance Methods
    public String getLocalPart( );
    public String getNamespaceURI( );
// Public Methods Overriding Object
    public final boolean equals( Object obj);
    public final int hashCode( );
    public String toString( );
}
```

This class represents an XML-qualified name. The two-argument constructor creates a QName object with a given local part and namespace URI. The one-argument constructor creates a QName object that does not have an explicitly specified namespace.

An XML element associated with a QName that does not have an explicit namespace is considered to be in the default namespace that is in force for that element. The URI for the default namespace is determined by an xmlns attribute with no associated prefix, placed either on that element or on one of its ancestors.

The getLocalPart( ) and getNamespaceURI( ) methods return the local part and the namespace URI associated with the QName. In the case of a QName that does not have a namespace URI, the latter method returns an empty string. The toString( ) method creates a string representation of the QName as follows:

- If the name does not have a namespace URI, then the value returned by toString( ) is just the local part of the name.

- Otherwise, the value returned is {URI}localPart.

The static valueOf( ) method accepts a string representation of a qualified name in the form returned by toString( ) and converts it to a QName object. For example, the result of the call QName.valueOf("{URI}localPart") is the same as using the constructor QName("URI", "localPart"), whereas QName.valueOf("localPart") produces the same result as QName("localPart"). If the argument cannot be decoded as a QName, then a java.lang.IllegalArgumentException is thrown.

Passed To   Too many methods to list.

Returned By   QName.valueOf( ), javax.xml.rpc.Call.{getOperationName( ), getParameterTypeByName( ), getPortTypeName( ), getReturnType( )}, javax.xml.rpc.Service.getServiceName( ), javax.xml. rpc.handler.GenericHandler.getHeaders( ), javax.xml.rpc.handler.Handler.getHeaders( ), javax.xml.rpc.handler.HandlerInfo.getHeaders( ), javax.xml.rpc.soap.SOAPFaultException. getFaultCode( )

Type Of   javax.xml.rpc.encoding.XMLType.{SOAP_ARRAY, SOAP_BASE64, SOAP_BOOLEAN, SOAP_ BYTE, SOAP_DOUBLE, SOAP_FLOAT, SOAP_INT, SOAP_LONG, SOAP_SHORT, SOAP_STRING, XSD_BASE64, XSD_BOOLEAN, XSD_BYTE, XSD_DATETIME, XSD_DECIMAL, XSD_DOUBLE, XSD_FLOAT, XSD_HEXBINARY, XSD_INT, XSD_INTEGER, XSD_LONG, XSD_QNAME, XSD_ SHORT, XSD_STRING}, javax.xml.rpc.holders.QNameHolder.value

11

The javax.xml.registry Package

Package javax.xml.registry
JAXR 1.0; JWSDP 1.0, J2EE 1.4

The javax.xml.registry and javax.xml.registry.infomodel packages contain the classes and interfaces that make up the Java API for XML-based Registries (JAXR). The javax.xml.registry. infomodel package (described in the next chapter), defines the programming interface for the objects that reside in a registry, while the javax.xml.registry package (the subject of this chapter), provides the means to connect to a registry, submit queries, and update and delete objects within the registry.

In the JAXR API, a client application connects to a JAXR provider that is usually co-resident with it. The JAXR provider is specific to a particular type of registry, but provides a programming model that is entirely independent of the way in which the target registry stores and manages its content. There are currently two major registry types in common use: the UDDI registry and the ebXML registry/repository. Although these registries have a lot of common functionality, the ebXML registry/repository also provides features that have no counterpart in the UDDI registry and that cannot reasonably be emulated by a UDDI-based JAXR provider. The JAXR API deals with this situation by allocating each method to a capability level. There are currently two such levels: level 0, which broadly corresponds to the functionality provided by a UDDI registry, and level 1, which extends level 0 to include functionality from the ebXML registry specification. All JAXR providers are required to implement level 0. The JAXR reference implementation includes a level 0 provider that works with a UDDI registry. The level to which each method in the API is allocated is shown in the reference sections in both this and the next chapter.

The core interface of the JAXR API is RegistryService. Each JAXR provider is represented by a single instance of this interface, which can be retrieved by creating a Connection-Factory, then obtaining a Connection to the JAXR provider and calling its getRegistryService() method. The RegistryService object provides access to the query managers and the life-cycle manager that can be used to query and update the registry itself.

Querying a registry and updating a registry are modeled as two separate activities. This is appropriate because registry queries can usually (depending on the policy of the registry) be performed by any user, without the need for authentication. Registry updates, on the other hand, almost always require prior authentication and are typically carried out only over a secure transport protocol, such as HTTPS. The JAXR API provides the QueryManager and BusinessQueryManager interfaces to handle registry queries and the LifeCycleManager and BusinessLifeCycleManager interfaces for registry updates. In addition, level 1 registries may support registry queries written using SQL-92 or XQuery (and possibly other query languages) via the DeclarativeQueryManager interface.

Interfaces

public interface **BulkResponse** extends JAXRResponse;
public interface **BusinessLifeCycleManager** extends LifeCycleManager;
public interface **BusinessQueryManager** extends QueryManager;
public interface **CapabilityProfile**;
public interface **Connection**;
public interface **DeclarativeQueryManager** extends QueryManager;
public interface **FederatedConnection** extends Connection;
public interface **FindQualifier**;
public interface **JAXRResponse**;
public interface **LifeCycleManager**;
public interface **Query**;
public interface **QueryManager**;
public interface **RegistryService**;

Classes

public abstract class **ConnectionFactory**;

Exceptions

public class **JAXRException** extends Exception implements JAXRResponse;
public class **InvalidRequestException** extends JAXRException;
public class **RegistryException** extends JAXRException;
public class **DeleteException** extends RegistryException;
public class **FindException** extends RegistryException;
public class **SaveException** extends RegistryException;
public class **UnexpectedObjectException** extends JAXRException;
public class **UnsupportedCapabilityException** extends JAXRException;

BulkResponse
javax.xml.registry

JAXR 1.0; JWSDP 1.0, J2EE 1.4

```
public interface BulkResponse extends JAXRResponse {
// Public Instance Methods
    public abstract Collection getCollection() throws JAXRException;          //L0
    public abstract Collection getExceptions() throws JAXRException;          //L0
    public abstract boolean isPartialResponse() throws JAXRException;         //L0
}
```

BulkResponse is an interface derived from JAXRResponse that is returned by the JAXR API methods that perform registry queries and by some of the registry update methods. A BulkResponse contains a set of RegistryObjects that represent the results of a search or of an update operation such as a delete, where the objects that were deleted are returned. These objects can be obtained by calling the getCollection() method. If any errors are encountered while the operation is in progress, one or more RegistryExceptions may also be included in the response. These exceptions can be retrieved using the getExceptions() method. It is possible for an operation to succeed in respect to some objects, but fail for others. In this case, both the getCollection() and getExceptions() methods return nonempty collections. The isPartialResponse() method returns true if the registry did not return all possible responses.

If a request is made on a synchronous connection, the caller is blocked until the JAXR provider receives a reply, at which point the content of the BulkResponse is valid. In the case of an asynchronous response, the getCollection() and getExceptions() methods block until the operation is complete. To avoid being blocked, the caller may use the isAvailable() method, which returns false until the results of the operation are available. An alternative is to monitor the return value of the getStatus() method, which returns STATUS_UNAVAILABLE while the operation is in progress. Once the operation has completed according to the isAvailable() method, the caller may use the value returned by getStatus() to determine its success or failure, before retrieving the results or exceptions, as appropriate. The status is set to STATUS_SUCCESS to indicate that the operation fully succeeded. STATUS_FAILURE indicates that there is at least one exception in the collection returned by getExceptions(); there may also be RegistryObjects available from the getCollection() method. In other words, this status may represent partial success. STATUS_WARNING is used to indicate that the request was successful, but may only contain a partial response (i.e., isPartial() would return true).

When an asynchronous request is initiated, the JAXR provider allocates a unique identifier to it. This identifier is of use mainly to the provider itself, but application code can retrieve its value from the getRequestId() method.

Returned By   Too many methods to list.

BusinessLifeCycleManager   javax.xml.registry

JAXR 1.0; JWSDP 1.0, J2EE 1.4

```
public interface BusinessLifeCycleManager extends LifeCycleManager {
// Public Instance Methods
    public abstract void confirmAssociation(javax.xml.registry.infomodel.Association assoc)
        throws JAXRExceptionInvalidRequestException;                                        //LO
    public abstract BulkResponse deleteAssociations(Collection associationKeys) throws JAXRException;      //LO
    public abstract BulkResponse deleteClassificationSchemes(Collection schemeKeys) throws JAXRException;  //LO
    public abstract BulkResponse deleteConcepts(Collection conceptKeys) throws JAXRException;              //LO
    public abstract BulkResponse deleteOrganizations(Collection organizationKeys) throws JAXRException;    //LO
    public abstract BulkResponse deleteServiceBindings(Collection bindingKeys) throws JAXRException;       //LO
    public abstract BulkResponse deleteServices(Collection serviceKeys) throws JAXRException;              //LO
    public abstract BulkResponse saveAssociations(Collection associations, boolean replace) throws JAXRException;  //LO
    public abstract BulkResponse saveClassificationSchemes(Collection schemes) throws JAXRException;       //LO
    public abstract BulkResponse saveConcepts(Collection concepts) throws JAXRException;                   //LO
    public abstract BulkResponse saveOrganizations(Collection organizations) throws JAXRException;         //LO
    public abstract BulkResponse saveServiceBindings(Collection bindings) throws JAXRException;            //LO
    public abstract BulkResponse saveServices(Collection services) throws JAXRException;                   //LO
    public abstract void unConfirmAssociation(javax.xml.registry.infomodel.Association assoc)
        throws JAXRExceptionInvalidRequestException;                                        //LO
}
```

BusinessLifeCycleManager is a derived interface of LifeCycleManager that provides additional methods to allow registry objects to be saved and deleted by reference to their type rather than by using the generic methods provided by LifeCycleManager itself. Additionally, the confirmAssociation( ) and unConfirmAssociation( ) methods allow the caller to change the confirmed state of an extramural association (see the description of javax.xml.registry.info-model.Association in the next chapter for the meaning of this term). These two methods can only be called by the owner of either the source or the target object in the association, as indicated by the credentials associated with the connection to the provider, or an InvalidRequestException is thrown.

All of the delete methods in this interface require a Collection argument, which must contain the Keys for the registry objects to be deleted. The BulkResponse returned by these methods contains the Keys of the deleted objects. If an error occurs, a DeleteException is added to the response, along with the keys of all objects that have been deleted. A registry may refuse to allow the removal of an object that is referenced from another object, but is not obliged to do so. If this error is detected, an InvalidRequestException is placed in the BulkResponse.

The save methods in this interface all accept a Collection containing the objects to be saved. Objects in this collection that did not already exist in the registry are created and a new key is assigned. Objects that already exist are updated from the instance provided in the collection. When an object refers to other objects, those dependent objects are also updated or created as a result of saving the first object. Therefore, if a new Organization is created in memory, the act of saving that Organization also saves any Classifications and other objects that become associated with it. The BulkResponse returned by these methods contains the Keys that are associated with the created or updated objects, together with any SaveExceptions that result from failures to save or create individual objects. When an object is created using a factory method of the LifeCycleManager interface, it does not necessarily have a valid key, but the process of saving it does not install a key in the client's view of the object, even though one will have been allocated and returned in the BulkResponse.

Returned By   RegistryService.getBusinessLifeCycleManager( )

BusinessQueryManager   javax.xml.registry

JAXR 1.0; JWSDP 1.0, J2EE 1.4

```
public interface BusinessQueryManager extends QueryManager {
// Public Instance Methods
    public abstract BulkResponse findAssociations(Collection findQualifiers, String sourceObjectId,
        String targetObjectId, Collection associationTypes) throws JAXRException;          //LO
    public abstract BulkResponse findCallerAssociations(                                   //LO
    Boolean confirmedByCaller,
    Boolean confirmedByOtherParty,
    Collection associationTypes) throws JAXRException;
        public abstract javax.xml.registry.infomodel.ClassificationScheme findClassificationSchemeByName
        Collection findQualifiers, String namePattern) throws JAXRException;               //LO
    public abstract BulkResponse findClassificationSchemes(Collection findQualifiers, Collection namePatterns,
        Collection classifications, Collection externalLinks) throws JAXRException;        //LO
    public abstract javax.xml.registry.infomodel.Concept findConceptByPath(String path) throws JAXRException;    //LO
    public abstract BulkResponse findConcepts(Collection findQualifiers, Collection namePatterns,Collection classifications,
        Collection externalIdentifiers, Collection externalLinks) throws JAXRException;    //LO
```

```
public abstract BulkResponse findOrganizations(Collection findQualifiers, Collection namePatterns,
    Collection classifications, Collection specifications, Collection externalIdentifiers,Collection externalLinks)
    throws JAXRException;                                                                    // L0
public abstract BulkResponse findRegistryPackages(Collection findQualifiers, Collection namePatterns,
    Collection classifications, Collection externalLinks) throws JAXRException;              // L1
public abstract BulkResponse findServiceBindings(javax.xml.registry.infomodel.Key serviceKey,
    Collection findQualifiers, Collection classifications, Collection specifications) throws JAXRException;   // L0
public abstract BulkResponse findServices(javax.xml.registry.infomodel.Key orgKey, Collection findQualifiers,
    Collection namePatterns, Collection classifications, Collection specifications) throws JAXRException;     // L0
}
```

BusinessQueryManager is a derived interface of QueryManager that provides convenience methods allowing registry searches to be performed based on registry object type, together with various criteria that allow filtering of the objects contained in the response. A search may also specify a sort order for the results that are returned. Most of the methods in this interface require a set of Collections that contain the filtering and sorting criteria. Where no criterion of a given type is to be applied, the corresponding collection may be supplied as null. The filter and sorting arguments that may be supplied are as follows; note that not all of these arguments are valid for every method.

findQualifiers

> A collection of filters and sorting criteria as defined by the FindQualifier interface. Values such as AND_ALL_KEYS specified here override the default methods of combining multiple criteria described in each of the following paragraphs.

name patterns

> A collection of strings that completely or partially specify the names of the registry objects to be returned. The syntax defined for the SQL-92 LIKE clause may be used to specify wildcards. By default, these names are combined using an OR operator, so that objects whose names matching any of the supplied patterns are returned.

classifications

> A collection of Classifications that are required to be attached to the registry objects returned. These values are combined using an AND operator, so that only those objects that have all of the Classifications specified are returned.

specifications

> A ServiceBinding may have associated with it any number of specifications that provide information of use to the developers writing applications that will invoke the service. The connection between a ServiceBinding and a specification is made via a SpecificationLink that must point to another object in the registry—typically, a Concept. This search criterion uses any object that might be linked to by a SpecificationLink and, if more than one criterion is supplied, requires a match on all of them.

external identifiers

> Specifies a collection of objects of type ExternalIdentifier that must be associated with the registry object. The specified external identifiers are combined with an AND operator; therefore, the returned objects will have all of the requested external identifiers.

external link

> Specifies a collection of objects of type ExternalLink that must be associated with the registry object. The specified links are combined with an AND operator; therefore, the returned objects will have all of the requested links.

association type

A collection of association types. This filter is applied only to the findAssociations( ) method and is combined using an OR operator, so that Associations with any of the types in the collection are returned.

The query operations provided by this interface may be performed either synchronously (the default) or asynchronously. In either case, the BulkResponse object returned is valid immediately, but may not contain valid data. An attempt to access either the object collection or the exception set results in the calling thread being blocked until the operation completes. See the reference section for BulkResponse earlier in this chapter for a discussion of asynchronous operations.

Returned By   RegistryService.getBusinessQueryManager( )

CapabilityProfile

JAXR 1.0; JWSDP 1.0, J2EE 1.4

```
public interface CapabilityProfile {
// Public Instance Methods
  public abstract int getCapabilityLevel( ) throws JAXRException;            // LO
  public abstract String getVersion( ) throws JAXRException;                 // LO
}
```

CapabilityProfile provides two methods that return information about the JAXR provider. The getCapabilityLevel( ) methods return the highest capability level that the provider implements. A UDDI provider, like the one provided with the JAXR reference implementation, returns 0, while an ebXML provider returns 1. The getVersion( ) method returns the version of the JAXR specification that the provider implements, such as JAXR Version 1.0.

Returned By   RegistryService.getCapabilityProfile( )

Connection

JAXR 1.0; JWSDP 1.0, J2EE 1.4

```
public interface Connection {
// Public Instance Methods
  public abstract void close( ) throws JAXRException;                                    // LO
  public abstract Set getCredentials( ) throws JAXRException;                             // LO
  public abstract RegistryService getRegistryService( ) throws JAXRException;             // LO
  public abstract boolean isClosed( ) throws JAXRException;                               // LO
  public abstract boolean isSynchronous( ) throws JAXRException;                          // LO
  public abstract void setCredentials(Set credentials) throws JAXRException;              // LO
  public abstract void setSynchronous(boolean sync) throws JAXRException;                 // LO
}
```

The Connection interface represents a logical connection between a JAXR client and a JAXR provider. Although the client and provider may reside in separate processes or separate systems, in general, they are co-located; therefore, method calls made by a JAXR client are handled directly by the provider. The provider, however, is not normally in the same Java VM as the registry itself and is responsible for using whatever communication mechanism is necessary to access the registry. This is typically

JAX-RPC or SAAJ, using SOAP as the underlying messaging protocol. A Connection object is obtained from a ConnectionFactory and is specific to one type of registry. That is, all Connection objects returned from a UDDI implementation of ConnectionFactory support only communication with a UDDI registry.

Once you have a Connection, if the registry that you wish to communicate with requires authentication of its users, you should use the setCredentials() method to supply the required authentication information. This method takes an argument of type Set, which may contain authentication information for more than one authentication scheme. For basic authentication, credentials are supplied in the form of a java.net.PasswordAuthentication object containing a username and password, whereas certificate authentication requires an object of type javax.security.auth.x500.X500PrivateCredential. The credentials set for a Connection can be retrieved by calling the getCredentials() method.

A Connection may operate in either synchronous or asynchronous mode, as described in the reference section for the BulkResponse interface earlier in this chapter. The setSynchronous() and isSynchronous() methods can be used to set and query this setting. It is possible to change this setting on a per-request basis, if desired. The getRegistryService method returns the RegistryService associated with the connection. Multiple calls to this method return the same object. The RegistryService object is used to obtain the query and the life-cycle managers that are used to send query and update requests to the registry.

When you no longer need access to a Connection object, call its close() method to allow the provider to release resources it may have allocated. You can determine whether a Connection is already closed by calling the isClosed() method.

Implementations FederatedConnection

Returned By ConnectionFactory.createConnection( )

ConnectionFactory   javax.xml.registry

JAXR 1.0; JWSDP 1.0, J2EE 1.4

```
public abstract class ConnectionFactory {
// Public Constructors
    public ConnectionFactory( );
// Public Class Methods
    public static ConnectionFactory newInstance( ) throws JAXRException;
// Public Instance Methods
    public abstract javax.xml.registry.Connection createConnection( ) throws JAXRException;          //LO
    public abstract FederatedConnection createFederatedConnection(Collection connections)
        throws JAXRException;                                                            // LO (optional)
    public abstract Properties getProperties( ) throws JAXRException;                                 // LO
    public abstract void setProperties(Properties properties) throws JAXRException;                   // LO
}
```

The abstract ConnectionFactory class can be used to connect to JAXR registry providers. An instance of ConnectionFactory may be obtained by calling newInstance( ) method, which uses a four-step process to locate a suitable concrete implementation class, as follows:

1. Looks in the system properties for a property called javax.xml.registry.ConnectionFactory-Class. If this property is defined, its value is assumed to be the class name of a concrete implementation of ConnectionFactory.

2. Looks for the same property in a file called ${JAVA_HOME}/lib/jaxr.properties. If the property is found, its value is assumed to be the required class name.

3. Looks for a resource called META-INF/services/javax.xml.registry.ConnectionFactoryClass in the classpath. If such a resource exists, it is opened and a single line is read from it. If the line is not empty, it is used as the required class name.

4. Finally, an implementation-dependent default class is used. In the case of the reference implementation, this class is called com.sun.xml.registry.common. ConnectionFactoryImpl.

A container-resident client may also be able to obtain a ConnectionFactory instance from its JNDI environment.

A ConnectionFactory supports only one type of registry—at the present time, there are providers available for both UDDI and ebXML registries. In order to ensure you create an instance of the appropriate ConnectionFactory, set the system property javax.xml.registry. ConnectionFactoryClass to the appropriate value, or make sure that the ConnectionFactory class for the registry implementation that you need appears on your classpath before any other implementations and that none of the first three steps in the previous list locates another implementation.

Once you have a ConnectionFactory, use the setProperties() method to set property values and then call either the createConnection() method or the createFederatedConnection() method to get a connection to a JAXR provider. The following properties must be supported by all JAXR providers:

javax.xml.registry.queryManagerURL

The URL required to connect to the query service provided by a registry. The query service is usually an open, insecure service accessed over HTTP.

javax.xml.registry.lifeCycleManagerURL

The URL required to connect to the registry update service. The registry update service typically requires a user to obtain a user ID and to authenticate when connecting. Registries may require the use of a secure transport, such as HTTPS, to perform registry updates. If this property is not specified, it defaults to the value of the javax.xml.registry.queryManagerURL property.

javax.xml.registry.semanticEquivalences

Allows pairs of Concepts to be made equivalent in the view of the registry provider. This facility is used in the handling of postal addresses, as described in Chapter 7.

javax.xml.registry.security.authenticationMethod

Specifies the authentication mechanism that the client would like to use when connecting to the registry. Not all registries insist on authentication for queries, but most do so before allowing registry updates. The JAXR specification defines property values for several possible authentication schemes. JAXR providers and registries are not expected to support all of these schemes, which are UDDI_GET_ AUTHTOKEN, HTTP_BASIC, CLIENT_CERTIFICATE, and MS_PASSPORT. You'll find a description of each of these schemes in Chapter 7.

javax.xml.registry.uddi.maxRows

As its name suggests, this property is specific to UDDI registry providers and specifies the maximum number of rows that should be returned in the result of a query operation.

javax.xml.registry.postalAddressScheme

Different registry types use different representations of postal addresses. The JAXR API, on the other hand, provides an abstract view of a postal address that allows application code to be independent of any specific registry. This property provides the identifier of a ClassificationScheme that specifies the mapping between the fields of the postal address scheme used by the registry and the virtual scheme provided by JAXR.

The createConnection() method creates a Connection object that can be used to communicate with a single registry via a JAXR provider. The provider uses the values of the javax.xml. registry.queryManagerURL and javax.xml.registry.lifeCycleManagerURL properties to access the target registry when the JAXR client makes requests that require communication with the registry itself. The createFederatedConnection() method returns a FederatedConnection object that can be used to send the same query to more than one registry at the same time and combine the responses that are received into a single result set. The createFederatedConnection() method requires a Collection containing one or more Connection objects that correspond to the registries to which the queries should be sent. Support for FederatedConnections is optional despite the fact that it is a level 0 feature, although this may change in a future revision of the JAXR specification. A provider that does not support this feature throws an UnsupportedCapabilityException from its createFederatedConnection() method.

Returned By   ConnectionFactory.newInstance( )

DeclarativeQueryManager   javax.xml.registry

JAXR 1.0; JWSDP 1.0, J2EE 1.4

```
public interface DeclarativeQueryManager extends QueryManager {
// Public Instance Methods
    public abstract Query createQuery(int queryType, String queryString) throws InvalidRequestExceptionJAXRException; //L1
    public abstract BulkResponse executeQuery(Query query) throws JAXRException;                                        //L1
}
```

DeclarativeQueryManager is a derived interface of QueryManager that provides the ability to search the registry using queries expressed directly in one of the query languages that it supports, rather than using a query generated as a result of calling one of the methods of the QueryManager or BusinessQueryManager interfaces. A DeclarativeQueryManager can be obtained from the RegistryService object of a level 1 JAXR provider.

The query languages that a DeclarativeQueryManager supports are implementation-dependent and might include SQL-92, the ebXML filter query language, or XQuery. The createQuery() method returns a Query object that encapsulates a specified query expressed in a given query language. An InvalidRequestType exception is thrown if the JAXR provider does not support the requested query language or if the query string appears to be invalid. Validation of the query string is optional. The executeQuery() method performs a query described by a Query object and returns the results in the form of a BulkResponse.

Returned By   RegistryService.getDeclarativeQueryManager( )

DeleteException   javax.xml.registry

JAXR 1.0; JWSDP 1.0, J2EE 1.4   serializable checked

```
public class DeleteException extends RegistryException {
// Public Constructors
    public DeleteException( );
    public DeleteException( Throwable cause);
    public DeleteException( String reason);
    public DeleteException( String reason, Throwable cause);
}
```

DeleteException is a subclass of RegistryException that is used to indicate a failure during a registry delete operation. DeleteException is not thrown by any method—instead, it is stored within a BulkResponse object returned from a method such as the deleteOrganizations() method of BusinessLifeCycleManager. The affected object may be identified using the getErrorObjectKey() method inherited from RegistryException.

FederatedConnection

JAXR 1.0; JWSDP 1.0, J2EE 1.4

```
public interface FederatedConnection extends javax.xml.registry.Connection {
}
```

A FederatedConnection is a Connection that represents a collection of other Connections, some of which may also be FederatedConnections. The FederatedConnection interface defines exactly the same methods as Connection, but differs in the following respects:

- It is created by calling the createFederatedConnection() method of ConnectionFactory, which requires a Collection containing the Connection objects that will be grouped together by the FederatedConnection.
- When a request is made of a QueryManager obtained from a RegistryService corresponding to a FederatedConnection, the query is sent to all of the individual registries and the results are combined into a single BulkResponse, thus allowing the set of registries to be treated as one.
- Updates to multiple registries grouped into a FederatedConnection are not allowed. An attempt to get a reference to a LifeCycleManager using the methods of a RegistryService corresponding to a FederatedConnection results in an UnsupportedCapabilityException.

JAXR providers are not required to support FederatedConnections despite the fact that it is a level 0 feature, although this may change in a future revision of the JAXR specification. Such providers throw an UnsupportedCapabilityException from the createFederatedConnection() method of its ConnectionFactory method.

Returned By   ConnectionFactory.createFederatedConnection()

FindException

JAXR 1.0; JWSDP 1.0, J2EE 1.4   serializable checked

```
public class FindException extends RegistryException {
// Public Constructors
  public FindException();
  public FindException( Throwable cause);
  public FindException( String reason);
  public FindException( String reason, Throwable cause);
}
```

FindException is a subclass of RegistryException that is used to indicate a failure during a registry search operation. FindException is not thrown by any method—instead, it is stored within a BulkResponse object returned from a method such as the findOrganizations() method of BusinessQueryManager.

JAXR 1.0; JWSDP 1.0, J2EE 1.4

```
public interface FindQualifier {
// Public Constants
  public static final String AND_ALL_KEYS;                                        // ="andAllKeys"
  public static final String CASE_SENSITIVE_MATCH;                                // ="caseSensitiveMatch"
  public static final String COMBINE_CLASSIFICATIONS;                             // ="combineClassifications"
  public static final String EXACT_NAME_MATCH;                                    // ="exactNameMatch"
  public static final String OR_ALL_KEYS;                                         // ="orAllKeys"
  public static final String OR_LIKE_KEYS;                                        // ="orLikeKeys"
  public static final String SERVICE_SUBSET;                                      // ="serviceSubset"
  public static final String SORT_BY_DATE_ASC;                                    // ="sortByDateAsc"
  public static final String SORT_BY_DATE_DESC;                                   // ="sortByDateDesc"
  public static final String SORT_BY_NAME_ASC;                                    // ="sortByNameAsc"
  public static final String SORT_BY_NAME_DESC;                                   // ="sortByNameDesc"
  public static final String SOUNDEX;                                             // ="soundex"
}
```

The FindQualifier interface defines constants that are used when performing registry search operations to specify criteria such has how to combine multiple keys, whether the operation should consider case, and whether the results should be sorted. Registry providers are required to implement all qualifiers, apart from SOUNDEX, while non-UDDI providers are not required to implement SERVICE_SUBSET and COMBINE_CLASSIFICATIONS.

InvalidRequestException   javax.xml.registry

JAXR 1.0; JWSDP 1.0, J2EE 1.4   serializable checked

```
public class InvalidRequestException extends JAXRException {
// Public Constructors
  public InvalidRequestException( );
  public InvalidRequestException( Throwable cause);
  public InvalidRequestException( String reason);
  public InvalidRequestException(String reason, Throwable cause);
}
```

InvalidRequestException is thrown to report an invalid request. For example, the JAXR reference implementation throws this exception from the ConnectionFactory createConnection( ) method if the property that specifies the authentication method is set to any value other than null or UDDI_GET_AUTHTOKEN.

Thrown By   BusinessLifeCycleManager.{confirmAssociation( ), unConfirmAssociation( )},
                     DeclarativeQueryManager.createQuery( ), LifeCycleManager.{createClassification( ),
                     createClassificationScheme( ), createObject( )}, RegistryService.getBulkResponse( )

```
public class JAXRException extends Exception implements JAXRResponse {
// Public Constructors
    public JAXRException( );
    public JAXRException( Throwable cause);
    public JAXRException( String reason);
    public JAXRException( String reason, Throwable cause);
// Methods Implementing JAXRResponse
    public String getRequestId( );                          // constant default:null LO
    public int getStatus( );                                // constant default:0 LO
    public boolean isAvailable( ) throws JAXRException;     // constant default:true
// Public Methods Overriding Throwable
    public Throwable getCause( );                           // default:null
    public String getMessage( );                           // default:null
    public Throwable initCause( Throwable cause);          // synchronized
// Protected Instance Fields
    protected Throwable cause;
}
```

JAXRException is a checked exception that can be thrown from many of the methods in the JAXR API. JAXRException also implements the methods of the JAXRResponse interface, although there is no clear reason why it should do so. In the reference implementation, these methods return fixed values that indicate a completed request. Registry exceptions that result from errors detected by the JAXR provider (that is, on the client side of the operation) are derived from JAXRException, while those that occur on the registry side are reported as subclasses of RegistryException, which is itself derived from JAXRException.

A JAXRException contains a text message that describes the reason for the exception, and an optional Throwable that can be used to link to another exception as the root cause of this one. Both of these attributes may be set at construction time. The initCause( ) method may be used to associate a Throwable with a JAXRException after it is created, but may be called at most once and may not be called at all if a non-null Throwable is supplied to the constructor. The getMessage( ) method returns the message text set at construction time, or it returns the result of invoking the getMessage( ) of the Throwable if no message text is supplied to the constructor. If, in this case, there is no associated Throwable, then getMessage( ) returns null.

Subclasses InvalidRequestException, RegistryException, UnexpectedObjectException, UnsupportedCapabilityException

Thrown By Too many methods to list.

JAXRResponse

```
public interface JAXRResponse {
// Public Constants
    public static final int STATUS_FAILURE;                // =2
```

```
    public static final int STATUS_SUCCESS;                                          // =0
    public static final int STATUS_UNAVAILABLE;                                      // =3
    public static final int STATUS_WARNING;                                          // =1
// Public Instance Methods
    public abstract String getRequestId( ) throws JAXRException;                     // LO
    public abstract int getStatus( ) throws JAXRException;                           // LO
    public abstract boolean isAvailable( ) throws JAXRException;                     // LO
}
```

JAXRResponse is an interface that defines methods and constants that provide information about a response to a JAXR query or update operation. Application code does not deal with JAXRResponse directly, but rather with JAXRException or BulkResponse, which both implement its methods. How these methods are used depends on whether the Connection on which the original request was made is set to operate in synchronous or asynchronous mode. Refer to the description of the BulkResponse interface for details.

Implementations BulkResponse, JAXRException

LifeCycleManager   javax.xml.registry

JAXR 1.0; JWSDP 1.0, J2EE 1.4

```
public interface LifeCycleManager {
// Public Constants
    public static final String ASSOCIATION;                              // ="Association"
    public static final String AUDITABLE_EVENT;                          // ="AuditableEvent"
    public static final String CLASSIFICATION;                           // ="Classification"
    public static final String CLASSIFICATION_SCHEME;                    // ="ClassificationScheme"
    public static final String CONCEPT;                                  // ="Concept"
    public static final String EMAIL_ADDRESS;                            // ="EmailAddress"
    public static final String EXTERNAL_IDENTIFIER;                      // ="ExternalIdentifier"
    public static final String EXTERNAL_LINK;                            // ="ExternalLink"
    public static final String EXTRINSIC_OBJECT;                         // ="ExtrinsicObject"
    public static final String INTERNATIONAL_STRING;                     // ="InternationalString"
    public static final String KEY;                                      // ="Key"
    public static final String LOCALIZED_STRING;                         // ="LocalizedString"
    public static final String ORGANIZATION;                             // ="Organization"
    public static final String PERSON_NAME;                              // ="PersonName"
    public static final String POSTAL_ADDRESS;                           // ="PostalAddress"
    public static final String REGISTRY_ENTRY;                           // ="RegistryEntry"
    public static final String REGISTRY_PACKAGE;                         // ="RegistryPackage"
    public static final String SERVICE;                                  // ="Service"
    public static final String SERVICE_BINDING;                          // ="ServiceBinding"
    public static final String SLOT;                                     // ="Slot"
    public static final String SPECIFICATION_LINK;                       // ="SpecificationLink"
    public static final String TELEPHONE_NUMBER;                         // ="TelephoneNumber"
    public static final String USER;                                     // ="User"
    public static final String VERSIONABLE;                              // ="Versionable"
// Public Instance Methods
    public abstract javax.xml.registry.infomodel.Association createAssociation
       (javax.xml.registry.infomodel.RegistryObject targetObject, javax.xml.registry.infomodel.Concept associationType)
       throws JAXRException;                                             // LO
```

```
public abstract javax.xml.registry.infomodel.Classification createClassification
  (javax.xml.registry.infomodel.Concept concept) throws JAXRExceptionInvalidRequestException;      //L0
public abstract javax.xml.registry.infomodel.Classification createClassification
  (javax.xml.registry.infomodel.ClassificationScheme scheme, javax.xml.registry.infomodel.InternationalString name,
    String value) throws JAXRException;                                                             //L0
public abstract javax.xml.registry.infomodel.Classification createClassification
  (javax.xml.registry.infomodel.ClassificationScheme scheme, String name, String value) throws JAXRException;  //L0
public abstract javax.xml.registry.infomodel.ClassificationScheme createClassificationScheme
  (javax.xml.registry.infomodel.Concept concept) throws JAXRExceptionInvalidRequestException;       //L0
public abstract javax.xml.registry.infomodel.ClassificationScheme createClassificationScheme
  (javax.xml.registry.infomodel.InternationalString name, javax.xml.registry.infomodel.InternationalString description)
    throws JAXRExceptionInvalidRequestException;                                                    //L0
public abstract javax.xml.registry.infomodel.ClassificationScheme createClassificationScheme
  (String name, String description) throws JAXRExceptionInvalidRequestException;                    //L0
public abstract javax.xml.registry.infomodel.Concept createConcept
  (javax.xml.registry.infomodel.RegistryObject parent, String name, String value) throws JAXRException;  //L0
public abstract javax.xml.registry.infomodel.Concept createConcept
  (javax.xml.registry.infomodel.RegistryObject parent, javax.xml.registry.infomodel.InternationalString name,
    String value) throws JAXRException;                                                             //L0
public abstract javax.xml.registry.infomodel.EmailAddress createEmailAddress
  (String address) throws JAXRException;                                                            //L0
public abstract javax.xml.registry.infomodel.EmailAddress createEmailAddress
  (String address, String type) throws JAXRException;                                               //L0
public abstract javax.xml.registry.infomodel.ExternalIdentifier createExternalIdentifier
  (javax.xml.registry.infomodel.ClassificationScheme identificationScheme, javax.xml.registry.infomodel.
    InternationalString name, String value) throws JAXRException;                                   //L0
public abstract javax.xml.registry.infomodel.ExternalIdentifier createExternalIdentifier
  (javax.xml.registry.infomodel.ClassificationScheme identificationScheme, String name, String value)
    throws JAXRException;                                                                            //L0
public abstract javax.xml.registry.infomodel.ExternalLink createExternalLink(String externalURI,
  javax.xml.registry.infomodel.InternationalString description) throws JAXRException;               //L0
public abstract javax.xml.registry.infomodel.ExternalLink createExternalLink(String externalURI, String description)
  throws JAXRException;                                                                             //L0
public abstract javax.xml.registry.infomodel.ExtrinsicObject createExtrinsicObject
  (javax.activation.DataHandler repositoryItem) throws JAXRException;                               //L1
public abstract javax.xml.registry.infomodel.InternationalString createInternationalString( )
  throws JAXRException;                                                                             //L0
public abstract javax.xml.registry.infomodel.InternationalString createInternationalString(String s)
  throws JAXRException;                                                                             //L0
public abstract javax.xml.registry.infomodel.InternationalString createInternationalString
  (Locale l, String s) throws JAXRException;                                                        //L0
public abstract javax.xml.registry.infomodel.Key createKey(String id) throws JAXRException;         //L0
public abstract javax.xml.registry.infomodel.LocalizedString createLocalizedString
  (Locale l, String s) throws JAXRException;                                                        //L0
public abstract javax.xml.registry.infomodel.LocalizedString createLocalizedString
  (Locale l, String s, String charSetName) throws JAXRException;                                    //L0
public abstract Object createObject(String interfaceName)
  throws JAXRExceptionInvalidRequestExceptionUnsupportedCapabilityException;                        //L0
public abstract javax.xml.registry.infomodel.Organization createOrganization
  (javax.xml.registry.infomodel.InternationalString name) throws JAXRException;                     //L0
public abstract javax.xml.registry.infomodel.Organization createOrganization(String name) throws JAXRException;  //L0
```

public abstract javax.xml.registry.infomodel.PersonName **createPersonName**(String *fullName*) throws JAXRException;	//L0
public abstract javax.xml.registry.infomodel.PersonName **createPersonName** (String *firstName*, String *middleName*, String *lastName*) throws JAXRException;	//L0
public abstract javax.xml.registry.infomodel.PostalAddress **createPostalAddress**(String *streetNumber*, String *street*, String *city*,String *stateOrProvince*, String *country*, String *postalCode*, String *type*) throws JAXRException;	//L0
public abstract javax.xml.registry.infomodel.RegistryPackage **createRegistryPackage** (javax.xml.registry.infomodel.InternationalString *name*) throws JAXRException;	//L1
public abstract javax.xml.registry.infomodel.RegistryPackage **createRegistryPackage** (String *name*) throws JAXRException;	//L1
public abstract javax.xml.registry.infomodel.Service **createService** (javax.xml.registry.infomodel.InternationalString *name*) throws JAXRException;	//L0
public abstract javax.xml.registry.infomodel.Service **createService**(String *name*) throws JAXRException;	//L0
public abstract javax.xml.registry.infomodel.ServiceBinding **createServiceBinding**( ) throws JAXRException;	//L0
public abstract javax.xml.registry.infomodel.Slot **createSlot** (String *name*, Collection *values*, String *slotType*) throws JAXRException;	//L0
public abstract javax.xml.registry.infomodel.Slot **createSlot** (String *name*, String *value*, String *slotType*) throws JAXRException;	//L0
public abstract javax.xml.registry.infomodel.SpecificationLink **createSpecificationLink**( ) throws JAXRException;	//L0
public abstract javax.xml.registry.infomodel.TelephoneNumber **createTelephoneNumber**( ) throws JAXRException;	//L0
public abstract javax.xml.registry.infomodel.User **createUser**( ) throws JAXRException;	//L0
public abstract BulkResponse **deleteObjects**(Collection *keys*) throws JAXRException;	//L1
public abstract BulkResponse **deleteObjects**(Collection *keys*, String *objectType*) throws JAXRException;	//L0
public abstract BulkResponse **deprecateObjects**(Collection *keys*) throws JAXRException;	//L1
public abstract RegistryService **getRegistryService**( ) throws JAXRException;	//L0
public abstract BulkResponse **saveObjects**(Collection *objects*) throws JAXRException;	//L0
public abstract BulkResponse **unDeprecateObjects**(Collection *keys*) throws JAXRException;	//L1

}

The LifeCycleManager interface provides the methods necessary to create, update, remove, and deprecate objects in the registry. JAXR clients that make use of these methods usually need to authenticate to the registry by supplying valid credentials using the setCredentials( ) method of ConnectionFactory, and may be required to use a secure transport, such as HTTPS.

The createXXX( ) methods allow you to create an in-memory representation of a new object of a given type. In order to build a set of related registry objects, you would use the appropriate factory methods to create the objects and then link them together using the methods that they provide for this purpose. None of these operations affect the registry until the saveObjects( ) method is called. This method requires a Collection of RegistryObjects that are to be saved. For each object in this collection, a new registry entry is created if it did not already exist, or an existing entry is updated to reflect the state of the object supplied in the collection. In cases in which one object points to another (such as an Organization referring to a Service), the process of saving the first object also creates or updates all of its dependents. The BulkResponse returned by the saveObjects( ) method contains the keys for the objects that were saved. Note that the RegistryObjects themselves are not automatically updated with these keys. If an error occurs while saving an object, a SaveException is included in the BulkResponse to indicate the error. The BusinessLifeCycleManager interface provides additional methods that let you save objects by type.

The deleteObjects( ) method requires a Collection containing the keys of registry objects to be deleted. The BulkResponse returned from this method contains the keys of those objects that were deleted and possibly DeleteExceptions indicating deletion failures. The BusinessLife-CycleManager interface provides additional methods that let you delete objects by type.

The level 1 deprecateObjects( ) and undeprecateObjects( ) methods allow a registry client to change the deprecation status of one or more registry objects given by their keys. An object that is deprecated may still be used and referred to by other registry objects, but the creation of new links to them from other objects in the registry results in a JAXRException with a java.lang.IllegalStateException as its root cause.

The LifeCycleManager interface also defines constants that represent each of the types of registry object defined in the javax.xml.registry.infomodel package. These constants are required as arguments to some method calls, such as the getRegistryObject( ) and getRegistryObjects( ) methods in the QueryManager interface.

Implementations BusinessLifeCycleManager

Returned By javax.xml.registry.infomodel.RegistryObject.getLifeCycleManager( )

Query

javax.xml.registry

JAXR 1.0; JWSDP 1.0, J2EE 1.4

```
public interface Query {
// Public Constants
    public static final int QUERY_TYPE_EBXML_FILTER_QUERY;          // =2
    public static final int QUERY_TYPE_SQL;                          // =0
    public static final int QUERY_TYPE_XQUERY;                       // =1
// Public Instance Methods
    public abstract int getType( ) throws JAXRException;             //L1
    public abstract String toString( );                              //L1
}
```

The Query interface provides a way to encapsulate a registry query to be handled by a DeclarativeQueryManager. A Query object is created by calling the createQuery( ) method of the DeclarativeQueryManager whose executeQuery( ) method is eventually used to perform the search operation that it specifies. The query manager may choose to return a private object implementing Query that represents the query string in a form that is suitable for the means that are eventually used to action it. The getType( ) methods return the type of query that the Query object represents (such as QUERY_TYPE_SQL), while toString( ) returns a string representation of the query. DeclarativeQueryManagers are supported only by level 1 providers, but only queries of type QUERY_TYPE_EBXML_FILTER_QUERY are required to be supported.

Passed To DeclarativeQueryManager.executeQuery( )

Returned By DeclarativeQueryManager.createQuery( )

QueryManager

javax.xml.registry

JAXR 1.0; JWSDP 1.0, J2EE 1.4

```
public interface QueryManager {
// Public Instance Methods
    public abstract javax.xml.registry.infomodel.RegistryObject getRegistryObject(String id) throws JAXRException;    //L1
```

```
public abstract javax.xml.registry.infomodel.RegistryObject getRegistryObject(String id, String objectType)
    throws JAXRException;                                                                          // L0
public abstract BulkResponse getRegistryObjects() throws JAXRException;                            // L0
public abstract BulkResponse getRegistryObjects(String objectType) throws JAXRException;           // L0
public abstract BulkResponse getRegistryObjects(Collection objectKeys) throws JAXRException;        // L1
public abstract BulkResponse getRegistryObjects(Collection objectKeys, String objectTypes) throws JAXRException;  // L0
public abstract RegistryService getRegistryService() throws JAXRException;                          // L0
}
```

QueryManager provides methods that allow objects in the registry to be retrieved based on type and/or identifier. The only way to obtain a QueryManager object is by calling the getBusinessQueryManager() or the getDeclarativeQueryManager() method on RegistryService, which both return one of the two derived interfaces of QueryManager defined by the API. The QueryManager getRegistryService() method returns the RegistryService object from which it was obtained.

The zero-argument getRegistryObjects() returns a BulkResponse containing all of the objects in the registry belonging to the calling user, while getRegistryObject(String objectType) returns the subset of those objects that are of a given type (such as LifeCycleManager.ORGANIZATION). Both of these methods throw a JAXRException if the connection does not have valid credentials associated with it, allowing the calling user to be identified. The getRegistryObjects(Collection keys) method returns all of the objects in the registry whose javax.xml.registry.infomodel.Key values appear in the collection passed as its argument, while the getRegistryObject(String id) method returns the single object whose identifier (i.e., the result of calling the getId() method on the object's Key) is supplied. Neither of these methods uses the caller's identity as an implicit filter. However, they can be used only with a level 1 registry provider. To get similar functionality from a level 0 provider, you need to specify the type of registry object to be retrieved, in the form of a constant defined by the LifeCycleManager interface, as well as the keys or registry object identifier.

Implementations BusinessQueryManager, DeclarativeQueryManager

RegistryException   javax.xml.registry

JAXR 1.0; JWSDP 1.0, J2EE 1.4   serializable checked

```
public class RegistryException extends JAXRException {
// Public Constructors
    public RegistryException();
    public RegistryException( Throwable cause);
    public RegistryException( String reason);
    public RegistryException( String reason, Throwable cause);
// Public Instance Methods
    public javax.xml.registry.infomodel.Key getErrorObjectKey() throws JAXRException;      // default:null
    public void setErrorObjectKey(javax.xml.registry.infomodel.Key key) throws JAXRException;
}
```

RegistryException is a subclass of JAXRException that is used to report errors that occur on the registry side of a connection during a JAXR query or update operation. RegistryExceptions are returned to a JAXR client as part of a BulkResponse rather than being thrown from a JAXR API method. When a RegistryException reports an error relating to a single object in the registry (such as a failure to save or delete that object), the provider may use the setErrorObjectKey() key method to associate the javax.xml.registry.infomodel.Key that uniquely

---

identifies the object with the exception. The getErrorObjectKey() method may be used to retrieve the key, but returns null if it has not been set, as would be the case, for example, if an error were detected during a find operation.

Subclasses   DeleteException, FindException, SaveException

RegistryService

javax.xml.registry

JAXR 1.0; JWSDP 1.0, J2EE 1.4

```
public interface RegistryService {
// Property Accessor Methods (by property name)
    public abstract BusinessLifeCycleManager getBusinessLifeCycleManager() throws JAXRException;         // L0
    public abstract BusinessQueryManager getBusinessQueryManager() throws JAXRException;                 // L0
    public abstract CapabilityProfile getCapabilityProfile() throws JAXRException;                       // L0
    public abstract DeclarativeQueryManager getDeclarativeQueryManager()
        throws JAXRExceptionUnsupportedCapabilityException;                                              // L1
    public abstract javax.xml.registry.infomodel.ClassificationScheme getDefaultPostalScheme()
        throws JAXRException;                                                                            // L0
// Public Instance Methods
    public abstract BulkResponse getBulkResponse(String requestId) throws InvalidRequestExceptionJAXRException;   // L0
    public abstract String makeRegistrySpecificRequest(String request) throws JAXRException;             // L0
}
```

This interface provides methods that are used to access the principal services provided by a registry provider. To obtain a RegistryService object, first get a Connection or FederatedConnection from a ConnectionFactory, then call its getRegistryService() method.

The most important methods in this interface are getBusinessQueryManager() and getBusinessLifeCycleManager(). The former returns a BusinessQueryManager object associated with the registry whose URL is given by the javax.xml.registry.queryManagerURL property of the ConnectionFactory used when creating the RegistryService. BusinessQueryManager lets you query the content of the registry. The latter method returns a BusinessLifeCycleManager that can be used to make changes to the registry whose URL is given by the javax.xml.registry.lifeCycleManagerURL property. The getDeclarativeQueryManager method, which is supported only by level 1 providers, returns an object that you can use to form and send queries expressed in a query language such as SQL-92 or the ebXML filter query language.

The getCapabilityProfile() method returns an object that can be used to find out which version of the JAXR specification the provider implements and its capability level. The getDefaultPostalScheme() method returns a ClassificationScheme that describes the mapping of fields in a postal address as used within the registry to the fields of the generic postal address used by the JAXR provider itself. Refer to Chapter 7 for a discussion of postal addresses. The getBulkResponse() method is supplied the unique identifier of a previously initiated asynchronous request, and returns the BulkResponse that contains the responses from that request, which may still be in progress and therefore incomplete. See the description of the BulkResponse for a discussion of asynchronous request handling. The makeRegistrySpecificRequest() method can be used to send a request expressed as an XML message in the format expected by the target registry, and to receive the XML response.

Returned By   javax.xml.registry.Connection.getRegistryService(), LifeCycleManager.getRegistryService(), QueryManager.getRegistryService()

JAXR 1.0; JWSDP 1.0, J2EE 1.4

serializable checked

```
public class SaveException extends RegistryException {
// Public Constructors
  public SaveException( );
  public SaveException( Throwable cause);
  public SaveException( String reason);
  public SaveException( String reason, Throwable cause);
}
```

SaveException is a subclass of RegistryException that is used to indicate a failure to save an object in the registry. SaveException is not thrown by any method—instead, it is stored within a BulkResponse object returned from a method such as the saveOrganizations( ) method of BusinessLifeCycleManager. The affected object may be identified using the getErrorObjectKey( ) method inherited from RegistryException.

UnexpectedObjectException

javax.xml.registry

JAXR 1.0; JWSDP 1.0, J2EE 1.4

serializable checked

```
public class UnexpectedObjectException extends JAXRException {
// Public Constructors
  public UnexpectedObjectException( );
  public UnexpectedObjectException( Throwable cause);
  public UnexpectedObjectException( String reason);
  public UnexpectedObjectException(String reason, Throwable cause);
}
```

UnexpectedObjectException is an exception that is thrown by a JAXR provider when asked to perform an operation using a collection of objects that are not of the type that the operation requires. For example, the saveOrganizations( ) method of BusinessLifeCycleManager requires a Collection of objects of type Organization. If an object in the Collection is not of this type, an UnexpectedObjectException is thrown.

UnsupportedCapabilityException

javax.xml.registry

JAXR 1.0; JWSDP 1.0, J2EE 1.4

serializable checked

```
public class UnsupportedCapabilityException extends JAXRException {
// Public Constructors
  public UnsupportedCapabilityException( );
  public UnsupportedCapabilityException( Throwable cause);
  public UnsupportedCapabilityException( String reason);
  public UnsupportedCapabilityException(String reason, Throwable cause);
}
```

UnsupportedCapabilityException is thrown when an optional method that a JAXR provider does not implement is invoked. For example, the createFederatedConnection( ) method of ConnectionFactory may throw this exception, since support for FederatedConnections is optional.

Thrown By   LifeCycleManager.createObject( ), RegistryService.getDeclarativeQueryManager( )

12

The javax.xml.registry. infomodel Package

Package javax.xml.registry.infomodel
JAXR 1.0; JWSDP 1.0, J2EE 1.4

The javax.xml.registry.infomodel package contains the interfaces that represent the objects in the registry information model provided by a JAXR provider. The information model is transparently mapped by the provider to the real information model used by the registry to which a JAXR client is connected. Instances of registry objects, which are realized by concrete classes supplied by JAXR implementations, can be created using methods of the BusinessLifeCycleManager interface or returned as the result of a registry search performed using a BusinessQueryManager. Both of these interfaces are defined in the javax.xml.registry package.

From an inheritance point of view, RegistryObject is the most important interface in this package, since it is the base from which all other objects in the registry are derived. The method of this interface allows an object to have a name, a description, a unique key used by the registry to identify it, and a set of optional attributes that can be used as search criteria by JAXR clients, such as classifications and external identifiers. From a structural viewpoint, the registry data for a business is rooted in its Organization object, from which a registry client can obtain contact information and discover the services provided by the Organization. A business publishes its details in the registry by creating a new Organization object and adding to it the required Services, Classifications, contact information, and other attributes, and then realizing the same structure in the registry using the saveOrganizations( ) method of BusinessLifeCycleManager. Each object in the registry is tagged with an identifier for the user that created it and can only be modified by its owner. In a level 1 registry, the life cycle of an object can be tracked by viewing an audit trail that is automatically created by the registry as changes are made to the object.

Interfaces

public interface **Association** extends RegistryObject;
public interface **AuditableEvent** extends RegistryObject;
public interface **Classification** extends RegistryObject;
public interface **ClassificationScheme** extends RegistryEntry;
public interface **Concept** extends RegistryObject;

```
public interface EmailAddress;
public interface ExtensibleObject;
public interface ExternalIdentifier extends RegistryObject;
public interface ExternalLink extends RegistryObject, URIValidator;
public interface ExtrinsicObject extends RegistryEntry;
public interface InternationalString;
public interface Key;
public interface LocalizedString;
public interface Organization extends RegistryObject;
public interface PersonName;
public interface PostalAddress extends ExtensibleObject;
public interface RegistryEntry extends RegistryObject, Versionable;
public interface RegistryObject extends ExtensibleObject;
public interface RegistryPackage extends RegistryEntry;
public interface Service extends RegistryEntry;
public interface ServiceBinding extends RegistryObject, URIValidator;
public interface Slot;
public interface SpecificationLink extends RegistryObject;
public interface TelephoneNumber;
public interface URIValidator;
public interface User extends RegistryObject;
public interface Versionable;
```

Association   javax.xml.registry.infomode

JAXR 1.0; JWSDP 1.0, J2EE 1.4

```
public interface Association extends RegistryObject {
// Property Accessor Methods (by property name)
    public abstract Concept getAssociationType( ) throws javax.xml.registry.JAXRException;          //LO
    public abstract void setAssociationType(Concept associationType) throws javax.xml.registry.JAXRException;   //LO
    public abstract boolean isConfirmed( ) throws javax.xml.registry.JAXRException;                 //LO
    public abstract boolean isConfirmedBySourceOwner( ) throws javax.xml.registry.JAXRException;    //LO
    public abstract boolean isConfirmedByTargetOwner( ) throws javax.xml.registry.JAXRException;    //LO
    public abstract boolean isExtramural( ) throws javax.xml.registry.JAXRException;                //LO
    public abstract RegistryObject getSourceObject( ) throws javax.xml.registry.JAXRException;      //LO
    public abstract void setSourceObject(RegistryObject srcObject) throws javax.xml.registry.JAXRException;   //LO
    public abstract RegistryObject getTargetObject( ) throws javax.xml.registry.JAXRException;      //LO
    public abstract void setTargetObject(RegistryObject targetObject) throws javax.xml.registry.JAXRException;  //LO
}
```

An Association represents an assertion of a relationship of some kind between two objects in the registry, one of which is referred to as the source object, and the other as the target object. To create an Association, use the LifeCycleManager createAssociation( ) method, which requires a reference to the target object and an association type. The source object is set by adding the Association to it using the RegistryObject addAssociation( ) method. As with other registry objects, an Association is not visible in the registry until it has been saved using the BusinessLifeCycleManager saveAssociations( ) method; in some cases, this is not sufficient to make the association visible, as described shortly.

The Association type is specified using a Concept. The JAXR specification defines an enumerated type containing a set of standard Association types. There is a full list of these types listed under "Associations" in Chapter 7. You can obtain the appropriate Concept for the type of association you would like to create using the findConceptByPath() method of BusinessQueryManager, which is described in the reference section for the Concept interface, later in this chapter. To form the path needed to locate the Concept, you must have the identifier of a ClassificationScheme called AssociationType, which represents the enumeration that defines all of the types. The following code extract demonstrates how to get this ClassificationScheme and then use it to find the Concept that represents the association type Uses. It is assumed that the variable bqm refers to an instance of BusinessQueryManager.

```
ClassificationScheme types = bqm.findClassificationSchemeByName(null,
"AssociationType");
String path = "/" + types.getKey().getId() + "/Uses";
Concept uses = bqm.findConceptByPath(path);
```

Some JAXR providers allow you to use the name of the enumeration in the path supplied to the findConceptByPath() method, thus removing the need to search for the ID of the ClassificationScheme. In this case, you can use the following, much simpler code:

```
Concept uses = bqm.findConceptByPath("/AssociationType/Uses");
```

The next step is to create an Association by specifying the type and the target object. The following code uses the BusinessLifeCycleManager referred to by the variable blcm to create an association of type uses with an object referred to by the variable targetObject as its target:

```
Association association = blcm.createAssociation(targetObject, uses);
```

Finally, to complete the association, add the Association object to the source object:

```
sourceObject.addAssociation(association);
```

There is a distinction made in the API between the source and target objects because associations are directional. The Uses association type is an example of this — the Assocation just created conveys the fact that the source object "uses" the target object, rather than the other way around. If, at some point in the future, the association needs to be broken, this can be done by removing it from the source object using the removeAssociation() method. The source and target objects and the association type can be obtained by calling the getSourceObject(), getTargetObject(), and getAssociationType() methods, respectively, and can be changed using the corresponding setter methods. Changing the source object using setSourceObject() implicitly removes the Association from the original source. Note that a registry object may be the source and/or target of any number of Associations at the same time. You can search for existing Associations using the findAssociations() and findCallerAssociations() methods of BusinessQueryManager.

Associations can be categorized as either intramural or extramural. An intramural Association is formed when the source and target objects are owned by the same registry User and the Association is created by that same User. Such an Association can be considered a correct factual assertion, and is therefore said to be confirmed as soon as it is created. An extramural Association is one in which at least one of the source and target objects in not owned by the User that creates it. Such an Association is unconfirmed, since it has not been agreed to by the owner of both objects and is not visible to other registry users until it is confirmed by them. The isExtramural() method can be used to determine the intramural or extramural status of an Association. An Association can be confirmed using the confirmAssociation() method of BusinessLifeCycleManager, and confirmation can be withdrawn using the unconfirmAssociation() method. To find out whether an extramural Association is confirmed, use the isConfirmed(), isConfirmedBySourceOwner(), and isConfirmedByTargetOwner() methods, which all return true when applied to an intramural Association.

Passed To	javax.xml.registry.BusinessLifeCycleManager.{confirmAssociation( ), unConfirmAssociation( )}, RegistryObject.{addAssociation( ), removeAssociation( )}
Returned By	javax.xml.registry.LifeCycleManager.createAssociation( )

AuditableEvent

javax.xml.registry.infomodel

JAXR 1.0; JWSDP 1.0, J2EE 1.4

```
public interface AuditableEvent extends RegistryObject {
// Public Constants
    public static final int EVENT_TYPE_CREATED;                                    //=0
    public static final int EVENT_TYPE_DELETED;                                    //=1
    public static final int EVENT_TYPE_DEPRECATED;                                 //=2
    public static final int EVENT_TYPE_UNDEPRECATED;                               //=5
    public static final int EVENT_TYPE_UPDATED;                                    //=3
    public static final int EVENT_TYPE_VERSIONED;                                  //=4
// Public Instance Methods
    public abstract int getEventType( ) throws javax.xml.registry.JAXRException;    //L1
    public abstract RegistryObject getRegistryObject( ) throws javax.xml.registry.JAXRException;
    public abstract java.sql.Timestamp getTimestamp( ) throws javax.xml.registry.JAXRException;  //L1
    public abstract User getUser( ) throws javax.xml.registry.JAXRException;        //L1
}
```

Level 1 registries support the use of an audit trail that records changes made to objects in the registry. Each RegistryObject has its own audit trail that is composed of AuditableEvents. To retrieve the audit trail for a particular RegistryObject, use the getAuditTrail( ) method. The audit trail is managed by the registry itself; therefore, there is no API that allows client programs to explicitly create or remove entries.

The getEventType( ) method returns a value that indicates the type of event that the AuditableEvent represents. The JAXR API provides for auditing of object creation, deletion, deprecation, undeprecation, versioning, and updates. The getRegistryObject( ) method returns a reference to the object that the event relates to, while the getTimestamp( ) method gets the time at which the event occurred, in the form of a java.sql.Timestamp object. The getUser( ) method returns the User object for the user that causes the event to be generated. Since registry updates require authentication, it is always possible to record the identity of any user that causes a registry object to be modified.

Classification

javax.xml.registry.infomodel

JAXR 1.0; JWSDP 1.0, J2EE 1.4

```
public interface Classification extends RegistryObject {
// Property Accessor Methods (by property name)
    public abstract ClassificationScheme getClassificationScheme( ) throws javax.xml.registry.JAXRException;   //LO
    public abstract void setClassificationScheme(ClassificationScheme classificationScheme)
        throws javax.xml.registry.JAXRException;                                                              //LO
    public abstract RegistryObject getClassifiedObject( ) throws javax.xml.registry.JAXRException;             //LO
    public abstract void setClassifiedObject(RegistryObject classifiedObject) throws javax.xml.registry.JAXRException;  //LO
    public abstract Concept getConcept( ) throws javax.xml.registry.JAXRException;                             //LO
    public abstract void setConcept(Concept concept) throws javax.xml.registry.JAXRException;                  //LO
    public abstract boolean isExternal( ) throws javax.xml.registry.JAXRException;                             //LO
```

```
    public abstract String getValue() throws javax.xml.registry.JAXRException;              //LO
    public abstract void setValue(String value) throws javax.xml.registry.JAXRException;     //LO
}
```

A Classification is an object that categorizes the RegistryObject to which it is attached according to the ClassificationScheme to which it belongs. There are several standard classification schemes in use, such as NAICS and UNSPSC, which are widely supported by registries and can be used by businesses to make it easier for registry searches to locate their services. For example, a book publisher might label its Organization entry and its services with the classification Book Publisher, which is part of the NAICS classification scheme.

In order to categorize a RegistryObject, use one of the LifeCycleManager createClassification() methods and then call the addClassification() or addClassifications() method of the target RegistryObject. Note that a Classification instance can be associated with only one object in the registry at any given time, so it is necessary to create a new instance for each object to be classified. The object that a Classification is associated with can be obtained from its getClassifiedObject() method and set using setClassifiedObject(), which is called on your behalf when you use addClassification() or addClassifications().

There are two types of Classification: internal and external. The *type* of a Classification is the same as that of the scheme to which it belongs, as described in the reference section for the ClassificationScheme interface later in this chapter. An internal Classification is defined by the Concept from the ClassificationScheme that appears as the node in which it corresponds to the classification hierarchy. Given a ClassificationScheme, you can use the findConceptByPath() method of BusinessQueryManager to obtain the required Concept and then use the single-argument variant of the LifeCycleManager createClassification() method to create the corresponding Classification object. The following code extract illustrates this: bqm and blcm are instances of BusinessQueryManager and BusinessLifeCycleManager, respectively:

```
ClassificationScheme naics = bqm.findClassificationSchemeByName(null,
"%naics%");
String path = "/" + naics.getKey().getId() + "/51/511/5111/51113";
Concept publisherConcept = bqm.findConceptByPath(path);
Classification bookPublishers = blcm.createClassification(publisherConcept);
```

This code creates a Classification that refers to the "Book Publishers" category of the NAICS classification scheme, which is supported as an internal classification scheme by the JAXR provider in the reference implementation.

An external Classification simply has an associated name and value, and is created using one of the other two createClassification() methods of LifeCycleManager:

```
// Create external classification
ClassificationScheme naics = bqm.findClassificationSchemeByName(null,
"%naics%");
Classification bookPublishers = blcm.createClassification(naics, "Book
Publishers", "51113");
```

Here, you need only to specify the name of the classification ("Book Publishers") and its value ("51113"). Using external classifications is more error-prone than internal classifications because there is no way for the registry to verify that the values supplied are valid, whereas an internal classification can only be created from a Concept that is part of a (presumably trusted) internal ClassificationScheme.

You can get or set the Concept associated with an internal Classification using the getConcept() and setConcept() methods. For an external Classification, use the getValue() and setValue()

methods instead. In the case of the external Classification created previously, the getValue( ) method returns "51113". The name attribute ("Book Publishers") can be retrieved using the getName( ) method inherited from RegistryObject. You can use the isExternal( ) method to determine whether a Classification is external or internal and, hence, which of these sets of methods you need to use.

Passed To   RegistryObject.{addClassification( ), removeClassification( )}

Returned By   javax.xml.registry.LifeCycleManager.createClassification( )

ClassificationScheme   javax.xml.registry.infomodel

JAXR 1.0; JWSDP 1.0, J2EE 1.4

```
public interface ClassificationScheme extends RegistryEntry {
// Public Constants
    public static final int VALUE_TYPE_EMBEDDED_PATH;                              //=1
    public static final int VALUE_TYPE_NON_UNIQUE;                                 //=2
    public static final int VALUE_TYPE_UNIQUE;                                     //=0
// Property Accessor Methods (by property name)
    public abstract int getChildConceptCount( ) throws javax.xml.registry.JAXRException;            //LO
    public abstract Collection getChildrenConcepts( ) throws javax.xml.registry.JAXRException;       //LO
    public abstract Collection getDescendantConcepts( ) throws javax.xml.registry.JAXRException;     //LO
    public abstract boolean isExternal( ) throws javax.xml.registry.JAXRException;                   //LO
    public abstract int getValueType( ) throws javax.xml.registry.JAXRException;                     //L1
    public abstract void setValueType(int valueType) throws javax.xml.registry.JAXRException;        //L1
// Public Instance Methods
    public abstract void addChildConcept(Concept concept) throws javax.xml.registry.JAXRException;       //LO
    public abstract void addChildConcepts(Collection concepts) throws javax.xml.registry.JAXRException;  //LO
    public abstract void removeChildConcept(Concept concept) throws javax.xml.registry.JAXRException;    //LO
    public abstract void removeChildConcepts(Collection concepts) throws javax.xml.registry.JAXRException; //LO
}
```

A ClassificationScheme represents a hierarchy of related classifications that can be used to categorize objects in a registry. There are several commonly used classification schemes, such as NAICS, ISO-3166, and UNSPSC, that can be used to describe a business or service in various different ways. The NAICS scheme, for example, is used to categorize objects by their business type, such as "Book Publisher," whereas the ISO-3166 is used to denote geographical location. By associating elements of both schemes (represented in the JAXR model by Classification objects) with a business, it is possible to indicate that your Organization is a U.S.-based book publisher in such a way that potential clients could search for items tagged with these attributes.

A ClassificationScheme is hierarchical, with broader classifications appearing toward the root of the hierarchy and more specific ones toward the leaf nodes. The structure of the hierarchy may be known to the registry and represented as a hierarchy of Concepts, in which each Concept represents a single classification node. Such a ClassificationScheme is referred to as an *internal scheme*. An internal scheme has the advantage that you can use the JAXR API to navigate the Concept hierarchy to find out what classifications are available, and you can check whether a classification that claims to be within the scheme actually exists. By contrast, an external ClassificationScheme's existence is known to the registry, but its structure is not. As a result, the registry cannot check whether classifications that claim to be part of an external scheme are valid, and cannot provide a way to discover all of the valid classifications.

You can use the findClassificationSchemes() and findClassificationSchemeByName() methods of BusinessLifeCycleManager to look up a ClassificationScheme, as the following code extract illustrates for the NAICS scheme:

```
ClassificationScheme naics = bqm.findClassificationSchemeByName(null,
"%naics%");
```

To create a new scheme, use one of the createClassificationScheme() methods of LifeCycleManager:

```
ClassificationScheme myScheme = blcm.
createClassificationSchemeByName("MyScheme", "My Private Scheme");
```

If your scheme is going to be internal, you need to create the Concepts that represent the classification nodes and link them together to form the required structure. The top-level nodes can then be added to the ClassificationScheme using the addChildConcept() or addChildConcepts() methods. You can navigate the structure of an internal scheme using its getChildrenConcepts() and getDescendentConcepts() methods, together with the methods of Concept that allow its children and parents to be discovered. An external scheme has no internal structure known to the registry and therefore does not need to be constructed in the same way. Note that some registries, in particular the UDDI V2 registry, do not support the dynamic definition of internal classification schemes so that, although you can use the JAXR API to build one, you cannot save it. JAXR providers are required instead to provide a client-side mechanism that simulates the existence of custom internal classification schemes, although the exact mechanism is implementation-dependent. The reference implementation uses an XML file to represent such a classification scheme, as described in Chapter 7. Custom internal classification schemes can be created and stored in an ebXML registry as just described.

The getValueType() and setValueType() methods can be used to get and set an attribute that describes the value parts of the nodes in the scheme hierarchy. The following values are defined:

VALUE_TYPE_UNIQUE
Each node in the ClassificationScheme hierarchy has a unique value.

VALUE_TYPE_NON_UNIQUE
More than one node in the hierarchy may have the same value, although any two nodes belonging to the same parent must still have distinct values. As a result, to uniquely identify a classification within such a scheme, you may need the entire path from the node to the root.

VALUE_TYPE_EMBEDDED_PATH
The value embeds the path from its node to the root of the scheme. This guarantees, of course, that the value is unique.

Passed To   javax.xml.registry.LifeCycleManager.{createClassification( ), createExternalIdentifier( )},
Classification.setClassificationScheme( ), ExternalIdentifier.setIdentificationScheme( ), Postal-
Address.setPostalScheme( )

Returned By   javax.xml.registry.BusinessQueryManager.findClassificationSchemeByName( ), javax.xml.
registry.LifeCycleManager.createClassificationScheme( ), javax.xml.registry.RegistryService.
getDefaultPostalScheme( ), Classification.getClassificationScheme( ), Concept.
getClassificationScheme( ), ExternalIdentifier.getIdentificationScheme( ), PostalAddress.
getPostalScheme( )

```
public interface Concept extends RegistryObject {
// Property Accessor Methods (by property name)
    public abstract int getChildConceptCount( ) throws javax.xml.registry.JAXRException;                    //LO
    public abstract Collection getChildrenConcepts( ) throws javax.xml.registry.JAXRException;              //LO
    public abstract ClassificationScheme getClassificationScheme( ) throws javax.xml.registry.JAXRException; //LO
    public abstract Collection getDescendantConcepts( ) throws javax.xml.registry.JAXRException;            //LO
    public abstract RegistryObject getParent( ) throws javax.xml.registry.JAXRException;                    //LO
    public abstract Concept getParentConcept( ) throws javax.xml.registry.JAXRException;                    //LO
    public abstract String getPath( ) throws javax.xml.registry.JAXRException;                              //LO
    public abstract String getValue( ) throws javax.xml.registry.JAXRException;                             //LO
    public abstract void setValue(String value) throws javax.xml.registry.JAXRException;                    //LO
// Public Instance Methods
    public abstract void addChildConcept(Concept concept) throws javax.xml.registry.JAXRException;          //LO
    public abstract void addChildConcepts(Collection concepts) throws javax.xml.registry.JAXRException;     //LO
    public abstract void removeChildConcept(Concept concept) throws javax.xml.registry.JAXRException;       //LO
    public abstract void removeChildConcepts(Collection concepts) throws javax.xml.registry.JAXRException;  //LO
}
```

Concepts are used in various different ways within the JAXR API. A Concept can be thought of as a useful item that is given meaning by the context in which it is used. Some typical uses for Concepts are:

- To represent a member of an enumerated type. The JAXR API defines several enumerated types that represent the different types of objects in the registry, the various types of Association that are available, and so on.

- As a node in an internal ClassificationScheme either stored within the registry or emulated by the JAXR provider. In the NAICS scheme, for example, there is a Concept that represents the node for "Publishing Industries," and another for a subclassification called "Newspaper, Periodical, Book, and Database Publishers." The hierarchical relation between the classification nodes is represented using the parent-child relationship between the corresponding Concepts.

- As the target of a SpecificationLink when storing a reference to a WSDL document in the registry. When used in this way, the Concept is acting simply as an anonymous registry object and making use of its inherited ability to be classified and to refer to external content using an ExternalLink. Refer to "Storing a WSDL document reference in a UDDI registry" in Chapter 7 for more details of this use.

Create a Concept using the createConcept( ) method of LifeCycleManager, which requires a name and a value (both of which are strings), and a parent RegistryObject, which must be either another Concept or a ClassificationScheme. In terms of the methods that it defines, a Concept is a simple object that has a string value and resides in a hierarchy. The addChildConcept( ) and addChildConcepts( ) methods can be used to add one or more children to a Concept, while removeChildConcept( ) and removeChildConcepts( ) can be used to remove them. You can navigate around a Concept by using the methods getParentConcept( ) (which returns null if there is no parent), getChildrenConcepts( ) (which returns all of the immediate children of a Concept), and getDescendentConcepts( ) (which returns all of the descendents of a Concept).

As noted earlier, Concepts often appear as nodes in a classification scheme. When this is the case, you can find the ClassificationScheme of which a Concept is part by calling its getClassificationScheme( ) method. Although you can build a new classification scheme hierarchy by creating a new ClassificationScheme object and linking a hierarchy of Concepts beneath it, you cannot store such a scheme in a UDDI V2.0 registry (although you can do so in an ebXML registry). To compensate for this, the JAXR provider allows you to simulate the creation of a custom classification scheme using configuration information stored locally to the provider, as described in Chapter 7.

Since Concepts are hierarchical, they have an associated path that can be obtained using the getPath() method. The path is formed from the identifier of the ClassificationScheme beneath which the Concept resides, followed by the value (not the name) of each Concept in the path leading down to the target Concept, where the path components are separated using the "/" character. For example, a Concept with the value "3" linked three levels below a ClassificationScheme with identifier uuid:f1ef390d-08f1-ef39-3f48-e3438b38f908, with intervening Concepts having values "1" and "2", returns the string /uuid:f1ef390d-08f1-ef39-3f48-e3438b38f908/1/2/3 from its getPath() method. Conversely, if you know the path of a Concept, you can use the findConceptByPath() method of BusinessQueryManager to look it up:

```
Concept c = bqm.findConceptByPath("/uuid:f1ef390d-08f1-ef39-3f48-
    e3438b38f908/1/2/3");
```

Code like this is commonly used when looking up members of enumerated types. In this case, the JAXR provider typically allows you to use one of the enumerated type names listed in the JAXR specification in place of the long-winded identifier used with ClassificationSchemes as the first part of the path. For example, the following code returns the Concept that represents the object type for the Classification object:

```
Concept c = bqm.findConceptByPath("/ObjectType/Classification");
```

javax.xml. registry

Passed To	javax.xml.registry.LifeCycleManager.{createAssociation( ), createClassification( ), createClassificationScheme( )}, Association.setAssociationType( ), Classification.setConcept( ), ClassificationScheme.{addChildConcept( ), removeChildConcept( )}, Concept. {addChildConcept( ), removeChildConcept( )}
Returned By	javax.xml.registry.BusinessQueryManager.findConceptByPath( ), javax.xml.registry.Life-CycleManager.createConcept( ), Association.getAssociationType( ), Classification.getConcept( ), Concept.getParentConcept( ), RegistryObject.getObjectType( )

EmailAddress

javax.xml.registry.infomodel

JAXR 1.0; JWSDP 1.0, J2EE 1.4

```
public interface EmailAddress {
// Public Instance Methods
    public abstract String getAddress( ) throws javax.xml.registry.JAXRException;         //L0
    public abstract String getType( ) throws javax.xml.registry.JAXRException;            //L0
    public abstract void setAddress(String address) throws javax.xml.registry.JAXRException;  //L0
    public abstract void setType(String type) throws javax.xml.registry.JAXRException;     //L0
}
```

EmailAddress is a simple interface that is intended to designate a string value as the email address of a user. A User object in the registry may have one or more associated Email-Address objects, created using the LifeCycleManager createEmailAddress() method and added as a group by calling setEmailAddresses(). The actual address required to contact the user can be obtained by calling the getAddress() method, whereas the type attribute available from getType() is an arbitrary qualifier that might be used to indicate that the address reaches the person at home, in the office, and so on.

Returned By	javax.xml.registry.LifeCycleManager.createEmailAddress( )

JAXR 1.0; JWSDP 1.0, J2EE 1.4

```
public interface ExtensibleObject {
// Public Instance Methods
    public abstract void addSlot(Slot slot) throws javax.xml.registry.JAXRException;                         //LO
    public abstract void addSlots(Collection slots) throws javax.xml.registry.JAXRException;                 //LO
    public abstract Slot getSlot(String slotName) throws javax.xml.registry.JAXRException;                   //LO
    public abstract Collection getSlots( ) throws javax.xml.registry.JAXRException;                          //LO
    public abstract void removeSlot(String slotName) throws javax.xml.registry.JAXRException;                //LO
    public abstract void removeSlots(Collection slotNames) throws javax.xml.registry.JAXRException;          //LO
}
```

ExtensibleObject is the interface from which all objects that reside in the registry are derived. The methods of this interface provide for the association with a registry object of attributes that are not explicitly defined in the JAXR API. An ExtensibleObject may have any number of these attributes, which are represented by the Slot interface. Slots are created and added by the JAXR provider and may also be used by application code, although not all JAXR providers will store application-created Slots in the registry.

Slots can be added to an ExtensibleObject either singly using the addSlot() method or as a group by calling addSlots(); they can be removed using removeSlot() or removeSlots(). Both of these methods use the name of the Slot as the key. The getSlot() method locates a Slot given its name and returns null if no slot with the supplied name is associated with the ExtensibleObject. Finally, the getSlots() method returns a Collection containing all of an object's Slots.

Implementations PostalAddress, RegistryObject

ExternalIdentifier

javax.xml.registry.infomodel

JAXR 1.0; JWSDP 1.0, J2EE 1.4

```
public interface ExternalIdentifier extends RegistryObject {
// Public Instance Methods
    public abstract ClassificationScheme getIdentificationScheme( ) throws javax.xml.registry.JAXRException;     //LO
    public abstract RegistryObject getRegistryObject( ) throws javax.xml.registry.JAXRException;                 //LO
    public abstract String getValue( ) throws javax.xml.registry.JAXRException;                                  //LO
    public abstract void setIdentificationScheme(ClassificationScheme identificationScheme)
        throws javax.xml.registry.JAXRException;                                                                 //LO
    public abstract void setValue(String value) throws javax.xml.registry.JAXRException;                         //LO
}
```

An ExternalIdentifer is a value assigned by an external authority that can be associated with a RegistryObject. An example of ExternalIdentifiers that is widely recognized is a Dun and Bradstreet number (D-U-N-S), which a business can obtain following a process of registration. The value of the identifier can be obtained from the getValue() method, but its meaning can be interpreted only in relation to the scheme under which the value is classified, which can be obtained using the getClassificationScheme() method. A RegistryObject can have any number of ExternalIdentifiers, which are created using the BusinessLifeCycleManager createExternalIdentifier() method and added by calling addExternalIdentifier().

Passed To   RegistryObject.{addExternalIdentifier( ), removeExternalIdentifier( )}

Returned By   javax.xml.registry.LifeCycleManager.createExternalIdentifier( )

JAXR 1.0; JWSDP 1.0, J2EE 1.4

```
public interface ExternalLink extends RegistryObject, URIValidator {
// Public Instance Methods
    public abstract String getExternalURI( ) throws javax.xml.registry.JAXRException;          //L0
    public abstract Collection getLinkedObjects( ) throws javax.xml.registry.JAXRException;     //L0
    public abstract void setExternalURI(String uri) throws javax.xml.registry.JAXRException;    //L0
}
```

A RegistryObject may have any number of ExternalLinks that act as references to information related to the object that resides outside of the registry. The location of the referenced information is given by a URI that can be set using the setExternalURI() method and retrieved by calling getExternalURI(). The getLinkedObjects() method returns a Collection containing all of the RegistryObjects to which the ExternalLink has been applied using the RegistryObject addExternalLink() or addExternalLinks() methods. Compare this level 0 facility to ExtrinsicObject, which stores a copy of the information in a repository linked to the registry (but is available only with a level 1 JAXR provider).

Passed To   RegistryObject.{addExternalLink( ), removeExternalLink( )}

Returned By   javax.xml.registry.LifeCycleManager.createExternalLink( )

ExtrinsicObject   **javax.xml.registry.infomodel**

JAXR 1.0; JWSDP 1.0, J2EE 1.4

```
public interface ExtrinsicObject extends RegistryEntry {
// Public Instance Methods
    public abstract String getMimeType( ) throws javax.xml.registry.JAXRException;                          //L1
    public abstract javax.activation.DataHandler getRepositoryItem( ) throws javax.xml.registry.JAXRException;  //L1
    public abstract boolean isOpaque( ) throws javax.xml.registry.JAXRException;                             //L1
    public abstract void setMimeType(String mimeType) throws javax.xml.registry.JAXRException;              //L1
    public abstract void setOpaque(boolean isOpaque) throws javax.xml.registry.JAXRException;               //L1
    public abstract void setRepositoryItem(javax.activation.DataHandler repositoryItem)
        throws javax.xml.registry.JAXRException;                                                            //L1
}
```

Most of the interfaces in the javax.xml.registry.infomodel package represent data that is held within the registry itself and is of a type that the registry understands. This is not the case for an ExtrinsicObject. The ExtrinsicObject interface represents information that does not have any meaning to and is not interpreted by the registry, which treats it simply as data and stores it in an associated repository from which it can be retrieved on demand. To add an ExtrinsicObject to the registry, use the LifeCycleManager createExtrinsicObject() method, which requires a DataHandler that can be used to retrieve the data to be written to the repository as a byte stream. Once a ExtrinsicObject is created, you can use the getRepositoryItem() method to get a DataHandler that retrieves its content from the repository and the getMimeType() method to get the MIME type of the data. The setOpaque() method can be used to mark the data as opaque, so that the registry should not attempt to interpret it in any way. This might be done if the data is encrypted before being submitted to the registry.

Since ExtrinsicObjects require storage outside the registry, they represent a level 1 feature.

InternationalString   javax.xml.registry.infomodel

JAXR 1.0; JWSDP 1.0, J2EE 1.4

```
public interface InternationalString {
// Public Instance Methods
    public abstract void addLocalizedString(LocalizedString localizedString) throws javax.xml.registry.JAXRException;    //LO
    public abstract void addLocalizedStrings(Collection localizedStrings) throws javax.xml.registry.JAXRException;    //LO
    public abstract LocalizedString getLocalizedString(Locale locale, String charsetName)
        throws javax.xml.registry.JAXRException;    //LO
    public abstract Collection getLocalizedStrings( ) throws javax.xml.registry.JAXRException;    //LO
    public abstract String getValue( ) throws javax.xml.registry.JAXRException;    //LO
    public abstract String getValue(Locale locale) throws javax.xml.registry.JAXRException;    //LO
    public abstract void removeLocalizedString(LocalizedString localizedString)
        throws javax.xml.registry.JAXRException;    //LO
    public abstract void removeLocalizedStrings(Collection localizedStrings) throws javax.xml.registry.JAXRException;    //LO
    public abstract void setValue(String value) throws javax.xml.registry.JAXRException;    //LO
    public abstract void setValue(Locale locale, String value) throws javax.xml.registry.JAXRException;    //LO
}
```

An InternationalString contains a string that has been translated for one or more locales, in which each translation is represented by a LocalizedString object that specifies a locale, the text to be used in that locale and, optionally, the character set that the locale requires. The LifeCycleManager createInternationalString( ) method can be used to create an InternationalString and optionally to add a LocalizedString for a single locale. The name attribute of RegistryObject is of type InternationalString; therefore, all of the factory methods of LifeCycleManager that create objects in the registry either accept a name argument of this type, or allow you to specify the name as a String that is then converted to an InternationalString associated with the current locale.

Once you have an InternationalString object, you can add translations for additional locales by creating the appropriate LocalizedString and using the addLocalizedString( ) or addLocalizedStrings( ) methods. In the unlikely event that you need to remove translations, use the removeLocalizedString( ) or removeLocalizedStrings( ) methods. The getLocalizedStrings( ) method returns a Collection of all of the LocalizedStrings that the InternationalString contains, while getLocalizedString( ) returns the appropriate LocalizedString for a given locale and character set, or null if there isn't one.

If you don't want to deal directly with LocalizedStrings, you can use one of the setValue( ) methods instead. The setValue(Locale locale, String value) method creates and adds a Localized-String with the given value and locale, using the default character set (which is UTF-8). The setValue(String value) does the same, but defaults to the system's default locale. The getValue(Locale locale) method retrieves the string that is appropriate for the given locale, while getValue( ) returns the value for the system's default locale. These methods return null if there is no value stored for the given locale.

Passed To   javax.xml.registry.LifeCycleManager.{createClassification( ), createClassificationScheme( ), createConcept( ), createExternalIdentifier( ), createExternalLink( ), createOrganization( ), createRegistryPackage( ), createService( )}, RegistryObject.{setDescription( ), setName( )}, SpecificationLink.setUsageDescription( )

Returned By   javax.xml.registry.LifeCycleManager.createInternationalString( ), RegistryObject. {getDescription( ), getName( )}, SpecificationLink.getUsageDescription( )

JAXR 1.0; JWSDP 1.0, J2EE 1.4

```
public interface Key {
// Public Instance Methods
    public abstract String getId( ) throws javax.xml.registry.JAXRException;                    //LO
    public abstract void setId(String id) throws javax.xml.registry.JAXRException;              //LO
}
```

A Key object represents the unique key allocated to a RegistryObject when it is first added to the registry. The Key contains a string-valued identifier that can be retrieved using the getId() method and set using setId(). Changing the identifier has the effect of changing the object in the registry with which the RegistryObject is associated. In general, you should allow the registry to assign the key for a new registry object. However, ebXML registries also allow the registry client to specify the key.

Passed To   javax.xml.registry.BusinessQueryManager.{findServiceBindings( ), findServices( )}, javax.xml.registry.RegistryException.setErrorObjectKey( ), RegistryObject.setKey( )

Returned By   javax.xml.registry.LifeCycleManager.createKey( ), javax.xml.registry.RegistryException.getErrorObjectKey( ), RegistryObject.getKey( )

LocalizedString

javax.xml.registry.infomodel

JAXR 1.0; JWSDP 1.0, J2EE 1.4

```
public interface LocalizedString {
// Public Constants
    public static final String DEFAULT_CHARSET_NAME;                                            //="UTF-8"
// Public Instance Methods
    public abstract String getCharsetName( ) throws javax.xml.registry.JAXRException;          //LO
    public abstract Locale getLocale( ) throws javax.xml.registry.JAXRException;               //LO
    public abstract String getValue( ) throws javax.xml.registry.JAXRException;                //LO
    public abstract void setCharsetName(String charsetName) throws javax.xml.registry.JAXRException;  //LO
    public abstract void setLocale(Locale locale) throws javax.xml.registry.JAXRException;     //LO
    public abstract void setValue(String value) throws javax.xml.registry.JAXRException;       //LO
}
```

LocalizedString is a container for a string together with a locale and a character set. One or more LocalizedStrings are typically combined in an InternationalString to provide a single object that can provide a localized variant of a text string for several locales. To create a new LocalizedString(), use the LifeCycleManager createLocalizedString() method, which requires at least the locale for which the object is being created and the text to be used in that locale. Optionally, a character set may also be specified; if no value is supplied, then UTF-8 is assumed.

The getValue(), getLocale(), and getCharsetName() methods return the text, locale, and character set associated with the LocalizedString. If no explicit character set is specified, then the getCharsetName() method returns "UTF-8". The values of any of these attributes can be changed at any time by calling setValue(), setLocale(), or setCharsetName().

Returned By   javax.xml.registry.LifeCycleManager.createLocalizedString( ), InternationalString. getLocalizedString( )

Organization

javax.xml.registry.infomodel

JAXR 1.0; JWSDP 1.0, J2EE 1.4

```
public interface Organization extends RegistryObject {
// Property Accessor Methods (by property name)
    public abstract int getChildOrganizationCount( ) throws javax.xml.registry.JAXRException;          //L1
    public abstract Collection getChildOrganizations( ) throws javax.xml.registry.JAXRException;        //L1
    public abstract Collection getDescendantOrganizations( ) throws javax.xml.registry.JAXRException;   //L1
    public abstract Organization getParentOrganization( ) throws javax.xml.registry.JAXRException;      //L1
    public abstract PostalAddress getPostalAddress( ) throws javax.xml.registry.JAXRException;          //L1
    public abstract void setPostalAddress(PostalAddress address) throws javax.xml.registry.JAXRException; //L1
    public abstract User getPrimaryContact( ) throws javax.xml.registry.JAXRException;                  //L0
    public abstract void setPrimaryContact(User primaryContact) throws javax.xml.registry.JAXRException; //L0
    public abstract Organization getRootOrganization( ) throws javax.xml.registry.JAXRException;        //L1
    public abstract Collection getServices( ) throws javax.xml.registry.JAXRException;                  //L0
    public abstract Collection getUsers( ) throws javax.xml.registry.JAXRException;                     //L0
// Public Instance Methods
    public abstract void addChildOrganization(Organization organization) throws javax.xml.registry.JAXRException;   //L1
    public abstract void addChildOrganizations(Collection organizations) throws javax.xml.registry.JAXRException;   //L1
    public abstract void addService(javax.xml.registry.infomodel.Service service)
        throws javax.xml.registry.JAXRException;                                                        //L0
    public abstract void addServices(Collection services) throws javax.xml.registry.JAXRException;      //L0
    public abstract void addUser(User user) throws javax.xml.registry.JAXRException;                    //L0
    public abstract void addUsers(Collection users) throws javax.xml.registry.JAXRException;            //L0
    public abstract Collection getTelephoneNumbers(String phoneType) throws javax.xml.registry.JAXRException; //L0
    public abstract void removeChildOrganization(Organization organization) throws javax.xml.registry.JAXRException; //L1
    public abstract void removeChildOrganizations(Collection organizations) throws javax.xml.registry.JAXRException; //L1
    public abstract void removeService(javax.xml.registry.infomodel.Service service)
        throws javax.xml.registry.JAXRException;                                                        //L0
    public abstract void removeServices(Collection services) throws javax.xml.registry.JAXRException;   //L0
    public abstract void removeUser(User user) throws javax.xml.registry.JAXRException;                 //L0
    public abstract void removeUsers(Collection users) throws javax.xml.registry.JAXRException;         //L0
    public abstract void setTelephoneNumbers(Collection phoneNumbers) throws javax.xml.registry.JAXRException; //L0
}
```

The Organization interface represents a company or another type of provider that wants to publish details about itself and its services in the registry. The Organization object, an instance of which can be created by calling the createOrganization( ) method of LifeCycleManager, is the root from which all other information regarding the organization can be found. Like all RegistryObjects, it has an associated name and description, and can have associated Classifications that should be chosen to allow potential clients to locate it based on searches that use criteria that relate to its activities, along with links to external specifications and so on. The following information can be accessed directly from the Organization object:

Services

The Service objects representing the services that the organization wishes to publish. The getServices( ) method returns a Collection containing all of the services, whereas addService( ), addServices( ), removeService( ), and removeServices( ) can be used to add to or remove from this set.

Primary Contact

A User object that represents the person responsible for maintaining the information published by the Organization in the registry. Use the getPrimaryContact( ) method to access this attribute and the setPrimaryContact( ) method to change it.

Users

An additional set of Users associated with the Organization. This set should always contain at least the user designated as the primary contact. When the primary contact is set, her entry is automatically included in this list. Note that the JAXR reference implementation does not prevent duplicate entries from appearing in this list, which can be modified using the addUser( ), addUsers( ), removeUser( ), and removeUsers( ) methods.

Telephone Numbers

A collection of TelephoneNumbers for the organization, manipulated as a group using the getTelephoneNumbers( ) and setTelephoneNumbers( ) methods.

Postal Address

A postal address for the organization, set using setPostalAddress( ) and read using getPostalAddress( ), which are both level 1 methods. The principal address for an organization in a level 0 registry is that of the primary contact.

Level 1 registry providers allow hierarchies of Organizations to be constructed that mirror the business or ownership relationships between parent and subsidiary organizations, or other business structures that should be visible to the outside world. The addChildOrganization( ) and addChildOrganizations( ) methods let you add subsidiary organization nodes below their parent, while getParentOrganization( ), getChildOrganizations( ), and getDescendentOrganizations( ) allow you to traverse the hierarchy from any node or from the root, which can be obtained by calling getRootOrganization( ) on any of its nodes. To remove nodes, use the removeChildOrganization( ) or removeChildOrganizations( ) method.

Passed To   Organization.{addChildOrganization( ), removeChildOrganization( )}, javax.xml.registry.info-model.Service.setProvidingOrganization( )

Returned By   javax.xml.registry.LifeCycleManager.createOrganization( ), Organization. {getParentOrganization( ), getRootOrganization( )}, RegistryObject. getSubmittingOrganization( ), javax.xml.registry.infomodel.Service. getProvidingOrganization( ), User.getOrganization( )

PersonName   javax.xml.registry.infomodel

JAXR 1.0; JWSDP 1.0, J2EE 1.4

```
public interface PersonName {
// Public Instance Methods
    public abstract String getFirstName( ) throws javax.xml.registry.JAXRException;      //L1
    public abstract String getFullName( ) throws javax.xml.registry.JAXRException;       //L0
    public abstract String getLastName( ) throws javax.xml.registry.JAXRException;       //L1
    public abstract String getMiddleName( ) throws javax.xml.registry.JAXRException;     //L1
    public abstract void setFirstName(String firstName) throws javax.xml.registry.JAXRException;  //L1
```

public abstract void **setFullName**(String *fullName*) throws javax.xml.registry.JAXRException;	//L0
public abstract void **setLastName**(String *lastName*) throws javax.xml.registry.JAXRException;	//L1
public abstract void **setMiddleName**(String *middleName*) throws javax.xml.registry.JAXRException;	//L1
}	

The PersonName interface represents the name of a registry User. A level 0 registry provides only the ability to store the user's full name as a free-form string using the setFullName() method and to retrieve it by calling getFullName(). A level 1 JAXR provider additionally implements the methods that let you get and set a first name, middle name, and last name. The specification does not describe how to resolve the possible conflicts caused by using these additional methods together with the setFullName() method, or what getFullName() should return if both setFullName() and the methods that set part of the name have been used, as in the following code extract:

```
personName.setFullName("John D. Doe");
personName.setFirstName("Jane");
String name = personName.getFullName( );
//Result is undefined
```

Passed To   User.setPersonName( )

Returned By   javax.xml.registry.LifeCycleManager.createPersonName( ), User.getPersonName( )

PostalAddress   javax.xml.registry.infomodel

JAXR 1.0; JWSDP 1.0, J2EE 1.4

public interface **PostalAddress** extends ExtensibleObject {	
// Property Accessor Methods (by property name)	
public abstract String **getCity**( ) throws javax.xml.registry.JAXRException;	//L0
public abstract void **setCity**(String *city*) throws javax.xml.registry.JAXRException;	//L0
public abstract String **getCountry**( ) throws javax.xml.registry.JAXRException;	//L0
String *country*) throws javax.xml.registry.JAXRException;	
public abstract String **getPostalCode**( ) throws javax.xml.registry.JAXRException;	//L0
public abstract void **setPostalCode**(String *postalCode*) throws javax.xml.registry.JAXRException;	//L0
public abstract ClassificationScheme **getPostalScheme**( ) throws javax.xml.registry.JAXRException;	//L0
public abstract void **setPostalScheme**(ClassificationScheme *scheme*) throws javax.xml.registry.JAXRException;	//L0
public abstract String **getStateOrProvince**( ) throws javax.xml.registry.JAXRException;	//L0
public abstract void **setStateOrProvince**(String *stateOrProvince*) throws javax.xml.registry.JAXRException;	//L0
public abstract String **getStreet**( ) throws javax.xml.registry.JAXRException;	//L0
public abstract void **setStreet**(String *street*) throws javax.xml.registry.JAXRException;	//L0
public abstract String **getStreetNumber**( ) throws javax.xml.registry.JAXRException;	//L0
public abstract void **setStreetNumber**(String *streetNumber*) throws javax.xml.registry.JAXRException;	//L0
public abstract String **getType**( ) throws javax.xml.registry.JAXRException;	//L0
public abstract void **setType**(String *type*) throws javax.xml.registry.JAXRException;	//L0
}	

A PostalAddress object can be used as the contact address of a User and, in the case of a level 1 registry, an Organization. To obtain a PostalAddress object, use the createPostalAddress() method of LifeCycleManager. The PostalAddress interface is composed entirely of methods that allow you to get and set the various fields that make up the address, with the exception of the getPostalScheme() and setPostalScheme() methods. These methods allow you to specify the ClassificationScheme that describes how the fields in the PostalAddress should be mapped to specific fields in the object in the registry that represents it. This mapping is necessary because UDDI registries do not have a fixed representation of a postal address. As a result, each individual registry may have its own particular way of holding the street address, city, ZIP code, and so on. Obviously, in order to be portable, the JAXR provider has to be independent of the addressing scheme chosen for any particular registry. It achieves this by putting the onus on the user, with knowledge of the target registry, to describe how the mapping is to be performed. For a detailed description of how this mapping is performed, along with examples, refer to "Postal Addresses" in Chapter 7.

Passed To   Organization.setPostalAddress( )

Returned By   javax.xml.registry.LifeCycleManager.createPostalAddress( ), Organization.getPostalAddress( )

RegistryEntry

javax.xml.registry.infomodel

JAXR 1.0; JWSDP 1.0, J2EE 1.4

**javax.xml.
registry**

```
public interface RegistryEntry extends RegistryObject, Versionable {
// Public Constants
    public static final int STABILITY_DYNAMIC;                                           //=0
    public static final int STABILITY_DYNAMIC_COMPATIBLE;                                //=1
    public static final int STABILITY_STATIC;                                           //=2
    public static final int STATUS_APPROVED;                                            //=1
    public static final int STATUS_DEPRECATED;                                          //=2
    public static final int STATUS_SUBMITTED;                                           //=0
    public static final int STATUS_WITHDRAWN;                                           //=3
// Public Instance Methods
    public abstract java.util.Date getExpiration( ) throws javax.xml.registry.JAXRException;     //L1
    public abstract int getStability( ) throws javax.xml.registry.JAXRException;                 //L1
    public abstract int getStatus( ) throws javax.xml.registry.JAXRException;                    //L1
    public abstract void setExpiration(java.util.Date expiration) throws javax.xml.registry.JAXRException;  //L1
    public abstract void setStability(int stability) throws javax.xml.registry.JAXRException;     //L1
}
```

RegistryEntry is an interface that acts as a base for objects within the registry that require metadata beyond that provided by RegistryObject, of which it is an extension. The following additional attributes are provided:

Versioning

ExtensibleObject implements the Versionable interface, which allows a RegistryEntry to have major, minor, and user version numbers. See the description of the Versionable interface later in this chapter for further details.

Stability

The getStability( ) and setStability( ) methods manipulate a value that indicates whether the registry object is permitted to change. If this attribute has the value STABILITY_ STATIC, no changes can occur. The value STABILITY_DYNAMIC means that a change of any type may occur, whereas STABILITY_DYNAMIC_COMPATIBLE means that changes can be made, but will be backward-compatible with previous versions of the object. The validity of the stability attribute may be bounded by an expiration date, available from the getExpiration( ) method. If this is not null, then the object is free to change arbitrarily after the returned Date.

Status

The getStatus( ) and setStatus( ) methods retrieve and set the attribute that gives the state of the object within its overall lifecycle. There are several defined values for this attribute, although it is only possible for clients using the JAXR API to move an object to STATE_SUBMITTED or STATE_DEPRECATED. The other values might still be seen, however, since they could be set as a result of administrative action by the registry operator or by a client using a more capable API.

Although there are objects derived from RegistryEntry in the registry API that are available to clients of both level 0 and level 1 providers, the attributes themselves are supported only in level 1 registries and therefore are not available to level 0 clients.

Implementations ClassificationScheme, ExtrinsicObject, RegistryPackage, javax.xml.registry.infomodel.Service

RegistryObject

javax.xml.registry.infomodel

JAXR 1.0; JWSDP 1.0, J2EE 1.4

```
public interface RegistryObject extends ExtensibleObject {
// Property Accessor Methods (by property name)
    public abstract Collection getAssociatedObjects( ) throws javax.xml.registry.JAXRException;              //L1
    public abstract Collection getAssociations( ) throws javax.xml.registry.JAXRException;                   //L0
    public abstract void setAssociations(Collection associations) throws javax.xml.registry.JAXRException;    //L0
    public abstract Collection getAuditTrail( ) throws javax.xml.registry.JAXRException;                     //L1
    public abstract Collection getClassifications( ) throws javax.xml.registry.JAXRException;                //L0
    public abstract void setClassifications(Collection classifications) throws javax.xml.registry.JAXRException;  //L0
    public abstract InternationalString getDescription( ) throws javax.xml.registry.JAXRException;           //L0
    public abstract void setDescription(InternationalString description) throws javax.xml.registry.JAXRException;  //L0
    public abstract Collection getExternalIdentifiers( ) throws javax.xml.registry.JAXRException;            //L0
    public abstract void setExternalIdentifiers(Collection externalIdentifiers) throws javax.xml.registry.JAXRException;  //L0
    public abstract Collection getExternalLinks( ) throws javax.xml.registry.JAXRException;                  //L0
    public abstract void setExternalLinks(Collection externalLinks) throws javax.xml.registry.JAXRException;  //L0
    public abstract javax.xml.registry.infomodel.Key getKey( ) throws javax.xml.registry.JAXRException;      //L0
    public abstract void setKey(javax.xml.registry.infomodel.Key key) throws javax.xml.registry.JAXRException;  //L0
    public abstract javax.xml.registry.LifeCycleManager getLifeCycleManager( )
        throws javax.xml.registry.JAXRException;                                                             //L0
    public abstract InternationalString getName( ) throws javax.xml.registry.JAXRException;                  //L0
    public abstract void setName(InternationalString name) throws javax.xml.registry.JAXRException;          //L0
    public abstract Concept getObjectType( ) throws javax.xml.registry.JAXRException;                        //L1
    public abstract Collection getRegistryPackages( ) throws javax.xml.registry.JAXRException;               //L1
    public abstract Organization getSubmittingOrganization( ) throws javax.xml.registry.JAXRException;
// Public Instance Methods
    public abstract void addAssociation(Association association) throws javax.xml.registry.JAXRException;     //L0
    public abstract void addAssociations(Collection associations) throws javax.xml.registry.JAXRException;    //L0
    public abstract void addClassification(Classification classification) throws javax.xml.registry.JAXRException;  //L0
    public abstract void addClassifications(Collection classifications) throws javax.xml.registry.JAXRException;  //L0
    public abstract void addExternalIdentifier(ExternalIdentifier externalIdentifier)
        throws javax.xml.registry.JAXRException;                                                             //L0
    public abstract void addExternalIdentifiers(Collection externalIdentifiers) throws javax.xml.registry.JAXRException;  //L0
    public abstract void addExternalLink(ExternalLink externalLink) throws javax.xml.registry.JAXRException;  //L0
    public abstract void addExternalLinks(Collection externalLinks) throws javax.xml.registry.JAXRException;  //L0
    public abstract void removeAssociation(Association association) throws javax.xml.registry.JAXRException;  //L0
```

```
public abstract void removeAssociations(Collection associations) throws javax.xml.registry.JAXRException;     //LO
public abstract void removeClassification(Classification classification) throws javax.xml.registry.JAXRException;     //LO
public abstract void removeClassifications(Collection classifications) throws javax.xml.registry.JAXRException;     //LO
public abstract void removeExternalIdentifier(ExternalIdentifier externalIdentifier)
    throws javax.xml.registry.JAXRException;     //LO
public abstract void removeExternalIdentifiers(Collection externalIdentifiers)
    throws javax.xml.registry.JAXRException;     //LO
public abstract void removeExternalLink(ExternalLink externalLink) throws javax.xml.registry.JAXRException;     //LO
Collection externalLinks) throws javax.xml.registry.JAXRException;
public abstract String toXML() throws javax.xml.registry.JAXRException;     //LO
}
```

With the exception of a very small number of helper classes, every object that can be stored in the registry and accessed using the JAXR API is derived from the RegistryObject interface. RegistryObject provides very little functionality of its own—instead, it is composed mainly of accessor and mutator methods that allow JAXR clients to work with the attributes of a RegistryObject. The following paragraphs provide an overview of each of these attributes; for more detailed information, refer to the appropriate reference section in this chapter.

Name

A human-readable name for the object. This value, along with the description, is typically used to represent the object in a user interface and is of type International-String so that it can be presented in the appropriate way for the locale of the viewing client. This attribute is accessed using the getName() and setName() methods.

Description

A free-form description of the object, which can be accessed using the getDescription and setDescription() methods. Like the Name attribute, this is intended for human consumption and is therefore of type InternationalString.

Key

A value that identifies the object in the registry. The Key contains a unique identifier that is usually a 128-bit DCE UUID. To guarantee uniqueness, this value is generally allocated by the registry when the object is created, but ebXML registries allow clients to select the identifier for objects that they create.

LifeCycleManager

A reference to the LifeCycleManager that was used to create this instance of the object. This refers to the instance of the object currently being used by the JAXR client, rather than the instance used to initially create the registry's version of the object.

Object Type

A Concept that describes the type of the registry object. The JAXR specification defines an enumeration of object types called "ObjectType" from which these values are taken. Refer to Chapter 7 for the list of valid object types. This attribute can be read using the getObjectType() method, which is available only with a level 1 JAXR provider.

Submitting Organization

A reference to the Organization object for the organization that created the object. This attribute can be retrieved using the getSubmittingOrganization() method.

Audit Trail

A set of AuditableEvent objects that record changes to the object made by authorized users. Audit trails are maintained only by level 1 registries, The complete set of audited events for an object can be obtained from the getAuditTrail() method.

Associations

A RegistryObject can be associated with other objects in order to express some kind of relationship between them, such as "Uses" or "Supersedes." Methods are provided to add and remove associations, and to list the set of associations that involve the object on which they are invoked. See the reference section for the Assocation interface, earlier in this chapter, for further details.

Associated Objects

The getAssociatedObjects( ) method returns the Collection of RegistryObjects that are related to this object via an Association. This is a level 1 method.

Classifications

A set of Classification objects that allow a RegistryObject to be categorized according to one or more classification schemes such as NAICS, which describes the industry to which an object relates, or ISO-3166, which indicates a geographical location. Refer to the reference sections for Classification and ClassificationScheme, earlier in this chapter, for more information.

External Identifiers

A RegistryObject can have any number of associated ExternalIdentifier objects that represent an identifier from an external numbering or tagging scheme such as D-U-N-S. See the reference section for the ExternalIdentifier interface, earlier in this chapter, for more details.

External Links

An ExternalLink object provides the means to link a RegistryObject to information that resides outside the registry via a URI. Refer to the description of the ExternalLink interface, earlier in this chapter, for further information.

The toXML( ) method is provided to allow a registry to return its native XML representation of the RegistryObject to allow access to attributes that are not exposed via the JAXR API. Although this is a level 0 method, JAXR providers are not required to support it and may throw an UnsupportedCapabilityException if they do not.

Implementations Association, AuditableEvent, Classification, Concept, ExternalIdentifier, ExternalLink, Organization, RegistryEntry, ServiceBinding, SpecificationLink, User

Passed To javax.xml.registry.LifeCycleManager.{createAssociation( ), createConcept( )}, Association. {setSourceObject( ), setTargetObject( )}, Classification.setClassifiedObject( ), RegistryPackage. {addRegistryObject( ), removeRegistryObject( )}, SpecificationLink.setSpecificationObject( )

Returned By javax.xml.registry.QueryManager.getRegistryObject( ), Association.{getSourceObject( ), getTargetObject( )}, AuditableEvent.getRegistryObject( ), Classification.getClassifiedObject( ), Concept.getParent( ), ExternalIdentifier.getRegistryObject( ), SpecificationLink. getSpecificationObject( )

RegistryPackage   javax.xml.registry.infomodel

JAXR 1.0; JWSDP 1.0, J2EE 1.4

```
public interface RegistryPackage extends RegistryEntry {
// Public Instance Methods
   public abstract void addRegistryObject(RegistryObject registryObject) throws javax.xml.registry.JAXRException;    //L1
   public abstract void addRegistryObjects(Collection registryObjects) throws javax.xml.registry.JAXRException;      //L1
   public abstract Set getRegistryObjects( ) throws javax.xml.registry.JAXRException;                               //L1
```

```
public abstract void removeRegistryObject(RegistryObject registryObject) throws javax.xml.registry.JAXRException;   //L1
public abstract void removeRegistryObjects(Collection registryObjects) throws javax.xml.registry.JAXRException;   //L1
}
```

RegistryPackage is an interface supported by level 1 JAXR providers. It allows a set of RegistryObjects to be logically grouped together. An empty RegistryPackage can be created using the LifeCycleManager createRegistryPackage() method, and entries can be added to it by calling addRegistryObject() or addRegistryObjects(). To remove items from the package, use removeRegistryObject() or removeRegistryObjects(). The benefits of a RegistryPackage include the ability to version it or to indicate its stability, using methods provided by the RegistryEntry interface, which it extends. You can also use the getRegistryObjects() method to get a list of the objects that it contains. Since a RegistryPackage is a RegistryObject, it is possible to nest one package inside another.

Returned By   javax.xml.registry.LifeCycleManager.createRegistryPackage()

Service   javax.xml.registry.infomodel

JAXR 1.0; JWSDP 1.0, J2EE 1.4

```
public interface Service extends RegistryEntry {
// Public Instance Methods
    public abstract void addServiceBinding(ServiceBinding serviceBinding) throws javax.xml.registry.JAXRException;   //L0
    public abstract void addServiceBindings(Collection serviceBindings) throws javax.xml.registry.JAXRException;   //L0
    public abstract Organization getProvidingOrganization() throws javax.xml.registry.JAXRException;   //L0
    public abstract Collection getServiceBindings() throws javax.xml.registry.JAXRException;   //L0
    public abstract void removeServiceBinding(ServiceBinding serviceBinding) throws javax.xml.registry.JAXRException;  //L0
    public abstract void removeServiceBindings(Collection serviceBindings) throws javax.xml.registry.JAXRException;   //L0
    public abstract void setProvidingOrganization(Organization providingOrganization)
        throws javax.xml.registry.JAXRException;   //L0
}
```

Service is a simple container object that holds a set of ServiceBindings. A Service object is created by an Organization to describe a service that it wants to publish in the registry. An Organization may have any number of associated Service objects, which are created using the createService() method of LifeCycleManager and added using the addService() or addServices() methods of the Organization interface. A registry client can locate a Service using the findServices() method of BusinessQueryManager. When the target registry is UDDI, it is only possible to search for services provided by a specified Organization; ebXML registries allow searching for Services over all Organizations. In most cases, a service query is based on a set of classifications that describe the nature of the service required. Once a suitable service is found, the getProvidingOrganization() method can be used to discover the service provider (which is, of course, obvious in the case of a UDDI registry), and the getServiceBindings() method can be used to obtain ServiceBinding objects that describe how to access and use the service. The creating Organization can install and remove these bindings using the addServiceBinding(), addServiceBindings(), removeServiceBinding(), and removeServiceBindings() methods.

Passed To   Organization.{addService(), removeService()}

Returned By   javax.xml.registry.LifeCycleManager.createService(), ServiceBinding.getService()

JAXR 1.0; JWSDP 1.0, J2EE 1.4

```
public interface ServiceBinding extends RegistryObject, URIValidator {
// Public Instance Methods
  public abstract void addSpecificationLink(SpecificationLink specificationLink)
    throws javax.xml.registry.JAXRException;                                                    //LO
  public abstract void addSpecificationLinks(Collection specificationLinks) throws javax.xml.registry.JAXRException;  //LO
  public abstract String getAccessURI( ) throws javax.xml.registry.JAXRException;                //LO
  public abstract javax.xml.registry.infomodel.Service getService( ) throws javax.xml.registry.JAXRException;        //LO
  public abstract Collection getSpecificationLinks( ) throws javax.xml.registry.JAXRException;    //LO
  public abstract ServiceBinding getTargetBinding( ) throws javax.xml.registry.JAXRException;     //LO
  public abstract void removeSpecificationLink(SpecificationLink specificationLink)
    throws javax.xml.registry.JAXRException;                                                    //LO
  public abstract void removeSpecificationLinks(Collection specificationLinks)
    throws javax.xml.registry.JAXRException;                                                    //LO
  public abstract void setAccessURI(String uri) throws javax.xml.registry.JAXRException;          //LO
  public abstract void setTargetBinding(ServiceBinding binding) throws javax.xml.registry.JAXRException;  //LO
}
```

A Service has one or more associated ServiceBindings that provide the information necessary for a developer to discover how to use and access the service. A Service that can be accessed using more than one protocol or that is available at several different locations requires a separate ServiceBinding for each. The Service object to which a binding corresponds can be obtained from its getService( ) method, while the URI at which the service instance resides can be found by calling the getAccessURI( ) method.

Information that describes the service can be linked to the binding using a SpecificationLink, which may point to a WSDL document stored in an associated repository or at a location given by its URL. Refer to the description of the SpecificationLink interface, later in this chapter, for a description of the ways in which it can be used to refer to service documentation.

In some cases, a ServiceBinding may not refer directly to an instance of the service but to another ServiceBinding. When this is true, the target binding can be retrieved using the getTargetBinding( ) method.

Passed To   javax.xml.registry.infomodel.Service.{addServiceBinding( ), removeServiceBinding( )}, ServiceBinding.setTargetBinding( )

Returned By   javax.xml.registry.LifeCycleManager.createServiceBinding( ),
                   ServiceBinding.getTargetBinding( ), SpecificationLink.getServiceBinding( )

Slot   javax.xml.registry.infomodel

JAXR 1.0; JWSDP 1.0, J2EE 1.4

```
public interface Slot {
// Public Constants
  public static final String ADDRESS_LINES_SLOT;       //="addressLines"
  public static final String AUTHORIZED_NAME_SLOT;      //="authorizedName"
  public static final String OPERATOR_SLOT;             //="operator"
```

```
public static final String SORT_CODE_SLOT;                                    //="sortCode"
// Public Instance Methods
  public abstract String getName( ) throws javax.xml.registry.JAXRException;            //LO
  public abstract String getSlotType( ) throws javax.xml.registry.JAXRException;         //LO
  public abstract Collection getValues( ) throws javax.xml.registry.JAXRException;        //LO
  public abstract void setName(String name) throws javax.xml.registry.JAXRException;      //LO
  public abstract void setSlotType(String slotType) throws javax.xml.registry.JAXRException;  //LO
  public abstract void setValues(Collection values) throws javax.xml.registry.JAXRException;  //LO
}
```

A Slot is an object with a name, a type, and a collection of string values, no two of which may be the same. Slots are used to add arbitrary attributes to a RegistryObject without requiring an extension to the JAXR API. Every RegistryObject inherits the ability to handle Slots from the ExtensibleObject interface, which defines the methods necessary to store and retrieve them. A Slot is uniquely identified by its name; the result of attempting to add a Slot to an object that already has one with the same name is not defined by the JAXR specification.

The JAXR provider uses Slots to represent a small number of registry object attributes that are not explicitly recognized by the JAXR API because they are registry-type specific; refer to Chapter 7 for examples. Application code can create a Slot using one of the createSlot( ) methods of LifeCycleManager, and it can associate it with a RegistryObject using its addSlot( ) or addSlots( ) methods. It should be noted, however, that the JAXR reference implementation for the UDDI registry does not store Slots created by application code, although it does allow them to be created and attached to an object.

The getName( ), getSlotType( ), and getValues( ) methods of Slot allow you to fetch the attributes of a Slot, while the corresponding setter methods let you change them. Note that the meaning of the slot type attribute is not defined by the specification and there is no predefined set of valid values.

Passed To   ExtensibleObject.addSlot( )

Returned By   javax.xml.registry.LifeCycleManager.createSlot( ), ExtensibleObject.getSlot( )

SpecificationLink   javax.xml.registry.infomodel

JAXR 1.0; JWSDP 1.0, J2EE 1.4

```
public interface SpecificationLink extends RegistryObject {
// Public Instance Methods
  public abstract ServiceBinding getServiceBinding( ) throws javax.xml.registry.JAXRException;       //LO
  public abstract RegistryObject getSpecificationObject( ) throws javax.xml.registry.JAXRException;   //LO
  public abstract InternationalString getUsageDescription( ) throws javax.xml.registry.JAXRException; //LO
  public abstract Collection getUsageParameters( ) throws javax.xml.registry.JAXRException;           //LO
  public abstract void setSpecificationObject(RegistryObject obj) throws javax.xml.registry.JAXRException; //LO
    public abstract void setUsageDescription(InternationalString usageDescription)
    throws javax.xml.registry.JAXRException;                                                         //LO
  public abstract void setUsageParameters(Collection usageParameters) throws javax.xml.registry.JAXRException; //LO
}
```

A SpecificationLink is an attribute of a ServiceBinding that is used to link the binding to another RegistryObject that either is or refers to technical documentation for the service.

The link to the information itself is provided by the object obtained from the getSpecificationObject( ) object method. In an ebXML registry, this is likely to be an Extrinsic-Object that refers directly to a copy of the specification in the repository, which can be obtained using the getRepositoryItem( ) method. In the case of the UDDI registry, the target object is most likely to be a Concept with an associated ExternalLink that points to the location at which the specification can be found. Refer to Chapter 7 for an example that shows how to link a ServiceBinding to the WSDL document that describes how to access the service. Additional information can be provided in the form of usage parameters, which can be obtained in the form of a Collection of String objects using the getUsageParameters( ) method and set using setUsageParameters( ). Note that the UDDI registry allows only a single entry to be present in this collection. The getUsageDescription( ) method returns an InternationalString that describes how the usage parameters should be used. Both of these attributes are meant for human use and are therefore only loosely described in the JAXR specification.

Passed To   ServiceBinding.{addSpecificationLink( ), removeSpecificationLink( )}

Returned By   javax.xml.registry.LifeCycleManager.createSpecificationLink( )

TelephoneNumber   javax.xml.registry.infomodel

JAXR 1.0; JWSDP 1.0, J2EE 1.4

public interface **TelephoneNumber** {	
// Property Accessor Methods (by property name)	
public abstract String **getAreaCode**( ) throws javax.xml.registry.JAXRException;	//L1
public abstract void **setAreaCode**(String areaCode) throws javax.xml.registry.JAXRException;	//L1
public abstract String **getCountryCode**( ) throws javax.xml.registry.JAXRException;	//L1
public abstract void **setCountryCode**(String countryCode) throws javax.xml.registry.JAXRException;	//L1
public abstract String **getExtension**( ) throws javax.xml.registry.JAXRException;	//L1
public abstract void **setExtension**(String extension) throws javax.xml.registry.JAXRException;	//L1
public abstract String **getNumber**( ) throws javax.xml.registry.JAXRException;	//L0
public abstract void **setNumber**(String number) throws javax.xml.registry.JAXRException;	//L0
public abstract String **getType**( ) throws javax.xml.registry.JAXRException;	//L0
public abstract void **setType**(String type) throws javax.xml.registry.JAXRException;	//L0
public abstract String **getUrl**( ) throws javax.xml.registry.JAXRException;	//L1
public abstract void **setUrl**(String url) throws javax.xml.registry.JAXRException;	//L1
}	

The TelephoneNumber interface represents the telephone number of a user or an organization. Create one or more TelephoneNumbers using the LifeCycleManager createTelephoneNumber method and then add them, as a group, to either a User or an Organization object by calling their setTelephoneNumbers( ) method.

The functionality provided by this interface depends on the JAXR provider. A level 0 provider implements a type field, which is set to an arbitrary value such as "Home," "Office," or "Mobile," and a single string to hold the number as dialed, which can be obtained using the getNumber( ) method. A level 1 registry provider adds to this the ability to specify a URL that can dial the telephone number automatically, and the ability to get and set each field of the number separately using methods such as getCountryCode( ), getExtension, and so on. In this case, the value returned by getNumber( ) is the local part of the number. No validity checking is performed on the content of this object.

Returned By   javax.xml.registry.LifeCycleManager.createTelephoneNumber( )

JAXR 1.0; JWSDP 1.0, J2EE 1.4

```
public interface URIValidator {
// Public Instance Methods
    public abstract boolean getValidateURI( ) throws javax.xml.registry.JAXRException;          //L0
    boolean (validate) throws javax.xml.registry.JAXRException;
}
```

URIValidator is an interface implemented by objects that contain a URI and provide the ability to check that the URI is valid. In the JAXR registry model, both ExternalLink and ServiceBinding implement this interface and, as a result, may attempt to check the validity of URIs that they contain when their state is written to the registry. In some cases, this is not convenient, perhaps because the referred content is not available at the time that the registry is updated. The setValidateURI( ) method can be used to enable or disable verification of the URI associated with an object that implements this interface. To determine whether checking is enabled, use getValidateURI( ).

Implementations ExternalLink, ServiceBinding

JAXR 1.0; JWSDP 1.0, J2EE 1.4

```
public interface User extends RegistryObject {
// Property Accessor Methods (by property name)
    public abstract Collection getEmailAddresses( ) throws javax.xml.registry.JAXRException;                          //L0
    public abstract void setEmailAddresses(Collection emailAddresses) throws javax.xml.registry.JAXRException;        //L0
    public abstract Organization getOrganization( ) throws javax.xml.registry.JAXRException;                          //L0
    public abstract PersonName getPersonName( ) throws javax.xml.registry.JAXRException;                              //L0
    public abstract void setPersonName(PersonName personName) throws javax.xml.registry.JAXRException;                //L0
    public abstract Collection getPostalAddresses( ) throws javax.xml.registry.JAXRException;                         //L0
    public abstract void setPostalAddresses(Collection addresses) throws javax.xml.registry.JAXRException;            //L0
    public abstract String getType( ) throws javax.xml.registry.JAXRException;                                        //L0
    public abstract void setType(String type) throws javax.xml.registry.JAXRException; //L0
    public abstract java.net.URL getUrl( ) throws javax.xml.registry.JAXRException;                                   //L1
    public abstract void setUrl(java.net.URL url) throws javax.xml.registry.JAXRException;                            //L1
// Public Instance Methods
    public abstract Collection getTelephoneNumbers( String phoneType) throws javax.xml.registry.JAXRException;        //L0
    public abstract void setTelephoneNumbers(Collection phoneNumbers) throws javax.xml.registry.JAXRException;        //L0
}
```

The User interface represents a registry user. Every object in the registry is associated with the User object of the user that created it and, in a level 1 registry, changes to registry content are audited using the User object of the authenticated user that made the change in order to preserve accountability. The User object is also used to ensure that updates can only be made by the owner of the object being modified.

When used by the registry for auditing and authorization checks, the User object is created from authentication supplied when the user connected to the registry. It is also possible for a registry client to create a User object by calling the createUser( ) method of LifeCycleManager. An object created in this way is used to assign the primary contact for or to add a user to an Organization.

Like many other objects in this package, the User interface consists mainly of getter and setter methods that access attributes of the object. A User object has the following attributes:

- The Organization with which the user is associated. Unlike the other attributes, this one cannot be modified. It is set when the user is added to the Organization object either as the primary contact or as an ordinary user.

- A name, held in the form of a PersonName object.

- A type, which is an arbitrary string that probably has some specific meaning within the organization that assigned it.

- A collection of postal addresses, represented by objects of type PostalAddress.

- A collection of TelephoneNumber objects supplying contact numbers of various types (home, office, mobile, fax, etc.) for the user.

- A collection of email addresses, represented by objects of type EmailAddress.

- For level 1 registries only, a URL that is owned by the user in some way. This might, for example, be the URL of the user's home page or, in the case of the primary contact for an Organization, the URL of a page that is relevant to the services that it has published in the registry.

Passed To Organization.{addUser( ), removeUser( ), setPrimaryContact( )}

Returned By javax.xml.registry.LifeCycleManager.createUser( ), AuditableEvent.getUser( ), Organization.getPrimaryContact( )

Versionable   javax.xml.registry.infomodel

JAXR 1.0; JWSDP 1.0, J2EE 1.4

```
public interface Versionable {
// Public Instance Methods
    public abstract int getMajorVersion( ) throws javax.xml.registry.JAXRException;        //L1
    public abstract int getMinorVersion( ) throws javax.xml.registry.JAXRException;        //L1
    public abstract String getUserVersion( ) throws javax.xml.registry.JAXRException;      //L1
    public abstract void setMajorVersion(int majorVersion) throws javax.xml.registry.JAXRException;   //L1
    public abstract void setMinorVersion(int minorVersion) throws javax.xml.registry.JAXRException;   //L1
    public abstract void setUserVersion(String userVersion) throws javax.xml.registry.JAXRException;  //L1
}
```

Some RegistryObjects, specifically those derived from RegistryEntry, include version information, access to which is possible using the methods of the Versionable interface. The major and minor version numbers, which can be read and set using the getMajorVersion( ), getMinorVersion( ), setMajorVersion( ), and setMinorVersion( ) methods, are intended to be maintained by the registry and may be modified by the registry as changes are made to the object. By contrast, there is also a user version number, which is intended to be a number that might be quoted to a registry user. This value is manipulated using the getUserVersion( ) and setUserVersion( ) methods and is not modified by the registry itself. Versioning is a level 1 registry feature.

Implementations RegistryEntry

13

The javax.xml.rpc Package

Package javax.xml.rpc

JAX-RPC 1.0; JWSDP 1.0, J2EE 1.4

The javax.xml.rpc package contains the client-side API for the Java API for XML-based RPC (JAX-RPC). Applications use the classes and interfaces in this package to invoke the methods of a web service, the definition for which may be obtained in the form of either a WSDL document or a Java interface. A simple JAX-RPC application uses stub classes generated from either of these sources by a tool such as wscompile and may have to only deal directly with the Service and Stubs interfaces. A more advanced application may choose to build its own method calls without involving a code generator by making use of the Call interface, which provides the JAX-RPC Dynamic Invocation Interface (DII) feature.

Interfaces

public interface **Call**;
public interface **Service**;
public interface **Stub**;

Classes

public class **NamespaceConstants**;
public class **ParameterMode**;
public abstract class **ServiceFactory**;

Exceptions

public class **JAXRPCException** extends RuntimeException;
public class **ServiceException** extends Exception;

JAX-RPC 1.0; JWSDP 1.0, J2EE 1.4

```
public interface Call {
// Public Constants
    public static final String ENCODINGSTYLE_URI_PROPERTY;       // ="javax.xml.rpc.encodingstyle.namespace.uri"
    public static final String OPERATION_STYLE_PROPERTY;          // ="javax.xml.rpc.soap.operation.style"
    public static final String PASSWORD_PROPERTY;                 // ="javax.xml.rpc.security.auth.password"
    public static final String SESSION_MAINTAIN_PROPERTY;         // ="javax.xml.rpc.session.maintain"
    public static final String SOAPACTION_URI_PROPERTY;           // ="javax.xml.rpc.soap.http.soapaction.uri"
    public static final String SOAPACTION_USE_PROPERTY;           // ="javax.xml.rpc.soap.http.soapaction.use"
    public static final String USERNAME_PROPERTY;                 // ="javax.xml.rpc.security.auth.username"
// Property Accessor Methods (by property name)
    public abstract javax.xml.namespace.QName getOperationName( );
    public abstract void setOperationName(javax.xml.namespace.QName operationName);
    public abstract Map getOutputParams();
    public abstract java.util.List getOutputValues();
    public abstract javax.xml.namespace.QName getPortTypeName( );
    public abstract void setPortTypeName(javax.xml.namespace.QName portType);
    public abstract Iterator getPropertyNames( );
    public abstract javax.xml.namespace.QName getReturnType( );
    public abstract void setReturnType(javax.xml.namespace.QName xmlType);
    public abstract void setReturnType(javax.xml.namespace.QName xmlType, Class javaType);
    public abstract String getTargetEndpointAddress( );
    public abstract void setTargetEndpointAddress(
// Public Instance Methods
    public abstract void addParameter(String paramName, javax.xml.namespace.QName xmlType,
        ParameterMode parameterMode);
    public abstract void addParameter(String paramName, javax.xml.namespace.QName xmlType, Class javaType,
        ParameterMode parameterMode);
    public abstract javax.xml.namespace.QName getParameterTypeByName(String paramName);
    public abstract Object getProperty( String name);
    public abstract Object invoke(Object[] inputParams) throws java.rmi.RemoteException;
    public abstract Object invoke(javax.xml.namespace.QName operationName, Object[] inputParams)
        throws java.rmi.RemoteException;
    public abstract void invokeOneWay(Object[] inputParams);
    public abstract boolean isParameterAndReturnSpecRequired(javax.xml.namespace.QName operationName);
    public abstract void removeAllParameters( );
    public abstract void removeProperty( String name);
    public abstract void setProperty(String name, Object value);
}
```

The Call interface allows you to construct and make a call to a method in a web service endpoint interface without using a generated stub class or a dynamic proxy. In order to make a call, you need to obtain a Call object and configure the names of the port and operation that you want to invoke, together with the types of the input and output arguments and the return value, if there is one. Once the Call object is properly initialized, set the address of the service using the setTargetEndpointAddress( ) method, and use the invoke( ) or invokeOneWay( ) methods to make the method call. Depending on exactly how the Call object is obtained, some or all of the required information may already be set up, leaving you with less to do. The Call interface provides the JAX-RPC Dynamic Invocation Interface (DII). This is primarily intended as an internal implementation mechanism for dynamic proxies and for service brokers, which dynamically discover services and construct method calls given suitable parameters obtained from a human or from other software. It is not the preferred mechanism for creating web service clients.

An instance of Call is obtained from a Service object and is therefore already associated with a specific web service. Depending on how it was created, it may already be configured for a specific port and even a particular method within that port. If the port is not configured, the setPortTypeName() method must be used to set it, using its fully qualified name from the WSDL definition, before a call can be made. If the operation name is not configured, you may choose to set (or change) it using the setOperationName() method (which also requires a fully qualified name), or you can supply the operation name when you make the method call.

If the Call object is obtained from a Service object that was built from a WSDL definition (perhaps by passing a WSDL document URL to the ServiceFactory createService() method), then it is already fully initialized with information regarding the input and output arguments and the return value of the target method, and you may not change them. You can use the isParameterAndReturnSpecRequired() to determine whether this is the case—if false is returned, the Call object is fully initialized and you cannot use the calls described in the following two paragraphs. Otherwise, you are required to initialize the Call object as described next.

If the method requires input or output parameters, you must use one of the addParameter() methods to declare at least the name, XML type, and mode of each parameter. This information can, of course, be obtained directly from the WSDL definition of the operation. The XML type is an XML schema or SOAP data type, and is declared using one of the constants defined by the javax.xml.rpc.encoding.XMLType interface. In most cases, an XML type implies a corresponding Java type, but, where there are ambiguities, you may supply an explicit Java class in addition to the XML type. An example of such is XSD_DATETIME, which could be mapped to either java.util.Date or java.util. Calendar. Note that if you supply both the XML type and the Java class, then they must be compatible. The parameter modes are defined by the ParameterMode interface and may be IN, OUT, or INOUT. You do not set the argument values using these methods—these are supplied at invocation time. Note also that once you have built and used a Call object, you can reuse it either unchanged to make another call to the same method, or to make a call to a different method by resetting it by using removeAllParameters().

The type of the value returned by the method is set using setReturnType(), which has two variants that specify either just the XML type (again using a value defined by the javax. xml.rpc.encoding.XMLType interface) or both the type and the corresponding Java class. If the method does not return anything (i.e., the Java return type is void), use setReturnType(null).

To call the web service method, use either invoke() or invokeOneWay(). There are two variants of invoke(), one of which requires the fully qualified name of the operation and the argument values, while the other requires only the arguments and relies on the operation already configured in the Call object. invoke() is a synchronous operation that blocks until the server sends a reply. The value returned from the remote operation is also the return value of the invoke() call. By contrast, invokeOneWay() simply calls the web service method and does not return anything. This is not necessarily the same as an asynchronous operation, since the caller may still be blocked until the server completes the operation, even though there is no return value from the method call.

The order of argument values in the list passed to both invoke() and invokeOneWay() must match the order in which the corresponding method parameters are declared and, of course, the data type of each argument must be compatible with that of its matching method parameter. Values should not be supplied for method parameters that are declared to have mode OUT. The values returned for output and input/output parameters can be obtained using the getOutputValues() and getOutputParams() methods. The first of these methods returns a java.util.List containing the output values in the order in which they appear in the WSDL definition of the operation (and the same order as that used with the addParameter() method). The second method returns a java.util.Map in which the key to each entry is the fully qualified name (QName) of an argument, and the value is its returned value.

The Call interface defines a small number of properties, the values of which can be set and read using the setProperty() and getProperty() methods. Only property names defined in the JAX-RPC specification can be used with these methods, and not all properties need be supported by all implementations. The getPropertyNames() method can be used to get the complete set of supported names. To unset a property, use the removeProperty() method. The properties defined by the specification are as follows:

USERNAME_PROPERTY
>   Holds the username associated with the caller. This property need only be set if the service being called is protected by HTTP basic authentication. All implementations must support this property.

PASSWORD_PROPERTY
>   The caller's password. This property, which must be supported by all implementations, is used together with USERNAME_PROPERTY.

SESSION_MAINTAIN_PROPERTY
>   A value of type Boolean that specifies whether the client will allow the service to maintain HTTP session information for the client between calls. A service implementation that implements the javax.xml.rpc.server.ServiceLifecycle interface can make use of sessions to store state between method calls if this property is set to true. Support for this property is mandatory.

OPERATION_STYLE_PROPERTY
>   Indicates whether the operation is rpc- or document-style using the values rpc and document, respectively. Support for this property is optional.

SOAPACTION_USE_PROPERTY
>   A Boolean value that indicates whether a SOAPAction header should be included in the message. Defaults to Boolean.FALSE. Support for this property is optional.

SOAPACTION_URI_PROPERTY
>   The URI to be included as the value of the SOAPAction header if the SOAPACTION_USE_ PROPERTY has the value Boolean.TRUE. Support for this property is optional.

ENCODINGSTYLE_URI_PROPERTY
>   The encoding style to be used for elements in the generated SOAP message that do not have an explicitly specified style. Defaults to the standard SOAP encoding rules. Support for this property is optional.

Returned By

javax.xml.rpc.Service.{createCall( ), getCalls( )}

```
public class JAXRPCException extends RuntimeException {
// Public Constructors
    public JAXRPCException( );
    public JAXRPCException( Throwable cause);
    public JAXRPCException( String message);
    public JAXRPCException( String message, Throwable cause);
// Public Instance Methods
    public Throwable getLinkedCause( );                                    // default:null
}
```

JAXRPCException is an unchecked exception that is thrown to report an error condition that arises during the invocation of a method in JAX-RPC client-side API. In most cases, this exception reports incorrect use of a parameter in a client-side API, but may also be thrown to report an operational exception, such as a communication failure when attempting to send a SOAP message to the server-side implementation.

A JAXRPCException object has two attributes, both of which may only be set at construction time. The message attribute contains a human-readable string that describes the cause of the error. The cause attribute, of type java.lang.Throwable, is used if the JAXRPCException is being used to report an error that was originally caused by another exception. If a JAXRPCException is constructed with a non-null cause and a null message, then the message attribute is set to the value of the message associated with Throwable supplied as the cause.

NamespaceConstants

javax.xml.rpc

```
public class NamespaceConstants {
// Public Constructors
    public NamespaceConstants( );
// Public Constants
    public static final String NSPREFIX_SCHEMA_XSD;                 // ="xsd"
    public static final String NSPREFIX_SCHEMA_XSI;                 // ="xsi"
    public static final String NSPREFIX_SOAP_ENCODING;             // ="soapenc"
    public static final String NSPREFIX_SOAP_ENVELOPE;             // ="soapenv"
    public static final String NSURI_SCHEMA_XSD;            // ="http://www.w3.org/2001/XMLSchema"
    public static final String NSURI_SCHEMA_XSI;       // ="http://www.w3.org/2001/XMLSchema-instance"
    public static final String NSURI_SOAP_ENCODING;     // ="http://schemas.xmlsoap.org/soap/encoding/"
    public static final String NSURI_SOAP_ENVELOPE;     // ="http://schemas.xmlsoap.org/soap/envelope/"
    public static final String NSURI_SOAP_NEXT_ACTOR;    // ="http://schemas.xmlsoap.org/soap/actor/next"
}
```

The NamespaceConstants class contains symbolic names that map to several well-known XML namespaces that are used by the JAX-RPC implementation. This may be useful to application code that needs to directly create or manipulate XML fragments passed to and from JAX-RPC method calls.

JAX-RPC 1.0; JWSDP 1.0, J2EE 1.4

```
public class ParameterMode {
// No Constructor
// Public Constants
    public static final ParameterMode IN;
    public static final ParameterMode INOUT;
    public static final ParameterMode OUT;
// Public Methods Overriding Object
    public String toString( );
}
```

The ParameterMode class provides symbolic constants that are used to specify whether a
JAX-RPC method parameter is input-only (i.e., set before the call and not modified),
output-only (undefined before the call, and modified as a result of the call), or both
input and output. These constants are used in conjunction with the addParameter( )
methods of the javax.xml.rpc.Call when building a method call using the DII. See the
description of the Call interface, earlier in this chapter, for further information.

Passed To   Call.addParameter( )

Type Of   ParameterMode.{IN, INOUT, OUT}

Service   javax.xml.rpc

JAX-RPC 1.0; JWSDP 1.0, J2EE 1.4

```
public interface Service {
// Property Accessor Methods (by property name)
    public abstract javax.xml.rpc.handler.HandlerRegistry getHandlerRegistry( );
    public abstract Iterator getPorts( ) throws ServiceException;
    public abstract javax.xml.namespace.QName getServiceName( );
    public abstract javax.xml.rpc.encoding.TypeMappingRegistry getTypeMappingRegistry( );
    public abstract java.net.URL getWSDLDocumentLocation( );
// Public Instance Methods
    public abstract Call createCall( ) throws ServiceException;
    public abstract Call createCall(javax.xml.namespace.QName portName) throws ServiceException;
    public abstract Call createCall(javax.xml.namespace.QName portName, javax.xml.namespace.QName operationName)
        throws ServiceException;
    public abstract Call createCall(javax.xml.namespace.QName portName,
    String operationName) throws ServiceException;
    public abstract Call[] getCalls(javax.xml.namespace.QName portName) throws ServiceException;
    public abstract java.rmi.Remote getPort(Class serviceEndpointInterface) throws ServiceException;
    public abstract java.rmi.Remote getPort(javax.xml.namespace.QName portName, Class serviceEndpointInterface)
        throws ServiceException;
}
```

Service is the core interface of the JAX-RPC client-side API, representing a service element
in a WSDL definition of a web service. There are several ways to obtain a Service object,
which are discussed in the following list.

- By using a tool such as wscompile to generate stubs from a WSDL file or an equivalent Java interface definition. This process also creates a class that implements the Service interface.

- From a ServiceFactory, either with or without the help of a WSDL document that describes the service. A Service object that is created by a ServiceFactory without the use of a WSDL document is simply a skeleton that has no information about the service other than its qualified name, and can be used only in conjunction with the Dynamic Invocation Interface (DII), which is described in the reference section for the Call interface. I'll refer to this type of Service as *unconfigured*.

- For container-resident clients only, from the JNDI environment. A Service obtained from the environment normally is generated from a WSDL definition and is therefore fully configured with service information. Sometimes, however, the WSDL document may not contain a service; element. In such a case, the Service object contains information about the operations that the service provides, but does not contain the service address.

The getWSDLDcoumentLocation() method returns the URL for the WSDL document from which the Service is generated, or null if it is not created from a WSDL document. The getServiceName() method returns the fully qualified name of the service in the form of a javax.xml.namespace.QName object.

A web service is composed of one or more ports, each of which is an access point for an instance of the service with an associated address. A single web service might be accessible at more than one address (and therefore have multiple ports) if it supports more than one transport protocol, or perhaps for load-balancing or mirroring reasons. You can use the getPorts() method to get an Iterator over all of the ports of the service. In the case of an unconfigured Service object, this Iterator does not contain any elements.

To get an object that can be used to invoke the methods of a specific service endpoint interface, use one of the getPort() methods and cast it to the service endpoint interface type. These methods throw a ServiceException if invoked on an unconfigured Service object. The two-argument getPort() method returns an object that can be used to invoke the methods of a port given the fully qualified name of the port from the WSDL definition, and a Class object that represents the Java interface created from the port definition. The returned value can be cast to the given class type. The one-argument variant supplies only the Java interface, and does not specify the qualified name of the port. Use of this method is not recommended in circumstances in which it can be avoided because it requires a search of the WSDL definition to locate a port whose operations match the methods defined by the Java interface. This requires not only a comparison of method and operation names, but also their argument types. The getPort() methods may return an instance of a pregenerated stub class or a dynamic proxy, which is a class generated on-the-fly that implements the methods of the service endpoint interface accessible through the named port. Dynamic proxies are actually implemented using the DII, as described in the reference section for Call earlier in this chapter.

The createCall() methods return a Call object that can be used to construct a DII call to one of the methods provided by the service. The two-argument variants create a Call object that is fully configured to invoke a specific method, whereas the one-argument variant requires you to additionally specify the operation name using the methods of the Call interface. The zero-argument variant of this method requires you to specify both the port name and the operation name before attempting to make a call. The getCalls() method returns an array of Call objects, each of which is fully configured to invoke one method of the service endpoint interface. Each time this method is called, it generates and returns a new set of Call objects and is therefore a relatively expensive operation. A ServiceException is thrown if this method is called on an unconfigured Service object.

The getTypeMappingRegistry( ) method returns a reference to the type mapping information relating to the service. This information, which determines how Java data types are mapped to and from their corresponding XML representation in SOAP messages, is created dynamically from the WSDL definition of the service or the equivalent Java interface. Some implementations may also allow you to add additional mappings, as described in Chapter 6 of this book. The getHandlerRegistry( ) method returns a HandlerRegistry object that contains the configuration of SOAP handlers that will appear in the processing pipeline for messages sent to the service. SOAP handlers can modify or extract information from a SOAP message before it is sent or after it is received. Refer to Chapter 6 or Chapter 15 for further information.

Returned By   ServiceFactory.createService( )

ServiceException   javax.xml.rpc

JAX-RPC 1.0; JWSDP 1.0, J2EE 1.4   serializable checked

```
public class ServiceException extends Exception {
// Public Constructors
    public ServiceException( );
    public ServiceException( Throwable cause);
    public ServiceException( String message);
    public ServiceException( String message, Throwable cause);
// Public Instance Methods
    public Throwable getLinkedCause( );                           // default:null
}
```

ServiceException is a checked exception that is thrown to report an error condition that arises during the invocation of a method of the javax.xml.rpc.Service interface. It may also be thrown from the init( ) method of a service implementation class that implements the javax.xml.rpc.server.ServiceLifecycle interface.

Like JAXRPCException, ServiceException may have either or both a text message and a linked Throwable that describe the cause of the error. These can only be set at construction time and are retrieved using the getMessage( ) and getLinkedCause( ) methods, respectively.

Thrown By   javax.xml.rpc.Service.{createCall( ), getCalls( ), getPort( ), getPorts( )}, ServiceFactory. {createService( ), newInstance( )}, javax.xml.rpc.server.ServiceLifecycle.init( )

ServiceFactory   javax.xml.rpc

JAX-RPC 1.0; JWSDP 1.0, J2EE 1.4

```
public abstract class ServiceFactory {
// Protected Constructors
    protected ServiceFactory( );
// Public Constants
    public static final String SERVICEFACTORY_PROPERTY;           // ="javax.xml.rpc.ServiceFactory"
```

```
// Public Class Methods
    public static ServiceFactory newInstance( ) throws ServiceException;
// Public Instance Methods
    public abstract javax.xml.rpc.Service createService(javax.xml.namespace.QName serviceName) throws ServiceException;
    public abstract javax.xml.rpc.Service createService(java.net.URL wsdlDocumentLocation,
    javax.xml.namespace.QName serviceName) throws ServiceException;
}
```

ServiceFactory is a factory object used to create Service objects. To obtain an instance of this abstract class, use the static newInstance( ) method, which attempts to locate a suitable concrete implementation as follows:

- Looks in the system properties for a property called javax.xml.rpc.ServiceFactory. If this property is defined, its value is assumed to be the class name of a concrete implementation of ServiceFactory.

- Looks for the same property in a file called ${JAVA_HOME}/lib/jaxrpc.properties. If the property is found, its value is assumed to be the required class name.

- Looks for a resource called META-INF/services/javax.xml.rpc.ServiceFactory in the classpath. If such a resource exists, it is opened and a single line is read from it. If the line is not empty, it is used as the required class name.

- Uses an implementation-dependent default class. In the case of the reference implementation, this class is called com.sun.xml.rpc.client.ServiceFactoryImpl.

The two createService( ) methods return Service objects that are intended to be used in different ways. The two-argument variant requires the location of a WSDL document and the fully qualified name of a service defined within that document. The Service object that it returns has access to all of the service information in the WSDL document and can be used to make calls on the remote methods of the service using either dynamic proxies or the DII, both of which are covered in Chapter 6. The single-argument variant accepts only a service name and therefore has no information at all about the service (including whether it exists). A Service object created using this latter method can only be used to construct a service endpoint interface call using the DII and is not able to validate the correctness of these calls before they are made. Refer to the description of the Call interface earlier in this chapter for further information.

ServiceFactory is intended to be used by J2SE clients that have no container support. Container-resident JAX-RPC clients, such as servlets or JSP pages, are not expected to use ServiceFactory. Instead, they typically obtain a reference to a Service object that has been configured into their JNDI environment.

Returned By   ServiceFactory.newInstance( )

Stub   javax.xml.rpc

JAX-RPC 1.0; JWSDP 1.0, J2EE 1.4

```
public interface Stub {
// Public Constants
    public static final String ENDPOINT_ADDRESS_PROPERTY;       // ="javax.xml.rpc.service.endpoint.address"
    public static final String PASSWORD_PROPERTY;               // ="javax.xml.rpc.security.auth.password"
    public static final String SESSION_MAINTAIN_PROPERTY;       // ="javax.xml.rpc.session.maintain"
    public static final String USERNAME_PROPERTY;               // ="javax.xml.rpc.security.auth.username"
// Public Instance Methods
```

```
public abstract Object _getProperty( String name);
public abstract Iterator _getPropertyNames( );
public abstract void _setProperty(String name,  Object value);
}
```

Stub is an interface implemented by all client-side stub classes generated by the wscompile tool or a vendor-specific equivalent. The task of a Stub object is to marshall the parameters for a remote method call made on the client into a SOAP message, to unmarshall the reply to create the return value from the call, if there is one, and to update any output parameters supplied in the form of Holder objects. The code for a stub class is entirely generated by wscompile; the only methods that are of interest to application code are declared in the Stub interface.

A Stub contains a collection of properties that application code can set to control the operation of the JAX-RPC runtime when invoking the remote method. To set a property, use the _setProperty() method. Use the _getProperty() method to retrieve the value of a named property and the _getPropertyNames() method to get the names of the properties that may be used. (Note, however, that the JAX-RPC 1.0 reference implementation implements this method differently—it returns the names of the properties for which values have actually been set. The text here reflects the specification.)

Only the property names defined by the interface may be used with the _getProperty() and _setProperty() methods; not all implementations are required to support all of the properties. A JAXRPCException is thrown for a property that is not recognized or not supported. The properties defined by the interface are as follows:

USERNAME_PROPERTY

Holds the username associated with the caller. This property need only be set if the service is protected by HTTP basic authentication. All implementations must support this property.

PASSWORD_PROPERTY

The caller's password. This property, which must be supported by all implementations, is used together with USERNAME_PROPERTY.

ENDPOINT_ADDRESS_PROPERTY

A string containing the address of the service endpoint interface (i.e., the port address) as a URI. For services accessed over HTTP, this is a URL. Support of this property is optional.

SESSION_MAINTAIN_PROPERTY

A value of type Boolean that specifies whether the client will allow the service to maintain HTTP session information for the client between calls. A service implementation that implements the javax.xml.rpc.server.ServiceLifecycle interface can make use of sessions to store state between method calls if this property is set to true. Support for this property is mandatory.

14

The javax.xml.rpc.encoding Package

Package javax.xml.rpc.encoding

JAX-RPC 1.0; JWSDP 1.0, J2EE 1.4

The javax.xml.rpc.encoding package contains the classes and interfaces that form the portable part of the serialization framework used to convert between Java language types and XML messages. Although the rules for mapping between these two representations are well-defined by the JAX-RPC specification, only a minimal interface to the serialization framework is defined, leaving most of the details to be determined by vendors that implement the specification. This has two consequences:

- Although a minimal serialization interface is defined, it is far from sufficient to allow developers to create their own serializers that would work across different JAX-RPC implementations. Serializer portability was not an aim of the JAX-RPC 1.0 specification.

- Although the JAX-RPC reference implementation contains a serialization framework, it is not part of the public API and there is no documentation available for it. Therefore, in practice, even if you don't mind the fact that your custom serializers will be nonportable, it is very difficult to even get started writing one. Furthermore, the nonpublic nature of the API means that incompatible changes may be made at any time, which may cause your serializers to stop working.

As a result, this book does not describe how to write custom serializers, and this chapter documents only the minimal public API.

The XMLType class defines constants that represent various XML Schema and SOAP data types. This class is probably the only one in this package that application developers will be likely to use. The TypeMappingRegistry and TypeMapping interfaces provide groupings of serializers for specific XML data types using one or more encoding schemes. The serializers themselves implement the Serializer and Deserializer interfaces, which, at least in the current version of the specification, are marker interfaces that define no methods. Serializers are obtained from a SerializerFactory or a DeserializerFactory, and use instances of the SerializationContext and DeserializationContext interfaces to maintain state during the serialization or deserialization of a message.

Interfaces

public interface **DeserializationContext**;
public interface **Deserializer** extends Serializable;
public interface **DeserializerFactory** extends Serializable;
public interface **SerializationContext**;
public interface **Serializer** extends Serializable;
public interface **SerializerFactory** extends Serializable;
public interface **TypeMapping**;
public interface **TypeMappingRegistry** extends Serializable;

Classes   public class **XMLType**;

DeserializationContext   javax.xml.rpc.encoding

JAX-RPC 1.0; JWSDP 1.0, J2EE 1.4

```
public interface DeserializationContext {
}
```

DeserializationContext is a marker interface containing no methods that indicates an object that can be used to store state the deserialization process requires. Although this interface is used internally by the JAX-RPC reference implementation, the JAX-RPC 1.0 specification does not include any public API that refers to it.

Deserializer   javax.xml.rpc.encoding

JAX-RPC 1.0; JWSDP 1.0, J2EE 1.4   serializable

```
public interface Deserializer extends java.io.Serializable {
// Public Instance Methods
  public abstract String getMechanismType( );
}
```

A **Deserializer** is a class that can convert from an XML fragment into a corresponding Java object or Java primitive. The deserialization process might accept XML in the form of a SAX stream, a DOM model, or in some other form. The JAX-RPC specification does not give a list of supported input types (which it refers to as mechanism types), but the reference implementation supports deserialization from a raw input stream of XML characters. The getMechanismType( ) method returns an identifier for the input type that the deserializer supports.

The **Deserializer** interface does not actually contain a method that causes deserialization to occur. The JAX-RPC 1.0 specification does not attempt to create a standard or portable deserialization mechanism and therefore does not specify the means by which deserialization is actually performed. The reference implementation uses private deserializers that implement the **Deserializer** interface and uses methods that are not part of the public API to invoke them.

Returned By   DeserializerFactory.getDeserializerAs( )

```
public interface DeserializerFactory extends java.io.Serializable {
// Public Instance Methods
   public abstract Deserializer getDeserializerAs(String mechanismType);
   public abstract Iterator getSupportedMechanismTypes( );
}
```

A DeserializerFactory returns Deserializers that can convert from an XML type to a corresponding Java object or primitive. A DeserializerFactory for a given (Java type, XML type) pairing is registered with, and can be obtained from, a TypeMapping object. Once you have a DeserializerFactory, you can obtain a Deserializer instance by calling its getDeserializerAs( ) method, which requires an argument that specifies a serialization mechanism type. The mechanism type describes the style of the underlying XML processing model with which the serializer works, examples of which might be a DOM model or a character stream containing XML to be decoded. A factory might be able to supply deserializers for more than one mechanism type. The JAX-RPC specification does not define standard mechanism types, but the reference implementation supports a single, private type identified by the URI http://java.sun.com/jax-rpc-ri/1.0/streaming/. The URIs for the mechanism types for which the factory can return a suitable Deserializer can be obtained by calling the getSupportedMechanismTypes( ) method.

Passed To   TypeMapping.register( )

Returned By   TypeMapping.getDeserializer( )

SerializationContext

javax.xml.rpc.encoding

JAX-RPC 1.0; JWSDP 1.0, J2EE 1.4

```
public interface SerializationContext {
}
```

SerializationContext is a marker interface containing no methods, that indicates an object that can be used to store state the serialization process requires. Although this interface is used internally by the JAX-RPC reference implementation, the JAX-RPC 1.0 specification does not include any public API that refers to it.

Serializer

javax.xml.rpc.encoding

JAX-RPC 1.0; JWSDP 1.0, J2EE 1.4

serializable

```
public interface Serializer extends java.io.Serializable {
// Public Instance Methods
   public abstract String getMechanismType( );
}
```

A Serializer is a class that can convert from a Java object or primitive into a corresponding XML representation. The serialization process might result in a stream of characters that form an XML tag with associated attributes and text, or a fragment of a DOM model. The JAX-RPC specification does not give a list of supported output types (which it refers to as mechanism types), but the reference implementation supports the creation of an XML output stream. The getMechanismType( ) method returns an identifier for the mechanism that the serializer supports.

The Serializer interface does not actually contain a method that causes serialization to occur. The JAX-RPC 1.0 specification does not attempt to create a standard or portable serialization mechanism and therefore does not specify the means by which serialization is actually performed. The reference implementation uses private serialization classes that implement the Serializer interface, and uses methods that are not part of the public API to invoke them.

Returned By   SerializerFactory.getSerializerAs( )

SerializerFactory   javax.xml.rpc.encoding

JAX-RPC 1.0; JWSDP 1.0, J2EE 1.4   serializable

```
public interface SerializerFactory extends java.io.Serializable {
// Public Instance Methods
    public abstract Serializer getSerializerAs(String mechanismType);
    public abstract Iterator getSupportedMechanismTypes( );
}
```

A SerializerFactory returns Serializers that can convert from a specific Java type to a corresponding XML type. A SerializerFactory for a given (Java type, XML type) pairing is registered with, and can be obtained from, a TypeMapping object. Once you have a Serializer-Factory, you can obtain a Serializer instance by calling its getSerializerAs( ) method, which requires an argument that specifies a serialization mechanism type. The mechanism type describes the style of the underlying XML processing model with which the serializer works—for example, a DOM model or a character stream containing the generated XML. A factory might be able to supply serializers for more than one mechanism type. The JAX-RPC specification does not define standard mechanism types, but the reference implementation supports a single, private type identified by the URI http://java.sun.com/jax-rpc-ri/1.0/streaming/. The URIs for the mechanism types for which the factory can return a suitable Serializer can be obtained by calling the getSupportedMechanismTypes( ) method.

Passed To   TypeMapping.register( )

Returned By   TypeMapping.getSerializer( )

TypeMapping   javax.xml.rpc.encoding

JAX-RPC 1.0; JWSDP 1.0, J2EE 1.4

```
public interface TypeMapping {
// Public Instance Methods
    javax.xml.namespace.QName xmlType);
    public abstract SerializerFactory getSerializer(Class javaType, javax.xml.namespace.QName xmlType);
    public abstract String[] getSupportedEncodings( );
    public abstract boolean isRegistered(Class javaType, javax.xml.namespace.QName xmlType);
    public abstract void register(Class javaType, javax.xml.namespace.QName xmlType,
        SerializerFactory sf, DeserializerFactory dsf);
```

```
    public abstract void removeDeserializer(Class javaType, javax.xml.namespace.QName xmlType);
    public abstract void removeSerializer(Class javaType, javax.xml.namespace.QName xmlType);
    public abstract void setSupportedEncodings(String[] encodingStyleURIs);
}
```

A TypeMapping object contains serializers and deserializers that can convert between Java objects or primitive types and a corresponding XML representation. A single TypeMapping may support one or several encoding styles. The supported encodings may be obtained by calling the getSupportedEncodings( ) method and set using setSupportedEncodings( ), both of which deal with an array of strings that represent encoding scheme URIs (such as http://schemas.xmlsoap.org/soap/encoding/, which represents the SOAP section 5 encoding rules).

The register( ) method is used to associate a SerializerFactory and a DeserializerFactory with a (Java object, XML type) pair that represents the start and endpoints of the conversion process that the serializers and deserializers obtained from those factories can perform. The XML type is specified using constants defined by the javax.xml.rpc.encoding.XMLType class, whereas the Java type is represented by its Class object. Although it is most likely that both a SerializerFactory and a DeserializerFactory will be registered together, it is possible to register only one of the pair by specifying the argument for the other as null. The removeSerializer( ) method removes the SerializerFactory mapping for a specified Java type to XML type mapping, and throws a JAXRPCException if there is no mapping for the given combination. The removeDeserializer( ) similarly removes a DeserializerFactory.

The getSerializer( ) and getDeserializer( ) methods return a SerializerFactory or DeserializerFactory for a given (Java type, XML type) pair, or returns null if none is registered. You can determine whether either a SerializerFactory or DeserializerFactory is registered for a given pairing using the isRegistered( ) method. This method does not, however, tell you which of these objects is registered if only one of them is.

Passed To TypeMappingRegistry.{register( ), registerDefault( ), removeTypeMapping( )}

Returned By TypeMappingRegistry.{createTypeMapping( ), getDefaultTypeMapping( ),
                 getTypeMapping( ), register( ), unregisterTypeMapping( )}

TypeMappingRegistry   javax.xml.rpc.encoding

JAX-RPC 1.0; JWSDP 1.0, J2EE 1.4   serializable

```
public interface TypeMappingRegistry extends java.io.Serializable {
// Public Instance Methods
    public abstract void clear( );
    public abstract TypeMapping createTypeMapping( );
    public abstract TypeMapping getDefaultTypeMapping( );
    public abstract String[] getRegisteredEncodingStyleURIs( );
    public abstract TypeMapping getTypeMapping(String encodingStyleURI);
    public abstract TypeMapping register(String encodingStyleURI, TypeMapping mapping);
    public abstract void registerDefault(TypeMapping mapping);
    public abstract boolean removeTypeMapping(TypeMapping mapping);
    public abstract TypeMapping unregisterTypeMapping(String encodingStyleURI);
}
```

As its name suggests, the TypeMappingRegistry interface represents a registry for TypeMapping objects. On the client side, a TypeMappingRegistry is associated with a Service object, and a reference to the single instance for that Service can be obtained by calling its getTypeMappingRegistry( ) method. On the server side, each service implementation has its own TypeMappingRegistry that is created by the code for the tie classes that is generated by utilities such as wsdeploy or j2eec, which are described in Chapter 8.

A TypeMappingRegistry maintains a set of mappings from URIs that represent encoding styles to the TypeMapping objects that know how to encode and decode Java types using the rules of that encoding. A typical example of an encoding style URI is http://schemas. xmlsoap.org/soap/encoding/, which represents the SOAP section 5 encoding rules. A TypeMapping can be registered by calling the register( ) method, which supplies the encoding style URI that the TypeMapping handles. Stubs, ties, dynamic proxies, and Call objects created by the JAX-RPC reference implementation all have a registry that is initialized with a TypeMapping that can handle the SOAP section 5 encoding rules, and another that handles encoding for document-style operations, which maps the URI equal to the empty string. To get a type mapping for a given encoding style, use the getTypeMapping( ) method, passing the appropriate URI. If no mapping is registered for the given URI, null is returned, unless a default mapping has been installed using the registerDefault( ) method. To determine which encoding styles have configured mappings, use the getRegisteredEncodingStyleURIs( ) method.

To create a TypeMapping, use the createTypeMapping( ) method, and then use the methods of the TypeMapping interface to configure it. The objects returned by this method must subsequently be registered using the register( ) method before they can be used. A mapping can be removed by using the removeTypeMapping( ) method, which requires a reference to the TypeMapping object. It returns false if the mapping was not present in the registry. Since a single TypeMapping can be registered more than once if it supports more than one encoding style, this method may remove the type mapping capability for more than one encoding style. To remove the association between a TypeMapping and a single encoding-style URI, use the unregisterTypeMapping( ) method, which affects only the encoding style whose URI is supplied as its argument. The clear( ) method removes all useful content in the registry.

Returned By   javax.xml.rpc.Service.getTypeMappingRegistry( )

XMLType   javax.xml.rpc.encoding

JAX-RPC 1.0; JWSDP 1.0, J2EE 1.4

```
public class XMLType {
// Public Constructors
  public XMLType( );
// Public Constants
  public static final javax.xml.namespace.QName SOAP_ARRAY;
  public static final javax.xml.namespace.QName SOAP_BASE64;
  public static final javax.xml.namespace.QName SOAP_BOOLEAN;
  public static final javax.xml.namespace.QName SOAP_BYTE;
  public static final javax.xml.namespace.QName SOAP_DOUBLE;
  public static final javax.xml.namespace.QName SOAP_FLOAT;
  public static final javax.xml.namespace.QName SOAP_INT;
  public static final javax.xml.namespace.QName SOAP_LONG;
  public static final javax.xml.namespace.QName SOAP_SHORT;
```

```
public static final javax.xml.namespace.QName SOAP_STRING;
public static final javax.xml.namespace.QName XSD_BASE64;
public static final javax.xml.namespace.QName XSD_BOOLEAN;
public static final javax.xml.namespace.QName XSD_BYTE;
public static final javax.xml.namespace.QName XSD_DATETIME;
public static final javax.xml.namespace.QName XSD_DECIMAL;
public static final javax.xml.namespace.QName XSD_DOUBLE;
public static final javax.xml.namespace.QName XSD_FLOAT;
public static final javax.xml.namespace.QName XSD_HEXBINARY;
public static final javax.xml.namespace.QName XSD_INT;
public static final javax.xml.namespace.QName XSD_INTEGER;
public static final javax.xml.namespace.QName XSD_LONG;
public static final javax.xml.namespace.QName XSD_QNAME;
public static final javax.xml.namespace.QName XSD_SHORT;
public static final javax.xml.namespace.QName XSD_STRING;
}
```

The XMLType class defines constants of type javax.xml.namespace.QName that represent various XML Schema and SOAP data types. The values defined by this class are used in the JAX-RPC API where it is necessary to refer to the XML representation of particular data types—for example, the addParameter() method of the javax.xml.rpc.Call interface, which uses these constants as the value of an argument that describes the XML data type of a method call to be made using the JAX-RPC dynamic invocation interface.

15

The javax.xml.rpc.handler
Package

Package javax.xml.rpc.handler JAX-RPC 1.0; JWSDP 1.0, J2EE 1.4

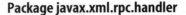

The javax.xml.rpc.handler package contains the classes and interfaces used to create and manage handler chains on both the client and server sides of a JAX-RPC method call. A JAX-RPC message handler is a class that is placed on the message path between the sender of a message and the network on the client side, or between the network and the service implementation on the server side. A handler receives and may process any SOAP message that is sent along the message path in either direction; therefore it is somewhat akin to servlet filters. Any number of handlers may be grouped together to form a handler chain. The handlers in a chain may be related or completely independent of each other and/or the sender or recipient of the message. Typical uses for handlers include the processing and removal or insertion of message headers (so that they are not seen by the message sender or receiver), logging, encryption of some or all of a message, and so on. A message handler implements the **Handler** interface, and may, for convenience, be derived from **GenericHandler**, which provides dummy implementations of most of the interface methods.

A handler chain is associated with a **Service** object on the client side and with a service endpoint on the server side. The handlers that make up a chain are typically set in advance in the configuration files used by the **wscompile** utility on the client side and the **wsdeploy** or **j2eec** utilities on the server side. It is also possible to configure handler chains at runtime—in some cases, this is the only way to achieve the desired effect. See the description of the **HandlerRegistry** interface, later in this chapter, for further information.

Interfaces
public interface **Handler**;
public interface **HandlerRegistry** extends Serializable;
public interface **MessageContext**;

Collections
public interface **HandlerChain** extends java.util.List;

Other Classes

public abstract class **GenericHandler** implements Handler;
public class **HandlerInfo** implements Serializable;

GenericHandler

JAX-RPC 1.0; JWSDP 1.0, J2EE 1.4

```
public abstract class GenericHandler implements javax.xml.rpc.handler.Handler {
// Protected Constructors
  protected GenericHandler( );
// Methods Implementing Handler
  public void destroy( );                                              // empty
  public abstract javax.xml.namespace.QName[] getHeaders( );
  public boolean handleFault( MessageContext context);                 // constant
  public boolean handleRequest( MessageContext context);               // constant
  public boolean handleResponse( MessageContext context);              // constant
  public void init( HandlerInfo config);                               // empty
}
```

GenericHandler is a convenience class that can optionally be used as a base class for message handlers. MessageHandler provides default implementations of all of the methods of the Handler interface apart from getHeaders( ), which must be provided by subclasses. The default implementations do the following:

- The handleRequest( ), handleResponse( ), and handleFault( ) methods all return true, indicating the processing of the message should continue.
- The init( ) and destroy( ) methods do nothing.

Handler

JAX-RPC 1.0; JWSDP 1.0, J2EE 1.4

```
public interface Handler {
// Public Instance Methods
  public abstract void destroy( );
  public abstract javax.xml.namespace.QName[] getHeaders( );
  public abstract boolean handleFault(MessageContext context);
  public abstract boolean handleRequest(MessageContext context);
  public abstract boolean handleResponse(MessageContext context);
  public abstract void init( HandlerInfo config);
}
```

The Handler interface defines the methods that must be implemented by a message handler. The init( ) and destroy( ) methods mark the beginning and end of the handler's life cycle. The init( ) method receives a Map containing property values that are typically set from a configuration file such as the jaxrpc-ri.xml file used by wsdeploy, the config.xml used by wscompile, or the webservices.xml file supplied to the J2EE 1.4 j2eec utility. The getHeaders( ) method returns the URIs of all of the headers that the handler can process, in the form of an array of javax.xml.namespace.QName objects. A handler whose processing is not directly related to a header should return an empty array.

javax.xml.rpc.
handler

The handler processing is carried out by the handleRequest( ), handleResponse( ), and handleFault( ) methods, which are called for an outgoing message, an incoming message that is not a fault, and a fault, respectively. Each of these methods is passed a Message-Context object that handlers can use to store state that can then be read by other handlers in the chain. The MessageContext object can also be used to retrieve the message itself. If a handler successfully processes a message, it should return true from these methods. If an error occurs that should result in message processing being inter-rupted, the handler should substitute a fault message for the original and return false. A handler may also throw an exception from one of its handleXXX( ) methods to report an exceptional condition. This exception is thrown to the application that sent the message. There are also cases in which a handler might wish to terminate handling of a message without reporting an error. For example, a handler might cache the replies to requests that it has already seen. In this case, the handler should replace the message with its cached response and return false. For examples that illustrate the possible uses of a handler, refer to Chapter 6.

Implementations GenericHandler

HandlerChain   javax.xml.rpc.handler

JAX-RPC 1.0; JWSDP 1.0, J2EE 1.4   collection

```
public interface HandlerChain extends java.util.List {
// Public Instance Methods
    public abstract void destroy( );
    public abstract String[] getRoles( );
    public abstract boolean handleFault(MessageContext context);
    public abstract boolean handleRequest(MessageContext context);
    public abstract boolean handleResponse( MessageContext context);
    public abstract void init( Map config);
    public abstract void setRoles(String[] soapActorNames);
}
```

A HandlerChain is a list of Handlers configured to operate on either the client or server side of a SOAP message path. The configuration information required to build a HandlerChain is held in a HandlerRegistry, the content of which may be created at the same time as client-side tools or server-side ties are generated, or which may be installed by applica-tion code at runtime.

The handleFault( ), handleRequest( ), and handleResponse( ) methods are called to pass a SOAP fault, request, or response message to each Handler within the chain in turn, resulting in the Handler methods of the same name being called in sequence. Under some circum-stances, the message does not fully traverse the message path, as described in the reference entry for Handler, earlier in this chapter. These methods return true if the message is completely processed, or false if a handler in the chain caused message processing to be aborted.

The getRoles( ) method returns an array of strings that correspond to the URIs of the SOAP actors on behalf of which the handlers in the chain claim to act. This list is initialized from configuration information by calling the setRoles( ) method. The init( ) and destroy() methods are intended to mark the beginning and end of the life cycle of a HandlerChain. However, in the reference implementation, these methods are never called.

```
public class HandlerInfo implements java.io.Serializable {
// Public Constructors
    public HandlerInfo( );
    public HandlerInfo(Class handlerClass, Map config, javax.xml.namespace.QName[] headers);
// Property Accessor Methods (by property name)
    public Class getHandlerClass( );                                        // default:null
    public void setHandlerClass( Class handlerClass);
    public Map getHandlerConfig( );                                         // default:HashMap
    public void setHandlerConfig( Map config);
    public javax.xml.namespace.QName[] getHeaders( );                       // default:null
    public void setHeaders(javax.xml.namespace.QName[] headers);
}
```

The HandlerInfo class contains all of the information needed to describe and construct a Handler. HandlerInfo objects are stored in a HandlerRegistry and may be created by application code or, more commonly, by code generated by a tool such as wscompile, wsdeploy, or j2eec, based on the content of a configuration file.

A HandlerInfo object contains three attributes, all of which may be set at construction time or using setter methods:

Handler class

    The fully qualified name of the Java class that contains the handler functionality. This class must have a no-argument constructor and must implement the Handler interface. This attribute may be read using the getHandlerClass( ) method and changed by calling setHandlerClass( ).

Header list

    The set of headers that the handler processes, specified as an array of QName objects. If the handler does not operate on headers, then an empty array may be supplied. This attribute can be accessed using the getHeaders( ) and setHeaders( ) methods.

Configuration information

    A handler may be given configuration information in the form of a Map containing key/value pairs, the meaning of which is of interest only to the handler. The content of this map, which is accessed using the getHandlerConfig() and setHandlerConfig( ) methods, is set from property definitions in the configuration files used by the wsdeploy, wscompile, and j2eec utilities, as described in Chapter 8.

Passed To   GenericHandler.init( ), javax.xml.rpc.handler.Handler.init( )

HandlerRegistry

javax.xml.rpc.handler

JAX-RPC 1.0; JWSDP 1.0, J2EE 1.4   serializable

```
public interface HandlerRegistry extends java.io.Serializable {
// Public Instance Methods
    public abstract java.util.List getHandlerChain( javax.xml.namespace.QName portName);
    public abstract void setHandlerChain(javax.xml.namespace.QName portName, java.util.List chain);
}
```

HandlerRegistry is a container that holds the information necessary to build a handler chain. Handler chains are defined for a port within a service endpoint interface. Each HandlerRegistry is therefore associated with a service and contains one or more entries that are keyed on the javax.xml.namespace.QName of a port within the service, as defined in the service's WSDL document. The getHandlerChain() method can be used to retrieve the handler chain definition for a port given its QName, while setHandlerChain() is used to install a chain definition. Both of these methods represent a handler chain as a java.util.List containing a HandlerInfo object for each handler in the chain.

On the client side, the HandlerRegistry for an endpoint is associated with its Service object and can be retrieved using the getHandlerRegistry() method. When the Service object is generated from a WSDL file or a Java interface definition, the code required to initialize the Handler-Registry is generated from the configuration information passed to wscompile. However, in the case of a Service object obtained from a ServiceFactory, the HandlerRegistry is not initialized. A client application that needs to use handlers with a Service obtained in this way needs to programmatically initialize the registry by constructing the appropriate HandlerInfo objects, and by using the setHandlerChain() method to install them on each port for which the handlers are required. This must be done before the getPort(), createCall(), or createCalls() methods are used.

The code required to create the handler registry used with the server-side implementation of a service endpoint interface is generated at the same time as the tie classes for the service are generated.

Returned By   javax.xml.rpc.Service.getHandlerRegistry()

MessageContext   javax.xml.rpc.handler

JAX-RPC 1.0; JWSDP 1.0, J2EE 1.4

```
public interface MessageContext {
// Public Instance Methods
   public abstract boolean containsProperty( String name);
   public abstract Object getProperty( String name);
   public abstract Iterator getPropertyNames( );
   public abstract void removeProperty( String name);
   public abstract void setProperty(String name,  Object value);
}
```

A MessageContext object contains the state that accompanies a message as it traverses the pipeline from the sender to the network when being sent from the network to its eventual recipient for an inbound message. The MessageContext object is passed to the handleRequest(), handleResponse(), or handleFault() method of each handler in the handler chain on the message path (if there is one), depending on the message type and the direction in which it is moving. In addition, a service implementation that implements the javax.xml.rpc.server.ServiceLifecycle interface can access the MessageContext associated with the message that caused a service endpoint interface method to be invoked by calling the getMessageContext() method of the javax.xml.rpc.server.ServletEndpointContext object passed to its init() method.

The MessageContext interface is concerned only with providing a mechanism for information to be propagated along the message path. Since all message handlers in the chain receive a reference to the same MessageContext object during the processing of a single message, one handler can insert objects that another handler or the web service implementation class (in the case of a server-side message chain) can extract and possibly modify further. A client application, however, cannot access the MessageContext.

The setProperty() method can be used to store an object in the context using any string as the key. Calling setProperty() a second time with the same key has the effect of replacing the original value. The getProperty() method returns the object stored under the given key, or returns null if the key is not in use. To get a list of all of the property names in use, employ the getPropertyNames() method. To determine whether a property with a given name has been set, use the containsProperty() method; to remove a property, use removeProperty(). Refer to Chapter 6 for an example that demonstrates how to use properties to communicate information from a SOAP message header to the web service implementation that receives the message, without requiring the service implementation to know anything about SOAP messages.

Since message handlers deal with messages, it might at first sight be surprising that MessageContext does not have a method that provides access to the message itself. In order to preserve a degree of independence of the underlying messaging protocol, MessageContext delegates the responsibility for providing access to the message to derived interfaces that are specific to individual messaging protocols. In the case of SOAP, the MessageContext object is actually an instance of the derived interface javax.xml.rpc.soap.SOAP-MessageContext, which does contain a method that allows access to the SOAP message being sent or received.

Implementations javax.xml.rpc.handler.soap.SOAPMessageContext

Passed To   GenericHandler.{handleFault( ), handleRequest( ), handleResponse( )}, javax.xml.rpc.handler. Handler.{handleFault( ), handleRequest( ), handleResponse( )}, HandlerChain.{handleFault( ), handleRequest( ), handleResponse( )}

Returned By   javax.xml.rpc.server.ServletEndpointContext.getMessageContext( )

16

The javax.xml.rpc.handler. soap Package

Package javax.xml.rpc.handler.soap

JAX-RPC 1.0; JWSDP 1.0, J2EE 1.4

This package contains a single interface that provides an additional API for JAX-RPC message handlers that work specifically with SOAP messages.

Interfaces
public interface **SOAPMessageContext** extends javax.xml.rpc.handler.MessageContext;

SOAPMessageContext

javax.xml.rpc.handler.soap

JAX-RPC 1.0; JWSDP 1.0, J2EE 1.4

```
public interface SOAPMessageContext extends javax.xml.rpc.handler.MessageContext {
// Public Instance Methods
    public abstract javax.xml.soap.SOAPMessage getMessage( );
    public abstract String[ ] getRoles( );
    public abstract void setMessage( javax.xml.soap.SOAPMessage message)
}
```

The SOAPMessageContext interface represents the context information passed between JAX-RPC message handlers that are placed in the processing pipeline for an incoming or outgoing message, when that message is constructed according to the rules of the SOAP 1.1 specification. An instance of this interface is passed as an argument to the handleRequest( ), handleResponse( ), and handleFault( ) methods of each SOAP message handler in the pipeline.

Most of the functionality of this interface is inherited from MessageContext, from which it is derived. The SOAPMessageContext interface adds only three methods, all of which are specific to SOAP as the underlying message protocol. The getRoles( ) method returns the set of SOAP roles that apply to the handler chain within which the SOAPMessageContext object is being used. This information is obtained by the runtime system from configuration information associated with the handler chain. The setMessage( ) method is used by the JAX-RPC runtime to store a reference to the message being processed so that handlers can retrieve it by calling **getMessage()**. A handler may also use the **setMessage()** method to change the message being processed. This is typically done when a handler detects an error and wishes to prevent the original message from being sent, and to substitute a SOAP fault message that is returned to the client. A substitution of the response message for a fault or other message may also take place on the server side.

17

The javax.xml.rpc.holders Package

Package javax.xml.rpc.holders

JAX-RPC 1.0; JWSDP 1.0, J2EE 1.4

This package contains a set of classes that are used to simulate method arguments that can be used to receive output values, a feature that is not directly supported by the Java programming language. A holder argument is used wherever the WSDL definition calls for an output or input/output argument. In terms of method call syntax, a service endpoint interface method that uses a holder class looks like this:

```
public void methodName(IntHolder arg) throws RemoteException;
```

All holders implement the Holder interface, which is a marker that does not declare any methods. Each holder class can contain a value of a specific type. There are 21 predefined holder classes in the javax.xml.rpc.holders package, which correspond to the Java primitive types (such as int), their object wrapper counterparts (such as Integer), and a small number of special cases (such as QNameHolder). A simple naming convention applies to the standard wrapper classes:

- For a Java primitive type, the class name is formed by capitalizing the first letter of the type name and appending Holder. Hence, the IntHolder class is the holder class for a primitive int, ByteHolder corresponds to byte, and so on.

- For a primitive wrapper type, the class name consists of the wrapper class name followed by WrapperHolder. The holder for the Integer class is therefore IntegerWrapperHolder

JAX-RPC is capable of generating additional holder classes for method arguments of other types that are defined to have either output or input/output semantics. For the reference implementation, this task is performed by the wscompile utility described in Chapter 2 and Chapter 8. Since the Holder interface does not define any methods, there is no standard way to get or set the value in a holder. Instead, the predefined classes all follow a coding convention as follows:

- The class provides a constructor that accepts a value of the appropriate type. For example, the constructor of the IntHolder class requires an argument of type int.

- The value itself is held in a public variable called value.

Assuming that the argument of the methodName() method just shown has input/output semantics, the following code extract shows how it might be used:

```
IntHolder arg = new IntHolder(10);     // Use 10 as the argument value
port.methodName(arg);                  // Invoke the method...
int result = arg.value;                //  ... and get the result
```

Customized holders can be created by writing a class that declares that it implements the Holder and follows these coding conventions. Refer to Chapter 2 for an example.

Interfaces

public interface **Holder**;

Classes

public final class **BigDecimalHolder** implements Holder;
public final class **BigIntegerHolder** implements Holder;
public final class **BooleanHolder** implements Holder;
public final class **BooleanWrapperHolder** implements Holder;
public final class **ByteArrayHolder** implements Holder;
public final class **ByteHolder** implements Holder;
public final class **ByteWrapperHolder** implements Holder;
public final class **CalendarHolder** implements Holder;
public final class **DoubleHolder** implements Holder;
public final class **DoubleWrapperHolder** implements Holder;
public final class **FloatHolder** implements Holder;
public final class **FloatWrapperHolder** implements Holder;
public final class **IntegerWrapperHolder** implements Holder;
public final class **IntHolder** implements Holder;
public final class **LongHolder** implements Holder;
public final class **LongWrapperHolder** implements Holder;
public final class **ObjectHolder** implements Holder;
public final class **QNameHolder** implements Holder;
public final class **ShortHolder** implements Holder;
public final class **ShortWrapperHolder** implements Holder;
public final class **StringHolder** implements Holder;

BigDecimalHolder

JAX-RPC 1.0; JWSDP 1.0, J2EE 1.4

```
public final class BigDecimalHolder implements Holder {
// Public Constructors
   public BigDecimalHolder( );
   public BigDecimalHolder(java.math.BigDecimal myBigDecimal);
// Public Instance Fields
   public java.math.BigDecimal value;
}
```

A Holder class that contains a value of type java.math.BigDecimal.

BigIntegerHolder

JAX-RPC 1.0; JWSDP 1.0, J2EE 1.4

```
public final class BigIntegerHolder implements Holder {
// Public Constructors
  public BigIntegerHolder( );
  public BigIntegerHolder( java.math.BigInteger myBigInteger);
// Public Instance Fields
  public java.math.BigInteger value;
}
```

A Holder class that contains a value of type java.math.BigInteger.

BooleanHolder

JAX-RPC 1.0; JWSDP 1.0, J2EE 1.4

```
public final class BooleanHolder implements Holder {
// Public Constructors
  public BooleanHolder( );
  public BooleanHolder( boolean myboolean);
// Public Instance Fields
  public boolean value;
}
```

A Holder class that contains a primitive Java boolean value.

BooleanWrapperHolder

JAX-RPC 1.0; JWSDP 1.0, J2EE 1.4

```
public final class BooleanWrapperHolder implements Holder {
// Public Constructors
  public BooleanWrapperHolder( );
  public BooleanWrapperHolder( Boolean myboolean);
// Public Instance Fields
  public Boolean value;
}
```

A Holder class that contains a java.lang.Boolean value.

ByteArrayHolder

JAX-RPC 1.0; JWSDP 1.0, J2EE 1.4

```
public final class ByteArrayHolder implements Holder {
// Public Constructors
  public ByteArrayHolder( );
  public ByteArrayHolder( byte[] mybyteArray);
// Public Instance Fields
  public byte[] value;
}
```

A Holder class that contains an array of bytes (i.e., byte[ ]).

ByteHolder

JAX-RPC 1.0; JWSDP 1.0, J2EE 1.4

```
public final class ByteHolder implements Holder {
// Public Constructors
  public ByteHolder( );
  public ByteHolder( byte mybyte);
// Public Instance Fields
  public byte value;
}
```

A Holder class that contains a single byte.

ByteWrapperHolder

JAX-RPC 1.0; JWSDP 1.0, J2EE 1.4

```
public final class ByteWrapperHolder implements Holder {
// Public Constructors
  public ByteWrapperHolder( );
  public ByteWrapperHolder( Byte mybyte);
// Public Instance Fields
  public Byte value;
}
```

A Holder class that contains an object of type java.lang.Byte.

CalendarHolder

JAX-RPC 1.0; JWSDP 1.0, J2EE 1.4

```
public final class CalendarHolder implements Holder {
// Public Constructors
  public CalendarHolder( );
  public CalendarHolder( Calendar myCalendar);
// Public Instance Fields
  public Calendar value;
}
```

A Holder class that contains holds a value of type java.util.Calendar.

DoubleHolder

JAX-RPC 1.0; JWSDP 1.0, J2EE 1.4

```
public final class DoubleHolder implements Holder {
// Public Constructors
  public DoubleHolder( );
  public DoubleHolder( double mydouble);
```

```
// Public Instance Fields
    public double value;
}
```

A Holder class that contains a value of type double.

DoubleWrapperHolder

JAX-RPC 1.0; JWSDP 1.0, J2EE 1.4

```
public final class DoubleWrapperHolder implements Holder {
// Public Constructors
    public DoubleWrapperHolder( );
    public DoubleWrapperHolder( Double mydouble);
// Public Instance Fields
    public Double value;
}
```

A Holder class that contains a value of type java.lang.Double.

FloatHolder

JAX-RPC 1.0; JWSDP 1.0, J2EE 1.4

```
public final class FloatHolder implements Holder {
// Public Constructors
    public FloatHolder( );
    public FloatHolder( float myfloat);
// Public Instance Fields
    public float value;
}
```

A Holder class that contains a value of type float.

FloatWrapperHolder

JAX-RPC 1.0; JWSDP 1.0, J2EE 1.4

```
public final class FloatWrapperHolder implements Holder {
// Public Constructors
    public FloatWrapperHolder( );
    public FloatWrapperHolder( Float myfloat);
// Public Instance Fields
    public Float value;
}
```

A Holder class that contains a value of type java.lang.Float.

Holder

JAX-RPC 1.0; JWSDP 1.0, J2EE 1.4

```
public interface Holder {
}
```

Holder is a marker interface that is implemented by all standard and custom holder classes. It does not define any methods or constants. Instead, holder classes follow a coding convention described in the package overview.

Implementations

BigDecimalHolder, BigIntegerHolder, BooleanHolder, BooleanWrapperHolder, ByteArrayHolder, ByteHolder, Byte-WrapperHolder, CalendarHolder, DoubleHolder, DoubleWrapperHolder, FloatHolder, FloatWrapperHolder, IntegerWrapperHolder, IntHolder, LongHolder, LongWrapperHolder, ObjectHolder, QNameHolder, ShortHolder, ShortWrapperHolder, StringHolder

IntegerWrapperHolder

JAX-RPC 1.0; JWSDP 1.0, J2EE 1.4

```
public final class IntegerWrapperHolder implements Holder {
// Public Constructors
  public IntegerWrapperHolder( );
  public IntegerWrapperHolder( Integer myint);
// Public Instance Fields
  public Integer value;
}
```

A Holder class that contains a value of type java.lang.Integer.

IntHolder

JAX-RPC 1.0; JWSDP 1.0, J2EE 1.4

```
public final class IntHolder implements Holder {
// Public Constructors
  public IntHolder( );
  public IntHolder( int myint);
// Public Instance Fields
  public int value;
}
```

A Holder class that contains a value of type int.

LongHolder

JAX-RPC 1.0; JWSDP 1.0, J2EE 1.4

```
public final class LongHolder implements Holder {
// Public Constructors
  public LongHolder( );
  public LongHolder( long mylong);
// Public Instance Fields
  public long value;
}
```

A Holder class that contains a value of type long.

LongWrapperHolder

JAX-RPC 1.0; JWSDP 1.0, J2EE 1.4

```
public final class LongWrapperHolder implements Holder {
// Public Constructors
  public LongWrapperHolder( );
  public LongWrapperHolder( Long mylong);
// Public Instance Fields
  public Long value;
}
```

A Holder class that contains a value of type java.lang.Long.

ObjectHolder

JAX-RPC 1.0; JWSDP 1.0, J2EE 1.4

```
public final class ObjectHolder implements Holder {
// Public Constructors
  public ObjectHolder( );
  public ObjectHolder( Object value);
// Public Instance Fields
  public Object value;
}
```

A Holder class that contains a value of type java.lang.Object.

QNameHolder

JAX-RPC 1.0; JWSDP 1.0, J2EE 1.4

```
public final class QNameHolder implements Holder {
// Public Constructors
  public QNameHolder( );
  public QNameHolder( javax.xml.namespace.QName myQName);
// Public Instance Fields
  public javax.xml.namespace.QName value;
}
```

A Holder class that contains a value of type javax.xml.namespace.QName.

ShortHolder

JAX-RPC 1.0; JWSDP 1.0, J2EE 1.4

```
public final class ShortHolder implements Holder {
// Public Constructors
  public ShortHolder( );
  public ShortHolder( short myshort);
// Public Instance Fields
  public short value;
}
```

A Holder class that contains a value of type short.

ShortWrapperHolder

JAX-RPC 1.0; JWSDP 1.0, J2EE 1.4

```
public final class ShortWrapperHolder implements Holder {
// Public Constructors
   public ShortWrapperHolder( );
   public ShortWrapperHolder( Short myshort);
// Public Instance Fields
   public Short value;
}
```

A Holder class that contains a value of type java.lang.Short.

StringHolder

JAX-RPC 1.0; JWSDP 1.0, J2EE 1.4

```
public final class StringHolder implements Holder {
// Public Constructors
   public StringHolder( );
   public StringHolder( String myString);
// Public Instance Fields
   public String value;
}
```

A Holder class that contains a value of type java.lang.String.

18

The javax.xml.rpc.server Package

This package contains two interfaces that define the server-side API for JAX-RPC. These interfaces allow a JAX-RPC service implementation to detect the beginning and end of its life cycle in order to perform appropriate initialization and cleanup as well as to gain access to its execution environment.

Both interfaces are relevant only to a service that is hosted within a web container. Services implemented as stateless session beans have access to similar facilities via the life cycle methods of the bean itself and the SessionContext object passed as an argument to its setSessionContext( ) method.

The server-side programming model for JAX-RPC is, in part, dependent on the container in which the service is hosted. For example, a service implemented as a stateless session bean can assume that methods invoked on a given instance are executed serialized with respect to each other, and therefore need not be concerned about threading issues. By contrast, a servlet-hosted service must assume that any of its methods may be called concurrently in separate threads and must, therefore, be thread-safe, unless it implements the javax.servlet.SingleThreadModel interface. Note, however, that while the J2EE specification requires that the container honor this interface, the JAX-RPC specification does not. Therefore, services written for web containers that implement only the JAX-RPC specification (such as the one provided by JWSDP 1.0) must be thread-safe.

Interfaces
public interface **ServiceLifecycle**;
public interface **ServletEndpointContext**;

JAX-RPC 1.0; JWSDP 1.0, J2EE 1.4

```
public interface ServiceLifecycle {
// Public Instance Methods
    public abstract void destroy( );
    public abstract void init( Object context) throws javax.xml.rpc.ServiceException;
}
```

This interface is implemented by a web service implementation class that wishes to be notified of the start and end of its life cycle.

The init( ) method is called when an instance of the service implementation class is created and before its first service endpoint interface method is invoked. The argument passed to this method is of unspecified type and is intended to be dependent on the nature of the container within which the service is running. In fact, the ServiceLifecycle interface is provided only by web containers; in this case, the object passed to the init( ) method is of type javax.xml.rpc.server.ServletEndpointContext.

The init( ) method is permitted to report an unrecoverable error or an illegal context object by throwing a javax.xml.rpc.ServiceException. The container typically responds to this exception by discarding the instance.

The destroy( ) method is called to notify a service instance of the end of its life cycle. Once this method completes, the container does not dispatch any further web service interface method calls to the instance and may make the instance eligible for garbage collection.

The J2EE specification does not require an EJB container to honor the ServiceLifecycle interface; therefore, a service implemented as a stateless session bean should not implement it. Such a service can detect the start and end of its life cycle by implementing the ejbCreate( ) and ejbRemove( ) methods of the SessionBean interface, and can access the container environment by using the SessionContext object passed to its setSessionContext( ) method. Additionally, the service can access its JNDI naming context in the usual way by instantiating a javax.naming.InitialContext object.

ServletEndpointContext

javax.xml.rpc.server

JAX-RPC 1.0; JWSDP 1.0, J2EE 1.4

```
public interface ServletEndpointContext {
// Public Instance Methods
    public abstract javax.servlet.http.HttpSession getHttpSession( );
    public abstract javax.xml.rpc.handler.MessageContext getMessageContext( );
    public abstract javax.servlet.ServletContext getServletContext( );
    public abstract java.security.Principal getUserPrincipal( );
}
```

A servlet container that provides a server-side implementation of JAX-RPC must create an object of type ServletEndpointContext and pass it to the init( ) method of any service that declares that it implements the ServiceLifecyle interface. The service class typically stores the object passed to it, and uses it to obtain context information as necessary during the invocation of its service endpoint interface methods.

The getServletContext( ) method returns the ServletContext for the web application of which the web service implementation is a part. The ServletContext provides methods that allow the service to access initialization parameters, delegate service implementation to other servlets or JSPs, and so on. This is the only method that returns a meaningful value if called outside of a service endpoint interface method (e.g., in init( )).

The getHttpSession( ) method returns the HttpSession object that corresponds to the active session maintained by the hosting web container for the client invoking a remote service endpoint interface method, or null if the client is not in a session with the server. A JAX-RPC client must explicitly enable the use of sessions by setting the SESSION_ MAINTAIN_PROPERTY of its javax.xml.rpc.Stub or javax.xml.rpc.Call object to true. The ability of other types of clients to establish a session is dependent on the client's software environment.

The getUserPrincipal( ) method returns a java.security.Principal that identifies the caller of a service endpoint interface method. A meaningful value is returned only if the web container has authenticated the calling user as the result of the use of an auth-constraint element in the *web.xml* file for the hosting servlet. If authentication is not performed, then null is returned.

The getMessageContext( ) method returns the javax.xml.rpc.handler.MessageContext object for the SOAP message that caused the service's executing service endpoint interface method to be invoked. The MessageContext can be used to allow a service implementation class to share property values with SOAP message handlers that are designated to be included on the server-side processing path. A service implementation might make use of this facility by reading a value extracted by a message handler from a SOAP header that was part of the incoming message, or by saving a value that a handler should write into the reply message, while not itself becoming dependent on the actual message structure. If the MessageContext is an instance of javax.xml.rpc.handler.soap.SOAPMessageContext, the service implementation class may use it to gain direct access to the message itself, although this is not recommended.

Even though a single ServletEndpointContext object is passed to a given servlet instance, the values that it returns depend on the execution context of the service endpoint interface method within which it is used. For example, the same ServletEndpointContext object used concurrently in two different threads by the same service instance might return different values from the getHttpSession( ) method if the callers are in separate sessions with the web container. This is possible because the ServletEndpointContext methods return information obtained from context that is held within the servlet container on a per-thread basis.

19

The javax.xml.rpc.soap Package

Package javax.xml.rpc.soap

JAX-RPC 1.0; JWSDP 1.0, J2EE 1.4

This package contains classes from the client-side JAX-RPC API that are specific to the use of this API when SOAP is used as the underlying message transport (which, at the time of this writing, is exclusively the case). In JAX-RPC 1.0, there is only one class in this package.

Exceptions

public class **SOAPFaultException** extends RuntimeException;

SOAPFaultException

javax.xml.rpc.soap

JAX-RPC 1.0; JWSDP 1.0, J2EE 1.4

serializable unchecked

```
public class SOAPFaultException extends RuntimeException {
// Public Constructors
    public SOAPFaultException( javax.xml.namespace.QName faultcode,
        String faultstring, String faultactor, javax.xml.soap.Detail faultdetail);
// Public Instance Methods
    public javax.xml.soap.Detail getDetail( );
    public String getFaultActor( );
    public javax.xml.namespace.QName getFaultCode( );
    public String getFaultString( );
}
```

SOAPFaultException is an unchecked exception that is thrown from a method call on the client side that results in the server returning a SOAP message that contains a fault element. The methods from which such a fault can be thrown are the invoke( ) method of the Call interface, and any method in the service endpoint interface of a web service for which the WSDL definition allows the response to contain a fault element.

The methods of SOAPFaultException allow the client application to retrieve the information conveyed in the fault message (for a discussion of this, refer to the description of the

SOAPFault element in the SAAJ API in Chapter 20). The getFaultCode() and getFaultString() methods retrieve the reason for the fault as an error code and a human-readable string, respectively, while the getFaultActor() method returns a URI that identifies the system that detected the fault. The getDetail() returns additional information, which is application-specific, that the sender stored in the SOAP fault element. The value returned by this method is of type javax.xml.soap.Detail (see Chapter 20) and can, therefore, contain arbitrary XML elements.

The javax.xml.soap Package

Package javax.xml.soap SAAJ 1.1; JWSDP 1.0, J2EE 1.4

The javax.xml.soap package contains the classes and interfaces that make up the Soap with Attachments API for Java (SAAJ). This package can be divided into two major parts: a small number of classes and interfaces that obtain a SOAP message and send it, and a much larger set that deal with the structure of the message itself.

In order to send a message, you need to get an instance of the SOAPConnection class. As is the case with most of the classes in this package, this class is abstract in order to allow vendors to provide their own implementations. You can obtain a SOAPConnection object from the SOAPConnectionFactory class, which is another abstract class that you can get an instance of by calling its newInstance() method. A SOAP message is represented by the SOAPMessage class, which can be obtained from a MessageFactory.

SOAP messages are built from elements that are represented in the API by the SOAPElement interface. This interface provides methods that allow you to add other elements and text nodes to form a tree structure that is serialized to XML form when the message is transmitted. Similarly, on receipt, a SOAP message is converted from XML form to a SOAPMessage consisting of SOAPElements and Text nodes. SOAPElement has various subinterfaces that represent different parts of the SOAP message, such as SOAP-Header, SOAPBody, and SOAPFault.

The body of a SOAP message can only contain valid XML data. Non-XML data can be included by adding one or more attachments. SAAJ supports the use of attachments that contain MIME-encoded data. To add such an attachment, create an AttachmentPart object, specifying the data content and its MIME type, and attach it to the message.

Interfaces
public interface **Detail** extends SOAPFaultElement;
public interface **DetailEntry** extends SOAPElement;
public interface **Name**;
public interface **Node**;
public interface **SOAPBody** extends SOAPElement;
public interface **SOAPBodyElement** extends SOAPElement;

public interface **SOAPConstants**;
public interface **SOAPElement** extends Node;
public interface **SOAPEnvelope** extends SOAPElement;
public interface **SOAPFault** extends SOAPBodyElement;
public interface **SOAPFaultElement** extends SOAPElement;
public interface **SOAPHeader** extends SOAPElement;
public interface **SOAPHeaderElement** extends SOAPElement;
public interface **Text** extends Node;

Classes

public abstract class **AttachmentPart**;
public abstract class **MessageFactory**;
public class **MimeHeader**;
public class **MimeHeaders**;
public abstract class **SOAPConnection**;
public abstract class **SOAPConnectionFactory**;
public class **SOAPElementFactory**;
public abstract class **SOAPFactory**;
public abstract class **SOAPMessage**;
public abstract class **SOAPPart**;

Exceptions

public class **SOAPException** extends Exception;

AttachmentPart

javax.xml.soap

SAAJ 1.1; JWSDP 1.0, J2EE 1.4

```
public abstract class AttachmentPart {
// Public Constructors
  public AttachmentPart( );
// Property Accessor Methods (by property name)
  public abstract Iterator getAllMimeHeaders( );
  public abstract Object getContent( ) throws SOAPException;
  public String getContentId( );
  public void setContentId( String contentId);
  public String getContentLocation( );
  public void setContentLocation( String contentLocation);
  public String getContentType( );
  public void setContentType( String contentType);
  public abstract javax.activation.DataHandler getDataHandler( ) throws SOAPException;
  public abstract void setDataHandler( javax.activation.DataHandler dataHandler);
  public abstract int getSize( ) throws SOAPException;
// Public Instance Methods
  public abstract void addMimeHeader(String name, String value);
  public abstract void clearContent( );
  public abstract Iterator getMatchingMimeHeaders(String[] names);
  public abstract String[] getMimeHeader(String name);
  public abstract Iterator getNonMatchingMimeHeaders(String[] names);
  public abstract void removeAllMimeHeaders( );
  public abstract void removeMimeHeader( String header);
```

```
public abstract void setContent(Object object, String contentType);
   public abstract void setMimeHeader(String name, String value);
}
```

The AttachmentPart class represents an attachment to a SOAP message. Attachments are created using the createAttachment() method of the SOAPMessage class and are composed of MIME-encoded content and a set of MIME headers. The content can be associated with the attachment either when it is constructed or when subsequently using the setContent() or setDataHandler() methods.

The content of an attachment can be added using either the setContent() or the setDataHandler() method, both of which automatically set the Content-Type MIME header to match the type of data provided. The setContent() method supplies the content as a Java object together with a string that indicates its MIME type. When the SOAPMessage is serialized to XML, the content of the attachment is converted to a byte stream using a DataHandler that is specialized for that object's MIME type. The SAAJ reference implementation provides handlers that work for a small number of MIME types, including plain text and XML and JPEG images. However, these handlers require the source object to be of a specific type, which is not always convenient. For example, if you want to include a JPEG image as an attachment, you need to supply it in the form of a java.awt.Image object. This is inconvenient if you already have it in the form of a byte array. The setDataHandler() method lets you supply the attachment data in the form of a DataHandler object that encapsulates both the MIME type and the data, and also allows you to provide the code required to handle the conversion into byte stream form, which is, of course, trivial if you already have a byte stream. Except for a small number of special cases, the setDataHandler() method is the better choice. For a more complete discussion of this topic, refer to Chapter 3.

You can discover the size of the data in an attachment by calling the getSize() method. The actual content can be retrieved using either the getContent() or the getDataHandler() method. The getContent() method returns the data in the form of an object that is determined by its MIME type and the data content handlers that are installed. The getDataHandler() method returns the content in the form of a DataHandler object instead, which potentially allows you to retrieve it in various different forms or as a raw byte stream. The clearContent() method removes the data content of the attachment, but does not affect any of the MIME headers.

Each attachment has its own set of MIME headers that are distinct from those associated with the SOAPMessage of which it forms a part. The AttachmentPart class provides a group of methods that allow you to access or set the MIME headers. The addMimeHeader(), setMimeHeader(), removeMimeHeader(), and removeAllMimeHeaders() methods all change the set of headers, whereas getMimeHeader(), getAllMimeHeaders(), getMatchingMimeHeaders(), and getNonMatchingMimeHeaders() return some or all of the existing headers. These methods are the same as the similarly named methods of the MimeHeaders class, which is described later in this section, apart from the fact that the MimeHeaders method does not include Mime in the method name (e.g., getAllMimeHeaders() corresponds to the MimeHeaders getAllHeaders() method). AttachmentPart also provides a small number of convenience methods, such as getContentType() and setContentType(), that provide access to commonly used MIME headers without requiring the use of the header name. As noted earlier, the appropriate Content-Type is set automatically when the attachment data is installed, and should not usually be changed.

Passed To   SOAPMessage.addAttachmentPart()

Returned By   SOAPMessage.createAttachmentPart()

```
javax.xml.soap
```

SAAJ 1.1; JWSDP 1.0, J2EE 1.4

```
public interface Detail extends SOAPFaultElement {
// Public Instance Methods
    public abstract DetailEntry addDetailEntry( Name name) throws SOAPException;
    public abstract Iterator getDetailEntries( );
}
```

Detail is a SOAPElement that supplies application-specific information relating to a SOAP fault. A SOAPFault element that reports an error while processing the body part of an earlier message must contain a Detail element. Conversely, a SOAPFault reporting an error in the header of the message must not contain this element. The Detail element, when present, contains one or more detail entries that are represented in the SAAJ API by the DetailEntry element and contain the useful information relating to the fault.

To create a Detail element, use the addDetail( ) method of the SOAPFault object within which it is to appear. Once you have a Detail object, you can add entries to it by calling its addDetailEntry( ) method. To examine the entries contained in a Detail object, use the getDetailEntries( ) method, which returns an Iterator in which each item is of type DetailEntry.

Passed To	javax.xml.rpc.soap.SOAPFaultException.SOAPFaultException( )
Returned By	javax.xml.rpc.soap.SOAPFaultException.getDetail( ), SOAPFactory.createDetail( ), SOAPFault. {addDetail( ), getDetail( )}

DetailEntry   **javax.xml.soap**

SAAJ 1.1; JWSDP 1.0, J2EE 1.4

```
public interface DetailEntry extends SOAPElement {
}
```

DetailEntry is a SOAPElement that provides application-specific information relating to a SOAP fault. A DetailEntry is always contained by and can only be created from a Detail element. There is no predefined SOAP element that corresponds to a DetailEntry—instead, the element name and its namespace are supplied when it is created.

Since the DetailEntry interface is derived from SOAPElement, applications may nest Text nodes or other SOAPElements inside a DetailEntry and may also attach attributes and namespace declarations to it. The following code extract creates a DetailEntry and adds to it a single Text node. In this code, detail is assumed to be a reference to a Detail object, and factory is assumed to be a reference to a SOAPFactory:

```
DetailEntry entry = detail.addDetailEntry(
        factory.createName("BookError", "books", "urn:BookService"));
entry.addTextNode("Book title not known");
```

Here is how this would look in the resulting SOAP message, where the <detail> tag corresponds to the containing Detail element:

```
<detail>
        <books:BookError xmlns:books="urn:BookService">Book title not known
        </books:BookError>
</detail>
```

Returned By	Detail.addDetailEntry( )

SAAJ 1.1; JWSDP 1.0, J2EE 1.4

```
public abstract class MessageFactory {
// Public Constructors
  public MessageFactory( );
// Public Class Methods
  public static MessageFactory newInstance( ) throws SOAPException;
// Public Instance Methods
  public abstract SOAPMessage createMessage( ) throws SOAPException;
  public abstract SOAPMessage createMessage(MimeHeaders headers,
  java.io.InputStream in) throws java.io.IOExceptionSOAPException;
}
```

MessageFactory is an abstract base class that provides the methods used by application code to construct SOAP messages. A SAAJ application obtains an instance of this class by calling the static newInstance( ) method, which looks for a suitable concrete implementation using the following algorithm:

- Looks in the system properties for a property called javax.xml.soap.MessageFactory. If this property is defined, its value is assumed to be the class name of a concrete implementation of MessageFactory.

- Looks for the same property in a file called ${JAVA_HOME}/lib/jaxm.properties. If the property is found, its value is assumed to be the required class name.

- Looks for a resource called META-INF/services/javax.xml.soap.MessageFactory in the classpath. If such a resource exists, it is opened and a single line is read from it. If the line is not empty, it is used as the class name.

- Finally, an implementation-dependent default class is used. In the case of the reference implementation, this class is called com.sun.xml.messaging.saaj.soap. MessageFactoryImpl.

Once you have a MessageFactory, use its zero-argument createMessage( ) method to obtain a basic SOAPMessage object to which you can then add content and attachments. The default MessageFactory provided by the SAAJ reference implementation returns a message that contains the following:

- A SOAPEnvelope within a SOAPPart object

- An empty SOAPHeader, followed by an empty SOAPBody, inside the SOAPEnvelope

Since the MessageFactory is found using a lookup process, it is possible to plug in a custom factory that will return a SOAPMessage that is partially populated with elements that a particular application or suite of applications might require, without modifying application code.

The other variant of createMessage( ) is intended to be used to deserialize a SOAP message received from an HTTP connection or some other communications mechanism into a SOAPMessage object and therefore is most commonly used by servlets. The in argument provides an InputStream from which the raw XML message can be read, while the headers argument is a MimeHeaders object containing the MIME headers that accompanied the message and therefore accessible from the SOAPPart object within the resulting SOAPMessage. Refer to Chapter 6 for an example that shows how to use this method to handle a SOAP message from within a servlet.

Passed To	javax.xml.messaging.JAXMServlet.setMessageFactory( )
Returned By	javax.xml.messaging.ProviderConnection.createMessageFactory( ), MessageFactory. newInstance( )
Type Of	javax.xml.messaging.JAXMServlet.msgFactory

MimeHeader
javax.xml.soap

SAAJ 1.1; JWSDP 1.0, J2EE 1.4

```
public class MimeHeader {
// Public Constructors
   public MimeHeader( String name, String value);
// Public Instance Methods
   public String getName( );
   public String getValue( );
}
```

MimeHeader is a simple class that acts as a container for the name and value of a MIME header. A SOAP message may have MIME headers associated with its SOAPMessage object and, if it has any attachments, the SOAPPart and each AttachmentPart may have its own MIME headers. MimeHeader objects are usually grouped together and stored in a MimeHeaders object.

The getName( ) and getValue( ) methods return the name and value of the MIME header, respectively. Typical values for these attributes might be Content-Type and text/xml. A SOAP message may have multiple headers with the same name but different values. In this case, each individual name/value pair has its own MimeHeader object. The Mime-Headers class provides methods that allow all of the values for a given header to be retrieved.

MimeHeaders
javax.xml.soap

SAAJ 1.1; JWSDP 1.0, J2EE 1.4

```
public class MimeHeaders {
// Public Constructors
   public MimeHeaders( );
// Public Instance Methods
   public void addHeader( String name, String value);
   public Iterator getAllHeaders( );                                    // default:Itr
   public String[] getHeader( String name);
   public Iterator getMatchingHeaders(String[] names);
   public Iterator getNonMatchingHeaders(String[] names);
   public void removeAllHeaders( );
   public void removeHeader( String name);
   public void setHeader( String name, String value);
}
```

MimeHeaders is a container class that represents a group of MIME headers associated with a SOAP message. A message that has no attachments has a single set of MIME headers that can be obtained by calling the getMimeHeaders( ) method of its SOAPMessage object. A message with attachments has additional sets of independent MIME headers associated with the SOAP envelope (available from the SOAPPart object) and with each attachment.

MimeHeaders manages a set of MimeHeader objects, each of which represents a single header name/value combination. It is possible for a header to have multiple values, in which case each value has its own MimeHeader object. The addHeader() method creates a new entry with a given name and value, leaving all existing entries with the same name intact. The setHeader() method adds a new entry if a header with the given name does not already exist; otherwise, it replaces the value of the first header in the collection with the given name, as illustrated by the following code snippet, in which headers is a reference to a MimeHeaders object:

```
headers.setHeader("Content-Length", "1024");
headers.setHeader("Content-Type", "text/plain");
headers.setHeader("Content-Length", "2048");
// Replaces the value added earlier
```

This code creates a Content-Type header with the value text/plain and a Content-Length header with the value 2048.

The removeHeader() method removes all MIME headers whose name matches the supplied value. Note that the name comparison performed by this method (and all MimeHeaders methods) is case-insensitive. The removeAllHeaders() method removes all headers, leaving an empty container.

There are four methods that let you obtain some or all of the headers in a MimeHeaders object. The getHeader() method accepts a header name and returns an array containing all of the values associated with that header, or null if there are none. The other three methods all return an Iterator containing objects of type MimeHeader. The getAllHeaders() method returns all headers and their values. getMatchingHeaders() accepts a list of header names and returns the MimeHeader objects for all headers whose names appear in the given list. getNonMatchingHeaders() returns the MimeHeader objects for all headers whose names do not appear in the list; if an empty list of names is supplied, then all headers and their associated values are returned.

Passed To   javax.xml.messaging.JAXMServlet.putHeaders( ), MessageFactory.createMessage( ), SOAPMessage.getAttachments( )

Returned By   javax.xml.messaging.JAXMServlet.getHeaders( ), SOAPMessage.getMimeHeaders( )

Name   javax.xml.soap

SAAJ 1.1; JWSDP 1.0, J2EE 1.4

```
public interface Name {
// Public Instance Methods
    public abstract String getLocalName( );
    public abstract String getPrefix( );
    public abstract String getQualifiedName( );
    public abstract String getURI( );
}
```

Name is an interface that encapsulates the concept of an XML element name that may be namespace-qualified. It is used whenever such a name is required by the SAAJ API instead of the javax.xml.namespace.QName class, which is used by JAX-RPC. A Name has three attributes:

- A local name, which all Name objects are required to have
- A namespace URI, which uniquely identifies the namespace within which the local name is defined
- The prefix that is used as a shorthand identifier for the namespace and that appears along with the local name in XML tags

Name objects can be obtained by calling one of the createName( ) methods of the SOAPFactory class or the SOAPEnvelope interface. These methods have two variants:

```
public Name createName(String localName) throws SOAPException;
public Name createName(String localName, String prefix, String uri)
       throws SOAPException;
```

The first method creates a Name that is not explicitly associated with a namespace, as in the following example:

```
SOAPFactory factory = SOAPFactory.newInstance;
Name bookTitle = factory.createName("BookTitle");
SOAPElement bookTitleElement = factory.createElement(bookTitle);
```

If bookTitleElement is added to a SOAPMessage and serialized, it appears as BookTitle. The fact that the Name object does not have an explicit namespace does not, however, mean that an element created from it is not in a namespace. In fact, the element is in the default namespace assigned either by itself or by the nearest ancestor element that has an xmlns with no namespace prefix, if there is one.

The second method returns a Name element that has an explicit namespace defined by the uri argument. Wherever the Name object is used to create a SOAPElement and then serialized, both the local name and the prefix appear. The following code creates an element called BookTitle in a namespace defined by the URI urn:BookService:

```
SOAPFactory factory = SOAPFactory.newInstance();
Name bookTitle = factory.createName("BookTitle", "book", "urn:BookService");
SOAPElement bookTitleElement = factory.createElement(bookTitle);
```

When the bookTitleElement is serialized, it appears as book:BookTitle, and a namespace declaration mapping the prefix book to the URI urn:BookService is added:

```
<book:BookTitle xmlns:book="urn:BookService">
```

The getLocalPart( ), getPrefix, and getURI( ) methods return the values of the three independent attributes of the Name object. The getQualifiedName( ) method returns a string that shows how the element will appear within the serialized SOAP message. For the two examples shown previously, this method returns either BookTitle or book:BookTitle.

It is important to note that two Name objects are considered to be equal if they have the same local part and the same namespace URI. In other words, the prefix is not a factor in the comparison.

Passed To	Detail.addDetailEntry( ), SOAPBody.addBodyElement( ), SOAPElement.{addAttribute( ), addChildElement( ), getAttributeValue( ), getChildElements( ), removeAttribute( )}, SOAPElementFactory.create( ), SOAPFactory.createElement( ), SOAPHeader.addHeaderElement( )
Returned By	SOAPElement.getElementName( ), SOAPEnvelope.createName( ), SOAPFactory.createName( )

SAAJ 1.1; JWSDP 1.0, J2EE 1.4

```
public interface Node {
// Public Instance Methods
    public abstract void detachNode( );
    public abstract SOAPElement getParentElement( );
    public abstract String getValue( );
    public abstract void recycleNode( );
    public abstract void setParentElement(SOAPElement parent) throws SOAPException;
}
```

Node is an interface that represents a node in a DOM-like tree representation of a SOAP message. In particular, Node owns the reference required to maintain the linkage between a SOAP element and its single parent. In the SAAJ API, Node is never used directly. Instead, the API deals with its two derived interfaces: SOAPElement, which adds the capability to attach attributes and namespace declarations, and Text, which represents textual content.

The getParentElement( ) method returns a reference to the SOAPElement that resides above this Node in the element hierarchy, whereas setParentElement( ) links the node beneath a given SOAPElement. The detachNode( ) method can be used to remove the Node from the tree. If the application code knows that it no longer needs a particular Node, it should use the recycleNode( ) method to allow it to be garbage-collected once all hard references to it are removed. As a side effect, the Node is removed from its parent if it is still linked when this method is called.

getValue( ) is a convenience method that returns a string that is the value associated with a Text child of this Node. It returns null if the node does not have such a child. Text can be associated with a Node using the addTextNode( ) method of SOAPElement, which actually creates a Text node and adds it as a child of the element.

Interestingly, although a Node may have a parent, it does not have any methods that allow access to other Nodes that are its direct descendents, since the concept of child elements belongs to SOAPElement instead. However, since every SOAPElement is also a Node, it is incorrect to regard Node as simply a leaf in a tree structure.

Implementations SOAPElement, Text

SOAPBody

javax.xml.soap

SAAJ 1.1; JWSDP 1.0, J2EE 1.4

```
public interface SOAPBody extends SOAPElement {
// Public Instance Methods
    public abstract SOAPBodyElement addBodyElement(Name name) throws SOAPException;
    public abstract SOAPFault addFault( ) throws SOAPException;
    public abstract SOAPFault getFault( );
    public abstract boolean hasFault( );
}
```

SOAPBody is a subinterface of SOAPElement that represents the body of a SOAP message. A single SOAPBody element will always be found as either the first or second element of the SOAPEnvelope, depending on whether the enclosing message has associated headers.

A SOAPBody element may contain any number of SOAPBodyElements that represent the information to be sent to the message recipient. These elements can be created and added to the body in a single operation by calling addBodyElement() or the addChildElement() method inherited from SOAPElement. SOAPElements obtained from a SOAPFactory or from the SOAPElementFactory class may also be added to the message body. However, in this case, since every immediate child of SOAPBody must be a SOAPBodyElement, a copy of the element (and any child elements it may contain) is made in which the original element is replaced by a SOAPBodyElement, and the copied hierarchy is added to the message body.

SOAPBody may also contain a single SOAPFault element if the message is reporting an error encountered while processing the headers or body of an earlier message. The addFault() method creates and adds a SOAPFault element to the message body. Application code is responsible for properly initializing this object, as described in the reference entry for SOAPFault, later in this chapter. A message recipient can determine whether the body contains a fault element by calling hasFault(), and can obtain a reference to it from the getFault() method, which returns null if there is no such element in the body.

Returned By   SOAPEnvelope.{addBody( ), getBody( )}

SOAPBodyElement   javax.xml.soap

SAAJ 1.1; JWSDP 1.0, J2EE 1.4

```
public interface SOAPBodyElement extends SOAPElement {
}
```

SOAPBodyElement is a subinterface of SOAPElement that represents an element that has been added directly to the body of a SOAP message. In all other respects, a SOAPBodyElement is the same as a SOAPElement.

The most direct way to create a SOAPBodyElement is to use the addBodyElement() method of SOAPBody, supplying the element name in the form of a Name object:

```
SOAPFacctory factory = SOAPFactory.newInstance();
Name elementName = factory.createName("BookSearch", "book",
                                        "urn:BookService");
SOAPBodyElement bodyElement = soapBody.addBodyElement(elementName);
bodyElement.addTextNode("Java Web Services");
```

Since SOAPBody is itself a SOAPElement, it inherits its addChildElement() methods. It is therefore possible to use these methods to directly add elements to a SOAPBody like this:

```
SOAPElement element = body.addChildElement(
                              "BookSearch", "book",
                              "urn:BookService");
```

This code actually creates a SOAPBodyElement rather than an ordinary SOAPElement. Additionally, SOAPElements created using factory methods and added directly to the SOAP body are replaced by SOAPBodyElements. Therefore, in the following code extract:

```
SOAPElement element = factory.createElement("BookSearch", "book",
    "urn:BookService");
SOAPElement textElement = element.addTextNode("J2ME");
SOAPElement bodyElement = body.addChildElement(element);
```

the result of the addChildElement() method called on the third line is that a new SOAPBodyElement is created and added to the body in place of the original element and a reference to that SOAPBodyElement is returned. Any elements below the original element (in this case, the Text node) are copied and placed below the newly created SOAPBodyElement.

Implementations SOAPFault

Returned By SOAPBody.addBodyElement( )

SOAPConnection

SAAJ 1.1; JWSDP 1.0, J2EE 1.4

```
public abstract class SOAPConnection {
// Public Constructors
    public SOAPConnection( );
// Public Instance Methods
    public abstract SOAPMessage call(SOAPMessage request, Object to)
    throws SOAPException;
    public abstract void close( ) throws SOAPException;
}
```

SOAPConnection is an object that can be used to send SOAP messages. Despite its name, it does not represent a connection in the traditional sense, since it does not have a fixed association with a peer object. Instead, it is better thought of as an access point that can be used to send any number of individually addressed SOAP messages to arbitrary receivers.

To obtain a SOAPConnection, you need to use a SOAPConnectionFactory:

```
SOAPConnectionFactory factory = SOAPConnectionFactory.newInstance;
SOAPConnection conn = factory.createConnection;
```

Both SOAPConnectionFactory and SOAPConnection are abstract classes, concrete instances of which are provided by your SAAJ implementation. The fact that the SOAPConnectionFactory newInstance( ) method searches for a suitable implementation class (as described in its reference section in this chapter) means that you can plug in different SAAJ implementations without changing your application code. When a SOAPConnection is no longer required, it should be released by calling its close( ) method.

The call( ) method takes a SOAPMessage object, serializes it into XML, and sends it to the destination given by its to argument. This argument is declared to be of type Object, which allows implementations to support various different forms of destination addresses. At a minimum, the following types must be supported:

java.net.URL

This is the simplest case: the URL directly specifies the location of the message recipient.

java.lang.String

When a string is supplied, it is expected to be the string representation of a valid URL.

javax.xml.messaging.URLEndpoint

This is a special case that is supported for compatibility with the JAXM API. The URLEndpoint is a simple wrapper for a URL, which is obtained by calling its getURL( ) method and treated as the message destination. This form of address is available only on systems that have JAXM installed. Note that JAXM is not part of the J2EE 1.4 platform; therefore, it cannot be assumed to be universally available.

Once the message is sent, the call( ) method blocks until a reply is received. The reply is unmarshalled from XML into a SOAPMessage, which is then returned to the caller. call( )

therefore represents a synchronous message exchange between a client and a server. SAAJ does not support asynchronous operation; if you need this functionality, you may either simulate it by starting a new thread to deliver a message, or by using JAXM if it is available.

Returned By   SOAPConnectionFactory.createConnection( )

SOAPConnectionFactory

SAAJ 1.1; JWSDP 1.0, J2EE 1.4

```
public abstract class SOAPConnectionFactory {
// Public Constructors
  public SOAPConnectionFactory( );
// Public Class Methods
  public static SOAPConnectionFactory newInstance()
    throws SOAPExceptionUnsupportedOperationException;
// Public Instance Methods
  public abstract SOAPConnection createConnection( ) throws SOAPException;
}
```

SOAPConnectionFactory is a factory object used to create SOAPConnections. To obtain an instance of this class, which is abstract, use the static newInstance( ) method, which uses the following algorithm to locate a suitable concrete implementation:

- Looks in the system properties for a property called javax.xml.soap.SOAPConnectionFactory. If this property is defined, its value is assumed to be the class name of a concrete implementation of SOAPConnectionFactory.
- Looks for the same property in a file called ${JAVA_HOME}/lib/jaxm.properties. If the property is found, its value is assumed to be the required class name.
- Looks for a resource called META-INF/services/javax.xml.soap.SOAPConnectionFactory in the classpath. If such a resource exists, it is opened and a single line is read from it. If the line is not empty, it is used as the required class name.
- Finally, an implementation-dependent default class is used. In the case of the reference implementation, this class is called com.sun.xml.messaging.saaj.client.p2p. HttpSOAPConnectionFactory.

Once you have a SOAPConnectionFactory, you can use its createConnection( ) method to obtain any number of SOAPConnection objects.

Returned By   SOAPConnectionFactory.newInstance( )

SOAPConstants

SAAJ 1.1; JWSDP 1.0, J2EE 1.4

```
public interface SOAPConstants {
// Public Constants
  public static final String URI_NS_SOAP_ENCODING;     // ="http://schemas.xmlsoap.org/soap/encoding/"
  public static final String URI_NS_SOAP_ENVELOPE;     // ="http://schemas.xmlsoap.org/soap/envelope/"
  public static final String URI_SOAP_ACTOR_NEXT;      // ="http://schemas.xmlsoap.org/soap/actor/next"
}
```

This interface defines three string-valued constants that are used within the SAAJ API:

URI_NS_SOAP_ENVELOPE

The URI of the namespace that is associated with the XML elements that make up the SOAP envelope (http://schemas.xmlsoap.org/soap/envelope/).

URI_NS_SOAP_ENCODING

The URI of the namespace that corresponds to the standard encoding rules defined in the SOAP specification (http://schemas.xmlsoap.org/soap/encoding/), usually referred to as the SOAP section 5 rules. This constant is used in conjunction with the SOAPElement setEncodingStyle( ) and getEncodingStyle( ) methods.

URI_SOAP_ACTOR_NEXT

This constant holds the well-known URI that is the distinguished value of the actor attribute of the SOAP header used to indicate that the header is intended to be processed by the next recipient of the message. This value can be supplied as the argument of the setActor( ) method of the SOAPHeaderElement interface and may be the return value of the getActor( ) method.

SOAPElement

javax.xml.soap

SAAJ 1.1; JWSDP 1.0, J2EE 1.4

```
public interface SOAPElement extends Node {
// Property Accessor Methods (by property name)
    public abstract Iterator getAllAttributes( );
    public abstract Iterator getChildElements( );
    public abstract Iterator getChildElements( Name name);
    public abstract Name getElementName( );
    public abstract String getEncodingStyle( );
    public abstract void setEncodingStyle(
    String encodingStyle) throws SOAPException;
    public abstract Iterator getNamespacePrefixes( );
// Public Instance Methods
    public abstract SOAPElement addAttribute(Name name, String value) throws SOAPException;
    public abstract SOAPElement addChildElement(SOAPElement element) throws SOAPException;
    public abstract SOAPElement addChildElement(String localName) throws SOAPException;
    public abstract SOAPElement addChildElement(Name name) throws SOAPException;
    public abstract SOAPElement addChildElement(String localName, String prefix) throws SOAPException;
    public abstract SOAPElement addChildElement(String localName, String prefix, String uri) throws SOAPException;
    public abstract SOAPElement addNamespaceDeclaration(String prefix, String uri) throws SOAPException;
    public abstract SOAPElement addTextNode(String text) throws SOAPException;
    public abstract String getAttributeValue( Name name);
    public abstract String getNamespaceURI( String prefix);
    public abstract boolean removeAttribute( Name name);
    public abstract boolean removeNamespaceDeclaration(String prefix);
}
```

A SOAPElement represents an element within a SOAPMessage. SOAPElement is derived from Node and inherits its ability to be associated with a parent node, thus allowing the construction of a message as a tree of objects representing the elements and attributes that will eventually be serialized into XML tags. With the exception of Text, SOAPPart, and AttachmentPart, all of the nodes within a SOAPMessage are SOAPElements. SOAPElement has a number of derived interfaces that are used to form particular parts of a SOAP message. For example, SOAPHeaderElement is a SOAPElement that appears only as a direct child of a SOAP-Header. Where these special interfaces exist, they are the only type of element that can be added to their particular parent. An attempt to add a SOAPElement where a more specialized type is required does not, however, result in an exception. Instead, the element and any child elements it might have are copied, and the root element is converted to the correct specialized type before being added to the parent. An attempt to add a SOAPElement to a SOAPHeader, for example, would result in an equivalent SOAPHeaderElement being added instead.

There are several ways to create a SOAPElement. The simplest way is to use one of the addChildElement() methods of an existing SOAPElement, such as SOAPBody, which both creates a new element and makes it a child of the original element. There are five variants of this method.

- The addChildElement(Name name) method creates a new element whose name and namespace prefix are taken from the supplied Name object. A namespace declaration linking the namespace prefix to the namespace URI from the Name object is also added to the element. If the Name object does not have an explicit namespace, then neither the namespace prefix nor the namespace declaration appears on the element.

- The addChildElement(String localName) method creates an element whose name is supplied by the localName argument and has no explicit namespace. The element is therefore in the default namespace declared by the nearest ancestor that has an xlmns: namespace declaration, or it is declared by itself if such a declaration is added using the addNamespaceDeclaration() method.

- The addChildElement(String localName, String prefix, String uri) method creates an element in which the name, namespace prefix, and namespace URI are obtained from the method arguments. A namespace declaration linking the prefix and URI are included. For example, the method call addChildElement("BookQuery", "book", "urn:BookService") would create an element that would be serialized as book:BookQuery xmlns:book="urn:BookService".

- The addChildElement(String localName, String prefix) method creates an element with the given local name and namespace prefix. A mapping from the given prefix to a URI must have been provided by an ancestor of the newly created element, or a SOAPException is thrown.

- The addChildElement(SOAPElement element) method adds either an existing element or a copy of that element (and any child elements it might have) as a child of the element on which it is invoked. The specification of this method warns that application code should not assume that the element itself is added, and a copy is actually added in the reference implementation.

All of the addChildElement() methods return a reference to the SOAPElement that was created and/or added. This can be useful if you want to create several nested elements in a single line of code:

```
body.addChildElement("Level1").addChildElement("Level2").
addChildElement("Level3").addTextNode("Text");
```

This code adds three levels of nested elements. The addTextNode() adds the text passed to it below the SOAPElement on which it is called and returns a reference to that SOAPElement. The result of executing this code is the following:

```
<Level1>
    <Level2>
        <Level3>Text</Level3>
    </Level2>
</Level1>
```

SOAPElement provides a group of methods that allow you to add and manipulate attributes. The addAttribute() method adds an attribute whose name and namespace prefix are given by the Name argument and equates it to the supplied attribute value. If the Name object does not have an associated namespace, then no namespace prefix appears in the serialized XML. The setEncodingStyle() method is a convenience method that allows you to set the attribute that represents the SOAP encoding style that applies to an element and its descendents without having to explicitly name the attribute. The following code extract sets the default SOAP encoding rules:

```
element.setEncodingStyle(SOAPConstants.URI_NS_SOAP_ENCODING);
```

The getEncodingStyle() method returns the encoding style set for the element on which it is invoked. Note that this method does not search the ancestors of the element for an inherited encoding style if the element itself does not specify one—it simply returns null. The getAttributeValue() method can be used to obtain the value of an attribute given its Name. If the given attribute is not present, then null is returned. You can get an Iterator containing a Name object for each attribute attached to an element by calling the getAllAttributes() method, and you can remove an attribute with removeAttribute().

The final group of SOAPElement methods handles namespaces. addNamespaceDeclaration() adds a namespace declaration to the element that links the given namespace prefix to its URI. For example, the following code links the namespace prefix book to the URI urn:BookService for the scope of the element referred to by the element variable and its child elements:

```
element.addNamespaceDeclaration("book", "urn:BookService");
```

The serialized XML for this element looks like this, assuming the element is called BookName:

```
<BookName xmlns:book="urn:BookService"/>
```

If the prefix is supplied as the empty string, then a declaration of the default namespace is being made (i.e., xmlns="urn:BookService"). The removeNamespaceDeclaration() method removes a namespace declaration from an element given its namespace prefix. The getNamespacePrefixes() method returns an Iterator in which each element is a string that represents the prefix of a namespace declaration attached to the element on which it is invoked. To get the namespace URI for a given prefix, use the getNamespaceURI() method.

Implementations   DetailEntry, SOAPBody, SOAPBodyElement, SOAPEnvelope, SOAPFaultElement, SOAPHeader, SOAPHeaderElement

Passed To   Node.setParentElement( ), SOAPElement.addChildElement( )

Returned By   Node.getParentElement( ), SOAPElement.{addAttribute( ), addChildElement( ), addNamespaceDeclaration( ), addTextNode( )}, SOAPElementFactory.create( ), SOAPFactory.createElement( )

SOAPElementFactory

SAAJ 1.1; JWSDP 1.0, J2EE 1.4

```
public class SOAPElementFactory {
// No Constructor
// Public Class Methods
    public static SOAPElementFactory newInstance( ) throws SOAPException;
```

```
    public SOAPElement create(String localName) throws SOAPException;                              // #
    public SOAPElement create(Name name) throws SOAPException;                                     // #
    public SOAPElement create(String localName, String prefix, String uri) throws SOAPException;   // #
}
```

SOAPElementFactory is an obsolete class that was used in the early releases of the SAAJ API to create SOAPElements and is now supported only for backward-compatibility. As of SAAJ Version 1.1, application code should use the SOAPFactory class to create SOAPElement objects.

Returned By   SOAPElementFactory.newInstance( )

SOAPEnvelope   javax.xml.soap

SAAJ 1.1; JWSDP 1.0, J2EE 1.4

```
public interface SOAPEnvelope extends SOAPElement {
// Public Instance Methods
    public abstract SOAPBody addBody( ) throws SOAPException;
    public abstract SOAPHeader addHeader( )( ) throws SOAPException;
    public abstract Name createName(String localName) throws SOAPException;
    public abstract Name createName(String localName, String prefix, String uri) throws SOAPException;
    public abstract SOAPBody getBody( ) throws SOAPException;
    public abstract SOAPHeader getHeader( ) throws SOAPException;
}
```

SOAPEnvelope is a subinterface of SOAPElement that maps to the envelope of a SOAP message. A reference to the SOAPEnvelope can be obtained from the SOAPPart of a message:

```
MessageFactory factory = MessageFactory .newInstance;
SOAPMessage msg = factory.createMessage;
SOAPEnvelope envelope = msg.getSOAPPart.getEnvelope;
```

SOAPEnvelope is a container for the header and body parts of the SOAP message, references to which can be obtained from the getHeader() and getBody() methods. A newly created SOAPMessage contains an empty header and an empty body. The addHeader() and addBody() methods can be used to create and add a new SOAPHeader or SOAPBody body element to the envelope. However, since only one object of each type can be present in the envelope at any time, the existing instance must be removed by calling the detachNode() method before a new one is created.

SOAPEnvelope also acts as a factory for Name objects. The single-argument createName() method creates a Name object with a given local part and no explicit namespace, while the three-argument variant additionally includes the namespace URI and prefix. Refer to the discussion of the Name interface earlier in this chapter for a description of these methods.

Returned By   SOAPPart.getEnvelope( )

```
public class SOAPException extends Exception {
// Public Constructors
    public SOAPException( );
    public SOAPException( String reason);
    public SOAPException( Throwable cause);
    public SOAPException( String reason, Throwable cause);
// Public Methods Overriding Throwable
    public Throwable getCause( );                              // default:null
    public String getMessage( );                              // default:null
    public Throwable initCause( Throwable cause);             // synchronized
}
```

SOAPException is a checked exception that is used to report errors encountered during the execution of methods of the SAAJ API.

A SOAPException typically includes a text string giving a human-readable description of the error and, in some cases, may have an associated Throwable that represents the root cause of the problem. The four constructors allow a SOAPException to be created with any combination of text message and Throwable, which may subsequently be retrieved using the getMessage( ) and getCause( ) methods. Note that the Throwable attribute can be set either at construction time or by using the initCause( ) method. However, a java.lang.IllegalStateException is thrown if this method is called when the Throwable attribute has already been set.

Subclasses   javax.xml.messaging.JAXMException

Thrown By   Too many methods to list.

SOAPFactory

javax.xml.soap

SAAJ 1.1; JWSDP 1.0, J2EE 1.4

```
public abstract class SOAPFactory {
// Public Constructors
    public SOAPFactory( );
// Public Class Methods
    public static SOAPFactory newInstance( ) throws SOAPException;
// Public Instance Methods
    public abstract Detail createDetail( ) throws SOAPException;
    public abstract SOAPElement createElement(String localName) throws SOAPException;
    public abstract SOAPElement createElement(Name name) throws SOAPException;
    public abstract SOAPElement createElement(String localName, String prefix, String uri) throws SOAPException;
    public abstract Name createName(String localName) throws SOAPException;
    public abstract Name createName(String localName, String prefix, String uri) throws SOAPException;
}
```

SOAPFactory is an abstract factory that can be used to create Detail, Name, and SOAPElement objects. Although all of these elements can be created using methods provided by various objects that are part of a SOAP message (such as SOAPEnvelope), it is often convenient to be able to construct message parts without having a reference to a SOAPMessage. In such cases, you should use the SOAPFactory class.

To get a reference to a SOAPFactory object, use the static newInstance() method, which uses an algorithm similar to that described for the SOAPConnectionFactory class to locate a concrete implementation. By default, the reference implementation returns an object of type com.sun.xml.messaging.saaj.soap.SOAPFactoryImpl.

The createElement() method that accepts a single argument of type String returns a SOAPElement whose local name is given by the argument, and that does not have a namespace qualifier. An element created in this way is qualified by the default namespace, which can be designated by adding a suitable namespace declaration to the element itself or to one of its ancestors. You can create an element with an explicit namespace by using the three-argument variant of createElement(), which requires the namespace URI and the namespace prefix in addition to the local part of the element name. Here's a typical example of the usage of this method:

```
SOAPElement element = factory.createElement("BookTitle", "book",
                                            "urn:BookService");
```

The serialized form of this element, when incorporated into a SOAP message, is book:BookTitle xmlns:book="urn:BookService".

The variant of createElement() that accepts an argument of type Name returns a SOAPElement, the name of which is taken from the local part of the supplied argument. The element may or may not be explicitly namespace-qualified, depending on whether the Name contains a namespace.

The createName() methods return instances of the Name interface that have a specified local part and an optional namespace URI and namespace prefix. Refer to the description of the Name interface in this chapter for a discussion of the use of Name objects and namespaces.

Returned By   SOAPFactory.newInstance()

SOAPFault   javax.xml.soap

SAAJ 1.1; JWSDP 1.0, J2EE 1.4

```
public interface SOAPFault extends SOAPBodyElement {
// Public Instance Methods
   public abstract Detail addDetail( ) throws SOAPException;
   public abstract Detail getDetail( );
   public abstract String getFaultActor( );
   public abstract String getFaultCode( );
   public abstract String getFaultString( );
   public abstract void setFaultActor(String faultActor) throws SOAPException;
   public abstract void setFaultCode(String faultCode) throws SOAPException;
   public abstract void setFaultString(String faultString) throws SOAPException;
}
```

SOAPFault is a subinterface of SOAPBodyElement that is used to report an error encountered while processing the body or headers of an earlier message. A SOAPFault element can be created and added to a message by calling the addFault() method of the SOAPBody element of the message. Only one SOAPFault element may be present in a SOAP message body; a SOAPException is thrown if an attempt is made to add a second SOAPFault.

When created, a SOAPFault element is empty. Application code should use SOAPFault methods to add the following nested elements, as appropriate:

Fault code

This mandatory element contains a value intended to be used by software to identify the cause of the error being reported. The SOAP specification defines a small number of standard fault codes that should be used where applicable. For further information on SOAP fault codes, refer to Chapter 6. The fault code is a string value that can be set using the setFaultCode( ) method and read by calling getFaultCode( ).

Fault string

This mandatory element provides a human-readable description of the fault. It can be set using the setFaultString( ) method and read using getFaultString( ).

Fault actor

This element contains the URI of the system that detected and is reporting the fault described by the containing SOAPFault element. It must be present if the error was detected by an intermediate system, and is optional if the fault is being reported by the intended message recipient. Use the setFaultActor( ) and getFaultActor( ) methods to set and read this value.

Details

A SOAPFault element may also contain additional information that describes the fault, the nature of which is application-specific but might, for example, include some or all of the failing message. This optional information is included within a Detail element, which can be created using the addDetail( ) method. Refer to the description of DetailEntry earlier in this chapter for an example that shows how to include detailed fault information in a SOAP message. Fault reports that relate to the content of a message header may not have an associated Detail element, whereas those that report errors in processing the body content may have no more than one nested Detail element. A SOAPException is thrown if an attempt is made to add a second Detail element to a SOAPFault.

Additionally, application-dependent elements may also be added to a SOAPFault by using the addChildElement( ) method inherited from SOAPElement. These elements, which must be namespace-qualified, will all be of type SOAPFaultElement.

Returned By   SOAPBody.{addFault( ), getFault( )}

SOAPFaultElement   *javax.xml.soap*

SAAJ 1.1; JWSDP 1.0, J2EE 1.4

```
public interface SOAPFaultElement extends SOAPElement {
}
```

SOAPFaultElement is a subinterface of SOAPElement that represents an element that has been added directly to a SOAPFault. In all other respects, a SOAPFaultElement is the same as a SOAPElement. The Detail element, described earlier in this chapter, is an example of a SOAP-FaultElement that can be created using the addDetail( ) method of the SOAPFault interface. There are two other ways to create a SOAPFaultElement:

- Using the addChildElement( ) method that SOAPFault inherits from SOAPElement. For example, fault.addChildElement("BookError", "books", "urn:BookService") creates and returns a SOAPFaultElement called BookError in the namespace urn:BookService, and also adds it to the SOAPFault element referenced by the variable fault.

- Creating a SOAPElement using the methods of SOAPFactory or SOAPElementFactory and using addChildElement( ) to add it to a SOAPFault. In this case, the SOAPElement is replaced by an equivalent SOAPFaultElement, and any nested elements are copied.

Implementations Detail

SAAJ 1.1; JWSDP 1.0, J2EE 1.4

```
public interface SOAPHeader extends SOAPElement {
// Public Instance Methods
    public abstract SOAPHeaderElement addHeaderElement(Name name) throws SOAPException;
    public abstract Iterator examineHeaderElements(String actor);
    public abstract Iterator extractHeaderElements(String actor);
}
```

SOAPHeader is a subinterface of SOAPElement that acts as a container for SOAP message headers. A single SOAPHeader element is always found as the first element of the SOAPEnvelope within a SOAPMessage returned by the default MessageFactory provided by the SAAJ reference implementation. However, since the use of headers is optional, if it is not required, it may be removed by calling its detachNode() method:

```
SOAPMessage msg = factory.createMessage;
SOAPPart part = msg.getSOAPPart;
SOAPHeader header = part.getEnvelope.getHeader;
header.detachNode;
```

A SOAPHeader may contain any number of SOAP headers, which are represented by SOAPHeaderElements. The most direct way to add a header is to use the addHeaderElement() method, which requires a Name object as its argument. Other elements may be nested within the SOAPHeaderElement as required. The following code adds the header code BookHeader to a SOAP message:

```
SOAPHeader header = part.getEnvelope.getHeader;
SOAPHeaderElement e = header.addHeaderElement(
        factory.createName("BookHeader", "book", "urn:BookService"));
```

Alternatively, the addChildElement() methods that SOAPHeader inherits from SOAPElement can be used to achieve the same result. The following code extract is equivalent to that shown previously, and also results in the creation of a SOAPHeaderElement:

```
SOAPHeader header = part.getEnvelope.getHeader;
SOAPElement e = header.addChildElement(factory.createName("BookHeader",
                                    "book", "urn:BookService"));
```

Elements created using SOAPFactory or SOAPElementFactory that are added to a SOAPHeader using the addChildElement() method are copied and converted to instances of SOAPHeaderElement before being included in the header.

The extractHeaderElements() method returns an Iterator over the set of nested SOAPHeaderElements for which the actor attribute matches the supplied argument and removes those elements from the header. By default, a SOAPHeaderElement is created with an actor attribute that indicates that it should be processed by the next system that receives it. The following code extract therefore retrieves all headers intended for the system that has received the message, which is assumed to be identified by the URI urn:thisSystem:

```
Iterator iter1 = header.extractHeaderElements(
    SOAPConstants.URI_SOAP_ACTOR_NEXT);
Iterator iter2 = header.extractHeaderElements("urn:thisSystem");
```

Removal of header elements intended for the system that is processing a message is required by the SOAP specification. However, if you just want to look at the headers with a given actor URI without removing them, use the examineHeaderElements() method instead.

Returned By   SOAPEnvelope.{addHeader( ), getHeader( )}

SAAJ 1.1; JWSDP 1.0, J2EE 1.4

```
public interface SOAPHeaderElement extends SOAPElement {
// Public Instance Methods
   public abstract String getActor( );
   public abstract boolean getMustUnderstand( );
   public abstract void setActor( String actorURI);
   public abstract void setMustUnderstand(boolean mustUnderstand);
}
```

SOAPHeaderElement is a subinterface of SOAPElement that represents the root element of a SOAP header. A SOAPHeaderElement can be created using the addHeaderElement( ) or addChildElement( ) methods of SOAPHeader, or by adding a SOAPElement directly to a SOAPHeader.

The setActor( ) method can be used to set the URI of the intermediate system that is expected to process the header; the special value SOAPConstants.URI_SOAP_ACTOR_NEXT should be used to indicate that the header is intended for the next recipient of the message. The setMustUnderstand( ) method sets the header attribute that determines whether the actor to which the header is addressed must be able to understand and process it; the method returns a reply containing a SOAPFault if the actor does not understand the attribute.

Returned By   SOAPHeader.addHeaderElement( )

SOAPMessage   javax.xml.soap

SAAJ 1.1; JWSDP 1.0, J2EE 1.4

```
public abstract class SOAPMessage {
// Public Constructors
   public SOAPMessage( );
// Property Accessor Methods (by property name)
   public abstract Iterator getAttachments( );
   public abstract Iterator getAttachments MimeHeaders headers);
   public abstract String getContentDescription( );
   public abstract void setContentDescription(String description);
   public abstract MimeHeaders getMimeHeaders( );
   public abstract SOAPPart getSOAPPart( );
// Public Instance Methods
   public abstract void addAttachmentPart(AttachmentPart AttachmentPart);
   public abstract int countAttachments( );
   public abstract AttachmentPart createAttachmentPart( );
   public AttachmentPart createAttachmentPart(javax.activation.DataHandler dataHandler);
   public AttachmentPart createAttachmentPart(Object content, String contentType);
   public abstract void removeAllAttachments( );
   public abstract void saveChanges( ) throws SOAPException;
   public abstract boolean saveRequired( );
   public abstract void writeTo( java.io.OutputStream out)
      throws SOAPExceptionjava.io.IOException;
}
```

SOAPMessage is an abstract class that represents a complete SOAP message. A SOAPMessage object can be obtained from the createMessage() method of the MessageFactory class, and consists of several parts:

MIME headers

When a SOAP message is transmitted using a protocol such as HTTP or SMTP, it requires a set of MIME headers that specify, at a minimum, the type of the protocol payload and its length. In the case of a SOAP message with no attachments, the content type is always text/xml. A message with attachments has content type multipart/related as well as additional MIME headers associated with the SOAPPart and with each attachment.

A SOAPPart

SOAPPart is a wrapper for the XML part of the SOAP message. Nested inside the SOAPPart is a SOAPEnvelope object that itself wraps an empty SOAPHeader and an empty SOAPBody. In the case of a SOAP message with attachments, the SOAPPart has MIME headers, one of which specifies the content type of text/xml. The getSOAPPart() method returns a reference to the SOAPPart element of a SOAP message.

AttachmentParts

When a message has attachments, each is represented by an AttachmentPart. This object contains not only the data embedded within the attachment, but also the MIME headers that specify its type, length, and other attributes. The SOAPMessage created by the default MessageFactory implementation does not have any attachments.

The methods of the SOAPMessage class can be divided into three groups:

- Methods that deal with the MIME headers
- Methods that manage attachments
- Miscellaneous methods that handle the message itself

The getMimeHeaders() method can be used to get a reference to the MimeHeaders object that contains the message-level MIME headers. You can use the methods of this object to add or remove headers as required. The setContentDescription() and getContentDescription() methods are wrappers that allow you to quickly access or set the Content-Description header, although it is not obvious why this header deserves special treatment. In general, application code does not attempt to set either the Content-Type or Content-Length headers, since these are set appropriately by the saveChanges() method (discussed shortly) before the message is transmitted.

The addAttachmentPart() method allows you to add an attachment given as an Attachment-Part object to a SOAP message. There are three methods that you can use to create attachments. The zero-argument createAttachment() method creates an attachment that has no associated data and returns an AttachmentPart object. The content and MIME headers for an attachment created in this way can be set using methods of the AttachmentPart class, described earlier in this chapter. The two-argument variant of this method creates an attachment whose content is supplied by the first argument and whose MIME type is given by the second argument. The MIME type must be compatible with the type of the object itself, and SAAJ implementations may place restrictions on the data types that are handled properly by this method. Refer to the discussion of attachments in Chapter 6 for further information. The final version of this method specifies both the data content and its MIME type using a DataHandler object. This method allows you to include almost any type of data in the attachment, and also lets you determine the way in which it is represented.

The countAttachments( ) method returns the number of attachments in the message. There are two methods that allow you to get access to these attachments. The zero-argument getAttachments( ) method returns an Iterator over the AttachmentPart object for all of the attachments. The other variant of getAttachments( ) returns an Iterator over all of the attachments that have MIME headers that include all of those in the given MimeHeaders object. The removeAllAttachments( ) method removes all of the attachments from the message. Note that there is no way to remove individual attachments.

The final group of SOAPMessage methods deals with the message itself. A SOAPMessage is constructed by building a tree made up of SOAPElements and other node types. This tree is then serialized into XML for transmission, and the appropriate MIME headers are added. The serialization process can be performed by calling the saveChanges( ) method, which stores a copy of the generated XML as part of the SOAPMessage object. Subsequent changes to the node tree or to attachment data or MIME headers invalidates the XML representation and necessitates another call to the saveChanges( ) method. Since serialization is expensive, unnecessary calls to this method should be avoided by first calling saveRequired( ), which returns true only if the XML representation and the node tree are not synchronized.

The writeTo( ) method creates an XML representation of a SOAPMessage and writes it to a given output stream. writeTo( ) uses the saveRequired( ) and saveChanges( ) methods to create the XML if necessary. This method can be useful as a debugging aid, and is also used internally by the SOAPConnection call( ) method to generate the XML that is actually sent to a remote system.

Passed To   javax.xml.messaging.OnewayListener.onMessage( ), javax.xml.messaging.ProviderConnection.send( ), javax.xml.messaging.ReqRespListener.onMessage( ), javax.xml.rpc.handler.soap.SOAPMessageContext.setMessage( ), SOAPConnection.call( )

Returned By   javax.xml.messaging.ReqRespListener.onMessage( ), javax.xml.rpc.handler.soap.SOAPMessageContext.getMessage( ), MessageFactory.createMessage( ), SOAPConnection.call( )

SOAPPart   javax.xml.soap

SAAJ 1.1; JWSDP 1.0, J2EE 1.4

```
public abstract class SOAPPart {
// Public Constructors
    public SOAPPart( );
// Property Accessor Methods (by property name)
    public abstract Iterator getAllMimeHeaders( );
    public abstract javax.xml.transform.Source getContent( ) throws SOAPException;
    public abstract void setContent(javax.xml.transform.Source source) throws SOAPException;
    public String getContentId( );
    public void setContentId( String contentId);
    public String getContentLocation( );
    public void setContentLocation(String contentLocation);
    public abstract SOAPEnvelope getEnvelope( ) throws SOAPException;
// Public Instance Methods
    public abstract void addMimeHeader(String name, String value);
    public abstract Iterator getMatchingMimeHeaders(String[] names);
    public abstract String[] getMimeHeader(String name);
    public abstract Iterator getNonMatchingMimeHeaders(String[] names);
```

```
public abstract void removeAllMimeHeaders( );
public abstract void removeMimeHeader( String header);
public abstract void setMimeHeader(String name, String value);
}
```

SOAPPart is a container that wraps the envelope of a SOAP message. To get a reference to the SOAPPart, use the getSOAPPart( ) method of the containing SOAPMessage. Aside from getEnvelope( ), all of the methods of the SOAPPart interface are concerned with manipulating its associated MIME headers, which are used only if the SOAP message has one or more MIME attachments. Refer to the reference section for AttachmentPart, earlier in this chapter for a description of these methods.

Note that, unlike most interfaces that represent parts of a SOAP message, SOAPPart is not a subinterface of SOAPElement, and therefore does not have methods that allow content to be added to or removed from it. However, you can change the entire content of the SOAPPart by calling the setContent( ) method, which requires an argument of type javax.xml.transform.Source and supplies the XML representation of a complete SOAP message starting from the Envelope tag (but excluding attachments). The message content can be supplied in the form of a DOM tree, a SAX parser stream, or an input stream reading from a file or some other source.

Returned By   SOAPMessage.getSOAPPart( )

Text   javax.xml.soap

SAAJ 1.1; JWSDP 1.0, J2EE 1.4

```
public interface Text extends Node {
// Public Instance Methods
  public abstract boolean isComment( );
}
```

Text is a subinterface of Node that holds the text parts of a SOAP message. A Text node can only be created by using the addTextNode( ) method of SOAPElement, as shown in the following code extract:

```
SOAPElement element = body.addChildElement("BookTitle");
SOAPElement element2 = element.addTextNode("J2ME in a Nutshell");
```

This code creates an element called BookTitle and adds the given text as its value, resulting in the following XML when the message is serialized:

```
<BookTitle>J2ME in a Nutshell</BookTitle>
```

The value returned by the addTextNode( ) method is actually a reference to the SOAPElement beneath which the Text node was added. In the code extract shown previously, therefore, element2 is set to the same value as element. The value of the text associated with a SOAPElement can be obtained by calling getValue( ) on the element itself, rather than by first obtaining a reference to the intervening Text object:

```
// Returns "J2ME in a Nutshell"
String text = element.getValue
```

In fact, there is no direct way to get a reference to the Text element itself. The only way to do this is to use the getChildElements( ) method of the parent SOAPElement and search for a child of type Text:

```
Iterator iter = element.getChildElements;
while (iter.hasNext() {
```

```
        Node node = (Node)iter.next();
        if (node instanceof Text) {
            // This also prints "J2ME in a Nutshell"
            System.out.println("Value of Text node " + node.getValue());
            break;
        }
    }
```

In theory, a Text node may also represent an XML comment, although it is unlikely that a SOAP message would contain one. The isComment() method can be used to detect comments.

Class, Method, and Field Index

The following index allows you to look up a class or interface and find which package it is defined in. It also allows you to look up a method or field and find which class it is defined in. Use it when you want to look up a class but don't know its package, or when you want to look up a method but don't know its class..

addSlot( ): ExtensibleObject
addSlots( ): ExtensibleObject
addSpecificationLink( ): ServiceBinding
addSpecificationLinks( ): ServiceBinding
addTextNode( ): SOAPElement
addUser( ): Organization
addUsers( ): Organization
AND_ALL_KEYS: FindQualifier
Association: javax.xml.registry.infomodel
ASSOCIATION: LifeCycleManager
AttachmentPart: javax.xml.soap
AUDITABLE_EVENT: LifeCycleManager
AuditableEvent: javax.xml.registry.infomodel
AUTHORIZED_NAME_SLOT: Slot

B

BigDecimalHolder: javax.xml.rpc.holders
BigIntegerHolder: javax.xml.rpc.holders
BooleanHolder: javax.xml.rpc.holders
BooleanWrapperHolder: javax.xml.rpc.holders
BulkResponse: javax.xml.registry
BusinessLifeCycleManager: javax.xml.registry
BusinessQueryManager: javax.xml.registry
ByteArrayHolder: javax.xml.rpc.holders
ByteHolder: javax.xml.rpc.holders
ByteWrapperHolder: javax.xml.rpc.holders

C

CalendarHolder: javax.xml.rpc.holders
Call: javax.xml.rpc
call( ): SOAPConnection
CapabilityProfile: javax.xml.registry
CASE_SENSITIVE_MATCH: FindQualifier
cause: JAXRException
Classification: javax.xml.registry.infomodel
CLASSIFICATION: LifeCycleManager
CLASSIFICATION_SCHEME: LifeCycleManager
ClassificationScheme: javax.xml.registry.
    infomodel
clear( ): TypeMappingRegistry
clearContent( ): AttachmentPart
close( ): Connection, ProviderConnection,
    SOAPConnection

COMBINE_CLASSIFICATIONS: FindQualifier
CONCEPT: LifeCycleManager
Concept: javax.xml.registry.infomodel
confirmAssociation( ): BusinessLifeCycleMan-
    ager
Connection: javax.xml.registry
ConnectionFactory: javax.xml.registry
containsProperty( ): MessageContext
countAttachments( ): SOAPMessage
create( ): SOAPElementFactory
createAssociation( ): LifeCycleManager
createAttachmentPart( ): SOAPMessage
createCall( ): Service
createClassification( ): LifeCycleManager
createClassificationScheme( ): LifeCycleMan-
    ager
createConcept( ): LifeCycleManager
createConnection( ): ConnectionFactory,
    ProviderConnectionFactory,
    SOAPConnectionFactory
createDetail( ): SOAPFactory
createElement( ): SOAPFactory
createEmailAddress( ): LifeCycleManager
createExternalIdentifier( ): LifeCycleManager
createExternalLink( ): LifeCycleManager
createExtrinsicObject( ): LifeCycleManager
createFederatedConnection( ): ConnectionFac-
    tory
createInternationalString( ): LifeCycleManager
createKey( ): LifeCycleManager
createLocalizedString( ): LifeCycleManager
createMessage( ): MessageFactory
createMessageFactory( ): ProviderConnection
createName( ): SOAPEnvelope, SOAPFactory
createObject( ): LifeCycleManager
createOrganization( ): LifeCycleManager
createPersonName( ): LifeCycleManager
createPostalAddress( ): LifeCycleManager
createQuery( ): DeclarativeQueryManager
createRegistryPackage( ): LifeCycleManager
createService( ): LifeCycleManager,
    ServiceFactory
createServiceBinding( ): LifeCycleManager
createSlot( ): LifeCycleManager

---

getAreaCode( ): TelephoneNumber

getAssociatedObjects( ): RegistryObject

getAssociations( ): RegistryObject

getAssociationType( ): Association

getAttachments( ): SOAPMessage

getAttributeValue( ): SOAPElement

getAuditTrail( ): RegistryObject

getBody( ): SOAPEnvelope

getBulkResponse( ): RegistryService

getBusinessLifeCycleManager( ): RegistryService

getBusinessQueryManager( ): RegistryService

getCalls( ): Service

getCapabilityLevel( ): CapabilityProfile

getCapabilityProfile( ): RegistryService

getCause( ): JAXRException, SOAPException

getCharsetName( ): LocalizedString

getChildConceptCount( ): Classification-Scheme, Concept

getChildElements( ): SOAPElement

getChildOrganizationCount( ): Organization

getChildOrganizations( ): Organization

getChildrenConcepts( ): ClassificationScheme, Concept

getCity( ): PostalAddress

getClassifications( ): RegistryObject

getClassificationScheme( ): Classification, Concept

getClassifiedObject( ): Classification

getCollection( ): BulkResponse

getConcept( ): Classification

getContent( ): AttachmentPart, SOAPPart

getContentDescription( ): SOAPMessage

getContentId( ): AttachmentPart, SOAPPart

getContentLocation( ): AttachmentPart, SOAPPart

getContentType( ): AttachmentPart

getCountry( ): PostalAddress

getCountryCode( ): TelephoneNumber

getCredentials( ): Connection

getDataHandler( ): AttachmentPart

getDeclarativeQueryManager( ): RegistryService

getDefaultPostalScheme( ): RegistryService

getDefaultTypeMapping( ): TypeMappingRegistry

getDescendantConcepts( ): Classification-Scheme, Concept

getDescendantOrganizations( ): Organization

getDescription( ): RegistryObject

getDeserializer( ): TypeMapping

getDeserializerAs( ): DeserializerFactory

getDetail( ): SOAPFault, SOAPFaultException

getDetailEntries( ): Detail

getElementName( ): SOAPElement

getEmailAddresses( ): User

getEncodingStyle( ): SOAPElement

getEnvelope( ): SOAPPart

getErrorObjectKey( ): RegistryException

getEventType( ): AuditableEvent

getExceptions( ): BulkResponse

getExpiration( ): RegistryEntry

getExtension( ): TelephoneNumber

getExternalIdentifiers( ): RegistryObject

getExternalLinks( ): RegistryObject

getExternalURI( ): ExternalLink

getFault( ): SOAPBody

getFaultActor( ): SOAPFault, SOAPFaultException

getFaultCode( ): SOAPFault, SOAPFaultException

getFaultString( ): SOAPFault, SOAPFaultException

getFirstName( ): PersonName

getFullName( ): PersonName

getHandlerChain( ): HandlerRegistry

getHandlerClass( ): HandlerInfo

getHandlerConfig( ): HandlerInfo

getHandlerRegistry( ): Service

getHeader( ): MimeHeaders, SOAPEnvelope

getHeaders( ): GenericHandler, Handler, HandlerInfo, JAXMServlet

getHttpSession( ): ServletEndpointContext

getId( ): Key

getIdentificationScheme( ): ExternalIdentifier

getKey( ): RegistryObject

getLastName( ): PersonName

getLifeCycleManager( ): RegistryObject

Class Index

removeAllAttachments( ): SOAPMessage

removeAllHeaders( ): MimeHeaders

removeAllMimeHeaders( ): AttachmentPart, SOAPPart

removeAllParameters( ): Call

removeAssociation( ): RegistryObject

removeAssociations( ): RegistryObject

removeAttribute( ): SOAPElement

removeChildConcept( ): ClassificationScheme, Concept

removeChildConcepts( ): ClassificationScheme, Concept

removeChildOrganization( ): Organization

removeChildOrganizations( ): Organization

removeClassification( ): RegistryObject

removeClassifications( ): RegistryObject

removeDeserializer( ): TypeMapping

removeExternalIdentifier( ): RegistryObject

removeExternalIdentifiers( ): RegistryObject

removeExternalLink( ): RegistryObject

removeExternalLinks( ): RegistryObject

removeHeader( ): MimeHeaders

removeLocalizedString( ): InternationalString

removeLocalizedStrings( ): InternationalString

removeMimeHeader( ): AttachmentPart, SOAPPart

removeNamespaceDeclaration( ): SOAPElement

removeProperty( ): Call, MessageContext

removeRegistryObject( ): RegistryPackage

removeRegistryObjects( ): RegistryPackage

removeSerializer( ): TypeMapping

removeService( ): Organization

removeServiceBinding( ): Service

removeServiceBindings( ): Service

removeServices( ): Organization

removeSlot( ): ExtensibleObject

removeSlots( ): ExtensibleObject

removeSpecificationLink( ): ServiceBinding

removeSpecificationLinks( ): ServiceBinding

removeTypeMapping( ): TypeMappingRegistry

removeUser( ): Organization

removeUsers( ): Organization

ReqRespListener: javax.xml.messaging

S

saveAssociations( ): BusinessLifeCycleManager

saveChanges( ): SOAPMessage

saveClassificationSchemes( ): BusinessLifeCycleManager

saveConcepts( ): BusinessLifeCycleManager

SaveException: javax.xml.registry

saveObjects( ): LifeCycleManager

saveOrganizations( ): BusinessLifeCycleManager

saveRequired( ): SOAPMessage

saveServiceBindings( ): BusinessLifeCycleManager

saveServices( ): BusinessLifeCycleManager

send( ): ProviderConnection

SerializationContext: javax.xml.rpc.encoding

Serializer: javax.xml.rpc.encoding

SerializerFactory: javax.xml.rpc.encoding

Service: javax.xml.registry.infomodel, javax.xml.rpc

SERVICE: LifeCycleManager

SERVICE_BINDING: LifeCycleManager

SERVICE_SUBSET: FindQualifier

ServiceBinding: javax.xml.registry.infomodel

ServiceException: javax.xml.rpc

ServiceFactory: javax.xml.rpc

SERVICEFACTORY_PROPERTY: ServiceFactory

ServiceLifecycle: javax.xml.rpc.server

ServletEndpointContext: javax.xml.rpc.server

SESSION_MAINTAIN_PROPERTY: Call, Stub

setAccessURI( ): ServiceBinding

setActor( ): SOAPHeaderElement

setAddress( ): EmailAddress

setAreaCode( ): TelephoneNumber

setAssociations( ): RegistryObject

setAssociationType( ): Association

setCharsetName( ): LocalizedString

setCity( ): PostalAddress

setClassifications( ): RegistryObject

setClassificationScheme( ): Classification

setClassifiedObject( ): Classification

setConcept( ): Classification

setContent( ): AttachmentPart, SOAPPart

Class Index

V

value: BigDecimalHolder, BigIntegerHolder, BooleanHolder, BooleanWrapperHolder, ByteArrayHolder, ByteHolder, ByteWrapperHolder, CalendarHolder, DoubleHolder, DoubleWrapperHolder, FloatHolder, FloatWrapperHolder, IntegerWrapperHolder, IntHolder, LongHolder, LongWrapperHolder, ObjectHolder, QNameHolder, ShortHolder, ShortWrapperHolder, StringHolder

VALUE_TYPE_EMBEDDED_PATH: ClassificationScheme

VALUE_TYPE_NON_UNIQUE: ClassificationScheme

VALUE_TYPE_UNIQUE: ClassificationScheme

valueOf( ): QName

Versionable: javax.xml.registry.infomodel

VERSIONABLE: LifeCycleManager

W

writeTo( ): SOAPMessage

X

XMLType: javax.xml.rpc.encoding

XSD_BASE64: XMLType

XSD_BOOLEAN: XMLType

XSD_BYTE: XMLType

XSD_DATETIME: XMLType

XSD_DECIMAL: XMLType

XSD_DOUBLE: XMLType

XSD_FLOAT: XMLType

XSD_HEXBINARY: XMLType

XSD_INT: XMLType

XSD_INTEGER: XMLType

XSD_LONG: XMLType

XSD_QNAME: XMLType

XSD_SHORT: XMLType

XSD_STRING: XMLType

Class Index

III

Appendix

Part III of this book consists of a single chapter containing listings of the WSDL files for the JAX-RPC based book web service used in Chapter 2, Chapter 5, and Chapter 6. A glance at these files will probably be enough to convince you that the availability of tools that convert between WSDL and Java interfaces (and therefore relieve of the task of decoding WSDL or creating files manually) is a very good thing!

Appendix: WSDL Files for the Example Source Code

This appendix contains the full listing of the WSDL files for some of the web services developed in this book.

WSDL File for the Book Web Service

This WSDL file corresponds to the book web service used in Chapter 2, Chapter 5, and Chapter 6.

```
<?xml version="1.0" encoding="UTF-8"?>

<definitions name="BookService"
    targetNamespace="urn:jwsnut.chapter2.bookservice/wsdl/BookQuery"
    xmlns:tns="urn:jwsnut.chapter2.bookservice/wsdl/BookQuery"
    xmlns="http://schemas.xmlsoap.org/wsdl/"
    xmlns:soap="http://schemas.xmlsoap.org/wsdl/soap/"
    xmlns:xsd="http://www.w3.org/2001/XMLSchema"
    xmlns:ns2="urn:jwsnut.chapter2.bookservice/types/BookQuery"
    xmlns:ns3="http://java.sun.com/jax-rpc-ri/internal">
  <types>
    <schema
      targetNamespace="urn:jwsnut.chapter2.bookservice/types/BookQuery"
      xmlns:xsi="http://www.w3.org/2001/XMLSchema-instance"
      xmlns:tns="urn:jwsnut.chapter2.bookservice/types/BookQuery"
      xmlns:soap-enc="http://schemas.xmlsoap.org/soap/encoding/"
      xmlns:wsdl="http://schemas.xmlsoap.org/wsdl/"
      xmlns="http://www.w3.org/2001/XMLSchema">
      <import namespace="http://schemas.xmlsoap.org/soap/encoding/"/>
      <import namespace="http://java.sun.com/jax-rpc-ri/internal"/>
      <complexType name="ArrayOfBookInfo">
        <complexContent>
          <restriction base="soap-enc:Array">
```

```
              <attribute ref="soap-enc:arrayType"
                         wsdl:arrayType="tns:BookInfo[]"/>
        </restriction>
      </complexContent>
    </complexType>
    <complexType name="BookInfo">
      <sequence>
        <element name="author" type="string"/>
        <element name="editor" type="string"/>
        <element name="price" type="double"/>
        <element name="title" type="string"/>
      </sequence>
    </complexType>
    <complexType name="BookServiceException">
      <sequence>
        <element name="message" type="string"/>
      </sequence>
    </complexType>
  </schema>
  <schema targetNamespace="http://java.sun.com/jax-rpc-ri/internal"
        xmlns:xsi="http://www.w3.org/2001/XMLSchema-instance"
        xmlns:tns="http://java.sun.com/jax-rpc-ri/internal"
        xmlns:soap-enc="http://schemas.xmlsoap.org/soap/encoding/"
        xmlns:wsdl="http://schemas.xmlsoap.org/wsdl/"
        xmlns="http://www.w3.org/2001/XMLSchema">
    <import namespace="http://schemas.xmlsoap.org/soap/encoding/"/>
    <import namespace="urn:jwsnut.chapter2.bookservice/types/BookQuery"/>
    <complexType name="hashMap">
      <complexContent>
        <extension base="tns:map">
          <sequence/>
        </extension>
      </complexContent>
    </complexType>
    <complexType name="map">
      <complexContent>
        <restriction base="soap-enc:Array">
          <attribute ref="soap-enc:arrayType"
                     wsdl:arrayType="tns:mapEntry[]"/>
        </restriction>
      </complexContent>
    </complexType>
    <complexType name="mapEntry">
      <sequence>
        <element name="key" type="anyType"/>
        <element name="value" type="anyType"/>
      </sequence>
    </complexType>
  </schema>
</types>
<message name="BookQuery_getAuthor">
  <part name="String_1" type="xsd:string"/>
</message>
<message name="BookQuery_getAuthorResponse">
```

```
    <part name="result" type="xsd:string"/>
</message>
<message name="BookQuery_getBookCount"/>
<message name="BookQuery_getBookCountResponse">
  <part name="result" type="xsd:int"/>
</message>
<message name="BookQuery_getBookInfo"/>
<message name="BookQuery_getBookInfoResponse">
  <part name="result" type="ns2:ArrayOfBookInfo"/>
</message>
<message name="BookQuery_getBookMap"/>
<message name="BookQuery_getBookMapResponse">
  <part name="result" type="ns3:hashMap"/>
</message>
<message name="BookQuery_getEditor">
  <part name="String_1" type="xsd:string"/>
</message>
<message name="BookQuery_getEditorResponse">
  <part name="result" type="xsd:string"/>
</message>
<message name="BookQuery_getPrice">
  <part name="String_1" type="xsd:string"/>
</message>
<message name="BookQuery_getPriceResponse">
  <part name="result" type="xsd:double"/>
</message>
<message name="BookServiceException">
  <part name="BookServiceException" type="ns2:BookServiceException"/>
</message>
<portType name="BookQuery">
  <operation name="getAuthor" parameterOrder="String_1">
    <input message="tns:BookQuery_getAuthor"/>
    <output message="tns:BookQuery_getAuthorResponse"/>
  </operation>
  <operation name="getBookCount" parameterOrder="">
    <input message="tns:BookQuery_getBookCount"/>
    <output message="tns:BookQuery_getBookCountResponse"/>
  </operation>
  <operation name="getBookInfo" parameterOrder="">
    <input message="tns:BookQuery_getBookInfo"/>
    <output message="tns:BookQuery_getBookInfoResponse"/>
  </operation>
  <operation name="getBookMap" parameterOrder="">
    <input message="tns:BookQuery_getBookMap"/>
    <output message="tns:BookQuery_getBookMapResponse"/>
  </operation>
  <operation name="getEditor" parameterOrder="String_1">
    <input message="tns:BookQuery_getEditor"/>
    <output message="tns:BookQuery_getEditorResponse"/>
  </operation>
  <operation name="getPrice" parameterOrder="String_1">
    <input message="tns:BookQuery_getPrice"/>
    <output message="tns:BookQuery_getPriceResponse"/>
```

```
        <fault name="BookServiceException"
              message="tns:BookServiceException"/>
    </operation>
</portType>
<binding name="BookQueryBinding" type="tns:BookQuery">
    <operation name="getAuthor">
      <input>
        <soap:body encodingStyle="http://schemas.xmlsoap.org/soap/encoding/"
                   use="encoded"
          namespace="urn:jwsnut.chapter2.bookservice/wsdl/BookQuery"/>
      </input>
      <output>
        <soap:body encodingStyle="http://schemas.xmlsoap.org/soap/encoding/"
                   use="encoded"
          namespace="urn:jwsnut.chapter2.bookservice/wsdl/BookQuery"/>
      </output>
      <soap:operation soapAction=""/>
    </operation>
    <operation name="getBookCount">
      <input>
        <soap:body encodingStyle="http://schemas.xmlsoap.org/soap/encoding/"
                   use="encoded"
          namespace="urn:jwsnut.chapter2.bookservice/wsdl/BookQuery"/>
      </input>
      <output>
        <soap:body encodingStyle="http://schemas.xmlsoap.org/soap/encoding/"
                   use="encoded"
          namespace="urn:jwsnut.chapter2.bookservice/wsdl/BookQuery"/>
      </output>
      <soap:operation soapAction=""/>
    </operation>
    <operation name="getBookInfo">
      <input>
        <soap:body encodingStyle="http://schemas.xmlsoap.org/soap/encoding/"
                   use="encoded"
           namespace="urn:jwsnut.chapter2.bookservice/wsdl/BookQuery"/>
      </input>
      <output>
        <soap:body encodingStyle="http://schemas.xmlsoap.org/soap/encoding/"
                   use="encoded"
           namespace="urn:jwsnut.chapter2.bookservice/wsdl/BookQuery"/>
                                                      </output>
      <soap:operation soapAction=""/>
    </operation>
    <operation name="getBookMap">
      <input>
        <soap:body encodingStyle="http://schemas.xmlsoap.org/soap/encoding/"
                   use="encoded"
          namespace="urn:jwsnut.chapter2.bookservice/wsdl/BookQuery"/>
      </input>
      <output>
        <soap:body encodingStyle="http://schemas.xmlsoap.org/soap/encoding/"
                   use="encoded"
          namespace="urn:jwsnut.chapter2.bookservice/wsdl/BookQuery"/>
```

```
      </output>
      <soap:operation soapAction=""/>
    </operation>
    <operation name="getEditor">
      <input>
        <soap:body encodingStyle="http://schemas.xmlsoap.org/soap/encoding/"
                   use="encoded"
          namespace="urn:jwsnut.chapter2.bookservice/wsdl/BookQuery"/>
      </input>
      <output>
        <soap:body encodingStyle="http://schemas.xmlsoap.org/soap/encoding/"
                   use="encoded"
          namespace="urn:jwsnut.chapter2.bookservice/wsdl/BookQuery"/>
      </output>
      <soap:operation soapAction=""/>
    </operation>
    <operation name="getPrice">
      <input>
        <soap:body encodingStyle="http://schemas.xmlsoap.org/soap/encoding/"
                   use="encoded"
          namespace="urn:jwsnut.chapter2.bookservice/wsdl/BookQuery"/>
      </input>
      <output>
        <soap:body encodingStyle="http://schemas.xmlsoap.org/soap/encoding/"
                   use="encoded"
          namespace="urn:jwsnut.chapter2.bookservice/wsdl/BookQuery"/>
      </output>
      <fault name="BookServiceException">
        <soap:fault encodingStyle=
            "http://schemas.xmlsoap.org/soap/encoding/" use="encoded"
            namespace="urn:jwsnut.chapter2.bookservice/wsdl/BookQuery"/>
      </fault>
      <soap:operation soapAction=""/>
    </operation>
    <soap:binding transport="http://schemas.xmlsoap.org/soap/http"
                  style="rpc"/>
                  </binding>
  <service name="BookService">
    <port name="BookQueryPort" binding="tns:BookQueryBinding">
      <soap:address location="REPLACE_WITH_ACTUAL_URL"/>
    </port>
  </service>
</definitions>
```

WSDL File for the Document-Style Book Web Service

This WSDL file describes a document-style variant of the book web service. It forms the basis of the example in "JAX-RPC support for document-style operations" in Chapter 6.

```xml
<?xml version="1.0" encoding="UTF-8"?>
<definitions xmlns="http://schemas.xmlsoap.org/wsdl/"
    xmlns:tns="urn:jwsnut.chapter6.docbookservice/wsdl/DocBookQuery"
    xmlns:typesns="urn:jwsnut.chapter6.docbookservice/types/DocBookQuery"
    xmlns:soap="http://schemas.xmlsoap.org/wsdl/soap/"
    xmlns:xsd="http://www.w3.org/2001/XMLSchema"
    name="DocBookQuery"
    targetNamespace="urn:jwsnut.chapter6.docbookservice/wsdl/DocBookQuery">
  <types>
    <schema xmlns="http://www.w3.org/2001/XMLSchema"
            xmlns:xsi="http://www.w3.org/2001/XMLSchema-instance"
            xmlns:soap-enc="http://schemas.xmlsoap.org/soap/encoding/"
            xmlns:wsdl="http://schemas.xmlsoap.org/wsdl/"
            targetNamespace=
              "urn:jwsnut.chapter6.docbookservice/types/DocBookQuery">
      <element name="BookCountRequest">
        <complexType>
          <sequence/>
        </complexType>
      </element>
      <element name="BookCountResponse">
        <complexType>
          <sequence>
            <element name="result" type="xsd:int"/>
          </sequence>
        </complexType>
      </element>
      <element name="BookTitleRequest">
        <complexType>
          <sequence>
            <element name="index" type="xsd:int"/>
          </sequence>
        </complexType>
      </element>
      <element name="BookTitleResponse">
        <complexType>
          <sequence>
            <element name="result" type="xsd:string"/>
          </sequence>
        </complexType>
      </element>
      <element name="BookAuthorRequest">
        <complexType>
          <sequence>
            <element name="title" type="xsd:string"/>
          </sequence>
        </complexType>
      </element>
      <element name="BookAuthorResponse">
        <complexType>
          <sequence>
            <element name="author" type="xsd:string"/>
          </sequence>
        </complexType>
```

```
      </element>
      <element name="BookInfoRequest">
        <complexType>
          <sequence>
            <element name="title" type="xsd:string"/>
          </sequence>
        </complexType>
      </element>
      <element name="BookInfo">
        <complexType>
          <sequence>
            <element name="title" type="xsd:string"/>
            <element name="author" type="xsd:string"/>
            <element name="editor" type="xsd:string"/>
            <element name="price" type="xsd:double"/>
            <element name="stock" type="xsd:int"/>
          </sequence>
        </complexType>
      </element>
      <element name="StockInfoRequest">
        <complexType>
          <sequence>
            <element name="title" type="xsd:string"/>
          </sequence>
        </complexType>
      </element>
      <element name="StockInfoResponse">
        <complexType>
          <sequence>
            <element name="stock" type="xsd:nonNegativeInteger"/>
          </sequence>
        </complexType>
      </element>
    </schema>
  </types>
  <message name="DocBookQuery_getBookCount">
    <part name="body" element="typesns:BookCountRequest"/>
  </message>
  <message name="DocBookQuery_getBookCountResponse">
    <part name="result" element="typesns:BookCountResponse"/>
  </message>
  <message name="DocBookQuery_getBookTitle">
    <part name="body" element="typesns:BookTitleRequest"/>
  </message>
  <message name="DocBookQuery_getBookTitleResponse">
    <part name="result" element="typesns:BookTitleResponse"/>
  </message>
  <message name="DocBookQuery_getBookAuthor">
    <part name="title" element="typesns:BookAuthorRequest"/>
  </message>
  <message name="DocBookQuery_getBookAuthorResponse">
    <part name="author" element="typesns:BookAuthorResponse"/>
  </message>
  <message name="DocBookQuery_getBookInfo">
```

```xml
      <part name="title" element="typesns:BookInfoRequest"/>
    </message>
    <message name="DocBookQuery_getBookInfoResponse">
      <part name="result" element="typesns:BookInfo"/>
    </message>
    <message name="DocBookQuery_getStockInfo">
      <part name="title" element="typesns:StockInfoRequest"/>
    </message>
    <message name="DocBookQuery_getStockInfoResponse">
      <part name="result" element="typesns:StockInfoResponse"/>
    </message>
    <portType name="DocBookQuery">
      <operation name="getBookCount" parameterOrder="">
        <input message="tns:DocBookQuery_getBookCount"/>
        <output message="tns:DocBookQuery_getBookCountResponse"/>
      </operation>
      <operation name="getBookTitle" parameterOrder="index">
        <input message="tns:DocBookQuery_getBookTitle"/>
        <output message="tns:DocBookQuery_getBookTitleResponse"/>
      </operation>
      <operation name="getBookAuthor" parameterOrder="title author">
        <input message="tns:DocBookQuery_getBookAuthor"/>
        <output message="tns:DocBookQuery_getBookAuthorResponse"/>
      </operation>
      <operation name="getBookInfo" parameterOrder="title result">
        <input message="tns:DocBookQuery_getBookInfo"/>
        <output message="tns:DocBookQuery_getBookInfoResponse"/>
      </operation>
      <operation name="getStockInfo" parameterOrder="title">
        <input message="tns:DocBookQuery_getStockInfo"/>
        <output message="tns:DocBookQuery_getStockInfoResponse"/>
      </operation>
    </portType>
    <binding name="DocBookQueryBinding" type="tns:DocBookQuery">
      <soap:binding transport="http://schemas.xmlsoap.org/soap/http"
                    style="document"/>
      <operation name="getBookCount">
        <soap:operation soapAction=""/>
        <input>
          <soap:body use="literal"
            namespace="urn:jwsnut.chapter6.docbookservice/wsdl/DocBookQuery"/>
        </input>
        <output>
          <soap:body use="literal" namespace="urn:jwsnut.chapter6.
            docbookservice/wsdl/DocBookQuery"/>
        </output>
      </operation>
      <operation name="getBookTitle">
        <soap:operation soapAction=""/>
        <input>
          <soap:body use="literal" namespace="urn:jwsnut.chapter6.
            docbookservice/wsdl/DocBookQuery"/>
        </input>
        <output>
```

```
          <soap:body use="literal" namespace="urn:jwsnut.chapter6.
             docbookservice/wsdl/DocBookQuery"/>
        </output>
      </operation>
      <operation name="getBookAuthor">
        <soap:operation soapAction=""/>
        <input>
          <soap:body use="literal" namespace="urn:jwsnut.chapter6.
             docbookservice/wsdl/DocBookQuery"/>
        </input>
        <output>
          <soap:body use="literal" namespace="urn:jwsnut.chapter6.
             docbookservice/wsdl/DocBookQuery"/>
        </output>
      </operation>
      <operation name="getBookInfo">
        <soap:operation soapAction=""/>
        <input>
          <soap:body use="literal" namespace="urn:jwsnut.chapter6.
docbookservice/wsdl/DocBookQuery"/>
        </input>
        <output>
          <soap:body use="literal" namespace="urn:jwsnut.chapter6.
             docbookservice/wsdl/DocBookQuery"/>
        </output>
      </operation>
      <operation name="getStockInfo">
        <soap:operation soapAction=""/>
        <input>
          <soap:body use="literal" namespace="urn:jwsnut.chapter6.
             docbookservice/wsdl/DocBookQuery"/>
        </input>
        <output>
          <soap:body use="literal" namespace="urn:jwsnut.chapter6.
             docbookservice/wsdl/DocBookQuery"/>
        </output>
      </operation>
    </binding>
    <service name="DocBookService">
      <port name="DocBookQueryPort" binding="tns:DocBookQueryBinding">
        <soap:address location="http://localhost:8080/DocBooks/DocBookQuery"/>
      </port>
    </service>
</definitions>
```

Index

Symbols

We'd like to hear your suggestions for improving our indexes. Send email to *index@oreilly.com*.

W

W3C (World Wide Web
    Consortium), 3
wait( ) method
    doGet( ) method and, 174
WAR files, 63
    book web service, 64
    created by wsdeploy, 444–445
    creating for J2EE 1.4
        platform, 65–69
        required files, 65
    creating for JWSDP, 70–72
    deployable
        creating for JWSDP, 72–75
    deployed to J2EE 1.4 platform and to
        a web container hosting the
        JWSDP reference
        implementation, 65
    deploying, 76–78
    deploying to J2EE 1.4 platform, 70
    packaging web service containing
        document-style
        operations, 292
    portable, 64
WDSL
    documents and port elements, 238
web archive files (see WAR files)
web containers (see servlets)
web server
    enabling HTTPS, 154
web service APIs
    JAXM (see JAXM), 12
    JAXR (see JAXR), 12
    JAX-RPC (see JAX-RPC), 12
    SAAJ (see SAAJ), 12
    WSDL (see WSDL), 11
Web Service Description Language (see
    WSDL)
web service endpoint interface
    getting a stub for, 239
    rules, 44
web services, 3–7
    adding protected URLs to, 151–152
    clients and servers (JAX-
        RPC), 20–23
    client-side view, 241
    containing document-style
        operations
        packaging, 292–294
    creating clients from a WSDL
        file, 234

defined, 4
deployed on J2EE 1.4 platform, 62
deployment and testing, 38
describing and discovering, 10–11
discovered at runtime (see DII)
document-style, 282
document-style operations and JAX-
    RPC summary, 286
EJBs, 78–86
examples, 4, 12–17
full listing of WSDL files, 605–613
mapping
    (see also binding), 221
    to more than one protocol, 221
profiles, 9
references for servlets and EJBs, 268
remote procedure call–based (see
    JAX-RPC)
remote procedure calls (see JAX-
    RPC)
security for, 150
servlet-hosted
    deploying, 63–65
session beans (see session beans)
standards, 10
tools and configuration
    files, 427–459
versus screen scraping, 7
writing a client with only a WSDL
    definition, 237
(see also JAX-RPC)
(see also WSDL)
Web Services Architecture document, 3
Web Services Interoperability (WS-I)
    profile, 9
web-package (Ant buildfile target), 39
web-package target (Ant buildfile), 72
webservice-description element in
    webservices.xml file, 68
webservice-description element
    (webservices.xml file), 455
webServices element (jaxrpc-ri.xml
    file), 74
webServices element (wsdeploy
    configuration file), 441
webservicesclient.xml file
    adding a web service reference to
        JNDI environment, 262
    jaxrpc-mapping-file element, 263
    service-interface element, 263
    service-ref element, 263

About the Author

Kim Topley is a freelance Java developer with his own consulting company, based near London, England. By day, he develops Java applications for a variety of prominent companies in the financial and telecommunications marketplaces. He spends most evenings and weekends keeping abreast of the latest developments in the Java world by reading or writing about aspects of Java that he finds topical or interesting. Out of these long nights have come three other books: *J2ME in a Nutshell* (O'Reilly), and two editions of *Core JFC* and *Core Swing: Advanced Programming* (Prentice-Hall). Prior to being caught up with the Java phenomenon, Kim was a Unix kernel developer; even further back, he created microcode for mainframe computers. Kim has a B.A. degree in mathematics from the University of Cambridge, England.

When he's not working, Kim enjoys playing golf (badly, unfortunately), traveling abroad with his family, and flying Microsoft Flight Simulator with his son Andrew, contesting periodic flight challenges to prove who is the better virtual pilot. He is currently in second place and extremely proud of it. In September 2002, Kim landed a Boeing 747-400 at New York's John F. Kennedy airport (while in reality sitting in a British Airways full-motion simulator at London Heathrow) without losing any passengers.

Colophon

Our look is the result of reader comments, our own experimentation, and feedback from distribution channels. Distinctive covers complement our distinctive approach to technical topics, breathing personality and life into potentially dry subjects.

The animal on the cover of *Java Web Services in a Nutshell* is a European ibex. The animal, which is also known as the Alpine ibex, is a medium-sized mountain goat that can grow to 70 inches as an adult. It has very muscular legs, which allow it to move easily about the mountains in which it lives. Its coat is brown; it is a darker shade of brown in the winter months, but the color becomes lighter during the summer. The major defining characteristic of the ibex is its long horns, which grow up and then curl back slightly. The male horns, which are typically about 40 inches in length, are much longer than the female horns, which are only about 14 inches in length. The ibex eats mostly greens such as grass and plant leaves. The European ibex primarily lives in the Alps; over the spring and summer, it continuously moves up to higher altitudes, looking for more grazing land. Females and males do not interact except during mating season.

Mary Brady was the production editor and the copyeditor for *Java Web Services in a Nutshell*. Genevieve d'Entremont was the proofreader. Colleen Gorman and Claire Cloutier provided quality control. Derek Di Matteo, Darren Kelly, Linley Dolby, and Reg Aubry provided production support. Julie Hawks wrote the index.

Hanna Dyer designed the cover of this book, based on a series design by Edie Freedman. The cover image is a 19th-century engraving from the Dover Pictorial Archive. Emma Colby produced the cover layout with QuarkXPress 4.1 using Adobe's ITC Garamond font.

Ellie Volckhausen and David Futato designed the interior layout, based on a series design by David Futato. This book was converted by Andrew Savikas to FrameMaker 5.5.6 with a format conversion tool created by Erik Ray, Jason McIntosh, Neil Walls, and Mike Sierra that uses Perl and XML technologies. The text font is Linotype Birka; the heading font is Adobe Myriad Condensed; and the code font is LucasFont's TheSans Mono Condensed. The illustrations that appear in the book were produced by Robert Romano and Jessamyn Read using Macromedia FreeHand 9 and Adobe Photoshop 6. This colophon was written by Mary Brady.

Other Titles Available from O'Reilly

Java

Java Performance Tuning, 2nd Edition

By Jack Shirazi
2nd Edition January 2003
588 pages, ISBN 0-596-00377-3

Significantly revised and expanded, this second edition not only covers Java 1.4, but adds new coverage of JDBC, NIO, Servlets, EJB and JavaServer Pages. The book remains a valuable resource for teaching developers how to create a tuning strategy, how to use profiling tools to understand a program's behavior, and how to avoid performance penalties from inefficient code, making them more efficient and effective. The result is code that's robust, maintainable and fast!

Java Security, 2nd Edition

By Scott Oaks
2nd Edition May 2001
618 pages, ISBN 0-596-00157-6

The second edition focuses on the platform features of Java that provide security—the class loader, bytecode verifier, and security manager—and recent additions to Java that enhance this security model: digital signatures, security providers, and the access controller. The book covers in depth the security model of Java 2, version 1.3, including the two new security APIs: JAAS and JSSE.

Java Database Best Practices

By George Reese
1st Edition June 2003
304 pages, ISBN 0-596-00522-9

Java Database Best Practices rescues developers from having to slog through books on each of the various APIs before they figure out which method to use! This guide introduces each of the dominant APIs, explores the methodology and design components that use those APIs, and then offers practices most appropriate for different types and makes of databases, and different types of applications.

Java RMI

By William Grosso
1st Edition November 2001
576 pages, ISBN 1-56592-452-5

Enterprise Java developers, especially those working with Enterprise JavaBeans, and Jini, need to understand RMI technology in order to write today's complex, distributed applications. O'Reilly's *Java RMI* thoroughly explores and explains this powerful but often overlooked technology. Included is a wealth of real-world examples that developers can implement and customize.

Java Data Objects

By David Jordan & Craig Russell
1st Edition April 2003
384 pages, ISBN 0-596-00276-9

This book, written by the JDO Specification Lead and one of the key contributors to the JDO Specification, is the definitive work on the JDO API. It gives you a thorough introduction to JDO, starting with a simple application that demonstrates many of JDO's capabilities. It shows you how to make classes persistent, how JDO maps persistent classes to the database, how to configure JDO at runtime, how to perform transactions, and how to make queries.

Java Swing, 2nd Edition

By Marc Loy, Robert Eckstein, David Wood, James Elliott & Brian Cole
2nd Edition November 2002
1278 pages, ISBN 0-596-00408-7

This second edition of *Java Swing* thoroughly covers all the features available in Java 2 SDK 1.3 and 1.4. More than simply a reference, this new edition takes a practical approach. It is a book by developers for developers, with hundreds of useful examples, from beginning level to advanced, covering every component available in Swing. Whether you're a seasoned Java developer or just trying to find out what Java can do, you'll find *Java Swing*, 2nd edition an indispensable guide.

O'REILLY®

To order: *800-998-9938* • *order@oreilly.com* • *www.oreilly.com*
Online editions of most O'Reilly titles are available by subscription at *safari.oreilly.com*
Also available at most retail and online bookstores.

Java

Java Extreme Programming Cookbook

By Eric M. Burke & Brian M. Coyner
1st Edition March 2003
288 pages, ISBN0-596-00387-0

Brimming with over 100 "recipes" for getting down to business and actually doing XP, the *Java Extreme Programming Cookbook* doesn't try to "sell" you on XP; it succinctly documents the most important features of popular open source tools for XP in Java—including Ant, Junit, HttpUnit, Cactus, Tomcat, XDoclet—and then digs right in, providing recipes for implementing the tools in real-world environments.

Java Enterprise Best Practices

By The O'Reilly Java Authors,
edited by Robert Eckstein
1st Edition December 2002
288 pages, ISBN 0-596-00384-6

This book is for intermediate and advanced Java developers, the ones who have been around the block enough times to understand just how complex—and unruly—an enterprise system can get. Each chapter in this collection contains several rules that provide insight into the "best practices" for creating and maintaining projects using the Java Enterprise APIs. Written by the world's leading Java experts, this book covers JDBC, RMI/-CORBA, Servlets, JavaServer Pages and custom tag libraries, XML, Internationalization, JavaMail, Enterprise JavaBeans, and performance tuning.

Java Cookbook

By Ian Darwin
1st Edition June 2001
882 pages, ISBN 0-59600-170-3

This book offers Java developers short, focused pieces of code that are easy to incorporate into other programs. The idea is to focus on things that are useful, tricky, or both. The book's code segments cover all of the dominant APIs and many specialized APIs and should serve as a great "jumping-off place" for Java developers who want to get started in areas outside their specialization.

Learning Java, 2nd Edition

By Pat Niemeyer &
Jonathan Knudsen
2nd Edition June 2002
832 pages, ISBN 0-596-00285-8

This new edition of *Learning Java* comprehensively addresses important topics such as web applications, servlets, and XML. It provides full coverage of all Java 1.4 language features including assertions and exception chaining as well as new APIs such as regular expressions and NIO, the new I/O package. New Swing features and components are described along with updated coverage of the JavaBeans component architecture using the open source NetBeans IDE the latest information about Applets and the Java Plug-in for all major browsers.

Mac OS X for Java Geeks

By Will Iverson
1st Edition April 2003
304 pages, ISBN 0-596-00400-1

Mac OS X for Java Geeks delivers a complete and detailed look at the OS X platform for Java development. Based on the new 1.4 JDK and the 10.2 release of Mac OS X from Apple Computer, this is the most thorough guide available for both new and experienced Java developers who want to create cross-platform applications that take advantage of Mac OS X's unique functionality.

Java Management Extensions

By J. Steven Perry
1st Edition June 2002
312 pages, ISBN 0-596-00245-9

Java Management Extensions is a practical, hands-on guide to using the JMX APIs. This one-of-a kind book is a complete treatment of the JMX architecture (both the instrumentation level and the agent level), and it's loaded with real-world examples for implementing Management Extensions. It also contains useful information at the higher level about JMX (the "big picture") to help technical managers and architects who are evaluating various application management approaches and are considering JMX.

O'REILLY®

To order: *800-998-9938* • *order@oreilly.com* • *www.oreilly.com*
Online editions of most O'Reilly titles are available by subscription at *safari.oreilly.com*
Also available at most retail and online bookstores.

Java

Java Servlet Programming, 2nd Edition

By Jason Hunter with
William Crawford
2nd Edition April 2001
780 pages, ISBN 0-596-00040-5

The second edition of this popular book has been completely
updated to add the new features of the Java Servlet
API Version 2.2, and new chapters on servlet security and advanced communication. In addition to complete coverage of the 2.2 specification, we have included bonus material on the new 2.3 version of the specification.

Java & XML, 2nd Edition

By Brett McLaughlin
2nd Edition September 2001
528 pages, ISBN 0-596-000197-5

New chapters on Advanced SAX, Advanced DOM, SOAP, and data binding, as well as new examples throughout, bring the second edition of *Java & XML* thoroughly up to date. Except for a concise introduction to XML basics, the book focuses entirely on using XML from Java applications. It's a worthy companion for Java developers working with XML or involved in messaging, web services, or the new peer-to-peer movement.

JavaServer Pages, 2nd Edition

By Hans Bergsten
2nd Edition August 2002
712 pages, ISBN 0-596-00317-X

Filled with useful examples and the depth, clarity, and attention to detail that made the first edition so popular with web developers, *JavaServer Pages*, 2nd Edition is completely revised and updated to cover the substantial changes in the 1.2 version of the JSP specifications, and includes coverage of the new JSTL Tag libraries—an eagerly anticipated standard set of JSP elements for the tasks needed in most JSP applications, as well as thorough coverage of Custom Tag Libraries.

J2EE Design Patterns

By William C.R. Crawford
& Jonathan Kaplan
1st Edition July 2003 (est.)
352 pages (est.), ISBN 0-596-00427-3

Crawford and Kaplan's *J2EE Design Patterns* takes a different approach than just simply presenting another catalog of design patterns. The authors broaden the scope by discussing ways to choose design patterns when building an enterprise application from scratch, looking closely at the real world tradeoffs that Java developers must weigh when architecting their applications. They also extend design patterns into areas not covered in other books, presenting original patterns for data modeling, transaction/process modeling, and interoperability. This design pattern book breaks the mold.

Enterprise JavaBeans, 3rd Edition

By Richard Monson-Haefel
3rd Edition September 2001
592 pages, ISBN 0-596-00226-2

Enterprise JavaBeans has been thoroughly updated for the new EJB Specification. Important changes in Version 2.0 include a completely new CMP (container-managed persistence) model that allows for much more complex business function modeling; local interfaces that will significantly improve performance of EJB applications; and the "message driven bean," an entirely new kind of Java bean based on asynchronous messaging and the Java Message Service.

Java Message Service

By Richard Monson-Haefel &
David Chappell
1st Edition December 2000
238 pages, ISBN 0-596-00068-5

This book is a thorough introduction to Java Message Service (JMS) from Sun Microsystems. It shows how to build applications using the point-to-point and publish-and-subscribe models; use features like transactions and durable subscriptions to make applications reliable; and use messaging within Enterprise JavaBeans. It also introduces a new EJB type, the MessageDrivenBean, that is part of EJB 2.0, and discusses integration of messaging into J2EE.

Java

Java and SOAP

By Robert Englander
1st Edition May 2002
276 pages, ISBN 0-596-00175-4

Java and SOAP provides Java developers with an in-depth look at SOAP (the Simple Object Access Protocol). Of course, it covers the basics: what SOAP is, why it's soared to a spot on the Buzzwords' Top Ten list, and what its features and capabilities are. And it shows you how to work with some of the more common Java APIs in the SOAP world: Apache SOAP and GLUE.

Ant: The Definitive Guide

By Eric M. Burke & Jesse E. Tilly
1st Edition May 2002
288 pages, ISBN 0-596-00184-3

Ant is the premier build-management tool for Java environments. Ant is part of Jakarta, the Apache Software Foundation's open source Java project repository. Ant is written entirely in Java, and is platform independent. Using XML, a Java developer describes the modules involved in a build, and the dependencies between those modules. Ant then does the rest, compiling components as necessary in order to build the application.

Java & XML Data Binding

By Brett McLaughlin
1st Edition May 2002
214 pages, ISBN 0-596-00278-5

This new title provides an in-depth technical look at XML Data Binding. The book offers complete documentation of all features in both the Sun Microsystems JAXB API and popular open source alternative implementations (Enhydra Zeus, Exolabs Castor and Quick). It also gets into significant detail about when data binding is appropriate to use, and provides numerous practical examples of using data binding in applications.

NetBeans: The Definitive Guide

By Tim Boudreau, Jesse Glick, Simeon Greene, Vaughn Spurlin & Jack Woehr
1st Edition October 2002
696 pages, ISBN 0-596-00280-7

O'Reilly's NetBeans: The Definitive Guide is the authoritative reference for understanding and using the NetBeans Integrated Development Environment for creating new software with Java. Through a detailed tutorial, the book explains the capabilities of the NetBeans IDE, and compares it with competing software such as Borland's JBuilder. Then the authors go further, covering ways to expand NetBeans' basic capabilities by writing new modules for adding languages, new kinds of file storage, and collaborative capabilities, etc.

Programming Jakarta Struts

By Chuck Cavaness
1st Edition November 2002
462 pages, ISBN 0-596-00328-5

O'Reilly's Programming Jakarta Struts was written by Chuck Cavaness after his internet company decided to adopt the framework, then spent months really figuring out how to use it to its fullest potential. Readers will benefit from the real-world, "this is how to do it" approach Cavaness takes to developing complex enterprise applications using Struts, and his focus on the 1.1 version of the Framework makes this the most up-to-date book available.

Java NIO

By Ron Hitchens
1st Edition August 2002
312 pages, ISBN 0-596-00288-2

Java NIO explores the new I/O capabilities of version 1.4 in detail and shows you how to put these features to work to greatly improve the efficiency of the Java code you write. This compact volume examines the typical challenges that Java programmers face with I/O and shows you how to take advantage of the capabilities of the new I/O features. You'll learn how to put these tools to work using examples of common, real-world I/O problems and see how the new features have a direct impact on responsiveness, scalability, and reliability.

Java In a Nutshell Quick References

Java in a Nutshell, 4th Edition

By David Flanagan
4th Edition March 2002
992 pages, ISBN 0-596-00283-1

This bestselling quick reference contains an accelerated introduction to the Java programming language and its key APIs, so seasoned programmers can start writing Java code right away. The fourth edition of *Java in a Nutshell* covers the new Java 1.4 beta edition, which contains significant changes from the 1.3 version.

Java Enterprise in a Nutshell, 2nd Edition

By David Flanagan, Jim Farley &
William Crawford
2nd Edition April 2002
992 pages, ISBN 0-596-00152-5

Completely revised and updated to cover the new 2.0 version of Sun Microsystems Java Enterprise Edition software, *Java Enterprise in a Nutshell* 2nd edition covers the RMI, Java IDL, JDBC, JNDI, Java Servlet, and Enterprise JavaBeans APIs, with a fast-paced tutorial and compact reference material on each technology.

JXTA in a Nutshell

By Scott Oaks, Bernard Traversat
& Li Gong
1st Edition September 2002
416 pages, ISBN 0-596-00236-X

O'Reilly's pioneering reference is the first and last word on this powerful distributed computing technology. *JXTA in a Nutshell* delivers all the information you need to get started, including an overview of P2P distributed computing, an explanation of the JXTA Project's new platform, and ways that developers can become a part of the development effort. *JXTA in a Nutshell* introduces major concepts in a hands-on way by explaining them in context to the shell, and contains a complete reference to the JXTA application bindings. Also included is the full JXTA protocol specification. The book covers important topics such as security, and how the JXTA technology fits into the standard Java classes.

J2ME in a Nutshell

By Kim Topley
1st Edition, March 2002
468 pages, ISBN 0-596-00253-X

O'Reilly's *J2ME in a Nutshell* is as definitive a reference to the heart of the J2ME platform as the classic *Java in a Nutshell* is for the Standard Java platform. Its solid introduction to J2ME covers the essential APIs for different types of devices and deployments; the profiles (specifications of the minimum sets of APIs useful for a set-top box, wireless phone, PDA, or other device); and the Java virtual machine functions that support those APIs. The meat of the book is its classic O'Reilly-style quick reference to all the core Micro Edition classes.

Java Examples in a Nutshell, 2nd Edition

By David Flanagan
2nd Edition September 2000
584 pages, ISBN 0-596-00039-1

In *Java Examples in a Nutshell*, the author of Java in a Nutshell has created an entire book of example programs that not only serve as great learning tools, but can also be modified for individual use. The second edition of this best-selling book covers Java 1.3, and includes new chapters on JSP and servlets, XML, Swing, and Java 2D. This is the book for those who learn best "by example."

O'REILLY®

To order: *800-998-9938* • *order@oreilly.com* • *www.oreilly.com*
Online editions of most O'Reilly titles are available by subscription at *safari.oreilly.com*
Also available at most retail and online bookstores.

How to stay in touch with O'Reilly

1. Visit our award-winning web site

http://www.oreilly.com/

★ "Top 100 Sites on the Web"—PC Magazine
★ CIO Magazine's Web Business 50 Awards

Our web site contains a library of comprehensive product information (including book excerpts and tables of contents), downloadable software, background articles, interviews with technology leaders, links to relevant sites, book cover art, and more. File us in your bookmarks or favorites!

2. Join our email mailing lists

Sign up to get email announcements of new books and conferences, special offers, and O'Reilly Network technology newsletters at:

http://elists.oreilly.com

It's easy to customize your free elists subscription so you'll get exactly the O'Reilly news you want.

3. Get examples from our books

To find example files for a book, go to:

http://www.oreilly.com/catalog

select the book, and follow the "Examples" link.

4. Work with us

Check out our web site for current employment opportunites:

http://jobs.oreilly.com/

5. Register your book

Register your book at:
http://register.oreilly.com

6. Contact us

O'Reilly & Associates, Inc.
1005 Gravenstein Hwy North
Sebastopol, CA 95472 USA
TEL: 707-827-7000 or 800-998-9938
(6am to 5pm PST)
FAX: 707-829-0104

order@oreilly.com
For answers to problems regarding your order or our products. To place a book order online visit:

http://www.oreilly.com/order_new/

catalog@oreilly.com
To request a copy of our latest catalog.

booktech@oreilly.com
For book content technical questions or corrections.

corporate@oreilly.com
For educational, library, government, and corporate sales.

proposals@oreilly.com
To submit new book proposals to our editors and product managers.

international@oreilly.com
For information about our international distributors or translation queries. For a list of our distributors outside of North America check out:

http://international.oreilly.com/distributors.html

adoption@oreilly.com
For information about academic use of O'Reilly books, visit:

http://academic.oreilly.com

O'REILLY®

To order: *800-998-9938* • *order@oreilly.com* • *www.oreilly.com*
Online editions of most O'Reilly titles are available by subscription at *safari.oreilly.com*
Also available at most retail and online bookstores.